Organizational Behavior

SUNY Binghamton, MGMT 311

Debra L. Nelson | James Campbell Quick

CENGAGE
Learning™

Australia • Brazil • Japan • Korea • Mexico • Singapore • Spain • United Kingdom • United States

CENGAGE
Learning™

Organizational Behavior
SUNY Binghamton, MGMT 311

Debra L. Nelson | James Campbell Quick

Executive Editors:
Michele Baird

Maureen Staudt

Michael Stranz

Project Development Manager:
Linda deStefano

Senior Marketing Coordinators:
Sara Mercurio

Lindsay Shapiro

Senior Production / Manufacturing Manager:
Donna M. Brown

PreMedia Services Supervisor:
Rebecca A. Walker

Rights & Permissions Specialist:
Kalina Hintz

Cover Image:
Getty Images*

* Unless otherwise noted, all cover images used by Custom Solutions, a part of Cengage Learning, have been supplied courtesy of Getty Images with the exception of the Earthview cover image, which has been supplied by the National Aeronautics and Space Administration (NASA).

For product information and technology assistance, contact us at
Cengage Learning Customer & Sales Support, 1-800-354-9706

For permission to use material from this text or product, submit all requests online at **cengage.com/permissions**
Further permissions questions can be emailed to
permissionrequest@cengage.com

ISBN-13: 978-0-324-83144-3

ISBN-10: 0-324-83144-

Cengage Learning
5191 Natorp Boulevard
Mason, Ohio 45040
USA

Cengage Learning is a leading provider of customized learning solutions with office locations around the globe, including Singapore, the United Kingdom, Australia, Mexico, Brazil, and Japan. Locate your local office at:
international.cengage.com/region

Cengage Learning products are represented in Canada by Nelson Education, Ltd.

For your lifelong learning solutions, visit **custom.cengage.com**

Visit our corporate website at **cengage.com**

Printed in the United States of America

Brief Table of Contents

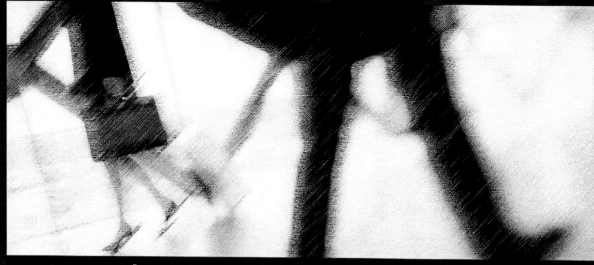

© DIGITAL VISION

Introduction

PART 1

CHAPTER 1

Organizational Behavior and Opportunity

LEARNING OBJECTIVES

After reading this chapter, you should be able to do the following:

1 Define *organizational behavior.*

2 Identify four action steps for responding positively in times of change.

3 Identify the important system components of an organization.

4 Describe the formal and informal elements of an organization.

5 Understand the diversity of organizations in the economy, as exemplified by the six focus organizations.

6 Recognize the opportunities that change creates for organizational behavior.

7 Demonstrate the value of objective knowledge and skill development in the study of organizational behavior.

THINKING AHEAD: CARIBOU COFFEE

Competing on Experience . . . for the Hearts of Customers

Caribou Coffee's chief competitor is Starbucks. Every organization has a chief competitor or set of competitors operating within its business environment, just as Starbucks is Caribou Coffee's chief competitor. Competitive markets increase the need for change and innovation within the firm as well as across the industry. When well managed and legally operated, they benefit the customer by delivering better products and services at lower rates. In addition, they benefit the competitors by challenging them to engage in innovations and serve their customers better without gouging, abusing, or shortchanging them. The rules of the competition need to be clear, the competitors well matched, and regulators engaged appropriately to insure competition that is fair to all concerned, including the public and society at large.[1]

Competition can be head-to-head or asymmetrical. Head-to-head competition occurs when two companies are competing for the same customers and on the same basis, such as price or size. Caribou Coffee's Michael Coles aims to compete with Starbucks asymmetrically, not head-to-head. That is, he is not trying to compete with Starbucks on the basis of size, and to keep up with his chief competitor on that basis. Size is only one dimension along which competition may occur. Competition may occur along other dimensions too, such as market share, quality of product or service, or a specialized, niche-customer strategy. Using asymmetrical competition, a company surrenders certain advantages or territory to the competition while capitalizing on their own distinctive strengths and advantages. Asymmetrical competition changes the rules of the game.

In the case of Caribou Coffee, Michael Coles has set the goal of being number one in "experience." Thus, Caribou has defined the competition in terms of a quality rather than a number, be that number of stores, number of customers, number of dollars earned in revenue, or number of profit dollars earned. This goes to the heart of the marketplace and to the heart of customer satisfaction. Customers, one at a time, are the ones who define experience for Caribou Coffee, Starbucks, and any other coffee chain. That is how Southwest Airlines succeeded and grew in the airline industry, by focusing on customer satisfaction and the traveler's experience, not on the size of their airline. When organizations like Caribou Coffee define the rules of the competition and state clearly what their goal is, they are engaging in asymmetrical competition and changing the game to how they want to play it. Can they win that way?

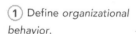

HUMAN BEHAVIOR IN ORGANIZATIONS

(1) Define *organizational behavior.*

Human behavior in organizations is complex and often difficult to understand. Organizations have been described as clockworks in which human behavior is logical and rational, but they often seem like snake pits to those who work in them.[2] The clockwork metaphor reflects an orderly, idealized view of organizational behavior devoid of conflict or dilemma because all the working parts (the people) mesh smoothly. The snake pit metaphor conveys the daily conflict, stress, and struggle in organizations. Each metaphor reflects reality from a different perspective—the organization's versus the individual's point of view. These metaphors reflect the complexity of human behavior, the dark side of which is seen in cases of air rage and workplace violence. On the positive side, the Gallup Organization's Marcus Buckingham suggests that people's psychological makeup is at the heart of the emotional economy.[3]

This chapter is an introduction to organizational behavior. The first section provides an overview of human behavior in organizations, its interdisciplinary origins, and behavior in times of change. The second section presents an organizational context within which behavior occurs and briefly introduces the six focus companies used selectively in the book. The third section highlights the *opportunities* that exist in times of *change* and *challenge* for people at work.[4] The fourth section addresses the ways people learn about organizational behavior and explains how the text's pedagogical features relate to the various ways of learning. The final section of the chapter presents the plan for the book.

Organizational behavior is individual behavior and group dynamics in organizations. The study of organizational behavior is primarily concerned with the psychosocial, interpersonal, and behavioral dynamics in organizations. However, organizational variables that affect human behavior at work are also relevant to

opportunities
Favorable times or chances for progress and advancement.

change
The transformation or modification of an organization and/or its stakeholders.

challenge
The call to competition, contest, or battle.

organizational behavior
The study of individual behavior and group dynamics in organizations.

the study of organizational behavior. These organizational variables include jobs, the design of work, communication, performance appraisal, organizational design, and organizational structure. Therefore, although individual behavior and group dynamics are the primary concerns in the study of organizational behavior, organizational variables are also important.

This section briefly contrasts two perspectives for understanding human behavior, the external and the internal perspectives. The section then discusses six scientific disciplines from which the study of organizational behavior has emerged and concludes with a discussion of behavior in times of change.

Understanding Human Behavior

The vast majority of theories and models of human behavior fall into one of two basic categories. One category has an internal perspective, and the other has an external perspective. The internal perspective considers factors inside the person to understand behavior. This view is psychodynamically oriented. People who subscribe to this view understand human behavior in terms of the thoughts, feelings, past experiences, and needs of the individual. The internal perspective explains people's actions and behavior in terms of their history and personal value systems. The internal processes of thinking, feeling, perceiving, and judging lead people to act in specific ways. The internal perspective has given rise to a wide range of motivational and leadership theories. This perspective implies that people are best understood from the inside and that their behavior is best interpreted after understanding their thoughts and feelings.

The other category of theories and models of human behavior takes an external perspective. This perspective focuses on factors outside the person to understand behavior. People who subscribe to this view understand human behavior in terms of external events, consequences of behavior, and the environmental forces to which a person is subject. From the external perspective, a person's history, feelings, thoughts, and personal value systems are not very important in interpreting actions and behavior. This perspective has given rise to an alternative set of motivational and leadership theories, which are covered in Chapters 5 and 12 of the text. The external perspective implies that a person's behavior is best understood by examining the surrounding external events and environmental forces.

The internal and external perspectives offer alternative explanations for human behavior. For example, the internal perspective might say Mary is an outstanding employee because she has a high need for achievement, whereas the external perspective might say Mary is an outstanding employee because she is paid extremely well for her work. Kurt Lewin captured both perspectives in saying that behavior is a function of both the person and the environment.[5]

Interdisciplinary Influences

Organizational behavior is a blended discipline that has grown out of contributions from numerous earlier fields of study, only one of which is the psychological discipline from which Kurt Lewin came. These interdisciplinary influences are the roots for what is increasingly recognized as the independent discipline of organizational behavior. The sciences of psychology, sociology, engineering, anthropology, management, and medicine have each contributed to our understanding of human behavior in organizations.

Psychology is the science of human behavior and dates back to the closing decades of the nineteenth century. Psychology traces its own origins to philosophy and the science of physiology. One of the most prominent early psychologists,

psychology
The science of human behavior.

William James, actually held a degree in medicine (M.D.). Since its origin, psychology has itself become differentiated into a number of specialized fields, such as clinical, experimental, military, organizational, and social psychology. Organizational psychology includes the study of many topics, such as work motivation, which are also covered by organizational behavior.[6] Early psychological research for the American military during World War I had later implications for sophisticated personnel selection methods used by corporations such as Johnson & Johnson, Valero Energy, and Texas Instruments.[7]

Sociology, the science of society, has made important contributions to knowledge about group and intergroup dynamics in the study of organizational behavior. Because sociology takes society rather than the individual as its point of departure, the sociologist is concerned with the variety of roles within a society or culture, the norms and standards of behavior in groups, and the consequences of compliant and deviant behavior. For example, the concept of *role set*, a key contribution to role theory in 1957 by Robert Merton, was used by a team of Harvard educators to study the school superintendent role in Massachusetts.[8] More recently, the role set concept has been used to study the effects of codes of ethics in organizations.[9]

Engineering is the applied science of energy and matter. Engineering has made important contributions to our understanding of the design of work. By taking basic engineering ideas and applying them to human behavior at work, Frederick Taylor had a profound influence on the early years of the study of organizational behavior.[10] Taylor's engineering background led him to place special emphasis on human productivity and efficiency in work behavior. His notions of performance standards and differential piece-rate systems have had lasting impact. Taylor's original ideas are embedded in organizational goal-setting programs, such as those at Black & Decker, IBM, and Weyerhaeuser.[11]

Anthropology, the science of human learned behavior, is especially important to understanding organizational culture. Cultural anthropology focuses on the origins of culture and the patterns of behavior as culture is communicated symbolically. Research in this tradition has examined the effects of efficient cultures on organization performance[12] and how pathological personalities may lead to dysfunctional organizational cultures.[13] Schwartz used a psychodynamic, anthropological mode of inquiry in exploring corporate decay at General Motors and NASA.[14]

Management, originally called administrative science, is a discipline concerned with the study of overseeing activities and supervising people in organizations. It emphasizes the design, implementation, and management of various administrative and organizational systems. March and Simon take the human organization as their point of departure and concern themselves with the administrative practices that will enhance the effectiveness of the system.[15] Management is the first discipline to take the modern corporation as the unit of analysis, and this viewpoint distinguishes the discipline's contribution to the study of organizational behavior.

Medicine is the applied science of healing or treatment of diseases to enhance an individual's health and well-being. Medicine has long-standing concern for both physical and psychological health, as well as for industrial mental health.[16] More recently, as the war against acute diseases is being won, medical attention has shifted to more chronic diseases, such as hypertension, and to occupational health and well-being.[17] Individual behavior and lifestyle patterns play important roles in treating chronic diseases.[18] These trends have contributed to the growth of corporate wellness programs, such as Johnson & Johnson's "Live for Life Program." The surge in health care costs over the past two decades has contributed to increased organizational concern with medicine and health care in the workplace.[19]

sociology
The science of society.

engineering
The applied science of energy and matter.

anthropology
The science of the learned behavior of human beings.

management
The study of overseeing activities and supervising people in organizations.

medicine
The applied science of healing or treatment of diseases to enhance an individual's health and well-being.

Behavior in Times of Change

Early research with individuals, groups, and organizations in the midst of environmental change found that change is often experienced as a threat that leads to a reliance on well-learned and dominant forms of behavior.[20] That is, in the midst of change, people often become rigid and reactive, rather than open and responsive. This may be useful if the change is neither dramatic nor rapid because we are often effective at coping with incremental change. However, if significant change occurs, then rigid and well-learned behavior may be counterproductive. The practice of outsourcing is a significant change in American industry that has been facilitated by dramatic advances in the Internet and networking technology.[21] Big changes disrupt people's habitual behavior and require learning if they are to be managed successfully. Eric Brown, ProLine International's VP of Global Business Development, offers some sage words of advice to see the opportunity in change.[22] He recommends adapting to change by seeing it as positive and seeing challenge as good rather than bad. His action steps for doing this are to (1) have a positive attitude, (2) ask questions, (3) listen to the answers, and (4) be committed to success.

However, success is never guaranteed, and change sometimes results in failure. If this happens, do not despair. Some of the world's greatest leaders, such as Winston Churchill, experienced dramatic failure before achieving lasting success. The key to their eventual success was their capacity to learn from the failure and to respond positively to the opportunities presented to them. One venture capitalist with whom the authors have worked likes to ask those seeking to build a business to tell him about their greatest failure. What the venture capitalist is looking for in the answer is how the executive responded to the failure and what he or she learned from the experience. While change carries with it the risk of failure as well as the opportunity for success, it is often how we behave in the midst of change that determines which outcome results. Success can come through the accumulation of small wins and through the micro-processes, as has been found with middle managers engaged in institutional change.[23]

2 Identify four action steps for responding positively in times of change.

THE ORGANIZATIONAL CONTEXT

A complete understanding of organizational behavior requires an understanding of both human behavior and the organizational context where behavior is enacted. This section discusses the organizational context. First, organizations are presented as systems. Second, the formal and informal organizations are discussed. Finally, six focus companies are presented as contemporary examples and drawn on throughout the text.

3 Identify the important system components of an organization.

Organizations as Open Systems

As with human behavior, two different perspectives offer complementary explanations of organizations. Organizations are open systems of interacting components, which are people, tasks, technology, and structure. These internal components also interact with components in the organization's task environment. Organizations as open systems have people, technology, structure, and purpose, which interact with elements in the organization's environment.

What, exactly, is an organization? Today, the corporation is the dominant organizational form for much of the Western world, but other organizational forms have dominated other times and societies. Some societies have been dominated by religious organizations, such as the temple corporations of ancient Mesopotamia and the churches in colonial America.[24] Other societies have been dominated by military organizations, such as the clans of the Scottish Highlands and the regional armies of the People's Republic of China.[25, 26] All of these societies are woven together by family organizations, which themselves may vary from nuclear and extended families to small, collective communities.[27, 28] The purpose and structure of the religious, military, and family organizational forms may vary, but people's behavior in these organizations may be very similar. In fact, early discoveries about power and leadership in work organizations were remarkably similar to findings about power and leadership within families.[29]

Organizations may manufacture products, such as aircraft components or steel, or deliver services, such as managing money or providing insurance protection. To understand how organizations do these things requires an understanding of the open system components of the organization and the components of its task environment.

Katz, Kahn, and Leavitt set out open system frameworks for understanding organizations.[30] The four major internal components—task, people, technology, and structure—along with the organization's inputs, outputs, and key elements in the task environment, are depicted in Figure 1.1. The *task* of the organization is its mission, purpose, or goal for existing. The *people* are the human resources of the organization. The *technology* is the wide range of tools, knowledge, and/or techniques used to transform the inputs into outputs. The *structure* is the systems of communication, the systems of authority, and the systems of workflow.

In addition to these major internal components, the organization as a system also has an external task environment. The task environment is composed of different constituents, such as suppliers, customers, and federal regulators. Thompson describes the task environment as that element of the environment related to the

task

An organization's mission, purpose, or goal for existing.

people

The human resources of the organization.

technology

The tools, knowledge, and/or techniques used to transform inputs into outputs.

structure

The systems of communication, authority and roles, and workflow.

FIGURE   An Open Systems View of Organization

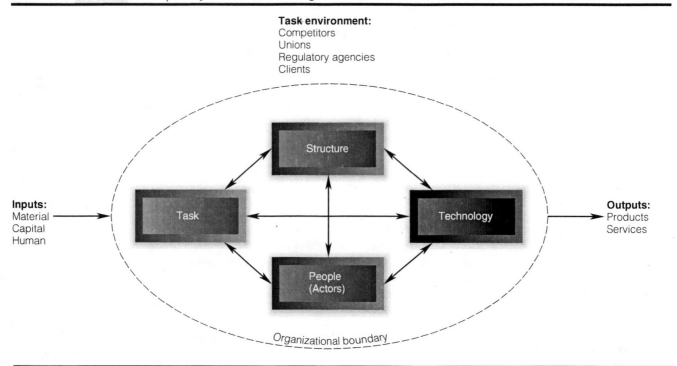

SOURCE: Based on Harold Leavitt, "Applied Organizational Change in Industry: Structural, Technological, and Humanistic Approaches," in J. G. March, ed., *Handbook of Organizations* (Chicago: Rand McNally, 1965), 1145. Reprinted by permission of James G. March.

organization's degree of goal attainment; that is, it is composed of those elements of the environment related to the organization's basic task.[31] For example, competitors are part of any organization's task environment, as we saw in Thinking Ahead with Caribou Coffee. Starbucks is the chief competitor for Caribou and thus a key element in Caribou's task environment. Therefore, Caribou has to develop a business strategy and approach to succeed that considers the actions and activities of Starbucks.

The organization system works by taking inputs, converting them into throughputs, and delivering outputs to its task environment. Inputs consist of the human, informational, material, and financial resources used by the organization. Throughputs are the materials and resources as they are transformed by the organization's technology component. Once the transformation is complete, they become outputs for customers, consumers, and clients. The actions of suppliers, customers, regulators, and other elements of the task environment affect the organization and the behavior of people at work. For example, Onsite Engineering and Management experienced a threat to its survival in the mid-1980s by being totally dependent on one large utility for its outputs. By broadening its client base and improving the quality of its services (that is, its outputs) over the next several years, Onsite became a healthier, more successful small company. Transforming inputs into high-quality outputs is critical to an organization's success.

The Formal and Informal Organization

The open systems view of organization may lead one to see the design of an organization as a clockwork with a neat, precise, interrelated functioning. The *formal organization* is the official, legitimate, and most visible part that enables people to think of organizations in logical and rational ways. The snake pit organizational metaphor mentioned earlier has its roots in the study and examination of the *informal organization*, which is unofficial and less visible. The informal elements were first fully appreciated as a result of the *Hawthorne studies,* conducted during the 1920s and 1930s. It was during the interview study, the third of the four Hawthorne studies, that the researchers began to develop a deeper understanding of the informal elements of the Hawthorne Works as an organization.[32] The formal and informal elements of the organization are depicted in Figure 1.2.

Potential conflict between the formal and informal organization makes an understanding of both important. Conflicts between these two elements erupted in many organizations during the early years of the twentieth century and were embodied in the union–management strife of that era. The conflicts escalated into violence in a number of cases. For example, during the 1920s, supervisors at the Homestead Works of U.S. Steel were issued pistols and boxes of ammunition "just in case" it became necessary to shoot unruly, dangerous steelworkers. Such potential formal–informal, management–labor conflict does not characterize all organizations. During the same era, Eastman Kodak was very progressive. The company helped with financial backing for employees' neighborhood communities, such as Meadowbrook in Rochester, New York. Kodak's concern for employees and attention to informal issues made unions unnecessary within the company.

The informal elements of the organization are frequent points of diagnostic and intervention activities in organization development, though the formal elements must always be considered as well because they provide the context for the informal.[33] These informal elements are important because people's feelings, thoughts, and attitudes about their work do make a difference in their behavior and performance. Individual behavior plays out in the context of the formal and informal elements of the system, becoming organizational behavior. The uncovering

4 Describe the formal and informal elements of an organization.

formal organization
The official, legitimate, and most visible part of the system.

informal organization
The unofficial and less visible part of the system.

Hawthorne studies
Studies conducted during the 1920s and 1930s that discovered the existence of the informal organization.

FIGURE 1.2   Formal and Informal Organization

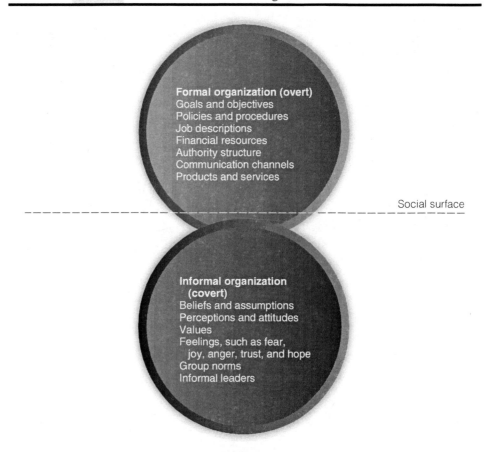

Social surface

of the informal elements in an organization was one of the major discoveries of the Hawthorne studies. The importance of employees' moods, emotions, and dispositional affect is being re-recognized as a key influence on critical organizational outcomes, such as job performance, decision making, creativity, turnover, teamwork, negotiation, and leadership.[34]

Six Focus Organizations

(5) Understand the diversity of organizations in the economy, as exemplified by the six focus organizations.

Organizational behavior always occurs in the context of a specific organizational setting. Most attempts at explaining or predicting organizational behavior rely heavily on factors within the organization and give less weight to external environmental considerations.[35] Students can benefit from being sensitive to the industrial context of organizations and from developing an appreciation for each organization as a whole.[36] In this vein, six organizations each appear three times for a total of eighteen Thinking Ahead and Looking Back features. Caribou Coffee is illustrated in this chapter. We challenge you in each chapter to anticipate what is in the Looking Back feature once you read Thinking Ahead.

The U.S. economy is the largest in the world, with a gross domestic product of more than $13.2 trillion in 2006. Figure 1.3 shows the major sectors of the economy. The largest sectors are service (41 percent) and product manufacture of nondurable goods (20 percent) and durable goods (8 percent). Taken together, the manufacture of products and the delivery of services account for 69 percent of

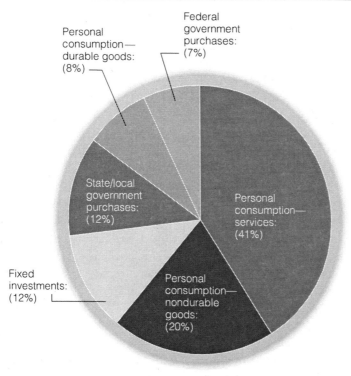

the U.S. economy. Government and fixed investments account for the remaining 31 percent. Large and small organizations operate in each sector of the economy shown in Figure 1.3.

The private sectors are an important part of the economy. The manufacturing sector includes the production of basic materials, such as steel, and the production of finished products, such as automobiles and electronic equipment. The service sector includes transportation, financial services, insurance, and retail sales. The government sectors, which provide essential infrastructure, and nonprofit organizations are also important to our collective well-being because they meet needs not addressed in these economic sectors. We have chosen organizations that reflect the manufacturing service, retail, and nonprofit sections of business: Caribou Coffee, Genentech, Inc., Google, The Timberland Company, American Express, and Toyota Motor Corporation.

Each of these six organizations makes an important and unique contribution to the manufacturing or service sectors of the national economy and/or to our national well-being. These organizations are not alone, however. Hundreds of other small, medium, and large organizations are making valuable and significant contributions to the economic health and human welfare of the United States. Brief examples from many organizations are used throughout the book. We hope that by better understanding these organizations, you may have a greater appreciation for your own organization and others within the diverse world of private business enterprises and nonprofit organizations.

Caribou Coffee. Caribou Coffee is the second largest retailer of specialty and gourmet coffee in the United States. It was born out of an entrepreneurial dream of newlyweds John and Kim Puckett on a trip through Alaska. They went through an arduous climb to the top of Sable Mountain and took in the breathtaking view of the beautiful countryside and a herd of caribou passing through the valley. In that moment, the Pucketts realized that life is short and anything worth having takes a lot of hard work. That has been the defining vision for Caribou Coffee as they pride themselves with creating an experience for anyone who walks into one of their thousands of stores in eighteen states.

Caribou Coffee is headquartered in Minneapolis, Minnesota. The company currently employs over 5,000 employees across the United States. Caribou also offers its specialty coffee products through several grocery chain outlets, college campuses, airlines, sports venues, and other vendors. Recently, the Rainforest Alliance awarded the prestigious Corporate Green Globe Award to Caribou. This award highlights the company's socially responsible practices, focusing on growing coffee in a way that balances ecological, social, and economic considerations.

Caribou's corporate culture is relaxed and informal. Employees are seen as a real asset and encouraged to hone their entrepreneurial spirit. New ideas are always encouraged and most of the company's offices are set in scenic mountain lodge locations. Caribou offers very attractive benefits packages to attract and retain the best talent. They also place a huge emphasis on diversity and recently appointed a woman to their Chief Operating Officer (COO) position.[37]

Genentech, Inc. Led by its chairman and CEO, Arthur D. Levinson, Ph.D., Genentech was founded in 1976 by two venture capitalists to develop, manufacture, and commercialize biotherapeutics for "significant unmet medical needs." And meet unmet medical needs the company has done. Through their basic and applied research, Genentech's more than 800 scientists have amassed a pipeline of over 50 projects in the areas of oncology, immunology, and tissue growth and repair. While Genentech is known for its new product development, it has also had great success in identifying multiple uses for existing drugs to fight not just a particular disease but evolving forms of it.

Genentech is headquartered in San Francisco, California, and has research facilities in Vacaville and Oceanside, California. With over 10,600 full-time employees, Genentech has been recognized as a top employer by *Fortune*, *Working Mother*, and *Science* magazines. Genentech was named one of *Fortune's* "100 Best Companies to Work For" in the United States for the ninth consecutive year in 2007. The company is also known for its commitment to making sure that the patients who need their products can afford them, donating nearly $205 million in free drugs to uninsured patients in 2006 and capping the price of per patient costs of certain drugs in 2007.

Genentech is publicly traded on the NYSE and reported total operating revenues of $2.84 million for the first quarter of 2007. The company's total cash and investments portfolio totaled nearly $4.9 billion as of March 31, 2007.[38]

Google. Founded in September 1998 by two Stanford University doctoral students, Larry Page and Sergey Brin, Google is currently home to one of the most popular search engines in the country, Google .com. Referred to by *FastCompany* in 2003 as having been "founded by geeks and run by geeks," Google has developed

At the Google headquarters in Mountain View, California, the lobby is complete with lava lamps, a piano, and live projections of Google.com queries from around the world.

© AP PHOTO/PAUL SAKUMA

a product that has changed the lives of more than 380 million Internet users a month by providing information that is fast, accurate, and easy to use.

Google employs more than 7,900 full-time employees ("Googlers" as they call themselves) worldwide. The company's corporate culture is relatively intimate and uniquely "geek." Its Mountain View, California, headquarters lobby is complete with lava lamps, a piano, and live projections of Google.com queries from around the world. Rather than expensive Porsches, most of the cars in the parking lot are beat-up Volvos and Subarus. Googlers seem to be driven by an impossible quest for perfection—in speed, relevant content, and user trust.

While online search continues to be the heart of Google, the company has developed a number of other Internet-related products including Google Maps, Google Earth, Google Book Search, and Google Video. In 2006, the company acquired YouTube, the enormously popular repository of commercial and user-generated video content. Google reported over $10.6 billion in total revenue and a net income of over $3 billion for the year ending December 31, 2006.[39]

The Timberland Company. The birth of Timberland can be traced back to when Nathan Schwartz bought a part of the Abington Shoe Company in 1952. It was in 1978 that the official Timberland company name took shape after the introduction of their first Timberland boot. Since then, the company has never looked back. Today it exports to several foreign locations.

In 1998, Jeffrey Schwartz, grandson of founder Nathan Schwartz, took over as the President and CEO of Timberland. He has been instrumental in creating the company's distinct corporate image. For example, in 2001, they introduced the Path of Service program for employees. This allows employees to take a sabbatical and engage in long-term service projects. Timberland ranked 78 in the *Fortune* "100 Best Companies to Work For" list in 2007. It employs just over 2,000 employees and is headquartered in Stratham, New Hampshire. Timberland encourages employees to give back to the communities they live in. It gives employees 40 hours of paid time per year to volunteer.

Today, the race to engage in socially responsible business practices seems to be more heated than ever for people at Timberland. The company recruited 9,000 volunteers across the globe to celebrate Earth Day. These service hours totaling about 53,000 hours were invested in activities such as planting tress and restoration of native species. Jeff Schwartz claims that such activities help achieve Timberland's larger corporate goal of being carbon neutral by 2010.[40]

American Express (AMEX). Founded in 1850 in New York, American Express started out as a business delivery service for large financial corporations. They specialized in delivering small bank parcels such as money orders, checks, and financial certificates. It was only much later in the late 1800s and early 1900s that they began to focus on financial services. Soon American Express evolved into a banking and financial services conglomerate with locations all over the world. In 1958, the company issued its first charge card and since then has been known for its credit card products and services.

American Express ranked 74 on *Fortune*'s "100 Best Companies to Work For" in America in 2007. With over 29,000 employees in the United States and over 35,000 outside the United States, the company has a strong corporate culture founded and built on values such as trust, integrity, and teamwork. During the 9/11 attacks, employees of the company, headquartered directly across from Ground Zero, demonstrated undeniable courage and commitment by continuing to work from temporary locations to help customers and colleagues get through the difficult time.

Fully realizing that investors care as much about company image as they do about bottom-line numbers, AMEX has transformed itself into a model corporate citizen. It heavily invests in three major themes related to corporate social responsibility: preservation and enrichment of cultural heritage; development of leadership; and encouragement of community service in the communities where it operates.[41]

Toyota Motor Corporation. The Toyota Motor Corporation was born when Kiichiro Toyoda completed his A1 prototype passenger car in 1935. More than seven decades later, Toyota has become a force in the automobile industry and is the fourth largest automaker in North America, having sold over 7.4 million passenger cars, trucks, and buses in 2005.

Since its founding, Toyota's aim has been to "enrich society through car making." To that end, the company has made good on its commitment to develop vehicles that are safe, environmentally advanced, and fun to drive. To date, Toyota has sold over 500,000 hybrid vehicles worldwide including the Lexus RX and GS, Highlander, Prius, and Camry models. Under the leadership of its chairman, Fujio Cho, and its president, Katsuaki Watanabe, Toyota deploys *monozukuri*—the manufacturing of value-added products—to help achieve its goals of creating a more prosperous society and innovating into the future.

Along with its subsidiaries, Toyota manufactures in 27 countries and sells vehicles in more than 170 countries. In addition to its worldwide presence, Toyota's economic impact in North America continues to grow. Nearly two-thirds of all its vehicles sold in the United States are built in the United States. The North American operations group expects that by 2008, it will have the capacity to build over 1.8 million cars and trucks. Toyota employs approximately 300,000 people worldwide; it has net sales of 23.95 billion yen ($194.08 million) and a net income of 1.64 billion yen ($13.32 million) for the fiscal year ending March 31, 2007.[42]

CHANGE CREATES OPPORTUNITIES

(6) Recognize the opportunities that change creates for organizational behavior.

Change creates opportunities and risks, as mentioned earlier in the chapter. Global competition is a leading force driving change at work. Competition in the United States and world economies has increased significantly during the past couple of decades, especially in industries such as banking, finance, and air transportation. Corporate competition creates performance and cost pressures, which have a ripple effect on people and their behavior at work. While one risk for employees is the marginalization of part-time professionals, good management practice can ensure the integration of these part-time professionals.[43] The competition may lead to downsizing and restructuring, yet it provides the opportunity for revitalization as well.[44] Further, small companies are not necessarily the losers in this competitive environment. Scientech, a small power and energy company, found it had to enhance its managerial talent and service quality to meet the challenges of growth and big-company competitors. Product and service quality is one tool that can help companies become winners in a competitive environment. Problem-solving skills are another tool used by IBM, Control Data Services, Inc., Northwest Airlines, and Southwest Airlines to help achieve high-quality products and services.

Too much change leads to chaos; too little change leads to stagnation. Change in the coffee industry is a key stimulus for both Caribou Coffee and for Starbucks as they innovate and improve as organizations. Winning in a competitive industry can be a transient victory however; continuous change is required to stay ahead of the

Nintendo "Gets It" and Is Back in the Game

By the 1980s, Nintendo, which had ushered in the modern age of videogames, was the most successful company in the gaming world. However, over the next twenty years they watched Sony and Microsoft cut their market share of U.S. hardware sales in half by the introduction of newer, more powerful systems. This occurred within the context of a booming industry that grew to $30 billion globally.

© REUTERS/TORU HANAI/LANDOV

Nintendo's Wii game console was released abroad as well as in the United States. Here is a Wii display at a game shop in Tokyo's Akihabara electronic district.

engaging in the competition with Sony and Microsoft. Iwata and Miyamoto decided they needed to do something about the game controller, whose basic design had remained unchanged for decades. They made the risky decision to build the Wii around a chip similar to one of Nintendo's early entries in gaming, which meant success would not be on the strength of breathtaking graphics. Then they designed a sleek, small, white

Nintendo began its dramatic turnaround in the early 2000s when its top two strategists, CEO Satoru Iwata and legendary game designer Shigeru Miyamoto, identified two troubling trends. First, as young consumers started careers and families, they cut back on game time. Second, as consoles became more powerful, the games became more expensive. Nintendo needed a paradigm shift and an entirely new way of

exterior console that would sit right next to the TV. Finally, they went for a motion-sensitive wireless controller. While risky, the new controller paradigm paid off and demand well outstripped supply of Wiis during 2006. The Wii is reversing twenty years of declining Nintendo console sales.

SOURCE: J. Gaudiosi, "Why Wii Won," *Business 2.0* 8 (May 2007): 35–37.

competition. For example, in 2006 it looked like the game was over for Nintendo's storied console business. Then again, maybe not, as we see in The Real World 1.1. The gaming world is full of changes. What are your perceptions of change? Complete You 1.1 and see how you perceive change.

Four Challenges for Managers Related to Change

Chapter 2 develops four challenges for managers related to change in contemporary organizations: globalization, workforce diversity, ethics and character, and technological innovation. These are four driving forces creating and shaping changes at work. Further, success in global competition requires organizations to be more responsive to ethnic, religious, and gender diversity as well as personal integrity in the workforce, in addition to responding positively to the competition in the international marketplace. Workforce demographic change and diversity are critical challenges in themselves for the study and management of organizational behavior.[45] The theories of motivation, leadership, and group behavior based on research in a workforce of one composition may not be applicable in a workforce of a very different composition.[46] This may be especially problematic if ethnic, gender, and/or religious differences lead to conflict between leaders and followers in organizations. For example, the Russian military establishment has found ethnic and religious conflicts between the officers and enlisted corps a serious impediment to unit cohesion and performance at times.

Analyze Your Perceptions of a Change

Everyone perceives change differently. Think of a change situation you are currently experiencing. It can be any business, school-related, or personal experience that requires a significant change in your attitude or behavior. Rate your feelings about this change using the following scales. For instance, if you feel the change is more of a threat than an opportunity, you would circle 0, 2, or 4 on the first scale.

1.	Threat	0	2	4	6	8	10	Opportunity
2.	Holding on to the past	0	2	4	6	8	10	Reaching for the future
3.	Immobilized	0	2	4	6	8	10	Activated
4.	Rigid	0	2	4	6	8	10	Versatile
5.	A loss	0	2	4	6	8	10	A gain
6.	Victim of change	0	2	4	6	8	10	Agent of change
7.	Reactive	0	2	4	6	8	10	Proactive
8.	Focused on the past	0	2	4	6	8	10	Focused on the future
9.	Separate from change	0	2	4	6	8	10	Involved with change
10.	Confused	0	2	4	6	8	10	Clear

How positive are your perceptions of this change?

SOURCE: H. Woodward and S. Buchholz, *Aftershock: Helping People through Corporate Change*, 15. Copyright © 1987 John Wiley & Sons, Inc. Reprinted by permission of John Wiley & Sons, Inc.

Global Competition in Business

Managers and executives in the United States face radical change in response to increased global competition. According to noted economist Lester Thurow, this competition is characterized by intense rivalry between the United States, Japan, and Europe in core industries.[47] Economic competition places pressure on all categories of employees to be productive and to add value to the firm. The uncertainty of unemployment resulting from corporate warfare and competition is an ongoing feature of organizational life for people in companies or industries that pursue cost-cutting strategies to achieve economic success. The global competition in the automotive industry among the Japanese, U.S., and European car companies embodies the intensity that can be expected in other industries in the future.

Some people feel that the future must be the focus in coming to grips with this international competition; others believe we can deal with the future only by studying the past.[48] Global, economic, and organizational changes have dramatic effects on the study and management of organizational behavior. How positive were your perceptions of the change you analyzed in You 1.1? Are you an optimist who sees opportunity, or a pessimist who sees threat?

Customer Focused for High Quality

Global competition has challenged organizations to become more customer focused, to meet changing product and service demands, and to exceed customers' expectations of high quality. Quality has the potential for giving organizations in viable industries a competitive edge in meeting international competition. By striving to be number one in experience, Caribou Coffee aims to compete with a customer-focused, high-quality approach.

Is TQM a Fleeting Fashion?

This research studied the provision of TQM consulting services between 1992 and 2001, a period during which TQM consulting went from the limelight to the background of the management stage. TQM consulting was a fleeting fashion with a boom and a bust during this period, and yet it has staying power. This study helps us to understand the boom-to-bust cycle that occurred. As TQM consulting boomed, the demand for qualified consultants outstripped the supply and led more generalists into the arena of offering TQM consulting services. However, these generalists had weak links to the technical foundations of this type of consulting and, as a result, were often uncommitted, unprepared, and superficial providers of services. These "fashion surfers" damaged the credibility of the consulting services offered by all, tarnishing the industry. As a result, they

contributed to the downturn and eventual bust in TQM consulting services. TQM was a legitimate managerial innovation and the question became: how could it survive the collapse of a boom? The answer lay in the commitment of consulting specialists with strong links to quality control expertise. The emergence of a hard core of knowledgeable TQM providers of management consulting services helped this innovation to survive and will improve the average TQM program success, refine industry best practice, and increase the legitimacy of an innovation that went through a real bust. Yes, TQM was a fleeting fashion but one that is still here because of a solid technical foundation.

SOURCE: R. J. David and D. Strang, "When Fashion Is Fleeting: Transitory Collective Beliefs and the Dynamics of TQM Consulting," *Academy of Management Journal* 49 (2006): 215–233.

Quality became a rubric for products and services of high status. Total quality is defined in many ways.[49] Total quality management (TQM) is the complete dedication to continuous improvement and to customers so that their needs are met and their expectations exceeded. Quality is a customer-oriented philosophy of management with important implications for virtually all aspects of organizational behavior. Quality cannot be optimized, because customer needs and expectations are always changing. It is a cultural value embedded in highly successful organizations. Ford Motor Company's dramatic metamorphosis as an automotive leader is attributable to the decision to "make quality Job One" in all aspects of the design and manufacture of cars. As we see in the Science feature, while TQM management consulting went through a boom-to-bust cycle, it is here to stay.

Quality improvement enhances the probability of organizational success in increasingly competitive industries. One study of 193 general medical hospitals examined seven TQM practices and found them positively related to the financial performance of the hospitals.[50] Quality improvement is an enduring feature of an organization's culture and of the economic competition we face today. It leads to competitive advantage through customer responsiveness, results acceleration, and resource effectiveness.[51] The three key questions in evaluating quality-improvement ideas for people at work are these: (1) Does the idea improve customer response? (2) Does the idea accelerate results? (3) Does the idea increase the effectiveness of resources? A "yes" answer means the idea should be implemented to improve quality.

Six Sigma is a philosophy for company-wide quality improvement developed by Motorola and popularized by General Electric. The Six Sigma program is characterized by its customer-driven approach, its emphasis on decision making based on quantitative data, and its priority on saving money.[52] It has evolved into a high-performance system to execute business strategy. Part of its quality program is a 12-step problem-solving method specifically designed to lead a Six Sigma "Black Belt" to significant improvement within a defined process. It tackles problems in

Six Sigma

A high-performance system to execute business strategy that is customer driven, emphasizes quantitative decision making, and places a priority on saving money.

TABLE 1.1 Contrasting Six Sigma and Total Quality Management

Six Sigma	Total Quality Management
Executive ownership	Self-directed work teams
Business strategy execution system	Quality initiative
Truly cross-functional	Largely within a single function
Focused training with verifiable	No mass training in statistics and quality
return on investment	Return on investment
Business results oriented	Quality oriented

SOURCE: M. Barney, "Motorola's Second Generation," *Six Sigma Forum Magazine* (May 2002): 13.

four phases: (1) measure, (2) analyze, (3) improve, and (4) control. In addition, it demands that executives be aligned to the right objective and targets, quality improvement teams be mobilized for action, results be accelerated, and sustained improvement be monitored. Six Sigma is set up in a way that it can be applied to a range of problems and areas, from manufacturing settings to service work environments. Table 1.1 contrasts Six Sigma and TQM. One study compared Six Sigma to two other methods for quality improvement (specifically, Taguchi's methods and the Shainin system) and found it to be the most complete strategy of the three, with a strong emphasis on exploiting statistical modeling techniques.[53]

Behavior and Quality at Work

Whereas total quality may draw on reliability engineering or just-in-time management, total quality improvement can be successful only when employees have the skills and authority to respond to customer needs.[54] Total quality has direct and important effects on the behavior of employees at all levels in the organization, not just on employees working directly with customers. Chief executives can advance total quality by engaging in participative management, being willing to change everything, focusing quality efforts on customer service (not cost cutting), including quality as a criterion in reward systems, improving the flow of information regarding quality-improvement successes or failures, and being actively and personally involved in quality efforts. While serving as chairman of Motorola, George Fisher emphasized the behavioral attributes of leadership, cooperation, communication, and participation as important elements in the company's Six Sigma program.

Quality improvement continues to be important to our competitiveness. The U.S. Department of Commerce's sponsorship of an annual award in the name of Malcolm Baldrige, former secretary of commerce in the Reagan administration, recognizes companies excelling in quality improvement and management. The Malcolm Baldrige National Quality Award examination evaluates an organization in seven categories: leadership, information and analysis, strategic quality planning, human resource utilization, quality assurance of products and services, quality results, and customer satisfaction.

According to former President George H. W. Bush, quality management is not just a strategy. It must be a new style of working, even a new style of thinking. A dedication to quality and excellence is more than good business. It is a way of life, giving something back to society, offering your best to others.

Quality is one watchword for competitive success. Organizations that do not respond to customer needs find their customers choosing alternative product and service suppliers who are willing to exceed their expectations. With this said, you should not conclude that total quality is a panacea for all organizations or that it guarantees unqualified success.

Managing Organizational Behavior in Changing Times

Over and above the challenge of quality improvement to meet international competition, managing organizational behavior during changing times is challenging for at least four reasons: (1) the increasing globalization of organizations' operating territory, (2) the increasing diversity of organizational workforces, (3) the continuing demand for higher levels of moral and ethical behavior at work, and (4) continuing technological innovation with its companion need for skill enhancement. These are the important issues to address in managing people at work.

Each of these four issues is explored in detail in Chapter 2 and highlighted throughout the text because they are intertwined in the contemporary practice of organizational behavior. For example, the issue of women in the workplace concerns workforce diversity and at the same time overlaps the globalization issue. Gender roles are often defined differently in various cultures, and sexual harassment is a frequent ethical problem for organizations in the United States, Europe, Israel, and South Africa. For another example, process and technology innovations require attention to behavioral issues if they are to be successful. One study of innovation in 47 German companies found that organizational support and psychological safety were positively related to return on assets and goal achievement, suggesting that attention to behavioral factors along with technical factors in implementing successful process innovations is important.[55] Therefore, students of organizational behavior must appreciate and understand these important issues.

LEARNING ABOUT ORGANIZATIONAL BEHAVIOR

Organizational behavior is based on scientific knowledge and applied practice. It involves the study of abstract ideas, such as valence and expectancy in motivation, as well as the study of concrete matters, such as observable behaviors and medical symptoms of distress at work. Therefore, learning about organizational behavior includes at least three activities, as shown in Figure 1.4. First, the science of organizational behavior requires the mastery of a certain body of *objective knowledge*. Objective knowledge results from research and scientific activities, as reflected in the Science feature in each chapter. Second, the practice of organizational behavior requires *skill development* based on knowledge and an understanding of yourself in order to master the abilities essential to success. The You features in each chapter challenge you to know yourself and apply what you are learning. Third, both objective knowledge and skill development must be applied in real-world settings. The Real World features in each chapter open windows into organizational realities where science and skills are applied.

Learning is challenging and fun because we are all different. The Real World 1.2 feature shows that while diversity is very important, it does have its limits. Within learning environments, student diversity is best addressed in the learning process through more options for students and greater responsibility on the part of students as coproducers in the effort and fun of learning.[56] For those who are blind or have vision impairments, learning can be a special challenge. The alignment of teaching styles with learning styles is important for the best fit, and teaching is no longer just verbal and visual but also virtual with a new generation of students.[57] To gain a better understanding of yourself as a learner, thereby maximizing your potential and developing strategies in specific learning environments, you need to evaluate the way you prefer to learn and process information. You 1.2 offers a quick way

⑦ Demonstrate the value of objective knowledge and skill development in the study of organizational behavior.

objective knowledge
Knowledge that results from research and scientific activities.

skill development
The mastery of abilities essential to successful functioning in organizations.

The Limits of Diversity

Diversity is critically important in the real world just as it is in learning environments. Appreciating, understanding, and working effectively with those who are different from us have huge value in achieving great results by working together. However, one Florida city manager learned that even diversity tolerance has its limits. Largo, Florida, is a city whose motto is "The City of Progress." According to Susan Sinz, the city's human resources director, Largo created a diversity program in 2004 to respond to the small number of employees who were terminated for making racial slurs or using derogatory remarks. The program focused primarily on the appreciation of diversity in knowledge, skills, and abilities without taking on a specific demographic diversity dimension, such as race or gender. The result was substantive tolerance for diversity among the employees of the city of Largo. However, when city manager Steven Stanton began undergoing hormone therapy in preparation for a sex-change operation, a very active group of churches became involved and worked to set limits on how much diversity the city should tolerate. The city found that transgender issues are still on the periphery of most diversity initiatives. As a result, while it still preaches and practices tolerance, Largo fired Stanton after the story created a firestorm locally and broke nationwide. Tolerance and appreciation of diversity do have limits.

SOURCE: J. Marquez, "Limits of Diversity Program Revealed," *Workforce Management* 86 (2007): 1–4.

of assessing your learning style. If you are a visual learner, then use charts, maps, PowerPoint slides, videos, the Internet, notes, or flash cards, and write things out for visual review. If you are an auditory learner, then listen, take notes during lectures, and consider taping them so you can fill in gaps later; review your notes frequently; and recite key concepts out loud. If you are a tactile learner, trace words as you are saying them, write down facts several times, and make study sheets.

FIGURE 1.4 Learning about Organizational Behavior

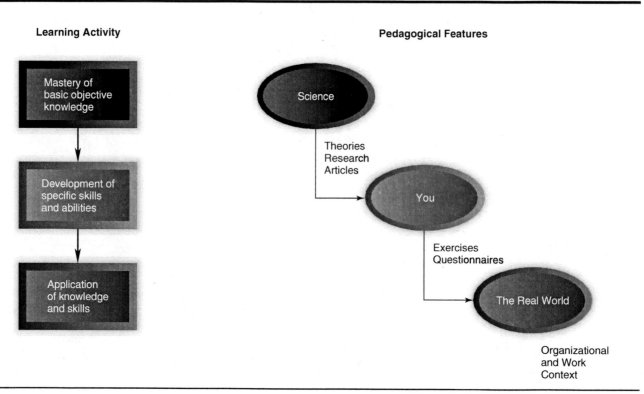

20

Learning Style Inventory

Directions: This 24-item survey is not timed. Answer each question as honestly as you can. Place a check on the appropriate line after each statement.

	OFTEN	SOMETIMES	SELDOM
1. Can remember more about a subject through the lecture method with information, explanations, and discussion.	____	____	____
2. Prefer information to be written on the chalkboard, with the use of visual aids and assigned readings.	____	____	____
3. Like to write things down or to take notes for visual review.	____	____	____
4. Prefer to use posters, models, or actual practice and some activities in class.	____	____	____
5. Require explanations of diagrams, graphs, or visual directions.	____	____	____
6. Enjoy working with my hands or making things.	____	____	____
7. Am skillful with and enjoy developing and making graphs and charts.	____	____	____
8. Can tell if sounds match when presented with pairs of sounds.	____	____	____
9. Remember best by writing things down several times.	____	____	____
10. Can understand and follow directions on maps.	____	____	____
11. Do better at academic subjects by listening to lectures and tapes.	____	____	____
12. Play with coins or keys in pockets.	____	____	____
13. Learn to spell better by repeating the word out loud than by writing the word on paper.	____	____	____
14. Can better understand a news development by reading about it in the paper than by listening to the radio.	____	____	____
15. Chew gum, smoke, or snack during studies.	____	____	____
16. Feel the best way to remember is to picture it in your head.	____	____	____
17. Learn spelling by "finger spelling" words.	____	____	____
18. Would rather listen to a good lecture or speech than read about the same material in a textbook.	____	____	____
19. Am good at working and solving jigsaw puzzles and mazes.	____	____	____
20. Grip objects in hands during learning period.	____	____	____
21. Prefer listening to the news on the radio rather than reading about it in the newspaper.	____	____	____
22. Obtain information on an interesting subject by reading relevant materials.	____	____	____
23. Feel very comfortable touching others, hugging, hand-shaking, etc.	____	____	____
24. Follow oral directions better than written ones.	____	____	____

Scoring Procedures

Score 5 points for each OFTEN, 3 points for each SOMETIMES, and 1 point for each SELDOM.

Visual Preference Score 5 Points for questions 2 + 3 + 7 + 10 + 14 + 16 + 19 + 22   = ____

Auditory Preference Score 5 Points for questions 1 + 5 + 8 + 11 + 13 + 18 + 21 + 24   = ____

Tactile Preference Score 5 Points for questions 4 + 6 + 9 + 12 + 15 + 17 + 20 + 23   = ____

SOURCE: Adapted from J. N. Gardner and A. J. Jewler, *Your College Experience: Strategies for Success, Third Concise Edition* (Belmont, Calif.: Wadsworth/ITP, 1998), pp. 62–63; E. Jensen, *Student Success Secrets*, 4th ed. (Hauppauge, N.Y.: Barron's, 1996), 33–36.

Objective Knowledge

Objective knowledge, in any field of study, is developed through basic and applied research. Research in organizational behavior has continued since early research on scientific management. Acquiring objective knowledge requires the cognitive mastery of theories, conceptual models, and research findings. In this book, the objective knowledge in each chapter is reflected in the notes that support the text and in the Science feature included in each chapter. Mastering the concepts and ideas that come from these notes enables you to intelligently discuss topics such as motivation, performance, leadership,[58] and executive stress.[59]

We encourage instructors and students of organizational behavior to think critically about the objective knowledge in organizational behavior. Only by engaging in critical thinking can one question or challenge the results of specific research and responsibly consider how to apply research results in a particular work setting. Rote memorization does not enable the student to appreciate the complexity of specific theories or the interrelationships among concepts, ideas, and topics. Good critical thinking, in contrast, enables the student to identify inconsistencies and limitations in the current body of objective knowledge.

Critical thinking, based on knowledge and understanding of basic ideas, leads to inquisitive exploration and is a key to accepting the responsibility of coproducer in the learning process. A questioning, probing attitude is at the core of critical thinking. The student of organizational behavior should evolve into a critical consumer of knowledge related to organizational behavior—one who is able to intelligently question the latest research results and distinguish plausible, sound new approaches from fads that lack substance or adequate foundation. Ideally, the student of organizational behavior develops into a scientific professional manager who is knowledgeable in the art and science of organizational behavior.

Skill Development

Learning about organizational behavior requires doing as well as knowing. The development of skills and abilities requires that students be challenged by the instructor and by themselves. Skill development is a very active component of the learning process. The You features in each chapter give you a chance to learn about yourself, challenge yourself, and developmentally apply what you are learning.

The U.S. Department of Labor wants people to achieve the necessary skills to be successful in the workplace.[60] The essential skills identified by the Department of Labor are (1) resource management skills, such as time management; (2) information management skills, such as data interpretation; (3) personal interaction skills, such as teamwork; (4) systems behavior and performance skills, such as cause–effect relationships; and (5) technology utilization skills, such as troubleshooting. Many of these skills, such as decision making and information management, are directly related to the study of organizational behavior.[61]

Developing skills is different from acquiring objective knowledge in that it requires structured practice and feedback. A key function of experiential learning is to engage the student in individual or group activities that are systematically reviewed, leading to new skills and understandings. Objective knowledge acquisition and skill development are interrelated. The process for learning from structured or experiential activities is depicted in Figure 1.5. The student engages in an individual or group-structured activity and systematically reviews that activity, which leads to new or modified knowledge and skills.

FIGURE 1.5 Learning from Structured Activity

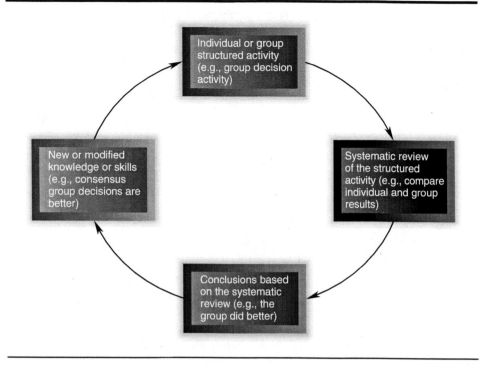

If skill development and structured learning occur in this way, there should be an inherently self-correcting element to learning because of the modification of the student's knowledge and skills over time.[62] To ensure that skill development does occur and that the learning is self-correcting as it occurs, three basic assumptions that underlie the previous model must be followed.

First, each student must accept responsibility for his or her own behavior, actions, and learning. This is a key to the coproducer role in the learning process. A group cannot learn for its members. Each member must accept responsibility for what he or she does and learns. Denial of responsibility helps no one, least of all the learner.

Second, each student must actively participate in the individual or group-structured learning activity. Structured learning is an active process. In group activities, everyone suffers if just one person adopts a passive attitude. Hence, all must actively participate.

Third, each student must be open to new information, new skills, new ideas, and experimentation. This does not mean that students should be indiscriminate. It does mean that they should have a nondefensive, open attitude so that change is possible through the learning process.

Participating in group activities helps to ensure skill development and that learning is self-correcting as it occurs.

Application of Knowledge and Skills

The Real World features in each chapter give you a window into organizational realities and help you assess your own knowledge of the real world at work. Understanding the real world is one essential aspect of appreciating organizational behavior, the other two being understanding scientific knowledge and understanding yourself.

One of the advantages of structured, experiential learning is that a person can explore new behaviors and skills in a comparatively safe environment. Losing your temper in a classroom activity and learning about the potential adverse impact on other people will have dramatically different consequences from doing so with an important customer in a tense work situation. Learning spaces that encourage the interface of student learning styles with institutional learning environments create safe spaces to engage the brain to form abstract hypotheses, to actively test these hypotheses through concrete experience, and to reflectively observe the outcomes in behavior and experience.[63] The ultimate objective of skill application and experiential learning is that students be able to transfer the learning process they employed in structured classroom activities and learning spaces to unstructured opportunities in the workplace.

Although organizational behavior is an applied discipline, students are not "trained" in organizational behavior. Rather, they are "educated" in organizational behavior and are a coproducer in learning. The distinction between these two modes of learning is found in the degree of direct and immediate applicability of either knowledge or skills. As an activity, training more nearly ties direct objective knowledge or skill development to specific applications. By contrast, education enhances a person's residual pool of objective knowledge and skills that may then be selectively applied later—sometimes significantly later—when the opportunity presents itself. Hence, education is highly consistent with the concept of lifelong learning. Especially in a growing area of knowledge such as organizational behavior, the student can think of the first course as the outset of lifelong learning about the topics and subject.

PLAN FOR THE BOOK

Challenge and opportunity are watchwords in organizations during these changing times. Managers and employees alike are challenged to meet change in positive and optimistic ways: change in how work gets done, change in psychological and legal contracts between individuals and organizations, change in who is working in the organization, and change in the basis for organization. Four challenges for managers are the global environment, workplace diversity, ethical issues at work, and technological innovation. These four challenges, which are discussed in detail in Chapter 2, are shaping the changes occurring in organizations throughout the world. For example, the increasing globalization of business has led to intense international competition in core industries, and the changing demographics of the workplace have led to gender, age, racial, and ethnic diversity among working populations.

The first two chapters compose Part 1 of the book, the introduction. Against the backdrop of the challenges discussed here, we develop and explore the specific subjects in organizational behavior. In addition to the introduction, the text has three major parts. Part 2 addresses individual processes and behavior. Part 3 addresses interpersonal processes and behavior. Part 4 addresses organizational processes and structure.

The five chapters in Part 2 are designed to help the reader understand specific aspects of human behavior. Chapter 3 discusses personality, perception, and attribution. Chapter 4 examines attitudes, values, and ethics. What was your attitude toward change in You 1.1? Chapters 5 and 6 address the broad range of motivational theories, learning, and performance management in organizations. Finally, Chapter 7 considers stress and well-being, including healthy aspects of life, at work.

Part 3 is composed of six chapters designed to help the reader better understand interpersonal and group dynamics in organizations. Chapter 8 addresses communication in organizations. Chapter 9 focuses on teamwork and groups as an increasingly prominent feature of the workplace. Chapter 10 examines how individuals and groups make decisions. Chapter 11 is about power and politics, one very dynamic aspect of organizational life. Chapter 12 addresses the companion topics of leadership and followership. Finally, Chapter 13 examines conflict at work, not all of which we consider bad.

The five chapters in Part 4 are designed to help the reader better understand organizational processes and the organizational context of behavior at work. Chapter 14 examines traditional and contemporary approaches to job design. Chapter 15 develops the topics of organizational design and structure, giving special attention to contemporary forces reshaping organizations and to emerging forms of organization. Chapter 16 addresses the culture of the organization. Chapter 17 focuses on the important issue of career management. Finally, Chapter 18 brings closure to the text and the main theme of change by addressing the topic of managing change.

MANAGERIAL IMPLICATIONS: FOUNDATIONS FOR THE FUTURE

Managers must consider personal and environmental factors to understand fully how people behave in organizations and to help them reach their maximum potential. Human behavior is complex and at times confusing. Characteristics of the organizational system and formal–informal dynamics at work are important environmental factors that influence people's behavior. Managers should look for similarities and differences in manufacturing, service-oriented, nonprofit, and governmental organizations.

Change may be seen as a threat or as an opportunity by contemporary managers. For example, hospital managers face not only clinical challenges but also organizational learning and the implementation of effective high involvement management practices with a professional workforce.[64] Changing customer demands for high-quality outputs in other industries challenges companies to beat the global competition. Globalization, workforce diversity, ethics, and technology are four challenges for managers that are developed in Chapter 2. Another aspect of meeting the competition is learning. Managers must continually upgrade their knowledge about all aspects of their businesses, to include especially the human side of the enterprise. They must hone both their technical and interpersonal skills, engaging in a lifelong educational process. This is a fun and somewhat unpredictable process that can at times be frustrating, while always challenging and exciting.

Several business trends and ongoing changes are affecting managers across the globe. These include continuing industrial restructuring, a dramatic increase in the amount and availability of information, a need to attract and retain the best employees, a need to understand a wide range of human and cultural differences, and a rapid shortening of response times in all aspects of business activities. Further, the old company towns are largely relics of the past, and managers are being called on to reintegrate their businesses with communities, cultures, and societies at a much broader level than has ever been required before. Trust, predictability, and a sense of security become important issues in this context. Reweaving the fabric of human relationships within, across, and outside the organization is a challenge for managers today.

Knowledge becomes power in tracking these trends and addressing these issues. Facts and information are two elements of knowledge in this context. Theories are a third element of a manager's knowledge base. Good theories are tools that help managers understand human and organizational behavior, help them make good business decisions, and inform them about actions to take or to refrain from taking. Managers always use theories, if not those generated from systematic research, then those evolved from the manager's implicit observation. Theories tell us how organizations, business, and people work—or do not work. Therefore, the student is challenged to master the theories in each topic area, and then apply and test the theory in the real world of organizational life. The challenge for the student and the manager is to see what works and what does not work in their specific work context.

LOOKING BACK: CARIBOU COFFEE

Winning the Experience Game

Consumer Reports rated Caribou Coffee's brew higher than their chief competitor's coffee in 2004, giving Caribou an argument that they offer better coffee. That is not their main claim to fame in the competition. Caribou believes that they offer a more inviting atmosphere and a broader lineup of coffee than does Starbucks. Caribou CEO Coles is clear that his company is not aiming to compete for location. They do not intend to have as many locations as Starbucks. However, this does not mean that Caribou does not plan to grow. It plans to open franchises in the United States as well as other countries. By 2014 Caribou expects to double the size of their chain and have 1,000 locations. This is still less than 10 percent of their chief competitor's base.

There are four dimensions of experience in which Caribou takes direct aim at its chief competitor to win the hearts of its customers.[65] These are the Internet, square tables, customer names, and coffee selection. Free wireless Internet service is a positive draw for the company, enabling every customer who wants to stay connected during a coffee break to do so. A stop at Caribou Coffee may be more than a coffee break, too. The company plans to stay with square tables and not go to the round ones of its chief competitor. This makes it possible to shuffle a couple or more together and have a meeting of the minds at Caribou, not just a coffee break on the Internet. The average Caribou customer visits one of its locations between three and five times per week. Hence, Caribou employees are expected to learn either a customer's name or drink by the second or third visit.

Winning in very competitive industries is challenging, hard, risky work to do. Setbacks occur too, and Caribou is still not a highly profitable business. In fact, the company continues to operate at a loss. However, they are in a booming industry of coffeehouses nationally, which is cause for optimism for the long term. Initially, the company underestimated how many new products would have to be launched to move ahead in the game, so for 2007 they plan to double the number of new product rollouts. Having large, strong, strategic partners helps, too. Caribou is partnering with Atlanta-based Coke to roll out a new iced coffee drink. Thus, being number one in experience does not mean ignoring size altogether.

Chapter Summary

1. Organizational behavior is individual behavior and group dynamics in organizations.

2. Change is an opportunity when one has a positive attitude, asks questions, listens, and is committed to succeed.

3. Organizations are open systems composed of people, structure, and technology committed to a task.

4. Organizations have formal and informal elements within them.

5. Manufacturing organizations, service organizations, privately owned companies, and nonprofit organizations all contribute to our national well-being.

6. The changes and challenges facing managers are driven by international competition and customer demands.

7. Learning about organizational behavior requires a mastery of objective knowledge, specific skill development, and thoughtful application.

Key Terms

anthropology (p. 6)
challenge (p. 4)
change (p. 4)
engineering (p. 6)
formal organization (p. 9)
Hawthorne studies (p. 9)
informal organization (p. 9)

management (p. 6)
medicine (p. 6)
objective knowledge (p. 19)
opportunities (p. 4)
organizational behavior (p. 4)
people (p. 8)
psychology (p. 5)

Six Sigma (p. 17)
skill development (p. 19)
sociology (p. 6)
structure (p. 8)
task (p. 8)
technology (p. 8)

Review Questions

1. Define *organizational behavior*. What is its focus?

2. Identify the four action steps for responding positively to change.

3. What is an organization? What are its four system components? Give an example of each.

4. Briefly describe the elements of the formal and the informal organization. Give examples of each.

5. Discuss the six focus organizations used in the book.

6. Describe how competition and total quality are affecting organizational behavior. Why is managing organizational behavior in changing times challenging?

Discussion and Communication Questions

1. How do the formal aspects of your work environment affect you? What informal aspects of your work environment are important?

2. What is the biggest competitive challenge or change facing the businesses in your industry today? Will that be different in the next five years?

3. Describe the next chief executive of your company and what she or he must do to succeed.

4. Discuss two ways people learn about organizational behavior.

5. Which of the focus companies is your own company most like? Do you work for one of these focus companies? Which company would you most like to work for?

6. *(communication question)* Prepare a memo about an organizational change occurring where you work or in your college or university. Write a 100-word description of the change and, using Figure 1.1, identify how it is affecting the people, structure, task, and/or technology of the organization.

7. *(communication question)* Develop an oral presentation about the changes and challenges facing your college or university based on an interview with a faculty member or administrator. Be prepared to describe the changes and challenges. Are these good or bad changes? Why?

8. *(communication question)* Prepare a brief description of a service or manufacturing company, entrepreneurial venture, or nonprofit organization of your choice. Go to the library and read about the organization from several sources; then use these multiple sources to write your description.

Ethical Dilemma

The afternoon was as gloomy as Brian's mood. It had not been a very productive day. All Brian could think about was the decision before him. He found the current situation interesting in that he had never before struggled with decisions. In the past, he had always been able to make quick and good decisions. His gut gave him the answer and he trusted his instincts. This time he felt nothing, and he was unsure how to proceed without that guiding force.

Brian Cowell was 62 years old and the CEO of Data Solutions, a company he had run for the last 20 years. Brian had been very successful at the helm. Data Solutions had grown from a small data processing business to one of the largest employers in the area. Brian's good instincts had guided them through the challenging times of the '80s and '90s, and the company was in just the right place to meet the challenges ahead. Or was it? This was the question that plagued Brian.

Changes in technology were providing some interesting possibilities for the future. A part of Brian said that he needed to step up and lead Data Solutions into the global environment. He could do that and continue the growth he had begun so many years ago. That was a big step and would take Brian down a very challenging road. The other option was to continue on the company's current path. Not a bad one; the company had its most profitable year last year and everyone was very happy. Deep inside, Brian knew the answer: move the company forward to the next logical step, globalization. But he was tired and really wanted to spend his last years at Data Solutions reaping the benefits of his hard work, not gearing up for the biggest challenge of his career. Didn't he deserve the right to enjoy his final years at the company he built?

Questions

1. Does Brian have an obligation to lead the company to globalization?
2. What is Brian's responsibility to himself and his family?
3. Consider Brian's decision in light of consequential, rule-based, and character theories.

Experiential Exercises

1.1 What's Changing at Work?

This exercise provides an opportunity to discuss changes occurring in your workplace and university. These changes may be for the better or the worse. However, rather than evaluating whether they are good or bad changes, begin by simply identifying the changes that are occurring. Later, you can evaluate whether they are good or bad.

Step 1. The class forms into groups of approximately six members each. Each group elects a spokesperson and answers the following questions. The group should spend at least five minutes on each question. Make sure that each member of the group makes a contribution to each question. The spokesperson for each group should be ready to share the group's collective responses.

a. *What are the changes occurring in your workplace and university?* Members should focus both on internal changes, such as reorganizations, and on external changes, such as new customers or competitors. Develop a list of the changes discussed in your group.

b. *What are the forces that are driving the changes?* To answer this question, look for the causes of the changes members of the group are observing. For example, a reorganization may be caused by new business opportunities, by new technologies, or by a combination of factors.

c. *What signs of resistance to change do you see occurring?* Change is not always easy for people or organizations. Do you see signs of resistance, such as frustration, anger, increased absences, or other forms of discomfort with the changes you observe?

Step 2. Once you have answered the three questions in Step 1, your group needs to spend some time evaluating whether these changes are good or bad. Decide whether each change on the list developed in Step 1a is good or bad. In addition, answer the question "Why?" That is, why is this change good? Why is that change bad?

Step 3. Each group shares the results of its answers to the questions in Step 1 and its evaluation of the changes completed in Step 2. Cross-team questions and discussion follow.

Step 4. Your instructor may allow a few minutes at the end of the class period to comment on his or her perceptions of changes occurring within the university, or businesses with which he or she is familiar.

1.2 My Absolute Worst Job

Purpose: To become acquainted with fellow classmates.
Group size: Any number of groups of two.
Exercise schedule:

1. Write answers to the following questions:

   a. What was the worst job you ever had? Describe the following:

      (1) The type of work you did

      (2) Your boss

      (3) Your coworkers

      (4) The organization and its policies

      (5) What made the job so bad

   b. What is your dream job?

2. Find someone you do not know, and share your responses.

3. Get together with another dyad (pair), preferably new people. Partner "a" of one dyad introduces partner "b" to the other dyad; then "b" introduces "a." The same process is followed by the other dyad. The introduction should follow this format: "This is Mary Cullen. Her very worst job was putting appliqués on bibs at a clothing factory, and she disliked it for the following reason. What she would rather do is be a financial analyst for a big corporation."

4. Each group of four meets with another quartet and is introduced, as before.

5. Your instructor asks for a show of hands on the number of people whose worst jobs fit into the following categories:

   a. Factory

   b. Restaurant

   c. Manual labor

   d. Driving or delivery

   e. Professional

   f. Health care

   g. Phone sales or communication

   h. Other

6. Your instructor gathers data on worst jobs from each group and asks the groups to answer these questions:

   a. What are the common characteristics of the worst jobs in your group?

   b. How did your coworkers feel about their jobs?

   c. What happens to morale and productivity when a worker hates the job?

   d. What was the difference between your own morale and productivity in your worst job and in a job you really enjoyed?

   e. Why do organizations continue to allow unpleasant working conditions to exist?

7. Your instructor leads a group discussion on Parts (a) through (e) of Question 6.

Biz Flix | 8 Mile

Jimmy "B-Rabbit" Smith, Jr., (Eminem) wants to succeed as a rapper and to prove that a white man can create moving sounds. His job at the North Detroit Stamping (NDS) plant fills his days while he pursues his music at night—and sometimes on the plant's grounds. The film's title refers to Detroit's northern city boundary, well known to local people. *8 Mile* is a gritty look at Detroit's hip-hop culture in 1995 and Jimmy's desire for acceptance by it. Eminem's original songs, "Lose Yourself" and "8 Mile," received several award nominations. "Lose Yourself" won the 2003 Academy Award for best original song.

The scene has two parts. It is an edited composite of two brief NDS plant sequences that appear in different places in the film. Part I of the scene appears early in the film in the sequence "The Franchise." Part II appears in the last twenty-five minutes of the film in the "Papa Doc Payback" sequence. Jimmy arrives late for work in the first part of the scene, after riding the city bus because his car did not start. The second part occurs after his beating by Papa Doc (Anthony Mackie) and Papa Doc's gang. The film continues to its end with Jimmy's last battle (a rapper competition).

What to Watch for and Ask Yourself:

> What is your perception of the quality of Jimmy's job and his work environment?
> What is the quality of Jimmy's relationship with Manny (Paul Bates), his foreman? Does it change? If it does, why?
> How would you react to this type of work experience?

Workplace Video | Managerial and Quality Control at Honda

When Honda announced in 1982 that it was building its first auto assembly plant in North America, many analysts felt that American labor could not produce the same quality automobiles as the Japanese. Quality had been a strategic focus of Japanese manufacturers since World War II, and automakers like Honda and Toyota were undisputed leaders of Japan's quality movement. Confident that American workers could produce award-winning Civics and Accords, Honda moved ahead with its plans and became the first Japanese company to establish manufacturing operations in the United States.

Relocating to North America was nearly inevitable for Honda's manufacturing division. Turbulent changes in the global economic environment had put a financial squeeze on the automaker, and moving overseas was the only way it could reduce transportation costs and counter unfavorable exchange rates, which had raised the price of materials in Japan.

Change proved favorable. Despite the cultural challenges involved in transplanting Japanese manufacturing methods to the United States, Honda's North American facilities have attained remarkable efficiency. Sam Kennedy, associate chief inspecting engineer at Honda, uses quality circles, statistical process control, and weekly managers' meetings to establish a culture of continuous improvement at Honda's Marysville, Ohio, plant. For

Kennedy, quality management means taking a proactive approach to problem solving. "If you simply wait and react to a problem," the inspection chief remarks, "you're going to be dealing with nothing but problems."

Honda's preventative approach to quality is apparent throughout the assembly process. The paint department, for example, places white protective film over vehicle frames to prevent assembly-line workers from chipping and scratching paint while installing parts and components. Likewise, Honda's welding zone, a bustling area formerly occupied by human workers, is now filled with speedy high-precision robots that make millions of welds but few errors. According to Kennedy, Honda's high-tech welding zone is emblematic of Honda's commitment to quality: "We have improved the accuracy of our product and the consistency of the product, which is really what quality is all about."

Discussion Questions

1. What opportunities and challenges would you expect Honda to encounter as a result of establishing manufacturing facilities in the United States?

2. What are some managerial techniques that help Honda's workers achieve higher quality and efficiency in their production tasks?

3. How might changes associated with Honda's move to the United States affect the behavior of plant workers and managers?

Johnson & Johnson:
Using a Credo for Business Guidance

Johnson & Johnson, founded by Robert Wood Johnson and his brothers James and Mead in 1886, has grown into the world's most comprehensive manufacturer of health care products and related services for the consumer, pharmaceutical, and medical devices and diagnostics markets. Today, Johnson & Johnson consists of more than 250 operating companies, employing approximately 121,000 employees, with more than 50,000 of those in the United States. The company has operations in 57 nations and sells products all around the world.[1] Product categories include, but are not limited to: allergy, colds, and flu; baby care; cardiology; dental care; diabetes care; first aid; medical devices and diagnostics; oncology; prescription drugs; skin and hair care; and vision care.[2] The company's sales have increased every year for since 1946, and in 2006, global sales were $53.9 billion and net earnings were $11.1 billion.[3] Moreover, Johnson & Johnson was ranked ninth on *Fortune's* 2006 "America's Most Admired Companies" list and fourth on the magazine's 2006 "Global Most Admired Companies."[4]

The worldwide success of Johnson & Johnson is widely attributed to an unwavering commitment to a business philosophy that puts customers first and stockholders last. Robert Wood Johnson II first articulated this philosophy in 1943; it was called the *Johnson & Johnson Credo*.[5] Like his father before him, Robert Wood Johnson II could be dogmatic, autocratic, and prone to micromanagement. Yet he was not inflexible; in fact, he encouraged innovation in every part of the company. There was, however, one thing about him that was inflexible—adherence to the Johnson & Johnson Credo. Even after the company went from being family owned to having public ownership and trading of its stock in the early 1960s, the Johnson & Johnson Credo has provided fundamental managerial and operational guidance to which the company has unwaveringly adhered.[6]

The key points of the Johnson & Johnson Credo address the company's four responsibilities. In descending order of emphasis, these responsibilities may be summarized as follows:

> The company's first responsibility is to meet the needs of everyone—doctors, nurses, patients, mothers, fathers, and others—who use its products. Johnson & Johnson does this by providing quality products that are reasonably priced, and by ensuring that suppliers and distributors have the opportunity to make a fair profit.

> The company's second responsibility is to its employees throughout the world, treating them fairly and with dignity, seeking to involve them, and providing them with competent and ethical management.

> The company's third responsibility is to the various communities where it operates, seeking to improve those communities and sharing in the burden of such improvements.

> The company's last responsibility is to the stockholders, seeking to make a sound profit in order to provide a fair return to the owners and to enable the company to innovate and grow so that fair returns are maintained in the future.[7]

The full credo was in a format that people could understand, and Robert Wood Johnson II demanded that people follow it. Very importantly, the company created appropriate organizational mechanisms to bring the credo to life, and to support and reinforce it. The credo "may sound a bit corny—and so may J&J's devotion to it: It's posted in every J&J facility around the world and carved in an eight-foot chunk of limestone at company headquarters in New Brunswick, N.J. But Johnson made sure everyone bought into it."[8]

The credo has served the company well during normal operating conditions and in times of crisis, such as in 1982 and 1986 when the Tylenol® acetaminophen product was adulterated with cyanide and used as a murder weapon. During the

Tylenol crises, Johnson & Johnson's "managers and employees made countless decisions that were inspired by the philosophy embedded in the credo."[9] Tylenol was immediately cleared from store shelves, and the company was very proactive and open in addressing each crisis. As a result, J&J's good reputation was maintained and the Tylenol business was reinvigorated.

The Johnson & Johnson Credo continues to guide the company's decisions and actions regarding its responsibilities to customers, employees, the community, and stockholders. The credo guides the company's operations in Africa, Asia and the Pacific Rim, Eastern and Western Europe, Latin America, the Middle East, and North America.[10] Ralph Larsen, a former chief executive officer of Johnson & Johnson, maintains that the credo provides a constant source of guidance for the company and that it is the foundation for everything the company does.[11] Although the credo has been revised and updated at different points throughout its existence, the essential responsibilities endure.[12] To help ensure the credo's continuing viability, Johnson & Johnson employees periodically participate in a survey to evaluate how the company performs its responsibilities.[13]

Discussion Questions

1. From your perspective, what role(s) should business play in the contemporary world?

2. What implications does the credo have for Johnson & Johnson's view of the role(s) it should play in the contemporary world?

3. What implications does the credo have for the attitudes and job behavior of the company's employees?

4. Would you like to work for a company like Johnson & Johnson? Why or why not?

SOURCE: This case was written by Michael K. McCuddy, The Louis S. and Mary L. Morgal Chair of Christian Business Ethics and Professor of Management, College of Business Administration, Valparaiso University.

Challenges for Managers

After reading this chapter, you should be able to do the following:

1 Describe the dimensions of cultural differences in societies that affect work-related attitudes.

2 Explain the social and demographic changes that are producing diversity in organizations.

3 Describe actions managers can take to help their employees value diversity.

4 Discuss the assumptions of consequential, rule-based, and character theories of ethics.

5 Explain six issues that pose ethical dilemmas for managers.

6 Understand the alternative work arrangements produced by technological advances.

7 Explain the ways managers can help employees adjust to technological change.

THINKING AHEAD: GENENTECH, INC.

Do Business and Science Mix?

Genentech, Inc. is the world's foremost biotechnology company and a leader in nurturing a culture of creativity. This combination has put the company in the top 25 most innovative companies along with Intel Corp. and GE. According to Chairman and Chief Executive Arthur Levinson, you can make it really complicated or really simple. Genentech does it simply; it hires innovative people, listens to them, and then does what they suggest. The company uses a unique approach to attracting and cultivating the best scientists to attain success in the world of business.[1]

First and foremost, Genentech is committed to doing great science. If a drug cannot be first in class or best in class, they do not pursue it. They do not work to achieve incremental advances or extend patents unless it is going to really matter to patients. Their most talented scientists are thus encouraged to do important basic and translational research.

Second, the company decided in the early 1990s that they would be committed to oncology, which at the time was new for them. By 2007 they were the leading producer of anticancer drugs in the United States. They did take a lot of risks, many of which paid off. That is a central tenet in business; knowing the right risks to take and then working extremely hard and wisely to make the risk pay off. The company has now broadened into immunology, where the role of management is to set broad direction, and then hire the best scientists, and to tell them: "Do your stuff." But there are always trade-offs in the short term between the cancer patient who needs treatment now and the immunology patient who needs long-term defense.

Third, Genentech places a huge emphasis on making the company a great place to work. In the late 1990s, it did not appear in the many lists of the best places to work. This led the company to begin employee surveys that asked some key questions: What do you like about the company? More importantly, what don't you like? What bothers you? By listening to employees and then taking action, Genentech management led the company to *Fortune*'s Top 20 list four years in a row. The firm was number one in 2006 and number two in 2007, just behind Google Inc. Genentech operates in the new industrial technology arena of biotechnology and has successfully mixed business with science. The company cannot do everything for everyone, so how do they address the ethical trade-offs?

MANAGEMENT CHALLENGES IN A NEW TIME

Most U.S. executives continue to believe that U.S. firms are encountering unprecedented global competition.[2] Globalization is being driven on the one hand by the spread of economic logics centered on freeing, opening, deregulating, and privatizing economies to make them more attractive for investment and, on the other hand, by the digitization of technologies that is revolutionizing communication.[3] The challenges for managers in this context are manifest in both opportunities and threats, as briefly touched upon in Chapter 1. The long, robust economic expansion in the United States during the 1990s led to a bubble that burst and several years of economic difficulty. Managers are challenged to lead people in the good times and the bad times, as Anne Mulcahy did in addressing Xerox's financial difficulties, because business cycles ultimately produce both. Over time, managers face both opportunities and threats.

What major challenges must managers overcome in order to remain competitive? Chief executive officers of U.S. corporations cite four issues that are paramount: (1) globalizing the firm's operations to compete in the global village; (2) leading a diverse workforce; (3) encouraging positive ethics, character, and personal integrity; and (4) advancing and implementing technological innovation in the workplace.[4,5]

Successful organizations and managers respond to these four challenges as opportunities rather than as threats. Our six focus companies—Caribou Coffee, Genentech, American Express, Toyota Motor Corporation, Timberland, and Google—and their managers have wrestled with one or more of these four challenges as they pursue success and achievement. We see in the Looking Back feature that some of the trade-offs that companies like Genentech face are not simple ethical dilemmas with simple solutions. While Caribou Coffee, as we detailed in Chapter 1, wanted to be number one in experience, Genentech's industry offers a different challenge. In this chapter, we focus on these four challenges that, when well managed, lead to success and healthy organizational outcomes.

Globalization has led to the emergence of the global village in the world economy. The Internet, along with rapid political and social changes, has broken down old national barriers to competition. What has emerged is a world characterized by an ongoing process of integration and interconnection of states, markets, technologies, and firms. This world as a global macroeconomic village is a boundaryless market in which all firms, large and small, must compete.[6]

Managing a diverse workforce is something organizations like Alcon Laboratories and Coors Brewing Company do extremely well. Both companies reap success from their efforts. The workforce of today is more diverse than ever before. Managers are challenged to bring together employees of different backgrounds in work teams. This requires going beyond the surface to deep-level diversity.[7]

Good character, ethical behavior, and *personal integrity* are hallmarks of managers in organizations like Johnson & Johnson. The company's credo guides employee behavior and has helped employees do the right thing in tough situations. Ethical behavior in business has been at the forefront of public consciousness for some time now. Insider trading scandals, influence peddling, and contract frauds are in the news daily. It need not be that way. Many executives lead with a spirit of personal integrity.[8]

Technological innovation is one of the keys to strategic competitiveness. Imagine yourself as a small business owner of a package delivery firm. You'll be competing with FedEx, which owns the most technologically advanced package tracking and delivery system in the world. Would you be able to compete? Technological change can be complex and risky. It may also create ethical dilemmas, as in the case of Genentech's biotechnology advances.

Organizations and managers who see opportunity in these four challenges will remain competitive, rather than just survive, in today's turbulent environment. Throughout the book, you'll see how organizational behavior can contribute to successfully managing the challenges.

THE GLOBAL VILLAGE

Only a few years ago, business conducted across national borders was referred to as "international" activity. The word *international* carries with it a connotation that the individual's or the organization's nationality is held strongly in consciousness.[9] *Globalization,* in contrast, implies that the world is free from national boundaries and that it is really a borderless world.[10] U.S. workers are now competing with workers in other countries. Foreign-based organizations are locating subsidiaries in the United States, such as the U.S. manufacturing locations of Honda, Toyota, Mazda, and Mercedes. The reverse is true as well, as we see in The Real World 2.1, which shows how Volkswagen's German workers had to come to grips with globalization.

Similarly, what were once referred to as multinational organizations (those doing business in several countries) are now called transnational companies. In *transnational organizations,* the global viewpoint supersedes national issues.[11] Transnational organizations operate over large global distances and are multicultural in terms of the people they employ. 3M, Dow Chemical, Coca-Cola, and other transnational organizations operate worldwide with diverse employee populations.

Changes in the Global Marketplace

Social and political upheavals have led organizations to change the way they conduct business and to encourage their members to think globally. Toyota is one Japanese company thinking big, thinking globally, and thinking differently by learning to speak to the 60-million-strong Generation Y, or millennials.[12] The collapse of Eastern Europe was followed quickly by the demise of the Berlin Wall. East and West

transnational organization
An organization in which the global viewpoint supersedes national issues.

Globalization Comes to Wolfsburg, Germany

Wolfsburg, Germany, is the home of Volkswagen (VW), Europe's largest automaker, and has a population of 125,000. Actually, VW has prospered greatly from globalization throughout its history, which began in 1938 when the town was formed with the mission to manufacture an affordable "people's car." After World War II, the company churned out millions of Beetles and exported them to every continent except Antarctica. The postwar years were a globalization boom for the company. By the early 2000s, it was saddled with some of the highest labor costs in the world, with factory employees generally working four-day weeks and earning as much as $50 per hour. The company was forced to slash 20,000 jobs and faced the prospect of being taken over by an international hedge fund or merge with an Asian competitor. Waves of panic swept through Wolfsburg. By 2007, however, the mood was good according to Hartmut Meine, a district manager for IG Metal, the metalworkers' union that represents 97 percent of VW's German employees. Negotiations have led to a pact that includes no more job cuts before 2011 in exchange for wage freezes and longer workweeks. The company is ramping up production on its all-time best-selling car, the Golf, and expecting a pretax profit of more than $6 billion for 2007. Thus, VW is doing well in the global automotive shakeout that has devastated the U.S. auto industry.

SOURCE: C. Whitlock, "VW's Home Town Finds Ways to Cope with Globalization," *The Washington Post* (June 5, 2007): A10.

Germany were united into a single country. In the Soviet Union, perestroika led to liberation and brought about many opportunities for U.S. businesses, as witnessed by the press releases showing extremely long waiting lines at Moscow's first McDonald's restaurant.

Business ventures in China have become increasingly attractive to U.S. companies. Coca-Cola has led the way. One challenge U.S. managers have faced is understanding the Chinese way of doing business. Chinese managers' business practices have been shaped by the Communist Party, socialism, feudalistic values, and *guanxi* (building networks for social exchange). Once *guanxi* is established, individuals can ask favors of each other with the expectation that the favor will be returned. For example, it is common in China to use *guanxi* to conduct business or to obtain jobs. *Guanxi* is sometimes a sensitive word, because Communist Party policies oppose the use of such practices to gain influence. In China, the family is regarded as being responsible for a worker's productivity, and in turn, the company is responsible for the worker's family. Because of socialism, Chinese managers have very little experience with rewards and punishments and are reluctant to use them in the workplace. The concept of *guanxi* is not unique to China. There are similar concepts in many other countries, including Russia and Haiti. It is a broad term that can mean anything from strongly loyal relationships to ceremonial gift-giving, sometimes seen as bribery. *Guanxi* is more common in societies with underdeveloped legal support for private businesses.[13]

To work with Chinese managers, Americans can learn to build their own *guanxi*; understand the Chinese chain of command; and negotiate slow, general agreements in order to interact effectively. Using the foreign government as the local franchisee may be effective in China. For example, KFC Corporation's operation in China is a joint venture between KFC (60 percent) and two Chinese government bodies (40 percent).[14]

guanxi
The Chinese practice of building networks for social exchange.

© AP PHOTO/GREG BAKER

One challenge that U.S. managers pursuing business ventures in China face is understanding the Chinese way of doing business.

In 1993, the European Union integrated fifteen nations into a single market by removing trade barriers. At that time, the member nations of the European Union were Belgium, Denmark, France, Germany, Greece, Ireland, Italy, Luxembourg, the Netherlands, Portugal, Spain, Austria, Finland, Sweden, and the United Kingdom. As of 2004, Estonia, Hungary, Latvia, Lithuania, Malta, Poland, Slovakia, and Slovenia were also members. The integration of Europe provides many opportunities for U.S. organizations, including 350 million potential customers. Companies like Ford Motor Company and IBM, which entered the market early with wholly owned subsidiaries, will have a head start on these opportunities.[15] Competition within the European Union will increase, however, as will competition from Japan and the former Soviet nations.

The United States, Canada, and Mexico have dramatically reduced trade barriers in accordance with the North American Free Trade Agreement (NAFTA), which took effect in 1994. Organizations have found promising new markets for their products, and many companies have located plants in Mexico to take advantage of low labor costs. DaimlerChrysler, for example, has a massive assembly plant in Saltillo. Prior to NAFTA, Mexico placed heavy tariffs on U.S. exports. The agreement immediately eliminated many of these tariffs and provided that the remaining tariffs be phased out over time.

All of these changes have brought about the need to think globally. Managers can benefit from global thinking by taking a long-term view. Entry into global markets requires long-term strategies.

Understanding Cultural Differences

One of the keys for any company competing in the global marketplace is to understand diverse cultures. Whether managing culturally diverse individuals within a single location or managing individuals at remote locations around the globe, an appreciation of the differences among cultures is crucial. Edgar Schein suggests that to understand an organization's culture, or more broadly any culture, it is important to dig below the surface of visible artifacts and uncover the basic underlying assumptions at the core of the culture.[16] His definition of organizational culture is the pattern of basic assumptions that a given group has invented, discovered, or developed in learning to cope with its problems of external adaptation and internal integration, and that have worked well enough to be considered valid. These basic assumptions are then taught to new members as the correct way to perceive, think, and feel in relation to those problems. We develop Schein's culture model of basic assumptions, values, visible artifacts, and creations more fully in Chapter 16.

Microcultural differences (i.e., differences within cultures) can play an important role in understanding the global work environment.[17] Knowing cultural differences in symbols is extremely important. Computer icons may not translate well in other cultures. The thumbs-up sign, for example, means approval in the United States. In Australia, however, it is an obscene gesture. And manila file folders, like the icons used in Windows applications, aren't used in many European countries and therefore aren't recognized.[18]

Do cultural differences translate into differences in work-related attitudes? The pioneering Dutch researcher Geert Hofstede focused on this question.[19] He and his colleagues surveyed 160,000 managers and employees of IBM who were working in 60 different countries.[20] In this way, the researchers were able to study individuals from the same company in the same jobs, but working in different countries. Hofstede's work is important because his studies showed that national culture explains more differences in work-related attitudes than do age, gender, profession, or position within the organization. Thus, cultural differences do affect individuals' work-related attitudes. Hofstede found five dimensions of cultural differences that

1 Describe the dimensions of cultural differences in societies that affect work-related attitudes.

FIGURE 2.1 Hofstede's Dimensions of Cultural Differences

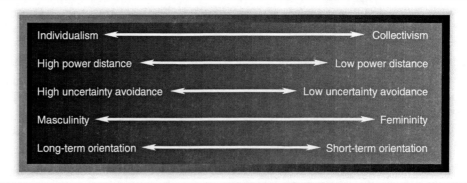

formed the basis for work-related attitudes. These dimensions are shown in Figure 2.1 and are described next.

Individualism versus Collectivism In cultures where *individualism* predominates, people belong to loose social frameworks, but their primary concern is for themselves and their families. People are responsible for taking care of their own interests. They believe that individuals should make decisions. Cultures characterized by *collectivism* are tightly knit social frameworks in which individual members depend strongly on extended families or clans. Group decisions are valued and accepted.

The North American culture is individualistic in orientation. It is a "can-do" culture that values individual freedom and responsibility. In contrast, collectivist cultures emphasize group welfare and harmony. Israeli kibbutzim and Japanese culture are examples of societies in which group loyalty and unity are paramount. Organization charts show these orientations. In Canada and the United States, which are individualistic cultures, organization charts show individual positions. In Malaysia, which is a collectivist culture, organization charts show only sections or departments.

This dimension of cultural differences has other workplace implications. Individualistic managers, as found in Great Britain and the Netherlands, emphasize and encourage individual achievement. In contrast, collectivistic managers, such as in Japan and Colombia, seek to fit harmoniously within the group. They also encourage these behaviors among their employees. Further, there are cultural differences within regions of the world. Arabs are more collectivist than Americans. Within the Arab culture, however, Egyptians are more individualistic than Arabs from the Gulf States (Saudi Arabia, Oman, Bahrain, Kuwait, Qatar, United Arab Emirates). This may be due to the fact that Egyptian businesspeople tend to have longer and more intensive exposures to Western culture.[21]

Power Distance The second dimension of cultural differences examines the acceptance of unequal distribution of power. In countries with a high *power distance*, bosses are afforded more power simply because they are the bosses. Titles are used, formality is the rule, and authority is seldom bypassed. Power holders are entitled to their privileges, and managers and employees see one another as fundamentally

individualism

A cultural orientation in which people belong to loose social frameworks, and their primary concern is for themselves and their families.

collectivism

A cultural orientation in which individuals belong to tightly knit social frameworks, and they depend strongly on large extended families or clans.

power distance

The degree to which a culture accepts unequal distribution of power.

different kinds of people. India is a country with a high power distance, as are Venezuela and Mexico.

In countries with a low power distance, people believe that inequality in society should be minimized. People at various power levels are less threatened by, and more willing to trust, one another. Managers and employees see one another as similar. Managers are given power only if they have expertise. Employees frequently bypass the boss in order to get work done in countries with a low power distance, such as Denmark and Australia.

Uncertainty Avoidance Some cultures are quite comfortable with ambiguity and uncertainty, whereas others do not tolerate these conditions well. Cultures with high *uncertainty avoidance* are concerned with security and tend to avoid conflict. People have a need for consensus. The inherent uncertainty in life is a threat against which people in such cultures constantly struggle.

Cultures with low uncertainty avoidance are more tolerant of ambiguity. People are more willing to take risks and are more tolerant of individual differences. Conflict is seen as constructive, and people accept dissenting viewpoints. Norway and Australia are characterized by low uncertainty avoidance, and this trait is seen in the value placed on job mobility. Japan and Italy are characterized by high uncertainty avoidance, so career stability is emphasized.

Masculinity versus Femininity In cultures that are characterized by *masculinity*, assertiveness and materialism are valued. Men are expected to be assertive, tough, and decisive, and women to be nurturing, modest, and tender.[22] Money and possessions are important, and performance is what counts. Achievement is admired. Cultures that are characterized by *femininity* emphasize relationships and concern for others. Men and women are expected to assume both assertive and nurturing roles. Quality of life is important, and people and the environment are emphasized.

Masculine societies, such as in Austria and Venezuela, define gender roles strictly. Feminine societies, in contrast, tend to blur gender roles. Women may be the providers, and men may stay home with the children. The Scandinavian countries of Norway, Sweden, and Denmark exemplify the feminine orientation.

Time Orientation Cultures also differ in *time orientation;* that is, whether the culture's values are oriented toward the future (long-term orientation) or toward the past and present (short-term orientation).[23] In China, a culture with a long-term orientation, values such as thrift and persistence, which focus on the future, are emphasized. In Russia, the orientation is short-term. Values such as respect for tradition (past) and meeting social obligations (present) are emphasized.

U.S. Culture The position of the United States on these five dimensions is interesting. Hofstede found the United States to be the most individualistic country of any studied. On the power distance dimension, it ranked among the countries with weak power distance. Its rank on uncertainty avoidance indicated a tolerance of uncertainty. The United States also ranked as a masculine culture with a short-term orientation. These values have shaped U.S. management theory, so Hofstede's work casts doubt on the universal applicability of U.S. management theories. Because cultures differ so widely on these dimensions, management practices should be adjusted to account for cultural differences. Managers in transnational organizations must learn as much as they can about other cultures in order to lead their culturally diverse organizations effectively.

uncertainty avoidance
The degree to which a culture tolerates ambiguity and uncertainty.

masculinity
The cultural orientation in which assertiveness and materialism are valued.

femininity
The cultural orientation in which relationships and concern for others are valued.

time orientation
Whether a culture's values are oriented toward the future (long-term orientation) or toward the past and present (short-term orientation).

Planning for a Global Career

Think of a country you would like to work in, do business in, or visit. Find out about its culture, using Hofstede's dimensions as guidelines. You can use a variety of sources to accomplish this, particularly your school library, government offices, faculty members, or others who have global experience. You will want to answer the following questions:

1. Is the culture individualistic or collectivist?
2. Is the power distance high or low?
3. Is uncertainty avoidance high or low?
4. Is the country masculine or feminine in its orientation?

5. Is the time orientation short-term or long-term?
6. How did you arrive at your answers to the first five questions?
7. How will these characteristics affect business practices in the country you chose to investigate?

Careers in management have taken on a global dimension. Working in transnational organizations may well give managers the opportunity to work in other countries. *Expatriate managers,* those who work outside their home country, benefit from having as much knowledge as possible about cultural differences. Because managers are increasingly exposed to global work experiences, it is never too early to begin planning for this aspect of your career. You 2.1 asks you to begin gathering information about a country in which you would like to work, including information on its culture.

International executives are executives whose jobs have international scope, whether in an expatriate assignment or in a job dealing with international issues. What kind of competencies should an individual develop in order to prepare for an international career? There seem to be several attributes, all of them centering on core competencies and the ability to learn from experience. Some of the key competencies are integrity, insightfulness, risk taking, courage to take a stand, and ability to bring out the best in people. Learning-oriented attributes of international executives include cultural adventurousness, flexibility, openness to criticism, desire to seek learning opportunities, and sensitivity to cultural differences.[24] Further, strong human capital has a generally positive effect on internationalization.[25]

Understanding cultural differences becomes especially important for companies that are considering opening foreign offices, because workplace customs can vary widely from one country to another. Carefully searching out this information in advance can help companies successfully manage foreign operations. Consulate offices and companies operating within the foreign country are excellent sources of information about national customs and legal requirements. Table 2.1 presents a business guide to cultural differences in three countries: Japan, Mexico, and Saudi Arabia.

Another reality that can affect global business practices is the cost of layoffs in other countries. The practice of downsizing is not unique to the United States. Dismissing a forty-five-year-old middle manager with twenty years of service and a $50,000 annual salary can vary in cost from a low of $13,000 in Ireland to a high of $130,000 in Italy.[26] The cost of laying off this manager in the United States would be approximately $19,000. The wide variability in costs stems from the various legal protections that certain countries give workers. In Italy, laid-off employees must receive a "notice period" payment (one year's pay if they have nine years or

expatriate manager
A manager who works in a country other than his or her home country.

TABLE 2.1 Business Guide to Cultural Differences

Country	Appointments	Dress	Gifts	Negotiations
Japan	Punctuality is necessary when doing business here. It is considered rude to be late.	Conservative for men and women in large to medium companies, though pastel shirts are common. May be expected to remove shoes in temples and homes, as well as in some *ryokan* (inn) style restaurants. In that case, slip-on shoes should be worn.	Important part of Japanese business protocol. Gifts are typically exchanged among colleagues on July 15 and January 1 to commemorate midyear and the year's end, respectively.	Business cards (*meishi*) are an important part of doing business in Japan and key for establishing credentials. One side of your card should be in English and the reverse in Japanese. It is an asset to include information such as membership in professional associations.
Mexico	Punctuality is not always as much of a priority in Mexican business culture. Nonetheless, Mexicans are accustomed to North Americans arriving on time, and most Mexicans in business, if not government, will try to return the favor.	Dark, conservative suits and ties are the norm for most men. Standard office attire for women includes dresses, skirted suits, or skirts and blouses. Femininity is strongly encouraged in women's dress. Women business travelers will want to bring hosiery and high heels.	Not usually a requirement in business dealings though presenting a small gift will generally be appreciated as a gesture of goodwill. If giving a gift, be aware that inquiring about what the receiver would like to receive can be offensive.	Mexicans avoid directly saying "no." A "no" is often disguised in responses such as "maybe" or "We'll see." You should also use this indirect approach in your dealings. Otherwise, your Mexican counterparts may perceive you as being rude and pushy.
Saudi Arabia	Customary to make appointments for times of day rather than precise hours. The importance Saudis attach to courtesy and hospitality can cause delays that prevent keeping to a strict schedule.	The only absolute requirement of dress code in Saudi Arabia is modesty. For men, this means covering everything from navel to knee. Females are required to cover everything except the face, hands, and feet in public; they can wear literally anything they want providing they cover it with an *abaya* (standard black cloak) and headscarf when they go out.	Should only be given to the most intimate of friends. For a Saudi to receive a present from a lesser acquaintance is so embarrassing that it is considered offensive.	Business cards are common but not essential. If used, the common practice is to have both English and Arabic printed, one on each side so that neither language is perceived as less important by being on the reverse of the same card.

SOURCE: Adapted from information obtained from business culture guides accessed online at http://www.executiveplanet.com.

more of service) plus a severance payment (based on pay and years of service). U.S. companies operating overseas often adopt the European tradition of training and retraining workers to avoid overstaffing and potential layoffs. An appreciation of the customs and rules for doing business in another country is essential if a company wants to go global.

Developing Cross-Cultural Sensitivity

As organizations compete in the global marketplace, employees must learn to deal with individuals from diverse cultural backgrounds. Stereotypes may pervade employees' perceptions of other cultures. In addition, employees may be unaware of others' perceptions of the employees' national culture. A potentially valuable exercise is to ask members of various cultures to describe one another's cultures. This provides a lesson on the misinterpretation of culture.

Intel wants interns and employees to understand the company's culture, but more importantly, it wants to understand the employees' cultures. In an effort to increase diversity, Intel's proportion of ethnic minorities in managerial positions increased from 13 percent in 1993 to 20 percent in 2003, and is still climbing.[27] Many individuals feel their cultural heritage is important and may walk into uncomfortable situations at work. To prevent this, Intel's new workers are paired carefully with mentors, and mentors and protégés learn about each others' cultures.

Cultural sensitivity training is a popular method for helping employees recognize and appreciate cultural differences. Another way of developing sensitivity is to use cross-cultural task forces or teams. The Milwaukee-based GE Medical Systems Group (GEMS) has 19,000 employees working worldwide. GEMS has developed a vehicle for bringing managers from each of its three regions (the Americas, Europe, and Asia) together to work on a variety of business projects. Under the Global Leadership Program, several work groups made up of managers from various regions of the world are formed. The teams work on important projects, such as worldwide employee integration to increase the employees' sense of belonging throughout the GEMS international organization.[28]

The globalization of business affects all parts of the organization, and human resource management is affected in particular. Companies have employees around the world, and human resource managers face the daunting task of effectively supporting a culturally diverse workforce. Human resource managers must adopt a global view of all functions, including human resource planning, recruitment and selection, compensation, and training and development. They must have a working knowledge of the legal systems in various countries, as well as of global economics, culture, and customs. Human resource managers must not only prepare U.S. workers to live outside their native country but also help foreign employees interact with U.S. culture. Global human resource management is a complex endeavor, but it is critical to the success of organizations in the global marketplace.

Globalization is one challenge managers must meet in order to remain competitive in the changing world. Related to globalization is the challenge of managing an increasingly diverse workforce. Cultural differences contribute a great deal to the diversity of the workforce, but there are other forms of diversity as well.

THE DIVERSE WORKFORCE

Workforce diversity is an important issue for organizations. The United States, as a melting pot nation, has always had a mix of individuals in its workforce. We once sought to be all alike, as in the melting pot, but we now recognize and appreciate individual differences. *Diversity* encompasses all forms of differences among individuals, including culture, gender, age, ability, religion, personality, social status, and sexual orientation. Catalyst's Sheila Wellington believed 2003 was the year in which business made the case for diversity and inclusion, and then matched it with action.

Attention to diversity has increased in recent years. This is largely because of the changing demographics of the working population. Managers feel that dealing with diversity successfully is a paramount concern for two reasons. First, managers need to know how to motivate diverse work groups. Second, managers need to know how to communicate effectively with employees who have different values and language skills.

Several demographic trends are affecting organizations. By the year 2020, the workforce will be more culturally diverse, more female, and older than ever. In addition, legislation and new technologies have brought more workers with disabilities into the workforce. Hence, learning to work together is an increasingly important skill, just as it is important to work with an open mind.[29] Alcon Laboratories, the Swiss-owned and Fort Worth–based international company whose mission is to improve and preserve eyesight and hearing, creates an opportunity for learning to work together through diversity training.[30] Valuing diversity in organizations is an important issue.[31]

Cultural Diversity

Cultural diversity in the workplace is growing because of the globalization of business, as we discussed earlier. People of diverse national origins—Koreans, Bolivians, Pakistanis, Vietnamese, Swedes, Australians, and others—find themselves cooperating in teams to perform the work of the organization. In addition, changing demographics within the United States significantly affect the cultural diversity in organizations. By 2020, minorities will constitute more than one-half of the new entrants to the U.S. workforce. The participation rates of African Americans and Hispanic Americans in the labor force increased dramatically in recent years. By 2020, white non-Hispanics will constitute 68 percent of the labor force (down from 83 percent in 2002); 14 percent of the workforce will be Hispanic (up from 12 percent); African Americans' share will remain at 11 percent; and 5 percent will be Asian.[32]

These trends have important implications for organizations. African Americans and Hispanic Americans are overrepresented in declining occupations, thus limiting their opportunities. Further, both groups tend to live in a small number of large cities that are facing severe economic difficulties and high crime rates. Because of these factors, minority workers are likely to be at a disadvantage within organizations. It does not have to be this way. For example, by monitoring its human resource systems, Coco-Cola has made substantial progress on diversity.[33]

The jobs available in the future will require more skill than has been the case in the past. Often, minority workers have not had opportunities to develop leading-edge skills. Minority skill deficits are large, and the proportions of African Americans and Hispanic Americans who are qualified for higher-level jobs are often much lower than the proportions of qualified whites and Asian Americans.[34] Minority workers are less likely to be prepared because they are less likely to have had satisfactory schooling and on-the-job training. Educational systems within the workplace are needed to supply minority workers the skills necessary for success. Companies such as Motorola are already recognizing and meeting this need by focusing on basic skills training.

The globalization of business and changing demographic trends present organizations with a tremendously culturally diverse workforce. This represents both a

2 Explain the social and demographic changes that are producing diversity in organizations.

diversity

All forms of individual differences, including culture, gender, age, ability, religion, personality, social status, and sexual orientation.

challenge and a risk. The challenge is to harness the wealth of differences that cultural diversity provides. The risk is that prejudices and stereotypes may prevent managers and employees from developing synergies that can benefit the organization.

Gender Diversity

The feminization of the workforce has increased substantially. The number of women in the labor force increased from 31.5 million in 1970 to 64 million in 2003. This increase accounts for almost 60 percent of the overall expansion of the entire labor force in the United States for this time period. In 2004, women made up over 60 percent of the labor force, and it is predicted that by the year 2010, 70 percent of new entrants into the workforce will be women and/or people of color. Women are better prepared to contribute in organizations than ever before. Women now earn 32 percent of all doctorates, 52 percent of master's degrees, and 50 percent of all undergraduate degrees. Thus, women are better educated, and more are electing to work. In 2004, almost 58 percent of U.S. women were employed.[35] However, women comprised only 14.7 percent of corporate board members in 2005.[36]

Women's participation in the workforce is increasing, but their share of the rewards of participation is not increasing commensurately. Women hold only 16.4 percent of corporate officer positions in the *Fortune* 500 companies.[37] In 2005, only eight *Fortune* 500 companies had women CEOs.[38] Xerox CEO Anne Mulcahy is a very positive example yet still the exception, not the rule. Median weekly earnings for women persist at a level of 81 percent of their male counterparts' earnings.[39] Furthermore, because benefits are tied to compensation, women also receive lower levels of benefits.

In addition to lower earnings, women face other obstacles at work. The *glass ceiling* is an intangible barrier that keeps women (and minorities) from rising above a certain level in organizations. In the United States, it is rare to find women in positions above middle management in corporations.[40] The ultimate glass ceiling may well be the corporate board room and the professional partnership. One study found no substantive increase in female corporate board members between 1996 and 2002.[41] While women account for 40 percent of the legal professionals, they are not 40 percent of the partners.

There is reason to believe that, on a global basis, the leadership picture for women is improving and will continue to improve. For example, the number of female political leaders around the world increased dramatically in recent decades. In the 1970s, there were only five such leaders. In the 1990s, twenty-one female leaders came into power. Countries such as Ireland, Sri Lanka, Iceland, and Norway all had female political leaders in the 1990s. Women around the world are leading major global companies, albeit not in the United States. These global female business leaders do not come predominantly from the West. In addition, a large number of women have founded entrepreneurial businesses. Women now own nearly 10.4 million of all American businesses, and these women-owned businesses employ more than 12.8 million people and generate $1.9 trillion in sales.[42]

Removing the glass ceiling and other obstacles to women's success represents a major challenge to organizations. Policies that promote equity in pay and benefits, encourage benefit programs of special interest to women, and provide equal starting salaries for jobs of equal value are needed in organizations. Corporations that shatter the glass ceiling have several practices in common. Upper managers clearly demonstrate support for the advancement of women, often with a statement of commitment issued by the CEO. Leaders incorporate practices into their diversity management programs to ensure that women perceive the organization as attractive.[43] Women are represented on standing committees that address strategic

glass ceiling

An intangible barrier that keeps women and minorities from rising above a certain level in organizations.

business issues of importance to the company. Women are targeted for participation in executive education programs, and systems are in place for identifying women with high potential for advancement.[44] Three of the best companies in terms of their advancement and development of women are Motorola, Deloitte & Touche, and the Bank of Montreal.[45]

Although women in our society have adopted the provider role, men have not been as quick to share domestic responsibilities. Managing the home and arranging for child care are still seen as the woman's domain. In addition, working women often find themselves having to care for their elderly parents. Because of their multiple roles, women are more likely than men to experience conflicts between work and home. Organizations can offer incentives such as flexible work schedules, child care, elder care, and work site health promotion programs to assist working women in managing the stress of their lives.[46]

More women in the workforce means that organizations must help them achieve their potential. To do less would be to underutilize the talents of half of the U.S. workforce.

The glass ceiling is not the only gender barrier in organizations. Males may suffer from discrimination when they are employed in traditionally female jobs such as nursing, elementary school teaching, and social work. Males may be overlooked as candidates for managerial positions in traditionally female occupations.[47]

Age Diversity

The graying of the U.S. workforce is another source of diversity in organizations. Aging baby boomers (those individuals born from 1946 through 1964) contributed to the rise of the median age in the United States to thirty-six in the year 2000—six years older than at any earlier time in history. This also means that the number of middle-aged Americans is rising dramatically. In the workforce, the number of younger workers is declining, as is the number of older workers (over age sixty-five). The net result will be a gain in workers aged thirty-five to fifty-four. By 2030, there will be 70 million older persons, more than twice their number in 1996. People over age sixty-five will comprise 13 percent of the population in 2010, and 20 percent of the population by 2030.[48]

This change in worker profile has profound implications for organizations. The job crunch among middle-aged workers will become more intense as companies seek flatter organizations and the elimination of middle-management jobs. Older workers are often higher paid, and companies that employ large numbers of aging baby boomers may find these pay scales a handicap to competitiveness.[49] However, a more experienced, stable, reliable, and healthy workforce can pay dividends to companies. The baby boomers are well trained and educated, and their knowledge can be a definite asset to organizations.

Another effect of the aging workforce is greater intergenerational contact in the workplace.[50] As organizations grow flatter, workers who were traditionally segregated by old corporate hierarchies (with older workers at the top and younger workers at the bottom) are working together. Four generations are cooperating: the silent generation (people born from 1930 through 1945), a small group that includes most organizations' top managers; the baby boomers, whose substantial numbers give them a strong influence; the baby bust generation, popularly known as Generation X (those born from 1965 through 1976); and the subsequent generation, tentatively called Generation Y, millennials, or the baby boomlet.[51] The millennials bring new challenges to the workplace because of their access to technology since a young age and a perpetual connection to parents.[52] While there is diversity among these various generations, there is diversity within each as well.

The differences in attitudes and values among these four generations can be substantial, and managers face the challenge of integrating these individuals into a cohesive group. Currently, as already noted, most positions of leadership are held by members of the silent generation. Baby boomers regard the silent generation as complacent and as having done little to reduce social inequities. Baby boomers strive for moral rights in the workplace and take a more activist position regarding employee rights. The baby busters, newer to the workplace, are impatient, want short-term gratification, and believe that family should come before work. They scorn the achievement orientation and materialism of the baby boomers. The millennials generate much controversy in both the definition of who they are and what constitute their distinguishing characteristics. Managing such diverse, conflicting perspectives is a challenge that must be addressed.

One company that is succeeding in accommodating the baby busters is Patagonia, a manufacturer of products for outdoor enthusiasts. Although the company does not actively recruit twenty-year-olds, approximately 20 percent of Patagonia's workers are in this age group because they are attracted to its products. To retain baby busters, the company offers several options, one of which is flextime. Employees can arrive at work as early as 6 a.m., and work as late as 6 p.m., as long as they work the core hours between 9 a.m. and 3 p.m. Workers also have the option of working at the office for five hours a day and at home for three hours.

Personal leaves of absence are also offered, generally unpaid, for as much as four months per year. This allows employees to take an extended summer break and prevents job burnout. Patagonia has taken into consideration the baby busters' desire for more time for personal concerns and has incorporated that desire into the company.[53]

Younger workers may have false impressions of older workers, viewing them as resistant to change, unable to learn new work methods, less physically capable, and less creative than younger employees. Research indicates, however, that older employees are more satisfied with their jobs, are more committed to the organization, and possess more internal work motivation than their younger cohorts.[54] Research also shows that direct experience with older workers reduces younger workers' negative beliefs.[55] Motivating aging workers and helping them maintain high levels of contribution to the organization is a key task for managers.

Ability Diversity

The workforce is full of individuals with different abilities, presenting another form of diversity. Individuals with disabilities are an underutilized human resource. An estimated 50 million individuals with disabilities live in the United States, and their unemployment rate is estimated to exceed 50 percent.[56] Nevertheless, the representation of individuals with disabilities in the workforce has increased because of the Americans with Disabilities Act, which went into effect in the summer of 1992. Under this law, employers are required to make reasonable accommodations to permit workers with disabilities to perform jobs. The act defines a person with a disability as "anyone possessing a physical or mental impairment that substantially limits one or more major life activities."[57] The law protects individuals with temporary, as well as permanent, disabilities. Its protection encompasses a broad range of illnesses that produce disabilities. Among these are acquired immune deficiency syndrome (AIDS), cancer, hypertension, anxiety disorders, dyslexia, blindness, and cerebral palsy, to name only a few. The Real World 2.2 examines an ability/disability debate in the case of a successful amputee sprinter.

Some companies recognized the value of employing workers with disabilities long before the legislation. Pizza Hut employs 3,000 workers with disabilities and

An Equalizer or an Edge?

Oscar Pistorius of South Africa is facing resistance from the track and field's world governing body to his desire to be the first amputee runner to compete in the Olympics. He wants to compete in the 2008 Beijing Games. Pistorius calls himself the fastest man on no legs; he sprints on a pair of j-shaped blades made of carbon fiber and known as Cheetahs. Born with a birth defect, he had both legs amputated below the knee when he was 11 months old. During 2007, Pistorius delivered startling record performances for disabled athletes at 100 meters (10.91 seconds), 200 meters (21.58 seconds), and 400 meters (46.34 seconds). He did win second place in the 2007 South African national championships against able-bodied runners with a 46.56 second finish in the 400. Do his prosthetic legs simply level the playing field for him by compensating for his disability, or do they give him an unfair edge via what some call techno-doping? Track and field's world governing body prohibited the use of technological aids like springs and wheels starting in 2007. Since 2004, transgender athletes have been allowed to compete in the Olympics. One scientist argues that Pistorius has no advantage, only that he competes at a disadvantage, because a prosthetic leg returns only about 80 percent of the energy absorbed in each stride compared to 240 percent for a natural leg. Overall, Pisotrius' success presents more questions than answers.

SOURCE: J. Longman, "Debate on Amputee Sprinter: Is He Disabled or Too-Abled?" The New York Times (May 15, 2007): 1.

plans to hire more. The turnover rate for Pizza Hut workers with disabilities is only one-fifth of the normal turnover rate.[58]

McDonald's created McJOBS, a program that has trained and hired more than 9,000 mentally and physically challenged individuals since 1981.[59] McJOBS is a corporate plan to recruit, train, and retain individuals with disabilities. Its participants include workers with visual, hearing, or orthopedic impairments; learning disabilities; and mental retardation. Through classroom and on-site training, the McJOBS program prepares individuals with disabilities for the work environment. Before McJOBS workers go on-site, sensitivity training sessions are held with store managers and crew members. These sessions help workers without disabilities understand what it means to be a worker with a disabling condition. Most McJOBS workers start part-time and advance according to their abilities and the opportunities available. Some McJOBS workers with visual impairments prefer to work on the back line, whereas others who use wheelchairs can work the drive-thru window.

Companies like Pizza Hut and McDonald's have led the way in hiring individuals with disabilities. One key to their success is helping able-bodied employees understand how workers with disabilities can contribute to the organization. In this way, ability diversity becomes an asset and helps organizations meet the challenge of unleashing the talents of workers with disabilities.

Differences Are Assets

Diversity involves much more than culture, gender, age, ability, or personality. It also encompasses religion, social status, and sexual orientation. The scope of diversity is broad and inclusive. All these types of diversity lend heterogeneity to the workforce. Some programs aimed at enhancing appreciation and understanding diversity are required while some are voluntary. As we see in the accompanying Science feature, not everyone participates equally in voluntary diversity training.

Diversity Training and Competence

Diversity training is an umbrella term that encompasses a wide array of specific programs designed to train and direct employees in behaviors aimed at displaying openness and receptiveness to diversity. Early on, diversity training focused specifically on race and gender. Because of its concern with human resource recruiting, hiring, and promotion practices that might limit opportunities for women and minorities, it was often described as equal opportunity training. More recently there has been an expansion to diversity dimensions such as disability status and culture. In a two-part study by Kulik and colleagues, interest and actual participation in voluntary diversity training were examined. The results found that demographic characteristics played no significant role in either a person's interest or participation in voluntary diversity training. That is, characteristics such as age, sex, and race made no difference. However, what did make a difference was the pretraining competence of the person. Specifically, persons with more competence in the diversity domain displayed significantly more interest in additional diversity training and were more likely to attend a voluntary training session. The researchers concluded that trainees with low competence in the diversity domain are unaware of their low competence levels and therefore are not motivated to participate in training designed to increase diversity competence. Hence, the competent become more competent and those low in competence miss the opportunity to increase their knowledge and awareness.

SOURCE: C. T. Kulik, M. B. Pepper, L. Robertson, and S. K. Parker, "The Rich Get Richer: Predicting Participation in Voluntary Diversity Training," *Journal of Organizational Behavior*. In press.

The issue of sexual orientation as a form of diversity has received increasing attention from organizations. Approximately 1.5 million households in the United States are identified as homosexual domestic partnerships.[60] Sexual orientation is an emotionally charged issue. Often, heterosexual resistance to accepting gay, lesbian, or bisexual workers is caused by moral beliefs. Although organizations must respect these beliefs, they must also send a message that all people are valued. The threat of job discrimination leads many gay men and lesbians to keep their sexual orientation secret at work. This secrecy has a cost, however. Closeted gay workers report lower job satisfaction and organizational commitment and more role conflict and conflict between work and home life issues than do openly gay workers or heterosexual workers.[61] To counteract these problems, companies like NCR are actively seeking gay job applicants. Other companies like IBM, Ford Motor Company, JPMorgan Chase, and American Airlines are offering benefits, training, support groups, and marketing strategies in support of gay rights. These initiatives help gay employees become more integrated and productive organizational members. Education and training can be supplemented by everyday practices like using inclusive language—for example, using the term "partner" instead of "spouse" in verbal and written communication.

Combating prejudice and discrimination is a challenge in managing diversity. Whereas prejudice is an attitude, discrimination is behavior. Both are detrimental to organizations that depend on productivity from every single worker. Often, in studies of ratings of promotion potential, minorities are rated lower than whites, and females are rated lower than males.[62] The disparity between the pay of women and minority-group members relative to white men increases with age.[63] It is to organizations' benefit to make sure that good workers are promoted and compensated fairly, but as the workforce becomes increasingly diverse, the potential for unfair treatment also increases.

Diversity is advantageous to the organization in a multitude of ways. Some organizations have recognized the potential benefits of aggressively working to increase the diversity of their workforces. Yum! Brands' Kentucky Fried Chicken (KFC) has a goal of attracting and retaining female and minority-group executives. A president of KFC's U.S. operations said, "We want to bring in the best people. If there are two equally qualified people, we'd clearly like to have diversity."[64]

3 Describe actions managers can take to help their employees value diversity.

In an effort to understand and encourage diversity, Alcon Laboratories developed a diversity training class called Working Together. The course takes advantage of two key ideas. First, people work best when they are valued and when diversity is taken into account. Second, when people feel valued, they build relationships and work together as a team.[65] Even majority group managers may be more supportive of diversity training if they appreciate their own ethnic identity. One evaluation of diversity training found that participants were more favorable if the training was framed with a traditional title and had a broad focus.[66] Further, women react more positively to diversity training than men. Companies can get positive payoffs from diversity training and should, therefore, measure the effect of training.

Managing diversity is one way a company can become more competitive. It is more than simply being a good corporate citizen or complying with affirmative action.[67] It is also more than assimilating women and minorities into a dominant male culture. Managing diversity includes a painful examination of hidden assumptions that employees hold. Biases and prejudices about people's differences must be uncovered and dealt with so that differences can be celebrated and exploited to their full advantage.

Diversity's Benefits and Problems

Diversity can enhance organizational performance. Table 2.2 summarizes the main benefits, as well as problems, with diversity at work. Organizations can reap five main benefits from diversity. First, diversity management can help firms attract and retain the best available talent. The companies that appear at the top of "Best Places to Work" lists are usually excellent at managing diversity. Second, diversity can enhance marketing efforts. Just as workforces are becoming more diverse, so are markets. Having a diverse workforce can help the company improve its marketing plans by drawing on insights of employees from various cultural backgrounds. Third, diversity promotes creativity and innovation. The most innovative companies, such as HP, deliberately put together diverse teams to foster creativity. Fourth, diversity results in better problem solving. Diverse groups bring more expertise and experience to bear on problems and decisions. They also encourage higher levels of critical thinking. Fifth, diversity enhances organizational flexibility. Inflexible organizations are characterized by narrow thinking, rigidity, and standard definitions of "good" work styles. In contrast, diversity makes an organization challenge old assumptions

TABLE 2.2 Diversity's Benefits and Problems

Benefits	Problems
• Attracts and retains the best human talent	• Resistance to change
• Improves marketing efforts	• Lack of cohesiveness
• Promotes creativity and innovation	• Communication problems
• Results in better problem solving	• Interpersonal conflicts
• Enhances organizational flexibility	• Slowed decision making

and become more adaptable. These five benefits can add up to competitive advantage for a company that manages diversity well.

Lest we paint an overly rosy picture of diversity, we must recognize its potential problems. Five problems are particularly important: resistance to change, lack of cohesiveness, communication problems, conflicts, and decision making. People are more highly attracted to, and feel more comfortable with, others like themselves. It stands to reason that diversity efforts may be met with considerable resistance when individuals are forced to interact with others unlike themselves. Managers should be prepared for this resistance rather than naively assuming that everybody supports diversity. (Managing resistance to change is presented at length in Chapter 18.) Another potential problem with diversity is the issue of cohesiveness, that invisible "glue" that holds a group together. Cohesive, or tightly knit, groups are preferred by most people. It takes longer for a diverse group of individuals to become cohesive. In addition, cohesive groups have higher morale and better communication. We can reason that it may take longer for diverse groups to develop high morale.

Another obstacle to performance in diverse groups is communication. Culturally diverse groups may encounter special challenges in terms of communication barriers. Misunderstandings can occur that can lower work group effectiveness. Conflicts can also arise, and decision making may take more time.[68]

In summary, diversity has several advantages that can lead to improved productivity and competitive advantage. In diverse groups, however, certain aspects of group functioning can become problematic. The key is to maximize the benefits of diversity and prevent or resolve the potential problems.

Pillsbury is one company that lays out the performance case for managing and valuing differences. Pillsbury's managers argue that the same business rationale for cross-functional teams is relevant to all kinds of diversity. Managing differences includes bringing race and gender, as well as marketing expertise, into a team. The company lacked the language expertise and cultural access to the Hispanic community. To open up a very profitable baked-goods market in a tough-to-crack niche, Pillsbury hired a group of Spanish-speaking Americans of Hispanic descent. Pillsbury's vice president of human resources conducted his own study of the food industry, asking an independent group to rate the diversity performance of ten companies and correlating it with financial performance over a ten-year period. Along with many other studies, the Pillsbury research suggests that diversity is a strong contributor to financial performance.[69]

Whereas the struggle for equal employment opportunity is a battle against racism and prejudice, managing diversity is a battle to value the differences that individuals bring to the workplace. Organizations that manage diversity effectively can reap the rewards of increased productivity and improved organizational health. Another aspect of a healthy organization is employees of good character, ethical behavior, and personal integrity.

ETHICS, CHARACTER, AND PERSONAL INTEGRITY

(4) Discuss the assumptions of consequential, rule-based, and character theories of ethics.

In addition to the challenges of globalization and workforce diversity, managers frequently face ethical dilemmas and trade-offs. Some organizations display good character and their executives are known for personal integrity. Johnson & Johnson employees operate with an organizational credo, presented later in this section. Merck & Company is another organization that manages ethical issues well; its emphasis on ethical behavior has earned it recognition as one of America's most admired companies in *Fortune*'s polls of CEOs. We saw that Genentech is a biotechnology company facing ethical dilemmas and trade-offs in its decision making between cancer patients and immunology patients.

Despite the positive way some organizations handle ethical issues, however, unethical conduct can still occur. A few of the ethical problems that managers report as toughest to resolve include employee theft, environmental issues, comparable worth of employees, conflicts of interest, and sexual harassment.[70]

How can people in organizations rationally think through ethical decisions so that they make the "right" choices? Ethical theories help us understand, evaluate, and classify moral arguments; make decisions; and then defend conclusions about what is right and wrong. Ethical theories can be classified as consequential, rule based, or character based.

Consequential theories of ethics emphasize the consequences or results of behavior. John Stuart Mill's utilitarianism, a well-known consequential theory, suggests that right and wrong are determined by the consequences of the action.[71] "Good" is the ultimate moral value, and we should maximize the most good for the greatest number of people. But do good ethics make for good business?[72] Right actions do not always produce good consequences, and good consequences do not always follow from right actions. And how do we determine the greatest good—in short-term or long-term consequences? Using the "greatest number" criterion can imply that minorities (less than 50 percent) might be excluded in evaluating the morality of actions. An issue that may be important for a minority but unimportant for the majority might be ignored. These are but a few of the dilemmas raised by utilitarianism.

In contrast, *rule-based theories* of ethics emphasize the character of the act itself, not its effects, in arriving at universal moral rights and wrongs.[73] Moral rights, the basis for legal rights, are associated with such theories. In a theological context, the Bible, the Talmud, and the Koran are rule-based guides to ethical behavior. Immanuel Kant worked toward the ultimate moral principle in formulating his categorical imperative, a universal standard of behavior.[74] Kant argued that individuals should be treated with respect and dignity and that they should not be used as a means to an end. He argued that we should put ourselves in the other person's position and ask if we would make the same decision if we were in his or her situation.

Corporations and business enterprises are more prone to subscribe to consequential ethics than rule-based ethics, in part due to the persuasive arguments of the Scottish political economist and moral philosopher Adam Smith.[75] He believed that the self-interest of human beings is God's providence, not the government's. Smith set forth a doctrine of natural liberty, presenting the classical argument for open market competition and free trade. Within this framework, people should be allowed to pursue what is in their economic self-interest, and the natural efficiency of the marketplace would serve the well-being of society. However, an alternative to those theories is offered through virtue-ethics.

Character theories of ethics emphasize the character of the individual and the intent of the actor, in contrast to either the character of the act itself or its consequences. These theories emphasize virtue-ethics and are based on an Aristotelian approach to character. Robert Solomon is the best-known advocate of this approach.[76] He supports a business ethics theory that centers on the individual within the corporation, thus emphasizing both corporate roles and personal virtues. The center of Aristotle's vision was on the inner character and virtuousness of the individual, not on her or his behavior or actions. Thus, the "good" person who acted out of virtuous and "right" intentions was one with integrity and ultimately good ethical standards. For Solomon, the six dimensions of virtue-ethics are community,

© AP PHOTO/DAVID J. PHILLIP

Despite the positive way some organizations handle ethical issues, unethical conduct does occur. Andrew S. Fastow, former chief financial officer of Enron Corp., was convicted on charges related to his role in the company's collapse.

consequential theory
An ethical theory that emphasizes the consequences or results of behavior.

rule-based theory
An ethical theory that emphasizes the character of the act itself rather than its effects.

character theory
An ethical theory that emphasizes the character, personal virtues, and integrity of the individual.

excellence, role identity, integrity, judgment (*phronesis*), and holism. Further, "the virtues" are a shorthand way of summarizing the ideals that define good character. These include honesty, loyalty, sincerity, courage, reliability, trustworthiness, benevolence, sensitivity, helpfulness, cooperativeness, civility, decency, modesty, openness, and gracefulness, to name a few.

Cultural relativism contends that there are no universal ethical principles and that people should not impose their own ethical standards on others. Local standards should be the guides for ethical behavior. Cultural relativism encourages individuals to operate under the old adage "When in Rome, do as the Romans do." Unfortunately, strict adherence to cultural relativism can lead individuals to deny accountability for their decisions and to avoid difficult ethical dilemmas.

(5) Explain six issues that pose ethical dilemmas for managers.

People need ethical theories to help them think through confusing, complex, difficult moral choices and ethical decisions. In contemporary organizations, people face ethical and moral dilemmas in many diverse areas. The key areas we address are employee rights, sexual harassment, romantic involvements, organizational justice, whistle-blowing, and social responsibility. We conclude with a discussion of professionalism and codes of ethics.

Employee Rights

Managing the rights of employees at work creates many ethical dilemmas in organizations. Some of these dilemmas are privacy issues related to technology. Computerized monitoring, discussed later in the chapter, constitutes an invasion of privacy in the minds of some individuals. The use of employee data from computerized information systems presents many ethical concerns. Safeguarding the employee's right to privacy and at the same time preserving access to the data for those who need it requires that the manager balance competing interests.

Drug testing, free speech, downsizing and layoffs, and due process are but a few of the issues involving employee rights that managers face. Perhaps no issue generates as much need for managers to balance the interests of employees and the interests of the organization as AIDS in the workplace. New drugs have shown the promise of extended lives for people with human immunodeficiency virus (HIV), and this means that HIV-infected individuals can remain in the workforce and stay productive. Managers may be caught in the middle of a conflict between the rights of HIV-infected workers and the rights of their coworkers who feel threatened.

Employers are not required to make concessions to coworkers but do have obligations to educate, reassure, and provide emotional support to them. Confidentiality may also be a difficult issue. Some employees with HIV or AIDS do not wish to waive confidentiality and do not want to reveal their condition to their coworkers because of fears of stigmatization or even reprisals. In any case, management should discuss with the affected employee the ramifications of trying to maintain confidentiality and should assure the employee that every effort will be made to prevent negative consequences for him or her in the workplace.[77]

Laws exist that protect HIV-infected workers. As mentioned earlier, the Americans with Disabilities Act requires employees to treat HIV-infected workers as disabled individuals and to make reasonable accommodations for them. The ethical dilemmas involved with this situation, however, go far beyond the legal issues. How does a manager protect the dignity of the person with AIDS and preserve the morale and productivity of the work group when so much prejudice and ignorance surround this disease? Many organizations, such as Wells Fargo, believe the answer is education.[78] Wells Fargo has a written AIDS policy because of the special issues associated with the disease—such as confidentiality, employee socialization, coworker education, and counseling—that must be addressed. The Body Shop's employee

How Much Do You Know about Sexual Harassment?

Indicate whether you believe each statement below is true (T) or false (F).

_____ 1. Sexual harassment is unprofessional behavior.

_____ 2. Sexual harassment is against the law in all fifty states.

_____ 3. Sexual advances are a form of sexual harassment.

_____ 4. A request for sexual activity is a form of sexual harassment.

_____ 5. Verbal or physical conduct of a sexual nature may be sexual harassment.

_____ 6. Sexual harassment occurs when submission to sex acts is a condition of employment.

_____ 7. Sexual harassment occurs when submission to or rejection of sexual acts is a basis for performance evaluation.

_____ 8. Sexual harassment occurs when such behavior interferes with an employee's performance or creates an intimidating, hostile, and offensive environment.

_____ 9. Sexual harassment includes physical contact of a sexual nature, such as touching.

_____ 10. Sexual harassment requires that a person have the intent to harass, harm, or intimidate.

All of the items are true except item 10, which is false. While somewhat ambiguous, sexual harassment is defined in the eyes of the beholder. Give yourself 1 point for each correct answer. This score reflects how much you know about sexual harassment. Scores can range from 0 (poorly informed) to 10 (well informed). If your score was less than 5, you need to learn more about sexual harassment.

SOURCE: See W. O'Donohue, ed., *Sexual Harassment* (Boston: Allyn and Bacon, 1997) for theory, research, and treatment. See http://www.eeoc.gov/stats/harass.html for the latest statistics.

education program consists of factual seminars combined with interactive theater workshops. The workshops depict a scenario in which an HIV-positive worker must make decisions, and the audience decides what the worker should do. This helps participants explore the emotional and social issues surrounding HIV.[79] Many fears arise because of a lack of knowledge about AIDS.

Sexual Harassment

According to the Equal Employment Opportunity Commission, sexual harassment is unwelcome sexual attention, whether verbal or physical, that affects an employee's job conditions or creates a hostile working environment.[80] Court rulings, too, have broadened the definition of sexual harassment beyond job-related abuse to include acts that create a hostile work environment. In addition, Supreme Court rulings presume companies are to blame when managers create a sexually hostile working environment. Some organizations are more tolerant of sexual harassment. Complaints are not taken seriously, it is risky to complain, and perpetrators are unlikely to be punished. In such organizations, sexual harassment is more likely to occur. It is also more likely to occur in male-dominated workplaces.[81] Managers can defend themselves by demonstrating that they took action to eliminate workplace harassment and that the complaining employee did not take advantage of company procedures to deal with it. Even the best sexual harassment policy, however, will not absolve a company when harassment leads to firing, demotions, or undesirable working assignments.[82] How much do you know about sexual harassment? Complete You 2.2 to get an idea.

There are three types of sexual harassment. *Gender harassment* includes crude comments or sexual jokes and behaviors that disparage someone's gender or convey hostility toward a particular gender. *Unwanted sexual attention* involves unwanted touching or repeated unwanted pressures for dates. *Sexual coercion* consists of implicit or explicit demands for sexual favors by threatening negative job-related consequences or promising job-related rewards.[83] Recent theory has focused attention on the aggressive behavior of sexual harassers.[84]

Sexual harassment costs the typical *Fortune* 500 company $6.7 million per year in absenteeism, turnover, and loss of productivity. Valeant Pharmaceuticals International has paid out millions to settle four sexual harassment complaints against former CEO Milan Panic. One U.S. airline reached a $2.6 million settlement with the EEOC in 2001 after the agency found widespread sexual harassment of female employees at the airline's New York JFK International Airport facility. Plaintiffs may now sue not only for back pay but also for compensatory and punitive damages. And these costs do not take into account the negative publicity that firms may encounter from sexual harassment cases, which can cost untold millions. Sexual harassment can have strong negative effects on victims. Victims are less satisfied with their work, supervisors, and coworkers and may psychologically withdraw at work. They may suffer poorer mental health and even exhibit symptoms of post-traumatic stress disorder in conjunction with the harassment experience. Some victims report alcohol abuse, depression, headaches, and nausea.[85]

Several companies have created comprehensive sexual harassment programs that seem to work. Atlantic Richfield (ARCO), owned by British Petroleum and a player in the male-dominated energy industry, has a handbook on preventing sexual harassment that includes phone numbers of state agencies where employees can file complaints. In essence, it gives employees a road map to the courthouse, and the openness seems to work. Lawsuits rarely happen at ARCO. When sexual harassment complaints come in, the company assumes the allegations are true and investigates thoroughly. The process has resulted in the firing of highly placed managers, including the captain of an oil tanker. Other companies believe in the power of training programs. Some of the best training programs use role-playing, videotapes, and group discussions of real cases to help supervisors recognize unlawful sexual harassment and investigate complaints properly.

Romantic Involvements

Hugging, sexual innuendos, and repeated requests for dates may constitute sexual harassment for some but a prelude to romance for others. This situation carries with it a different set of ethical dilemmas for organizations.

A recent fax poll indicated that three-fourths of the respondents felt it was okay to date a coworker, while three-fourths disapproved of dating a superior or subordinate. In *Meritor vs. Vinson*, the Supreme Court ruled that the agency principle applies to supervisor–subordinate relationships. Employers are liable for acts of their agents (supervisors) and can thus be held liable for sexual harassment. Other employees might claim that the subordinate who is romantically involved with the supervisor gets preferential treatment. Dating between coworkers poses less liability for the company because the agency principle does not apply. Policing coworker dating can also backfire: Wal-Mart lost a lawsuit when it tried to forbid coworkers from dating.

Workplace romances may result, for the participants, in experiences that can be positive or negative, temporary or permanent, exploitative to nonexploitative. The effects of office romances can similarly be positive or negative, or they can simply be mild diversions. Romances can be damaging to organizational effectiveness, or they can occasionally enhance effectiveness through their positive effects on participants. Two particular kinds of romances are hazardous in the workplace. Hierarchical romances, in which one person directly reports to another, can create tremendous conflicts of interest. Utilitarian romances, in which one person satisfies the needs of another in exchange for task-related or career-related favors, are potentially damaging in the workplace. Although most managers realize that workplace romance cannot be eliminated through rules and policies, they believe that intervention is a must when romance constitutes a serious threat to productivity or workplace morale.[86]

Organizational Justice

Another area in which moral and ethical dilemmas may arise for people at work concerns organizational justice, both distributive and procedural. *Distributive justice* concerns the fairness of outcomes individuals receive. For example, the salaries and bonuses of U.S. corporate executives became a central issue with Japanese executives when former President George H. W. Bush and American CEOs in key industries visited Japan in 1992. The Japanese CEOs questioned the distributive justice in keeping the American CEOs' salaries at high levels at a time when so many companies were having financial difficulty and laying off workers.

Procedural justice concerns the fairness of the process by which outcomes are allocated. The ethical questions here do not concern the just or unjust distribution of organizational resources but rather, the process. Has the organization used the correct procedures in allocating resources? Have the right considerations, such as competence and skill, been brought to bear in the decision process? And have the wrong considerations, such as race and gender, been excluded from the decision process? One study in a work-scheduling context found voluntary turnover negatively related to advance notice and consistency, two dimensions of procedural justice.[87] Some research found cultural differences in the effects of distributive and procedural justice, such as between Hong Kong and the United States.[88]

Whistle-Blowing

Whistle-blowers are employees who inform authorities of wrongdoings by their company or coworkers. Whistle-blowers can be perceived as either heroes or villains depending on the circumstances. For a whistle-blower to be considered a public hero, the situation the whistle-blower reports to authorities must be so serious as to be perceived as abhorrent by others.[89] In contrast, the whistle-blower is considered a villain if others see the act of whistle-blowing as more offensive than the situation being reported.

Whistle-blowing is important in the United States because workers sometimes engage in unethical behavior in an intense desire to succeed. Many examples of whistle-blowing can be found in corporate America. For example, one former Coca-Cola employee made a number of allegations against the company and issued an ultimatum: Coca-Cola must pay him nearly $45 million or he would go to the media.[90] While a Georgia state court dismissed most of the allegations, Coca-Cola still had to defend itself against claims related to wrongful termination. One of the former employee's allegations relating to a falsified marketing test did force Coca-Cola to make a public apology and offer to pay Burger King $21 million.

Organizations can manage whistle-blowing by communicating the conditions that are appropriate for the disclosure of wrongdoing. Clearly delineating wrongful behavior and the appropriate ways to respond are important organizational actions.

distributive justice
The fairness of the outcomes that individuals receive in an organization.

procedural justice
The fairness of the process by which outcomes are allocated in an organization.

whistle-blower
An employee who informs authorities of the wrongdoings of his or her company or coworkers.

Social Responsibility

Corporate *social responsibility* is the obligation of an organization to behave in ethical ways in the social environment in which it operates. Ethical conduct at the individual level can translate into social responsibility at the organizational level. When Malden Mills, the maker of Polartec, burned down in 1995, the company's president, Aaron Feuerstein, paid workers during the months it took to rebuild the company. Although doing so cost the company a lot of money and was not required by law, Feuerstein said his own values caused him to do the socially responsible thing. Malden Mills recovered financially and continues its success with Polartec.

Socially responsible actions are expected of organizations. Current concerns include protecting the environment, promoting worker safety, supporting social issues, and investing in the community, among others. Some organizations, like IBM, loan executives to inner-city schools to teach science and math. Other organizations, like Patagonia, demonstrate social responsibility through environmentalism. Firms that are seen as socially responsible have a competitive advantage in attracting applicants.[91]

Codes of Ethics

One of the characteristics of mature professions is the existence of a code of ethics to which the practitioners adhere in their actions and behavior. An example is the Hippocratic oath in medicine. Although some of the individual differences we address in Chapter 4 produce ethical or unethical orientations in specific people, a profession's code of ethics becomes a standard against which members can measure themselves in the absence of internalized standards.

No universal code of ethics or oath exists for business as it does for medicine. However, Paul Harris and four business colleagues, who founded Rotary International in 1905, made an effort to address ethical and moral behavior right from the beginning. They developed the four-way test, shown in Figure 2.2, which is now used in more than 166 nations throughout the world by the 1.2 million Rotarians in more than 30,000 Rotary clubs. Figure 2.2 focuses the questioner on key ethical and moral questions.

Beyond the individual and professional level, corporate culture is another excellent starting point for addressing ethics and morality. In Chapter 16 we examine how corporate culture and leader behavior trickle down the company, setting a standard for all below. In some cases, the corporate ethics may be captured in

FIGURE 2.2 The Four-Way Test

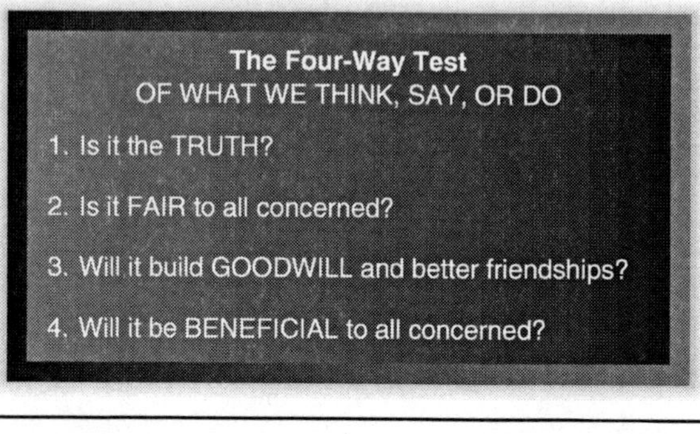

The Four-Way Test
OF WHAT WE THINK, SAY, OR DO

1. Is it the TRUTH?

2. Is it FAIR to all concerned?

3. Will it build GOODWILL and better friendships?

4. Will it be BENEFICIAL to all concerned?

social responsibility
The obligation of an organization to behave in ethical ways.

a regulation. For example, the Joint Ethics Regulation (DOD 5500.7-R, August 1993) specifies the ethical standards to which all U.S. military personnel are to adhere. In other cases, the corporate ethics may be in the form of a credo. Johnson & Johnson's credo, shown in Figure 2.3, helped hundreds of employees ethically address the criminal tampering with Tylenol products. In its 1986 centennial annual report, J & J attributed its success in this crisis, as well as its long-term business growth (a compound sales rate of 11.6 percent for 100 years), to "our unique form of decentralized management, our adherence to the ethical principles embodied in our credo, and our emphasis on managing the business for the long term."

Individual codes of ethics, professional oaths, and organizational credos all must be anchored in a moral, ethical framework. They are always open to question and continuous improvement using ethical theories as a tool for reexamining the soundness of the current standard. Although a universal right and wrong may exist, it would be hard to argue that there is only one code of ethics to which all individuals, professions, and organizations can subscribe.

FIGURE The Johnson & Johnson Credo

We believe our first responsibility is to the doctors, nurses, and patients,
to mothers and all others who use our products and services.
In meeting their needs everything we do must be of high quality.
We must constantly strive to reduce our costs
in order to maintain reasonable prices.
Customers' orders must be serviced promptly and accurately.
Our suppliers and distributors must have an opportunity
to make a fair profit.

We are responsible to our employees,
the men and women who work with us throughout the world.
Everyone must be considered as an individual.
We must respect their dignity and recognize their merit.
They must have a sense of security in their jobs.
Compensation must be fair and adequate,
and working conditions clean, orderly, and safe.
Employees must feel free to make suggestions and complaints.
There must be equal opportunity for employment, development
and advancement for those qualified.
We must provide competent management,
and their actions must be just and ethical.

We are responsible to the communities in which we live and work
and to the world community as well.
We must be good citizens—support good works and charities
and bear our fair share of taxes.
We must encourage civic improvements and better health and education.
We must maintain in good order
the property we are privileged to use,
protecting the environment and natural resources.

Our final responsibility is to our stockholders.
Business must make a sound profit.
We must experiment with new ideas.
Research must be carried on, innovative programs developed
and mistakes paid for.
New equipment must be purchased, new facilities provided,
and new products launched.
Reserves must be created to provide for adverse times.
When we operate according to these principles,
the stockholders should realize a fair return.

TECHNOLOGICAL INNOVATION

A fourth challenge that managers face is effectively managing technological innovation. *Technology* consists of the intellectual and mechanical processes used by an organization to transform inputs into products or services that meet organizational goals. Managers face the challenge of rapidly changing technology and of putting the technology to optimum use in organizations. The inability of managers to incorporate new technologies successfully into their organizations is a major factor that has limited economic growth in the United States.[92] Although the United States still leads the way in developing new technologies, it lags behind in making productive use of these new technologies in workplace settings.[93]

Good-to-great organizations avoid technology fads and bandwagons, yet become pioneers in the application of carefully selected technologies.[94]

The Internet has radically changed the way organizations communicate and perform work. By integrating computer, cable, and telecommunications technologies, businesses have learned new ways to compete. For example, Kmart takes advantage of the Internet through BlueLight.com for online retailing. In networked organizations, time, distance, and space become irrelevant. A networked organization can do business anytime and anywhere, which is essential in the global marketplace. This allows retailers to drastically cut their investments in inventories. The World Wide Web has created a virtual commercial district. Customers can book air travel, buy compact discs, and "surf the Net" to conduct business around the globe.[95]

Managers face the challenge of effectively managing technological innovation, such as Hitachi's electronic paper display.

© YOSHIKAZU TSUNG/AFP/GETTY IMAGES

The Internet and electronic innovation have made surveillance of employees more widespread. However, companies need to balance the use of spyware, monitoring of employee e-mails and Web sites, and video monitoring systems with respect for employee rights to privacy. Managers with excellent interpersonal skills go a long way in ensuring high productivity, commitment, and appropriate behavior on the part of employees versus the use of intense employee performance monitoring systems using electronic surveillance. Companies with clearly written policies that spell out their approach to monitoring employees may succeed better in walking the fine line between respecting employees' privacy and protecting the interests of the organization.

One fascinating technological change is the development of *expert systems*, computer-based applications that use a representation of human expertise in a specialized field of knowledge to solve problems. Expert systems can be used in many ways, including providing advice to nonexperts, offering assistance to experts, replacing experts, and serving as a training and development tool in organizations.[96] They are used in medical decision making, diagnosis, and medical informatics.[97] Anheuser-Busch has used an expert system to assist managers in ensuring that personnel decisions comply with antidiscrimination laws.[98]

Robots, another technological innovation, were invented in the United States, and advanced research on *robotics* is still conducted here. However, Japan leads

technology
The intellectual and mechanical processes used by an organization to transform inputs into products or services that meet organizational goals.

expert system
A computer-based application that uses a representation of human expertise in a specialized field of knowledge to solve problems.

robotics
The use of robots in organizations.

the world in the use of robotics in organizations. Organizations in the United States have fewer total robots than were added in 1989 alone in Japan.[99] Robots in Japan are treated like part of the family. They are even named after favorite celebrities, singers, and movie stars. Whereas Japanese workers are happy to let robots take over repetitive or dangerous work, Americans are more suspicious of labor-saving robots because employers often use them to cut jobs.[100] The main reason for the reluctance of U.S. organizations to use robots is their slow payout. Robotics represents a big investment that does not pay off in the short term. Japanese managers are more willing to use a long-term horizon to evaluate the effectiveness of robotics technology. Labor unions may also resist robotics because of the fear that robots will replace employees.

Some U.S. companies that experimented with robotics had bad experiences. Deere & Company originally used robots to paint its tractors, but the company scrapped them because programming the robots for the multitude of types of paint used took too long. Now Deere uses robots to torque cap screws on tractors, a repetitive job that once had a high degree of human error.

It is tempting to view technology from only the positive side; however, a reality check is in order. Some firms that have been disappointed with costly technologies are electing to *de*-engineer. And computer innovations often fail; 42 percent of information technology projects are abandoned before completion, and half of all technology projects fail to meet managers' expectations. Pacific Gas and Electric (part of PG&E Corporation) spent tens of millions of dollars on a new IBM-based system. Deregulation then hit the utility industry, and customers were permitted to choose among utility companies. Keeping up with multiple suppliers and fast-changing prices was too much, and the massive new system couldn't handle the additional burden quickly enough. It was scrapped in favor of a new project using the old first-generation computer system, which is being updated and gradually replaced. Because some innovations fail to live up to expectations, and some simply fail, it is important to effectively manage both revolutionary and evolutionary approaches to technological transitions.[101]

Alternative Work Arrangements

Technological advances have been responsible, to a large degree, for the advent of alternative work arrangements, the nontraditional work practices, settings, and locations that are now supplementing traditional workplaces. One alternative work arrangement is *telecommuting*, transmitting work from a home computer to the office using a modem. IBM, for example, was one of the first companies to experiment with the notion of installing computer terminals in employees' homes. By telecommuting, employees gain flexibility, save the commute to work, and enjoy the comforts of being at home. Telecommuting also has disadvantages, however, including distractions, lack of opportunities to socialize with other workers, lack of interaction with supervisors, and decreased identification with the organization. Despite these disadvantages, telecommuters still feel "plugged in" to the communication system at the office. Studies show that telecommuters often report higher satisfaction with office communication than do workers in traditional office environments.[102]

Estimates are that about 28 million Americans are telecommuting. Why do companies encourage telecommuting? Cost reductions are an obvious motivator. Since 1991, AT&T has gained $550 million in cash flow from eliminating office space and reducing overhead costs. Another reason is to increase productivity. At IBM, a survey of telecommuters indicated that 87 percent believed they were more

6 Understand the alternative work arrangements produced by technological advances.

telecommuting
Transmitting work from a home computer to the office using a modem.

productive in the alternative work arrangement. Telecommuting also allows companies access to workers with key skills regardless of their location. Alternative workplaces also give companies an advantage in hiring and keeping talented employees who find the flexibility of working at home very attractive.

There is a spectrum of other alternative work arrangements. *Hoteling* is a shared-office arrangement wherein employees have mobile file cabinets and lockers for personal storage, and "hotel" work spaces are furnished for them. These spaces must be reserved instead of being permanently assigned. The computer system routes phone calls and e-mail as necessary. Individuals' personal photos and memorabilia are stored electronically and "placed" on occupants' computer desktops upon arrival.

Satellite offices comprise another alternative work arrangement. In such offices, large facilities are broken into a network of smaller workplaces close to employees' homes. Satellites are often located in comparatively inexpensive cities and suburban areas. They usually have simpler and less costly furnishings and fixtures than the more centrally located offices. Satellites can save a company as much as 50 percent in real estate costs and can be quite appealing to employees who do not want to work in a large urban area. This can broaden the pool of potential employees, who can communicate with the home office via various technologies.[103]

All of these alternative work arrangements signal a trend toward *virtual offices*, in which people work anytime, anywhere, and with anyone. The concept involves work being where people are, rather than people moving to where the work is. Information technologies make connectivity, collaboration, and communication easy. Critical voice mails and messages can be delivered to and from the central office, a client's office, the airport, the car, or home. Wireless Internet access and online meeting software such as WebEx make it possible for employees to participate in meetings anywhere at any time.

Emerging Managerial Realities

Technological innovation affects the very nature of the management job. Managers who once had to coax workers back to their desks from coffee breaks now find that they need to encourage workers mesmerized by new technology to take more frequent breaks.[104] Working with a computer can be stressful, both physically and psychologically. Eyestrain, neck and back strain, and headaches can result from sitting at a computer terminal too long. In addition, workers can become accustomed to the fast response time of the computer and expect the same from their coworkers. When coworkers do not respond with the speed and accuracy of the computer, they may receive a harsh retort. New technology combined with globalization and intensified business pressures has led to the rise of extreme workers, pushing up the ranks of workaholics.[105] These extreme workers pay a price in relationships; other dimensions of a full, rich life; and levels of stress.

Computerized monitoring provides managers with a wealth of information about employee performance, and it holds great potential for misuse as mentioned earlier in this section. The telecommunications, airline, and mail-order merchandise industries make wide use of systems that secretly monitor employees' interactions with customers. Employers praise such systems because they improve customer service. Workers, however, are not so positive; they react with higher levels of depression, anxiety, and exhaustion from working under such secret scrutiny. At Bell Canada, operators were evaluated on a system that tabulated average working time with customers. Operators found the practice highly stressful, and they sabotaged the system by giving callers wrong directory assistance numbers rather than taking the time to look up the correct ones. As a result, Bell

Canada now uses average working time scores for entire offices rather than for individuals.[106]

New technologies and rapid innovation place a premium on a manager's technical skills. Early management theories rated technical skills as less important than human and conceptual skill. This is past reality. Managers today must develop technical competence in order to gain workers' respect. Computer-integrated manufacturing systems, for example, have been shown to require managers to use participative management styles, open communication, and greater technical expertise to be effective.[107] In a world of rapid technological innovation, managers must focus more carefully on helping workers manage the stress of their work. They must take advantage of the wealth of information at their disposal to motivate, coach, and counsel workers rather than try to control them more stringently or police them. The management of intellectual property, however, cannot be left to technology managers or corporate lawyers.[108] Roughly 75 percent of *Fortune* 100's total market capitalization is in intangible assets, such as patents, copyrights, and trademarks. Managers and companies with well-conceived strategies and policies for their intellectual property can use it for competitive advantage in the global marketplace.

Technological change occurs so rapidly that turbulence characterizes most organizations. Workers must constantly learn and adapt to changing technology so that organizations can remain competitive. Managers must grapple with the challenge of helping workers adapt and make effective use of new technologies.

Helping Employees Adjust to Technological Change

Most workers are well aware of the benefits of modern technologies. The availability of skilled jobs and improved working conditions have been by-products of innovation in many organizations. Technology is also bringing disadvantaged individuals into the workforce. Microchips have dramatically increased opportunities for workers with visual impairments. Information can be decoded into speech using a speech synthesizer, into braille using a hard-copy printer, or into enlarged print visible on a computer monitor. Workers with visual impairments are no longer dependent on sighted persons to translate printed information for them, and this has opened new doors of opportunity.[109] Engineers at Carnegie Mellon University have developed PizzaBot, a robot that individuals with disabilities can operate using a voice-recognition system. Despite these and other benefits of new technology in the workplace, however, employees may still resist change.

Technological innovations bring about changes in employees' work environments, and change has been described as the ultimate stressor. Many workers react negatively to change that they perceive as threatening to their work situation. Many of their fears center around loss—of freedom, of control, of the things they like about their jobs.[110] Employees may fear deterioration of their quality of work life and increased pressure at work. Further, they may fear being replaced by technology or being displaced into jobs of lower skill levels.

Managers can take several actions to help employees adjust to changing technology. The workers' participation in early phases of the decision-making process regarding technological changes is important. This helps them gain important information about the potential changes in their jobs, making them less resistant to the change. Workers are the users of the new technology. Their input in early stages can lead to a smoother transition into the new ways of performing work.

Managers should also keep in mind the effects that new technology has on the skill requirements of workers. Many employees support changes that increase the skill requirements of their jobs. Increased skill requirements often lead to increases

(7) Explain the ways managers can help employees adjust to technological change.

in job autonomy, more responsibility, and potential pay increases, all of which are received positively by employees. Whenever possible, managers should select technology that increases workers' skill requirements.

Providing effective training about ways to use the new technology also is essential. Training helps employees feel that they control the technology rather than being controlled by it. The training should be designed to match workers' needs, and it should increase the workers' sense of mastery of the new technology.

Support groups within the organization are another way of helping employees adjust to technological change. Such change is stressful, and support groups are important emotional outlets for workers. Support groups can also function as information exchanges so that workers can share advice on using the technology. Workers feel less alone with the problem when they know that other workers share their frustration.

A related challenge is to encourage workers to invent new uses for technology already in place. *Reinvention* is the term for creatively applying new technology.[111] Innovators should be rewarded for their efforts. Individuals who explore the boundaries of a new technology can personalize the technology and adapt it to their own job needs, as well as share this information with others in the work group. In one large public utility, service representatives, without their supervisor's knowledge, developed a personal note-passing system that later became the basis of a formal communication system that improved the efficiency of their work group.

Managers face a substantial challenge in leading organizations to adopt new technologies more humanely and effectively. Technological changes are essential for earnings growth and for expanded employment opportunities. The adoption of new technologies is a critical determinant of U.S. competitiveness in the global marketplace.

MANAGERIAL IMPLICATIONS: BEATING THE CHALLENGES

Organizational success depends on managers' ability to address the four challenges of globalization, workforce diversity, ethics, and technological innovation. Failure to address the challenges can be costly. Think about Pepsi's losses to Coke in the global cola wars. Coke is winning the battle and capitalizing on the huge opportunities and profits from global markets. A racial discrimination lawsuit against Texaco cost the company millions in a settlement and damaged its reputation. Managers' behavioral integrity (i.e., word-deed alignment) is judged by all employees, most especially African American employees.[112] Mitsubishi suffered a similar fate in a sexual harassment scandal. Failure to address these challenges can mean costly losses, damage to reputations, and ultimately an organization's demise.

These four challenges are important because the way managers handle them shapes employee behavior. Developing global mindsets among employees expands their worldview and puts competition on a larger scale. Knowing that diversity is valued and differences are assets causes employees to think twice about engaging in discriminatory behaviors. Valuing technological change leads employees to experiment with new technologies and develop innovative ways to perform their jobs. Sending a message that unethical behavior is not tolerated lets employees know that doing the right thing pays off.

These four challenges are recurring themes that you will see throughout our book. You will learn how companies are tackling these challenges and how organizational behavior can be used to create opportunity in organizations, which is a must if they are to remain competitive.

reinvention
The creative application of new technology.

"You're Hired!" . . . Not . . . if You're Over 40

Donald Trump's hugely popular reality series, *The Apprentice*, was mired in controversy at the beginning of its sixth and final season. R. Joseph Hewett, a 51-year-old technology manager, alleged in an age-discrimination lawsuit that he never got a chance to hear the words, "You're fired!" because the show's organizers and producers felt he was too old to compete.

Hewett maintained that he was unjustifiably turned down for the reality show given his "many years of experience managing large commercial properties." Among his qualifications, Hewett graduated magna cum laude from college and worked as a technology manager at a commercial real estate company. He was also 49 years old at the time he applied for the show in 2005. In his lawsuit, Hewett asserted that only two of the finalists in the first six seasons of show had been over 40 years of age, a claim that a Trump spokesman did not deny. According to the Trump organization,

while they actively sought participants from "all age groups," few applicants were over the age of 40.

Hewett reached a settlement with the Trump organization that in his words was "satisfactory to all." He stated that the lawsuit was never about a disgruntled applicant trying to get back at Trump's organization but rather an opportunity to advocate on behalf of an entire class of people he believed had been victimized.

1. Was Hewett justified in bringing age-discrimination litigation against *The Apprentice*? Why or why not?
2. What could the Trump organization have done to encourage more people over 40 to apply for the show?

SOURCE: M. Pratt. "Apprentice Reject Who Claimed Age Discrimination Settles Suit," *The Associated Press* (May 22, 2007).

LOOKING BACK: GENENTECH, INC.

You Can't Do Everything for Everybody

Science and business have their limitations. No company, no government, no agency can meet the needs of everyone; those are the constraints of reality. However, no one knows what the actual limits are until they push them. For example, in 2006, Genentech spent $1.8 billion in research and development. That is a significant budget for one company, but Genentech still had to do some serious prioritizing to decide where to spend those precious resources. The budget was large; it was not unlimited. Imagination is great, and reality provides a set of constraint limitations. As a result, trade-offs must be made both in the short term and the long term, giving rise to ethical dilemmas.

At the same time it wrestles with priorities of resource allocation, Genentech has nurtured a culture that fosters innovation, creativity, and new ideas. The company is committed to the proper treatment of employees and scientists in creative cultures, which takes more than training and lip service. Innovation and creativity need to be underscored at every turn. Within Genentech, the implication of this commitment has been, from the beginning, to allow its researchers to publish their findings in academic journals. Publication in leading scientific journals is an important career status marker for scientists.[113] The company's position is very different from most pharmaceutical companies that tightly guard their research secrets.

The good news for Genentech is that their "publish your research" policy allows them to compete with Harvard, Stanford, Lancaster, Cambridge, and other leading research universities of the world when recruiting top scientists. This is because these scientists know that they can continue to build their academic reputations while also doing important research and earning corporate salaries. They have helped lead Genentech to scientific and financial successes, for example with a drug like Lucetis, which treats the leading cause of blindness. Approved in mid-2006, Lucetis had sales of $380 million for the year, making it one of Genentech's most successful launches ever. Science and business can mix!

Chapter Summary

1. To ensure that their organizations meet the competition, managers must tackle four important challenges: globalization, workforce diversity, ethical behavior, and technological change at work.

2. The five cultural differences that affect work-related attitudes are individualism versus collectivism, power distance, uncertainty avoidance, masculinity versus femininity, and time orientation.

3. Diversity encompasses gender, culture, personality, sexual orientation, religion, ability, social status, and a host of other differences.

4. Managers must take a proactive approach to managing diversity so that differences are valued and capitalized upon.

5. Three types of ethical theories include consequential theories, rule-based theories, and character theories.

6. Ethical dilemmas emerge for people at work in the areas of employee rights, sexual harassment, romantic involvements, organizational justice, whistle-blowing, and social responsibility.

7. Alternative work arrangements, facilitated by technology, are changing the way work is performed.

8. Through supportive relationships and training, managers can help employees adjust to technological change.

Key Terms

character theory (p. 53)
collectivism (p. 40)
consequential theory (p. 53)
distributive justice (p. 57)
diversity (p. 45)
expatriate manager (p. 42)
expert system (p. 60)
femininity (p. 41)

glass ceiling (p. 46)
guanxi (p. 38)
individualism (p. 40)
masculinity (p. 41)
power distance (p. 40)
procedural justice (p. 57)
reinvention (p. 64)
robotics (p. 60)

rule-based theory (p. 53)
social responsibility (p. 58)
technology (p. 60)
telecommuting (p. 61)
time orientation (p. 41)
transnational organization (p. 37)
uncertainty avoidance (p. 41)
whistle-blower (p. 57)

Review Questions

1. What are Hofstede's five dimensions of cultural differences that affect work attitudes? Using these dimensions, describe the United States.

2. What are the primary sources of diversity in the U.S. workforce?

3. What are the potential benefits and problems of diversity?

4. What is the reality of the glass ceiling? What would it take to change this reality?

5. What are some of the ethical challenges encountered in organizations?

6. Describe the difference between distributive and procedural justice.

7. Why do employees fear technological innovations, and how can managers help employees adjust?

Discussion and Communication Questions

1. How can managers be encouraged to develop global thinking? How can managers dispel stereotypes about other cultures?

2. Some people have argued that in designing expert systems, human judgment is made obsolete. What do you think?

3. Why do some companies encourage alternative work arrangements?

4. What effects will the globalization of business have on a company's culture? How can an organization with a strong "made in America" identity compete in the global marketplace?

5. Why is diversity such an important issue? Is the workforce more diverse today than in the past?

6. How does a manager strike a balance between encouraging employees to celebrate their own cultures and forming a single unified culture within the organization?

7. Do you agree with Hofstede's findings about U.S. culture? Other cultures? On what do you base your agreement or disagreement?

8. (*communication question*) Select one of the four challenges (globalization, diversity, ethics, technology) and write a brief position paper arguing for its importance to managers.

9. (*communication question*) Find someone whose culture is different from your own. This could be a classmate or an international student at your university. Interview the person about his or her culture, using Hofstede's dimensions. Also ask what you might need to know about doing business in that person's culture (e.g., customs, etiquette). Be prepared to share this information in class.

Ethical Dilemma

Jill Warner, President of Ace Toys, sat looking at the monthly profit and loss statement. For the fifth month in a row, the company had lost money. Labor costs were killing them. Jill had done everything she could think of to reduce costs and still produce a quality product. She was beginning to face the fact that soon she would no longer be able to avoid the idea of outsourcing. It was a concept that Jill had done everything to avoid, but it was beginning to look inevitable.

Jill felt strongly about making a quality American product using American workers in an American factory. But if things continued the way they were, she was going to have to do something. She owed it to her stockholders and board of directors to keep the company financially

healthy. They had entrusted her with the future of the company, and she could not let them down. It was not her money or company to do with as she pleased. Her job was to make sure that Ace Toys flourished.

However, if she chose to outsource the production segment of the company, only management and the sales force would keep their jobs. How could she face the 500 people who would lose their jobs? How would the small community that depended on those 500 jobs survive? She also worried about the customers who had come to depend on Ace Toys to produce a safe product that they could give to their children with confidence. Would that quality suffer if she sent production halfway around the world? How could she ensure that the company she hired to produce their toys would live up to Ace's standards? Would the other company pay a fair wage and not employ children? The questions seemed endless, but Jill needed to decide how to save the company.

Experiential Exercises

2.1 International Orientations

1. Preparation (preclass)

Read the background on the International Orientation Scale and the case study "Office Supplies International— Marketing Associate," complete the ratings and questions, and fill out the self-assessment inventory.

2. Group Discussions

Groups of four to six people discuss their answers to the case study questions and their own responses to the self-assessment.

3. Class Discussion

Instructor leads a discussion on the International Orientation Scale and the difficulties and challenges of adjusting to a new culture. Why do some people adjust more easily than others? What can you do to adjust to a new culture? What can you regularly do that will help you adjust in the future to almost any new culture?

Office Supplies International—Marketing Associate*

Jonathan Fraser is a marketing associate for a large multinational corporation, Office Supplies International (OSI), in Buffalo, New York. He is being considered for a transfer to the international division of OSI. This position will require that he spend between one and three years working abroad in one of OSI's three foreign subsidiaries: OSI-France, OSI-Japan, or OSI-Australia. This transfer is considered a fast-track career move at OSI, and Jonathan feels honored to be in the running for the position.

Jonathan has been working at OSI since he graduated with his bachelor's degree in marketing ten years ago. He is married and has lived and worked in Buffalo all his life. Jonathan's parents are first-generation German Americans. His grandparents, although deceased, spoke only German at home and upheld many of their ethnic traditions. His parents, although quite "Americanized," have retained some of their German traditions. To communicate better with his grandparents, Jonathan took German in high school but never used it because his grandparents had passed away.

In college, Jonathan joined the German Club and was a club officer for two years. His other collegiate extracurricular activity was playing for the varsity baseball team. Jonathan

Questions

1. Is sending jobs out of the country unethical?

2. Using consequential, rule-based, and character theories, evaluate Jill's options.

still enjoys playing in a summer softball league with his college friends. Given his athletic interests, he volunteered to be the athletic programming coordinator at OSI, where he organizes the company's softball and volleyball teams. Jonathan has been making steady progress at OSI. Last year, he was named marketing associate of the year.

His wife, Sue, is also a Buffalo native. She teaches English literature at the high school in one of the middle-class suburbs of Buffalo. Sue took five years off after she had a baby but returned to teaching this year when Janine, their five-year-old daughter, started kindergarten. She is happy to be resuming her career. One or two nights a week, Sue volunteers at the city mission where she works as a career counselor and a basic skills trainer. For fun, she takes pottery and ethnic cooking classes.

Both Sue and Jonathan are excited about the potential transfer and accompanying pay raise. They are, however, also feeling apprehensive and cautious. Neither Sue nor Jonathan has ever lived away from their families in Buffalo, and Sue is concerned about giving up her newly reestablished career. Their daughter Janine has just started school, and Jonathan and Sue are uncertain whether living abroad is the best thing for her at her age.

Using the following three-point scale, try to rate Jonathan and Sue as potential expatriates. Write a sentence or two on why you gave the ratings you did.

Rating Scale

1. Based on this dimension, this person would adjust well to living abroad.

2. Based on this dimension, this person may or may not adjust well to living abroad.

3. Based on this dimension, this person would not adjust well to living abroad.

Jonathan's International Orientation

rating dimension	rating and reason for rating
International attitudes	
Foreign experiences	
Comfort with differences	
Participation in cultural events	

Sue's International Orientation

rating dimension	rating and reason for rating
International attitudes	
Foreign experiences	
Comfort with differences	
Participation in cultural events	

Discussion Questions: Office Supplies International

1. Imagine that you are the international human resource manager for OSI. Your job is to interview both Jonathan and Sue to determine whether they should be sent abroad. What are some of the questions you would ask? What critical information do you feel is missing? It might be helpful to role-play the three parts and evaluate your classmates' responses as Jonathan and Sue.

2. Suppose France is the country where they would be sent. To what extent would your ratings change? What else would you change about the way you are assessing the couple?

3. Now answer the same questions, except this time they are being sent to Japan. Repeat the exercise for Australia.

4. For those dimensions that you rated Sue and Jonathan either 2 or 3 (indicating that they might have a potential adjustment problem), what would you suggest for training and development? What might be included in a training program?

5. Reflect on your own life for a moment and give yourself a rating on each of the following dimensions. Try to justify why you rated yourself as you did. Do you feel that you would adjust well to living abroad? What might be difficult for you?

rating dimension	rating and reason for rating France, Japan, Australia (or other)
International attitudes	
Foreign experiences	
Comfort with differences	
Participation in cultural events	

6. Generally, what are some of the potential problems a dual-career couple might face? What are some of the solutions to those problems?

7. How would the ages of children affect the expatriate's assignment? At what age should the children's international orientations be assessed along with their parents?

International Orientation Scale

The following sample items are taken from the International Orientation Scale. Answer each question and give yourself a score for each dimension. The highest possible score for any dimension is 20 points.

Dimension 1: International Attitudes

Use the following scale to answer questions Q1 through Q4.

1	*Strongly agree*
2	*Agree somewhat*
3	*Maybe or unsure*
4	*Disagree somewhat*
5	*Strongly disagree*

Q1. Foreign language skills should be taught as early as elementary school. _____

Q2. Traveling the world is a priority in my life. _____

Q3. A yearlong overseas assignment (from my company) would be a fantastic opportunity for my family and me. _____

Q4. Other countries fascinate me. _____

Total Dimension 1 _____

Dimension 2: Foreign Experiences

Q1. I have studied a foreign language.

1	Never
2	For less than a year
3	For a year
4	For a few years
5	For several years

Q2. I am fluent in another language.

1	I don't know another language.
2	I am limited to very short and simple phrases.
3	I know basic grammatical structure and speak with a limited vocabulary.
4	I understand conversation on most topics.
5	I am very fluent in another language.

Q3. I have spent time overseas (traveling, studying abroad, etc.).

1	Never
2	About a week
3	A few weeks
4	A few months
5	Several months or years

Q4. I was overseas before the age of 18.

1	Never
2	About a week
3	A few weeks
4	A few months
5	Several months or years

Total Dimension 2 _____

Dimension 3: Comfort with Differences

Use the following scale for questions Q1 through Q4.

1	*Quite similar*
2	*Mostly similar*
3	*Somewhat different*
4	*Quite different*
5	*Extremely different*

Q1. My friends' career goals, interests, and education are . . . _____

Q2. My friends' ethnic backgrounds are . . . _____

Q3. My friends' religious affiliations are . . . _____

Q4. My friends' first languages are . . . _____

Total Dimension 3 _____

Dimension 4: Participation in Cultural Events

Use the following scale to answer questions Q1 through Q4.

1	*Never*
2	*Seldom*
3	*Sometimes*
4	*Frequently*
5	*As often as possible*

Q1. I eat at a variety of ethnic restaurants (e.g., Greek, Polynesian, Thai, German). _____

Q2. I watch the major networks' world news programs. _____

Q3. I attend ethnic festivals. _____

Q4. I visit art galleries and museums. _____

Total Dimension 4 _____

Self-Assessment Discussion Questions:

Do any of these scores suprise you?

Would you like to improve your international orientation?

If so, what could you do to change various aspects of your life?

*"Office Supplies International—Marketing Associate" by Paula Caligiuri. Copyright © 1994 by Paula Caligiuri, Ph.D. Information for the International Orientation Scale can be obtained by contacting Paula Caligiuri, Ph.D. at 732-445-5228 or e-mail: paula@caligiuri.com. Reprinted by permission of the author.

Dorothy Marcic and Sheila M. Puffer, *Management International: Cases, Exercises, and Readings* (Eagan, MN: West Publishing, 1994). *All rights reserved. May not be reproduced without written permission of the publisher.*

2.2 Ethical Dilemmas

Divide the class into five groups. Each group should choose one of the following scenarios and agree on a course of action.

1. Sam works for you. He is technically capable and a good worker, but he does not get along well with others in the work group. When Sam has an opportunity to transfer, you encourage him to take it. What would you say to Sam's potential supervisor when he asks about Sam?

2. Your boss has told you that you must reduce your work group by 30 percent. Which of the following criteria would you use to lay off workers?

   a. Lay off older, higher-paid employees.

   b. Lay off younger, lower-paid employees.

   c. Lay off workers based on seniority only.

   d. Lay off workers based on performance only.

3. You are an engineer, but you are not working on your company's Department of Transportation (DOT) project. One day you overhear a conversation in the cafeteria between the program manager and the project engineer that makes you reasonably sure a large contract will soon be given to the ABC Company to develop and manufacture a key DOT subsystem. ABC is a small firm, and its stock is traded over the counter. You feel sure that the stock will rise from its present $2.25 per share as soon as news of the DOT contract gets out. Would you go out and buy ABC's stock?

4. You are the project engineer working on the development of a small liquid rocket engine. You know that if you could achieve a throttling ratio greater than 8 to 1, your system would be considered a success and continue to receive funding support. To date, the best you have achieved is a 4-to-1 ratio. You have an unproven idea that you feel has a 50 percent chance of being successful. Your project is currently being reviewed to determine if it should be continued. You would like to continue it. How optimistically should you present the test results?

5. Imagine that you are the president of a company in a highly competitive industry. You learn that a competitor has made an important scientific discovery that is not patentable and will give that company an advantage that will substantially reduce the profits of your company for about a year. There is some hope of hiring one of the competitor's employees

who knows the details of the discovery. Would you try to hire this person?

Each group should present its scenario and chosen course of action to the class. The class should then evaluate the ethics of the course of action, using the following questions to guide discussion:

1. Are you following rules that are understood and accepted?

2. Are you comfortable discussing and defending your action?

3. Would you want someone to do this to you?

4. What if everyone acted this way?

5. Are there alternatives that rest on firmer ethical ground?

Scenarios adapted from R. A. DiBattista, "Providing a Rationale for Ethical Conduct from Alternatives Taken in Ethical Dilemmas," *Journal of General Psychology* 116 (1989): 207–214; discussion questions adapted with the permission of The Free Press, a Division of Simon & Schuster, Inc. from *The Manager as Negotiator: Bargaining for Cooperation and Competitive Gain* by David A. Lax and James K. Sebenius 0-02-918770-2. Copyright © 1986 by David A. Lax and James K. Sebenius.

TAKE 2

Biz Flix | Mr. Baseball

The New York Yankees trade aging baseball player Jack Elliot (Tom Selleck) to the Chunichi Dragons, a Japanese team. This lighthearted comedy traces Jack's bungling entry into Japanese culture and exposes his cultural misconceptions, which almost cost him everything—including his new girlfriend Hiroko Uchiyama (Aya Takanashi). Unknown to Jack, Hiroko's father is "The Chief" (Ken Takakura), the Chunichi Dragons' manager. After Jack slowly begins to understand Japanese culture and Japanese baseball, his team-mates finally accept him. This film shows many examples of Japanese culture, especially its love for baseball.

The *Mr. Baseball* scene takes place after "The Chief" has removed Jack from a base-ball game. It shows Jack dining with Hiroko and her grandmother (Mineko Yorozuya), grandfather (Jun Hamamura), and father. The film continues with a dispute between Jack and Hiroko. Jack also learns from "The Chief" what he must do to succeed on the team.

What to Watch for and Ask Yourself:

> Does Jack Elliot behave as if he had cross-cultural training before arriving in Japan?

> Is he culturally sensitive or insensitive?

> What do you propose that Jack Elliot do for the rest of his time in Japan?

Workplace Video | Meeting the Challenge of Diversity at Whirlpool

In today's global marketplace, managers must routinely interact with people of different cultures, languages, beliefs, and values. Recognizing diversity and the unique way people of different backgrounds communicate is essential to success in the international arena.

Whirlpool Corporation, the number-one name in home appliances, has a long history of managing diversity. Established in 1911, Whirlpool has become a global corporation with manufacturing locations on every major continent. Approximately 60 percent of Whirlpool's 68,000 employees work outside of North America, and those within North America represent a diverse mix of people.

Building a cohesive team of diverse individuals is one of the great challenges of man-agement. Whirlpool's leaders are committed to cultivating a broad workforce, and that means eliminating glass ceilings and biases that discourage certain groups from participat-ing fully in the company. Attaining these objectives is the job of Whirlpool's award-winning diversity program. To enter the program, workers join the particular employee-network group with which they self-identify. Once joined to a network, workers have access to career resources and training opportunities.

Although the diversity program is designed for employees, it also helps Whirlpool achieve specific business objectives, such as understanding the needs and desires of its global customer base. "Whirlpool has recognized that having diverse people making decisions and giving input to the factors that we consider on a daily basis is extremely important to the business," says Kathy Nelson, VP of Consumer & Appliance Care at Whirlpool. "It's important because we need to make sure that the people who are making business decisions are reflective of who our consumers are."

Mark McLane, director of Global Diversity and Inclusion, sees diversity as a vehicle through which Whirlpool can find innovative solutions to problems. "The greatest strength of our employee base today is its diversity—the diversity of thought and what that brings to our innovation processes," McLane remarks. "We've embedded innovation throughout the entire organization; we've really leveraged the strengths of each individual Whirlpool employee."

Discussion Questions

1. What are the three main objectives of Whirlpool's diversity networks?

2. What challenges do managers at Whirlpool face in establishing a diverse workplace? How might they respond to these challenges?

3. Do you think Whirlpool's encouragement of employee networks always leads to a culture of diversity and the formation of effective multicultural teams? Why or why not?

The Timberland Company:
Challenges and Opportunities

The Timberland Company, headquartered in Stratham, New Hampshire, makes and markets footwear, apparel, and accessories. Its footwear includes hiking boots, boat shoes, sandals, outdoor casual footwear, and dress shoes. The apparel line includes socks, shirts, pants, and outerwear, whereas accessories involve such products as watches, sunglasses, and belts. Timberland sells its products around the world through department stores and athletic stores and operates over 220 company-owned and franchised outlets in the United States, Canada, Latin America, Europe, the Middle East, and Asia.[1]

Timberland has a strong international operation with a growing market in China; however, it has experienced increased labor costs and tariffs in Europe. In 2006 the tariff issue became very important due to the sourcing of approximately 30 percent of Timberland's total volume from factories in China and Vietnam. The company's international strength has been offset somewhat by its declining market fortunes in the United States. Timberland also faces increased competition globally, particularly from Nike and Adidas. From 2001 to 2005, Timberland had an average annual revenue growth of 7.5 percent, compared to the industry average of 9 percent during the same period. Moreover, revenue growth has been decelerating.[2] In 2006, Timberland had $1.6 billion in revenues that reflected growth in the business segments serving casual, outdoor, and industrial consumers. However, the boot business declined due to significant fashion changes that diminished demand for those products.[3]

Although Timberland experienced some market difficulty in 2006, it was still recognized as a great place to work. The company was honored by *Working Mother* magazine as "One of the Best Places to Work" and by *Fortune* magazine as "One of the 100 Best Companies to Work For."[4]

Timberland develops and uses technology to further its business interests and to benefit its customers and distributors. For example, Timberland uses innovative technology that enables customers to customize their footwear online. The company's configuration software allows shoppers to "specify so many product details—including colors, hardware, laces and typefaces for monogramming—that more than one million combinations are possible for any one base [footwear] style."[5] The results are visualized instantaneously on the customer's own computer. A company spokesperson observed, "... no one else out there has this technology. It was really important to us to include that because the challenge in the online environment is trying to replicate that tactile-visual experience of an offline environment."[6]

Another application of innovative technology occurred in the summer of 2005 with Timberland's test of its PreciseFit System in 54 stores in Europe, Asia, and the United States. The PreciseFit System, tested in the men's casual footwear category, enables Timberland to exactly fit footwear for the 60 percent of men who can't get an optimal fit otherwise and for those men—about 35 percent of the market—who have a half-size or greater difference between their left foot and right foot. Each pair of shoes comes with inserts that fit full and half-sizes in narrow, medium, and wide widths, thereby enabling retailers to more easily service hard-to-fit customers, maintain a smaller inventory, and have fewer lost sales.[7]

In addition to its efforts to run the business more effectively and efficiently, to provide customers with continually improving service, and to meaningfully support suppliers and distributors, Timberland is also committed to social and environmental causes. Part of its mission is to use "the resources, energy, and profits of a publicly traded footwear-and-apparel company to combat social ills, help the environment, and improve conditions for laborers around the globe."[8] Jeffrey Swartz, Timberland's CEO, believes that the best way to pursue social objectives is through a publicly traded company rather than through a privately owned company or a nonprofit organization because it forces commerce and justice—business interests and social/

environmental interests—to be enacted in a public and transparent manner.[9]

Timberland's social and environmental commitments and efforts are evident in its products and operations as well as in its relationships with suppliers and customers. In terms of its products and operations, Timberland practices full-disclosure labeling on its footwear. Every footwear box has a label describing the ecological impact with respect to the amount of energy used in the manufacture and distribution of each product. Timberland's goal is to decrease its ecological footprint by increasing the use of wind or solar power in the manufacture and distribution of its products. Future plans for full-disclosure packaging include labeling that details the environmental impact of the chemicals and organic materials contained in Timberland's products.[10]

In dealing with suppliers around the world, Timberland promotes fair labor practices and human rights. According to the company's Global Human Rights Standards, "[W]e're equally committed to improving the quality of life for our business partners' employees. Through our Code of Conduct program, Timberland works to ensure that our products are made in workplaces that are fair, safe and nondiscriminatory. Beyond training factory management, educating factory workers, and auditing for compliance with our Code of Conduct, we also partner with nongovernmental organizations and international agencies such as Verité, CARE, and Social Accountability International to help us develop programs focused on continuous improvement and sustainable change."[11] How does Timberland operationalize these standards? One way is by constructively engaging suppliers who commit labor infractions. Rather than immediately discharging such suppliers, Timberland works at getting them to change their policies so as to keep the workers employed.[12]

Timberland engages in similar influence attempts with its customers. For instance, in making a sales presentation to executives from McDonald's Corporation regarding the possibility of Timberland becoming the contract supplier of new uniforms for the fast food giant, CEO Swartz used a novel approach. To the surprise of the McDonald's executives, he did not provide product prototypes or pitch the company's creativity or craftsmanship. Instead, he talked enthusiastically about Timberland's corporate culture and what the company was doing in terms of social, environmental, and labor commitments. Swartz's message was that he expected Timberland's culture would rub off on McDonald's, thereby helping McDonald's to build a unified, purposeful, motivated workforce.[13]

Can commerce and justice—business interests and social/environmental interests—peacefully coexist and mutually reinforce each other for Timberland and its stakeholders over the long term?

Discussion Questions

1. Jeffrey Swartz's approach to running Timberland is based on the belief that business success is compatible with a corporate social and environmental responsibility. Do you share this belief? Why or why not?

2. How does Timberland's commitment to social and environmental responsibility influence the ways in which it deals with the diversity, technology, and globalization challenges that it faces?

3. Consider the ethical, diversity, technology, and globalization challenges that have confronted Timberland. How has the company converted these challenges into opportunities?

4. What are some advantages and disadvantages of Timberland's attempts to influence suppliers and customers regarding corporate social and environmental responsibility? How can these influence efforts help Timberland as it seeks to deal with its own ethical, diversity, technology, and globalization challenges?

SOURCE: This case was written by Michael K. McCuddy, The Louis S. and Mary L. Morgal Chair of Christian Business Ethics and Professor of Management, College of Business Administration, Valparaiso University.

BP: Facing Multiple Challenges (A)

During its 100-year history, BP PLC has grown from a local oil company into a global energy group that employs over 96,000 people and, on a daily basis, serves approximately 13 million customers in over 100 nations.[1] In the early 1900s, struggling against the elements and a variety of disappointments, George Reynolds and a group of explorers searched for seven years before discovering oil in Persia. To capitalize on their discovery, the Anglo-Persian Oil Company was formed. This company would eventually become BP. In the years leading up to World War I, the British government sought to secure a reliable source of Oil for its navy, consequently becoming a major investor in the Anglo-Persian Oil Company. Although British Petroleum was created by a German firm to market products in Britain, Britain seized those assets during World War I and sold them to the Anglo-Persian oil Company. Thus, British Petroleum became a company largely owned by the British government.[2]

Over the ensuing decades, British Petroleum continued to grow. Then in the 1970s, political changes in the Middle East had profound effects on world oil supplies. Nearly every oil-rich nation in the Middle East announced the immediate or impending nationalization of their petroleum resources. These moves profoundly influenced BP's subsequent corporate strategy, which to that point had been entirely focused on the supply of Middle Eastern oil. About the same time, the company discovered and began developing a major oil field in Prudhoe Bay, Alaska, and an oil field off the coast of Scotland. Development of the Prudhoe Bay oil field and building the Trans-Alaska Pipeline System taught BP "the value of dealing with potentially contentious environmental considerations at the very start of major projects."[3]

With no refineries or distribution outlets in the United States, BP acquired a stake in Standard Oil of Ohio (Sohio) in order to bring Alaskan products to market. In 1987, two major events occurred for BP. First, the company acquired complete ownership and control of Sohio and incorporated it into BP America. Second, the British government completed privatization of the company, selling the last of the BP shares it owned.[4] As a government-owned entity, BP was a rigid, hierarchical company. However, this dramatically changed when the company was split into 150 business units with managers' pay being linked to their unit's profitability. In this milieu, an aggressive and entrepreneurial corporate culture was born.[5]

Enter John Browne

In 1995, John P. Browne became CEO of BP and began pursuing a strategy of vigorous growth through mergers and acquisitions. During the next several years, BP acquired Amoco, ARCO, and Burmah Castrol while also negotiating oil deals in Russia. In the process, BP was transformed into a global force in the oil industry, becoming the second largest major oil company in the world, behind ExxonMobil.[6] Browne was the first leader in the oil industry to acknowledge the problem of climate change and the need for the oil industry as a whole to recognize this problem and deal with it appropriately and effectively.[7] BP also became engaged in significant efforts to develop alternative energy sources, including biofuels, solar energy, and hydrogen fuels.[8] By 2003, under Browne's guidance and with the help of advertising company Ogilvy & Mather, BP rebranded itself—BP was to stand for *Beyond Petroleum*.[9] With this orientation, BP reinforced its commitment to the environment and the development of alternative energy sources.

Current Challenges and Opportunities

In the past few years, however, BP has encountered several challenges that have threatened its expressed commitments to the environment and the development of alternative energy sources. Some of these challenges are in the United States; others are elsewhere in the global community. Most prominent among the American challenges are safety issues, charges of market manipulation, and environmental pollution.

In March 2005, an explosion at BP's Texas City, Texas, refinery—the company's largest in the United States—claimed 15 lives and injured 180 people. An investigation by the United States Chemical Safety Board attributed the explosion to BP management's "check-book mentality" with its emphasis on cutting costs, and to the failure of management to acknowledge warnings of safety problems and provide effective safety oversight.[10] Another investigation, headed by James Baker, the noted American elder statesman and problem solver, concluded that the safety budget was inadequate and safety staff was overstretched.[11] BP was faulted for not learning the lessons of poor safety management following refinery accidents in Grangemouth, Scotland, in 2000.[12] To the company's credit, it has offered to settle all lawsuits arising from the Texas City disaster and initially set aside $1.6 billion for victim compensation. This is in contrast to ExxonMobil, which is still engaged in a legal battle over liability for the 1989 Alaskan oil spill from the *Exxon Valdez*.[13]

In March 2006, a significant oil spill occurred on BP's Prudhoe Bay pipeline due to its corrosion. Standard operating procedure in the industry is for pipelines to be inspected every five years with "a smart-pig"—a high-tech device used for testing the internal wear and tear of the pipeline.[14] Although BP had conducted external inspections, the company admitted that it had not conducted a smart-pig inspection of the Alaska pipeline since 1992, a test that would have enabled the company to monitor the pipeline's health over time.[15] Jon Birger, writing in *Fortune* magazine, observes that "BP's current pipeline woes are receiving disproportionate attention because of when and where they occurred—at a time of high prices and in a place where every accident is an argument against further Alaska drilling."[16]

In June 2006, the Commodity Futures Trading Commission (CFTC), which oversees energy trading in the United States, charged BP's North American subsidiary and traders with manipulating the propane market in February 2004. Although it denied any wrongdoing, BP nonetheless fired some of the traders who were involved in the alleged scandal.[17]

BP's refinery in Whiting, Indiana has been the scene of several major controversies in 2006 and 2007. In November 2006, U.S. health and safety regulators imposed a $384,000 fine on BP for deficient lights and wiring, wrongly set heat alarms, and untested fire hydrants.[18] In April 2007, a fire at the Whiting refinery cut daily production in half. The fire was caused by a compressor unit that was inspected shortly before the outbreak of the fire. Employees at the refinery had previously "complained of a 'run until it breaks' approach at the plant."[19]

The Whiting refinery, BP's second largest in the United States, is located along the shores of Lake Michigan in northwest Indiana, just a few miles east of the Indiana/Illinois border. In late spring of 2007, BP sought and received a permit from Indiana regulators to increase the amount of pollutants that the Whiting refinery discharges into Lake Michigan. The permit allows BP to discharge an average of 1,584 pounds of ammonia and 4,925 pounds of suspended solids into Lake Michigan on a daily basis, both significant increases over current discharge levels. The additional pollutants are viewed as a threat to human health as well as fish and wildlife. Chicago and numerous other communities take their drinking water from Lake Michigan. The Whiting refinery is already one of the largest sources of industrial pollution discharged into Lake Michigan. An Illinois Congressman commented that BP apparently stands for "Back to Pollution."[20]

In addition to its American challenges, BP faces significant energy supply challenges on a global basis. Perhaps the most notable are with respect to deals in Russia and Venezuela. Under Browne, BP partnered with TNK to develop energy resources in Eastern Siberia. Investors now worry that BP may be pressured by the Russian government into giving up some of its interests in the Kovykta gas fields.[21] Officials of the Russian government charge that TNK-BP has not fulfilled the terms of its license due to underproduction in the Kovykta fields. BP counters that since TNK-BP is barred from exporting gas from Russia, there is no market for the volume of production required by the license.[22] BP's energy exploration and oil supplies may also be significantly disrupted in Venezuela, as President Hugo Chavez implements his strategy of nationalizing that country's oil production. Although in late June 2007, ExxonMobil and Conoco Phillips decided to pull out of Venezuela, BP, along with three other international oil companies, decided to "stick it out [in Venezuela] despite the unilateral abrogation of their contracts."[23]

BP's handling of these challenges will determine whether they become opportunities for growth or threats to future success. The company's approach will be influenced, perhaps even complicated, by the mantle of executive leadership changing on May 1, 2007, with John Browne's resignation and Tony Hayward's assumption of the CEO position. As J. Robinson West, head of a Washington-based energy consulting firm, observed, "BP is the most challenged of the super majors at this time."[24]

Discussion Questions

1. What lessons about leading people and managing organizations does BP provide?

2. Which of the four management challenges—globalization; leading a diverse workforce; ethics, character, and personal integrity; or technological innovation—have had the greatest impact on BP in the past few years? Explain your answer.

3. Which of the management challenges are likely to have the greatest impact on BP's future operations? Explain your answer.

4. What advice would you give Tony Hayward as he takes over the helm of BP? Why would you give this advice?

5. What can BP do to transform its challenges into opportunities?

SOURCE: This case was written by Michael K. McCuddy, The Louis S. and Mary L. Morgal Chair of Christian Business Ethics and Professor of Management, College of Business Administration, Valparaiso University.

Individual Processes and Behavior

PART 2

CHAPTER 3

Personality, Perception, and Attribution

After reading this chapter, you should be able to do the following:

1 Describe individual differences and their importance in understanding behavior.

2 Define *personality*.

3 Identify several personality characteristics and their influences on behavior in organizations.

4 Give examples of each personality characteristic from your own work experience and how you would apply your knowledge in managing personality differences.

5 Discuss Carl Jung's contribution to our understanding of individual differences,

and explain how his theory is used in the Myers-Briggs Type Indicator.

6 Evaluate the importance of the MBTI to managers.

7 Define *social perception* and explain how characteristics of the perceiver, the target, and the situation affect it.

8 Identify five common barriers to social perception.

9 Explain the attribution process and how attributions affect managerial behavior.

10 Evaluate the accuracy of managerial attributions from the standpoint of attribution biases and errors.

THINKING AHEAD: SERGEY BRIN: A REBELLIOUS CHILD BECOMES ONE OF THE MOST IMPORTANT PERSONS ON THE WEB

Sergey Brin cofounded Google while he and Larry Page were students at Stanford. In 2006, *Forbes* magazine named Brin the twelfth richest person in the United States with a net worth of $14.1 billion. So what is the story behind the young entrepreneur's rise to the top?

Brin's parents emigrated from the Soviet Union in 1979. His father is a mathematics professor at University of Maryland, and his mother is a research scientist at NASA's Goddard Space Flight Center. Such educated parents undoubtedly passed on some of their appreciation for science and mathematics to their son. Brin himself contends that his Russian heritage and skepticism toward authority drove his rebellious side. This aspect of his personality may have led him and Page to create a company that invented a new way of finding information on the Internet.

Brin also defies the stereotypical image of a successful CEO. He and Page have consistently highlighted the relaxed corporate culture at Google. He rarely wears business suits to work, and his behavior is full of boyish enthusiasm and restless energy. He shares an office space with Larry Page that looks like a playroom full of gadgets and monitors instead of a sleek corporate office.

In the Looking Back feature, you'll see how Sergey Brin's personality affects the culture and tremendous success of Google.[1]

INDIVIDUAL DIFFERENCES AND ORGANIZATIONAL BEHAVIOR

(1) Describe individual differences and their importance in understanding behavior.

In this chapter and continuing in Chapter 4, we explore the concept of *individual differences*. Individuals are unique in terms of their skills, abilities, personalities, perceptions, attitudes, emotions, and ethics. These are just a few of the ways people may be similar to or different from one another. Individual differences represent the essence of the challenge of management, because no two people are completely alike. Managers face the challenge of working with people who possess a multitude of individual characteristics, so the more managers understand those differences, the better they can work with others. Figure 3.1 illustrates how individual differences affect human behavior.

The basis for understanding individual differences stems from Lewin's early contention that behavior is a function of the person and the environment.[2] Lewin

FIGURE 3.1 Variables Influencing Individual Behavior

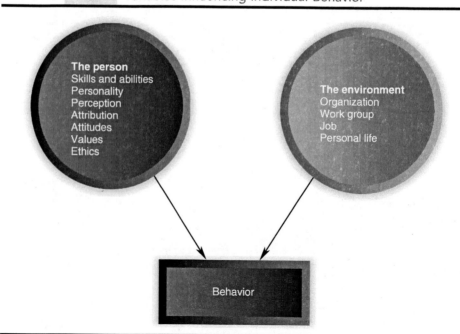

The person
Skills and abilities
Personality
Perception
Attribution
Attitudes
Values
Ethics

The environment
Organization
Work group
Job
Personal life

Behavior

individual differences
The way in which factors such as skills, abilities, personalities, perceptions, attitudes, values, and ethics differ from one individual to another.

expressed this idea in an equation: B = f(P, E), where B = behavior, P = person, and E = environment. This idea has been developed by the *interactional psychology* approach.[3] Basically, it says that in order to understand human behavior, we must know something about the person and the situation. There are four basic propositions of interactional psychology:

1. Behavior is a function of a continuous, multidirectional interaction between the person and the situation.
2. The person is active in this process and both changes, and is changed by, situations.
3. People vary in many characteristics, including cognitive, affective, motivational, and ability factors.
4. Two interpretations of situations are important: the objective situation and the person's subjective view of the situation.[4]

The interactional psychology approach points out the need to study both persons and situations. We will focus on personal and situational factors throughout the text. The person consists of individual differences such as those we emphasize in this chapter and Chapter 4: personality, perception, attribution, attitudes, emotions, and ethics. The situation consists of the environment the person operates in, and it can include things like the organization, work group, personal life situation, job characteristics, and many other environmental influences. One important and fascinating individual difference is personality.

SKILLS AND ABILITIES

There are many skills and abilities that relate to work outcomes. *General mental ability (GMA)* was introduced by Spearman (1904)[5] almost a hundred years ago. It is defined as an individual's innate cognitive intelligence. It was the single best predictor of work performance across many occupations studied both here in the United States[6] and across different cultures.[7]

PERSONALITY

What makes an individual behave in consistent ways in a variety of situations? Personality is an individual difference that lends consistency to a person's behavior. *Personality* is defined as a relatively stable set of characteristics that influence an individual's behavior. Although there is debate about the determinants of personality, there appear to be several origins. One determinant is heredity, and some interesting studies have supported this position. Identical twins who are separated at birth and raised apart in very different situations have been found to share personality traits and job preferences. For example, about half of the variation in traits like extraversion, impulsiveness, and flexibility was found to be genetically determined; that is, identical twins who grew up in different environments shared these traits.[8] For example, the opening discussion of Sergey Brin highlights his parents' penchant for the hard sciences that seems to have fed his own interest in computer sciences. In addition, the twins held similar jobs.[9] Thus, there does appear to be a genetic influence on personality.

Another determinant of personality is the environment a person is exposed to. Family, culture, education, and other environmental forces shape personality. Personality is therefore shaped by both heredity and environment.

(2) Define *personality*.

interactional psychology
The psychological approach that says in order to understand human behavior, we must know something about the person and about the situation.

personality
A relatively stable set of characteristics that influence an individual's behavior.

Personality Theories

Two major theories of personality are the trait theory and the integrative approach. Each theory has influenced the study of personality in organizations.

Trait Theory Some early personality researchers believed that to understand individuals, we must break down behavior patterns into a series of observable traits. According to *trait theory*, combining these traits into a group forms an individual's personality. Gordon Allport, a leading trait theorist, saw traits as broad, general guides that lend consistency to behavior.[10] Thousands of traits have been identified over the years. Raymond Cattell, another prominent trait theorist, identified sixteen traits that formed the basis for differences in individual behavior. He described traits in bipolar adjective combinations such as self-assured/apprehensive, reserved/outgoing, and submissive/dominant.[11]

Big Five Personality Model

Personality theorists have long argued that in order to understand individual behavior, people's behavioral patterns can be broken down into a series of observable traits. One popular personality classification is the "Big Five." The Big Five traits include extraversion, agreeableness, conscientiousness, emotional stability, and openness to experience.[12] These are broad, global traits that are associated with behaviors at work. Descriptions of the Big Five appear in Table 3.1.

From preliminary research, we know that introverted and conscientious employees are less likely to be absent from work.[13] In making peer evaluations, individuals with high agreeableness tend to rate others more leniently, while individuals with high conscientiousness tend to be tougher as raters.[14] Extraverts tend to have higher salaries, receive more promotions, and are more satisfied with their careers.[15] Across many occupations, people who are conscientious are more motivated and are high performers.[16] Viewing more specific occupations, however, shows that different patterns of the Big Five factors are related to high performance. For customer service jobs, individuals high in emotional stability, agreeableness, and openness to experience perform best. For managers, emotional stability and extraversion are traits of

TABLE 3.1   The Big Five Personality Traits

Extraversion	The person is gregarious, assertive, and sociable (as opposed to reserved, timid, and quiet).
Agreeableness	The person is cooperative, warm, and agreeable (rather than cold, disagreeable, and antagonistic).
Conscientiousness	The person is hardworking, organized, and dependable (as opposed to lazy, disorganized, and unreliable).
Emotional stability	The person is calm, self-confident, and cool (as opposed to insecure, anxious, and depressed).
Openness to experience	The person is creative, curious, and cultured (rather than practical with narrow interests).

SOURCES: P. T. Costa and R. R. McCrae, *The NEO-PI Personality Inventory* (Odessa, Fla.: Psychological Assessment Resources, 1992); J. F. Salgado, "The Five Factor Model of Personality and Job Performance in the European Community," *Journal of Applied Psychology* 82 (1997): 30–43.

trait theory

The personality theory that states that in order to understand individuals, we must break down behavior patterns into a series of observable traits.

Does Your Personality Affect Life Outcomes?

This question has long perplexed personality researchers. As noted earlier, some personality characteristics like conscientiousness and self efficacy have been shown to affect job performance. Are there more far-reaching impacts of an individuals' personality?

The answer seems to be a resounding yes. In a recent comprehensive review of research on the Big Five personality model, researchers predicted that personality characteristics could affect important individual outcomes (e.g., happiness, spirituality and virtues, depression, longevity, risky behavior), interpersonal outcomes (e.g., dating variety, attractiveness, status, family satisfaction) and social and institutional outcomes (e.g., occupational choice and performance, volunteerism, leadership, antisocial and criminal behavior).

They found that extraverts, for example, are happier, more satisfied with romantic relationships, and less likely to be depressed. Agreeable individuals are less likely to have heart disease, and more likely to have a positive leadership style. Conscientious people are healthier and enjoy greater occupational success, and they are less likely to engage in criminal or antisocial behaviors. Emotionally stable individuals experience greater job satisfaction, commitment, and occupational success. Those who are open to new experiences tend to choose occupations that involve creative and artistic skills, but they are also more likely to engage in substance abuse.

So it appears that the impact of the Big Five goes beyond the workplace and affects many facets of life.

SOURCE: D. J. Ozer and V. Benet-Martínez, "Personality and the Prediction of Consequential Outcomes," *Annual Review of Psychology* 57 (2006): 401–421.

---

top performers.[17] Recent research indicates that in work teams, the minimum level of agreeableness in a team as well as the mean levels of conscientiousness and openness to experience had a strong effect on overall team performance.[18]

Read about how the Big Five personality traits affect a broad range of personal and work outcomes in the Science feature above. The Big Five framework has also been applied across cultures. It has held up well among Spanish and Mexican populations.[19] It remains to be seen whether or not the Big Five traits will emerge in studies of cultures that are extremely different from Western cultures.[20]

The trait approach has been the subject of considerable criticism. Some theorists argue that simply identifying traits is not enough; instead, personality is dynamic and not completely stable. Further, early trait theorists tended to ignore the influence of situations.[21] Also, the trait theory tends to ignore process—that is, how we get from a trait to a particular outcome.

Integrative Approach Recently, researchers have taken a broader, more *integrative approach* to the study of personality.[22] To capture its influence on behavior, personality is described as a composite of the individual's psychological processes. Personality dispositions include emotions, cognitions, attitudes, expectancies, and fantasies.[23] *Dispositions*, in this approach, simply mean the tendencies of individuals to respond to situations in consistent ways. Influenced by both genetics and experiences, dispositions can be modified. The integrative approach focuses on both person (dispositions) and situational variables as combined predictors of behavior.

integrative approach
The broad theory that describes personality as a composite of an individual's psychological processes.

Personality Characteristics in Organizations

Managers should learn as much as possible about personality in order to understand their employees. Hundreds of personality characteristics have been identified. We have selected three characteristics because of their particular influences on individual behavior in organizations: core self-evaluations (CSE), self-monitoring, and

(3) Identify several personality characteristics and their influences on behavior in organizations.

What's Your Locus of Control?

Below is a short scale that can give you an idea of your locus of control. For each of the four items, circle either choice a or choice b.

1. a. Becoming a success is a matter of hard work; luck has little or nothing to do with it.
   b. Getting a good job depends mainly on being in the right place at the right time.
2. a. The average citizen can have an influence in government decisions.
   b. This world is run by the few people in power, and there is not much the little guy can do about it.

3. a. As far as world affairs are concerned, most of us are the victims of forces we can neither understand nor control.
   b. By taking an active part in political and social affairs, people can control world events.
4. a. With enough effort we can wipe out political corruption.
   b. It is difficult for people to have much control over the things politicians do in office.

Scoring Key:

The internal locus of control answers are:
1a, 2a, 3b, 4a
The external locus of control answers are:
1b, 2b, 3a, 4b

Determine which category you circled most frequently using the key to the left. This gives you an approximation of your locus of control.

SOURCES: T. Adeyemi-Bello, "Validating Rotter's Locus of Control Scale with a Sample of Not-for-Profit Leaders," *Management Research News* 24 (2001): 25–35; J. B. Rotter, "Generalized Expectancies for Internal vs. External Locus of Control of Reinforcement," *Psychological Monographs* 80, whole No. 609 (1966).

(4) Give examples of each personality characteristic from your own work experience and how you would apply your knowledge in managing personality differences.

positive/negative affect. Because these characteristics affect performance at work, managers need to have a working knowledge of them.

Core Self-Evaluation (CSE) Core self-evaluation (CSE) is a broad set of personality traits that refers to self-concept.[24] It is comprised of locus of control, self-esteem, generalized self-efficacy, and emotional stability. CSE has been found to predict both goal-directed behavior and performance,[25] even in non-U.S. cultures (e.g., Japan).[26] Each characteristic comprising CSE with the exception of emotional stability (as we discussed in the Big Five approach) is addressed next.

Locus of Control An individual's generalized belief about internal (self) versus external (situation or others) control is called *locus of control*. People who believe they control what happens to them are said to have an internal locus of control, whereas people who believe that circumstances or other people control their fate have an external locus of control.[27] Research on locus of control has strong implications for organizations. Internals (those with an internal locus of control) have been found to have higher job satisfaction and performance, to be more likely to assume managerial positions, and to prefer participative management styles.[28] For example, Sergey Brin's parents emigrated from Russia because they believed they would have greater control over their destinies in the United Sates. This action reflects internal locus of control. They believed they could have more control of their destiny here in the United States. You can assess your locus of control in You 3.1.

locus of control

An individual's generalized belief about internal control (self-control) versus external control (control by the situation or by others).

Internals and externals have similar positive reactions to being promoted, which include high job satisfaction, job involvement, and organizational commitment. The difference between the two is that internals continue to be happy long after the promotion, whereas externals' joy over the promotion is short-lived. This might occur because externals do not believe their own performance led to the promotion.[29]

Knowing about locus of control can prove valuable to managers. Because internals believe they control what happens to them, they will want to exercise control in their work environment. Allowing internals considerable voice in how work is performed is important. Internals will not react well to being closely supervised. Externals, in contrast, may prefer a more structured work setting, and they may be more reluctant to participate in decision making.

Self-Efficacy *General self-efficacy* is a person's overall view of himself/herself as being able to perform effectively in a wide variety of situations.[30] Employees with high general self-efficacy have more confidence in their job-related abilities and other personal resources (i.e., energy, influence over others, etc.) that help them function effectively on the job. People with low general self-efficacy often feel ineffective at work and may express doubts about performing a new task well. Previous success or performance is one of the most important determinants of self-efficacy. People who have positive beliefs about their efficacy for performance are more likely to attempt difficult tasks, to persist in overcoming obstacles, and to experience less anxiety when faced with adversity.[31] People with high self-efficacy also value the ability to provide input, or "voice," at work. Because they are confident in this capability, they value the opportunity to participate.[32] High self-efficacy has also been recently related to higher job satisfaction and performance.

There is another form of self-efficacy, called task-specific self-efficacy, which we will cover in Chapter 6. *Task-specific self-efficacy* is a person's belief that he or she can perform a specific task ("I believe I can do this sales presentation today"). In contrast, general self-efficacy is broader ("I believe I can perform well in just about any part of the job").

Employees with high general self-efficacy have more confidence in their job-related abilities and personal resources. This "I think I can" attitude helps them function effectively on the job.

COURTESY OF PENGUIN GROUPS (USA) INC.

Self-Esteem *Self-esteem* is an individual's general feeling of self-worth. Individuals with high self-esteem have positive feelings about themselves, perceive themselves to have strengths as well as weaknesses, and believe their strengths are more important than their weaknesses.[33] Individuals with low self-esteem view themselves negatively. They are more strongly affected by what other people think of them, and they compliment individuals who give them positive feedback while cutting down people who give them negative feedback.[34]

Evaluations from other people affect our self-esteem. For example, you might be liked for who you are or for your achievements. Being liked for who you are is more stable, and people who have this type of self-esteem are less defensive and more honest with themselves. Being liked for your achievement is more unstable; it waxes and wanes depending on how high your achievements are.[35]

A person's self-esteem affects a host of other attitudes and has important implications for behavior in organizations. People with high self-esteem perform better and are more satisfied with their jobs.[36] For example, a recent study of 288 R&D engineers from four organizations found that self-esteem predicted supervisor ratings of job performance. This research indicates that self-esteem might be important to performance in knowledge-based occupations.[37] When they are involved in a job search, those with high self-esteem seek out higher-status jobs.[38] A work team made up of such individuals is more likely to be successful than a team with low or average self-esteem.[39]

general self-efficacy
An individual's general belief that he or she is capable of meeting job demands in a wide variety of situations.

self-esteem
An individual's general feeling of self-worth.

Very high self-esteem may be too much of a good thing. When people with high self-esteem find themselves in stressful situations, they may brag inappropriately.[40] This may be viewed negatively by others, who see spontaneous boasting as egotistical. Very high self-esteem may also lead to overconfidence and to relationship conflicts with others who may not evaluate this behavior favorably.[41] Individuals with high self-esteem may shift their social identities to protect themselves when they do not live up to some standard. Take two students, Denise and Teresa, for example. If Denise outperforms Teresa on a statistics exam, Teresa may convince herself that Denise is not really a good person to compare against because Denise is an engineering major and Teresa is a physical education major. Teresa's high self-esteem is protecting her from this unfavorable comparison.[42]

Self-esteem may be strongly affected by situations. Success tends to raise self-esteem, whereas failure tends to lower it. Given that high self-esteem is generally a positive characteristic, managers should encourage employees to raise their self-esteem by giving them appropriate challenges and opportunities for success. These three characteristics, along with the effects of emotional stability as discussed in the section on the Big Five, then, constitute an important personality trait known as core self-evaluations. CSE is a strong predictor of both job satisfaction and job performance next only to GMA.[43]

Self-Monitoring A characteristic with great potential for affecting behavior in organizations is *self-monitoring*—the extent to which people base their behavior on cues from other people and situations.[44] High self-monitors pay attention to what is appropriate in particular situations and to the behavior of other people, and they behave accordingly. Low self-monitors, in contrast, are not as vigilant to situational cues and act from internal states rather than paying attention to the situation. As a result, the behavior of low self-monitors is consistent across situations. High self-monitors, because their behavior varies with the situation, appear to be more unpredictable and less consistent. One study amongst managers of a recruitment firm found that high self-monitors were more likely to offer emotional help to others in dealing with work related anxiety. Low self-monitors, on the hand, even when tasked with managerial responsibilities were less likely to offer such emotional support and help.[44a] You can use You 3.2 to assess your own self-monitoring tendencies.

Research is currently focusing on the effects of self-monitoring in organizations. In one study, the authors tracked the careers of 139 MBAs for five years to see whether high self-monitors were more likely to be promoted, change employers, or make a job-related geographic move. The results were "yes" to each question. High self-monitors get promoted because they accomplish tasks through meeting the expectations of others and because they seek out central positions in social networks.[45] They are also more likely to use self-promotion to make others aware of their skills and accomplishments.[46] However, the high self-monitor's flexibility may not be suited for every job, and the tendency to move may not fit every organization.[47] Because high self-monitors base their behavior on cues from others and from the situation, they demonstrate higher levels of managerial self-awareness. This means that, as managers, they assess their own workplace behavior accurately.[48] Managers who are high self-monitors are also good at reading their employees' needs and changing the way they interact with employees depending on those needs.[49]

Although research on self-monitoring in organizations is in its early stages, we can speculate that high self-monitors respond more readily to work group norms, organizational culture, and supervisory feedback than do low self-monitors, who

self-monitoring

The extent to which people base their behavior on cues from other people and situations.

Are You a High or Low Self-Monitor?

For the following items, circle T (true) if the statement is characteristic of your behavior. Circle F (false) if the statement does not reflect your behavior.

1. I find it hard to imitate the behavior of other people.   T F
2. At parties and social gatherings, I do not attempt to do or say things that others will like.   T F
3. I can only argue for ideas that I already believe.   T F
4. I can make impromptu speeches even on topics about which I have almost no information.   T F
5. I guess I put on a show to impress or entertain others.   T F
6. I would probably make a good actor.   T F
7. In a group of people, I am rarely the center of attention.   T F
8. In different situations and with different people, I often act like very different persons.   T F
9. I am not particularly good at making other people like me.   T F
10. I am not always the person I appear to be.   T F
11. I would not change my opinions (or the way I do things) in order to please others or win their favor. T F
12. I have considered being an entertainer.   T F
13. I have never been good at games like charades or at improvisational acting.   T F
14. I have trouble changing my behavior to suit different people and different situations.   T F
15. At a party, I let others keep the jokes and stories going.   T F
16. I feel a bit awkward in company and do not show up quite as well as I should.   T F
17. I can look anyone in the eye and tell a lie with a straight face (if it is for a good cause).   T F
18. I may deceive people by being friendly when I really dislike them.   T F

Scoring:

To score this questionnaire, give yourself 1 point for each of the following items that you answered T (true): 4, 5, 6, 8, 10, 12, 17, and 18. Now give yourself 1 point for each of the following items that you answered F (false): 1, 2, 3, 7, 9, 11, 13, 14, 15, and 16.

Add both subtotals to find your overall score. If you scored 11 or above, you are probably a *high self-monitor*. If you scored 10 or under, you are probably a *low self-monitor*.

SOURCE: From *Public Appearances, Private Realities: The Psychology of Self-Monitoring* by M. Snyder. Copyright © 1987 by W. H. Freeman and Company. Used with permission.

adhere more to internal guidelines for behavior ("I am who I am"). In addition, high self-monitors may be enthusiastic participants in the trend toward work teams because of their ability to assume flexible roles.

Positive/Negative Affect Recently, researchers have explored the effects of persistent mood dispositions at work. Individuals who focus on the positive aspects of themselves, other people, and the world in general are said to have *positive affect*.[50] In contrast, those who accentuate the negative in themselves, others, and the world are said to possess *negative affect* (also referred to as negative affectivity).[51] Positive affect is linked with job satisfaction, which we discuss at length in Chapter 4. Individuals with positive affect are more satisfied with their jobs.[52] In addition, those with positive affect are more likely to help others at work and also engage in more organizational citizenship behaviors (OCBs).[53] Employees with positive affect are also absent from work less often.[54] Positive affect has also been linked to more life satisfaction and better performance across a variety of life and work domains.[55]

positive affect
An individual's tendency to accentuate the positive aspects of himself or herself, other people, and the world in general.

negative affect
An individual's tendency to accentuate the negative aspects of himself or herself, other people, and the world in general.

Individuals with negative affect report more work stress.[56] Individual affect also influences the work group. Positive individual affect produces positive team affect, which leads to more cooperation and less conflict within the team.[57] Leader affectivity can have an impact on subordinate outcomes. For example, a recent study of leaders and subordinates found that leader negative affectivity had a negative effect on subordinate attitudinal outcomes such as organizational commitment, job satisfaction, and anxiety.[58]

Positive affect is a definite asset in work settings. Managers can do several things to promote this trait, including allowing participative decision making and providing pleasant working conditions. We need to know more about inducing positive affect in the workplace.

The characteristics previously described are but a few of the personality characteristics that affect behavior and performance in organizations. Negative affect, for example, affects work stress, as you'll see in Chapter 7. Another personality characteristic related to stress is Type A behavior, also presented in Chapter 7. Other personality characteristics are woven in throughout the book. Can managers predict the behavior of their employees by knowing their personalities? Not completely. You may recall that the interactional psychology model (Figure 3.1) requires both person and situation variables to predict behavior. Another idea to remember in predicting behavior is the strength of situational influences. Some situations are *strong situations* in that they overwhelm the effects of individual personalities. These situations are interpreted in the same way by different individuals, evoke agreement on the appropriate behavior in the situation, and provide cues to appropriate behavior. A performance appraisal session is an example of a strong situation. Employees know to listen to their boss and to contribute when asked to do so.

A weak situation, in contrast, is one that is open to many interpretations. It provides few cues to appropriate behavior and no obvious rewards for one behavior over another. Thus, individual personalities have a stronger influence in weak situations than in strong situations. An informal meeting without an agenda can be seen as a weak situation.

Organizations present combinations of strong and weak situations; therefore, personality has a stronger effect on behavior in some situations than in others.[59]

Measuring Personality

Several methods can be used to assess personality. These include projective tests, behavioral measures, and self-report questionnaires.

The *projective test* is one method used to measure personality. In these tests, individuals are shown a picture, abstract image, or photo and are asked to describe what they see or tell a story about it. The rationale behind projective tests is that each individual responds to the stimulus in a way that reflects his or her unique personality. The Rorschach inkblot test is a projective test commonly used to assess personality.[60] Like other projective tests, however, it has low reliability. The individual being assessed may look at the same picture and see different things at different times. Also, the assessor may apply his or her own biases in interpreting the information about the individual's personality.

There are *behavioral measures* of personality as well. Measuring an individual's behavior involves observing it in a controlled situation. We might assess a person's sociability, for example, by counting the number of times he or she approaches strangers at a party. The behavior is scored in some manner to produce an index of personality. Some potential problems with behavioral measures include the observer's ability

strong situation

A situation that overwhelms the effects of individual personalities by providing strong cues for appropriate behavior.

projective test

A personality test that elicits an individual's response to abstract stimuli.

behavioral measures

Personality assessments that involve observing an individual's behavior in a controlled situation.

to stay focused and the way the observer interprets the behavior. In addition, some people behave differently when they know they are being observed.

The most common method of assessing personality is the *self-report questionnaire*. Individuals respond to a series of questions, usually in an agree/disagree or true/false format. One of the more widely recognized questionnaires is the Minnesota Multiphasic Personality Inventory (MMPI). The MMPI is comprehensive and assesses a variety of traits, as well as various neurotic or psychotic disorders. Used extensively in psychological counseling to identify disorders, the MMPI is a long questionnaire. The Big Five traits we discussed earlier are measured by another self-report questionnaire, the NEO Personality Inventory. Self-report questionnaires also suffer from potential biases. It is difficult to be objective about your own personality. People often answer the questionnaires in terms of how they want to be seen, rather than as they really are.

Another approach to applying personality theory in organizations is the Jungian approach and its measurement tool, the MBTI® instrument. The Myers-Briggs Type Indicator® instrument has been developed to measure Jung's ideas about individual differences. Many organizations use the MBTI instrument, and we will focus on it as an example of how some organizations use personality concepts to help employees appreciate diversity.

APPLICATION OF PERSONALITY THEORY IN ORGANIZATIONS: THE MYERS-BRIGGS TYPE INDICATOR INSTRUMENT

One approach to applying personality theory in organizations is the Jungian approach and its measurement tool, the MBTI instrument.

Swiss psychiatrist Carl Jung built his work on the notion that people are fundamentally different, but also fundamentally alike. His classic treatise *Psychological Types* proposed that the population was made up of two basic types—Extraverted types and Introverted types.[61] He went on to identify two types of Perceiving (Sensing and Intuition) and two types of Judgment (Thinking and Feeling). Perceiving (how we gather information) and Judging (how we make decisions) represent the basic mental functions that everyone uses.

Jung suggested that human similarities and differences could be understood by combining preferences. We prefer and choose one way of doing things over another. We are not exclusively one way or another; rather, we have a preference for Extraversion or Introversion, just as we have a preference for right-handedness or left-handedness. We may use each hand equally well, but when a ball is thrown at us by surprise, we will reach to catch it with our preferred hand. Jung's type theory argues that no preferences are better than others. Differences are to be understood, celebrated, and appreciated.

During the 1940s, a mother–daughter team became fascinated with individual differences among people and with the work of Carl Jung. Katharine Briggs and her daughter, Isabel Briggs Myers, developed the *Myers-Briggs Type Indicator instrument* to put Jung's type theory into practical use. The MBTI instrument is used extensively in organizations as a basis for understanding individual differences. More than 3 million people complete the instrument per year in the United States.[62] The MBTI instrument has been used in career counseling, team building, conflict management, and understanding management styles.[63] In Experiential Exercise 3.1 at the end of this chapter, you can assess your own MBTI type. You might find it helpful to do this before reading on.

(5) Discuss Carl Jung's contribution to our understanding of individual differences, and explain how his theory is used in the Myers-Briggs Type Indicator instrument.

(6) Evaluate the importance of the MBTI to managers.

self-report questionnaire

A common personality assessment that involves an individual's responses to a series of questions.

Myers-Briggs Type Indicator (MBTI) instrument

An instrument developed to measure Carl Jung's theory of individual differences.

The Preferences

There are four scale dichotomies in type theory with two possible choices for each scale. Table 3.2 shows these preferences. The combination of these preferences makes up an individual's psychological type.

Extraversion/Introversion The *Extraversion/Introversion* preference represents where you get your energy. The Extraverted type (E) is energized by interaction with other people. The Introverted type (I) is energized by time alone. Extraverted types typically have a wide social network, whereas Introverted types have a more narrow range of relationships. As articulated by Jung, this preference has nothing to do with social skills. Many Introverted types have excellent social skills but prefer the internal world of ideas, thoughts, and concepts. Extraverted types represent approximately 70 percent of the U.S. population.[64] Our culture rewards Extraverted types and nurtures them. Jung contended that the Extraversion/Introversion preference reflects the most important distinction between individuals.

In work settings, Extraverted types prefer variety, and they do not mind the interruptions of the phone or visits from coworkers. They communicate freely but may say things that they regret later. Read the Real World 3.1 in which Doug Parker (CEO of US Airways) is known for extraversion, yet sometimes has to be reined in by his staff.

Introverted types prefer quiet for concentration, and they like to think things through in private. They do not mind working on a project for a long time and are careful with details. Introverted types dislike telephone interruptions, and they may have trouble recalling names and faces.

Sensing/Intuition The *Sensing/Intuition* preference represents perception, or how we prefer to gather information. In essence, it reflects what we pay attention to. The Sensing type (S) pays attention to information gathered through the five senses and

---

Extraversion

A preference indicating that an individual is energized by interaction with other people.

Introversion

A preference indicating that an individual is energized by time alone.

Sensing

Gathering information through the five senses.

Intuition

Gathering information through "sixth sense" and focusing on what could be rather than what actually exists.

TABLE 3.2   Type Theory Preferences and Descriptions

Extraversion	Introversion	Thinking	Feeling
Outgoing	Quiet	Analytical	Subjective
Publicly expressive	Reserved	Clarity	Harmony
Interacting	Concentrating	Head	Heart
Speaks, then thinks	Thinks, then speaks	Justice	Mercy
Gregarious	Reflective	Rules	Circumstances
Sensing	**Intuition**	**Judging**	**Perceiving**
Practical	General	Structured	Flexible
Specific	Abstract	Time oriented	Open ended
Feet on the ground	Head in the clouds	Decisive	Exploring
Details	Possibilities	Makes lists/uses them	Makes lists/loses them
Concrete	Theoretical	Organized	Spontaneous

Doug Parker: Extraversion in Business

Doug Parker is one of the most interesting yet contradictory top executives in American business today. He is credited with taking over the ailing America West Airlines just days before the 9/11 attacks. He also drew a lot of flak for merging America West with another fiscally unhealthy airline (US Airways). Industry analysts speculated that this would be the worst merger in airline history.

Parker proved the skeptics wrong. US Airways made more money than any other airline in 2006 except Southwest. Parker is described as an extroverted, gregarious guy with the tendency to talk a lot, and is also known for a sharp, analytical mind. For example, on one occasion when he was on a US Airways flight, he kept saying that the Washington airport where they were supposed to land was shut down due to weather. He speculated that they would have to land in Boston. His immediate staff had to rein him in and remind him that he should not be making such comments to passengers. Instead, any news of change in landing plans should come from the cockpit. His drinking habits are also well documented, and he was arrested for a DUI.

Yet Parker seems to be able to channel his extraverted personality into profitable business. He surrounds himself with talented executives at all times, whether for business or leisure activities. This helps him learn aspects of the business that he is not necessarily well versed in.

SOURCE: B. Gimbel, "Onboard the Wild Ride of Doug Parker." *Fortune* (April 30, 2007): 137–141.

---

to what actually exists. The Intuitive type (N) pays attention to a "sixth sense" and to what could be rather than what is.[65] Approximately 70 percent of people in the United States are Sensing types.[66]

At work, Sensing types prefer specific answers to questions and can become frustrated with vague instructions. They like jobs that yield tangible results, and they enjoy using established skills more than learning new ones. Intuitive types like solving new problems and are impatient with routine details. They enjoy learning new skills more than actually using them. Intuitive types tend to think about several things at once, and they may be seen by others as absentminded. They like figuring out how things work just for the fun of it.

Thinking/Feeling The *Thinking/Feeling* preference represents the way we prefer to make decisions. The Thinking type (T) makes decisions in a logical, objective fashion, whereas the Feeling type (F) makes decisions in a personal, value-oriented way. The general U.S. population is divided 50/50 on the Thinking/Feeling type preference, but it is interesting that two-thirds of all males are Thinking types, whereas two-thirds of all females are Feeling types. It is the one preference in type theory that has a strong gender difference. Thinking types tend to analyze decisions, whereas Feeling types sympathize. Thinking types try to be impersonal, while Feeling types base their decisions on how the outcome will affect the people involved.

In work settings, Thinking types tend to show less emotion, and they may become uncomfortable with more emotional people. They are likely to respond more readily to other people's thoughts. They tend to be firm minded and like putting things into a logical framework. Feeling types, in contrast, tend to be more comfortable with emotion in the workplace. They enjoy pleasing people as well as frequent praise and encouragement.

Thinking
Making decisions in a logical, objective fashion.

Feeling
Making decisions in a personal, value-oriented way.

Sensing Types		Intuitive Types	

ISTJ

Quiet, serious, earn success by thoroughness and dependability. Practical, matter-of-fact, realistic, and responsible. Decide logically what should be done and work toward it steadily, regardless of distractions. Take pleasure in making everything orderly and organized—their work, their home, their life. Value traditions and loyalty.

ISFJ

Quiet, friendly, responsible, and conscientious. Committed and steady in meeting their obligations. Thorough, painstaking, and accurate. Loyal, considerate, notice and remember specifics about people who are important to them, concerned with how others feel. Strive to create an orderly and harmonious environment at work and at home.

INFJ

Seek meaning and connection in ideas, relationships, and material possessions. Want to understand what motivates people and are insightful about others. Conscientious and committed to their firm values. Develop a clear vision about how best to serve the common good. Organized and decisive in implementing their vision.

INTJ

Have original minds and great drive for implementing their ideas and achieving their goals. Quickly see patterns in external events and develop long-range explanatory perspectives. When committed, organize a job and carry it through. Skeptical and independent, have high standards of competence and performance for themselves and others.

ISTP

Tolerant and flexible, quiet observers until a problem appears, then act quickly to find workable solutions. Analyze what makes things work and readily get through large amounts of data to isolate the core of practical problems. Interested in cause and effect, organize facts using logical principles, value efficiency.

ISFP

Quiet, friendly, sensitive, and kind. Enjoy the present moment, what's going on around them. Like to have their own space and to work within their own time frame. Loyal and committed to their values and to people who are important to them. Dislike disagreements and conflicts, do not force their opinions or values on others.

INFP

Idealistic, loyal to their values and to people who are important to them. Want an external life that is congruent with their values. Curious, quick to see possibilities, can be catalysts for implementing ideas. Seek to understand people and to help them fulfill their potential. Adaptable, flexible, and accepting unless a value is threatened.

INTP

Seek to develop logical explanations for everything that interests them. Theoretical and abstract, interested more in ideas than in social interaction. Quiet, contained, flexible, and adaptable. Have unusual ability to focus in depth to solve problems in their area of interest. Skeptical, sometimes critical, always analytical.

(Continues)

Judging/Perceiving The *Judging-Perceiving* dichotomy reflects one's orientation to the outer world. The Judging type (J) loves closure. Judging types prefer to lead a planned, organized life and like making decisions. A Perceiving type (P), in contrast, prefers a more flexible and spontaneous life and wants to keep options open. Imagine two people, one with a preference for Judging and the other for Perceiving, going out for dinner. The J asks the P to choose a restaurant, and the P suggests ten alternatives. The J just wants to decide and get on with it, whereas the P wants to explore all the options.

In all arenas of life, and especially at work, Judging types love getting things accomplished and delight in marking off the completed items on their calendars. Perceiving types tend to adopt a wait-and-see attitude and to collect new information rather than draw conclusions. Perceiving types are curious and welcome new information. They may start too many projects and not finish them.

Judging Preference

Preferring closure and completion in making decisions.

Perceiving Preference

Preferring to explore many alternatives and flexibility.

TABLE 3-3 Continued

Sensing Types		Intuitive Types	
ESTP Flexible and tolerant, they take a pragmatic approach focused on immediate results. Theories and conceptual explanations bore them—they want to act energetically to solve the problem. Focus on the here-and-now, spontaneous, enjoy each moment that they can be active with others. Enjoy material comforts and style. Learn best through doing.	**ESFP** Outgoing, friendly, and accepting. Exuberant lovers of life, people, and material comforts. Enjoy working with others to make things happen. Bring common sense and a realistic approach to their work and make work fun. Flexible and spontaneous, adapt readily to new people and environments. Learn best by trying a new skill with other people.	**ENFP** Warmly enthusiastic and imaginative. See life as full of possibilities. Make connections between events and information very quickly, and confidently proceed based on the patterns they see. Want a lot of affirmation from others, and readily give appreciation and support. Spontaneous and flexible, often rely on their ability to improvise and their verbal fluency.	**ENTP** Quick, ingenious, stimulating, alert, and outspoken. Resourceful in solving new and challenging problems. Adept at generating conceptual possibilities and then analyzing them strategically. Good at reading other people. Bored by routine, will seldom do the same thing the same way, apt to turn to one new interest after another.
ESTJ Practical, realistic, matter-of-fact. Decisive, quickly move to implement decisions. Organize projects and people to get things done, focus on getting results in the most efficient way possible. Take care of routine details. Have a clear set of logical standards, systematically follow them and want others to also. Forceful in implementing their plans.	**ESFJ** Warmhearted, conscientious, and cooperative. Want harmony in their environment, work with determination to establish it. Like to work with others to complete tasks accurately and on time. Loyal, follow through even in small matters. Notice what others need in their day-by-day lives and try to provide it. Want to be appreciated for who they are and for what they contribute.	**ENFJ** Warm, empathetic, responsive, and responsible. Highly attuned to the emotions, needs, and motivations of others. Find potential in everyone, want to help others fulfill their potential. May act as catalysts for individual and group growth. Loyal, responsive to praise and criticism. Sociable, facilitate others in a group, and provide inspiring leadership.	**ENTJ** Frank, decisive, assume leadership readily. Quickly see logical and inefficient procedures and policies, develop and implement comprehensive systems to solve organizational problems. Enjoy long-term planning and goal setting. Usually well informed, well read, enjoy expanding their knowledge and passing it on to others. Forceful in presenting their ideas.

NOTE: I = Introversion; E = Extraversion; S = Sensing; N = Intuition; T = Thinking; F = Feeling; J = Judging; and P = Perceiving.

SOURCE: Modified and reproduced by special permission of the publisher, CPP, Inc., Palo Alto, CA 94303 from *Introduction to Type, Sixth Edition* by Isabel Briggs-Myers. Copyright 1998 by CPP, Inc. All rights reserved. Further reproduction is prohibited without the publisher's written consent.

The Sixteen Types

The preferences combine to form sixteen distinct types, as shown in Table 3.3. For example, let's examine ESTJ. This type has Extraversion, Sensing, Thinking, and Judging preferences. ESTJs see the world as it is (S); make decisions objectively (T); and like structure, schedules, and order (J). Combining these qualities with their preference for interacting with others makes them natural managers. ESTJs are seen by others as dependable, practical, and able to get any job done. They are conscious of the chain of command and see work as a series of goals to be reached by following rules and regulations. They may have little tolerance for disorganization and have a high need for control. Research results from the *MBTI Atlas* show that most of the 7,463 managers studied were ESTJs.[67]

There are no good and bad types, and each type has its own strengths and weaknesses. There is a growing volume of research on type theory. The MBTI instrument has been found to have good reliability and validity as a measurement instrument for identifying type.[68, 69] Type has been found to be related to learning style, teaching style, and choice of occupation. For example, the MBTI types of engineering students at Georgia Tech were studied in order to see who was attracted to engineering and who was likely to leave the major. STs and NTs were more attracted to engineering. Es and Fs were more likely to withdraw from engineering courses.[70] Type has also been used to determine an individual's decision-making style and management style.

Recent studies have begun to focus on the relationship between type and specific managerial behaviors. The Introverted type (I) and the Feeling type (F), for example, have been shown to be more effective at participative management than their counterparts, the Extraverted type and the Thinking type.[71] Companies like AT&T, ExxonMobil, and Honeywell use the MBTI instrument in their management development programs to help employees understand the different viewpoints of others in the organization. The MBTI instrument can also be used for team building. Hewlett-Packard and Armstrong World Industries use the MBTI instrument to help teams realize that diversity and differences lead to successful performance.

Type theory is valued by managers for its simplicity and accuracy in depicting personalities. It is a useful tool for helping managers develop interpersonal skills. Managers also use type theory to build teams that capitalize on individuals' strengths and to help individual team members appreciate differences.

It should be recognized that there is the potential for individuals to misuse the information from the MBTI instrument in organizational settings.[72] Some inappropriate uses include labeling one another, providing a convenient excuse that they simply can't work with someone else, and avoiding responsibility for their own personal development with respect to working with others and becoming more flexible. One's type is not an excuse for inappropriate behavior.

We turn now to another psychological process that forms the basis for individual differences. Perception shapes the way we view the world, and it varies greatly among individuals.

SOCIAL PERCEPTION

(7) Define *social perception* and explain how characteristics of the perceiver, the target, and the situation affect it.

Perception involves the way we view the world around us. It adds meaning to information gathered via the five senses of touch, smell, hearing, vision, and taste. Perception is the primary vehicle through which we come to understand ourselves and our surroundings. *Social perception* is the process of interpreting information about another person. Virtually all management activities rely on perception. In appraising performance, managers use their perceptions of an employee's behavior as a basis for the evaluation.

One work situation that highlights the importance of perception is the selection interview. The consequences of a bad match between an individual and the organization can be devastating for both parties, so it is essential that the data gathered be accurate. Typical first interviews are brief, and the candidate is usually one of many seen by an interviewer during a day. How long does it take for the interviewer to reach a decision about a candidate? In the first four to five minutes, the interviewer often makes an accept or reject decision based on his or her perception of the candidate.[73]

In one study amongst CEOs and top management teams, it was found that perceptions of dissimilarity in values amongst CEOs and top management teams

social perception
The process of interpreting information about another person.

can lead to increased conflict. More interestingly, even if in reality there were no differences in values, just the perception thereof led to such increased conflict. This study highlights the importance of perception in organizations by recommending that managers pay attention to how their employees perceive organizational decisions because this (more than reality) might have an impact on behavior.[73a]

Perception is also culturally determined. Based on our cultural backgrounds, we tend to perceive things in certain ways. Read the following sentence:

Finished files are the result of years of scientific study combined with the experience of years.

Now quickly count the number of *f*s in the sentence. Individuals for whom English is their second language see all six *f*s. Most native English speakers report that there are three *f*s. Because of cultural conditioning, *of* is not an important word and is ignored.[74] Culture affects our interpretation of the data we gather, as well as the way we add meaning to it.

Valuing diversity, including cultural diversity, has been recognized as a key to international competitiveness.[75] This challenge and others make social perception skills essential to managerial success.

Three major categories of factors influence our perception of another person: characteristics of ourselves, as perceivers; characteristics of the target person we are perceiving; and characteristics of the situation in which the interaction takes place. Figure 3.2 shows a model of social perception.

FIGURE 3.2   A Model for Social Perception

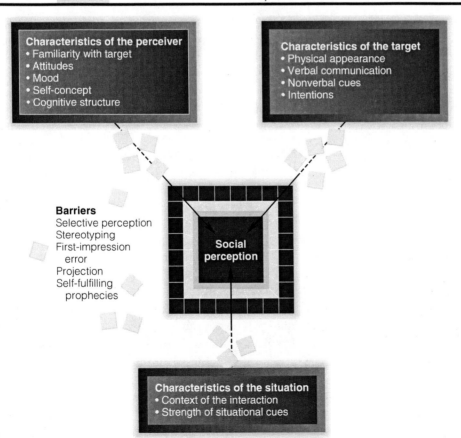

Characteristics of the perceiver
• Familiarity with target
• Attitudes
• Mood
• Self-concept
• Cognitive structure

Characteristics of the target
• Physical appearance
• Verbal communication
• Nonverbal cues
• Intentions

Barriers
Selective perception
Stereotyping
First-impression error
Projection
Self-fulfilling prophecies

Social perception

Characteristics of the situation
• Context of the interaction
• Strength of situational cues

Characteristics of the Perceiver

Several characteristics of the perceiver can affect social perception. One such characteristic is *familiarity* with the target (the person being perceived). When we are familiar with a person, we have multiple observations on which to base our impression of him or her. If the information we have gathered during these observations is accurate, we may have an accurate perception of the other person. Familiarity does not always mean accuracy, however. Sometimes, when we know a person well, we tend to screen out information that is inconsistent with what we believe the person is like. This is a particular danger in performance appraisals where the rater is familiar with the person being rated.

The perceiver's *attitudes* also affect social perception. Suppose you are interviewing candidates for a very important position in your organization—a position that requires negotiating contracts with suppliers, most of whom are male. You may feel that women are not capable of holding their own in tough negotiations. This attitude will doubtless affect your perceptions of the female candidates you interview. Read all about how Steve Jobs's perception of his life events has affected the success of Apple in the Real World feature.

Mood can have a strong influence on the way we perceive someone.[76] We think differently when we are happy than we do when we are depressed. In addition, we remember information that is consistent with our mood state better than information that is inconsistent with our mood state. When in a positive mood, we form more favorable impressions of others. When in a negative mood, we tend to evaluate others unfavorably.

Another factor that can affect social perception is the perceiver's *self-concept*. An individual with a positive self-concept tends to notice positive attributes in another person. In contrast, a negative self-concept can lead a perceiver to pick out negative traits in another person. Greater understanding of self provides more accurate perceptions of others.

Cognitive structure, an individual's pattern of thinking, also affects social perception. Some people have a tendency to perceive physical traits, such as height, weight, and appearance, more readily. Others tend to focus more on central traits, or personality dispositions. Cognitive complexity allows a person to perceive multiple characteristics of another person rather than attending to just a few traits.

Characteristics of the Target

Characteristics of the target—the person being perceived—influence social perception. *Physical appearance* plays a big role in our perception of others. The perceiver will notice the target's physical features like height, weight, estimated age, race, and gender. Clothing says a great deal about a person. Blue pin-striped suits, for example, are decoded to mean banking or Wall Street. Perceivers tend to notice physical appearance characteristics that contrast with the norm, that are intense, or that are new or unusual.[77] A loud person, one who dresses outlandishly, a very tall person, or a hyperactive child will be noticed because he or she provides a contrast to what is commonly encountered. In addition, people who are novel can attract attention. Newcomers or minorities in the organization are examples of novel individuals.

Physical attractiveness often colors our entire impression of another person. Interviewers rate attractive candidates more favorably, and attractive candidates are awarded higher starting salaries.[78, 79] People who are perceived as physically

Steve Jobs: Managerial Genius or Micromanager?

Steve Jobs is the cofounder and CEO of Apple and was the CEO of Pixar until it was acquired by Disney. Some have accused Jobs of being an egomaniac and very temperamental. Stories abound of his rash leadership style in which he recruited great talent yet belittled employees on a routine basis. Finally, the man he had hired to run Apple, John Sculley, fired Jobs from his own creation in 1984. In a recent commencement address at Stanford University, Jobs described this event as one of the best things that could have ever happened to him. He started another computer company called NeXT. This company was bought by Apple in 1996 and Jobs returned triumphantly to the helm of Apple.

Jobs's early life is a case in point for how individuals' life experiences shape personality and perception. Jobs dropped out of college but took calligraphy classes that eventually helped him design proportionally spaced fonts for the Mac. Jobs also backpacked around India in search of enlightenment and then returned to the States with a shaved head and wearing Indian clothing. In his Stanford commencement address, Jobs described his pancreatic cancer scare and battle as one of his most profound life lessons.

These experiences and Jobs's perception and attributions have changed his management style. Apple

© JUSTIN SULLIVAN/GETTY IMAGES

After a number of life-changing events, including being fired from his own company, Steve Jobs' management style has softened.

executives say that he is much calmer and more thoughtful. Perceiving a major crisis like being fired from your own company as a positive and life changing event is certainly unusual. However, that perception is what makes Steve Jobs one of the most enduring leaders in the business world today.

SOURCES: "Steve Jobs' Magic Kingdom: How Apple's Demanding Visionary Will Shake Up Disney and the World of Entertainment," http://www.businessweek.com/magazine/content/06_06/b3970001.htm; The Apple Museum, "Biography: Steve Jobs," by Darren Vader, http://www.theapplemuseum.com/index.php?id=49.

attractive face stereotypes as well. We will discuss these and other stereotypes later in this chapter.

Verbal communication from targets also affects our perception of them. We listen to the topics they speak about, their tone of voice, and their accent and make judgments based on this input.

Nonverbal communication conveys a great deal of information about the target. Eye contact, facial expressions, body movements, and posture all are deciphered by the perceiver in an attempt to form an impression of the target. It is interesting that some nonverbal signals mean very different things in different cultures. The "okay" sign in the United States (forming a circle with the thumb and forefinger) is an insult in South America. Facial expressions, however, seem to have universal meanings.

Individuals from different cultures are able to recognize and decipher such expressions the same way.[80]

The *intentions* of the target are inferred by the perceiver based on observation. We may see our boss appear in our office doorway and think, "Oh no! She's going to give me more work to do." Or we may perceive that her intention is to congratulate us on a recent success. In any case, the perceiver's interpretation of the target's intentions affects the way the perceiver views the target.

Characteristics of the Situation

The situation in which the interaction between the perceiver and the target takes place also influences the perceiver's impression of the target. The *social context* of the interaction is a major influence. Meeting a professor in his or her office affects your impression in a certain way that may contrast with the impression you would form had you met the professor in a local restaurant. In Japan, social context is very important. Business conversations after working hours or at lunch are taboo. If you try to talk business during these times, you may be perceived as rude.[81]

The *strength of situational cues* also affects social perception. As we discussed earlier in the chapter, some situations provide strong cues as to appropriate behavior. In these situations, we assume that the individual's behavior can be accounted for by the situation, and that it may not reflect her or his disposition. This is the *discounting principle* in social perception.[82] For example, you may encounter an automobile salesperson who has a warm and personable manner, asks about your work and hobbies, and seems genuinely interested in your taste in cars. Can you assume that this behavior reflects the salesperson's personality? You probably cannot, because of the influence of the situation. This person is trying to sell you a car, and in this particular situation he or she probably treats all customers in this manner.

You can see that characteristics of the perceiver, the target, and the situation all affect social perception. It would be wonderful if all of us had accurate social perception skills. Unfortunately, barriers often prevent us from perceiving another person accurately.

Barriers to Social Perception

(8) Identify five common barriers to social perception.

discounting principle
The assumption that an individual's behavior is accounted for by the situation.

selective perception
The process of selecting information that supports our individual viewpoints while discounting information that threatens our viewpoints.

stereotype
A generalization about a group of people.

Several factors lead us to form inaccurate impressions of others. Five of these barriers to social perception are selective perception, stereotyping, first-impression error, projection, and self-fulfilling prophecies.

We receive a vast amount of information. *Selective perception* is our tendency to choose information that supports our viewpoints. Individuals often ignore information that makes them feel uncomfortable or threatens their viewpoints. Suppose, for example, that a sales manager is evaluating the performance of his employees. One employee does not get along well with colleagues and rarely completes sales reports on time. This employee, however, generates the most new sales contracts in the office. The sales manager may ignore the negative information, choosing to evaluate the salesperson only on contracts generated. The manager is exercising selective perception.

A *stereotype* is a generalization about a group of people. Stereotypes reduce information about other people to a workable level, and they are efficient for compiling and using information. Stereotypes become even stronger when they are shared with and validated by others.[83] Stereotypes can be accurate; when they are accurate, they can be useful perceptual guidelines. Sometimes, however, stereotypes are inaccurate. They harm individuals when inaccurate impressions of them are inferred and are never tested or changed.[84]

In multicultural work teams, members often stereotype foreign coworkers rather than getting to know them before forming an impression. Team members from less developed countries are often assumed to have less knowledge simply because their homeland is economically or technologically less developed.[85] Stereotypes like these can deflate the productivity of the work team, as well as create low morale.

Attractiveness is a powerful stereotype. We assume that attractive individuals are also warm, kind, sensitive, poised, sociable, outgoing, independent, and strong. Are attractive people really like this? Certainly, all of them are not. A study of romantic relationships showed that most attractive individuals do not fit the stereotype, except for possessing good social skills and being popular.[86]

Some individuals may seem to us to fit the stereotype of attractiveness because our behavior elicits from them behavior that confirms the stereotype. Consider, for example, a situation in which you meet an attractive fellow student. Chances are that you respond positively to this person, because you assume he or she is warm, sociable, and so on. Even though the person may not possess these traits, your positive response may bring out these behaviors in the person. The interaction between the two of you may be channeled such that the stereotype confirms itself.[87]

Stereotyping pervades work life. When there is a contrast against a stereotype, the member of the stereotyped group is treated more positively (given more favorable comments or pats on the back). For example, a female softball player may be given more applause for a home run hit than a male teammate. This occurs because some people may stereotype women as less athletic than men, or because they hold female players to a lower standard. Either way, the contrast is still part of stereotyping.[88]

First impressions are lasting impressions, so the saying goes. Individuals place a good deal of importance on first impressions, and for good reason. We tend to remember what we perceive first about a person, and sometimes we are quite reluctant to change our initial impressions.[89] *First-impression error* occurs when we observe a very brief bit of a person's behavior in our first encounter and infer that this behavior reflects what the person is really like. Primacy effects can be particularly dangerous in interviews, given that we form first impressions quickly and that they may be the basis for long-term employment relationships.

What factors do interviewers rely on when forming first impressions? Perceptions of the candidate, such as whether they like the person, whether they trust the person, and whether or not the person seems credible, all influence the interviewer's decision. Something seemingly as unimportant as the pitch of your voice can leave a lasting impression. Speakers with higher vocal pitch are believed to be more competent, more dominant, and more assertive than those with lower voices. This belief can be carried too far; men whose voices are high enough that they sound feminine are judged the least favorably of all by interviewers. This finding is ironic, given that research has found that students with higher vocal pitch tend to earn better grades.[90]

Projection, also known as the false-consensus effect, is a cause of inaccurate perceptions of others. It is the misperception of the commonness of our own beliefs, values, and behaviors such that we overestimate the number of others who share these things. We assume that others are similar to us, and that our own values and beliefs are appropriate. People who are different are viewed as unusual and even

first-impression error
The tendency to form lasting opinions about an individual based on initial perceptions.

projection
Overestimating the number of people who share our own beliefs, values, and behaviors.

deviant. Projection occurs most often when you surround yourself with others similar to you. You may overlook important information about others when you assume everyone is alike and in agreement.[91]

Self-fulfilling prophecies are also barriers to social perception. Sometimes our expectations affect the way we interact with others such that we get what we wish for. Self-fulfilling prophecy is also known as the Pygmalion effect, named for the sculptor in Greek mythology who prayed that a statue of a woman he had carved would come to life, a wish that was granted by the gods.

Early studies of self-fulfilling prophecy were conducted in elementary school classrooms. Teachers were given bogus information that some of their pupils had high intellectual potential. These pupils were chosen randomly; there were really no differences among the students. Eight months later, the "gifted" pupils scored significantly higher on an IQ test. The teachers' expectations had elicited growth from these students, and the teachers had given them tougher assignments and more feedback on their performance.[92] Self-fulfilling prophecy has been studied in many settings, including at sea. The Israeli Defense Forces told one group of naval cadets that they probably wouldn't experience seasickness, and even if they did, it wouldn't affect their performance. The self-fulfilling prophecy worked! These cadets were rated better performers than other groups, and they also had less seasickness. The information improved the cadets' self-efficacy—they believed they could perform well even if they became seasick.[93]

The Pygmalion effect has been observed in work organizations as well.[94] A manager's expectations of an individual affect both the manager's behavior toward the individual and the individual's response. For example, suppose your initial impression is that an employee has the potential to move up within the organization. Chances are you will spend a great deal of time coaching and counseling the employee, providing challenging assignments, and grooming him or her for success.

Managers can harness the power of the Pygmalion effect to improve productivity in the organization. It appears that high expectations of individuals come true. Can a manager extend these high expectations to an entire group and have similar positive results? The answer is yes. When a manager expects positive things from a group, the group delivers.[95]

Impression Management

Most people want to make a favorable impression on others. This is particularly true in organizations, where individuals compete for jobs, favorable performance evaluations, and salary increases. The process by which people try to control the impressions others have of them is called *impression management*. Individuals use several techniques to control others' impressions of them.[96]

Some impression management techniques are self-enhancing. These techniques focus on enhancing others' impressions of the person using the technique. Name-dropping, which involves mentioning an association with important people in the hopes of improving one's image, is often used. Managing one's appearance is another technique for impression management. Individuals dress carefully for interviews because they want to "look the part" in order to get the job. Self-descriptions, or statements about one's characteristics, are used to manage impressions as well.

Another group of impression management techniques are *other-enhancing*. These techniques focus on the individual one is trying to impress rather than on one's self. Flattery is a common other-enhancing technique whereby compliments

self-fulfilling prophecy
The situation in which our expectations about people affect our interaction with them in such a way that our expectations are confirmed.

impression management
The process by which individuals try to control the impressions others have of them.

are given to an individual in order to win his or her approval. Favors are also used to gain the approval of others. Agreement with someone's opinion is a technique often used to gain a positive impression. People with disabilities, for example, often use other-enhancing techniques. They may feel that they must take it upon themselves to make others comfortable interacting with them. Impression management techniques are used by individuals with disabilities as a way of dealing with potential avoidance by others.[97]

Are impression management techniques effective? Most research on this topic has focused on employment interviews; the results indicate that candidates who engage in impression management by self-promoting performed better in interviews, were more likely to obtain site visits with potential employers, and were more likely to get hired.[98,99] In addition, employees who engage in impression management are rated more favorably in performance appraisals than those who do not.[100]

Impression management seems to have an impact on others' impressions. As long as the impressions conveyed are accurate, this process can be beneficial to organizations. If the impressions are found to be false, however, a strongly negative overall impression may result. Furthermore, excessive impression management can lead to the perception that the user is manipulative or insincere.[101] We have discussed the influences on social perception, the potential barriers to perceiving another person, and impression management. Another psychological process that managers should understand is attribution.

ATTRIBUTION IN ORGANIZATIONS

As human beings, we are innately curious. We are not content merely to observe the behavior of others; rather, we want to know why they behave the way they do. We also seek to understand and explain our own behavior. *Attribution theory* explains how we pinpoint the causes of our own behavior and that of other people.[102]

The attributions, or inferred causes, we provide for behavior have important implications in organizations. In explaining the causes of our performance, good or bad, we are asked to explain the behavior that was the basis for the performance.

Internal and External Attributions

Attributions can be made to an internal source of responsibility (something within the individual's control) or an external source (something outside the individual's control). Suppose you perform well on an exam in this course. You might say you aced the test because you are smart or because you studied hard. If you attribute your success to ability or effort, you are making an *internal attribution*.

Alternatively, you might make an *external attribution* for your performance. You might say it was an easy test (you would attribute your success to degree of task difficulty) or that you had good luck. In this case, you are attributing your performance to sources beyond your control, or external sources. You can see that internal attributions include such causes as ability and effort, whereas external attributions include causes like task difficulty or luck.

Attribution patterns differ among individuals.[103] Achievement-oriented individuals attribute their success to ability and their failures to lack of effort, both internal causes. Failure-oriented individuals attribute their failures to lack of ability, and they may develop feelings of incompetence as a result of their attributional pattern.

(9) Explain the attribution process and how attributions affect managerial behavior.

attribution theory

A theory that explains how individuals pinpoint the causes of their own behavior and that of others.

Evidence indicates that this attributional pattern also leads to depression.[104] Women managers, in contrast to men managers, are less likely to attribute their success to their own ability. This may be because they are adhering to social norms that compel women to be more modest about their accomplishments or because they believe that success has less to do with ability than with hard work.[105]

Attribution theory has many applications in the workplace. The way you explain your own behavior affects your motivation. For example, suppose you must give an important presentation to your executive management group. You believe you have performed well, and your boss tells you that you've done a good job. To what do you attribute your success? If you believe careful preparation and rehearsal were the cause, you're likely to take credit for the performance and to have a sense of self-efficacy about future presentations. If, however, you think you were just lucky, you may not be motivated to repeat the performance because you believe you had little influence on the outcome.

One situation in which a lot of attributions are made is the employment interview. Candidates are often asked to explain the causes of previous performance ("Why did you perform poorly in math classes?") to interviewers. In addition, candidates often feel they should justify why they should be hired ("I work well with people, so I'm looking for a managerial job"). Research shows that successful and unsuccessful candidates differ in the way they make attributions for negative outcomes. Successful candidates are less defensive and make internal attributions for negative events. Unsuccessful candidates attribute negative outcomes to things beyond their control (external attributions), which gives interviewers the impression that the candidate failed to learn from the event. In addition, interviewers fear that the individuals would be likely to blame others when something goes wrong in the workplace.[106]

Attributional Biases

(10) Evaluate the accuracy of managerial attributions from the standpoint of attribution biases and errors.

The attribution process may be affected by two very common errors: the fundamental attribution error and the self-serving bias. The tendency to make attributions to internal causes when focusing on someone else's behavior is known as the *fundamental attribution error*.[107] The other error, *self-serving bias*, occurs when focusing on one's own behavior. Individuals tend to make internal attributions for their own successes and external attributions for their own failures.[108] In other words, when we succeed, we take credit for it; when we fail, we blame it on other people.

Both of these biases were illustrated in a study of health care managers who were asked to cite the causes of their employees' poor performance.[109] The managers claimed that internal causes (their employees' lack of effort or lack of ability) were the problem. This is an example of the fundamental attribution error. When the employees were asked to pinpoint the cause of their own performance problems, they blamed a lack of support from the managers (an external cause), which illustrates self-serving bias.

There are cultural differences in these two attribution errors. As described previously, these biases apply to people from the United States. In more fatalistic cultures, such as India's, people tend to believe that fate is responsible for much that happens. People in such cultures tend to emphasize external causes of behavior.[110]

In China, people are taught that hard work is the route to accomplishment. When faced with either a success or a failure, Chinese individuals first introspect about whether they tried hard enough or whether their attitude was correct. In a

fundamental attribution error
The tendency to make attributions to internal causes when focusing on someone else's behavior.

self-serving bias
The tendency to attribute one's own successes to internal causes and one's failures to external causes.

study of attributions for performance in sports, Chinese athletes attributed both their successes and failures to internal causes. Even when the cause of poor athletic performance was clearly external, such as bad weather, the Chinese participants made internal attributions. In terms of the Chinese culture, this attributional pattern is a reflection of moral values that are used to evaluate behavior. The socialistic value of selfless morality dictates that individual striving must serve collective interests. Mao Zedong stressed that external causes function only through internal causes; therefore, the main cause of results lies within oneself. Chinese are taught this from childhood and form a corresponding attributional tendency. In analyzing a cause, they first look to their own effort.[111]

In a study of attributions for performance in sports, Chinese athletes attributed both their successes and failures to internal causes.

The way individuals interpret the events around them has a strong influence on their behavior. People try to understand the causes of behavior in order to gain predictability and control over future behavior. Managers use attributions in all aspects of their jobs. In evaluating performance and rewarding employees, managers must determine the causes of behavior and a perceived source of responsibility. One tough call managers often make is whether allegations of sexual harassment actually resulted from sexual conduct, and if harassment did occur, what should be done about it. To make such tough calls, managers use attributions.

Attribution theory can explain how performance evaluation judgments can lead to differential rewards. A supervisor attributing an employee's good performance to internal causes, such as effort or ability, may give a larger raise than a supervisor attributing the good performance to external causes, such as help from others or good training. Managers are often called on to explain their own actions as well, and in doing so they make attributions about the causes of their own behavior. We continue our discussion of attributions in Chapter 6 in terms of how they are used in managing employee performance by presenting Kelley's attribution theory.

MANAGERIAL IMPLICATIONS: USING PERSONALITY, PERCEPTION, AND ATTRIBUTION AT WORK

Managers need to know as much as possible about individual differences in order to understand themselves and those with whom they work. An understanding of personality characteristics can help a manager appreciate differences in employees. With the increased diversity of the workforce, tools like the MBTI can be used to help employees see someone else's point of view. These tools can also help make communication among diverse employees more effective.

Managers use social perception constantly on the job. Knowledge of the forces that affect perception and the barriers to accuracy can help the manager form more accurate impressions of others.

Determining the causes of job performance is a major task for the manager, and attribution theory can be used to explain how managers go about determining causality. In addition, knowledge of the fundamental attribution error and self-serving bias can help a manager guard against these biases in the processes of looking for causes of behavior on the job.

In this chapter, we have explored the psychological processes of personality, perception, and attribution as individual differences. In the next chapter, we will continue our discussion of individual differences in terms of attitudes, values, and ethics.

LOOKING BACK: SERGEY BRIN'S PERSONALITY AND GOOGLE'S IDENTITY

Like all corporations, Google has its set of catchphrases. However, unlike other corporations that have catchphrases designed to sell their product, Google's catchphrases are reflective of the life and personality of founders Sergey Brin and Larry Page. For example, one saying is "Don't Be Evil." Speculation abounds that this phrase is important at Google as a result of Brin's exposure to the atrocities of the Soviet Union against Jews and his natural dislike for set corporate dictums. In fact, his reputation at Stanford was that of a bright young man who at times appeared arrogant. He had a natural penchant for a variety of outdoor activities and focused on taking classes that interested him (such as advanced swimming) rather than what was required. To this day, he hasn't finished his doctorate at Stanford but holds a master's degree from the school.

Brin's youthful brashness has translated into several innovative policies at Google, where engineers are encouraged to devote 20 percent of their work time (one day per week) on projects that interest them. One senior vice president at Google stated that about half of their new products originated from this concept of 20 percent time.

Also, the "Don't Be Evil" principle had translated into numerous worker-friendly practices such as free laundry services, separate areas for nursing mothers, video games, foosball, and so on. Such practices have catapulted Google to number one in *Fortune's* 2007 list of the best places to work in America. Brin's personality and his perception of the business world have played a huge role in Google's success.[112, 113]

Chapter Summary

1. Individual differences are factors that make individuals unique. They include personalities, perceptions, skills and abilities, attitudes, values, and ethics.

2. The trait theory and integrative approach are two personality theories.

3. Managers should understand personality because of its effect on behavior. Several characteristics affect behavior in organizations, including locus of control, self-esteem, self-monitoring, and positive/negative affect.

4. Personality has a stronger influence in weak situations, where there are few cues to guide behavior.

5. One useful framework for understanding individual differences is type theory, developed by Carl Jung and measured by the Myers-Briggs Type Indicator (MBTI).

6. Social perception is the process of interpreting information about another person. It is influenced by characteristics of the perceiver, the target, and the situation.

7. Barriers to social perception include selective perception, stereotyping, first-impression error, projection, and self-fulfilling prophecies.

8. Impression management techniques such as name-dropping, managing one's appearance, self-descriptions, flattery, favors, and agreement are used by individuals to control others' impressions of them.

9. Attribution is the process of determining the cause of behavior. It is used extensively by managers, especially in evaluating performance.

Key Terms

attribution theory (p. 103)
behavioral measures (p. 90)
discounting principle (p. 100)
extraversion (p. 92)
Feeling (p. 93)
first-impression error (p. 101)
fundamental attribution error (p. 104)
general self-efficacy (p. 87)
impression management (p. 102)
individual differences (p. 82)
integrative approach (p. 85)
interactional psychology (p. 83)

introversion (p. 92)
intuition (p. 92)
Judging Preference (p. 94)
locus of control (p. 86)
Myers-Briggs Type Indicator (MBTI) (p. 91)
negative affect (p. 89)
Perceiving Preference (p. 94)
personality (p. 83)
positive affect (p. 89)
projection (p. 101)
projective test (p. 90)

selective perception (p. 100)
self-esteem (p. 87)
self-fulfilling prophecy (p. 102)
self-monitoring (p. 88)
self-report questionnaire (p. 91)
self-serving bias (p. 104)
sensing (p. 92)
social perception (p. 96)
stereotype (p. 100)
strong situation (p. 90)
Thinking (p. 93)
trait theory (p. 84)

Review Questions

1. What are individual differences, and why should managers understand them?

2. Define *personality* and describe its origins.

3. Describe two theories of personality and explain what each contributes to our knowledge of personality.

4. Describe the eight preferences of the Myers-Briggs Type Indicator. How does this instrument measure Carl Jung's ideas?

5. What factors influence social perception? What are the barriers to social perception?

6. Describe the errors that affect the attribution process.

Discussion and Communication Questions

1. What contributions can high self-monitors make in organizations? Low self-monitors?

2. How can managers improve their perceptual skills?

3. Which has the stronger impact on personality: heredity or environment?

4. How can managers make more accurate attributions?

5. How can managers encourage self-efficacy in employees?

6. How can self-serving bias and the fundamental attribution error be avoided?

7. *(communication question)* You have been asked to develop a training program for interviewers. An integral part of this program focuses on helping interviewers develop better social perception skills. Write an outline for this section of the training program. Be sure to address barriers to social perception and ways to avoid them.

8. *(communication question)* Form groups of four to six; then split each group in half. Debate the origins of personality, with one half taking the position that personality is inherited and the other half that personality is formed by the environment. Each half should also discuss the implications of its position for managers.

Ethical Dilemma

Alice loves to hire new people. As manager of the Medicare Reimbursement department of a large hospital, she sees it as a great responsibility to aggressively pursue and hire the best people. She has already experienced the challenges of hiring the wrong person. She knows a bad personality match could undermine the culture she has worked so hard to build. Alice plans to do everything in her power to never repeat the mistake of a bad hire.

Her latest hire, however, is proving to be a bigger challenge than she had expected. The problem is that the position requires a good deal of specialized knowledge. Alice needs someone who knows the current Medicare regulations and can decipher new ones. The pool of candidates with this knowledge is extremely small. Truthfully, she has interviewed only one person with the skills and knowledge that she needs.

Jana had interviewed two weeks ago. She knew the regulations better than anyone Alice has ever met. Every question Alice asked, Jana answered. What an asset Jana would be to the department. The dilemma is that Jana seems to be extremely extroverted, needing and wanting a lot of social involvement. This job would not offer that opportunity. Even worse, Mike, the main person with whom Jana would be working, is an extreme introvert. He rarely speaks to anyone and prefers that people speak to him as little as possible. Alice can see nothing but problems between these two employees.

Alice does not know what to do. She values Mike a great deal and does not want to do anything to make him unhappy in his job. But she desperately needs someone in this vacant position. She has been depending on everyone to pitch in and cover the workload for weeks now. She knows that has to stop. But is it fair to bring in someone she feels sure would be unhappy in the job and would ultimately quit? She may even end up losing both Jana and Mike. She has no idea what to do.

Questions

1. Who are the stakeholders affected by Alice's decisions?

2. How much importance should Alice place on Mike's needs and wants?

3. Using consequential, rule-based, and character theories, evaluate Alice's decision alternatives.

Experiential Exercises

3.1 MBTI Types and Management Styles

Part I. This questionnaire will help you determine your preferences. For each item, circle either a or b. If you feel both a and b are true, decide which one is more like you, even if it is only slightly more true.

1. I would rather
   a. solve a new and complicated problem.
   b. work on something I have done before.

2. I like to
   a. work alone in a quiet place.
   b. be where the action is.

3. I want a boss who
   a. establishes and applies criteria in decisions.
   b. considers individual needs and makes exceptions.

4. When I work on a project, I
   a. like to finish it and get some closure.
   b. often leave it open for possible changes.

5. When making a decision, the most important considerations are
   a. rational thoughts, ideas, and data.
   b. people's feelings and values.

6. On a project, I tend to
   a. think it over and over before deciding how to proceed.
   b. start working on it right away, thinking about it as I go along.

7. When working on a project, I prefer to
   a. maintain as much control as possible.
   b. explore various options.

8. In my work, I prefer to
   a. work on several projects at a time and learn as much as possible about each one.
   b. have one project that is challenging and keeps me busy.

9. I often
   a. make lists and plans whenever I start something and may hate to seriously alter my plans.
   b. avoid plans and just let things progress as I work on them.

10. When discussing a problem with colleagues, it is easy for me to
    a. see "the big picture."
    b. grasp the specifics of the situation.

11. When the phone rings in my office or at home, I usually
    a. consider it an interruption.
    b. do not mind answering it.

12. Which word describes you better?
    a. Analytical
    b. Empathetic

13. When I am working on an assignment, I tend to
    a. work steadily and consistently.
    b. work in bursts of energy with "downtime" in between.

14. When I listen to someone talk on a subject, I usually try to
    a. relate it to my own experience and see if it fits.
    b. assess and analyze the message.

15. When I come up with new ideas, I generally
    a. "go for it."
    b. like to contemplate the ideas some more.

16. When working on a project, I prefer to
    a. narrow the scope so it is clearly defined.
    b. broaden the scope to include related aspects.

17. When I read something, I usually
    a. confine my thoughts to what is written there.
    b. read between the lines and relate the words to other ideas.

18. When I have to make a decision in a hurry, I often
    a. feel uncomfortable and wish I had more information.
    b. am able to do so with available data.

19. In a meeting, I tend to
    a. continue formulating my ideas as I talk about them.
    b. only speak out after I have carefully thought the issue through.

20. In work, I prefer spending a great deal of time on issues of
    a. ideas.
    b. people.

21. In meetings, I am most often annoyed with people who
    a. come up with many sketchy ideas.
    b. lengthen meetings with many practical details.

22. I am a
    a. morning person.
    b. night owl.

23. What is your style in preparing for a meeting?
    a. I am willing to go in and be responsive.
    b. I like to be fully prepared and usually sketch an outline of the meeting.

24. In a meeting, I would prefer for people to
    a. display a fuller range of emotions.
    b. be more task oriented.

25. I would rather work for an organization where
    a. my job is intellectually stimulating.
    b. I am committed to its goals and mission.

26. On weekends, I tend to
    a. plan what I will do.
    b. just see what happens and decide as I go along.

27. I am more
    a. outgoing.
    b. contemplative.

28. I would rather work for a boss who is
    a. full of new ideas.
    b. practical.

In the following, choose the word in each pair that appeals to you more:

29. a. Social
    b. Theoretical

30. a. Ingenuity
    b. Practicality

31. a. Organized
    b. Adaptable

32. a. Active
    b. Concentration

Scoring Key

Count one point for each item listed below that you have circled in the inventory.

Score for I	Score for E	Score for S	Score for N
2a	2b	1b	1a
6a	6b	10b	10a
11a	11b	13a	13b
15b	15a	16a	16b
19b	19a	17a	17b
22a	22b	21a	21b
27b	27a	28b	28a
32b	32a	30b	30a

Total
Circle the one with more points—I or E.   Circle the one with more points—S or N.

Score for T	Score for F	Score for J	Score for P
3a	3b	4a	4b
5a	5b	7a	7b
12a	12b	8b	8a
14b	14a	9a	9b
20a	20b	18b	18a
24b	24a	23b	23a
25a	25b	26a	26b
29b	29a	31a	31b

Total
Circle the one with more points—T or F.   Circle the one with more points—J or P.

Your score is
I or E _____   T or F _____
S or N _____   J or P _____

Part II. The purpose of this part of the exercise is to give you experience in understanding some of the individual differences that were proposed by Carl Jung and are measured by the MBTI.

Step 1. Your instructor will assign you to a group.

Step 2. Your group is a team of individuals who want to start a business. You are to develop a mission statement and a name for your business.

Step 3. After you have completed Step 2, analyze the decision process that occurred within the group. How did you decide on your company's name and mission?

Step 4. Your instructor will have each group report to the class the name and mission of the company, and then the decision process used. Your instructor will also give you some additional information about the exercise and provide some interesting insights about your management style.

SOURCE: "MBTI Types and Management Styles" from D. Marcic and P. Nutt, "Personality Inventory," in D. Marcic, ed., *Organizational Behavior: Experiences and Cases* (St. Paul, Minn.: West, 1989), 9–16. Reprinted by permission.

3.2 Stereotypes in Employment Interviews

Step 1. Your instructor will give you a transcript that records an applicant's interview for a job as a laborer. Your task is to memorize as much of the interview as possible.

Step 2. Write down everything you can remember about the job candidate.

Step 3. Your instructor will lead you in a discussion.

SOURCE: Adapted from D. A. Sachau and M. Hussang, "How Interviewers' Stereotypes Influence Memory: An Exercise," *Journal of Management Education* 16 (1992): 391–396. Copyright © 1992 by Sage Publications. Reprinted with permission of Sage Publications, Inc.

Biz Flix | The Breakfast Club

John Hughes's careful look at teenage culture in a suburban Chicago high school focuses on a group of teenagers from the school's different subcultures. They start their Saturday detention with nothing in common, but over the course of a day, they learn each other's innermost secrets. The highly memorable characters—the Athlete, the Princess, the Criminal, the Basket Case, and the Brain—leave lasting impressions. If you have seen the film, try to recall which actor or actress played each character.

The scene from *The Breakfast Club* is an edited version of the "Lunchtime" sequence that appears in the first third of the film. Carefully study each character's behavior to answer the following questions. The rest of the film shows the growing relationships among the detainees as they try to understand each other's personality.

What to Watch for and Ask Yourself:

> Which Big Five personality dimensions describe each character in this scene?

> Which characters show positive affect? Which show negative affect?

> Refer to the Myers-Briggs Type Indicator (MBTI) section in this chapter. Which of the sixteen types shown in Table 3.3 best describes each character? Why?

Workplace Video | Managing Small Business Start-ups, Featuring The Little Guys

For many years David and Evie Wexler worked in a home-electronics store where their talents were not being utilized fully. Frustrated at not seeing their ideas put into action, the couple decided to leave the company and start a home-theater business with longtime associate Paul Gerrity. In just twelve years, the three partners grew their new venture, The Little Guys Home Electronics, into a thriving small business with $10 million in annual sales.

Like many entrepreneurs, the Wexlers felt limited by their former positions and wanted to strike out on their own. They had confidence that they could do things better than their previous employer, and they had a vision for opening an electronics business that could provide hands-on, personalized customer service. Above all, they believed in doing things differently from "the big guys"—hence the name.

The Wexlers and Gerrity possess a range of personality characteristics common to successful entrepreneurs. The partners are achievement-oriented extraverts who seek creative, rewarding enterprises. They thrive on overcoming the day-to-day challenges of operating a small business and demonstrate a high tolerance for ambiguity. Most importantly, they possess great confidence in their own abilities. "I knew we could pull it off," says cofounder David Wexler. "I was confident in our ability to succeed at some level. Failure was never something we accepted." Wexler's self-confidence was put to the test on numerous occasions—such as when the company moved up its grand opening a week ahead of schedule due to an advertising mistake—but the cofounders always found a way to keep The Little Guys on track.

Starting a new business is a risky venture, but the Wexlers and Gerrity had the personality, the openness to experience new things, and the internal motivation necessary to be successful. And while The Little Guys Home Electronics has already achieved enormous success, the company's owners don't rest on their laurels. Instead, they look forward to the next big challenge.

Discussion Questions

1. Describe the Wexlers' personality characteristics in terms of the partners' core self-evaluations (CSE).

2. Which of the Big Five personality traits do you consider the most important for small-business owners like the Wexlers? Explain.

3. Describe the three cofounders' social perceptions of each other, and explain how the characteristics of the perceiver, the target, and the situation influence those perceptions.

Sir Richard Branson:
Development of an Entrepreneur

Virgin is one of the most respected brands in Great Britain and is rapidly becoming an important global brand as well. The Virgin brand was started in the 1970s with a small mail-order record company that grew out of a student magazine.[1] Since then, Richard Branson has developed the Virgin brand into a veritable entrepreneurial empire, with businesses in travel and tourism (e.g., Virgin Atlantic Airways, Virgin Trains, Virgin Balloon Flights, Virgin Galactic, and Virgin Holidays); leisure and pleasure (e.g., Virgin Games, V2 Music, and Virgin Comics); social and environmental (e.g., Virgin Fuels and Virgin Earth); shopping (e.g., Virgin Books, Virgin Megastore, and Virgin Wines); media and telecommunications (e.g., Virgin Media, Virgin Mobile, and Virgin Radio); finance and money (Virgin Money); and health (Virgin Active and Virgin Health Bank).[2]

Branson: The Background

In the first chapter of his autobiography, Branson reminisces about some of his childhood experiences—ones that would have a profound effect on his development as an adult and an entrepreneur. He writes that his parents, especially his mother, continually set challenges for him and his sisters, Vanessa and Lindi, in order to make them independent. These challenges were physical in nature rather than academic. According to Branson, he and his sisters were soon setting physical challenges for themselves.[3]

A loving family played an important role in Branson's development. "We were a family that would have killed for each other—and we still are," he says.[4] Teamwork was also a hallmark of the family. Branson's parents treated him and his two sisters as equals. They valued their children's opinions and only provided advice when the children asked for it. Branson's mother was very entrepreneurial, as was his Aunt Clare. Each developed several different ways of making money.[5]

Despite his enormous entrepreneurial success, Branson still lacks a high school diploma.[6] In school, he was a mediocre student but a superb athlete.

Although he was dyslexic and had vision problems, his inability to read, write, and spell, and his poor performance on tests, were blamed on stupidity or laziness. In commenting on Branson's academic miseries as a child in relation to his athletic and future entrepreneurial successes, one observer noted: "In the end, it was the tests that failed. They totally missed his ability and passion for sports. They had no means to identify ambition, the fire inside that drives people to find a path to success that zigzags around the maze of standard doors that won't open. They never identified the most important talent of all. It's the ability to connect with people, mind to mind, soul to soul. It's that rare power to energize the ambitions of others so that they, too, rise to the level of their dreams."[7]

A passion for sports, adventure, family, and entrepreneurship define Sir Richard's life. Branson has broken several air and land speed and distance records while racing boats and hot air balloons in his pursuit of adventure. He structures his work schedule to leave ample time to spend with his family and friends. Indeed, Branson's efforts to synthesize work, play, and life seem to be the hallmark of his business model and business success.[8]

Branson: The Entrepreneur

Branson began building his entrepreneurial empire in his teenage years. At the age of 17, he became frustrated with the rules and regulations of schools. Brimming with activism, he and a friend, Jonny Gems, started a magazine called *Student*. The magazine tied many schools together and focused on the students themselves rather than the schools. After publishing the first issue, Branson received a note from the headmaster of the school that he and Gems attended. It read: "Congratulations, Branson. I predict that you will either go to prison or become a millionaire."[9]

Branson dropped out of school and continued to pursue his entrepreneurial interests. His next venture was a discount music business called Virgin Records. Then entrepreneurial venture after entrepreneurial venture developed, culminating in extraordinary success. Sir Richard—knighted by the Queen of England in 2000—has mostly majority stakes in over 200 companies that constitute his multibillion-dollar entrepreneurial empire.[10] Global revenues were approximately $20 billion in 2006.[11]

Branson is not a conventional businessperson—and he never intended to be one. In fact, he is about as far removed from the stereotypical CEO as one can imagine. "He continues to be a corporate iconoclast, defying conventional wisdom, pushing the envelope, poking fun at the big guys, saying exactly what he thinks and doing exactly what he wants."[12] Branson has irreverence for authority that he claims to have inherited from both parents. He relishes becoming involved in "industries that charge too much (music) or hold consumers hostage (cellular) or treat them badly and bore them to tears (airlines)."[13] His aim is to upset the status quo in such industries.

Branson also relishes teamwork and brings it into play in his entrepreneurial ventures. He has an "advisory team, whose job it is to capture his entrepreneurial ideas and wrestle them into some kind of corporate structure that is both attractive to investors and palatable to him."[14] He also gives others opportunities to develop their ideas into business ventures that he backs.

Sir Richard's entrepreneurial ventures and work pique his intellectual curiosity and provide the education he was never able to get in school. "What really sets him apart from other CEOs is that he doesn't mind surprises. He thrives on them. Startup problems don't bother him at all. Neither do unforeseen battles."[15]

Discussion Questions

1. Using the various personality characteristics discussed in this chapter, how would you describe Sir Richard Branson's personality?

2. What perceptions have you formed of Branson? How do you think your perceptions are affected by characteristics of you as the perceiver and Branson as the perceptual target? To what extent have the barriers to social perception influenced your view of him?

3. How do attributions factor into understanding the background of Branson's entrepreneurial development?

SOURCE: This case was written by Michael K. McCuddy, The Louis S. and Mary L. Morgal Chair of Christian Business Ethics and Professor of Management, College of Business Administration, Valparaiso University.

CASE

Attitudes, Emotions, and Ethics

LEARNING OBJECTIVES

After reading this chapter, you should be able to do the following:

1 Explain the ABC model of an attitude.

2 Describe how attitudes are formed.

3 Identify sources of job satisfaction and commitment and suggest tips for managers to help build these two attitudes among their employees.

4 Distinguish between organizational citizenship and workplace deviance behaviors.

5 Identify the characteristics of the source, target, and message that affect persuasion.

6 Discuss the definition and importance of emotions at work.

7 Justify the importance of emotional contagion at work.

8 Contrast the effects of individual and organizational influences on ethical behavior.

9 Discuss how value systems, locus of control, Machiavellianism, and cognitive moral development affect ethical behavior.

THINKING AHEAD: THE TIMBERLAND COMPANY TAKES ETHICAL BEHAVIOR TO THE NEXT LEVEL

The Timberland Company ranked 74th on *Fortune*'s "100 Best Companies to Work For" in 2007. Timberland was also ranked 8th among *CRO* magazine's "100 Best Corporate Citizens." *CRO* magazine is a publication of the organization for Corporate Responsibility Officers. In trying business times such as ours where more ethical scandals break out each day, how does Timberland do it?

The answer is building a strong culture based on ethical value systems. Timberland has a very clear set of values and corporate governance code of conduct. It also has set up a clear ethical guidelines section that employees and corporate officers can refer to when in doubt. In fact, Timberland's mission statement includes a statement of their values and emphasis on ethical behavior. The four values driving ethical behavior at the company are humility, humanity, integrity, and excellence.

Timberland's major competitor, Nike, faced criticism in the past for using child labor. In 2006, Timberland announced it would include a "nutritional label" on its products to create more awareness among its customers about their product. This label includes a manufacturing details section that describes the name and location of the factory where that product was produced. The environmental impact section describes how much energy was spent on manufacturing it, and the community involvement section assesses whether the shoe meets the Timberland code of conduct and whether any child labor was involved. While some organizations focus on product packaging and service only to market their products, companies like Timberland seem to derive success from their value systems as much as from the product itself. You'll find more on Timberland's values and ethics in the Looking Back feature at the end of the chapter.[1,2,3]

In this chapter, we continue the discussion of individual differences we began in Chapter 3 with personality, perception, and attribution. Persons and situations jointly influence behavior, and individual differences help us to better understand the influence of the person. Our focus now is on three other individual difference factors: attitudes, emotions, and ethics.

ATTITUDES

An *attitude* is a psychological tendency that is expressed by evaluating a particular entity with some degree of favor or disfavor.[4] We respond favorably or unfavorably toward many things: coworkers, our own appearance, and politics are some examples.

Attitudes are important because of their links to behavior. Attitudes are also an integral part of the world of work. Managers speak of workers who have a "bad attitude" and conduct "attitude adjustment" talks with employees. Often, poor performance attributed to bad attitude really stems from lack of motivation, minimal feedback, lack of trust in management, or other problems. These are areas that managers must explore.

It is important for managers to understand the antecedents to attitudes as well as their consequences. Managers also need to understand the different components of attitudes, how attitudes are formed, the major attitudes that affect work behavior, and how to use persuasion to change attitudes.

The ABC Model

Attitudes develop on the basis of evaluative responding. An individual does not have an attitude until he or she responds to an entity (person, object, situation, or issue) on an affective, cognitive, or behavioral basis. To understand the complexity of an attitude, we can break it down into three components, as depicted in Table 4.1.

These components—affect, behavioral intentions, and cognition—compose what we call the ABC model of an attitude.[5] *Affect* is the emotional component of an attitude. It refers to an individual's feeling about something or someone. Statements such as "I like this" or "I prefer that" reflect the affective component of an attitude. Affect is measured by physiological indicators such as galvanic skin response (changes in electrical resistance of skin that indicate emotional arousal) and blood pressure. These indicators show changes in emotions by measuring physiological arousal. An individual's attempt to hide his or her feelings might be shown by a change in arousal.

The second component is the intention to behave in a certain way toward an object or person. Our attitudes toward women in management, for example, may be inferred

1 Explain the ABC model of an attitude.

attitude
A psychological tendency expressed by evaluating an entity with some degree of favor or disfavor.

affect
The emotional component of an attitude.

TABLE 4.1   The ABC Model of an Attitude

	Component	Measured By	Example
A	Affect	Physiological indicators Verbal statements about feelings	I don't like my boss.
B	Behavioral intentions	Observed behavior Verbal statements about intentions	I want to transfer to another department.
C	Cognition	Attitude scales Verbal statements about beliefs	I believe my boss plays favorites at work.

SOURCE: Adapted from M. J. Rosenberg and C. I. Hovland, "Cognitive, Affective, and Behavioral Components of Attitude," in M. J. Rosenberg, C. I. Hovland, W. J. McGuire, R. P. Abelson, and J. H. Brehm, *Attitude Organization and Change* (New Haven, Conn.: Yale University Press, 1960). Copyright 1960 Yale University Press. Used with permission.

from observing the way we behave toward a female supervisor. We may be supportive, passive, or hostile, depending on our attitude. The behavioral component of an attitude is measured by observing behavior or by asking a person about behavior or intentions. The statement "If I were asked to speak at commencement, I'd be willing to try to do so, even though I'd be nervous" reflects a behavioral intention.

The third component of an attitude, cognition (thought), reflects a person's perceptions or beliefs. Cognitive elements are evaluative beliefs and are measured by attitude scales or by asking about thoughts. The statement "I believe Japanese workers are industrious" reflects the cognitive component of an attitude.

The ABC model shows that to thoroughly understand an attitude, we must assess all three components. Suppose, for example, you want to evaluate your employees' attitudes toward flextime (flexible work scheduling). You would want to determine how they feel about flextime (affect), whether they would use flextime (behavioral intention), and what they think about the policy (cognition). The most common method of attitude measurement, the attitude scale, measures only the cognitive component.

As rational beings, individuals try to be consistent in everything they believe in and do. They prefer consistency (consonance) between their attitudes and behavior. Anything that disrupts this consistency causes tension (dissonance), which motivates individuals to change either their attitudes or their behavior to return to a state of consistency. The tension produced when there is a conflict between attitudes and behavior is *cognitive dissonance*.[6]

Suppose, for example, a salesperson is required to sell damaged televisions for the full retail price, without revealing the damage to customers. She believes, however, that doing so constitutes unethical behavior. This creates a conflict between her attitude (concealing information from customers is unethical) and her behavior (selling defective TVs without informing customers about the damage).

The salesperson, experiencing the discomfort from dissonance, will try to resolve the conflict. She might change her behavior by refusing to sell the defective TV sets. Alternatively, she might rationalize that the defects are minor and that the customers will not be harmed by not knowing about them. These are attempts by the salesperson to restore equilibrium between her attitudes and behavior, thereby eliminating the tension from cognitive dissonance.

Managers need to understand cognitive dissonance because employees often find themselves in situations in which their attitudes conflict with their behavior. They manage the tension by changing their attitudes or behavior. Employees who display

cognitive dissonance
A state of tension that is produced when an individual experiences conflict between attitudes and behavior.

sudden shifts in behavior may be attempting to reduce dissonance. Some employees find the conflicts between strongly held attitudes and required work behavior so uncomfortable that they leave the organization to escape the dissonance.

Attitude Formation

(2) Describe how attitudes are formed.

Attitudes are learned. Our responses to people and issues evolve over time. Two major influences on attitudes are direct experience and social learning.

Direct experience with an object or person is a powerful influence on attitudes. How do you know that you like biology or dislike math? You have probably formed these attitudes from experience in studying the subjects. Research has shown that attitudes that are derived from direct experience are stronger, held more confidently, and more resistant to change than attitudes formed through indirect experience.[7] One reason attitudes derived from direct experience are so powerful is their availability. This means that the attitudes are easily accessed and are active in our cognitive processes.[8] When attitudes are available, we can call them quickly into consciousness. Attitudes that are not learned from direct experience are not as available, so we do not recall them as easily.

In *social learning*, the family, peer groups, religious organizations, and culture shape an individual's attitudes in an indirect manner.[9] Children learn to adopt certain attitudes by the reinforcement they are given by their parents when they display behaviors that reflect an appropriate attitude. This is evident when very young children express political preferences similar to their parents'. Peer pressure molds attitudes through group acceptance of individuals who express popular attitudes and through sanctions, such as exclusion from the group, placed on individuals who espouse unpopular attitudes.

Substantial social learning occurs through *modeling*, in which individuals acquire attitudes by merely observing others. After overhearing other individuals expressing an opinion or watching them engaging in a behavior that reflects an attitude, the observer adopts the attitude.

For an individual to learn from observing a model, four processes must take place:

1. The learner must focus attention on the model.
2. The learner must retain what was observed from the model. Retention is accomplished in two basic ways. In one, the learner "stamps in" what was observed by forming a verbal code for it. The other way is through symbolic rehearsal, by which the learner forms a mental image of himself or herself behaving like the model.
3. Behavioral reproduction must occur; that is, the learner must practice the behavior.
4. The learner must be motivated to learn from the model.

Culture also plays a definitive role in attitude development. Consider, for example, the contrast in the North American and European attitudes toward vacation and leisure. The typical vacation in the United States is two weeks, and some workers do not use all of their vacation time. In Europe, the norm is longer vacations; and in some countries, *holiday* means everyone taking a month off. The European attitude is that an investment in longer vacations is important to health and performance.

Attitudes and Behavior

If you have a favorable attitude toward participative management, will your management style be participative? As managers, if we know an employee's attitude, to what extent can we predict her or his behavior? These questions illustrate the fundamental issue of attitude–behavior correspondence, that is, the degree to which an attitude predicts behavior.

social learning
The process of deriving attitudes from family, peer groups, religious organizations, and culture.

This correspondence has concerned organizational behaviorists and social psychologists for quite some time. Can attitudes predict behaviors like being absent from work or quitting your job? Some studies suggested that attitudes and behavior are closely linked, while others found no relationship at all or a weak relationship at best. Attention then became focused on when attitudes predict behavior and when they do not. Attitude–behavior correspondence depends on five things: attitude specificity, attitude relevance, timing of measurement, personality factors, and social constraints.

Individuals possess both general and specific attitudes. You may favor women's right to reproductive freedom (a general attitude) and prefer pro-choice political candidates (a specific attitude) but not attend pro-choice rallies or send money to Planned Parenthood. That you don't perform these behaviors may make the link between your attitude and behaviors on this issue seem weak. However, given a choice between a pro-choice and an anti-abortion political candidate, you will probably vote for the pro-choice candidate. In this case, your attitude seems quite predictive of your behavior. The point is that the greater the attitude specificity, the stronger its link to behavior.[10]

Another factor that affects the attitude–behavior link is relevance.[11] Attitudes that address an issue in which we have some self-interest are more relevant for us, and our subsequent behavior is consistent with our expressed attitude. Suppose there is a proposal to raise income taxes for those who earn $150,000 or more. If you are a student, you may not find the issue of great personal relevance. Individuals in that income bracket, however, might find it highly relevant; their attitude toward the issue would be strongly predictive of whether they would vote for the tax increase.

The timing of the measurement also affects attitude–behavior correspondence. The shorter the time between the attitude measurement and the observed behavior, the stronger the relationship. For example, voter preference polls taken close to an election are more accurate than earlier polls.

Personality factors also influence the attitude–behavior link. One personality disposition that affects the consistency between attitudes and behavior is self-monitoring. Recall from Chapter 3 that low self-monitors rely on their internal states when making decisions about behavior, while high self-monitors are more responsive to situational cues. Low self-monitors therefore display greater correspondence between their attitudes and behaviors.[12] High self-monitors may display little correspondence between their attitudes and behavior because they behave according to signals from others and from the environment.

Finally, social constraints affect the relationship between attitudes and behavior.[13] The social context provides information about acceptable attitudes and behaviors.[14, 15] New employees in an organization, for example, are exposed to the attitudes of their work group. Suppose a newcomer from Afghanistan holds a negative attitude toward women in management because in his country the prevailing attitude is that women should not be in positions of power. He sees, however, that his work group members respond positively to their female supervisor. His own behavior may therefore be compliant because of social constraints. This behavior is inconsistent with his attitude and cultural belief system.

Work Attitudes

Attitudes at work are important because, directly or indirectly, they affect work behavior. Chief among the things that negatively affect employees' work attitudes are jobs that are very demanding, combined with a lack of control on the part of the employee.[16] A positive psychological climate at work, on the other hand, can lead to positive attitudes and good performance.[17] A study found that when hotel employees offered helpful, concerned service, hotel customers developed a warmer, more positive attitude toward the hotel itself. This attitude resulted in greater customer loyalty,

Assess Your Job Satisfaction

Think of the job you have now or a job you've had in the past. Indicate how satisfied you are with each aspect of your job below, using the following scale:

1 = Extremely dissatisfied
2 = Dissatisfied
3 = Slightly dissatisfied
4 = Neutral
5 = Slightly satisfied
6 = Satisfied
7 = Extremely satisfied

1. The amount of job security I have.
2. The amount of pay and fringe benefits I receive.
3. The amount of personal growth and development I get in doing my job.
4. The people I talk to and work with on my job.
5. The degree of respect and fair treatment I receive from my boss.
6. The feeling of worthwhile accomplishment I get from doing my job.
7. The chance to get to know other people while on the job.
8. The amount of support and guidance I receive from my supervisor.
9. The degree to which I am fairly paid for what I contribute to this organization.
10. The amount of independent thought and action I can exercise in my job.
11. How secure things look for me in the future in this organization.
12. The chance to help other people while at work.
13. The amount of challenge in my job.
14. The overall quality of the supervision I receive on my work.

Now compute your scores for the facets of job satisfaction.

Pay satisfaction:

Q2 + Q9   = Divided by 2:

Security satisfaction:

Q1 + Q1   = Divided by 2:

Social satisfaction:

Q4 + Q7 + Q12   = Divided by 3:

Supervisory satisfaction:

Q5 + Q8 + Q14   = Divided by 3:

Growth satisfaction:

Q3 + Q6 + Q10 + Q13 = Divided by 4:

Scores on the facets range from 1 to 7. (Scores lower than 4 suggest there is room for change.)

This questionnaire is an abbreviated version of the Job Diagnostic Survey, a widely used tool for assessing individuals' attitudes about their jobs. Compare your scores on each facet to the following norms for a large sample of managers.

Pay satisfaction:	4.6
Security satisfaction:	5.2
Social satisfaction:	5.6
Supervisory satisfaction:	5.2
Growth satisfaction:	5.3

How do your scores compare? Are there actions you can take to improve your job satisfaction?

SOURCE: *Work Redesign* by Hackman/Oldham, © 1980. Reprinted by permission of Pearson Education, Inc., Upper Saddle River, N.J.

(3) Identify sources of job satisfaction and commitment and suggest tips for managers to help build these two attitudes among their employees.

job satisfaction

A pleasurable or positive emotional state resulting from the appraisal of one's job or job experiences.

greater likelihood that the customers would stay at the hotel, and even a willingness to pay more for the same service. Customer attitudes were strongly influenced by employee gestures, facial expressions, and words. In this study, customer attitudes were crucial to the success of the firm, and employee behaviors were crucial in forming customer attitudes, meaning firms can "train" their employees to "train" customers to have better attitudes![18]

Although many work attitudes are important, two attitudes in particular have been emphasized. Job satisfaction and organizational commitment are key attitudes of interest to managers and researchers.

Job Satisfaction Most of us believe that work should be a positive experience. *Job satisfaction* is a pleasurable or positive emotional state resulting from the appraisal of one's job or job experiences.[19] It has been treated both as a general attitude and as satisfaction with five specific dimensions of the job: pay, the work itself, promotion opportunities, supervision, and coworkers.[20] You can assess your own job satisfaction by completing You 4.1.

An individual may hold different attitudes toward various aspects of the job. For example, an employee may like her job responsibilities but be dissatisfied with the opportunities for promotion. Personal characteristics also affect job satisfaction.[21] Those with high negative affectivity are more likely to be dissatisfied with their jobs. Challenging work, valued rewards, opportunities for advancement, competent supervision, and supportive coworkers are dimensions of the job that can lead to satisfaction.

There are several measures of job satisfaction. One of the most widely used measures comes from the Job Descriptive Index (JDI). This index measures the specific facets of satisfaction by asking employees to respond yes, no, or cannot decide to a series of statements describing their jobs. Another popular measure is the Minnesota Satisfaction Questionnaire (MSQ).[22] This survey also asks employees to respond to statements about their jobs, using a five-point scale that ranges from very dissatisfied to very satisfied. Figure 4.1 presents some sample items from each questionnaire.

Managers and employees hold a common belief that happy or "satisfied" employees are more productive at work. Most of us feel more satisfied than usual when we believe that we are performing better than usual.[23] Interestingly, the relationship between job satisfaction and performance is quite a bit more complex than that. Are satisfied workers more productive? Or are more productive workers more satisfied? The link between satisfaction and performance has been widely explored. One view holds that satisfaction causes good performance. If this were true, the manager's job would simply be to keep workers happy. Although this may be the case for certain individuals, job satisfaction for most people is one of several causes of good performance. Read about one important consequence of low job satisfaction and employee morale at Yahoo in the Real World 4.1 feature.

Another view holds that good performance causes satisfaction. If this were true, managers would need to help employees perform well, and satisfaction would follow. However, some employees who are high performers are not satisfied with their jobs.

The research shows modest support for both views, but no simple, direct relationship between satisfaction and performance has been found.[24] One reason for these results may be the difficulty of demonstrating the attitude–behavior links we described earlier in this chapter. Future studies using specific, relevant attitudes and measuring personality variables and behavioral intentions may be able to demonstrate a link between job satisfaction and performance.

Another reason for the lack of a clear relationship between satisfaction and performance is the intervening role of rewards. Employees who receive valued rewards are more satisfied. In addition, employees who receive rewards that are contingent on performance (the higher the performance, the larger the reward) tend to perform better. Rewards thus influence both satisfaction and performance. The key to influencing both satisfaction and performance through rewards is that the rewards are valued by employees and are tied directly to performance.

Job satisfaction has been shown to be related to many other important personal and organizational outcomes. It is related to *organizational citizenship behavior*—behavior that is above and beyond the call of duty. Satisfied employees are more likely to make positive comments about the company, refrain from complaining when things at work do not go well, and help their coworkers.[25] Going beyond the call of duty is especially important to organizations using teams to get work done. Employees depend on extra help from each other to get things accomplished. When massive wildfires swept through California in 2003, most businesses in the San Diego

(4) Distinguish between organizational citizenship and workplace deviance behaviors.

organizational citizenship behavior
Behavior that is above and beyond the call of duty.

FIGURE 4.1 Sample Items from Satisfaction Questionnaires

Job Descriptive Index

Think of the work you do at present. How well does each of the following words or phrases describe your work? In the blank beside each word given below, write

_____Y_____ for "Yes" if it describes your work
_____N_____ for "No" if it does NOT describe it
_____?_____ if you cannot decide

WORK ON YOUR PRESENT JOB:

_____ Routine
_____ Satisfying
_____ Good

Think of the majority of the people that you work with now or the people you meet in connection with your work. How well does each of the following words or phrases describe these people? In the blank beside each word, write

_____Y_____ for "Yes" if it describes the people you work with
_____N_____ for "No" if it does NOT describe them
_____?_____ if you cannot decide

COWORKERS (PEOPLE):

_____ Boring
_____ Responsible
_____ Intelligent

Minnesota Satisfaction Questionnaire

1 = Very dissatisfied
2 = Dissatisfied
3 = I can't decide whether I am satisfied or not
4 = Satisfied
5 = Very satisfied

On my present job, this is how I feel about:

_____ The chance to work alone on the job (independence)
_____ My chances for advancement on this job (advancement)
_____ The chance to tell people what to do (authority)
_____ The praise I get for a good job (recognition)
_____ My pay and the amount of work I do (compensation)

SOURCES: The Job Descriptive Index is copyrighted by Bowling Green State University. The complete forms, scoring key, instructions, and norms can be obtained from Dr. Patricia C. Smith, Department of Psychology, Bowling Green State University, Bowling Green, OH 43403. Minnesota Satisfaction Questionnaire from D. J. Weiss, R. V. Davis, G. W. England, and L. H. Lofquist, *Manual for the Minnesota Satisfaction Questionnaire* (University of Minnesota Vocational Psychology Research, 1967).

area closed for one or more days as choking black smoke filled the air and thousands of homes were threatened. Aplus.net, an Internet service provider, chose to remain open; however, due to the danger involved, the company did not require its employees to report to work. Yet, in spite of thick smoke, most of the firm's employees came to work anyway, even though some were unsure if their homes would be waiting for them when they left work that evening.[26] Because of their willingness to go the extra mile, Aplus.net and its customers remained up and running throughout the fires. The firm reported in November that the massive fires had no negative impact on its financial results for the quarter.

Satisfied workers are more likely to want to give something back to the organization because they want to reciprocate their positive experiences.[27] Often, employees may feel that citizenship behaviors are not recognized because they occur outside the confines of normal job responsibilities. Organizational citizenship behaviors (OCBs) do, however, influence performance evaluations. Employees who exhibit behaviors such as helping others, making suggestions for innovations, and developing their skills receive higher performance ratings.[28] And different parts of

Yahoo: Down and Out?

Yahoo was recently plagued by rumors of takeovers by Microsoft or Google. It is consistently being outperformed by its rival Google and is reporting its worst revenues in years. Several industry analysts have started to speculate that if Yahoo doesn't cut costs or divest assets, there might indeed be a takeover.

These speculations fueled some negative behaviors within the organization, including turnover. Several top Yahoo executives and engineers who have been with the company for years have migrated to greener pastures at Google or Apple. Yahoo's troubles are manifested through three main symptoms: mass exodus of experienced executives from the company, taking with them years of knowledge and know-how; a bureaucratic organizational structure that slows down decision making; and employee complaints about the lack of passion from their CEO, Terry Semel.

Morale-related problems at Yahoo led to the downfall of former Yahoo CEO Terry Semel.

Such massive morale problems finally led to Semel's downfall at Yahoo. Now the company is headed by a woman president, Susan Decker, and a very young CEO, Jerry Yang, who is also its cofounder. Both executives are expected to bring a much-needed morale boost to Yahoo through their creative energy and expertise. For now, the rumors of a merger or takeover seem to have settled down. Only time will tell if Yahoo is able to pull itself out of its current morale problems.

SOURCES: R. D. Hof, "Even Yahoo! Gets the Blues." *Business Week* (2007): 37; M. Helft, "Can She Turn Yahoo into, Well, Google?" *The New York Times* (July 1, 2007), http://news.com.com/Can+she+turn+Yahoo+into%2C+well%2C+Google/2100-1024_3-6194437.html?tag=st.num.

an attitude relate to different targets of OCBs. Affect tends to direct OCBs toward other people, while job cognitions direct OCBs toward the organization.[29]

Individuals who identify strongly with the organization are more likely to perform OCBs.[30] High self-monitors, who base their behavior on cues from the situation, are also more likely to perform OCBs.[31] Good deeds, in the form of OCBs, can be contagious. One study found that when a person's close coworkers chose to perform OCBs, that person was more likely to reciprocate. When the norm among other team members was to engage in OCBs, the individual worker was more likely to offer them. The impact of one worker's OCBs can spread throughout an entire department.[32]

Although researchers have had a tough time demonstrating the link between job satisfaction and individual performance, this has not been the case for the link between job satisfaction and organizational performance. Companies with satisfied workers have better performance than companies with dissatisfied workers.[33] This may be due to the more intangible elements of performance, like organizational citizenship behavior, that contribute to organizational effectiveness but aren't necessarily captured by just measuring individual job performance.

Job satisfaction is related to some other important outcomes. People who are dissatisfied with their jobs are absent more frequently. The type of dissatisfaction that most often causes employee absenteeism is dissatisfaction with the work itself.

In addition, unhappy workers are more likely to quit their jobs, and turnover at work can be very costly to organizations. Such workers also report more psychological and medical problems than do satisfied employees.[34]

Researchers have consistently demonstrated a link between job satisfaction and turnover intentions; that is, unhappy employees tend to leave the organization. One thing that leads to dissatisfaction at work is a misfit between an individual's values and the organization's values, which is called a lack of person–organization fit. People who feel that their values don't mesh with the organization's experience job dissatisfaction and eventually leave the company when other job opportunities arise.[35]

Like all attitudes, job satisfaction is influenced by culture. American workers tend to hold to the "Protestant work ethic," which values work for its own sake and makes it a central part of their lives. Consistent with this basic view, American managers place a high value on outcomes such as autonomy, independence, and achievement. Koreans, in contrast to Americans, generally grow up in a more authoritarian system, which places greater value on family and less value on work for its own sake. Americans place greater value on and find greater job satisfaction through intrinsic job factors, whereas Koreans prefer extrinsic factors.[36]

This finding was echoed in a study comparing job satisfaction across 49 countries. Job characteristics and job satisfaction were more tightly linked in richer countries, more individualistic countries, and smaller power-distance countries. These findings suggest that cultural differences have strong influences on job satisfaction and the factors that produce it.[37]

Because organizations face the challenge of operating in the global environment, managers must understand that job satisfaction and other job attitudes are significantly affected by culture. Employees from different cultures may have differing expectations of their jobs; thus, there may be no single prescription for increasing the job satisfaction of a multicultural workforce. Researchers are currently studying job attitudes around the world. In China's hotel and restaurant industry, for example, researchers found that high-performance human resource practices led to service-oriented OCBs. Examples of such practices include promotions from within, flexibility in job assignments, long-term-results-oriented appraisals, and job security. Such OCBs were in turn linked to lower turnover and higher productivity at the organizational level.[38] So, it appears that high-performance human resource practices have very positive impacts in China.

Workplace deviance behavior (WDB)—counterproductive behavior that violates organizational norms and causes harm to others or the organization—is another outcome of attitudes at work.[39] Deviance is garnering attention due to negative events in the business world such as downsizing, technological insecurities, and other challenges being faced by many organizations. Layoffs, for example, may cause employees to develop negative attitudes and to feel anger and hostility toward the organization and to indulge in retaliatory behaviors. Even when an employee keeps his or her job but believes the procedure used to determine the layoff is unfair, workplace deviance such as bad-mouthing the employer or revenge against the manager may occur.[40, 41] Unfairness at work is a major cause of deviance, sabotage, and retaliation. Positive attitudes about the work environment lead to reduced deviance. Preventing and managing WDB is important because it harms department and organizational performance. You can assess your own workplace deviance behaviors with the questionnaire in You 4.2.

Organizational Commitment The strength of an individual's identification with an organization is known as *organizational commitment*. There are three kinds of organizational commitment: affective, continuance, and normative.

workplace deviance behavior
Any voluntary counterproductive behavior that violates organizational norms and causes some degree of harm to organizational functioning.

organizational commitment
The strength of an individual's identification with an organization.

Do You Engage in Workplace Deviance Behavior?

Think of the job you have now or a job you've had in the past. Indicate to what extent you engaged in the behaviors below. Use the following scale:

1 Very slightly or not at all
2 A little
3 Moderately
4 Quite a bit
5 Definitely

1. Worked on a personal matter instead of work for your employer.
2. Taken property from work without permission.
3. Spent too much time fantasizing or daydreaming instead of working.
4. Made fun of someone at work.
5. Falsified a receipt to get reimbursed for more money than you spent on business expenses.
6. Said something hurtful to someone at work.
7. Taken an additional or a longer break than is acceptable at your workplace.
8. Repeated a rumor or gossip about your company.
9. Made an ethnic, religious, or racial remark or joke at work.
10. Come in late to work without permission.
11. Littered your work environment.
12. Cursed at someone at work.
13. Called in sick when you were not.
14. Told someone about the lousy place where you work.
15. Lost your temper while at work.
16. Neglected to follow your boss's instructions.
17. Intentionally worked slower than you could have worked.
18. Discussed confidential company information with an unauthorized person.
19. Left work early without permission.
20. Played a mean prank on someone at work.
21. Left your work for someone else to finish.
22. Acted rudely toward someone at work.
23. Repeated a rumor or gossip about your boss or coworkers.
24. Made an obscene comment at work.
25. Used an illegal drug or consumed alcohol on the job.
26. Put little effort into your work.
27. Publicly embarrassed someone at work.
28. Dragged out work in order to get overtime.

SOURCE: R. J. Bennett and S. L. Robinson, S. L. "Development of a Measure of Workplace Deviance," *Journal of Applied Psychology* 85 (2000): 349–360.

Affective commitment is an employee's intention to remain in an organization because of a strong desire to do so. It consists of three factors:

> A belief in the goals and values of the organization.

> A willingness to put forth effort on behalf of the organization.

> A desire to remain a member of the organization.[42]

Affective commitment encompasses loyalty, but it is also a deep concern for the organization's welfare.

Continuance commitment is an employee's tendency to remain in an organization because he or she cannot afford to leave.[43] Sometimes employees believe that if they leave, they will lose a great deal of their investments in time, effort, and benefits and that they cannot replace these investments.

Normative commitment is a perceived obligation to remain with the organization. Individuals who experience normative commitment stay with the organization because they feel that they should.[44]

Certain organizational conditions encourage commitment. Participation in decision making and job security are two such conditions. Certain job characteristics also positively affect commitment. These include autonomy, responsibility, role clarity and interesting work.[45, 46]

affective commitment

A type of organizational commitment based on an individual's desire to remain in an organization.

continuance commitment

A type of organizational commitment based on the fact that an individual cannot afford to leave.

normative commitment

A type of organizational commitment based on an individual's perceived obligation to remain with an organization.

Affective and normative commitments are related to lower rates of absenteeism, higher quality of work, increased productivity, and several different types of performance.[47] Managers should encourage affective commitment because committed individuals expend more task-related effort and are less likely than others to leave the organization.[48]

Managers can increase affective commitment by communicating that they value employees' contributions, and that they care about employees' well-being.[49] Affective commitment also increases when the organization and employees share the same values, and when the organization emphasizes values like moral integrity, fairness, creativity, and openness.[50] Negative experiences at work can undoubtedly diminish affective commitment. One such experience is discrimination. Perceived age discrimination, whether for being too old or too young, can dampen affective commitment.[51]

Several researchers have examined organizational commitment in different countries. One study revealed that American workers displayed higher affective commitment than did Korean and Japanese workers.[52] Another study showed that Chinese workers place high value on social relationships at work and that those with stronger interpersonal relationships are more committed to their organizations.[53] The authors suggest that Chinese firms improve employee commitment and retention by organizing activities to help cultivate relationships among employees. This means that expatriate managers should be sensitive to the quality of relationships among their Chinese employees if they want to improve organizational commitment.

Job satisfaction and organizational commitment are two important work attitudes that managers can strive to improve among their employees. And these two attitudes are strongly related. Both affective and normative commitment are related to job satisfaction. Increasing job satisfaction is likely to increase commitment as well. To begin with, managers can use attitude surveys to reveal employees' satisfaction or dissatisfaction with specific facets of their jobs. Then they can take action to make the deficient aspects of the job more satisfying. Work attitudes are also important because they influence business outcomes. Job satisfaction and organizational citizenship behavior are linked to customer satisfaction and company profitability.[54]

Persuasion and Attitude Change

5 Identify the characteristics of the source, target, and message that affect persuasion

To understand how attitudes can change, it is necessary to understand the process of persuasion. The days of command-and-control management, in which executives simply told employees what do to, are long gone. Modern managers must be skilled in the art of persuasion.[55] Through persuasion, one individual (the source) tries to change the attitude of another person (the target). Certain characteristics of the source, target, and message affect the persuasion process. There are also two cognitive routes to persuasion.

Source Characteristics Three major characteristics of the source affect persuasion: expertise, trustworthiness, and attractiveness.[56] A source who is perceived as an expert is particularly persuasive. Trustworthiness is also important. John Mack, head of Credit Suisse First Boston (CSFB), understands the importance of trust. When he came to CSFB, the investment bank was a huge mess, but in a short time Mack achieved amazing results by persuading his employees to trust him. First, he told CSFB's bankers that their pay packages were excessive and the firm could not afford them. The bankers gave back more than $400 million in cash bonuses. Next, he asked CSFB's executives to give up some of the richest pay packages in the business. Mack was able to convince them to give up amounts that sometimes exceeded $20 million, all so that younger executives could receive bonuses and remain with the firm. And when lawyers discovered an e-mail suggesting a top CSFB employee had covered up wrongdoing from federal regulators, Mack immediately alerted federal regulators. His employees trust him because he doesn't just talk about teamwork, integrity, and trust; he demonstrates them in his own career. This trustworthiness allowed him to persuade his employees to help him save the firm.[57] Finally, attractiveness and likeability play a role in persuasion. Attractive communicators have long been used in advertising to persuade consumers to buy certain products. As a source of persuasion, managers who are perceived as being experts, who are trustworthy, or who are attractive or likable will have an edge in changing employee attitudes.

Target Characteristics Some people are more easily persuaded than others. Individuals with low self-esteem are more likely to change their attitudes in response to persuasion than are those with high self-esteem. People who hold very extreme attitudes are more resistant to persuasion, and those who are in a good mood are easier to persuade.[58] Undoubtedly, individuals differ widely in their susceptibility to persuasion. Managers must recognize these differences and realize that their attempts to change attitudes may not receive universal acceptance.

Message Characteristics Suppose you must implement an unpopular policy at work. You want to persuade your employees that the policy is a positive change. Should you present one side of the issue or both sides? Given that your employees are already negatively inclined toward the policy, you will have more success in changing their attitudes if you present both sides. This shows support for one side of the issue while acknowledging that another side does exist. Moreover, refuting the other side makes it more difficult for the targets to hang on to their negative attitudes.

Messages that are obviously designed to change the target's attitude may be met with considerable negative reaction. In fact, undisguised, deliberate attempts at changing attitudes may cause attitude change in the opposite direction! This is most likely to occur when the target of the persuasive communication feels her or his freedom is threatened.[59] Less threatening approaches are less likely to elicit negative reactions. The emotional tone of the message is also important. Persuasion is more successful when messages are framed with the same emotion as that felt by the receiver.[60]

Cognitive Routes to Persuasion When are message characteristics more important, and when are other characteristics more important in persuasion? The elaboration likelihood model of persuasion, presented in Figure 4.2, proposes that persuasion occurs over two routes: the central route and the peripheral route.[61] The routes are differentiated by the amount of elaboration, or scrutiny, the target is motivated to give the message.

The *central route* to persuasion involves direct cognitive processing of the message's content. When an issue is personally relevant, the individual is motivated to think carefully about it. The listener may nod his/her head when the argument is strong and shake his or her head if the argument is weak.[62] In the central route, the content of the message is very important. If the arguments presented are logical and convincing, attitude change will follow.

In the *peripheral route* to persuasion, the individual is not motivated to pay much attention to the message's content. This is because the message may not be perceived as personally relevant, or the target may be distracted. Instead, the individual is persuaded by characteristics of the persuader—for example, expertise, trustworthiness, and attractiveness. In addition, he or she may be persuaded by statistics, the number of arguments presented, or the method of presentation—all of which are nonsubstantial aspects of the message.

The elaboration likelihood model shows that the target's level of involvement with the issue is important. That involvement also determines which route to

FIGURE 4.2   The Elaboration Likelihood Model of Persuasion

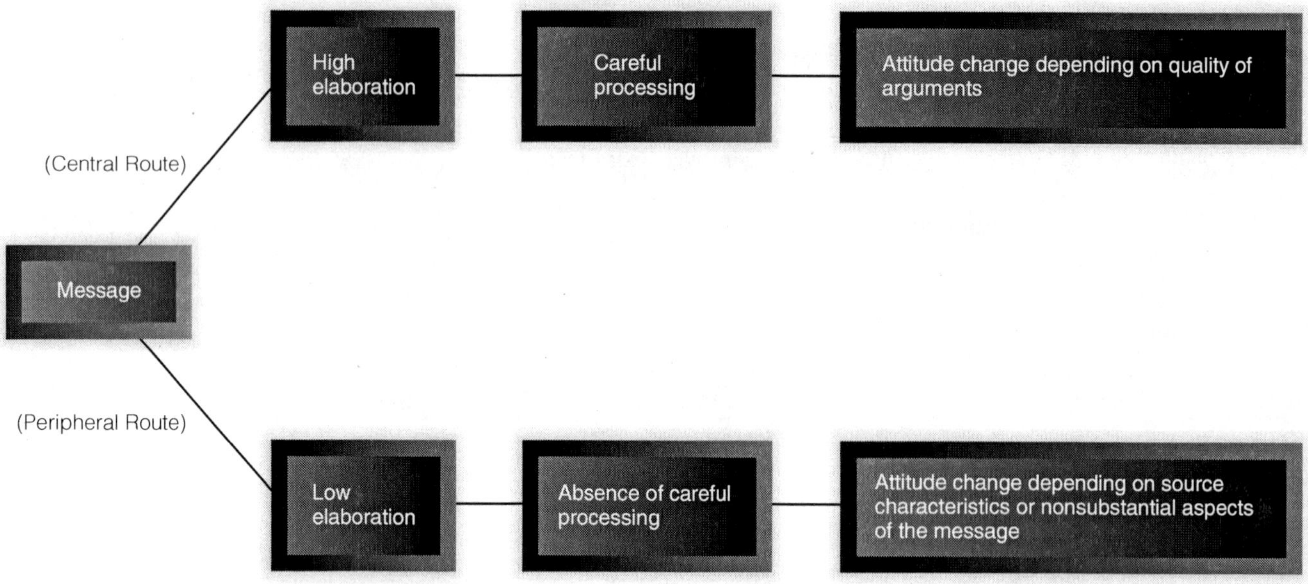

SOURCE: Adapted from R. E. Petty and J. T. Cacioppo, "The Elaboration Likelihood Model of Persuasion," in L. Berkowitz, ed., *Advances in Experimental Social Psychology*, vol. 19 (New York: Academic Press, 1986): 123–205.

persuasion will be more effective. In some cases, attitude change comes about through both the central and the peripheral routes. To cover all of the bases, managers should structure the content of their messages carefully, develop their own attributes that will help them be more persuasive, and choose a method of presentation that will be attractive to the audience.[63]

We have seen that the process of persuading individuals to change their attitudes is affected by the source, the target, the message, and the route. When all is said and done, however, managers are important catalysts for encouraging attitude change. This is a difficult process. Recently, researchers have proposed that people hold attitudes at two different levels.

EMOTIONS AT WORK

(6) Discuss the definition and importance of emotions at work

Traditional management theories did not place a premium on studying the effects of employee emotions at work. This was largely because emotions were thought to be "bad" for rational decision making. Ideas about management centered around the stereotypic ideal employee who kept her or his emotions in check and behaved in a totally rational rather than emotional manner. Because of recent research, we know that emotions and cognitions are intertwined and that both are normal parts of human functioning and decision making.

What are emotions? They are mental states that typically include feelings, physiological changes, and the inclination to act.[64]

Emotions (e.g., anger, joy, pride, hostility) are short-lived, intense reactions to an event that affect work behaviors. Individuals differ in their capacity to experience both positive emotions (e.g. happiness, pride) and negative emotions (e.g., anger, fear, guilt).[65] Employees have to cope with both positive and negative events at work almost daily, and these events lead to moods and emotions. When events at work are positive and goals are being met, employees experience positive emotions.[66] Events that threaten or thwart the achievement of goals cause negative emotions,

emotions

Mental states that typically include feelings, physiological changes, and the inclination to act.

The Inner Work Life and Impact of Emotions on Performance

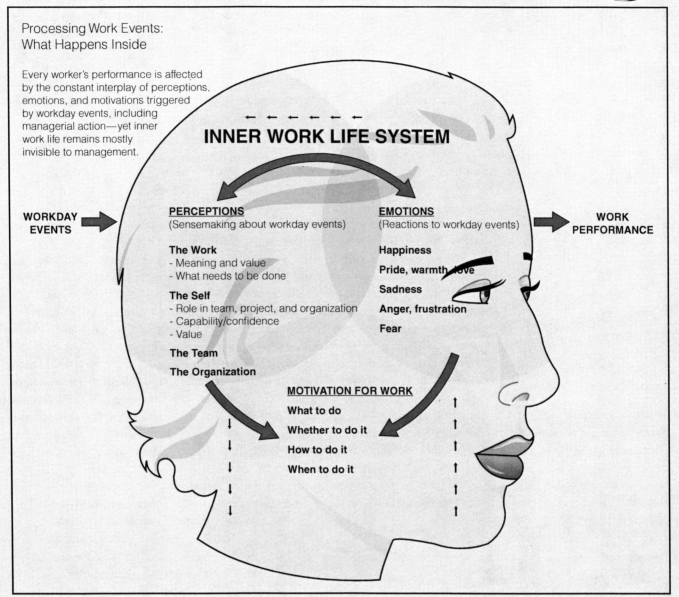

Processing Work Events:
What Happens Inside

Every worker's performance is affected by the constant interplay of perceptions, emotions, and motivations triggered by workday events, including managerial action—yet inner work life remains mostly invisible to management.

INNER WORK LIFE SYSTEM

WORKDAY EVENTS

PERCEPTIONS
(Sensemaking about workday events)

The Work
- Meaning and value
- What needs to be done

The Self
- Role in team, project, and organization
- Capability/confidence
- Value

The Team

The Organization

EMOTIONS
(Reactions to workday events)

Happiness

Pride, warmth, love

Sadness

Anger, frustration

Fear

WORK PERFORMANCE

MOTIVATION FOR WORK

What to do

Whether to do it

How to do it

When to do it

Do emotions matter to work life? This question led two researchers to explore the role of everyday emotion reactions in work behavior. In a comprehensive study involving 238 professionals from 28 project teams, these researchers uncovered the significant impact of emotions on team performance. They invited these knowledge professionals to keep diaries of their workday for the duration of a major project they were involved in. After 12,000 such diary entries later, these researchers were able to offer an insight into employees' inner work lives.

This study reveals that people perceive everyday work events (positive or negative) and immediately engage in a process of sense making. This sense making

is affected by both the rational part of the brain responsible for logical decisions and the emotional part responsible for feelings. People's sense-making processes in turn evoke emotions, which impact what they do at work and their motivation to perform. For example, one diary entry revealed that a team was working on a project that was very important to their organization with huge financial implications ($145 million was at stake). As the team was working late hours and through Memorial Day when the rest of the country was on holiday, one employee reported positive emotions (e.g., happiness) in response to a top management official bringing them pizza and bottled water after-hours. This event caused the team to view top management as

(Continued)

supportive and caring. This in turn made them more confident in their project and led to better team performance. Similarly, layoffs announced after an acquisition caused immense fear and anger, which in turn affected people's motivation to perform. This study further highlighted that most managers are not in sync with the inner work lives of their employees.

The practical implications of this research for managers are twofold: one, managers should enable rather than hinder subordinate progress. They can do so by making resources available viewing work progress or the lack of it as a learning mechanism in addition to just an evaluative process, and setting clear goals. Two, managers can really make a difference to the quality of employees' inner work lives by managing with a human touch. People's progress in this research was vastly facilitated by perceptions of a supervisor that was appreciative and fair in interpersonal interactions. Focusing on trifling events that highlight shortcomings can only hinder progress. Finally, these researchers offer the practical advice that such humane management can have a short-term as well as long-term effect on people's performance and the quality of their inner work lives. That is ultimately why an understanding of such perceptions and emotions matters in organizations.

SOURCE: T. M. Amabile and S. J. Kamer, "Inner Work Life: Understanding the Subtext of Business Performance," *Harvard Business Review* 85 (5): (2007): 72–83.

which then threaten job satisfaction and commitment. Positive emotions such as joy, attention, and interest lead employees to perform more OCBs.[67]

As we discussed earlier, negative emotions lead to workplace deviance. The use of power and influence in organizations, even if it is routine, can spark several forms of deviance. Such deviance could be targeted at both the organization and other individuals in the work environment.[68] Positive emotions produce better cognitive functioning, physical and psychological health, and coping mechanisms.[69] People who experience positive emotions tend to do so repeatedly, and they are more creative.[70] Overall, people who experience positive emotions are more successful across a variety of life domains and report higher life satisfaction. Negative emotions, on the other hand, lead to unhealthy coping behaviors and lowered cardiovascular function and physical health. The importance of managing emotions at work was highlighted in a recent comprehensive review of emotion research.[71] You can read all about how emotions affect the the daily work lives of employees and their performance in organizations in the Science feature.

What is emotional contagion? It is defined as a dynamic process through which the emotions of one person are transferred to another either consciously or unconsciously through nonverbal channels.

There is another reason why emotions need to be managed at work: emotions are very infectious. They spread through emotional contagion. This phenomenon occurs primarily through nonverbal cues, and is affected through a basic human tendency of mimicry. We tend to mimic each other's facial expressions, body language, speech patterns, and vocal tones. Emotional contagion is an important work process because most jobs today require some degree of interpersonal interaction. Examples of such interactions could be dealing with a customer who is angry, a coworker who is fearful of a layoff decision, a leader who praises an employee's work, and so on. Emotional contagion could occur in many of these instances and travel throughout the work group. Positive emotions that spread through a work group through this process

(7) Justify the importance of emotional contagion at work.

emotional contagion

A dynamic process through which the emotions of one person are transferred to another either consciously or unconsciously through nonverbal channels.

© DOUGLAS GRAHAM/CONGRESSIONAL QUARTERLY/GETTY IMAGES

An employee of Pike Place Fish, an open-air market in downtown Seattle, entertains customers by throwing a halibut to a co-worker for cleaning after selling the fish to a customer. Positive emotions that travel through a work group through emotional contagion produce cooperation and task performance.

produce cooperation and task performance.[72] The opposite can occur as well. Negative emotions can permeate a work group and destroy morale and performance.

When organizations and their employees go through change and/or huge losses, the pain caused by such trauma is not always eased by reason. Good leaders learn how to use compassion to heal and rebuild employee morale.[73] You will recall the tragedy of September 11th in New York City. Examples abound of organizational leaders who stood by their people with strength and empathy in times of tragedy. Yet other companies there refused, for example, to give their employees the next day off. These organizations failed to create a comfortable place for their employees to share their grief and trauma. Undoubtedly, these are not issues that could be resolved by a sound business strategy alone but by compassionate leaders who are not afraid to let their emotions show appropriately and are not disdainful of employee feelings.

The impact of emotion is far-reaching in workplace behavior. Much of our decision-making is driven by emotions. Emotions play a particularly important role in heated negotiations wherein some parties might benefit from the experience of certain emotions.[74]

ETHICAL BEHAVIOR

Ethics is the study of moral values and moral behavior. *Ethical behavior* is acting in ways consistent with one's personal values and the commonly held values of the organization and society.[75]

There is evidence that paying attention to ethical issues pays off for companies. In the early 1990s, James Burke, then the CEO of Johnson & Johnson, put together a list of companies that devoted a great deal of attention to ethics. The group included Johnson & Johnson, Coca-Cola, Gerber, Kodak, 3M, and Pitney Bowes. Over a forty-year period, the market value of these organizations grew at an annual rate of 11.3 percent, as compared to 6.2 percent for the Dow Jones industrials as a whole.[76] Doing the right thing can have a positive effect on an organization's performance.[77]

Ethical behavior in firms can also lead to practical benefits, particularly in attracting new talent. Firms with better reputations are able to attract more applicants, creating a larger pool from which to hire, and evidence suggests that respected firms are able to choose higher-quality applicants.[78] For example, Timberland is built on a strong system of values as noted in the Thinking Ahead feature on pages 117–118. This continually helps them attract and recruit the best talent as well as maintain a solid reputation with investors.

Failure to handle situations in an ethical manner can cost companies. Employees who are laid off or terminated are very concerned about the quality of treatment they receive. Honestly explaining the reasons for the dismissal and preserving the dignity of the employee will reduce the likelihood that she or he will initiate a claim against the company. One study showed that less than 1 percent of employees who felt the company was being honest filed a claim; more than 17 percent of those who felt the company was being less than honest filed claims.[79]

Unethical behavior by employees can affect individuals, work teams, and even the organization. Organizations thus depend on individuals to act ethically. For this reason, more and more firms are starting to monitor their employees' Internet usage. "Little Brother" and "SurfControl Web Filter" are just two of several software packages that allow system administrators to easily monitor employee Web usage, flagging visits to specific Web sites by using neural network technology to classify URL content and block Web traffic.

Although some employees have complained that this type of monitoring violates their privacy, the courts have generally disagreed, arguing that employees are using

ethical behavior
Acting in ways consistent with one's personal values and the commonly held values of the organization and society.

company hardware and software, hence the company is entitled to monitor what employees do with it. In one such case, Michael Smyth was fired from his job with Pillsbury Co. after company employees read inflammatory comments he made in several e-mails to his supervisor. Smyth sued for wrongful termination, claiming that his right to privacy was violated because the firm had told employees their e-mail would remain confidential. Despite these promises, the court ruled that Smyth had no reasonable expectation of privacy while using the firm's equipment; further, it said, Smyth's right to privacy was outweighed by the firm's need to conduct business in a professional manner. Only future court cases will clarify where a firm's effort to monitor potentially unethical behavior actually crosses its own ethical line.[80]

Today's high-intensity business environment makes it more important than ever to have a strong ethics program in place. In a survey of more than 4,000 employees conducted by the Washington, D.C.–based Ethics Resource Center, one-third of the employees said that they had witnessed ethical misconduct in the past year. If that many employees actually saw unethical acts, imagine how many unethical behaviors occurred behind closed doors! The most common unethical deeds witnessed were lying to supervisors (56 percent), lying on reports or falsifying records (41 percent), stealing or theft (35 percent), sexual harassment (35 percent), drug or alcohol abuse (31 percent), and conflicts of interest (31 percent).[81]

One of the toughest challenges managers face is aligning the ideal of ethical behavior with the reality of everyday business practices. Violations of the public's trust are costly. Since Jack in the Box restaurants' *E. coli* crisis, the company has faced image and financial problems. And Firestone Inc., after spending more than a third of a billion dollars replacing allegedly defective tires on Ford sport utility vehicles in 2000, still faces an uncertain future including billions of dollars in lawsuits. Studies show that firms experience lower accounting returns and slow sales growth for as long as five years after being convicted of a corporate illegality.[82]

The ethical issues that individuals face at work are complex. A review of articles appearing in *The Wall Street Journal* during just one week revealed more than sixty articles dealing with ethical issues in business.[83] As Table 4.2 shows, the themes

TABLE 4.2 Ethical Issues from One Week in *The Wall Street Journal*

1. **Stealing:** Taking things that don't belong to you.
2. **Lying:** Saying things you know aren't true.
3. **Fraud and deceit:** Creating or perpetuating false impressions.
4. **Conflict of interest and influence buying:** Bribes, payoffs, and kickbacks.
5. **Hiding versus divulging information:** Concealing information that another party has a right to know or failing to protect personal or proprietary information.
6. **Cheating:** Taking unfair advantage of a situation.
7. **Personal decadence:** Aiming below excellence in terms of work performance (e.g., careless or sloppy work).
8. **Interpersonal abuse:** Behaviors that are abusive of others (e.g., sexism, racism, emotional abuse).
9. **Organizational abuse:** Organizational practices that abuse members (e.g., inequitable compensation, misuses of power).
10. **Rule violations:** Breaking organizational rules.
11. **Accessory to unethical acts:** Knowing about unethical behavior and failing to report it.
12. **Ethical dilemmas:** Choosing between two equally desirable or undesirable options.

SOURCE: Kluwer Academic Publishers, by J. O. Cherrington and D. J. Cherrington, "A Menu of Moral Issues: One Week in the Life of *The Wall Street Journal*," *Journal of Business Ethics* 11 (1992): 255–265. Reprinted with kind permission of Springer Science and Business Media.

PepsiCo in India: The Impact of Cultural Differences in Perceptions of Ethical Behavior

PepsiCo recently named India as one of its topmost strategic priorities. Headed by a woman CEO with a Yale degree, this organization seems to be battling a strange and socially driven demon in India. Water is a scarce commodity in much of India, and PepsiCo CEO Indra K. Nooyi has firsthand experience in living with such scarcity. However, she might not have anticipated that this issue would resurface as one of the most important business challenges soon after she took over as the company's CEO last year.

Driven by activist and social worker Sunita Narain, also a woman, the issue of water contamination in bottled beverages caused PepsiCo's sales to fall dramatically over the last year. Locals accused the multinational giant of exhausting their already scarce water resources and also that pesticides made their way into such bottled beverages. This accusation by a well-known and highly respected social activist and environmentalist caused public protests against PepsiCo's beverages and led to a ban of bottled soft drinks in several states.

Much of this protest seems to be entangled in the bigger issue of local Indian consumers' perception that such corporate giants pollute and use natural

© REUTERS/B MATHUR/LANDOV

There was a protest in India against PepsiCo and Coca-Cola after reports that products sold in India were contaminated with pesticides.

resources indiscriminately. To make matters worse, Narain called for a test of water samples used in both Pepsi and Coke's bottled beverages in India. They found contamination levels that would not be acceptable in the United States. Narain accused the two corporate giants of selling subpar products that would never be sold in the United States. PepsiCo subsequently lost corporate sponsors in India.

Recently, the company launched several efforts to address these perceptions of lack of concern for local communities by digging wells in villages. CEO Narain traveled through India trying to promote the image of PepsiCo as a company with a soul. She talks about investing in local communities and educating people about sustainable water harvesting techniques. Such practices seem to have diminished the intensity of this scandal in India, at least for now, as PepsiCo's sales continue to slowly climb.

SOURCE: D. Brady, "Pepsi: Repairing a Poisoned Reputation In India," *Business Week online* (June 11, 2007). http://www .businessweek.com/magazine/content/07_24/b4038064 .htm?chan=search.

appearing throughout the articles were distilled into twelve major ethical issues. You can see that few of these issues are clear-cut. All of them depend on the specifics of the situation, and their interpretation depends on the characteristics of the individuals examining them. For example, look at issue 2: lying. We all know that "white lies" are told in business. Is this acceptable? The answer varies from person to person. Thus, the perception of what constitutes ethical versus unethical behavior in organizations varies among individuals. Check out Timberland's guidelines for ethical behavior at http://www.timberland.com/investorRelations/index.jsp. Moreover, corporate social responsibility might not be just a buzzword anymore. Check out the Real World 4.2 feature to learn about PepsiCo's troubles over water contamination in India.

Ethical behavior is influenced by two major categories of factors: individual characteristics and organizational factors.[84] This section looks at the individual influences. We examine organizational influences throughout the remainder of the

FIGURE 4.3 Individual/Organizational Model of Ethical Behavior

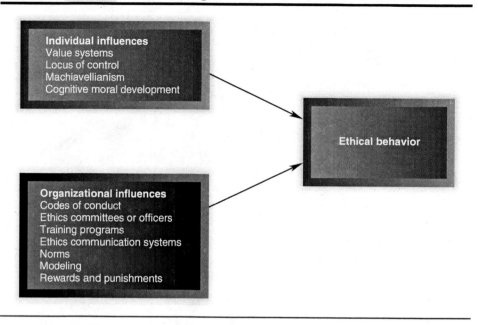

book—particularly in Chapter 15, where we focus on creating an organizational culture that reinforces ethical behavior.

The model that guides our discussion of individual influences on ethical behavior is presented in Figure 4.3. It shows both individual and organizational influences.

Making ethical decisions is part of each manager's job. It has been suggested that ethical decision making requires three qualities of individuals:[85]

1. The competence to identify ethical issues and evaluate the consequences of alternative courses of action.

2. The self-confidence to seek out different opinions about the issue and decide what is right in terms of a particular situation.

3. Toughmindedness—the willingness to make decisions when all that needs to be known cannot be known and when the ethical issue has no established, unambiguous solution.

What are the individual characteristics that lead to these qualities? Our model presents four major individual differences that affect ethical behavior: value systems, locus of control, Machiavellianism, and cognitive moral development.

VALUES

One important source of individual differences in ethical behavior is values. We use them to evaluate our own behavior and that of others. As such, they vary widely among individuals. *Values* are enduring beliefs that a specific mode of conduct or end state of existence is personally or socially preferable to an opposite or converse mode of conduct or end state of existence.[86] This definition was proposed by Rokeach, an early scholar of human values. As individuals grow and mature, they learn values, which may change over the life span as an individual develops a sense of self. Cultures, societies, and organizations shape values. Parents and others who are respected by the individual play crucial roles in value development by providing guidance about what is right and wrong. Because values are general beliefs about right and wrong, they form the basis for ethical behavior. For example, Whole Foods is committed to environmentally friendly causes

(8) Contrast the effects of individual and organizational influences on ethical behavior.

(9) Discuss how value systems, locus of control, Machiavellianism, and cognitive moral development affect ethical behavior.

values
Enduring beliefs that a specific mode of conduct or end state of existence is personally or socially preferable to an opposite or converse mode of conduct or end state of existence.

and has created a foundation for the compassionate treatment of animals. The CEO of Whole Foods, John Mackey, was recently named one of the top 30 corporate leaders in American businesses. Mackey has set an extraordinary example by ignoring conventional wisdom and refusing to compete with Wal-Mart. Instead he has led Whole Foods through five consecutive years of 21 percent sales gains by strongly adhering to what he believes in and being environmentally and socially responsible. Visit the wholefoods.com Web site to learn more about how being values driven can lead to success.

Instrumental and Terminal Values

Rokeach distinguished between two types of values: instrumental and terminal. *Instrumental values* reflect the means to achieving goals; that is, they represent the acceptable behaviors to be used in achieving some end state. Instrumental values identified by Rokeach include ambition, honesty, self-sufficiency, and courage. *Terminal values*, in contrast, represent the goals to be achieved or the end states of existence. Rokeach identified happiness, love, pleasure, self-respect, and freedom among the terminal values. A complete list of instrumental and terminal values is presented in Table 4.3. Terminal and instrumental values work in concert to provide individuals with goals to strive for and acceptable ways to achieve the goals.

This discussion of values is highlighted in our opening case of Timberland. The terminal values of Timberland include creating communities that are sustainable and manufacturing products that do not leave a footprint on the planet. Its instrumental values are concern for the environment and the communities that make its business happen. These instrumental values are shown in acts such as recruiting volunteers to engage in service in the communities in which they operate and displaying nutritional labels on their shoes.

Americans' rankings of instrumental and terminal values have shown remarkable stability over time.[87] The highest-ranked instrumental values were honesty, ambition, responsibility, forgiving nature, open-mindedness, and courage. The highest ranked terminal values were world peace, family security, freedom, happiness, self-respect, and wisdom.

TABLE 4.3 Instrumental and Terminal Values

Instrumental Values		
Honesty	Ambition	Responsibility
Forgiving nature	Open-mindedness	Courage
Helpfulness	Cleanliness	Competence
Self-control	Affection/love	Cheerfulness
Independence	Politeness	Intelligence
Obedience	Rationality	Imagination
Terminal Values		
World peace	Family security	Freedom
Happiness	Self-respect	Wisdom
Equality	Salvation	Prosperity
Achievement	Friendship	National security
Inner peace	Mature love	Social respect
Beauty in art and nature	Pleasure	Exciting, active life

SOURCE: Table adapted with the permission of The Free Press, a Division of Simon & Schuster, Inc., from *The Nature of Human Values* by Milton Rokeach. Copyright © 1973 by The Free Press.

instrumental values
Values that represent the acceptable behaviors to be used in achieving some end state.

terminal values
Values that represent the goals to be achieved or the end states of existence.

Age also affects values. Baby boomers' values contrast with those of the baby busters, who are beginning to enter the workforce. The baby busters value family life and time off from work and prefer a balance between work and home life. This contrasts with the more driven, work-oriented value system of the boomers. The baby boomers placed a huge emphasis on achievement values. Their successors in Generation X and Generation Y, however, are markedly different in what they value at work. For example, Generation X values self-reliance, individualism, and balance between family and work life. Generation Y, on the other hand, values freedom in scheduling so much that most are employed only part-time. Furthermore, they have a work-to-live mindset rather than the live-to-work philosophy of the baby boomers.[88]

Work Values

Work values are important because they affect how individuals behave on their jobs in terms of what is right and wrong.[89] Four work values relevant to individuals are achievement, concern for others, honesty, and fairness.[90] Achievement is a concern for the advancement of one's career. This is shown in such behaviors as working hard and seeking opportunities to develop new skills. Concern for others is shown in caring, compassionate behaviors such as encouraging other employees or helping others work on difficult tasks. These behaviors constitute organizational citizenship, as we discussed earlier. Honesty is providing accurate information and refusing to mislead others for personal gain. Fairness emphasizes impartiality and recognizes different points of view. Individuals can rank-order these values in terms of their importance in their work lives.[91] Although individuals' value systems differ, sharing similar values at work produces positive results. Employees who share their supervisor's values are more satisfied with their jobs and more committed to the organization.[92] Values also have profound effects on the choice of jobs. Traditionally, pay and advancement potential have been the strongest influences on job choice decisions. One study, however, found that three other work values—achievement, concern for others, and fairness—exerted more influence on job choice decisions than did pay and promotion opportunities.[93]

This means that organizations recruiting job candidates should pay careful attention to individuals' values and to the messages that organizations send about company values. A new "name and shame" report published in Australia by RepuTex is designed to embarrass companies that behave unethically. Nineteen groups graded each of Australia's top companies on corporate governance policies, environmental friendliness, and workplace practices. The 500-page report named Westpac, a major bank, as the most ethical firm in Australia. Westpac was the only company in the country's top 100 to receive the AAA rating.[94]

Cultural Differences in Values

As organizations face the challenges of an increasingly diverse workforce and a global marketplace, it becomes more important than ever for them to understand the influence of culture on values. Doing business in a global marketplace often means that managers encounter a clash of values among different cultures. Take the value of loyalty, for example. In Japan, loyalty means "compassionate overtime." Even though you have no work to do, you should stay late to give moral support to your peers who are working late.[95] In contrast, Koreans value loyalty to the person for whom one works.[96] In the United States, family and other personal loyalties are more highly valued than is loyalty to the company or one's supervisor.

Cultures differ in what they value in terms of an individual's contributions to work. Collectivist cultures such as China and Mexico value a person's contributions to relationships in the work team. In contrast, individualist cultures like the United States and the Netherlands value a person's contributions to task accomplishment. Both collectivist and individualist cultures value rewards based on individual performance.[97] Iran also represents a collectivist culture. Iranian managers' values, which include little tolerance for ambiguity, high need for structure, and willingness to sacrifice for the good of society, are greatly influenced by Islam. Belonging, harmony, humility, and simplicity are all values promoted by Islam.[98]

Values also affect individuals' views of what constitutes authority. French managers value authority as a right of office and rank. Their behavior reflects this value, as they tend to use power based on their position in the organization. In contrast, managers from the Netherlands and Scandinavia value group inputs to decisions and expect their decisions to be challenged and discussed by employees.[99]

Value differences between cultures must be acknowledged in today's global economy. We may be prone to judging the value systems of others, but we should resist the temptation to do so. Tolerating diversity in values can help us understand other cultures. Value systems of other nations are not necessarily right or wrong—merely different. The following suggestions can help managers understand and work with the diverse values that characterize the global environment:[100]

1. Learn more about and recognize the values of other peoples. They view their values and customs as moral, traditional, and practical.

2. Avoid prejudging the business customs of others as immoral or corrupt. Assume they are legitimate unless proved otherwise.

3. Find legitimate ways to operate within others' ethical points of view—do not demand that they operate within your value system.

4. Avoid rationalizing "borderline" actions with excuses such as the following:

   > "This isn't really illegal or immoral."
   > "This is in the organization's best interest."
   > "No one will find out about this."
   > "The organization will back me up on this."

5. Refuse to do business when stakeholder actions violate or compromise laws or fundamental organizational values.

6. Conduct relationships as openly and aboveboard as possible.

Locus of Control

Another individual influence on ethical behavior is locus of control. In Chapter 3, we introduced locus of control as a personality variable that affects individual behavior. Recall that people with an internal locus of control believe that they control events in their lives and that they are responsible for what happens to them. In contrast, people with an external locus of control believe that outside forces such as fate, chance, or other people control what happens to them.[101]

Internals are more likely than externals to take personal responsibility for the consequences of their ethical or unethical behavior. Externals are more apt to believe that external forces caused their ethical or unethical behavior. Research has shown that internals make more ethical decisions than do externals.[102] Internals also are more resistant to social pressure and are less willing to hurt another person, even if ordered to do so by an authority figure.[103]

Machiavellianism

Another individual difference that affects ethical behavior is Machiavellianism. Niccolò Machiavelli was a sixteenth-century Italian statesman. He wrote *The Prince*, a guide for acquiring and using power.[104] The primary method for achieving power that he suggested was manipulation of others. *Machiavellianism*, then, is a personality characteristic indicating one's willingness to do whatever it takes to get one's own way.

A high-Mach individual behaves in accordance with Machiavelli's ideas, which include the notion that it is better to be feared than loved. High-Machs tend to use deceit in relationships, have a cynical view of human nature, and have little concern for conventional notions of right and wrong.[105] They are skilled manipulators of other people, relying on their persuasive abilities. Low-Machs, in contrast, value loyalty and relationships. They are less willing to manipulate others for personal gain and are concerned with others' opinions.

High-Machs believe that the desired ends justify any means. They believe that manipulation of others is fine if it helps achieve a goal. Thus, high-Machs are likely to justify their manipulative behavior as ethical.[106] They are emotionally detached from other people and are oriented toward objective aspects of situations. And high-Machs are likelier than low-Machs to engage in behavior that is ethically questionable.[107] Employees can counter Machiavellian individuals by focusing on teamwork instead of on one-on-one relationships where high-Machs have the upper hand. It is also beneficial to make interpersonal agreements public and thus less susceptible to manipulation by high-Machs.

Cognitive Moral Development

An individual's level of *cognitive moral development* also affects ethical behavior. Psychologist Lawrence Kohlberg proposed that as individuals mature, they move through a series of six stages of moral development.[108] With each successive stage, they become less dependent on other people's opinions of right and wrong and less self-centered (acting in one's own interest). At higher levels of moral development, individuals are concerned with broad principles of justice and with their self-chosen ethical principles. Kohlberg's model focuses on the decision-making process and on how individuals justify ethical decisions. His model is a cognitive developmental theory about how people think about what is right and wrong and how the decision-making process changes through interaction with peers and the environment.

Cognitive moral development occurs at three levels, and each level consists of two stages. In Level I, called the premoral level, the person's ethical decisions are based on rewards, punishments, and self-interest. In Stage 1, the individual obeys rules to avoid punishment. In Stage 2, the individual follows the rules only if it is in his or her immediate interest to do so.

In Level II, the conventional level, the focus is on the expectations of others (parents, peers) or society. In Stage 3, individuals try to live up to the expectations of people close to them. In Stage 4, they broaden their perspective to include the laws of the larger society. They fulfill duties and obligations and want to contribute to society.

In Level III, the principled level, what is "right" is determined by universal values. The individual sees beyond laws, rules, and the expectations of other people. In Stage 5, individuals are aware that people have diverse value systems. They uphold their own values despite what others think. For a person to be classified as being in Stage 5, decisions must be based on principles of justice and rights. For example, a person who decides to picket an abortion clinic just because his religion says abortion is wrong is not a Stage 5 individual. A person who arrives at the same decision through a complex decision process based on justice and rights may be a Stage 5 individual. The key is the process rather than the decision itself. In Stage 6, the individual follows self-selected ethical principles. If there is a conflict between a law and a self-selected ethical principle, the individual acts according to the principle.

As people mature, their moral development passes through these stages in an irreversible sequence. Research suggests that most adults are in Stage 3 or 4. Most adults thus never reach the principled level of development (Stages 5 and 6).

Machiavellianism
A personality characteristic indicating one's willingness to do whatever it takes to get one's own way.

cognitive moral development
The process of moving through stages of maturity in terms of making ethical decisions.

Since it was proposed more than thirty years ago, Kohlberg's model of cognitive moral development has received a great deal of research support. Individuals at higher stages of development are less likely to cheat,[109] more likely to engage in whistle-blowing,[110] and more likely to make ethical business decisions.[111, 112]

Kohlberg's model has also been criticized. Gilligan, for example, has argued that the model does not take gender differences into account. Kohlberg's model was developed from a 20-year study of 84 boys.[113] Gilligan contends that women's moral development follows a different pattern—one that is based not on individual rights and rules but on responsibility and relationships. Women and men face the same moral dilemmas but approach them from different perspectives—men from the perspective of equal respect and women from the perspective of compassion and care. Researchers who reviewed the research on these gender differences concluded that the differences may not be as strong as originally stated by Gilligan. Some men use care reasoning, and some women may use justice reasoning when making moral judgments.[114]

There is evidence to support the idea that men and women view ethics differently. A large-scale review of 66 studies found that women were more likely than men to perceive certain business practices as unethical. Young women were more likely to see breaking the rules and acting on insider information as unethical. Both sexes agreed that collusion, conflicts of interest, and stealing are unethical. It takes about 21 years for the gender gap to disappear. Men seem to become more ethical with more work experience; the longer they are in the workforce, the more their attitudes become similar to those held by women. There is an age/experience effect for both sexes: experienced workers are more likely to think lying, bribing, stealing, and colluding are unethical.[115]

Individual differences in values, locus of control, Machiavellianism, and cognitive moral development are important influences on ethical behavior in organizations. Given that these influences vary widely from person to person, how can organizations use this knowledge to increase ethical behavior? One action would be to hire those who share the organization's values. Another would be to hire only internals, low-Machs, and individuals at higher stages of cognitive moral development. This strategy obviously presents practical and legal problems.

There is evidence that cognitive moral development can be increased through training.[116] Organizations could help individuals move to higher stages of moral development by providing educational seminars. However, values, locus of control, Machiavellianism, and cognitive moral development are fairly stable in adults.

The best way to use the knowledge of individual differences may be to recognize that they help explain why ethical behavior differs among individuals and to focus managerial efforts on creating a work situation that supports ethical behavior.

Most adults are susceptible to external influences; they do not act as independent ethical agents. Instead, they look to others and to the organization for guidance. Managers can offer such guidance by encouraging ethical behavior through codes of conduct, ethics committees, ethics communication systems, training, norms, modeling, and rewards and punishments, as shown in Figure 4.3. We discuss these areas further in Chapter 16.

MANAGERIAL IMPLICATIONS: ATTITUDES, VALUES, AND ETHICS AT WORK

Managers must understand attitudes because of their effects on work behavior. By understanding how attitudes are formed and how they can be changed, managers can shape employee attitudes. Attitudes are learned through observation of other employees and by the way they are reinforced. Job satisfaction and organizational commitment are important attitudes to encourage among employees, and participative management is an excellent tool for doing so.

Emotions are also important because of their influence on employee behaviors. Managers should be trained to perceive emotions in employees and manage them effectively. They should watch for burnout and emotional exhaustion, specifically in service occupations. Such emotion management can help foster organizational citizenship behaviors and prevent workplace deviance in the organization.

Ethical behavior at work is affected by individual and organizational influences. A knowledge of individual differences in value systems, locus of control, Machiavellianism, and cognitive moral development helps managers understand why individuals have diverse views about what constitutes ethical behavior.

This chapter concludes our discussion of individual differences that affect behavior in organizations. Attitudes, emotions, and ethics combine with personality, perception, and attribution to make people unique. Individual uniqueness is a major managerial challenge, and it is one reason there is no single best way to manage people.

LOOKING BACK: THE TIMBERLAND COMPANY

Walking the Talk and "Making It Better"

Jeffrey Schwartz, the CEO and president of the Timberland Company, seems to be adept at walking the talk. Since he took over in 1998, he has created a new corporate image for Timberland with renewed emphasis on ethical and environmental issues. Timberland employees recruited 9,000 volunteers to engage in about 54,000 hours of community service as a part of their Earth Day celebrations. Schwartz asserts that this is in line with the company's vision of becoming carbon neutral by the year 2010. Timberland also has a commitment to diversity and has a strong contingent of women and minorities on its board of directors. It also has several worker-friendly programs such as on-site childcare at its headquarters. Timberland's catchphrase "Make It Better" reflects such commitment to ethical standards in conduct of their business. They are also an industry leader in recruiting volunteers from the communities they operate in. Check out the following Web site to stay informed of the thousands of volunteer opportunities facilitated via Timberland.[117,118]

http://www.timberland.com/timberlandserve/timberlandserve_index.jsp

Chapter Summary

1. The ABC model of an attitude contends that an attitude has three components: affect, behavioral intentions, and cognition. Cognitive dissonance is the tension produced by a conflict between attitudes and behavior.

2. Attitudes are formed through direct experience and social learning. Direct experience creates strong attitudes because the attitudes are easily accessed and active in cognitive processes.

3. Attitude–behavior correspondence depends on attitude specificity, attitude relevance, timing of measurement, personality factors, and social constraints.

4. Two important work attitudes are job satisfaction and organizational commitment. There are cultural differences in these attitudes, and both attitudes can be improved by providing employees with opportunities for participation in decision making.

5. A manager's ability to persuade employees to change their attitudes depends on characteristics of the manager (expertise, trustworthiness, and attractiveness); the employees (self-esteem, original attitude, and mood); the message (one-sided versus two-sided); and the route (central versus peripheral).

6. Emotions can strongly affect an individual's behavior at work.

7. Instrumental values reflect the means to achieving goals; terminal values represent the goals to be achieved.

8. Ethical behavior is influenced by the individual's value system, locus of control, Machiavellianism, and cognitive moral development.

Key Terms

affect (p. 118)
affective commitment (p. 127)
attitude (p. 118)
cognitive dissonance (p. 119)
cognitive moral development (p. 140)
continuance commitment (p. 127)

emotions (p. 130)
emotional contagion (p. 132)
ethical behavior (p. 133)
instrumental values (p. 137)
job satisfaction (p. 122)
Machiavellianism (p. 140)
normative commitment (p. 127)

organizational citizenship behavior (p. 123)
organizational commitment (p. 126)
social learning (p. 120)
terminal values (p. 137)
values (p. 136)
workplace deviance behavior (p. 126)

Review Questions

1. How are attitudes formed? Which source is stronger?

2. Discuss cultural differences in job satisfaction and organizational commitment.

3. What are the major influences on attitude–behavior correspondence? Why do some individuals seem to exhibit behavior that is inconsistent with their attitudes?

4. What should managers know about the emotions at work?

5. Define *values*. Distinguish between instrumental values and terminal values. Are these values generally stable, or do they change over time?

6. What is the relationship between values and ethics?

7. How does locus of control affect ethical behavior?

8. What is Machiavellianism, and how does it relate to ethical behavior?

9. Describe the stages of cognitive moral development. How does this concept affect ethical behavior in organizations?

Discussion and Communication Questions

1. What jobs do you consider to be most satisfying? Why?

2. How can managers increase their employees' job satisfaction?

3. Suppose you have an employee whose lack of commitment is affecting others in the work group. How would you go about persuading the person to change this attitude?

4. In Rokeach's studies on values, the most recent data are from 1981. Do you think values have changed since then? If so, how?

5. What are the most important influences on an individual's perceptions of ethical behavior? Can organizations change these perceptions? If so, how?

6. How can managers encourage organizational citizenship?

7. *(communication question)* Suppose you are a manager in a customer service organization. Your group includes seven supervisors who report directly to you. Each supervisor manages a team of seven customer service representatives. One of your supervisors, Linda, has complained that Joe, one of her employees, has "an attitude problem." She has requested that Joe be transferred to another team. Write a memo to Linda explaining your position on this problem and what should be done.

8. *(communication question)* Select a company that you admire for its values. Use the resources of your university library to answer two questions. First, what are the company's values? Second, how do employees enact these values? Prepare an oral presentation to present in class.

9. *(communication question)* Think of a time when you have experienced cognitive dissonance. Analyze your experience in terms of the attitude and behavior involved. What did you do to resolve the cognitive dissonance? What other actions could you have taken? Write a brief description of your experience and your responses to the questions.

Ethical Dilemma

Sara, a manager in a large software development company, sits at her desk looking out the window. The challenge before her is to pick a project manager for a major new project just given to her department. She has narrowed her choice to two employees. Sara's first option is Paula, who is probably the most qualified candidate for this project. No one knows this area of software development better than Paula. She also has extensive knowledge of the client. Paula has one other attribute, which can be a positive or a negative factor: attitude. She is the best at her job and she knows it. She also lets everyone else know it. Because of this, she always gets the top projects. The problem is that Paula cares only about Paula and little else. She is not a team player and does little to contribute to the department as a whole. She can be arrogant and extremely self-centered.

Sara's other option is Mark. Mark is also talented with all the markings of becoming a great project manager if given the chance. In addition to his technical skills, Mark is an excellent coworker. He is a team player who cares as much about the success of the department as he does about his own personal success. He is well liked by everyone, especially Sara. As a manager, she always appreciates Mark's willingness to consider the department's needs and not just the work that would lead to personal success.

Sara's predicament needs to be resolved by the end of the day. She knows everyone expects her to again choose Paula to head this project. However, Sara really believes it is time to give Mark a chance. She realizes the fallout for not choosing Paula would be great, but she is really tired of doing what everyone, including Paula, expects her to do within her own department.

Questions

1. What is Sara's obligation to the client?
2. Does this obligation affect her decision?
3. Using consequential, rule-based, and character theories, evaluate Sara's decision options.

Experiential Exercises

4.1 Chinese, Indian, and American Values

Purpose

To learn some differences among Chinese, Indian, and American value systems.

Group size

Any number of groups of five to eight people.

Time required

50+ minutes

Exercise Schedule

1. **Complete rankings (preclass)**

   Students rank the fifteen values for either Chinese and American orientations or for Indian and American systems. If time permits, all three can be done.

	Unit time	Total time
2. **Small groups (optional)** | 15 min. | 15 min.

   Groups of five to eight members try to achieve consensus on the ranking values for both Chinese and American cultures.

3. **Group presentations (optional)** | 15 min. | 30 min.

   Each group presents its rankings and discusses reasons for making those decisions.

4. **Discussion** | 20+ min. | 50 min.

   Instructor leads a discussion on the differences between Chinese and American value systems and presents the correct rankings.

Value Rankings

Rank each of the fifteen values below according to what you think they are in the Chinese, Indian (from India), and American cultures. Use "1" as the most important value for the culture and "15" as the least important value for that culture.

Value	American	Chinese	Indian
Achievement			
Deference			
Order			
Exhibition			
Autonomy			
Affiliation			
Intraception			
Succorance			

Dominance	
Abasement	
Nurturance	
Change	
Endurance	
Heterosexuality	
Aggression	

Some Definitions

Intraception: The tendency to be governed by subjective factors, such as feelings, fantasies, speculations, and aspirations; the other side of extraception, where one is governed by concrete, clearly observable physical conditions.

Succorance: Willingness to help another or to offer relief.

Abasement: To lower oneself in rank, prestige, or esteem.

Internal/External Locus of Control

Consider American and Chinese groups. Which would tend to have more internal locus of control (tend to feel in control of one's destiny, that rewards come as a result of hard work, perseverance, and responsibility)? Which would be more external (fate, luck or other outside forces control destiny)?

Machiavellianism

This concept was defined by Christie and Geis as the belief that one can manipulate and deceive people for personal gain. Do you think Americans or Chinese would score higher on the Machiavellian scale?

Discussion Questions

1. What are some main differences among the cultures? Did any pattern emerge?

2. Were you surprised by the results?

3. What behaviors could you expect in business dealings with Chinese (or Indians) based on their value system?

4. How do American values dictate Americans' behaviors in business situations?

SOURCE: "Chinese, Indian, and American Values" by Dorothy Marcic, copyright 1993. Adapted from Michael Harris Bond, ed., *The Psychology of the Chinese People*, Hong Kong: Oxford University Press, 200 Madison Ave., NY 10016, 1986. The selection used here is a portion of "Chinese Personality and Its Change," by Kuo-Shu Yang, pp. 106–170. Reprinted by permission.

4.2 Is This Behavior Ethical?

The purpose of this exercise is to explore your opinions about ethical issues faced in organizations. The class should be divided into twelve groups. Each group will randomly be assigned one of the following issues, which reflect the twelve ethical themes found in *The Wall Street Journal* study shown in Table 4.3.

1. Is it ethical to take office supplies from work for home use? Make personal long-distance calls from the office? Use company time for personal business? Or do these behaviors constitute stealing?

2. If you exaggerate your credentials in an interview, is it lying? Is lying in order to protect a coworker acceptable?

3. If you pretend to be more successful than you are in order to impress your boss, are you being deceitful?

4. How do you differentiate between a bribe and a gift?

5. If there are slight defects in a product you are selling, are you obligated to tell the buyer? If an advertised "sale" price is really the everyday price, should you divulge the information to the customer?

6. Suppose you have a friend who works at the ticket office for the convention center where Shania Twain will be appearing. Is it cheating if you ask the friend to get you tickets so that you won't have to fight the crowd to get them? Is buying merchandise for your family at your company's cost cheating?

7. Is it immoral to do less than your best in terms of work performance? Is it immoral to accept workers' compensation when you are fully capable of working?

8. What behaviors constitute emotional abuse at work? What would you consider an abuse of one's position of power?

9. Are high-stress jobs a breach of ethics? What about transfers that break up families?

10. Are all rule violations equally important? Do employees have an ethical obligation to follow company rules?

11. To what extent are you responsible for the ethical behavior of your coworkers? If you witness unethical behavior and don't report it, are you an accessory?

12. Is it ethical to help one work group at the expense of another? For instance, suppose one group has excellent performance and you want to reward its members with an afternoon off. In that case, the other group will have to pick up the slack and work harder. Is this ethical?

Once your group has been assigned its issue, you have two tasks:

1. First, formulate your group's answer to the ethical dilemmas.

2. After you have formulated your group's position, discuss the individual differences that may have contributed to your position. You will want to discuss the individual differences presented in this chapter as well as any others that you feel affected your position on the ethical dilemma.

Your instructor will lead the class in a discussion of how individual differences may have influenced your positions on these ethical dilemmas.

SOURCE: Kluwer Academic Publishers, by J. O. Cherrington and D. J. Cherrington, "A Menu of Moral Issues: One Week in the Life of *The Wall Street Journal*," *Journal of Business Ethics* 11 (1992): 255–265. Reprinted with kind permission of Springer Science and Business Media.

Biz Flix | The Emperor's Club

William Hundert (Kevin Kline), a professor at Saint Benedict's Academy for Boys, believes in teaching his students about living a principled life. He also wants them to learn his beloved classical literature. New student Sedgewick Bell (Emile Hirsch) challenges Hundert's principled ways. Bell's behavior during the 73rd annual Mr. Julius Caesar Contest causes Hundert to suspect that Bell leads a less than principled life, a suspicion reinforced years later during a repeat of the competition.

This scene appears at the end of the film. It is an edited portion of the Mr. Julius Caesar Contest reenactment at former student Sedgewick Bell's (Joel Gretsch) estate. Bell wins the competition, but Hundert notices Bell's earpiece. Earlier in the film, Hundert had suspected that young Bell also wore an earpiece during the original competition. Bell announced his candidacy for the U.S. Senate just before talking to Hundert in the bathroom. In his announcement, he described his commitment to specific values he would pursue if elected.

What to Watch for and Ask Yourself:

> Does William Hundert describe a specific type of life that one should lead? If so, what are its elements?

> Does Sedgewick Bell lead that type of life? Is he committed to any specific ethics view or theory?

> What consequences or effects do you predict for Sedgewick Bell because of the way he chooses to live his life?

Workplace Video | Organizational Behavior at Zingerman's

For over 25 years Zingerman's has delighted its customers with traditionally made breads, cheeses, oils, vinegars, and other gourmet foods. While connoisseurs and everyday customers alike rave about the upscale-food retailer's flavorful menu items, cofounders Ari Weinzweig and Paul Saginaw know that a committed, enthusiastic staff is the key ingredient of great-tasting specialty foods at Zingerman's. The duo in charge of the deli, bakehouse, and other eateries in Zingerman's Community of Businesses foster a high level of job satisfaction among employees, and this has earned Zingerman's a reputation as "The Coolest Small Company in America," according to *Inc.* magazine.

Employees at Zingerman's have a positive attitude about the company and its leadership. "I wanted to come to work at Zingerman's," says ZingNet Marketing Manager Pete Sickman-Garner, "because I really wanted to work for a place where I respected the people above me and respected their ability to organize people and get them all to do what needed to be done." Human Resources Manager Pat McGraw claims that Zingerman's takes attitude to a new level: "People are excited about their jobs, and it is each person's enthusiasm for the job that creates that experience."

Zingerman's has many organizational qualities that interest workers and motivate them to do a great job. Some employees like what the company stands for; others admire the founders' focus on organizational citizenship—work behavior that goes beyond one's job requirements and contributes to the organization's success. "In many firms," says Ron Maurer, VP of administration, "you wait for somebody else to make a decision and then you implement it. In this particular organization, you have a chance to actually influence the decision that is being made about what you're going to do." Such employee empowerment creates a positive work environment—one that in turn influences the cognitive thoughts, affective feelings, and behavioral intentions of each individual staff member.

Above all, management's commitment to delivering outstanding service—both to internal and external customers—lies at the core of the Zingerman's experience. "Our mission," says Weinzweig, "is to bring a great experience to everybody that we interact with, whether that's customers, coworkers, the community, or even just people walking down the street."

Discussion Questions

1. What is "servant leadership," and what impact do you think this managerial approach has on organizational commitment at Zingerman's?

2. What are some ways in which Zingerman's promotes job satisfaction among employees?

3. What personal qualities and values does Zingerman's look for in a candidate who is interviewing for a job?

Canine Companions for Independence: Enhancing People's Lives

Founded in July 1975 in Santa Rosa, California, "Canine Companions for Independence [CCI] is a nonprofit organization that enhances the lives of people with [physical or developmental] disabilities by providing highly trained assistance dogs and ongoing support to ensure quality partnerships."[1] These assistance dogs, called Canine Companions, help enhance the independence or quality of life of disabled people.

CCI operates nationwide with centers in Santa Rosa and Oceanside, California; Delaware, Ohio; Farmingdale, New York; and Orlando, Florida; and satellite offices in Chicago, Illinois, and Colorado Springs, Colorado. Private contributions, donations from civic groups, service clubs, and businesses, and fundraising through special events and mailings cover all of the costs associated with breeding, raising, and training Canine Companions. CCI does not receive any governmental funding, and participants in the program do not absorb any of the breeding, raising, or training costs. However, participants are responsible for the feeding, housing, proper care, and medical needs of their Canine Companion after they become partnered.[2]

The breed stock for Canine Companions consists of golden retrievers, Labrador retrievers, or a crossbreed between the two. Participants in the CCI program complete a mandatory two-week training session wherein the human user is matched with a Canine Companion and both are prepared to work well with each other. People with physical or developmental disabilities who want an assistance dog must complete an application process, and if selected for the CCI program, they attend the Team Training course. Professionals who work for organizations that provide physical or mental health care to clients may also apply to the program. To be eligible, the professional must demonstrate that clients would benefit from having a Canine Companion in the facility where they care for disabled clients.[3]

Types of CCI Assistance Teams

CCI trains four types of assistance teams: service teams, skilled companion teams, facility teams, and hearing teams. A service team consists of a child or adult with physical disabilities and a Canine Companion that performs physical tasks, such as picking up dropped items, turning light switches on or off, pulling a wheelchair, or opening doors and drawers, on behalf of the disabled person. The skilled companion team consists of an adolescent or adult with physical, emotional, or developmental disabilities as well as a human primary caretaker and a Canine Companion. The role of the Canine Companion is to help the disabled person with physical tasks and to provide companionship and affection.[4] A facility team links a Canine Companion with a rehabilitation professional or caregiver to help improve the physical, mental, or emotional health of people for whom the professional provides care in a facility setting.[5] A hearing team utilizes a Canine Companion to alert deaf or hard-of-hearing adults to everyday sounds like alarm clocks, smoke alarms, telephones, and doorbells.[6]

Just over 2,500 teams have been developed and placed between CCI's founding in 1975 and late August 2007. The first Canine Companion teams were placed with program participants in 1978. In the summer of 2007, approximately 1,200 active teams were operating nationwide.[7]

CCI Volunteers

Many volunteers are involved in raising puppies for the Canine Companions program. Indeed, in mid-2007, there were 623 active puppy raisers.[8] The puppy raisers care for the CCI puppies, take them to puppy classes, and train them in appropriate behaviors and house manners. Upon reaching the required age, the CCI puppies enter a formal training program at one of the five regional CCI centers.

Famed former professional basketball player Bill Walton and his wife, Lori, are puppy raiser volunteers. For fourteen months they raised, trained, and socialized a puppy named Loma. At fourteen months of age, Loma was placed in advanced training for nine months at one of CCI's regional training centers. During this time the Waltons could not have any contact with Loma. Turning her over to the Oceanside,

California, regional training center was an emotional time for the Waltons, given the relationship they had established with the dog. Loma was destined to be the Canine Companion for David Grucca, a quadriplegic. Upon Loma's completion of the advanced training, the Waltons ceremonially presented Loma to David Grucca and began a friendship with him that is likely to be permanent. The Waltons are now raising another CCI puppy.[9]

Two other volunteers, both employees of Perot Systems Corp. in Plano, Texas, also raised puppies to become Canine Companions. Amy Witherel and Karissa White gave their puppies, Hilani and Orenda, lots of love and affection while training them to be well mannered and housebroken. To become effectively socialized, the puppies went everywhere with their raisers, including the grocery store, sporting events, restaurants, movies theaters, the beauty parlor, and even work. Neither Witherel nor White relished the thought of parting with their beloved puppies, but they recognized that ultimately they will help people who really need the Canine Companions.[10]

Joyce and Gordon Spainhower raised Hovan, a retriever mix breed, for CCI. They became hooked on the program when they attended a graduation ceremony for the two-week training program and saw how delighted children were with their service dogs. The Spainhowers' motto now is: "Price of raising a service puppy: $3,000. Seeing a smile on a child's face: priceless."[11]

Volunteerism for CCI is not limited to adults or to those interested in raising puppies. Consider, for ex-

ample, Kyle Orent, an eight-year-old boy from Northport, New York, who in 2005 asked his parents for a lemonade stand so he could raise money for charity. Kyle knew he wanted to help some charity but didn't know which one. A family friend who knew Kyle liked animals suggested that he visit the Northeast Regional Center of CCI. He did and was impressed. When Kyle saw the pictures of smiling people in wheelchairs, he knew he had found his charity. Since then he has raised over $20,000 on behalf of CCI.[12]

Discussion Questions

1. Using the five attributes of attitude-behavior correspondence that are discussed in the chapter, explain the linkage between the CCI volunteers' attitudes and their behaviors.

2. How can the concept of emotional contagion help in understanding the attitudes and behaviors of the CCI volunteers?

3. What instrumental values and terminal values become evident through the activities of Canine Companions for Independence? For the CCI volunteers?

4. What impact might the instrumental and terminal values of CCI volunteers have on their propensity to behave ethically or unethically?

SOURCE: This case was written by Michael K. McCuddy, The Louis S. and Mary L. Morgal Chair of Christian Business Ethics and Professor of Management, College of Business Administration, Valparaiso University.

Motivation at Work

LEARNING OBJECTIVES

After reading this chapter, you should be able to do the following:

1 Define motivation.
2 Explain how Theory X and Theory Y relate to Maslow's hierarchy of needs.
3 Discuss the needs for achievement, power, and affiliation.
4 Describe the two-factor theory of motivation.
5 Explain two new ideas in human motivation.
6 Describe how inequity influences motivation and can be resolved.
7 Describe the expectancy theory of motivation.
8 Describe the cultural differences in motivation.

THINKING AHEAD: AMERICAN EXPRESS COMPANY

The Working Mother Hall of Fame

Fewer than 20 companies have landed a spot on the *Working Mother* list of 100 Best Companies for 15 years or more. These very select companies constitute the Working Mother Hall of Fame, and 2006 saw three new honorees added to the roster: GlaxoSmith-Kline, Northern Trust, and The Phoenix Company. American Express is one of the established members of the Hall of Fame because of its family-friendly policies.[1] These include flextime, compressed weeks, telecommuting, job sharing, childcare, maternity leave, fitness centers, massage and physical therapy, and career counseling. The company even allows its employees to bring along their children when traveling on business to cities with available emergency childcare centers. These work/life benefits require an investment by the company, but the returns include attracting and retaining top talent while propelling profits.

American Express chairman and CEO Kenneth Chenault believes that having an inspired and engaged workforce is key to providing customers with exceptional products and service. He emphasizes the importance of acknowledging employee needs, both in the workplace and in their personal lives. Some American Express employees are earning advanced degrees, some are raising children, while others are caring for an elderly relative. Still others volunteer in their communities. With this wide variance in gifts, talents, and needs, Chenault believes the company needs to look for ways to support every one of its employees. That support begins with understanding employees' needs and is followed by providing the resources and opportunities to meet them.

What about the numbers? American Express has a lot of women workers. Of their 28,627 employees, 19,245 are women, which is approximately 68 percent. Of those 19,245 women, 4,822 are women leaders. Therefore, 25 percent of women are in leadership positions. One hundred percent of the company's women receive career counseling, and 54 percent receive management or leadership training. Of the 19,245 women in the company, 2,519 are in the top 20 percent by pay. That means that 13 percent of the women are in this top 20 percent. The 14-member board of directors includes 2 women, or 14 percent. These numbers tell a story about women at American Express—but not the whole story. What about the faces and people behind these numbers? In the Looking Back feature on page 173, we profile the people behind the numbers.

This is the first of two chapters about motivation, behavior, and performance at work. A comprehensive approach to understanding these topics must consider three elements of the work situation—the individual, the job, and the work environment—and how these elements interact.[2] This chapter emphasizes internal and process theories of motivation. It begins with individual need theories of motivation, turns to the two-factor theory of motivation, and finishes by examining two individual–environment interaction or process theories of motivation. Chapter 6 emphasizes external theories of motivation and focuses on factors in the environment to help understand good or bad performance.

MOTIVATION AND WORK BEHAVIOR

(1) Define *motivation*.

Motivation is the process of arousing and sustaining goal-directed behavior. It is one of the more complex topics in organizational behavior. *Motivation* comes from the Latin root word *movere*, which means "to move."

Motivation theories attempt to explain and predict observable behavior. The wide range and variety of motivation theories result from the great diversity of people and the complexity of their behavior in organizations. Motivation theories may be broadly classified into internal, process, and external theories of motivation. Internal theories of motivation give primary consideration to variables within the individual that give rise to motivation and behavior. The hierarchy of needs theory exemplifies the internal theories. Process theories of motivation emphasize the nature of the interaction between the individual and the environment. Expectancy theory exemplifies the process theories. External

motivation

The process of arousing and sustaining goal-directed behavior.

theories of motivation focus on the elements in the environment, including the consequences of behavior, as the basis for understanding and explaining people's behavior at work. Any single motivation theory explains only a small portion of the variance in human behavior. Therefore, alternative theories have developed over time in an effort to account for the unexplained portions of the variance in behavior.

Internal Needs

Philosophers and scholars have theorized for centuries about human needs and motives. During the past century, attention narrowed to understanding motivation in businesses and other organizations.[3] Max Weber, an early German organizational scholar, argued that the meaning of work lay not in the work itself but in its deeper potential for contributing to a person's ultimate salvation.[4] From this Calvinistic perspective, the Protestant ethic was the fuel for human industriousness. The Protestant ethic said people should work hard because those who prospered at work were more likely to find a place in heaven. You 5.1 lets you evaluate how strongly you have a pro-Protestant versus a non-Protestant ethic. Although Weber, and later Blood, both used the term *Protestant ethic*, many see the value elements of this work ethic in the broader Judeo-Christian tradition. We concur.

A more complex motivation theory was proposed by Sigmund Freud. For him, a person's organizational life was founded on the compulsion to work and the power of love.[5] He saw much of human motivation as unconscious by nature. *Psychoanalysis* was Freud's method for delving into the unconscious mind to better understand a person's motives and needs. Freud's psychodynamic theory offers explanations for irrational and self-destructive behavior, such as suicide or workplace violence. The motives underlying such traumatic work events may be understood by analyzing a person's unconscious needs and motives. The psychoanalytic approach also helps explain deviant workplace behavior, which can have a negative impact on business unit performance.[6] Freud's theorizing is important as the basis for subsequent need theories of motivation. Research suggests that people's deeper feelings may transcend culture, with most people caring deeply about the same few things.[7]

Internal needs and external incentives both play an important role in motivation. Although extrinsic motivation is important, so too is intrinsic motivation, which varies by the individual.[8] Intrinsic work motivation is linked to spillover effects from work to home, with mothers transmitting the emotions of happiness, anger, and anxiety from work to home.[9] Interestingly, fathers who have high intrinsic work motivation tended to report greater overall anxiety at home after the workday. Therefore, it is important for managers to consider both internal needs and external incentives when attempting to motivate their employees. Further, managers who are more supportive and less controlling appear to elicit more intrinsic motivation from their employees.

External Incentives

Early organizational scholars made economic assumptions about human motivation and developed differential piece-rate systems of pay that emphasized external incentives. They assumed that people were motivated by self-interest and economic gain. The Hawthorne studies confirmed the positive effects of pay incentives on productivity and also found that social and interpersonal motives were important.[10] However, there are those who raise the question about where self-interest ends

psychoanalysis

Sigmund Freud's method for delving into the unconscious mind to better understand a person's motives and needs.

Protestant Ethic

Rate the following statements from 1 (for *disagree completely*) to 6 (for *agree completely*).

____ 1. When the workday is finished, people should forget their jobs and enjoy themselves.

____ 2. Hard work makes us better people.

____ 3. The principal purpose of people's jobs is to provide them with the means for enjoying their free time.

____ 4. Wasting time is as bad as wasting money.

____ 5. Whenever possible, a person should relax and accept life as it is rather than always striving for unreachable goals.

____ 6. A good indication of a person's worth is how well he or she does his or her job.

____ 7. If all other things are equal, it is better to have a job with a lot of responsibility than one with little responsibility.

____ 8. People who "do things the easy way" are the smart ones.

____ Total your score for the pro-Protestant ethic items (2, 4, 6, and 7).

____ Total your score for the non-Protestant ethic items (1, 3, 5, and 8).

A pro-Protestant ethic score of 20 or over indicates you have a strong work ethic; 15–19 indicates a moderately strong work ethic; 9–14 indicates a moderately weak work ethic; 8 or less indicates a weak work ethic.

A non-Protestant ethic score of 20 or over indicates you have a strong non-work ethic; 15–19 indicates a moderately strong non-work ethic; 9–14 indicates a moderately weak non-work ethic; 8 or less indicates a weak non-work ethic.

SOURCE: M. R. Blood, "Work Values and Job Satisfaction," *Journal of Applied Psychology* 53 (1969): 456–459. Copyright © 1969 by the American Psychological Association. Reprinted with permission.

and the public interest begins. The Real World 5.1 looks at this interesting question.

Those who made economic assumptions about human motivation emphasized financial incentives for behavior. The Scottish political economist and moral philosopher Adam Smith argued that a person's *self-interest* was God's providence, not the government's.[11] More recently, executives have focused on "enlightened" self-interest. Self-interest is what is in the best interest and benefit to the individual; enlightened self-interest additionally recognizes the self-interest of other people. Adam Smith laid the cornerstone for the free enterprise system of economics when he formulated the "invisible hand" and the free market to explain the motivation for individual behavior. The "invisible hand" refers to the unseen forces of a free market system that shape the most efficient use of people, money, and resources for productive ends. Smith's basic assumption was that people are motivated by self-interest for economic gain to provide the necessities and conveniences of life. Thus, employees are most productive when motivated by self-interest.

Technology is an important concept in Smith's view, because he believed that a nation's wealth is determined primarily by the productivity of its labor force. Therefore, a more efficient and effective labor force yields greater abundance for the nation. Technology is important as a force multiplier for the productivity of labor.[12]

Frederick Taylor, the founder of scientific management, was also concerned with labor efficiency and effectiveness.[13] His central concern was to change the relationship between management and labor from one of conflict to one of cooperation.[14] Taylor believed the basis of their conflict was the division of the profits. Instead of

self-interest

What is in the best interest and benefit to an individual.

Whose Interests?

Increasingly philanthropists and donors are combining charitable giving with their profit-making enterprises. This creates a challenge to determine where the self-interest of the donor ends and the public interest of the community begins. A case in point was that of Wade Dokken, whose 11,000-acre Ameya Preserve in Paradise Valley, Montana, is about 45 miles from Yellowstone Park. Dokken bought the land in 2005 for $23.3 million. He plans 301 luxury homes and related commercial development. What is unusual is that he promises in addition a package of donations that he claims have a value of more than $70 million. This package includes a $2 million homesite given to a benefit auction for the high-powered Robin Hood Foundation in New York, an earmark of $10 million for local nonprofits, a payment for low-cost Habitat for Humanity housing, and $1 million for the country's "social needs" as well as other charitable gifts. Some do not want the Ameya land developed at all. Dokken sees both a business opportunity and a chance to turn his development plan into an engine for charity. Thus, all

Wade Dokken's purchase of the Ameya Preserve in Paradise Valley, Montana, challenges the line between the interests of the individual and of the public.

© DONOVAN REESE/GETTY IMAGES

land sales would be assessed a 0.5 percent donation to a nonprofit "community stewardship organization" dedicated to the environment, arts, and sciences. This initiative, which did receive the county commissioners' blessing, ignores traditional constituencies and challenges the line between the interests of the individual and the public.

SOURCE: S. Beatty, "Giving Back: Developer Blends Charity, Profit," *The Wall Street Journal* (May 11, 2007): W2.

continuing this conflict over the division of profits, labor and management should form a cooperative relationship aimed at enlarging the total profits.

Employee Recognition and Ownership

Modern management practices—such as employee recognition programs, flexible benefit packages, and stock ownership plans—build on Smith's and Taylor's original theories. These practices emphasize external incentives, which may take either strictly economic form or more material form, such as "outstanding employee" plaques, gold watches, and other organizational symbols of distinction. Whataburger has developed the WhataGames in which the best employees compete for bragging rights as well as cash, prizes, and even medals.[15] This corporate Olympics is a training-and-loyalty exercise that helps significantly reduce turnover and build commitment. One bridge approach to employee motivation that considers both psychological needs and external incentives is psychological ownership. An increasing number of scholars and managers emphasize the importance of "feelings of ownership" for the organization. One study of 800 managers and employees in three different organizations found that psychological ownership increased organizational citizenship behavior, a key contextual performance beyond the call of duty as discussed in Chapter 3.[16]

MASLOW'S NEED HIERARCHY

Psychologist Abraham Maslow proposed a theory of motivation emphasizing psychological and interpersonal needs in addition to physical needs and economic necessity. His theory was based on a need hierarchy later applied through Theory X and Theory Y, two sets of assumptions about people at work. In addition, his need hierarchy was reformulated in an ERG theory of motivation using a revised classification scheme for basic human needs.

The Hierarchy of Needs

The core of Maslow's theory of human motivation is a hierarchy of five need categories.[17] Although he recognized that there were factors other than one's needs (for example, culture) that were determinants of behavior, he focused his theoretical attention on specifying people's internal needs. Maslow labeled the five hierarchical categories as physiological needs, safety and security needs, love (social) needs, esteem needs, and the need for self-actualization. Maslow's *need hierarchy* is depicted in Figure 5.1, which also shows how the needs relate to Douglas McGregor's assumptions about people, which will be discussed next.

Maslow conceptually derived the five need categories from the early thoughts of William James[18] and John Dewey,[19] coupled with the psychodynamic thinking of Sigmund Freud and Alfred Adler.[20] Maslow's need theory was later tested in research with working populations. For example, one study reported that middle managers and lower-level managers had different perceptions of their need deficiencies and the importance of their needs.[21] One distinguishing feature of Maslow's need hierarchy is the following progression hypothesis. Although some research has challenged the assumption, the theory says that only ungratified needs motivate

FIGURE 5.1 Human Needs, Theory X, and Theory Y

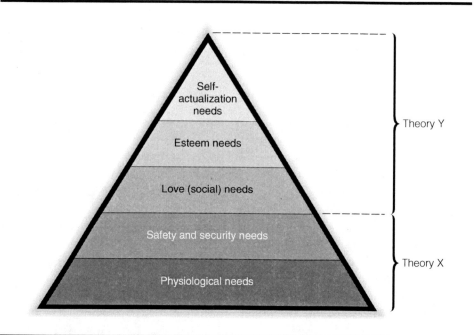

need hierarchy

The theory that behavior is determined by a progression of physical, social, and psychological needs, including lower-order needs and higher-order needs.

behavior.[22] Further, it is the lowest level of ungratified needs in the hierarchy that motivates behavior. As one level of need is met, a person progresses to the next higher level of need as a source of motivation. Hence, people progress up the hierarchy as they successively gratify each level of need.

Theory X and Theory Y

One important organizational implication of the need hierarchy concerns how to manage people at work (see Figure 5.1). Douglas McGregor understood people's motivation using Maslow's need theory. He grouped the physiological and safety needs as "lower order" needs and the social, esteem, and self-actualization needs as "higher order" needs, as shown in Figure 5.1. McGregor proposed two alternative sets of assumptions about people at work based on which set of needs were the motivators.[23] His *Theory X* and *Theory Y* assumptions are included in Table 5.1. McGregor saw the responsibility of management as the same under both sets of assumptions. Specifically, "management is responsible for organizing the elements of productive enterprise—money, materials, equipment, people—in the interest of economic ends."[24]

McGregor believed that Theory X assumptions are appropriate for employees motivated by lower order needs. Theory Y assumptions, in contrast, are appropriate for employees motivated by higher order needs. Employee participation programs are one consequence of McGregor's Theory Y assumptions. Therefore, *Fortune* 1000 corporations use employee involvement as one motivation strategy for achieving high performance.[25] Whole Foods founder and CEO John Mackey relies on Maslow's hierarchy of needs in leading the company.[26]

Gordon Forward, founding CEO of world-class Chaparral Steel Company, considered the assumptions made about people central to motivation and management.[27] He viewed employees as resources to be developed. Using Maslow's need hierarchy and Theory Y assumptions about people, he cultivated and developed a productive, loyal workforce in TXI's Chaparral Steel unit.

(2) Explain how Theory X and Theory Y relate to Maslow's hierarchy of needs.

Theory X

A set of assumptions of how to manage individuals who are motivated by lower-order needs.

Theory Y

A set of assumptions of how to manage individuals who are motivated by higher-order needs.

TABLE 5.1 McGregor's Assumptions about People

Theory X	Theory Y
▪ People are by nature indolent. That is, they work as little as possible.	▪ People are not by nature passive or resistant to organizational needs. They have become so as a result of experience in organizations.
▪ People lack ambition, dislike responsibility, and prefer to be led.	▪ The motivation, the potential for development, the capacity for assuming responsibility, and the readiness to direct behavior toward organizational goals are all present in people. Management does not put them there. It is a responsibility of management to make it possible for people to recognize and develop these human characteristics for themselves.
▪ People are inherently self-centered and indifferent to organizational needs.	
▪ People are by nature resistant to change.	
▪ People are gullible and not very bright, the ready dupes of the charlatan and the demagogue.	▪ The essential task of management is to arrange conditions and methods of operation so that people can achieve their own goals best by directing their own efforts toward organizational objectives.

SOURCE: From "The Human Side of Enterprise" by Douglas M. McGregor; reprinted from *Management Review*, November 1957. Copyright 1957 American Management Association International. Reprinted by permission of American Management Association International, New York, NY. All rights reserved. http://www.amanet.org.

ERG Theory

Clayton Alderfer recognized Maslow's contribution to understanding motivation, but believed that the original need hierarchy was not quite accurate in identifying and categorizing human needs.[28] As an evolutionary step, Alderfer proposed the ERG theory of motivation, which grouped human needs into only three basic categories: existence, relatedness, and growth.[29] Alderfer classified Maslow's physiological and physical safety needs in an existence need category; Maslow's interpersonal safety, love, and interpersonal esteem needs in a relatedness need category; and Maslow's self-actualization and self-esteem needs in a growth need category.

In addition to the differences in categorizing human needs, ERG theory added a regression hypothesis to go along with the progression hypothesis originally proposed by Maslow. Alderfer's regression hypothesis helped explain people's behavior when frustrated at meeting needs at the next higher level in the hierarchy. Specifically, the regression hypothesis states that people regress to the next lower category of needs and intensify their desire to gratify these needs. Hence, ERG theory explains both progressive need gratification and regression when people face frustration.

MCCLELLAND'S NEED THEORY

(3) Discuss the needs for achievement, power, and affiliation.

A second major need theory of motivation focuses on personality and learned needs. Henry Murray developed a long list of motives and manifest needs in his early studies of personality.[30] David McClelland was inspired by Murray's early work.[31] McClelland identified three learned or acquired needs, called *manifest needs*. These were the needs for achievement, for power, and for affiliation. Some individuals have a high need for achievement, whereas others have a moderate or low need for achievement. The same is true for the other two needs. Hence, it is important to emphasize that different needs are dominant in different people. American Express has recognized the importance of diverse employees needs through its family-friendly policies, as we saw in the Thinking Ahead feature on page 151. For example, a manager may have a strong need for power, a moderate need for achievement, and a weak need for affiliation. Each need has quite different implications for people's behavior. The Murray Thematic Apperception Test (TAT) was used as an early measure of the achievement motive and was further developed by McClelland and his associates.[32] The TAT is a projective test, and projective tests were discussed in Chapter 3.

Need for Achievement

The *need for achievement* concerns issues of excellence, competition, challenging goals, persistence, and overcoming difficulties.[33] A person with a high need for achievement seeks excellence in performance, enjoys difficult and challenging goals, and is persevering and competitive in work activities. Example questions that address the need for achievement are: Do you enjoy difficult, challenging work activities? Do you strive to exceed your performance objectives? Do you seek out new ways to overcome difficulties?

McClelland found that people with a high need for achievement perform better than those with a moderate or low need for achievement, and he has noted national differences in achievement motivation. Individuals with a high need for achievement have three unique characteristics. First, they set goals that are moderately difficult

need for achievement

A manifest (easily perceived) need that concerns individuals' issues of excellence, competition, challenging goals, persistence, and overcoming difficulties.

yet achievable. Second, they like to receive feedback on their progress toward these goals. Third, they do not like having external events or other people interfere with their progress toward the goals.

High achievers often hope and plan for success. They may be quite content to work alone or with other people—whichever is more appropriate to their task. High achievers like being very good at what they do, and they develop expertise and competence in their chosen endeavors. Research shows that need for achievement generalizes well across countries with adults who are employed full-time.[34] In addition, international differences in the tendency for achievement have been found. Specifically, achievement tendencies are highest for the United States, an individualistic culture, and lowest for Japan and Hungary, collectivistic societies.[35]

Need for Power

The *need for power* is concerned with the desire to make an impact on others, influence others, change people or events, and make a difference in life. The need for power is interpersonal, because it involves influence with other people. Individuals with a high need for power like to control people and events. McClelland makes an important distinction between socialized power, which is used for the benefit of many, and personalized power, which is used for individual gain. The former is a constructive force, whereas the latter may be a very disruptive, destructive force.

A high need for power was one distinguishing characteristic of managers rated the "best" in McClelland's research. Specifically, the best managers had a very high need for socialized power, as opposed to personalized power.[36] These managers are concerned for others; have an interest in organizational goals; and have a desire to be useful to the larger group, organization, and society.

While successful managers have the greatest upward velocity in an organization and rise to higher managerial levels more quickly than their contemporaries, they benefit their organizations most if they have a high socialized power need.[37] The need for power is discussed further in Chapter 11, on power and politics.

Need for Affiliation

The *need for affiliation* is concerned with establishing and maintaining warm, close, intimate relationships with other people.[38] Those with a high need for affiliation are motivated to express their emotions and feelings to others while expecting them to do the same in return. They find conflicts and complications in their relationships disturbing and are strongly motivated to work through any such barriers to closeness. The relationships they have with others are therefore close and personal, emphasizing friendship and companionship.

Over and above these three needs, Murray's manifest needs theory included the need for autonomy. This is the desire for independence and freedom from any constraints. People with a high need for autonomy prefer to work alone and to control the pace of their work. They dislike bureaucratic rules, regulations, and procedures. The need for relationships is important in each theory. A study of 555 nurses in specialized units found that intrinsic motivation increased with supportive relationships on the job.[39] Figure 5.2 summarizes Maslow's hierarchy of needs with its two extensions in the work of McGregor and Alderfer. The figure also summarizes McClelland's need theory of motivation. The figure shows the parallel structures of these four motivational theories.

need for power
A manifest (easily perceived) need that concerns an individual's need to make an impact on others, influence others, change people or events, and make a difference in life.

need for affiliation
A manifest (easily perceived) need that concerns an individual's need to establish and maintain warm, close, intimate relationships with other people.

FIGURE 5.2 Need Theories of Motivation

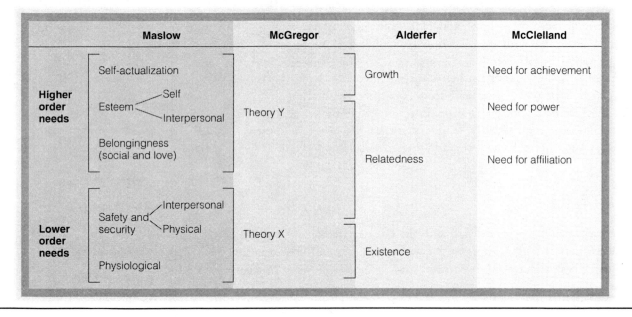

	Maslow	McGregor	Alderfer	McClelland
Higher order needs	Self-actualization Esteem — Self — Interpersonal Belongingness (social and love)	Theory Y	Growth Relatedness	Need for achievement Need for power Need for affiliation
Lower order needs	Safety and security — Interpersonal — Physical Physiological	Theory X	Existence	

HERZBERG'S TWO-FACTOR THEORY

(4) Describe the two-factor theory of motivation.

Frederick Herzberg departed from the need theories of motivation and examined the experiences that satisfied or dissatisfied people at work. This motivation theory became known as the two-factor theory.[40] Herzberg's original study included 200 engineers and accountants in western Pennsylvania during the 1950s. Herzberg asked these people to describe two important incidents at their jobs: one that was very satisfying and made them feel exceptionally good at work, and another that was very dissatisfying and made them feel exceptionally bad at work.

Herzberg and his colleagues believed that people had two sets of needs—one related to the avoidance of pain and one related to the desire for psychological growth. Conditions in the work environment would affect one or the other of these needs. Work conditions related to satisfaction of the need for psychological growth were labeled *motivation factors*. Work conditions related to dissatisfaction caused by discomfort or pain were labeled *hygiene factors*. Each set of factors related to one aspect of what Herzberg identified as the human being's dual nature regarding the work environment. Thus, motivation factors relate to job satisfaction, and hygiene factors relate to job dissatisfaction,[41] as shown in Figure 5.3.

Motivation Factors

motivation factor

A work condition related to satisfaction of the need for psychological growth.

hygiene factor

A work condition related to dissatisfaction caused by discomfort or pain.

Job satisfaction is produced by building motivation factors into a job, according to Herzberg. This process is known as job enrichment. In the original research, the motivation factors were identified as responsibility, achievement, recognition, advancement, and the work itself. When these factors are present, they lead to superior performance and effort on the part of job incumbents. As we saw in Thinking Ahead, American Express has clearly created growth and advancement opportunities for its women employees. Figure 5.3 also shows that salary is a motivational factor in some studies. Many organizational reward systems now include other financial benefits,

FIGURE 5.3 The Motivation–Hygiene Theory of Motivation

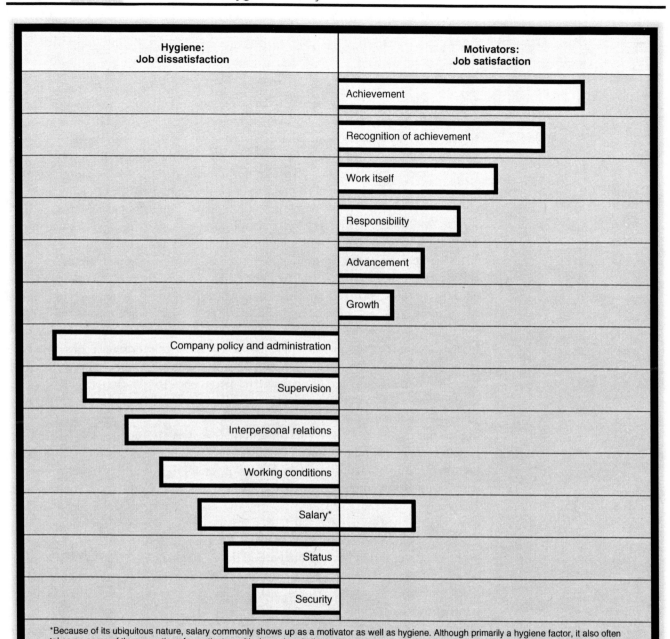

Hygiene: Job dissatisfaction	Motivators: Job satisfaction
	Achievement
	Recognition of achievement
	Work itself
	Responsibility
	Advancement
	Growth
Company policy and administration	
Supervision	
Interpersonal relations	
Working conditions	
Salary*	
Status	
Security	

*Because of its ubiquitous nature, salary commonly shows up as a motivator as well as hygiene. Although primarily a hygiene factor, it also often takes on some of the properties of a motivator, with dynamics similar to those of recognition for achievement.

SOURCE: Reprinted from Frederick Herzberg, *The Managerial Choice: To Be Efficient or to Be Human* (Salt Lake City: Olympus, 1982). Reprinted by permission.

such as stock options, as part of an employee's compensation package. A long-term study of young men in the United States and West Germany found job satisfaction positively linked to earnings and changes in earnings, as well as voluntary turnover.[42]

Motivation factors lead to positive mental health and challenge people to grow, contribute to the work environment, and invest themselves in the organization. According to the theory and original research, the absence of these factors does not lead to dissatisfaction. Rather, it leads to the lack of satisfaction. The motivation factors are the more important of the two sets of factors, because they directly affect a person's motivational drive to do a good job. When they are absent, the person is demotivated to perform well and achieve excellence. The hygiene factors are a completely distinct set of factors unrelated to the motivation to achieve and do excellent work.

Hygiene Factors

Job dissatisfaction occurs when the hygiene factors are either not present or not sufficient. In the original research, the hygiene factors were company policy and administration; technical supervision; salary; interpersonal relations with one's supervisor; working conditions; and status. These factors relate to the context of the job and may be considered support factors. They do not directly affect a person's motivation to work but influence the extent of the person's discontent. They cannot stimulate psychological growth or human development but may be thought of as maintenance factors. Excellent hygiene factors result in employees' being *not dissatisfied* and contribute to the absence of complaints about these contextual considerations.

When these hygiene factors are poor or absent, the person complains about "poor supervision," "poor medical benefits," or whatever hygiene factor is poor. Employees experience a deficit and are dissatisfied when the hygiene factors are not present. Many companies have initiated formal flextime policies as a way to reduce dissatisfaction and persuade women leaders to come back to work.[43] Even in the absence of good hygiene factors, employees may still be very motivated to perform their jobs well if the motivation factors are present. Although this may appear to be a paradox, it is not, because the motivation and hygiene factors are independent of each other.

The combination of motivation and hygiene factors can result in one of four possible job conditions. First, a job high in both motivation and hygiene factors leads to high motivation and few complaints among employees. Second, a job low in both factors leads to low motivation and many complaints among employees. Third, a job high in motivation factors and low in hygiene factors leads to high employee motivation to perform coupled with complaints about aspects of the work environment. Fourth, a job low in motivation factors and high in hygiene factors leads to low employee motivation to excel but few complaints about the work environment.

Two conclusions can be drawn at this point. First, hygiene factors are of some importance up to a threshold level, but beyond the threshold there is little value in improving them. Second, the presence of motivation factors is essential to enhancing employee motivation to excel at work. You 5.2 asks you to rank a set of ten job reward factors in terms of their importance to the average employee, to supervisors, and to you.

Critique of the Two-Factor Theory

Herzberg's two-factor theory has been critiqued. One criticism concerns the classification of the two factors. Data have not shown a clear dichotomization of incidents into hygiene and motivator factors. For example, employees almost equally classify pay as a hygiene factor and a motivation factor. A second criticism is the absence of individual differences in the theory. Specifically, individual differences such as age, sex, social status, education, or occupational level may influence the classification of factors. A third criticism is that intrinsic job factors, such as the work flow process, may be more important in determining satisfaction or dissatisfaction on the job. Finally, almost all of the supporting data for the theory come from Herzberg and his students using his peculiar critical-incident technique. These criticisms challenge and qualify, yet do not invalidate, the theory. Independent research found his theory valid in a government research and development environment.[44] Herzberg's two-factor theory has important implications for the design of work, as discussed in Chapter 14.

What's Important to Employees?

There are many possible job rewards that employees may receive. Listed below are ten possible job reward factors. Rank these factors three times. First, rank them as you think the average employee would rank them. Second, rank them as you think the average employee's supervisor would rank them for the employee. Finally, rank them according to what you consider important.

Your instructor has normative data for 1,000 employees and their supervisors that will help you interpret your results and put them in the context of Maslow's need hierarchy and Herzberg's two-factor theory of motivation.

Employee   Supervisor   You

1. job security
2. full appreciation of work done
3. promotion and growth in the organization
4. good wages
5. interesting work
6. good working conditions
7. tactful discipline
8. sympathetic help with personal problems
9. personal loyalty to employees
10. a feeling of being in on things

SOURCE: "Crossed Wires on Employee Motivation," *Training and Development* 49 (1995): 59–60. American Society for Training and Development. Reprinted with permission. All rights reserved.

TWO NEW IDEAS IN MOTIVATION

While executives like Whole Foods' CEO John Mackey value traditional motivation theories such as Maslow's, others like PepsiCo's CEO Steve Reinemund use new motivational ideas with their employees. Two new ideas in motivation have emerged in the past decade. One centers on eustress, strength, and hope. This idea comes from the new discipline of positive organizational behavior. The accompanying Science feature looks at core confidence in this regard. A second new idea centers on positive energy and full engagement. This idea translates what was learned from high-performance athletes for *Fortune* 500 executives and managers, such as those at PepsiCo. Both new ideas concern motivation, behavior, and performance at work.

(5) Explain two new ideas in human motivation.

Eustress, Strength, and Hope

Our detailed discussion of stress and health at work will come in Chapter 7. The positive side of stress discussed in Chapter 7 concerns its value as a motivational force, as in eustress. *Eustress* is healthy, normal stress.[45] Aligned with eustress in the new discipline of positive organizational scholarship are investing in strengths, finding positive meaning in work, displaying courage and principled action, and drawing on positive emotions at work.[46] This new, positive perspective on organizational life encourages optimism, hope, and health for people at work. Rather than focusing on the individual's needs, or alternatively on the rewards or punishment meted out

eustress

Healthy, normal stress.

Core Confidence and Employee Motivation

This study develops a new concept of core confidence as a higher order construct that is helpful in better understanding employee motivation in today's rapidly changing organizations. Globalization, advanced information technology, global sourcing, and new work structures and power distributions are now the norm instead of the exception. This dramatic change in organizations calls for development of new work motivation theories that fit the next work context. The purpose of this study is to develop new theory using new ideas from positive organizational behavior, the key construct of which is core confidence. Core confidence is manifested by hope, self-efficacy, optimism, and resilience. These four positive self-constructs share a common confidence core and thus, taken together, form the larger, higher-order construct of core confidence. The theory is that confidence is especially important in light of the new demands of the rapidly changing workplace that can trigger worrisome uncertainties for employees, giving them cause for doubt and anxiety. The ability to achieve and maintain high levels of motivation can therefore become a real challenge. In this context, core confidence can provide employees inner strength and help enhance their motivation by reducing their emotional experience of doubt, anxiety, and uncertainty. This positive experience leads then to both improved performance and positive subjective well-being.

SOURCE: A. D. Stajkovic, "Development of a Core Confidence–Higher Order Construct," *Journal of Applied Psychology* 91 (2006): 1208–1224.

in the work environment, this new idea in motivation focuses on the individual's interpretation of events.

Eustress is one manifestation of this broad, positive perspective. People are motivated by eustress when they see opportunities rather than obstacles, experience challenges rather than barriers, and feel energized rather than frustrated by the daily experiences of organizational life. Thus, eustress is a healthy and positive motivational force for individuals who harness its energy for productive work and organizational contributions.

Positive Energy and Full Engagement

The second new idea in motivation takes lessons learned from professional athletes and applies them in order to develop corporate athletes.[47] Jim Loehr's central tenets are the management of energy rather than time and the strategic use of disengagement to balance the power of full activity engagement.[48] This approach to motivation suggests that individuals do not need to be activated by unmet needs but are already activated by their own physical, emotional, mental, and spiritual energy. A manager's task is to help individuals learn to manage their energy so that they can experience periodic renewal and recovery and thus build positive energy and capacity for work.

A key to positive energy and full engagement is the concept that energy recovery is equally important to, if not more important than, energy expenditure. Individuals may be designed more as sprinters than long-distance runners, putting forth productive energy for short periods and then requiring time for recovery to reenergize. This approach to motivation and work is based on a balanced approach to the human body's potential to build or enhance its capacity, thus enabling the individual to sustain a high level of performance in the face of increasing work demands.

SOCIAL EXCHANGE AND EQUITY THEORY

Equity theory is a social exchange process theory of motivation that focuses on the individual–environment interaction. In contrast to internal needs theories of motivation, equity theory is concerned with the social processes that influence motivation and behavior. Power and exchange are important considerations in understanding human behavior.[49] In the same vein, Amitai Etzioni developed three categories of exchange relationships that people have with organizations: committed, calculated, and alienated involvements.[50] The implications of these relationships for power are discussed in detail in Chapter 11. Etzioni characterized committed relations as moral ones of high positive intensity, calculated relationships as ones of low positive or low negative intensity, and alienated relationships as ones of high negative intensity. Committed relationships may characterize a person's involvement with a religious group, and alienated relationships may characterize a person's incarceration in a prison. Social exchange theory may be the best way to understand effort–reward relationships and the sense of fairness at work as seen in a Dutch study.[51] Moral principles in workplace fairness are important because failures in fairness, or unfairness, lead to such things as theft, sabotage, and even violence.[52]

Demands and Contributions

Calculated involvements are based on the notion of social exchange in which each party in the relationship demands certain things of the other and contributes accordingly to the exchange. Business partnerships and commercial deals are excellent examples of calculated involvements. When they work well and both parties to the exchange benefit, the relationship has a positive orientation. When losses occur or conflicts arise, the relationship has a negative orientation. A model for examining these calculated exchange relationships is set out in Figure 5.4. We use this model to examine the nature of the relationship between a person and his or her employing organization.[53] The same basic model can be used to examine the relationship between two individuals or two organizations.

FIGURE 5.4 The Individual–Organizational Exchange Relationship

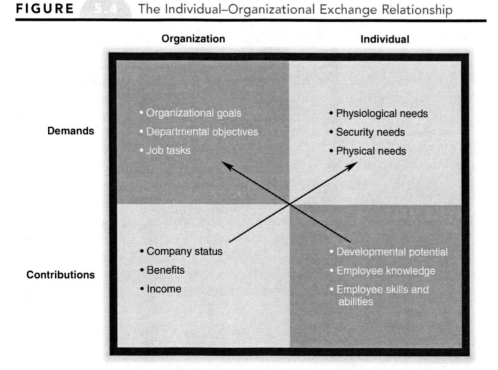

SOURCE: J. P. Campbell, M. D. Dunnette, E. E. Lawler III, and K. E. Weick, Jr., *Managerial Behavior, Performance, and Effectiveness* (New York: McGraw-Hill, Inc., 1970). Reproduced with permission from McGraw-Hill, Inc.

Demands Each party to the exchange makes demands upon the other. These demands express the expectations that each party has of the other in the relationship. The organization expresses its demands on the individual in the form of goal or mission statements, job expectations, performance objectives, and performance feedback. These are among the primary and formal mechanisms through which people learn about the organization's demands and expectations of them.

The organization is not alone in making demands of the relationship. The individual has needs to be satisfied as well, as we have previously discussed. These needs form the basis for the expectations or demands placed on the organization by the individual. Employee need fulfillment and the feeling of belonging are both important to a healthy exchange and to organizational membership.[54] These needs may be conceptualized from the perspective of Maslow, Alderfer, Herzberg, or McClelland. When employees are well taken care of by the company, then they take care of the business even in very difficult times, as discussed in The Real World 5.2.

Contributions Just as each party to the exchange makes demands upon the other, each also has contributions to make to the relationship. These contributions are the basis for satisfying the demands expressed by the other party in the relationship. Employees are able to satisfy organizational demands through a range of contributions, including their skills, abilities, knowledge, energy, professional contacts, and native talents. As people grow and develop over time, they are able to increasingly satisfy the range of demands and expectations placed upon them by the organization.

In a similar fashion, organizations have a range of contributions available to the exchange relationship to meet individual needs. These contributions include salary, benefits, advancement opportunities, security, status, and social affiliation. Some organizations are richer in resources and better able to meet employee needs than others. Thus, one of the concerns that individuals and organizations alike have is whether the relationship is a fair deal or an equitable arrangement for both members.

Adams's Theory of Inequity

6 Describe how inequity influences motivation and can be resolved.

Blau's and Etzioni's ideas about social process and exchange provide a context for understanding fairness, equity, and inequity in work relationships. Stacy Adams explicitly developed the idea that *inequity* in the social exchange process is an important motivator. Adams's theory of inequity suggests that people are motivated when they find themselves in situations of inequity or unfairness.[55] Inequity occurs when a person receives more, or less, than the person believes is deserved based on effort and/or contribution. Inequity leads to the experience of tension, and tension motivates a person to act in a manner to resolve the inequity.

When does a person know that the situation is inequitable or unfair? Adams suggests that people examine the contribution portion of the exchange relationship just discussed. Specifically, individuals consider their inputs (their own contributions to the relationship) and their outcomes (the organization's contributions to the relationship). They then calculate an input/outcome ratio, which they compare with that of a generalized or comparison other. Figure 5.5 shows one equity situation and two inequity situations, one negative and one positive. For example, inequity in (b) could occur if the comparison other earned a higher salary, and inequity in (c) could occur if the person had more vacation time, in both cases all else being equal. Although not illustrated in the example, nontangible inputs, like emotional investment, and nontangible outcomes, like job satisfaction, may well enter into a person's equity equation.

inequity
The situation in which a person perceives he or she is receiving less than he or she is giving, or is giving less than he or she is receiving.

Be Nice . . . to Your Customers and Employees

Gerald Grinstein brought Delta Air Lines out of bankruptcy and into competition with the leading airlines in the industry. The strategy he used was simple: Be nice to your customers and employees. Grinstein came out of retirement in 2004 to take on this turnaround challenge based on the chance that he could return the company to its glory days. Delta was weighed down by $21 billion in debts and gasping for air in 2005. The company emerged from bankruptcy with new routes, new planes, and new financing, which gave the number-three airline a chance to challenge industry leaders American Airlines and United while attempting to beat back low-fare rivals Southwest and JetBlue. Grinstein had to take drastic action that made a lot of people unhappy. He reduced the workforce to 47,000 from 70,000, slashed salaries, and dramatically cut executive incentives. Everyone was in the same boat. Once things began to turn around, he planned to plow money back into employee pockets if the company could meet its financial goals after coming out of bankruptcy. Was it ugly for employees? Absolutely! How-

© ERIK S. LESSER/BLOOMBERG NEWS/LANDOV

Gerald Grinstein brought Delta Air Lines out of bankruptcy and into competition with the airline industry's leaders with a simple strategy: Be nice to your customers and employees.

ever, employees are now working together at Delta, and Grinstein knew that the company needed happy workers in the long run. As he gets ready to retire—again—he is leaving a legacy of happier and more productive Delta employees who came through a tough challenge successfully.

SOURCE: M. Tatge, "Out of the Woods," *Forbes* 179 (May 21, 2007): 44.

FIGURE 5.5 Equity and Inequity at Work

	Person	Comparison other
(a) Equity	$\dfrac{\text{Outcomes}}{\text{Inputs}}$ =	$\dfrac{\text{Outcomes}}{\text{Inputs}}$
(b) Negative Inequity	$\dfrac{\text{Outcomes}}{\text{Inputs}}$ <	$\dfrac{\text{Outcomes}}{\text{Inputs}}$
(c) Positive Inequity	$\dfrac{\text{Outcomes}}{\text{Inputs}}$ >	$\dfrac{\text{Outcomes}}{\text{Inputs}}$

Pay inequity has been a particularly thorny issue for women in some professions and companies. Eastman Kodak and other companies have made real progress in addressing the problem through pay equity.[56] As organizations become increasingly international, it may be difficult to determine pay and benefit equity/inequity across national borders.

Adams would consider the inequity in Figure 5.5(b) to be a first level of inequity. A more severe, second level of inequity would occur if the comparison other's inputs were lower than the person's. Inequalities in one (inputs or outcomes) coupled with equality in the other (inputs or outcomes) are experienced as a less severe inequity than inequalities in both inputs and outcomes. Adams's theory, however, does not provide a way of determining if some inputs (such as effort or experience) or some outcomes are more important or weighted more than others, such as a degree or certification.

The Resolution of Inequity

Once a person establishes the existence of an inequity, a number of strategies can be used to restore equity to the situation. Adams's theory provides seven basic strategies: (1) alter the person's outcomes, (2) alter the person's inputs, (3) alter the comparison other's outcomes, (4) alter the comparison other's inputs, (5) change who is used as a comparison other, (6) rationalize the inequity, and (7) leave the organizational situation.

Within each of the first four strategies, a wide variety of tactics can be employed. For example, if an employee has a strategy to increase his or her income by $11,000 per year to restore equity, the tactic might be a meeting between the employee and his or her manager concerning the issue of salary equity. The person would present relevant data on the issue. Another tactic would be to work with the company's compensation specialists. A third tactic would be to bring the matter before an equity committee in the company. A fourth tactic would be to seek advice from the legal department.

The selection of a strategy and a set of tactics is a sensitive issue with possible long-term consequences. In this example, a strategy aimed at reducing the comparison other's outcomes may have the desired short-term effect of restoring equity while having adverse long-term consequences in terms of morale and productivity. Similarly, the choice of legal tactics may result in equity but have the long-term consequence of damaged relationships in the workplace. Therefore, as a person formulates the strategy and tactics to restore equity, the range of consequences of alternative actions must be taken into account. Hence, not all strategies or tactics are equally preferred. The equity theory does not include a hierarchy predicting which inequity reduction strategy a person will or should choose.

Field studies on equity theory suggest that it may help explain important organizational behaviors. For example, one study found that workers who perceived compensation decisions as equitable displayed greater job satisfaction and organizational commitment.[57] In addition, equity theory may play an important role in labor–management relationships with regard to union-negotiated benefits.

New Perspectives on Equity Theory

Since the original formulation of the theory of inequity, now usually referred to as equity theory, a number of revisions have been made in light of new theories and research. One important theoretical revision proposes three types of individuals based on preferences for equity.[58] *Equity sensitives* are those people who prefer equity

equity sensitive

An individual who prefers an equity ratio equal to that of his or her comparison other.

based on the originally formed theory. Equity sensitivity contributes significantly to variation in free time spent working.[59] *Benevolents* are people who are comfortable with an equity ratio less than that of their comparison other, as exhibited in the Calvinistic heritage of the Dutch.[60] These people may be thought of as givers. *Entitleds* are people who are comfortable with an equity ratio greater than that of their comparison other, as exhibited by some offspring of the affluent who want and expect more.[61] These people may be thought of as takers. Females and minorities have not always been equitably treated in business and commerce.

Research on organizational justice has a long history.[62] One study suggests that a person's organizational position influences self-imposed performance expectations.[63] Specifically, a two-level move up in an organization with no additional pay creates a higher self-imposed performance expectation than a one-level move up with modest additional pay. Similarly, a two-level move down in an organization with no reduction in pay creates a lower self-imposed performance expectation than a one-level move down with a modest decrease in pay. This suggests that organizational position may be more important than pay in determining the level of a person's performance expectations.

One of the unintended consequences of inequity and organizational injustice is dysfunctional behavior. Organizational injustice caused by payment inequity can even lead to insomnia, though the effects are reduced by training in interactional justice.[64] More seriously, workplace injustice can trigger aggressive reactions or other forms of violent and deviant behavior that do harm to both individuals and the organization. Fortunately, only a small number of individuals respond to such unfairness through dysfunctional behavior.[65]

Although most studies of equity theory take a short-term perspective, equity comparisons over the long term should be considered as well. Increasing, decreasing, or constant experiences of inequity over time may have very different consequences for people.[66] For example, do increasing experiences of inequity have a debilitating effect on people? In addition, equity theory may help companies implement two-tiered wage structures, such as the one used by American Airlines in the early 1990s. In a two-tiered system, one group of employees receives different pay and benefits than another group. A study of 1,935 rank-and-file members in one retail chain using a two-tiered wage structure confirmed the predictions of equity theory.[67] The researchers suggest that unions and management may want to consider work location and employment status (part-time versus full-time) prior to the implementation of a two-tiered system.

© DYNAMIC GRAPHICS/JUPITERIMAGES

One study on organizational justice suggests that a person's organizational position influences self-imposed performance expectations.

EXPECTANCY THEORY OF MOTIVATION

Whereas equity theory focuses on a social exchange process, Vroom's expectancy theory of motivation focuses on personal perceptions of the performance process. His theory is founded on the basic notions that people desire certain outcomes of behavior and performance, which may be thought of as rewards or consequences of behavior, and that they believe there are relationships between the effort they put forth, the performance they achieve, and the outcomes they receive. Expectancy theory is a cognitive process theory of motivation.

The key constructs in the expectancy theory of motivation are the *valence* of an outcome, *expectancy*, and *instrumentality*.[68] Valence is the value or importance one places on a particular reward. Expectancy is the belief that effort leads to performance (for example, "If I try harder, I can do better"). Instrumentality is the belief that performance is related to rewards (for example, "If I perform better, I will get

benevolent

An individual who is comfortable with an equity ratio less than that of his or her comparison other.

entitled

An individual who is comfortable with an equity ratio greater than that of his or her comparison other.

(7) Describe the expectancy theory of motivation.

valence

The value or importance one places on a particular reward.

expectancy

The belief that effort leads to performance.

instrumentality

The belief that performance is related to rewards.

FIGURE 5.6 An Expectancy Model for Motivation

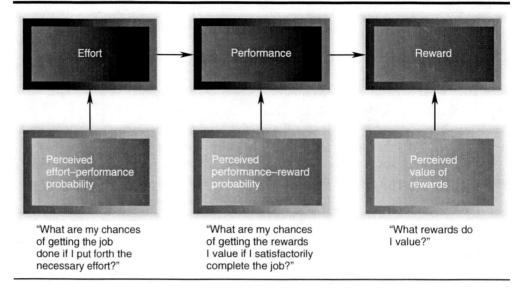

"What are my chances of getting the job done if I put forth the necessary effort?"

"What are my chances of getting the rewards I value if I satisfactorily complete the job?"

"What rewards do I value?"

more pay"). A model for the expectancy theory notions of effort, performance, and rewards is depicted in Figure 5.6.

Valence, expectancy, and instrumentality are all important to a person's motivation. Expectancy and instrumentality concern a person's beliefs about how effort, performance, and rewards are related. For example, a person may firmly believe that an increase in effort has a direct, positive effect on performance and that a reduced amount of effort results in a commensurate reduction in performance. Another person may have a very different set of beliefs about the effort–performance link. The person might believe that regardless of the amount of additional effort put forth, no improvement in performance is possible. Therefore, the perceived relationship between effort and performance varies from person to person and from activity to activity.

In a similar fashion, people's beliefs about the performance–reward link vary. One person may believe that an improvement in performance has a direct, positive effect on the rewards received, whereas another person may believe that an improvement in performance has no effect on the rewards received. Again, the perceived relationship between performance and rewards varies from person to person and from situation to situation. From a motivation perspective, it is the person's belief about the relationships between these constructs that is important, not the actual nature of the relationship. During volatile times in business, the performance–reward linkage may be confusing.

Expectancy theory has been used by managers and companies to design motivation programs.[69] Sometimes called *performance planning and evaluation systems,* these motivation programs are designed to enhance a person's belief that effort would lead to better performance and that better performance would lead to merit pay increases and other rewards. Valence and expectancy are particularly important in establishing priorities for people pursuing multiple goals.[70]

A person's motivation increases along with his or her belief that effort leads to performance and that performance leads to rewards, assuming the person wants the rewards. This is the third key idea within the expectancy theory of motivation. It is the idea that the valence, or value, that people place on various rewards varies. One person prefers salary to benefits, whereas another person prefers the reverse. All people do not place the same value on each reward. Expectancy theory has been used in a wide variety of contexts, including test-taking motivation among students.[71]

Motivational Problems

Within the expectancy theory framework, motivational problems stem from three basic causes: disbelief in a relationship between effort and performance, disbelief in a relationship between performance and rewards, and lack of desire for the rewards offered.

If the motivational problem is related to the person's belief that effort will not result in performance, the solution lies in altering this belief. The person can be shown how an increase in effort, or an alteration in the kind of effort put forth, can be converted into improved performance. For example, the textbook salesperson who does not believe more calls (effort) will result in greater sales (performance) might be shown how to distinguish departments with high-probability sales opportunities from those with low-probability sales opportunities. Hence, more calls (effort) can be converted into greater sales (performance).

If the motivational problem is related to the person's belief that performance will not result in rewards, the solution lies in altering this belief. The person can be shown how an increase in performance or a somewhat altered form of performance will be converted into rewards. For example, the textbook salesperson who does not believe greater sales (performance) will result in overall higher commissions (rewards) might be shown computationally or graphically that a direct relationship does exist. Hence, greater sales (performance) are directly converted into higher commissions (rewards).

If the motivational problem is related to the value the person places on, or the preference the person has for, certain rewards, the solution lies in influencing the value placed on the rewards or altering the rewards themselves. For example, the textbook salesperson may not particularly want higher commissions, given the small incremental gain he would receive at his tax level. In this case, the company might establish a mechanism for sheltering commissions from being taxed or alternative mechanisms for deferred compensation.

Research results on expectancy theory have been mixed.[72] The theory has been shown to predict job satisfaction accurately.[73] However, the theory's complexity makes it difficult to test the full model, and the measures of instrumentality, valence, and expectancy have only weak validity.[74] In addition, measuring the expectancy constructs is time consuming, and the values for each construct change over time for an individual. Finally, a theory assumes the individual is totally rational and acts as a minicomputer, calculating probabilities and values. In reality, the theory may be more complex than people as they typically function.

Motivation and Moral Maturity

Expectancy theory would predict that people work to maximize their personal outcomes. This is consistent with Adam Smith's ideas of working for one's own self-interest. Ultimately, Smith and expectancy theories believe that people work to benefit themselves alone. Expectancy theory would not explain altruistic behavior for the benefit of others. Therefore, it may be necessary to consider an individual's *moral maturity* in order to better understand altruistic, fair, and equitable behavior. Moral maturity is the measure of a person's cognitive moral development, which was discussed in Chapter 4. Morally mature people act and behave based on universal ethical principles, whereas morally immature people act and behave based on egocentric motivations.[75]

moral maturity
The measure of a person's cognitive moral development.

Cultural Differences in Motivation

(8) Describe the cultural differences in motivation.

Most motivation theories in use today have been developed by, and are about, Americans.[76] When researchers have examined the universality of these theories, they have found cultural differences, at least with regard to Maslow's, McClelland's, and Herzberg's theories. For example, while self-actualization may be the pinnacle need for Americans in Maslow's need hierarchy, security may be the most important need for people in cultures such as Greece and Japan who have a high need to avoid uncertainty.[77] Although achievement is an important need for Americans, research noted earlier in the chapter suggested that other cultures do not value achievement as much as Americans do.

The two-factor theory has been tested in other countries as well. Results in New Zealand did not replicate the results found in the United States; supervision and interpersonal relationships were important motivators in New Zealand rather than hygienic factors as in America.[78] Equity theory is being examined in cross-cultural contexts, leading to a reexamination of equity preferences, selection of referent others, and reactions to inequity.[79] Finally, expectancy theory may hold up very nicely in cultures that value individualism but break down in more collectivist cultures that value cooperative efforts. In collectivist cultures, rewards are more closely tied to group and team efforts, thus rendering unnecessary the utility of expectancy theory.

MANAGERIAL IMPLICATIONS: MANY WAYS TO MOTIVATE PEOPLE

Managers must realize that all motivation theories are not equally good or equally useful. The later motivation theories, such as the equity and expectancy theories, may be more scientifically sound than earlier theories, such as the two-factor theory. Nevertheless, the older theories of motivation have conceptual value, show us the importance of human needs, and provide a basis for the later theories. The individual, internal theories of motivation and the individual–environment interaction process theories uniquely contribute to our overall understanding of human behavior and motivation at work.

Managers cannot assume they understand employees' needs. They should recognize the variety of needs that motivate employee behavior and ask employees for input to better understand their needs. Individual employees differ in their needs, and managers should be sensitive to ethnic, national, gender, and age differences in this regard. Employees with high needs for power must be given opportunities to exercise influence, and employees with high needs for achievement must be allowed to excel at work.

Managers can increase employee motivation by training (increased perceptions of success because of increased ability), coaching (increased confidence), and task assignments (increased perceptions of success because of more experience). Managers should ensure that rewards are contingent on good performance and that valued rewards, such as time off or flexible work schedules, are available. Managers must understand what their employees want.

Finally, managers should be aware that morally mature employees are more likely to be sensitive to inequities at work. At the same time, these employees are less likely to be selfish or self-centered and more likely to be concerned about equity issues for all employees. Morally mature employees will act ethically for the common good of all employees and the organization.

Balance: Not Just for Working Moms Anymore

"Once upon a time—several decades ago—there was a clear divide between the roles of mothers and fathers. Mothers stayed home and took care of the kids and fathers went to work." That was the lead-in to an ABC television news story in June 2007. According to the story, the number of mothers working outside the home doubled to 80 percent in the past 40 years. This increase of women in the workforce has led many men to break from their traditional roles as the sole breadwinners of the family and embrace their new roles as "co-parents."

Bryan and Lisa Levey of Lexington, Massachusetts, are prime examples of how gender roles have converged. They both have careers yet they both share equally in the household duties—cooking, doing the laundry, helping with homework, and chauffeuring their two young children. Sharing the responsibilities takes the pressure off Lisa to be the primary caregiver and Bryan to be the primary breadwinner. Says Bryan,

"Having the work/life balance is very critical to both of our [his and Lisa's] happiness."

Bryan's happiness has not come without a price, however. He has had to forgo at least one promotion in order to spend less time at the office and more time at home with his family. Bryan is fine with the choices that he's made. "Maybe I could have been at the top of a business at a young age, but I probably wouldn't have been very happy, so what's the point?"

1. What effect will gender convergence have on the ways in which companies motivate and reward its employees?
2. Do you think men who have chosen to spend more time at home will be stigmatized at work for the choice they've made? Why or why not? If so, how can they address such stigmatization?

SOURCE: B. Stark, "Dad: 'I Can't Stay for That Meeting,'" *ABC News*, June 16, 2007. http://abcnews.go.com.

LOOKING BACK: AMERICAN EXPRESS

Wanji Walcott, VP and Mother of Two

Wanji Walcott is an American Express Vice President and Chief Technology Counsel.[80] She is one of the company's many women leaders who has grown, developed, and advanced professionally. Walcott is a mother of two and lives in New York City. In addition to her professional and personal lives, she has a life of community service as well, whether coordinating pro bono corporate counsel services for those in need or fighting heart disease. She led American Express's 18-member team in the 2006–2007 Wall Street Run and Heart Walk, which made a contribution of $1,410,000 to fight heart disease, the leading cause of death for American women and men. She is an active, caring, contributing leader on many fronts. She did not start as a leader.

Walcott credits American Express's culture with providing the flexibility she needed to balance work and family, primarily through her telecommuting arrangements. In addition, the company's leadership development and talent assessment programs had a direct impact on her career advancement through the ranks. At American Express, women, including the company's general counsel, fill key executive positions. As a result, Walcott had lots of positive role models as she formed and advanced her career plan. Because the company encourages networking, she got involved in employee networks that afforded her valuable opportunities for informal mentoring and networking. While formal mentoring programs can add value to individual careers, informal mentoring has always been a powerful help for rising leaders in all industries and professions.

While informal mentoring and networking are essential, American Express works to ensure fairness and equity within its family-friendly systems. To do this, the company provides managers with detailed selection criteria, user guides, and a sample case study of successful flexible work arrangements. It's important to assess in determining whether a flexible schedule is the right fit for the employee and the company. The objective is to create a win-win dynamic through which employee needs are met and the company's goals are achieved. Because Walcott has two children, the company's child-care initiatives are important to her as well. American Express boasts eight free backup-care facilities throughout the United States while, as noted in Thinking Ahead, supporting appropriate business travel with children. In addition, new moms can take up to twelve weeks off after the birth of their child, receiving full pay for four weeks and partial pay for two.

Chapter Summary

1. Early economic theories of motivation emphasized extrinsic incentives as the basis for motivation and technology as a force multiplier.

2. Maslow's hierarchy of needs theory of motivation was the basis for McGregor's Theory X and Theory Y assumptions about people at work.

3. According to McClelland, the needs for achievement, power, and affiliation are learned needs that differ among diverse cultures.

4. The two-factor theory found that the presence of motivation factors led to job satisfaction, and the presence of hygiene factors prevented job dissatisfaction.

5. New ideas in motivation emphasize eustress, hope, positive energy, and full engagement.

6. Social exchange theory holds that people form calculated working relationships and expect fair, equitable, ethical treatment.

7. Expectancy theory says that effort is the basis for motivation and that people want their effort to lead to performance and rewards.

8. Theories of motivation are culturally bound, and differences occur among nations.

Key Terms

benevolent (p. 169)
entitled (p. 169)
equity sensitive (p. 168)
eustress (p. 163)
expectancy (p. 169)
hygiene factor (p. 160)
inequity (p. 166)

instrumentality (p. 169)
moral maturity (p. 171)
motivation (p. 152)
motivation factor (p. 160)
need for achievement (p. 158)
need for affiliation (p. 159)
need for power (p. 159)

need hierarchy (p. 156)
psychoanalysis (p. 153)
self-interest (p. 154)
Theory X (p. 157)
Theory Y (p. 157)
valence (p. 169)

Review Questions

1. How can knowledge of motivation theories help managers?

2. What are the five categories of motivational needs described by Maslow? Give an example of how each can be satisfied.

3. What are the Theory X and Theory Y assumptions about people at work? How do they relate to the hierarchy of needs?

4. What three manifest needs does McClelland identify?

5. How do hygiene and motivational factors differ? What are the implications of the two-factor theory for managers?

6. What are two new ideas in motivation that managers are using?

7. How is inequity determined by a person in an organization? How can inequity be resolved if it exists?

8. What are the key concepts in the expectancy theory of motivation?

Discussion and Communication Questions

1. What do you think are the most important motivational needs for the majority of people? Do you think your needs differ from those of most people?

2. At what level in Maslow's hierarchy of needs are you living? Are you basically satisfied at this level?

3. Assume you are leaving your current job to look for employment elsewhere. What will you look for that you do not have now? If you do not have a job, assume you will be looking for one soon. What are the most important factors you will seek?

4. If you were being inequitably paid in your job, which strategy do you think would be the most helpful to you in resolving the inequity? What tactics would you consider using?

5. Do you believe you can do a better job of working or studying than you are currently doing? Do you think you would get more pay and benefits or better grades if you did a better job? Do you care about the rewards (or grades) in your organization (or university)?

6. What important experiences have contributed to your moral and ethical development? Are you working to further your own moral maturity at this time?

7. *(communication question)* Prepare a memo describing the two employees you work with who most closely operate according to Theory X and Theory Y assumptions about human nature. Be as specific and detailed in your description as you can, using quotes and/or observational examples.

8. *(communication question)* Develop an oral presentation about the most current management practices in employee motivation. Find out what at least four different companies are doing in this area. Be prepared to compare these practices with the theory and research in the chapter.

9. *(communication question)* Interview a manager and prepare a memo summarizing the relative importance she or he places on the needs for achievement, power, and affiliation. Include (a) whether these needs have changed over time and (b) what job aspects satisfy these needs.

Ethical Dilemma

Mitch heard the alarm blaring. "It couldn't be 5:00 a.m. already," he thought. He sat on the edge of the bed wondering how he had gotten himself into this mess. Mitch graduated from a good school with a bachelor's degree in management and a good GPA. He had dreams of a great job and a wonderful life. Instead, he found himself working 60 or more hours per week and feeling constantly pressured to work more.

Mitch started working at Acme, an electronics retailer, right out of college. At the time, the company recruiter had painted a picture of great opportunity for

the "right" people. Acme wanted employees who had a high need for achievement and a desire to attain positions of power and authority. It sounded perfect for Mitch. He knew he was executive material. The problem was that the company hired only people who were willing to go the extra mile.

Now, two years later, Mitch realized that the company was using his own personal needs against him. When he was hired by Acme, Mitch was told that the average workweek would be 50 hours. It was not the cushy job he had envisioned, but if it led to the advancement the company alluded to, it was well worth it. Although he was not required to go beyond the stated 50 hours, Mitch had never worked less than 60 hours and often approached 70. From day one, the company had pushed for full commitment. "The only way to advance is to prove yourself and your commitment to the company," was heard more than once. It was the mantra to every unit manager in the organization. Mitch was beginning to believe that the whole process had been a game. Acme hired employees who were highly motivated to achieve and then used that internal motivation against them to get as much pro-

ductivity from them as possible. The company caused managers to burn out and simply hired new ones when they left. Mitch had never felt so deceived and used.

Questions

1. Did Acme mislead Mitch and the other managers?

2. Does Acme have an obligation to its shareholders to maximize productivity and profitability?

3. Using consequential, rule-based, and character theories, evaluate Acme's hiring practices.

Experiential Exercises

5.1 What Do You Need from Work?

This exercise provides an opportunity to discuss your basic needs and those of other students in your class. Refer back to You 5.2, and look over your ranking of the ten possible job reward factors. Think about basic needs you may have that are possibly work related and yet would not be satisfied by one or another of these ten job reward factors.

Step 1. The class will form into groups of approximately six members each. Each group elects a spokesperson and answers the following questions. The group should spend at least five minutes on the first question and make sure each member of the group makes a contribution. The second question will probably take longer for your group to answer, up to fifteen minutes. The spokesperson should be ready to share the group's answers.

a. *What important basic needs do you have that are not addressed by one or another of these ten job reward factors?* Members should focus on the whole range of needs discussed in the different need theories of motivation covered in Chapter 5. Develop a list of the basic needs overlooked by these ten factors.

b. *What is important to members of your group?* Rank-order all job reward factors (the original ten and any new ones your group came up with in Step 1) in terms of their importance for your group. If group members disagree about the rankings, take time to discuss the differences among group members. Work for consensus and also note points of disagreement.

Step 2. Each group will share the results of its answers to the questions in Step 1. Cross-team questions and discussion follow.

Step 3. If your instructor has not already shared the normative data for 1,000 employees and their supervisors mentioned in You 5.2, the instructor may do that at this time.

Step 4 (Optional). Your instructor may ask you to discuss the similarities and differences in your group's rankings with the employee and supervisory normative rankings. If so, spend some time addressing two questions.

a. *What underlying reasons do you think may account for the differences that exist?*

b. *How have the needs of employees and supervisors changed over the past 20 years? Are they likely to change in the future?*

5.2 What to Do?

According to Stacy Adams, the experience of inequity or social injustice is a motivating force for human behavior. This exercise provides you and your group with a brief scenario of an inequity at work. Your task is to consider feasible actions for redress of this inequity.

John and Mary are full professors in the same medical school department of a large private university. As a private institution, neither the school nor the university makes the salaries and benefits of its faculty a matter of public record. Mary has pursued a long-term (fourteen years) career in the medical school, rising through the academic ranks while married to a successful businessman with whom she has raised three children. Her research and teaching contributions have been broad ranging and award winning. John joined the medical school within the last three years and was recruited for his leading-edge contribution to a novel line of research on a new procedure. Mary thought he was probably attracted with a comprehensive compensation package, yet she had no details until an administrative assistant gave her some information about salary and benefits a month ago. Mary learned that John's base contract salary is 16 percent higher than hers ($250,000 versus $215,000), that he was awarded an incentive pay component for the commercialization of his new procedure, and that he was given an annual discretionary travel budget of $35,000 and a membership in an exclusive private club. Mary is in a quandary about what to do. Given pressures from the board of trustees to hold down costs associated with public and private pressure to keep tuition increases low, Mary wonders how to begin to close this $70,000 inequity gap.

Step 1. Working in groups of six, discuss the equity issues in this medical school department situation using the text material on social exchange and equity theory. Do the outcome differences here appear to be based on gender, age, performance, or marital status? Do you need more information? If so, what would it be?

Step 2. Consider each of the seven strategies for the resolution of inequity as portrayed in this situation. Which ones are feasible to pursue based on what you know? Which ones are not feasible? Why? What are the likely consequences of each strategy or course of action? What would you advise Mary to do?

Step 3. Once your group has identified feasible resolution strategies, choose the best strategy. Next, develop a specific plan of action for Mary to follow in attempting to resolve the inequity so that she can achieve the experience and reality of fair treatment at work.

Step 4 (Optional). Your group may be asked to share its preferred strategy for this situation and your rationale for it.

Biz Flix | For Love of the Game

Billy Chapel (Kevin Costner), a 20-year veteran pitcher for the Detroit Tigers, learns just before the season's last game that the team's new owners want to trade him. He also learns that his partner, Jane Aubrey (Kelly Preston), intends to leave him. Faced with these daunting blows, Chapel wants to pitch a perfect final game. Director Sam Raimi's love of baseball shines through in some striking visual effects.

The scene from *For Love of the Game* is a slightly edited version of the "Just Throw" sequence that begins the film's exciting closing scenes. In this scene, Tigers' catcher Gus Sinski (John C. Reilly) comes out to the pitching mound to talk to Chapel. It is the beginning of Chapel's last game.

What to Watch for and Ask Yourself:

> At what level are Billy Chapel's esteem needs at this point in the game?

> Do you expect Gus Sinski's talk to have any effect on Chapel? If it will, what effect do you expect it to have?

> What rewards potentially exist for Billy Chapel? Remember, this is the last baseball game of his career.

Workplace Video | Motivation, Featuring Washburn Guitar

Washburn Guitar has been making high-quality musical instruments since 1883. The Chicago-based manufacturer sells 50,000 acoustic and electric guitars each year, totaling $40 million in annual revenues. At the heart of Washburn's enduring success is a rich guitar-making tradition developed and maintained by the company's skilled craftsmen.

Manufacturing quality instruments is labor-intensive work, and crafting guitars that look, play, and sound just right is the job of Washburn's highly motivated production teams. Some employees in the guitar shop are motivated by a kind of rock 'n' roll "cool factor"—a personal satisfaction that comes from being connected to rock music culture. Other Washburn shop workers are passionate about their jobs because they, like their customers, play guitar and can appreciate well-made instruments. "I would say 95 percent of the employees play an instrument," states Kevin Lello, VP of marketing at Washburn. "It really improves the quality of all of our instruments because they have a passion for what they are doing."

Although many intrinsic and extrinsic factors motivate Washburn employees to give their all on the job, watching a guitar progress from the design phase to the manufacturing floor to the artist on stage may be the ultimate thrill for a guitar maker. "One of the biggest motivational factors for me," says Washburn Production Manager Gil Vasquez, "is when you're done with a guitar and have taken it from the drawing board to the manufacturing point and have given it to the artist. Watching him play it on stage, it's like validation."

Many well-known performing artists have played Washburn guitars over the years, including Greg Allman, George Harrison, and Robert Plant. More recent Washburn strummers include members of Weezer, The All-American Rejects, and Modest Mouse. Dan Donegan, the hard-rocking axe-player of Disturbed, plays his very own signature-series model, the Maya Pro DD75.

While Washburn guitars occupy an esteemed place in rock history, it's the behind-the-scenes effort from Washburn's dedicated craftsmen that makes the brand tops with customers. The company's custom shop output has grown from 20 guitars to 300 guitars per month, and a recent merger with Parker Guitars has added even more quality and volume to the production process. Washburn employees relish their role in the company's success. "It's a labor of love," says Vasquez.

Discussion Questions

1. What motivates Washburn's employees to produce high-quality guitars?

2. Do rock star endorsements of Washburn guitars constitute a motivation factor or a hygiene factor, according to Herzberg's two-factor theory of motivation?

3. Should managers at Washburn adopt Theory X assumptions or Theory Y assumptions when seeking new ways to motivate employees? Explain.

High Expectations for
the Disney–Pixar Merger

On January 24, 2006, Pixar Animation Studios and The Walt Disney Company entered into a merger agreement to make Pixar a wholly owned subsidiary of Disney. The deal was consummated on May 5, 2006 for a purchase price of $7.4 billion.[1] Previously, the two companies had a business arrangement wherein Disney marketed and distributed Pixar's animated feature films, including *Toy Story 2*, *Finding Nemo*, *Cars*, *A Bug's Life*, and *The Incredibles*, among others.[2] As part of the merger agreement, Steve Jobs, Pixar's chairman and CEO, became Disney's largest stockholder and assumed a seat on Disney's board of directors. Another key part of the deal included installing two key Pixar executives into positions at Disney. John Lasseter, Pixar's top creative executive, now oversees development of movies at both Pixar's and Disney's animation studios, and Edwin Catmull, Pixar's president and technology chief, runs the business side for both studios.[3]

The merger is expected to have far-reaching results. Writing in *Business Week,* Peter Burrows and his colleagues observe that if Steve Jobs "can bring to Disney the same kind of industry-shaking, boundary-busting energy that has lifted Apple and Pixar sky-high, he could help the staid company become the leading laboratory for media convergence."[4] Jobs himself thinks the future will be very exciting for the Disney–Pixar merger.

What did Jobs, Lasseter, and Catmull accomplish at Pixar that brings so much excitement and high expectations to the merger? The three men are visionaries. In the mid-1980s, Jobs saw the potential when "Catmull and Lasseter believed they could use computer animation to create full-length movies, even though many in Hollywood and at Disney thought computers could never deliver the nuance and emotion of hand-drawn animation."[5] In continually achieving this vision, Pixar executives ensure that every movie gets the best efforts of the company's "brainy staff of animators, storytellers, and technologists."[6]

The creative staff is responsible for creating, writing, and animating all of Pixar's films. "Pixar strives to hire animators who have superior acting ability—those able to bring characters and inanimate objects to life, as though they have their own thought processes."[7] Lasseter, who guides the creative inspiration, maintains that good animated filmmaking is more about good storytelling than it is about innovative technology. Pixar makes films with a story that both make people laugh and grab their emotions. Technology helps to tell the story; it supports and enhances creativity. However, Lasseter maintains that animated film failures are never about bad technology but are always about bad storytelling.[8]

Pixar brings to the merger some very innovative proprietary technology that both reflects technical creativity and enables and supports animation creativity. With the technology side being led by Catmull, Pixar has developed several animation software packages including Marionette™, Ringmaster™, RenderMan®, and Luxo. Each is a proprietary software system that supports different aspects of computerized animation. RenderMan, for instance, is used to synthesize high-quality, photo-realistic images. Luxo allows fewer people to do more work, thus enhancing productivity. It also promotes creativity by automatically making adjustments to the animation environment when changes are made, for example, in the appearance of animated characters.[9]

Pixar's technological and creative genius has resulted in widespread acclaim and numerous film industry awards. The Academy of Motion Picture Arts and Sciences recognized the technical and creative advancements exemplified by RenderMan by awarding an Oscar to Catmull, Loren Carpenter, (senior scientist), and Rob Cook (vice president of software engineering). In total, Catmull has won three Scientific and Technical Engineering Awards. The Producer's Guild of America honored Pixar for achievement in new media and technology with its first Vanguard Award in 2002. Lasseter has won two Oscars for his direction of animated films. In 2004, the Art Directors Guild also honored Lasseter with its Outstanding Contribution to Cinematic Imagery award.[10] Over the years, "Pixar Animation Studios and its employees have received more than 100 awards and nominations for animated films, commercials and technical contributions."[11]

While Pixar's key employees receive significant financial incentives, this does not seem to be the force that drives them; rather, it is the creative freedom they are granted. Andrew Stanton, one of the cowriters and codirectors of *Finding Nemo*, is impressed with the creativity and quality of people at Pixar. He observes that people outside of Pixar "pale in comparison."[12] Pixar has created a working environment and working conditions that help to attract, motivate, and retain quality employees. "The enviably progressive working environment nurtures and sustains creativity, and the dividend has been a box-office winning streak that stands in notable contrast to the hit-and-miss model of almost every other movie studio."[13]

Discussion Questions

1. What needs does Pixar appeal to through its commitment to creative innovation and excellence?

2. What is important to you in terms of your personal work motivation? How do the things that motivate you fit with Pixar's approach to motivating employees?

3. Using the model of the individual–organizational exchange relationship shown in Figure 5.4, explain the relationship that Pixar seeks to develop with its employees. How might this exchange relationship influence the employees' perceptions of equity?

SOURCE: This case was written by Michael K. McCuddy, The Louis S. and Mary L. Morgal Chair of Christian Business Ethics and Professor of Management, College of Business Administration, Valparaiso University.

CASE

Learning and Performance Management

After reading this chapter, you should be able to do the following:

1 Define *learning, reinforcement, punishment, extinction,* and *goal setting.*

2 Distinguish between classical and operant conditioning.

3 Explain the use of positive and negative consequences of behavior in strategies of reinforcement and punishment.

4 Identify the purposes of goal setting and five characteristics of effective goals.

5 Describe 360-degree feedback.

6 Compare individual and team-oriented reward systems.

7 Describe strategies for correcting poor performance.

THINKING AHEAD: TOYOTA

Details, Corrective Adjustment, and Frugality

In the first quarter of 2007, Toyota surpassed General Motors (GM) as the top seller of cars and trucks for the first time ever.[1] This was a ground-shifting, trend-breaking milestone for the Japanese automotive manufacturer, as it sold 2,350,000 vehicles worldwide during the period of January through March 2007, a 9 percent increase. This is compared to 2,260,000 vehicles for GM during the same period, a 3 percent gain. Thus, Toyota outsold GM by 90,000 vehicles. While GM CEO Rick Wagoner continuously vows that his company has no intention of ceding industry leadership to Toyota, the Japanese company pursues continuous improvement through its fanatical attention to detail, corrective adjustment, frugality, process redesign, and market adaptation. These learning-based principles have made the company very competitive and led to world-class performance in manufacturing. Toyota was not always so successful; it has earned and learned its way into its position of leadership.

Toyota's trajectory has not always been a smooth one. The company nearly went bankrupt in the early 1950s, and its first export to the United States (the Crown) was not well received. Toyota faced two hot blasts of protectionist sentiment in the late 1980s and mid-1990s. In this challenging context, the company's legendary production system leader

Taiichi Ohno established a set of in-house precepts that have paid off handsomely. Toyota's efficient and lean manufacturing system includes just-in-time delivery; continuous improvement (*kaizen*); mistake proofing (*pokayoke*); and *obeya*, or face-to-face brainstorming sessions between engineers, designers, marketing pros, and suppliers. These precepts helped to revolutionize car making in general, not just within Toyota but more broadly in global manufacturing. Quite a legacy!

Being number one is no guarantee of continuing success, as GM well knows and is still learning. The company is handicapped in its ability to engage in lean, rapid change and advancement by massive retiree pension obligations and a staggering health care tab. These are burdens that Toyota does not have. Toyota, however, is neither a flawless organization nor an untouchable one. The company knows this and does fear the "big-company disease" whose scariest symptom is complacency within the ranks. The disease includes a sense of satisfaction at becoming the industry leader and a sense of arrogance or entitlement from that success. Mindful of these risks associated with the successful culmination of its decades-long efforts, Toyota is concerned about losing its way. Safeguards include employing in-house gurus at its local plants and standardizing the act of immediately signaling superiors when things go wrong. Can Toyota keep learning and changing to ensure continuous advancement?

This is the second of two chapters addressing motivation and behavior. Chapter 5 emphasized internal and process theories of motivation. This chapter focuses on external theories of motivation and factors in the work environment that influence good and bad performance. The first section addresses learning theory and the use of reinforcement, punishment, and extinction at work. It also touches on Bandura's social learning theory and Jung's personality approach to learning. The second section presents theory, research, and practice related to goal setting in organizations. The third section addresses the definition and measurement of performance. The fourth section is concerned with rewarding performance. The fifth and concluding section addresses how to correct poor performance.

LEARNING IN ORGANIZATIONS

① Define *learning, reinforcement, punishment, extinction,* and *goal setting.*

learning

A change in behavior acquired through experience.

② Distinguish between classical and operant conditioning.

Learning is a change in behavior acquired through experience. Learning may begin with the cognitive activity of developing knowledge about a subject, which then leads to a change in behavior. Alternatively, the behaviorist approach to learning assumes that observable behavior is a function of its consequences. According to the behaviorists, learning has its basis in classical and operant conditioning. Learning helps guide and direct motivated behavior.

Classical Conditioning

Classical conditioning is the process of modifying behavior so that a conditioned stimulus is paired with an unconditioned stimulus and elicits an unconditioned response. It is largely the result of the research on animals (primarily dogs) by the Russian physiologist Ivan Pavlov.[2] Pavlov's professional exchanges with Walter B. Cannon and other American researchers during the early 1900s led to the application of his ideas in the United States.[3] Classical conditioning builds on the natural consequence of an unconditioned response to an unconditioned stimulus. In dogs, this might be the natural production of saliva (unconditioned response) in response to the presentation of meat (unconditioned stimulus). By presenting a conditioned stimulus (for example, a bell) simultaneously with the unconditioned stimulus (the meat), the researcher caused the dog to develop a conditioned response (salivation in response to the bell).

Classical conditioning may occur in a similar fashion in humans.[4] For example, a person working at a computer terminal may get lower back tension (unconditioned response) as a result of poor posture (unconditioned stimulus). If the person becomes aware of that tension only when the manager enters the work area (conditioned stimulus), then the person may develop a conditioned response (lower back tension) to the appearance of the manager.

Although this example is logical, classical conditioning has real limitations in its applicability to human behavior in organizations for at least three reasons. First, humans are more complex than dogs and less amenable to simple cause-and-effect conditioning. Second, the behavioral environments in organizations are complex and not very amenable to single stimulus–response manipulations. Third, complex human decision making makes it possible to override simple conditioning.

Operant Conditioning

Operant conditioning is the process of modifying behavior through the use of positive or negative consequences following specific behaviors. It is based on the notion that behavior is a function of its consequences,[5] which may be either positive or negative. The consequences of behavior are used to influence, or shape, behavior through three strategies: reinforcement, punishment, and extinction.

Organizational behavior modification (O.B. Mod., commonly known as OBM) is a form of operant conditioning used successfully in a variety of organizations to shape behavior by Luthans and his colleagues.[6] The three types of consequences used in OBM to influence behavior are financial reinforcement, nonfinancial reinforcement, and social reinforcement. A major review of the research on the influence of OBM in organizations found that it had significant and positive influence on task performance in both manufacturing and service organizations, but that the effects were most powerful in manufacturing organizations.[7] In a study of pay for performance, more productive employees chose pay for performance over fixed compensation when given a choice.[8] However, regardless of which pay scheme employees chose, all produced more under a pay for performance scheme.

classical conditioning
Modifying behavior so that a conditioned stimulus is paired with an unconditioned stimulus and elicits an unconditioned response.

operant conditioning
Modifying behavior through the use of positive or negative consequences following specific behaviors.

The Strategies of Reinforcement, Punishment, and Extinction

Reinforcement is used to enhance desirable behavior, and punishment and extinction are used to diminish undesirable behavior. The application of reinforcement theory is central to the design and administration of organizational reward systems. Well-designed reward systems help attract and retain the very best employees. Strategic rewards help motivate behavior, actions, and accomplishments, which advance the organization toward specific business goals.[9] Strategic rewards go beyond

(3) Explain the use of positive and negative consequences of behavior in strategies of reinforcement and punishment.

cash to include training and educational opportunities, stock options, and recognition awards such as travel. Strategic rewards are important positive consequences of people's work behavior.

Reinforcement and punishment are administered through the management of positive and negative consequences of behavior. *Positive consequences* are the results of a person's behavior that he or she finds attractive or pleasurable. They might include a pay increase, a bonus, a promotion, a transfer to a more desirable geographic location, or praise from a supervisor. *Negative consequences* are the results of a person's behavior that she or he finds unattractive or aversive. They might include disciplinary action, an undesirable transfer, a demotion, or harsh criticism from a supervisor. Positive and negative consequences must be defined for the person receiving them. Therefore, individual, gender, and cultural differences may be important in their classification.

The use of positive and negative consequences following a specific behavior either reinforces or punishes that behavior.[10] Thorndike's law of effect states that behaviors followed by positive consequences are more likely to recur, and behaviors followed by negative consequences are less likely to recur.[11] Figure 6.1 shows how positive and negative consequences may be applied or withheld in the strategies of reinforcement and punishment.

Reinforcement   *Reinforcement* is the attempt to develop or strengthen desirable behavior by either bestowing positive consequences or withholding negative consequences. Positive reinforcement results from the application of a positive consequence following a desirable behavior. Bonuses paid at the end of successful business years are an example of positive reinforcement. Marriott International provides positive reinforcement by honoring ten to twenty employees each year with its J. Willard Marriott Award of Excellence. Each awardee receives a medallion engraved with the words that express the basic values of the company: dedication, achievement, character, ideals, effort, and perseverance.

Negative reinforcement results from withholding a negative consequence when a desirable behavior occurs. For example, a manager who reduces an employee's

FIGURE **6.1**   Reinforcement and Punishment Strategies

	Reinforcement (desirable behavior)	**Punishment** (undesirable behavior)
Positive consequences	Apply	Withhold
Negative consequences	Withhold	Apply

pay (negative consequence) if the employee comes to work late (undesirable behavior) and refrains from doing so when the employee is on time (desirable behavior) has negatively reinforced the employee's on-time behavior. The employee avoids the negative consequence (a reduction in pay) by exhibiting the desirable behavior (being on time to work).

Either continuous or intermittent schedules of reinforcement may be used. These reinforcement schedules are described in Table 6.1. When managers design organizational reward systems, they consider not only the type of reinforcement but also how often the reinforcement should be provided.

Punishment *Punishment* is the attempt to eliminate or weaken undesirable behavior. It is used in two ways. One way to punish a person is to apply a negative consequence following an undesirable behavior. For example, a professional athlete who is excessively offensive to an official (undesirable behavior) may be ejected from a game (negative consequence). The other way to punish a person is to withhold a positive consequence following an undesirable behavior. For example, a salesperson

punishment
The attempt to eliminate or weaken undesirable behavior by either bestowing negative consequences or withholding positive consequences.

TABLE 6.1 Schedules of Reinforcement

Schedule	Description	Effects on Responding
Continuous	Reinforcer follows every response.	1. Steady high rate of performance as long as reinforcement follows every response
		2. High frequency of reinforcement may lead to early satiation
		3. Behavior weakens rapidly (undergoes extinction) when reinforcers are withheld
		4. Appropriate for newly emitted, unstable, low-frequency responses
Intermittent	Reinforcer does not follow every response.	1. Capable of producing high frequencies of responding
		2. Low frequency of reinforcement precludes early satiation
		3. Appropriate for stable or high-frequency responses
Fixed Ratio	A fixed number of responses must be emitted before reinforcement occurs.	1. A fixed ratio of 1:1 (reinforcement occurs after every response) is the same as a continuous schedule
		2. Tends to produce a high rate of response that is vigorous and steady
Variable Ratio	A varying or random number of responses must be emitted before reinforcement occurs.	Capable of producing a high rate of response that is vigorous, steady, and resistant to extinction
Fixed Interval	The first response after a specific period of time has elasped is reinforced.	Produces an uneven response pattern varying from a very slow, unenergetic response immediately following reinforcement to a very fast, vigorous response immediately preceding reinforcement
Variable Interval	The first response after varying or random periods of time have elapsed is reinforced.	Tends to produce a high rate of response that is vigorous, steady, and resistant to extinction

SOURCE: Table from *Organizational Behavior Modification* by Fred Luthans and Robert Kreitner. Copyright © 1985, p. 58, by Scott Foresman and Company and the authors. Reprinted by permission of the authors.

who makes few visits to companies (undesirable behavior) and whose sales are well below the quota (undesirable behavior) is likely to receive a very small commission check (positive consequence) at the end of the month.

One problem with punishment is that it may have unintended results. Because punishment is discomforting to the individual being punished, the experience of punishment may result in negative psychological, emotional, performance, or behavioral consequences. For example, the person being punished may become angry, hostile, depressed, or despondent. From an organizational standpoint, this result becomes important when the punished person translates negative emotional and psychological responses into negative actions. Threat of punishment can elicit fear, a management tool used by some leaders but not at Southwest Airlines, a company that emphasizes positive relationships.[12] Some fears are legitimate, as seen in Thinking Ahead with Toyota's fear of "big-company disease."

Extinction   An alternative to punishing undesirable behavior is *extinction*—the attempt to weaken a behavior by attaching no consequences (either positive or negative) to it. It is equivalent to ignoring the behavior. The rationale for using extinction is that a behavior not followed by any consequence is weakened. However, some patience and time may be needed for extinction to be effective.

Extinction may be practiced, for example, by not responding (no consequence) to the sarcasm (behavior) of a colleague. Extinction may be most effective when used in conjunction with the positive reinforcement of desirable behaviors. Therefore, in the example, the best approach might be to compliment the sarcastic colleague for constructive comments (reinforcing desirable behavior) while ignoring mocking comments (extinguishing undesirable behavior).

Extinction is not always the best strategy, however. In cases of dangerous behavior, punishment might be preferable to deliver a swift, clear lesson. It might also be preferable in cases of seriously undesirable behavior, such as employee embezzlement and other illegal or unethical behavior.

Bandura's Social Learning Theory

A social learning theory proposed by Albert Bandura is an alternative and complement to the behaviorist approaches of Pavlov and Skinner.[13] Bandura believes learning occurs through the observation of other people and the modeling of their behavior. Executives might teach their subordinates a wide range of behaviors, such as leader–follower interactions and stress management, by exhibiting these behaviors. Since employees look to their supervisors for acceptable norms of behavior, they are likely to pattern their own responses on the supervisor's.

Central to Bandura's social learning theory is the notion of *task-specific self-efficacy*, an individual's beliefs and expectancies about his or her ability to perform a specific task effectively. (Generalized self-efficacy was discussed in Chapter 3.) Individuals with high self-efficacy believe that they have the ability to get things done, that they are capable of putting forth the effort to accomplish the task, and that they can overcome any obstacles to their success. Self-efficacy is higher in a learning context than in a performance context, especially for individuals with a high learning orientation.[14] There are four sources of task-specific self-efficacy: prior experiences, behavior models (witnessing the success of others), persuasion from other people, and assessment of current physical and emotional capabilities.[15] Believing in one's own capability to get something done is an important facilitator of success. There is strong evidence that self-efficacy leads to high performance on a wide variety of physical and mental tasks.[16] High self-efficacy has also led to success in breaking addictions, increasing pain tolerance, and recovering from illnesses. Conversely,

extinction
The attempt to weaken a behavior by attaching no consequences to it.

task-specific self-efficacy
An individual's beliefs and expectancies about his or her ability to perform a specific task effectively.

success can enhance one's self-efficacy. For example, women who trained in physical self-defense increased their self-efficacy, both for specific defense skills and for coping in new situations.[17]

Alexander Stajkovic and Fred Luthans draw on Bandura's ideas of self-efficacy and social learning in expanding their original work in behavioral management and OBM into a more comprehensive framework for performance management.[18] Bandura saw the power of social reinforcement, recognizing that financial and material rewards often occur following or in conjunction with the approval of others, whereas undesirable experiences often follow social disapproval. Thus, self-efficacy and social reinforcement can be powerful influences over behavior and performance at work. A comprehensive review of 114 studies found that self-efficacy is positively and strongly related to work performance, especially for tasks that are not too complex.[19] Stajkovic and Luthans suggest that managers and supervisors can be confident that employees with high self-efficacy are going to perform well. The challenge managers face is how to select and develop employees so that they achieve high self-efficacy.

Managers can help employees in this process. The strongest way for an employee to develop self-efficacy is to succeed at a challenging task. Managers can help by providing job challenges, coaching and counseling for improved performance, and rewarding employees' achievements. Empowerment, or sharing power with employees, can be accomplished by interventions that help employees increase their self-esteem and self-efficacy. Given the increasing diversity of the workforce, managers may want to target their efforts toward women and minorities in particular. Research has indicated that these groups tend to have lower than average self-efficacy.[20] Counterintuitively in a training context, self-efficacy was negatively related to motivation and exam performance for students taking a series of five class exams despite a significant positive relationship with exam performance at the between-person level for these students.[21]

Learning and Personality Differences

The cognitive approach to learning mentioned at the beginning of the chapter is based on the *Gestalt* school of thought and draws on Jung's theory of personality differences (discussed in Chapter 3). Two elements of Jung's theory have important implications for learning and subsequent behavior.

The first element is the distinction between introverted and extraverted people. Introverts need quiet time to study, concentrate, and reflect on what they are learning. They think best when they are alone. Extraverts need to interact with other people, learning through the process of expressing and exchanging ideas with others. They think best in groups and while they are talking.

The second element is the personality functions of intuition, sensing, thinking, and feeling. These functions are listed in Table 6.2, along with their implications for learning by individuals. The functions of intuition and sensing determine the individual's preference for information gathering. The functions of thinking and feeling determine how the individual evaluates and makes decisions about newly acquired information.[22] Each person has a preferred mode of gathering information and a preferred mode of evaluating and making decisions about that information. For example, an intuitive thinker may want to skim research reports about implementing total quality programs and then, based on hunches, decide how to apply the research findings to the organization. A sensing feeler may prefer viewing videotaped interviews with people in companies that implemented total quality programs and then identify people in the organization most likely to be receptive to the approaches presented.

TABLE 6.2 Personality Functions and Learning

Personality Preference	Implications for Learning by Individuals
Information Gathering	
Intuitors	Prefer theoretical frameworks.
	Look for the meaning in material.
	Attempt to understand the grand scheme.
	Look for possibilities and interrelations.
Sensors	Prefer specific, empirical data.
	Look for practical applications.
	Attempt to master details of a subject.
	Look for what is realistic and doable.
Decision Making	
Thinkers	Prefer analysis of data and information.
	Work to be fair-minded and evenhanded.
	Seek logical, just conclusions.
	Do not like to be too personally involved.
Feelers	Prefer interpersonal involvement.
	Work to be tenderhearted and harmonious.
	Seek subjective, merciful results.
	Do not like objective, factual analysis.

SOURCE: O. Kroeger and J. M. Thuesen, *Type Talk: The 16 Personality Types That Determine How We Live, Love, and Work* (New York: Dell Publishing Co., 1989).

GOAL SETTING AT WORK

4 Identify the purposes of goal setting and five characteristics of effective goals.

Goal setting is the process of establishing desired results that guide and direct behavior. Goal-setting theory is based on laboratory studies, field research experiments, and comparative investigations by Edwin Locke, Gary Latham, John M. Ivancevich, and others.[23] Goals help crystallize the sense of purpose and mission that is essential to success at work. Priorities, purpose, and goals are important sources of motivation for people at work, often leading to collective achievement, even in difficult times. Managing yourself and setting your own work goals can contribute to a productive U.S. government management career as we see in The Real World 6.1.

Characteristics of Effective Goals

Various organizations define the characteristics of effective goals differently. For the former Sanger-Harris, a retail organization, the acronym SMART communicated the approach to effective goals. SMART stands for *S*pecific, *M*easurable, *A*ttainable, *R*ealistic, and *T*ime-bound. Five commonly accepted characteristics of effective goals are specific, challenging, measurable, time-bound, and prioritized.

Specific and challenging goals serve to cue or focus the person's attention on exactly what is to be accomplished and to arouse the person to peak performance. In a wide range of occupations, people who set specific, challenging goals consistently outperform those who have easy or unspecified goals, as Figure 6.2 shows. The unconscious may have a positive effect here too. Two studies of subconscious goal motivation found that subconscious goals significantly enhanced task performance

goal setting

The process of establishing desired results that guide and direct behavior.

Set Work Goals and Manage Yourself

The U.S. government can provide a great career, but if it is to be a productive one, you cannot rely solely on your boss. You have to manage yourself, set your own work goals, reward yourself when you do well, and penalize yourself when you do a poor job. This is especially true for mid-level federal managers, one of the most challenging positions in any organization and one that often gets overlooked. Underperformance frequently triggers immediate negative feedback and punishment while there may be little or no response to good performance. If a manager helps her or his employees set goals and provides feedback on goal progress, why not do the same for herself or himself? Setting work goals provides the standards for job performance and the necessary clarity concerning the most important work to be done. Once you set your own work goals, you can set up measures and feedback systems that allow you to know if you are making positive progress toward these goals. Any performance problems related to your work goals are likely to come quickly and clearly. Therefore, do not be worried about being overly self-critical concerning performance problems; think more about rewarding yourself. When federal managers perform well, do a great job, and achieve their work goals, they are encouraged to praise themselves. Praise breeds confidence, which breeds better performance. It begins with work goals and good self-management.

SOURCE: B. Friel, "Manage Yourself," *Government Executive* (May 1, 2007), http://www.govexec.com/features/0507-01/0507-01admm.htm.

for conscious difficult and do-best goals, though not for easy goals.[24] How difficult and challenging are your work or school goals? You 6.1 gives you an opportunity to evaluate your goals for five dimensions.

Measurable, quantitative goals are useful as a basis for feedback about goal progress. Qualitative goals are also valuable. The Western Company of North America (now part of BJ Services Company) allowed about 15 percent of a manager's goals to be of a qualitative nature.[25] A qualitative goal might be to improve relationships with customers. Further work might convert the qualitative goal into quantitative measures such as number of complaints or frequency of complimentary letters. In this case, however, the qualitative goal may well be sufficient and most meaningful.

FIGURE 6.2 Goal Level and Task Performance

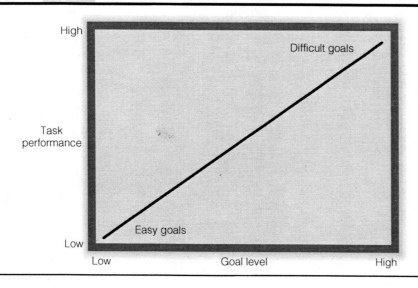

Task–Goal Attribute Questionnaire

Listed below is a set of statements that may or may not describe the job or school objectives toward which you are presently working. Please read each statement carefully and rate each on a scale from 1 (agree completely) to 7 (disagree completely) to describe your level of agreement or disagreement with the statement. *Please answer all questions.*

____ 1. I am allowed a high degree of influence in the determination of my work/school objectives.

____ 2. I should not have too much difficulty in reaching my work/school objectives; they appear to be fairly easy.

____ 3. I receive a considerable amount of feedback concerning my quantity of output on the job/in school.

____ 4. Most of my coworkers and peers try to outperform one another on their assigned work/school goals.

____ 5. My work/school objectives are very clear and specific; I know exactly what my job/assignment is.

____ 6. My work/school objectives will require a great deal of effort from me to complete them.

____ 7. I really have little voice in the formulation of my work/school objectives.

____ 8. I am provided with a great deal of feedback and guidance on the quality of my work.

____ 9. I think my work/school objectives are ambiguous and unclear.

____ 10. It will take a high degree of skill and know-how on my part to attain fully my work/school objectives.

____ 11. The setting of my work/school goals is pretty much under my own control.

____ 12. My boss/instructors seldom let(s) me know how well I am doing on my work toward my work/school objectives.

____ 13. A very competitive atmosphere exists among my peers and me with regard to attaining our respective work/school goals; we all want to do better than anyone else in attaining our goals.

____ 14. I understand fully which of my work/school objectives are more important than others; I have a clear sense of priorities on these goals.

____ 15. My work/school objectives are quite difficult to attain.

____ 16. My supervisor/instructors usually ask(s) for my opinions and thoughts when determining my work/school objectives.

Scoring:

Place your response (1 through 7) in the space provided. For questions 7, 12, 9, and 2, subtract your response from 8 to determine your adjusted score.

For each scale (e.g., participation in goal setting), add the responses and divide by the number of questions in the scale.

Participation in Goal Setting:
- Question 1 _____
- Question 7 (8 – _____) = _____
- Question 11 _____
- Question 16 _____
- Total divided by 4 = _____

Feedback on Goal Effort:
- Question 3 _____
- Question 8 _____
- Question 12 (8 – _____) = _____
- Total divided by 3 = _____

Peer Competition:
- Question 4 _____
- Question 13 _____
- Total divided by 2 = _____

Goal Specificity:
- Question 5 _____
- Question 9 (8 – _____) = _____
- Question 14 _____
- Total divided by 3 = _____

Goal Difficulty:
- Question 2 (8 – _____) = _____
- Question 6 _____
- Question 10 _____
- Question 15 _____
- Total divided by 4 = _____

Interpreting your average scale scores:

6 or 7 is very high on this task–goal attribute.

4 is a moderate level on this task–goal attribute.

1 or 2 is very low on this task–goal attribute.

SOURCE: Adapted from R. M. Steers, "Factors Affecting Job Attitudes in a Goal-Setting Environment," *Academy of Management Journal* 19 (1976): 9. Permission conveyed through Copyright Clearance Center, Inc.

Time-bound goals enhance measurability. The time limit may be implicit in the goal, or it may need to be made explicit. For example, without the six-month time limit, an insurance salesperson might think the sales goal is for the whole year rather than for six months. Many organizations work on standardized cycles, such as quarters or years, where very explicit time limits are assumed. If there is any uncertainty about the time period of the goal effort, the time limit should be explicitly stated.

The priority ordering of goals allows for effective decision making about resource allocation.[26] As time, energy, or other resources become available, a person can move down the list of goals in descending order. The key concern is with achieving the top-priority goals. Priority helps direct a person's efforts and behavior. Although these characteristics help increase motivation and performance, that is not the only function of goal setting in organizations. One new study of goal setting suggests that it may be a theory of ability as well as a theory of motivation, especially in a learning context versus a performance context.[27]

Goal setting serves one or more of three functions. First, it can increase work motivation and task performance.[28] Second, it can reduce the role stress that is associated with conflicting or confusing expectations.[29] Third, it can improve the accuracy and validity of performance evaluation.[30]

Increasing Work Motivation and Task Performance

Goals are often used to increase employee effort and motivation, which in turn improve task performance. The higher the goal, the better the performance; that is, people work harder to reach difficult goals. The positive relationship between goal difficulty and task performance is depicted in Figure 6.2.

Three important behavioral aspects of enhancing performance motivation through goal setting are employee participation, supervisory commitment, and useful performance feedback. Employee participation in goal setting leads to goal acceptance by employees. Goal acceptance is thought to lead to goal commitment and then to goal accomplishment. Special attention has been given to factors that influence commitment to difficult goals, such as participation in the process of setting the difficult goals.[31] Even in the case of assigned goals, goal acceptance and commitment are considered essential prerequisites to goal accomplishment.

Supervisory goal commitment is a reflection of the organization's commitment to goal setting. Organizational commitment is a prerequisite for successful goal-setting programs, such as management by objectives (MBO) programs.[32] The organization must be committed to the program, and the employee and supervisors must be committed to specific work goals as well as to the program. (MBO is discussed in more detail later in the chapter.)

The supervisor plays a second important role by providing employees with interim performance feedback on progress toward goals. Performance feedback is most useful when the goals are specific, and specific goals improve performance most when interim feedback is given.[33] When done correctly, negative performance feedback can lead to performance improvement.[34] For example, assume an insurance salesperson has a goal of selling $500,000 worth of insurance in six months but has sold only $200,000 after three months. During an interim performance feedback session, the supervisor may help the salesperson identify his problem—that he is not focusing his calls on the likeliest prospects. This useful feedback coupled with the specific goal helps the salesperson better focus his efforts to achieve the goal. Feedback is most helpful when it is useful (helping the salesperson identify high-probability prospects) and timely (halfway through the performance period).

Reducing Role Stress, Conflict, and Ambiguity

A second function of goal setting is to reduce the role stress associated with conflicting and confusing expectations. This is done by clarifying the task–role expectations communicated to employees. Supervisors, coworkers, and employees are all important sources of task-related information. A fourteen-month evaluation of goal setting in reducing role stress found that conflict, confusion, and absenteeism were all reduced through the use of goal setting.[35]

The improved role clarity resulting from goal setting may be attributable to improved communication between managers and employees. An early study of the MBO goal-setting program at Ford Motor Company found an initial 25 percent lack of agreement between managers and their bosses concerning the definition of the managers' jobs. Through effective goal-setting activities, this lack of agreement was reduced to about 5 percent.[36] At FedEx, managers are encouraged to include communication-related targets in their annual MBO goal-setting process.[37]

Improving Performance Evaluation

The third major function of goal setting is improving the accuracy and validity of performance evaluation. One of the best methods of doing so is to use *management by objectives (MBO)*—a goal-setting program based on interaction and negotiation between employees and managers. MBO programs have been pervasive in organizations for nearly 30 years.[38]

According to Peter Drucker, who originated the concept, the objectives-setting process begins with the employee writing an "employee's letter" to the manager. The letter explains the employee's general understanding of the scope of the manager's job, as well as the scope of the employee's own job, and lays out a set of specific objectives to be pursued over the next six months or year. After some discussion and negotiation, the manager and the employee finalize these items into a performance plan.

Drucker considers MBO a participative and interactive process. This does not mean that goal setting begins at the bottom of the organization. It means that goal setting is applicable to all employees, with lower-level organizational members and professional staff having a clear influence over the goal-setting process.[39] (The performance aspect of goal setting is discussed in the next section of the chapter.)

Goal-setting programs have operated under a variety of names, including goals and controls at Purex (now part of Dial Corporation), work planning and review at Black & Decker and General Electric, and performance planning and evaluation at IBM. Most of these programs are designed to enhance performance,[40] especially when incentives are associated with goal achievement.

The two central ingredients in goal-setting programs are planning and evaluation. The planning component consists of organizational and individual goal setting. Organizational goal setting is an essential prerequisite to individual goal setting; the two must be closely linked for the success of both.[41] At FedEx, all individual objectives must be tied to the overall corporate objectives of people, service, and profit.

In planning, discretionary control is usually given to individuals and departments to develop operational and tactical plans to support the corporate objectives. The emphasis is on formulating a clear, consistent, measurable, and ordered set of goals to articulate *what* to do. It is also assumed that operational support planning helps determine *how* to do it. The concept of intention is used to encompass both the goal (*what*) and the set of pathways that lead to goal attainment (*how*), thus recognizing the importance of both what and how.[42]

The evaluation component consists of interim reviews of goal progress, conducted by managers and employees, and formal performance evaluation. The reviews are midterm assessments designed to help employees take self-corrective action. They are not designed as final or formal performance evaluations. The formal performance evaluation occurs at the close of a reporting period, usually once a year. To be effective, performance reviews need to be tailored to the business, capture what goes on in the business, and easily changed when the business changes.[43]

Because goal-setting programs are somewhat mechanical by nature, they are most easily implemented in stable, predictable industrial settings. Although most programs allow for some flexibility and change, they are less useful in organizations where high levels of unpredictability exist, as in basic research and development, or where the organization requires substantial adaptation or adjustment. Finally, individual, gender, and cultural differences do not appear to threaten the success of goal-setting programs.[44] Thus, goal-setting programs may be widely applied and effective in a diverse workforce.

PERFORMANCE: A KEY CONSTRUCT

Goal setting is designed to improve work performance, an important organizational behavior directly related to the production of goods or the delivery of services. Performance is most often thought of as task accomplishment, the term *task* coming from Taylor's early notion of a worker's required activity.[45] Some early management research found performance standards and differential piece-rate pay to be key ingredients in achieving high levels of performance, while other early research found stress helpful in improving performance up to an optimum point.[46] Hence, outcomes and effort are both important for good performance. That is not all that is needed to excel in talent management at General Electric, as we see in The Real World 6.2.

Predicting job performance has been a concern for over 100 years. Early theories around the time of World War I focused on the importance of intelligence and general mental ability (GMA). Research has found GMA highly predictive of job knowledge in both civilian and military jobs.[47] Equally important to predicting job performance is defining the term.

Performance Management

Performance management is a process of defining, measuring, appraising, providing feedback on, and improving performance.[48] The skill of defining performance in behavioral terms is an essential first step in the performance management process. Once defined, performance can be measured and assessed. This information about performance can then be fed back to the individual and used as a basis for setting goals and establishing plans for improving performance. Positive performance behaviors should be rewarded, and poor performance behaviors should be corrected. This section of the chapter focuses on defining, measuring, appraising, and providing feedback on performance. The last two sections of the chapter focus on rewarding, correcting, and improving performance.

Defining Performance

Performance must be clearly defined and understood by the employees who are expected to perform well at work. Performance in most lines of work is multidimensional. For example, a sales executive's performance may require administrative and financial skills along with the interpersonal skills needed to motivate a sales force. Or a medical doctor's performance may demand the positive interpersonal

performance management
A process of defining, measuring, appraising, providing feedback on, and improving performance.

Seven Keys for Talent Management at GE

General Electric's legendary reputation for talent management owes much to one man, William J. Conaty, who retired in 2007 after 13 years as head of human resources and 40 years at GE. The company is known for having a deep bench of great leaders and emerging leaders as well as a relentless focus on continuous leadership development. Conaty has seven keys to share in nurturing leaders and achieving superior performance.

- Dare to differentiate the best from the rest by constantly judging, ranking, rewarding, and punishing employees for their performance.
- Constantly raise the bar to improve performance, which leaders do both among their own team members and for themselves.
- Do not be friends with the boss but establish your own trustworthiness and integrity as a confidant to all.

- Become easy to replace by developing great succession plans, especially when you do not need them, and mentoring the next generation.
- Be inclusive and do not favor people that you know because it can undermine your success.
- Free up others to do their jobs, especially by taking things off your boss' desk that are better done by you or others.
- Keep it simple by being consistent and straightforward because most organizations require simple, focused, and disciplined communications.

These seven keys are neither magic nor a panacea, yet they have served GE and Conaty well over the years.

SOURCE: D. Brady, "Secrets of an HR Superstar," *BusinessWeek* 4029 (April 9, 2007): 66.

---

skills of a bedside manner to complement the necessary technical diagnostic and treatment skills for enhancing the healing process. Each specific job in an organization requires the definition of skills and behaviors essential to excellent performance. Defining performance is a prerequisite to measuring and evaluating performance on the job.

Although different jobs require different skills and behaviors, organizational citizenship behavior (OCB) is one dimension of individual performance that spans many jobs. OCB was defined in Chapter 4 as behavior that is above and beyond the call of duty. OCB involves individual discretionary behavior that promotes the organization and is not explicitly rewarded; it includes helping behavior, sportsmanship, and civic virtue. According to supervisors, OCB is enhanced most through employee involvement programs aimed at engaging employees in the work organization rather than through employee involvement in employment decisions in nonunion operations.[49] OCB emphasizes collective performance in contrast to individual performance or achievement. OCB is just one of a number of performance dimensions to consider when defining performance for a specific job within an organization.

Performance appraisal is the evaluation of a person's performance once it is well defined. Accurate appraisals help supervisors fulfill their dual roles as evaluators and coaches. As a coach, a supervisor is responsible for encouraging employee growth and development. As an evaluator, a supervisor is responsible for making judgments that influence employees' roles in the organization. Although procedural justice is often thought of as a unidimensional construct, recent research shows that in the performance appraisal content it can be conceptualized as two-dimensional.[50]

Cross-cultural research has found that North American, Asian, and Latin American managers' perceptions of their employees' motivation are different and that their perceptions affect their appraisals of employee performance.[51]

performance appraisal
The evaluation of a person's performance.

The major purposes of performance appraisals are to give employees feedback on performance, identify the employees' developmental needs, make promotion and reward decisions, make demotion and termination decisions, and develop information about the organization's selection and placement decisions. For example, a review of 57,775 performance appraisals found higher ratings on appraisals done for administrative reasons and lower ratings on appraisals done for research or for employee development.[52]

Measuring Performance

Ideally, actual performance and measured performance are the same. Practically, this is seldom the case. Measuring operational performance is easier than measuring managerial performance because of the availability of quantifiable data. Measuring production performance is easier than measuring research and development performance because of the reliability of the measures. Recent research has focused on measuring motivation for task performance and has found that wording and context may influence the validity of direct self-reports.[53]

Performance appraisal systems are intended to improve the accuracy of measured performance and increase its agreement with actual performance. The extent of agreement is called the true assessment, as Figure 6.3 shows. The figure also identifies the performance measurement problems that contribute to inaccuracy. These

One major purpose of performance appraisals is to give employees feedback on performance. A supervisor is responsible for making judgments that influence employees' roles in the organization.

FIGURE 6.3   Actual and Measured Performance

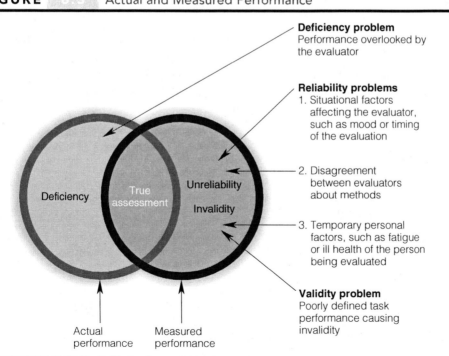

Deficiency problem
Performance overlooked by the evaluator

Reliability problems
1. Situational factors affecting the evaluator, such as mood or timing of the evaluation
2. Disagreement between evaluators about methods
3. Temporary personal factors, such as fatigue or ill health of the person being evaluated

Validity problem
Poorly defined task performance causing invalidity

Deficiency · True assessment · Unreliability · Invalidity

Actual performance · Measured performance

TABLE 6.3   Officer Effectiveness Reports, Circa 1813

Alexander Brown—Lt. Col., Comdg.—A good natured man.

Clark Crowell—first Major—A good man, but no officer.

Jess B. Wordsworth—2nd Major—An excellent officer.

Captain Shaw—A man of whom all unite in speaking ill. A knave despised by all.

Captain Thomas Lord—Indifferent, but promises well.

Captain Rockwell—An officer of capacity, but imprudent and a man of violent passions.

1st Lt. Jas. Kearns—Merely good, nothing promising.

1st Lt. Robert Cross—Willing enough—has much to learn—with small capacity.

2nd Lt. Stewart Berry—An ignorant unoffending fellow.

Ensign North—A good young man who does well.

SOURCE: Table from *The Air Officer's Guide*, 6th ed., Copyright © 1952 Stackpole Books. Used with permission.

include deficiency, unreliability, and invalidity. Deficiency results from overlooking important aspects of a person's actual performance. Unreliability results from poor-quality performance measures. Invalidity results from inaccurate definition of the expected job performance.

Early performance appraisal systems were often quite biased. See, for example, Table 6.3, which is a sample of officer effectiveness reports from an infantry company in the early 1800s. Even contemporary executive appraisals have a dark side, arousing managers' and executives' defenses. Addressing emotions and defenses is important to making appraisal sessions developmental.[54] Some performance review systems lead to forced rankings of employees, which may be controversial.

Performance-monitoring systems using modern electronic technology are sometimes used to measure the performance of vehicle operators, computer technicians, and customer service representatives. For example, such systems might record the rate of keystrokes or the total number of keystrokes for a computer technician. The people subject to this type of monitoring are in some cases unaware that their performance is being measured. What is appropriate performance monitoring? What constitutes inappropriate electronic spying on the employee? Are people entitled to know when their performance is being measured? The ethics of monitoring performance may differ by culture. The United States and Sweden, for example, respect individual freedom more than Japan and China do. The overriding issue, however, is how far organizations should go in using modern technology to measure human performance.

Goal setting and MBO are results-oriented methods of performance appraisal that do not necessarily rely on modern technology. Like performance-monitoring systems, they shift the emphasis from subjective, judgmental performance dimensions to observable, verifiable results. Goals established in the planning phase of goal setting become the standard against which to measure subsequent performance. However, rigid adherence to a results-oriented approach may risk overlooking performance opportunities.

FedEx has incorporated a novel and challenging approach to evaluation in its blueprint for service quality. All managers at FedEx are evaluated by their employees through a survey-feedback-action system. Employees evaluate their managers using a five-point scale on twenty-nine standard statements and ten local option ones. Low ratings suggest problem areas requiring management attention. For example, the following statement received low ratings from employees in 1990: "Upper management pays attention to ideas and suggestions from people at my level." CEO Fred Smith became directly involved in addressing this problem area. One of the actions he took to correct the problem was the development of a bi-weekly employee newsletter.

Performance Feedback: A Communication Challenge

Once clearly defined and accurate performance measures are developed, there is still the challenge of performance feedback. Feedback sessions are among the more stressful events for supervisors and employees. Early research at General Electric found employees responded constructively to positive feedback and were defensive over half the time in response to critical or negative feedback. Typical responses to negative feedback included shifting responsibility for the shortcoming or behavior, denying it outright, or providing a wide range of excuses for it.[55] In a study of 499 Chinese supervisor-subordinate dyads, supervisors responded positively to employees who sought performance feedback if their motive was performance enhancement or improvement.[56] However, if the employee's motive was impression management, supervisors responded less positively.

Both parties to a performance feedback session should try to make it a constructive learning experience, since positive and negative performance feedback has long-term implications for the employee's performance and for the working relationship. American Airlines follows three guidelines in providing evaluative feedback so that the experience is constructive for supervisor and employee alike.[57] First, refer to specific, verbatim statements and specific, observable behaviors displayed by the person receiving the feedback. This enhances the acceptance of the feedback while reducing the chances of denial. Second, focus on changeable behaviors, as opposed to intrinsic or personality-based attributes. People are often more defensive about who they are than about what they do. Third, plan and organize for the session ahead of time. Be sure to notify the person who will receive the feedback. Both the leader and the follower should be ready.

In addition to these ideas, many companies recommend beginning coaching and counseling sessions with something positive. The intent is to reduce defensiveness and enhance useful communication. There is almost always at least one positive element to emphasize. Once the session is underway and rapport is established, then the evaluator can introduce more difficult and negative material. Because people are not perfect, there is always an opportunity for them to learn and to grow through performance feedback sessions. Critical feedback is the basis for improvement and is essential to a performance feedback session. Specific feedback is beneficial for initial performance but discourages exploration and undermines the learning needed for later, more independent performance.[58]

360-Degree Feedback

Many organizations use *360-degree feedback* as a tactic to improve the accuracy of performance appraisals because it is based on multiple sources of information. When self-evaluations are included in this process, there is evidence that the evaluation interviews can be more satisfying, more constructive, and less defensive.[59] One of the criticisms of self-evaluations is their low level of agreement with supervisory evaluations.[60] However, high levels of agreement may not necessarily be desirable if the

360-degree feedback
A process of self-evaluation and evaluations by a manager, peers, direct reports, and possibly customers.

(5) Describe 360-degree feedback.

SCIENCE

360-Degree Feedback and Culture

An organization's capacity for sustainable growth hinges in part on the ability of its managers to learn better skills that improve performance. The 360-degree feedback process is one initiative used by companies to develop managerial skills in two ways: one, through its inherent ability to reinforce learning that has occurred through positive feedback and reinforcement; two, through the creation of actionable knowledge, which is scientifically rigorous knowledge that leads to implementing solutions to practical problems. Some global companies and multinationals have assumed that the 360-degree feedback process applies equally across cultures. These researchers have called this assumption into question and conducted a study with comparisons among five countries: Ireland, Israel, Malaysia, the Phillipines, and the U.S. The results revealed important differences among these countries. The study measured culture using the four work-related values that Hofstede's approach to culture proposed. The study results provided support for the overall effectiveness of the 360-degree feedback process. In addition, important between-group differences were found. Specifically, the 360-degree feedback process was found to be most effective in cultures with low power distance and individualistic values. These cultural context differences are important for managers and leaders to consider in the use of 360-degree feedback.

SOURCE: F. Shipper, R. C. Hoffman, and D. M. Rotondo, "Does the 360 Feedback Process Create Actionable Knowledge Equally Across Cultures?" *Academy of Management Learning & Education* 6 (2007): 33–50.

intent of the evaluation is to provide a full picture of the person's performance. This is a strength of the 360-degree feedback method, which provides a well-rounded view of performance from superiors, peers, followers, and customers.[61]

An example of a 360-degree feedback evaluation occurred in a large military organization for a mid-level civilian executive. The mid-level executive behaved very differently in dealing with superiors, peers, and followers. With superiors, he was positive, compliant, and deferential. With peers, he was largely indifferent, often ignoring them. With followers, he was tough and demanding, bordering on cruel and abusive. Without each of these perspectives, the executive's performance would not have been accurately assessed. When the executive received feedback, he was able to see the inconsistency in his behavior.

Two recommendations have been made to improve the effectiveness of the 360-degree feedback method. The first is to add a systematic coaching component to the 360-degree feedback.[62] By focusing on enhanced self-awareness and behavioral management, this feedback-coaching model can enhance performance as well as satisfaction and commitment, and reduce intent to turnover. The second is to separate the performance feedback component of the 360-degree appraisal from the management development component.[63] The feedback component should emphasize quantitative feedback and performance measures, while the management development component should emphasize qualitative feedback and competencies for development.

While 360-degree feedback generates actionable knowledge, its effectiveness has been found to vary across cultures. The accompanying Science feature examines one study of the importance of cultural context in the use of 360-degree feedback.

The 360-degree feedback method provides a well-rounded view of performance from superiors, peers, followers, and customers.

© STOCKBYTE/GETTY IMAGES

Developing People and Enhancing Careers

A key function of a good performance appraisal system is to develop people and enhance careers. Developmentally, performance appraisals should emphasize individual growth needs and future performance. If the supervisor is to coach and develop employees effectively, there must be mutual trust. The supervisor must be vulnerable and open to challenge from the subordinate while maintaining a position of responsibility for what is in the subordinate's best interests.[64] The supervisor must also be a skilled, empathetic listener who encourages the employee to talk about hopes and aspirations.[65]

The employee must be able to take active responsibility for future development and growth. This might mean challenging the supervisor's ideas about future development as well as expressing individual preferences and goals. Passive, compliant employees are unable to accept responsibility for themselves or to achieve full emotional development. Individual responsibility is a key characteristic of many organization work cultures that treat employees like adults and expect them to act and behave like adults. This contrasts with work cultures in which leaders treat employees more paternalistically.

Key Characteristics of an Effective Appraisal System

An effective performance appraisal system has five key characteristics: validity, reliability, responsiveness, flexibility, and equitability. Its validity comes from capturing multiple dimensions of a person's job performance. Its reliability comes from capturing evaluations from multiple sources and at different times over the course of the evaluation period. Its responsiveness allows the person being evaluated some input into the final outcome. Its flexibility leaves it open to modification based on new information, such as federal requirements. Its equitability results in fair evaluations against established performance criteria, regardless of individual differences.

REWARDING PERFORMANCE

One function of a performance appraisal system is to provide input for reward decisions. If an organization wants good performance, it must reward good performance. If it does not want bad performance, it must not reward bad performance. If companies talk "teamwork," "values," and "customer focus," they need to reward behaviors related to these ideas. Although this idea is conceptually simple, it can become very complicated in practice. Reward decisions are among the most difficult and complicated decisions made in organizations, and among the most important decisions. When leaders confront decisions about pay every day, they should know that it is a myth that people work for money.[66] While pay and rewards for performance have value, so too do trust, fun, and meaningful work. In addition, as we saw in The Real World 6.1, U.S. government managers are encouraged to reward themselves with self-praise when they know that they have performed well against their work goals.

A Key Organizational Decision Process

Reward and punishment decisions in organizations affect many people throughout the system, not just those being rewarded or punished. Reward allocation involves sequential decisions about which people to reward, how to reward them, and when to reward them. Taken together, these decisions shape the behavior of everyone in the organization because of the vicarious learning that occurs as people watch what happens to others, especially when new programs or initiatives are implemented.

People carefully watch what happens to peers who make mistakes or have problems with the new system; then they gauge their own behavior accordingly.

Individual versus Team Reward Systems

(6) Compare individual and team-oriented reward systems.

One of the distinguishing characteristics of Americans is the value they place on individualism. Systems that reward individuals are common in organizations in the United States. One strength of these systems is that they foster autonomous and independent behavior that leads to creativity, to novel solutions to old problems, and to distinctive contributions to the organization. Individual reward systems directly affect individual behavior and encourage competitive striving within a work team. However, different types of employees may have different reward preferences. For example, award seekers may prefer travel awards, nesters may prefer days off, bottom-liners may prefer cash bonuses, freedom yearners may prefer flextime, praise cravers may prefer written praise, and upward movers may prefer status awards.[67] Motivation and reward systems outside the United States are often group focused.[68]

Too much competition within a work environment, however, may be dysfunctional. At the Western Company of North America (now part of BJ Services Company), individual success in the MBO program was tied too tightly to rewards, and individual managers became divisively competitive. For example, some managers took last-minute interdepartmental financial actions in a quarter to meet their objectives, but by doing so, they caused other managers to miss their objectives. Actions such as these raise ethical questions about how far individual managers should go in serving their own self-interest at the expense of their peers.

Team reward systems solve the problems caused by individual competitive behavior. These systems emphasize cooperation, joint efforts, and the sharing of information, knowledge, and expertise. The Japanese and Chinese cultures, with their collectivist orientations, place greater emphasis than Americans on the individual as an element of the team, not a member apart from the team. Digital Equipment Corporation (now part of Hewlett-Packard) used a partnership approach to performance appraisals. Self-managed work group members participated in their own appraisal process. Such an approach emphasizes teamwork and responsibility.

Some organizations have experimented with individual and group alternative reward systems.[69] At the individual level, these include skill-based and pay-for-knowledge systems. Each emphasizes skills or knowledge possessed by an employee over and above the requirements for the basic job. At the group level, gain-sharing plans emphasize collective cost reduction and allow workers to share in the gains achieved by reducing production or other operating costs. In such plans, everyone shares equally in the collective gain. Avnet, Inc. found that collective profit sharing improved performance.

The Power of Earning

The purpose behind both individual and team reward systems is to shape productive behavior. Effective performance management can be the lever of change that boosts individual and team achievements in an organization. So, if one wants the rewards available in the organization, one should work to earn them. Performance management and reward systems assume a demonstrable connection between performance and rewards. Organizations get the performance they reward, not the performance they say they want.[70] Further, when there is no apparent link between performance and rewards, people may begin to believe they are entitled to rewards regardless of how they perform. The concept of entitlement is very different

Correcting Poor Performance

At one time or another, each of us has had a poor performance of some kind. It may have been a poor test result in school, a poor presentation at work, or a poor performance in an athletic event. Think of a poor performance event that you have experienced and work through the following three steps.

Step 1. Briefly describe the specific event in some detail. Include why you label it a poor performance (bad score? someone else's evaluation?).

Step 2. Analyze the Poor Performance

a. List all the possible contributing causes to the poor performance. Be specific, such as the room was too hot, you did not get enough sleep, you were not told how to perform the task, etc. You might ask other people for possible ideas, too.

1. _____
2. _____
3. _____
4. _____
5. _____
6. _____
7. _____

b. Is there a primary cause for the poor performance? What is it?

Step 3. Plan to Correct the Poor Performance
Develop a step-by-step plan of action that specifies what you can change or do differently to improve your performance the next time you have an opportunity. Include seeking help if it is needed. Once your plan is developed, look for an opportunity to execute it.

from the concept of earning, which assumes a performance–reward link. Toyota's frugality, mentioned in Thinking Ahead, places underlying value on the power of earning.

The notion of entitlement at work is counterproductive when taken to the extreme because it counteracts the power of earning.[71] People who believe they are entitled to rewards regardless of their behavior or performance are not motivated to behave constructively. Merit raises in some organizations, for example, have come to be viewed as entitlements, thus reducing their positive value in the organizational reward system. People believe they have a right to be taken care of by someone, whether that is the organization or a specific person. Entitlement engenders passive, irresponsible behavior, whereas earning engenders active, responsible, adult behavior. If rewards depend on performance, people must perform responsibly to receive them. The power of earning rests on a direct link between performance and rewards.

CORRECTING POOR PERFORMANCE

Often a complicated, difficult challenge for supervisors, correcting poor performance is a three-step process. First, the cause or primary responsibility for the poor performance must be identified. Second, if the primary responsibility is a person's, then the source of the personal problem must be determined. Third, a plan of action to correct the poor performance must be developed. You 6.2 gives you an opportunity to examine a poor performance you have experienced. As we saw in Thinking Ahead, Toyota is aggressive about making corrective adjustments when performance is not the best it can be.

Poor performance may result from a variety of causes, the more important being poorly designed work systems, poor selection processes, inadequate training and skills development, lack of personal motivation, and personal problems intruding

(7) Describe strategies for correcting poor performance.

on the work environment. Not all poor performance is self-motivated; some is induced by the work system. Therefore, a good diagnosis should precede corrective action. For example, it may be that an employee is subject to a work design or selection system that does not allow the person to exhibit good performance. Identifying the cause of the poor performance comes first and should be done in communication with the employee. If the problem is with the system and the supervisor can fix it, everyone wins as a result.

If the poor performance is not attributable to work design or organizational process problems, then attention should be focused on the employee. At least three possible causes of poor performance can be attributed to the employee. The problem may lie in (1) some aspect of the person's relationship to the organization or supervisor, (2) some area of the employee's personal life, or (3) a training or developmental deficiency. In the latter two cases, poor performance may be treated as a symptom as opposed to a motivated consequence. In such cases, identifying financial problems, family difficulties, or health disorders may enable the supervisor to help the employee solve problems before they become too extensive. Employee assistance programs (EAPs) can be helpful to employees managing personal problems. These are discussed in Chapter 7 in relation to managing stress.

Poor performance may also be motivated by an employee's displaced anger or conflict with the organization or supervisor. In such cases, the employee may or may not be aware of the internal reactions causing the problem. In either event, sabotage, work slowdowns, work stoppages, and similar forms of poor performance may result from such motivated behavior. The supervisor may attribute the cause of the problem to the employee, and the employee may attribute it to the supervisor or organization. To solve motivated performance problems requires treating the poor performance as a symptom with a deeper cause. Resolving the underlying anger or conflict results in the disappearance of the symptom (poor performance).

Performance and Kelley's Attribution Theory

According to attribution theory, managers make attributions (inferences) concerning employees' behavior and performance.[72] The attributions may not always be accurate. For example, an executive with Capital Cities Communications/ABC (now part of the Disney Company) who had a very positive relationship with his boss was not held responsible for profit problems in his district. The boss blamed the problem on the economy. Supervisors and employees who share perceptions and attitudes, as in the Capital Cities situation, tend to evaluate each other highly.[73] Supervisors and employees who do not share perceptions and attitudes are more likely to blame each other for performance problems.

Harold Kelley's attribution theory aims to help us explain the behavior of other people. He also extended attribution theory by trying to identify the antecedents of internal and external attributions. Kelley proposed that individuals make attributions based on information gathered in the form of three informational cues: consensus, distinctiveness, and consistency.[74,75] We observe an individual's behavior and then seek out information in the form of these three cues. *Consensus* is the extent to which peers in the same situation behave the same way. *Distinctiveness* is the degree to which the person behaves the same way in other situations. *Consistency* refers to the frequency of a particular behavior over time.

We form attributions based on whether these cues are low or high. Figure 6.4 shows how the combination of these cues helps us form internal or external attributions. Suppose you have received several complaints from customers regarding one of your customer service representatives, John. You have not received complaints

consensus

An informational cue indicating the extent to which peers in the same situation behave in a similar fashion.

distinctiveness

An informational cue indicating the degree to which an individual behaves the same way in other situations.

consistency

An informational cue indicating the frequency of behavior over time.

FIGURE 6.4 Informational Cues and Attributions

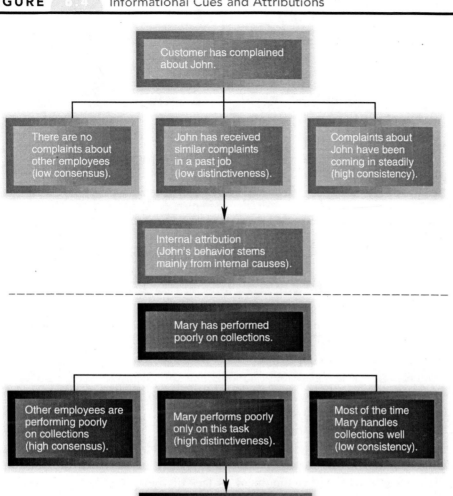

about your other service representatives (low consensus). Upon reviewing John's records, you note that he also received customer complaints during his previous job as a sales clerk (low distinctiveness). The complaints have been coming in steadily for about three months (high consistency). In this case, you would most likely make an internal attribution and conclude that the complaints must stem from John's behavior. The combination of low consensus, low distinctiveness, and high consistency leads to internal attributions.

Other combinations of these cues, however, produce external attributions. High consensus, high distinctiveness, and low consistency, for example, produce external attributions. Suppose one of your employees, Mary, is performing poorly on collecting overdue accounts. You find that the behavior is widespread within your work team (high consensus) and that Mary is performing poorly only on this aspect of the job (high distinctiveness), and that most of the time she handles this aspect of the job well (low consistency). You will probably decide that something about the work situation caused the poor performance—perhaps work overload or an unfair deadline.

FIGURE 6.5 Attribution Model

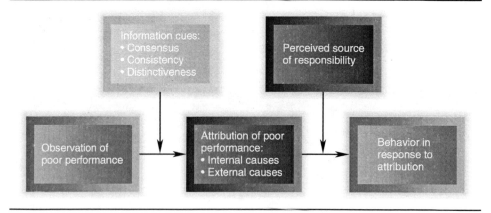

Consensus, distinctiveness, and consistency are the cues used to determine whether the cause of behavior is internal or external. The process of determining the cause of a behavior may not be simple and clear-cut, however, because of some biases that occur in forming attributions.

Figure 6.5 presents an attribution model that specifically addresses how supervisors respond to poor performance. A supervisor who observes poor performance seeks cues about the employee's behavior in the three forms discussed above: consensus, consistency, and distinctiveness.

On the basis of this information, the supervisor makes either an internal (personal) attribution or an external (situational) attribution. Internal attributions might include low effort, lack of commitment, or lack of ability. External attributions are outside the employee's control and might include equipment failure or unrealistic goals. The supervisor then determines the source of responsibility for the performance problem and tries to correct the problem.

Supervisors may choose from a wide range of responses. They can, for example, express personal concern, reprimand the employee, or provide training. Supervisors who attribute the cause of poor performance to a person (an internal cause) will respond more harshly than supervisors who attribute the cause to the work situation (an external cause). Supervisors should try not to make either of the two common attribution errors discussed in Chapter 3: the fundamental attribution error and the self-serving bias.

Coaching, Counseling, and Mentoring

Supervisors have important coaching, counseling, and mentoring responsibilities to their subordinates. Supervisors and coworkers have been found to be more effective in mentoring functions than assigned, formal mentors from higher up in the organizational hierarchy.[76] Success in the mentoring relationship also hinges on the presence of openness and trust.[77] This relationship may be one where performance-based deficiencies are addressed or one where personal problems that diminish employee performance, such as depression, are addressed.[78] In either case, supervisors can play a helpful role in employee problem-solving activities without accepting responsibility for

Coach Bill Walsh of the San Francisco 49ers talks to quarterback Joe Montana during an NFL game in 1981. Success in a coaching or mentoring relationship hinges on the presence of openness and trust.

© AL MESSERSCHMIDT/GETTY IMAGES

the employees' problems. One important form of help is to refer the employee to trained professionals.

Coaching and counseling are among the career and psychosocial functions of a mentoring relationship.[79] *Mentoring* is a work relationship that encourages development and career enhancement for people moving through the career cycle. Mentor relationships typically go through four phases: initiation, cultivation, separation, and redefinition. For protégés, mentoring offers a number of career benefits.[80] The relationship can significantly enhance the early development of a newcomer and the midcareer development of an experienced employee. One study found that good performance by newcomers resulted in leaders giving more delegation.[81] Career development can be enhanced through peer relationships as an alternative to traditional mentoring relationships.[82] Executive coaching is increasingly being used as a way of outsourcing the business mentoring functions.[83] Informational, collegial, and special peers aid the individual's development through information sharing, career strategizing, job-related feedback, emotional support, and friendship. Hence, mentors and peers may both play constructive roles in correcting an employee's poor performance and in enhancing overall career development.

MANAGERIAL IMPLICATIONS: PERFORMANCE MANAGEMENT IS A KEY TASK

People in organizations learn from the consequences of their actions. Therefore, managers must exercise care in applying positive and negative consequences to ensure that they are connected to the behaviors the managers intend to reward or punish. Managers should also be judicious in the use of punishment and should consider extinction coupled with positive reinforcement as an alternative to punishment for shaping employee behavior. The strategic use of training and educational opportunities, stock options, and recognition awards is instrumental to successful organizational reward systems. Managers can serve as positive role models for employees' vicarious learning about ethical behavior and high-quality performance.

Goal-setting activities may be valuable to managers in bringing out the best performance from employees. Managers can use challenging, specific goals for this purpose and must be prepared to provide employees with timely, useful feedback on goal progress so that employees will know how they are doing. Goal-setting activities that are misused may create dysfunctional competition in an organization and lead to lower performance.

Good performance management systems are a valuable tool for providing employees with clear feedback on their actions. Managers who rely on valid and reliable performance measures may use them in employee development and to correct poor performance. Managers who use high-technology performance monitoring systems must remember that employees are humans, not machines. Managers are responsible for creating a positive learning atmosphere in performance feedback sessions, and employees are responsible for learning from these sessions. 360-degree feedback is especially effective when combined with coaching.

Finally, managers can use rewards as one of the most powerful positive consequences for shaping employee behavior. If rewards are to improve performance, managers must make a clear connection between specific performance and the rewards. Employees should be expected to earn the rewards they receive; they should expect rewards to be related to performance quality and skill development.

mentoring

A work relationship that encourages development and career enhancement for people moving through the career cycle.

LOOKING BACK: TOYOTA

Learning and Change at the University of Toyota

Toyota's learning principles have been a driving force in the company's continuous rise to the top of the automotive industry.[84] Its in-house training has served the company well. In 2006 the company began teaching its "lean thinking" to other businesses as well as to police and the U.S. military at its in-house training center, known as the University of Toyota. The school occupies the Toyota Plaza building in Gardena, California, and banners displaying key Toyota principles hang on the walls. These principles include *kaizen* (continuous improvement) and *genchi genbutsu* (go look, go see). Toyota has leapfrogged its competition yet done so through *kaizen*, which is progress made with a million incremental ideas. While it charges most organizations for its training and educational services, it provides these to police and the U.S. military as a public service.

The Los Angeles Police Department's Captain Patrick Findley is one of the beneficiaries of this public service. When he took over the LAPD's jails in 2005, incoming prisoners stood in line for hours waiting to be booked while officers spent valuable time heating up frozen dinners to feed them each evening. That is the way it had always been done, and Captain Findley did not think to question the process—until he took a two-day class at the University of Toyota. As a result, Captain Findley did away with serving dinner hot and began serving sandwiches with an apple and milk, thus freeing more officers during one of the jail's busiest times. This public service advancement occurs courtesy of knowledge transfer from lean manufacturing in the automotive industry to lean thinking in a whole different context. The improvements resulting from learning at Toyota will save the LAPD over $1 million annually.

Toyota began this process of expanding its teaching to non-auto businesses in the United States when it looked for a business that had already devised some lean thinking of its own. They found Quadrant Homes, a Seattle home builder owned by forest-products giant Weyerhaeuser Company. Quadrant had built homes with features based on market trends for years, selling the finished products. This build-first approach left them with unsold inventory. So Quadrant flipped the process, started taking orders, and then built to buyers' specifications. This cut prices, cut average construction time (to 54 from 120 days), and nearly tripled sales closings over a five-year period. Hoping to ingrain that thinking more deeply, Quadrant began sending teams of employees to the University of Toyota as soon as it opened its doors to outsider businesses. What works for cars may be translated to home improvements, jail improvements, and even innovative thinking in military combat operations.

Chapter Summary

1. Learning is a change in behavior acquired through experience.

2. The operant conditioning approach to learning states that behavior is a function of positive and negative consequences.

3. Reinforcement is used to develop desirable behavior; punishment and extinction are used to decrease undesirable behavior.

4. Bandura's social learning theory suggests that task-specific self-efficacy is important to effective learning.

5. Goal setting improves work motivation and task performance, reduces role stress, and improves the accuracy and validity of performance appraisal.

6. Performance management and 360-degree feedback can lead to improved performance.

7. Making accurate attributions about the behavior of others is an essential prerequisite to correcting poor performance.

8. High-quality performance should be rewarded, and poor performance should be corrected.

9. Mentoring is a relationship for encouraging development and career enhancement for people moving through the career cycle.

Key Terms

classical conditioning (p. 185)
consensus (p. 204)
consistency (p. 204)
distinctiveness (p. 204)
extinction (p. 188)
goal setting (p. 190)
learning (p. 184)

management by objectives (MBO) (p. 194)
mentoring (p. 207)
negative consequences (p. 186)
operant conditioning (p. 185)
performance appraisal (p. 196)
performance management (p. 195)

positive consequences (p. 186)
punishment (p. 187)
reinforcement (p. 186)
task-specific self-efficacy (p. 188)
360-degree feedback (p. 199)

Review Questions

1. Define the terms *learning, reinforcement, punishment,* and *extinction.*

2. What are positive and negative consequences in shaping behavior? How should they be managed? Explain the value of extinction as a strategy.

3. How can task-specific self-efficacy be enhanced? What are the differences in the way introverted and extraverted and intuitive and sensing people learn?

4. What are the five characteristics of well-developed goals? Why is feedback on goal progress important?

5. What are the purposes of conducting performance appraisals? What are the benefits of 360-degree feedback?

6. What are the two possible attributions of poor performance? What are the implications of each?

7. How can managers and supervisors best provide useful performance feedback?

8. How do mentors and peers help people develop and enhance their careers?

Discussion and Communication Questions

1. Which learning approach—the behavioral approach or Bandura's social learning theory—do you find more appropriate for people?

2. Given your personality type, how do you learn best? Do you miss learning some things because of how they are taught?

3. What goals do you set for yourself at work? In your personal life? Will you know if you achieve them?

4. If a conflict occurred between your self-evaluation and the evaluation given to you by your supervisor or instructor, how would you respond? What, specifically, would you do? What have you learned

from your supervisor or instructor during the last reporting period?

5. What rewards are most important to you? How hard are you willing to work to receive them?

6. *(communication question)* Prepare a memo detailing the consequences of behavior in your work or university environment (e.g., grades, awards, suspensions, and scholarships). Include in your memo your classification of these consequences as positive or negative. Should your organization or university change the way it applies these consequences?

7. *(communication question)* Develop an oral presentation about the most current management practices in employee rewards and performance management. Find out what at least four different companies are doing in this area. Be prepared to discuss their fit with the text materials.

8. *(communication question)* Interview a manager or supervisor who is responsible for completing performance appraisals on people at work. Ask the manager which aspects of performance appraisal and the performance appraisal interview process are most difficult and how he or she manages these difficulties.

Ethical Dilemma

Donna Hermann shuffled the papers on her desk. She was very surprised by what she read. On her desk sat the annual evaluations of Julie Stringer, an employee in Donna's department. Both worked for Telecom Solutions, a large call center in the Midwest where it was the policy to do 360-degree annual evaluation on all employees. Each individual was evaluated by his or her supervisor, peers, and subordinates if the person was in a management position. As Julie's supervisor, Donna was looking at the evaluations completed by three of Julie's peers and three of her subordinates.

Julie's peers' opinion of her performance closely matched Donna's. Working at Telecom was intense, and the managers had worked hard to create an environment where they supported each other. They felt that Julie was not supporting this environment. She never got in anyone's way, but she never pitched in to help either. Julie came to Telecom every day to work, nothing else. She never cared to make friends or to be a part of the team. Donna felt this was not good for the morale of her department and had hoped this annual evaluation would help her start the process of replacing Julie. The problem was that Julie's employees loved her. Donna had never seen such glowing reviews by anyone's subordinates. Obviously, Julie was not remote with her team. One of Julie's highest ratings from her team was her willingness to pitch in at any time for any reason. This was a very different perception from the management team.

Donna had no personal problem with Julie; she was concerned about her entire department. Since Julie joined the company, things had not been the same. However, was it more important for Julie's peers to be happy or her employees? Her group was always productive. Also, was it fair to punish someone for coming to the office to work? But, was it right to let Julie's behaviors continue chipping away at the culture that Donna and the other managers had worked so hard to achieve?

Questions

1. What is Donna's primary responsibility?

2. Does Donna have a greater responsibility to her direct reports or to those one level down?

3. Using consequential, rule-based, and character theories, evaluate Donna's decision regarding Julie.

Experiential Exercises

6.1 Positive and Negative Reinforcement

Purpose: To examine the effects of positive and negative reinforcement on behavior change.

1. Two or three volunteers are selected to receive reinforcement from the class while performing a particular task. The volunteers leave the room.

2. The instructor identifies an object for the student volunteers to locate when they return to the room. (The object should be unobtrusive but clearly visible to the class. Some that have worked well are a small triangular piece of paper that was left behind when a notice was torn off a classroom bulletin board, a

smudge on the chalkboard, and a chip in the plaster of a classroom wall.)

3. The instructor specifies the reinforcement contingencies that will be in effect when the volunteers return to the room. For negative reinforcement, students should hiss, boo, and throw things (although you should not throw anything harmful) when the first volunteer is moving away from the object; cheer and applaud when the second volunteer is getting closer to the object; and if a third volunteer is used, use both negative and positive reinforcement.

4. The instructor should assign a student to keep a record of the time it takes each of the volunteers to locate the object.

5. Volunteer number one is brought back into the room and is instructed: "Your task is to locate and touch a particular object in the room, and the class has agreed to help you. You may begin."

6. Volunteer number one continues to look for the object until it is found while the class assists by giving negative reinforcement.

7. Volunteer number two is brought back into the room and is instructed: "Your task is to locate and touch a particular object in the room, and the class has agreed to help you. You may begin."

8. Volunteer number two continues to look for the object until it is found while the class assists by giving positive reinforcement.

9. Volunteer number three is brought back into the room and is instructed: "Your task is to locate and touch a particular object in the room, and the class has agreed to help you. You may begin."

10. Volunteer number three continues to look for the object until it is found while the class assists by giving both positive and negative reinforcement.

11. In a class discussion, answer the following questions:

    a. How did the behavior of the volunteers differ when different kinds of reinforcement (positive, negative, or both) were used?

    b. What were the emotional reactions of the volunteers to the different kinds of reinforcement?

    c. Which type of reinforcement—positive or negative—is most common in organizations? What effect do you think this has on motivation and productivity?

6.2 Correcting Poor Performance

This exercise provides an opportunity for you to engage in a performance diagnosis role-play as either the assistant director of the Academic Computing Service Center or as a member of a university committee appointed by the president of the university at the request of the center director. The instructor will form the class into groups of five or six students and either ask the group to select who is to be the assistant director or assign one group member to be the assistant director.

Performance diagnosis, especially where some poor performance exists, requires making attributions and determining causal factors as well as formulating a plan of action to correct any poor performance.

Step 1. (5 minutes) Once the class is formed into groups, the instructor provides the assistant director with a copy of the role description and each university committee member with a copy of the role context information. Group members are to read through the materials provided.

Step 2. (15 minutes) The university committee is to call in the assistant director of the Academic Computing Service Center for a performance diagnostic interview. This is an information-gathering interview, not an appraisal session. The purpose is to gather information for the center director.

Step 3. (15 minutes) The university committee is to agree on a statement that reflects their understanding of the assistant director's poor performance and to include a specification of the causes. Based on this problem statement, the committee is to formulate a plan of action to correct the poor performance. The assistant director is to do the same, again ending with a plan of action.

Step 4. (10–15 minutes, optional) The instructor may ask the groups to share the results of their work in Step 3 of the role-play exercise.

Biz Flix | Seabiscuit

Combine a jockey who is blind in one eye with an undersized, ill-tempered thoroughbred and an unusual trainer. The result: the Depression-era champion racehorse Seabiscuit. This engaging film shows the training and development of Seabiscuit by trainer "Silent" Tom Smith (Chris Cooper) and jockey Red Pollard (Tobey Maguire). The enduring commitment of owner Charles Howard (Jeff Bridges) ensures the ultimate success of Seabiscuit on the racing circuit. Based on *Seabiscuit: An American Legend,* the best selling book by Laura Hillenbrand, *Seabiscuit* received seven 2003 Academy Award nominations, including Best Picture.

The *Seabiscuit* scene is an edited composite from DVD Chapters 21 and 22 toward the end of the film. In earlier scenes, Red severely injured a leg and cannot ride Seabiscuit in the competition against War Admiral. Samuel Riddle (Eddie Jones), War Admiral's owner, described any new rider as immaterial to the race's result. The scene begins with Red giving George Wolff (Gary Stevens), Seabiscuit's new jockey, some tips about riding him. Red starts by saying to George, "He's got a strong left lead, Georgie. He banks like a frigg'n airplane." The film continues to its exciting and unexpected ending.

What to Watch for and Ask Yourself:

> Does Red set clear performance goals for George? If he does, what are they?

> Does Red help George reach those performance goals? How?

> Does Red give George any positive reinforcement while he tries to reach the performance goals?

Workplace Video | Managerial Planning and Goal Setting at Cold Stone Creamery

Donald and Susan Sutherland are serious about giving customers the "Ultimate Ice Cream Experience," as their slogan goes. In 1988, the couple turned their love of ice cream into the first Cold Stone Creamery in Tempe, Arizona, and today the franchise boasts more than 1,300 stores.

Cold Stone Creamery truly is "an experience." At every location, fresh ice cream is produced in a dizzying array of unusual flavors and mixed with tasty toppings—nuts, fruits, candy, cookies, and more. Crew members who serve up the gooey frozen treats offer an entertaining song and dance on the side—just for fun.

Careful planning and goal setting is the key to Cold Stone's success. The company's mission is to "make people happy around the world by selling the highest quality, most creative ice cream experience with passion, excellence, and innovation." Within that overarching mission, executives set a company-wide goal of becoming America's number-one-selling ice cream by 2010. Supporting this challenging goal is "Pyramid of Success 2010," a detailed strategic plan that informs employees at all levels of the organization about their role in achieving the companywide objective. By setting clear objectives and offering rewards for achievement, management lays the groundwork for top performance and unites all employees in the pursuit of a common cause.

In the race to be number one, Cold Stone Creamery remains true to the Sutherlands' original dream of providing the "Ultimate Ice Cream Experience." From the executive vice president to the first-line managers, all Cold Stone employees take pride in transforming ordinary ice cream into something extraordinary. In addition to signature creations like the Birthday Cake Remix and the ever-popular Founder's Favorite, Cold Stone experiments with new flavors, like French Toast and Cinnabon, while developing concepts such as Twinkie ice-cream sandwiches. Each new idea produces big smiles from ice cream lovers and moves the company ever closer to its 2010 target.

Discussion Questions

1. Do Cold Stone Creamery's goals possess the five characteristics of effective goals discussed in the chapter? Explain.

2. What makes the "Pyramid of Success 2010" graphic an effective tool for communicating Cold Stone Creamery's corporate mission and goals to all employees?

3. Should management at Cold Stone Creamery use the same reward system for employees in Japan as they do in the United States? Why or why not?

American Express:
Challenges in Managing Learning and Performance

American Express (AMEX) was founded in 1850 to provide freight forwarding and delivery services. Over the past 150-plus years, it has evolved into a global financial services company, with operations in over 130 countries.[1]

Like other organizations, AMEX is concerned with enhancing the performance capabilities of employees. Developing and maintaining employee competencies and skills can be daunting, as two different challenges in managing learning and performance at the company illustrate.

Learning to Manage the Managers of Learning

Not only must the learning operations of an organization address the training and development needs of other units within the organization, but the organizational unit responsible for employee learning must also be concerned with developing the talents of its own staff members. In 2005, this lesson came to the forefront at American Express as the company's Learning Network evaluated its practices. The AMEX Learning Network discovered that it was not doing a satisfactory job of addressing the training and development needs of its own staff members—those AMEX employees directly charged with providing training and development experiences for the rest of the organization. The Learning Network subsequently took appropriate steps to improve its performance and craft a new vision and mission.[2]

A crucial problem was that it "had been so focused on the learning and development of others that its members had not devoted enough attention to their own knowledge and skills development."[3] Consequently, it began to focus efforts on the development of its own staff members. The Learning Network staff participated in various programs designed to elevate their skill levels. They also earned additional certifications from appropriate professional organizations. The Network also reviewed its compensation policies and practices to ensure they were in line with AMEX's pay-for-performance compensation model. Finally, to better link its own activities with the rest of the AMEX organization, the Learning Network also improved its measurement of training metrics. To better respond to the needs of AMEX's managers, the training metrics technology team developed what it called "metrics central," a Web-enabled tool that can be accessed by both Learning Network staffers and other AMEX managers.[4]

Mode of Leadership Development at AMEX

Another learning and performance management issue at American Express involved the Learning Network's efforts in the leadership development arena. AMEX was seeking to ascertain the most effective manner in which to conduct leadership training.

In 2006, the company implemented a new model of leadership development across the entire organization. Three groups of trainees (or learners) were formed, each exposed to a different training venue. One group had only online delivery of learning materials, which were studied through self-direction without any supporting events like peer discussion, formal meetings, or talks by senior organizational leaders. Another group of learners experienced traditional classroom training without any support of online materials or other formal events. The third group of learners experienced a *blended learning* approach that combined classroom or Web-based interaction with senior leaders, self-directed online learning, and encouragement of discussion among learners.[5]

In evaluating the three different approaches, AMEX assessed employee training responses—called *learner responses*—at five different levels. Level 1 measured learner reaction, wherein the trainees indicated the level of satisfaction they had with the learning experience. Level 2 focused on learner knowledge, or an assessment of the acquisition of new knowledge and skills. Level 3 addressed the learners' behavior by evaluating their observed improvement in leadership skills three months after the training sessions. Level 4 focused on the business impact of the training on the learners in terms of improved productivity of the learners' direct reports (i.e., those people for whom the learner has immediate supervisory responsibility). Level 5 targeted return on investment (ROI) via a cost/benefit analysis of the sales productivity of the learners' direct reports over the preceding three-month period. Assessments at levels 1 and 2 were based on the learner's self-report; at levels 3 and 4 the assessments were conducted via self-report from the learners and reports from the learners' supervisor and direct reports; and at level 5 it was based on objective data.[6]

Little difference was found among the three learning approaches—online self-directed, traditional classroom, and blended—for levels 1 and 2. However, blended learning proved to be the superior training approach at evaluation levels 3, 4, and 5.[7]

Challenges to Organizational Learning

How to effectively manage the managers of organizational learning and ascertaining the most effective mode of leadership development are only two of many challenges that can influence the effectiveness of learning and performance management activities in an organization. The manner in which an organization addresses these challenges can make a major impact on the effectiveness of organizational learning within a company.

Discussion Questions

1. How has the American Express Learning Network utilized learning theory, goal setting, and reward systems in addressing the challenge of its own staff members' training and development needs?

2. How is the use of learning theory and goal-setting theory evident in the design of AMEX's leadership development program?

3. Using relevant concepts from Chapter 6, explain why you think the blended learning approach to leadership development produced the best results for evaluation levels 3, 4, and 5.

SOURCE: This case was written by Michael K. McCuddy, The Louis S. and Mary L. Morgal Chair of Christian Business Ethics and Professor of Management, College of Business Administration, Valparaiso University.

SB 15

13

14

S/B REPAIR
CONFIRMATION

Work Teams and Groups

LEARNING OBJECTIVES

After reading this chapter, you should be able to do the following:

1 Define *group* and *work team*.
2 Explain four important aspects of group behavior.
3 Describe group formation, the four stages of a group's development, and the characteristics of a mature group.
4 Explain the task and maintenance functions in groups.
5 Identify the social benefits of group and team membership.
6 Discuss diversity and creativity in teams.
7 Discuss empowerment, teamwork, and self-managed teams.
8 Explain the importance of upper echelons and top management teams.

THINKING AHEAD: TOYOTA

Trust Is Job One for Toyota

The Toyota Way to number one was not necessarily an easy one for the Japanese-based corporation.[1] The trend line that took the company past General Motors in worldwide sales globally in 2007 is likely to hold up over the coming years. As is often the case for a lead runner, Toyota is not complacent about its position. Being number two is often more comfortable because it allows a company to benchmark efforts, progress, and success against its more successful competitor. Being number one allows a company to set the standards and lead the way, but puts it risk by making it more vulnerable to change. The Toyota Way is constant improvement. While the company does not have a monopoly on this idea, it certainly exemplifies it.

In addition to constant striving for improvement, teamwork is a hallmark of both the Japanese way and the Toyota Way. At the heart of great teamwork is trust; trust in team members, in oneself, and in the system. Trust is more important than price for Toyota, though price is important as well. Trust is the basis of long-lasting relationships, it drives the teamwork that Toyota has with its suppliers, and it leads to win-win outcomes for all concerned. One supplier of axles for Toyota pickup trucks, for example, was flabbergasted when there was no mention of price during the negotiations. Toyota's entire focus was on the supplier's processes and quality. Were they acceptable to Toyota?

Much has been made of an uneven playing field between Toyota and General Motors, with key comparisons focusing on the cost structures. GM workers have enjoyed some of the best retirement and medical benefits in the American workforce. These benefits drive up the cost of GM cars. It is not all in the cost structure, however. Toyota has had its own challenges in overcoming the cultural barriers to understanding Americans and American needs. For example, the Camry's chief engineer is a Japanese man, and while the car does not sell well in Japan, it is a huge success in America. Why? Because the chief engineer and his team apply themselves to understanding American customer desires. Will Toyota always be a "Japanese" company?

---

(1) Define *group* and *work team*.

Northrop Grumman was able to achieve teamwork among employees, customers, and partners through knowledge sharing in integrated product teams.[2] Not all teams and groups work face to face. In today's information age, advanced computer and telecommunications technologies enable organizations to be more flexible through the use of virtual teams.[3] Virtual teams also address new workforce demographics, enabling companies to access expertise and the best employees who may be located anywhere in the world. Whether a traditional group or a virtual team, groups and teams continue to play a vital role in organizational behavior and performance at work.

A *group* is two or more people having common interests, objectives, and continuing interaction. Table 9.1 summarizes the characteristics of a well-functioning, effective group.[4] A *work team* is a group of people with complementary skills who are committed to a common mission, performance goals, and approach for which they hold themselves mutually accountable.[5] All work teams are groups, but not all groups are work teams. Groups emphasize individual leadership, individual accountability, and individual work products. Work teams emphasize shared leadership, mutual accountability, and collective work products.

group
Two or more people with common interests, objectives, and continuing interaction.

work team
A group of people with complementary skills who are committed to a common mission, performance goals, and approach for which they hold themselves mutually accountable.

TABLE 9.1   Characteristics of a Well-Functioning, Effective Group

- The atmosphere tends to be relaxed, comfortable, and informal.
- The group's task is well understood and accepted by the members.
- The members listen well to one another; most members participate in a good deal of task-relevant discussion.
- People express both their feelings and their ideas.
- Conflict and disagreement are present and centered around ideas or methods, not personalities or people.
- The group is aware and conscious of its own operation and function.
- Decisions are usually based on consensus, not majority vote.
- When actions are decided, clear assignments are made and accepted by members of the group.

The chapter begins with a traditional discussion of group behavior and group development in the first two sections. The third section discusses teams. The final two sections explore the contemporary team issues of empowerment, self-managed teams, and upper echelon teams.

GROUP BEHAVIOR

Group behavior has been a subject of interest in social psychology for a long time, and many different aspects of group behavior have been studied over the years. We now look at four topics relevant to groups functioning in organizations: norms of behavior, group cohesion, social loafing, and loss of individuality. Group behavior topics related to decision making, such as polarization and groupthink, are addressed in Chapter 10.

② Explain four important aspects of group behavior.

Norms of Behavior

The standards that a work group uses to evaluate the behavior of its members are its *norms of behavior*. These norms may be written or unwritten, verbalized or not, implicit or explicit. As long as individual members of the group understand them, the norms can be effective in influencing behavior. Norms may specify what members of a group should do (such as a stated dress code for men and women), or they may specify what members of a group should not do (such as executives not behaving arrogantly with employees).

Norms may exist in any aspect of work group life. They may evolve informally or unconsciously within a group, or they may arise in response to challenges, such as the norm of disciplined behavior by firefighters in responding to a three-alarm fire to protect the group.[6] Performance norms are among the most important group norms from the organization's perspective. Even when group members work in isolation on creative projects, they display conformity to group norms.[7] Group norms of cooperative behavior within a teams can lead to members working for mutual benefit, which in turn facilitate team performance.[8] We discuss performance standards further in a later section of this chapter. Organizational culture and corporate codes of ethics, such as Johnson & Johnson's credo (see Chapter 2), reflect behavioral norms expected within work groups. Finally, norms that create awareness of, and help regulate, emotions are critical to groups' effectiveness.[9]

Group Cohesion

The "interpersonal glue" that makes the members of a group stick together is *group cohesion*. Group cohesion can enhance job satisfaction for members and improve organizational productivity.[10] Highly cohesive groups are able to control and manage their membership better than work groups low in cohesion. In one study of 381 banking teams in Hong Kong and the United States, increased job complexity and task autonomy led to increased group cohesiveness, which translated into better performance.[11] In addition to performance, highly cohesive groups are strongly motivated to maintain good, close relationships among the members. We examine group cohesion in further detail, along with factors leading to high levels of it, when discussing the common characteristics of well-developed groups.

Social Loafing

Social loafing occurs when one or more group members rely on the efforts of other group members and fail to contribute their own time, effort, thoughts, or other

norms of behavior
The standards that a work group uses to evaluate the behavior of its members.

group cohesion
The "interpersonal glue" that makes members of a group stick together.

social loafing
The failure of a group member to contribute personal time, effort, thoughts, or other resources to the group.

resources to a group.[12] This may create a drag on the group's efforts and achievements. Some scholars argue that, from the individual's standpoint, social loafing, or free riding, is rational behavior in response to an experience of inequity or when individual efforts are hard to observe. However, it shortchanges the group, which loses potentially valuable resources possessed by individual members.[13]

A number of methods for countering social loafing exist, such as having identifiable individual contributions to the group product and member self-evaluation systems. For example, if each group member is responsible for a specific input to the group, a member's failure to contribute will be noticed by everyone. If members must formally evaluate their contributions to the group, they are less likely to loaf.

Loss of Individuality

Social loafing may be detrimental to group achievement, but it does not have the potentially explosive effects of *loss of individuality*. Loss of individuality, or deindividuation, is a social process in which individual group members lose self-awareness and its accompanying sense of accountability, inhibition, and responsibility for individual behavior.[14]

When individuality is lost, people may engage in morally reprehensible acts and even violent behavior as committed members of their group or organization. For example, loss of individuality was one of several contributing factors in the violent and aggressive acts that led to the riot that destroyed sections of Los Angeles following the Rodney King verdict in the early 1990s. Loss of individuality is not always negative or destructive, however. The loosening of normal ego control mechanisms in the individual may lead to prosocial behavior and heroic acts in dangerous situations.[15] A group that successfully matures may not encounter problems with loss of individuality.

GROUP FORMATION AND DEVELOPMENT

(3) Describe group formation, the four stages of a group's development, and the characteristics of a mature group.

After its formation, a group goes through predictable stages of development. If successful, it emerges as a mature group. One logical group development model proposes four stages following the group's formation:[16] mutual acceptance, decision making, motivation and commitment, and control and sanctions. To become a mature group, each of the stages in development must be successfully negotiated.

According to this group development model, a group addresses three issues: interpersonal issues, task issues, and authority issues.[17] The interpersonal issues include matters of trust, personal comfort, and security. As we saw in the Thinking Ahead feature, trust is a key issue for Toyota in its working relationships. The task issues include the mission or purpose of the group, the methods the group employs, and the outcomes expected of the group. The authority issues include decisions about who is in charge, how power and influence are managed, and who has the right to tell whom to do what. This section addresses group formation, each stage of group development, and the characteristics of a mature group.

Group Formation

loss of individuality

A social process in which individual group members lose self-awareness and its accompanying sense of accountability, inhibition, and responsibility for individual behavior.

Formal and informal groups form in organizations for different reasons. Formal groups are sometimes called official or assigned groups, and informal groups may be called unofficial or emergent groups. Formal groups gather to perform various tasks and include an executive and staff, standing committees of the board of directors, project task forces, and temporary committees. An example of a formal group was the task force assembled by the University of Texas at Arlington (UTA), whose mission was to design the Goolsby Leadership Academy that bridges academics and practice. Chaired by the associate dean of business, the task force was composed of seven members with diverse academic expertise and business experience. The task force envisioned a five-year developmental plan to create a national center of excellence in preparing Goolsby Scholars for authentic leadership in the twenty-first century.

Diversity is an important consideration in the formation of groups. For example, Monsanto Agricultural Company, now simply Monsanto Company, created a task force titled "Valuing Diversity" to address subtle discrimination resulting from workforce diversity.[18] The original task force was titled "Eliminating Subtle Discrimination (ESD)" and was composed of fifteen women, minorities, and white males. Subtle discrimination might include the use of gender- or culture-specific language. Monsanto and the task force's intent was to build on individual differences—whether in terms of gender, race, or culture—in developing a dominant heterogeneous culture. Diversity can enhance group performance. One study of gender diversity among U.S. workers found that men and women in gender-balanced groups had higher job satisfaction than those in homogeneous groups.[19]

Diversity is important in the workplace. PepsiCo President and CEO Indra Nooyi was born in India.

Ethnic diversity has characterized many industrial work groups in the United States since the 1800s. This was especially true during the early years of the 1900s, when waves of immigrant workers arrived from Germany, Yugoslavia, Italy, Poland, Scotland, the Scandinavian countries, and many other nations. Organizations were challenged to blend these culturally and linguistically diverse peoples into effective work groups.

In addition to ethnic, gender, and cultural diversity, there is interpersonal diversity. Highly effective work groups achieve compatibility through interpersonal diversity. Successful interpersonal relationships are the basis of group effort, a key foundation for business success. Effective, productive work groups often differ in their needs for inclusion in activities, control of people and events, and interpersonal affection from others. Although diverse in their interpersonal needs, the work group thus finds strength through balance and complementarity.

Informal groups evolve in the work setting to gratify a variety of member needs not met by formal groups. For example, organizational members' inclusion and affection needs might be satisfied through informal athletic or interest groups. Athletic teams representing a department, unit, or company may achieve semiofficial status, such as the AT&T National Running Team that uses the corporate logo on its race shirts.

Stages of Group Development

All groups, formal and informal, go through stages of development, from forming interpersonal relationships among the members to becoming a mature and productive unit. Mature groups are able to work through the necessary interpersonal, task, and authority issues to achieve at high levels. Demographic diversity and group fault lines (i.e., potential breaking points in a group) are two possible predictors of the sense-making process, subgroup formation patterns, and nature of group conflict at various stages of group development.[20] Hence, group development through these stages may not always be smooth.

There are a number of group development models in the literature and we look at two of these models in particular. These two well-known models are Tuckman's

FIGURE 9.1 Tuckman's Five-Stage Model of Group Development

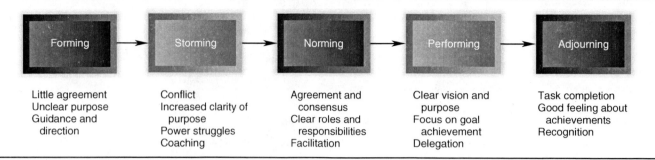

Forming	Storming	Norming	Performing	Adjourning
Little agreement Unclear purpose Guidance and direction	Conflict Increased clarity of purpose Power struggles Coaching	Agreement and consensus Clear roles and responsibilities Facilitation	Clear vision and purpose Focus on goal achievement Delegation	Task completion Good feeling about achievements Recognition

and Gersick's. Each of these models looks at the evolution of behavior in teams, and Tuckman's model also focuses on leadership.

The Five-Stage Model Bruce Tuckman's five-stage model of group development proposes that team behavior progresses through five stages: forming, storming, norming, performing, and adjourning.[21] These stages and the emphasis on relationships and leadership styles in each are shown in Figure 9.1.

Dependence on guidance and direction is the defining characteristic in the *forming* stage. Team members are unclear about individual roles and responsibilities and tend to rely heavily on the leader to answer questions about the team's purpose, objectives, and external relationships. Moving from this stage requires that team members feel they are part of the team.

Team members compete for position in the *storming* stage. As the name suggests, this is a stage of considerable conflict as power struggles, cliques, and factions within the group begin to form. Clarity of purpose increases, but uncertainties still exist. This is also the stage when members assess one another with regard to trustworthiness, emotional comfort, and evaluative acceptance. For the "Valuing Diversity" task force at Monsanto, trust was one of the early issues to be worked through. A coaching style by the leader is key during this stage of group development as team members may challenge him or her.

Agreement and consensus are characteristic of team members in the *norming* stage. It is in this stage that roles and responsibilities become clear and accepted with big decisions being made by group agreement. The focus turns from interpersonal relations to decision-making activities related to the group's task accomplishment. Small decisions may be delegated to individuals or small teams within the group. The group addresses authority questions like these: Who is responsible for what aspects of the group's work? Does the group need one primary leader and spokesperson? Wallace Supply Company, an industrial distributor of pipes, valves, and fittings, has found employee teams particularly valuable in this aspect of work life.[22] Leadership is facilitative with some leadership responsibilities being shared by the team.

As a team moves into the *performing* stage, it becomes more strategically aware and clear about its mission and purpose. In this stage of development, the group has successfully worked through the necessary interpersonal, task, and authority issues and can stand on its own with little interference from the leader. Primarily, the team makes decisions, and disagreements are resolved positively with necessary changes to structure and processes attended to by the team. A mature group is able to control its members through the judicious application of specific positive and negative sanctions based on the evaluation of specific member behaviors. Recent research shows that evaluation biases stemming from liking someone operate in face-to-face groups but not in electronic groups, such as virtual teams.[23] Members at this stage do not need to be instructed but may ask for assistance from the leader with personal or interpersonal development. The team requires a leader who delegates and oversees.

The final stage of group development is the *adjourning* stage. When the task is completed, everyone on the team can move on to new and different things. Team members have a sense of accomplishment and feel good knowing that their purpose is fulfilled. The leader's role is primarily one of recognition of the group's achievements. Unless the group is a task force or other informal team, most groups in organizations remain at the performing stage and do not disband as the adjourning stage suggests.

Punctuated Equilibrium Model Although it is still highly cited in team and group research, Tuckman's "forming–norming–storming–performing–adjourning" model may be unrealistic from an organizational perspective. In fact, research has shown that many teams experience relational conflicts at different times and in different contexts. Connie Gersick proposes that groups do not necessarily progress linearly from one step to another in a predetermined sequence but alternate between periods of inertia with little visible progress toward goal achievement *punctuated* by bursts of energy as work groups develop. It is in these periods of energy that the majority of a group's work is accomplished.[24] For example, a task force given nine months to complete a task may use the first four months to choose its norms, explore contextual issues, and determine how it will communicate.

Characteristics of a Mature Group

The description of a well-functioning, effective group in Table 9.1 characterizes a mature group. Such a group has four distinguishing characteristics: a clear purpose and mission, well-understood norms and standards of conduct, a high level of group cohesion, and a flexible status structure.

Purpose and Mission The purpose and mission may be assigned to a group (as in the previous example of the Goolsby Leadership Academy task force of UTA) or emerge from within the group (as in the case of the AT&T National Running Team). Even in the case of an assigned mission, the group may reexamine, modify, revise, or question the mission. It may also embrace the mission as stated. The importance of mission is exemplified in IBM's Process Quality Management, which requires that a process team of not more than twelve people develop a clear understanding of mission as the first step in the process.[25] The IBM approach demands that all members agree to go in the same direction. The mission statement is converted into a specific agenda, clear goals, and a set of critical success factors. Stating the purpose and mission in the form of specific goals enhances productivity over and above any performance benefits achieved through individual goal setting.[26]

Behavioral Norms Behavioral norms, which evolve over a period of time, are well-understood standards of behavior within a group.[27] They are benchmarks against which team members are evaluated and judged by other team members. Some behavioral norms become written rules, such as an attendance policy or an ethical code for a team. Other norms remain informal, although they are no less understood by team members. Dress codes and norms about after-hours socializing may fall into this category. Behavioral norms also evolve around performance and productivity.[28] Productivity norms even influence the performance of sports teams.[29] The group's productivity norm may or may not be consistent with, and supportive of, the organization's productivity standards. A high-performance team sets productivity standards above organizational expectations with the intent to excel. Average teams set productivity

Taking Care of All Concerned

Former Chairman Bill Greehey spun Valero Energy off of Coastal Corporation in 1980, and then worked to set a standard within the company of compassion and community service that has led to great market as well as human resource results. Valero Energy was ranked number three in the *Fortune* list of "100 Best Companies to Work For 2006." This success comes from hundreds of groups and teams throughout the company and the compassion of human resources professionals like Robert K. (Bob) Grimes. Grimes was encouraged by Greehey to take his message of compassion, caring, and community service to Corpus Christi from the headquarters in San Antonio, heading up human resources at their south Texas refinery. Grimes did just

COURTESY OF VALERO ENERGY CORPORATION

Valero Energy was ranked No. 3 on the list of "*Fortune* 100 Best Companies to Work For 2006," due in part to the compassion of human resource professionals like Robert Grimes, pictured here.

that and then took on public relations responsibilities too. He led by example, becoming president of the Rotary Club of Corpus Christi, being recognized for his committed community service as a Paul Harris Fellow for living the Rotary test: "Will it be beneficial to all concerned?" From a small group of caring and committed professionals, Valero has grown since 2002 into the largest refining company in North America. Bob Grimes' and other Valero leaders' challenge is to extend the norms of caring, compassion, and community service throughout the thousands of new employees who now make up 80 percent of the company.

SOURCE: B. Leonard, "Taking Care of Their Own," *HR Magazine* (June 2006): 112–115.

standards based on, and consistent with, organizational expectations. Noncompliant or counterproductive teams may set productivity standards below organizational expectations with the intent of damaging the organization or creating change. On the positive side, behavioral norms can permeate an entire organizational culture for the benefit of all, as we see in The Real World 9.1 discussion of Valero Energy.

Group Cohesion   Group cohesion was earlier described as the interpersonal attraction binding group members together. It enables a group to exercise effective control over its members in relation to its behavioral norms and standards. Goal conflict, unpleasant experiences, and domination of a subgroup are among the threats to a group's cohesion. Groups with low levels of cohesion have greater difficulty exercising control over their members and enforcing their standards of behavior. A classic study of cohesiveness in 238 industrial work groups found cohesion to be an important factor influencing anxiety, tension, and productivity within the groups.[30] Specifically, work-related tension and anxiety were lower in teams high in cohesion, and they were higher in teams low in cohesion, as depicted in Figure 9.2. This suggests that cohesion has a calming effect on team members, at least concerning work-related tension and anxiety. In addition, actual productivity was found to vary significantly less in highly cohesive teams, making these teams much more predictable with regard to their productivity. The actual productivity levels were primarily determined by the productivity norms within each work group. That is, highly cohesive groups with

FIGURE 9.2 Cohesiveness and Work-Related Tension*

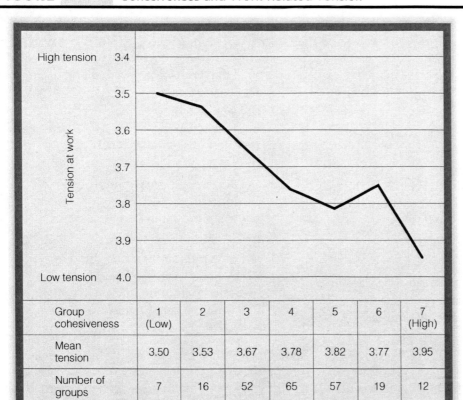

Note: Product–moment correlation is 0.28, and critical ratio is 4.20; the group cohesion–tension relationship is highly significant at the .001 level.

*The measure of tension at work is based on group mean response to the question "Does your work ever make you feel 'jumpy' or nervous?" A low numerical score represents relatively high tension.

SOURCE: From S. E. Seashore, *Group Cohesiveness in the Industrial Work Group*, 1954. Research conducted by Stanley E. Seashore at the Institute for Social Research, University of Michigan. Reprinted by permission.

high production standards are very productive. Similarly, highly cohesive groups with low productivity standards are unproductive. Member satisfaction, commitment, and communication are better in highly cohesive groups. Groupthink may be a problem in highly cohesive groups and is discussed in Chapter 10. You 9.1 includes the three group cohesion questions from this research project. Complete You 9.1 to determine the level of cohesion in a group of which you are a member.

Group cohesion is influenced by a number of factors, most notably time, size, the prestige of the team, external pressure, and internal competition. Group cohesion evolves gradually over time through a group's normal development. Smaller groups—those of five or seven members, for example—are more cohesive than those of more than twenty-five, although cohesion does not decline much with size after forty or more members. Prestige or social status also influences a group's cohesion, with more prestigious groups, such as the U.S. Air Force Thunderbirds or the U.S. Navy Blue Angels, being highly cohesive. However, even groups of very low prestige may be highly cohesive in how they stick together. Finally, external pressure and internal competition influence group cohesion. Although the mechanics' union, pilots, and other internal constituencies at Eastern Airlines had various differences of opinion, they all pulled together in a cohesive fashion in resisting Frank Lorenzo when he came in to reshape the airline before its demise. Whereas external pressures tend to enhance cohesion, internal competition usually decreases cohesion within a team. One study found that company-imposed work pressure disrupted group cohesion by increasing internal competition and reducing cooperative interpersonal activity.[31]

How Cohesive Is Your Group?

Think about a group of which you are a member. Answer each of the following questions in relation to this group by circling the number next to the alternative that most reflects your feelings.

1. Do you feel that you are really a part of your group?
   5—Really a part of the group.
   4—Included in most ways.
   3—Included in some ways, but not in others.
   2—Do not feel I really belong.
   1—Do not work with any one group of people.

2. If you had a chance to do the same activities in another group, for the same pay if it is a work group, how would you feel about moving?
   1—Would want very much to move.
   2—Would rather move than stay where I am.
   3—Would make no difference to me.
   4—Would rather stay where I am than move.
   5—Would want very much to stay where I am.

3. How does your group compare with other groups that you are familiar with on each of the following points?
   - The way people get along together.
     5—Better than most.
     3—About the same as most.
     1—Not as good as most.
   - The way people stick together.
     5—Better than most.
     3—About the same as most.
     1—Not as good as most.
   - The way people help one another on the job.
     5—Better than most.
     3—About the same as most.
     1—Not as good as most.

Add up your circled responses. If you have a number of 20 or above, you view your group as highly cohesive. If you have a number between 10 and 19, you view your group's cohesion as average. If you have a number of 7 or less, you view your group as very low in cohesion.

SOURCE: From S. E. Seashore, *Group Cohesiveness in the Industrial Work Group*, University of Michigan, 1954. Reprinted by permission.

Status Structure *Status structure* is the set of authority and task relations among a group's members. The status structure may be hierarchical or egalitarian (i.e., democratic), depending on the group. Successful resolution of the authority issue within a team results in a well-understood status structure of leader–follower relationships. Where leadership problems arise, it is important to find solutions and build team leader effectiveness.[32] Whereas groups tend to have one leader, teams tend to share leadership. For example, one person may be the team's task master who sets the agenda, initiates much of the work activity, and ensures that the team meets its deadlines. Another team member may take a leadership role in maintaining effective interpersonal relationships in the group. Hence, shared leadership is very feasible in teams. An effective status structure results in role interrelatedness among group members,[33] such as that displayed by Bill Perez and Bill Wrigley. Their tag-team style of cooperation in leading Wm. Wrigley Jr. Company has served the company well.

Diversity in a group is healthy, and members may contribute to the collective effort through one of four basic styles:[34] the contributor, the collaborator, the communicator, and the challenger. The contributor is data driven, supplies necessary information, and adheres to high performance standards. The collaborator sees the big picture and is able to keep a constant focus on the mission and urge other

status structure
The set of authority and task relations among a group's members.

members to join efforts for mission accomplishment. The communicator listens well, facilitates the group's process, and humanizes the collective effort. The challenger is the devil's advocate who questions everything from the group's mission, purpose, and methods to its ethics. Members may exhibit one or more of these four basic styles over a period of time. In addition, an effective group must have an integrator.[35] This can be especially important in cross-functional teams, where different perspectives carry the seeds of conflict. However, cross-functional teams are not necessarily a problem. Effectively managing cross-functional teams of artists, designers, printers, and financial experts enabled Hallmark Cards to cut its new-product development time in half.[36]

Emergent leadership in groups was studied among sixty-two men and sixty women.[37] Groups performed tasks not classified as either masculine or feminine, that is, "sex-neutral" tasks. Men and women both emerged as leaders, and neither gender had significantly more emergent leaders. However, group members who described themselves in masculine terms were significantly more likely to emerge as leaders than group members who described themselves in feminine, androgynous (both masculine and feminine), or undifferentiated (neither masculine nor feminine) terms. Hence, gender stereotypes may play a role in emergent leadership.

Task and Maintenance Functions

An effective group or team carries out various task functions to perform its work successfully and various maintenance functions to ensure member satisfaction and a sense of team spirit.[38] Teams that successfully fulfill these functions afford their members the potential for psychological intimacy and integrated involvement. Table 9.2 presents nine task and nine maintenance functions in teams or groups.

Task functions are those activities directly related to the effective completion of the team's work. For example, the task of initiating activity involves suggesting ideas, defining problems, and proposing approaches and/or solutions to problems. The task of seeking information involves asking for ideas, suggestions, information, or facts. Effective teams have members who fulfill various task functions as they are required.

Some task functions are more important at one time in the life of a group, and other functions are more important at other times. For example, during the engineering test periods for new technologies, the engineering team needs members who focus on testing the practical applications of suggestions and those who diagnose problems and suggest solutions.

(4) Explain the task and maintenance functions in groups.

TABLE 9.2 Task and Maintenance Functions in Teams or Groups

Task Functions	Maintenance Functions
Initiating activities	Supporting others
Seeking information	Following others' leads
Giving information	Gatekeeping communication
Elaborating concepts	Setting standards
Coordinating activities	Expressing member feelings
Summarizing ideas	Testing group decisions
Testing ideas	Consensus testing
Evaluating effectiveness	Harmonizing conflict
Diagnosing problems	Reducing tension

task function
An activity directly related to the effective completion of a team's work.

The effective use of task functions leads to the success of the group, and the failure to use them may lead to disaster. For example, the successful initiation and coordination of an emergency room (ER) team's activities by the senior resident saved the life of a knife wound victim.[39] The victim was stabbed one-quarter inch below the heart, and the ER team acted quickly to stem the bleeding, begin intravenous fluids, and monitor the victim's vital signs.

Maintenance functions are those activities essential to the effective, satisfying interpersonal relationships within a group or team. For example, following another group member's lead may be as important as leading others. Communication gatekeepers within a group ensure balanced contributions from all members. Because task activities build tension into teams and groups working together, tension-reduction activities are important to drain off negative or destructive feelings. For example, in a study of twenty-five work groups over a five-year period, humor and joking behavior were found to enhance the social relationships in the groups.[40] The researchers concluded that performance improvements in the twenty-five groups indirectly resulted from improved relationships attributable to the humor and joking behaviors. Maintenance functions enhance togetherness, cooperation, and teamwork, enabling members to achieve psychological intimacy while furthering the success of the team. Jody Grant's supportive attitude and comfortable demeanor as chairman and CEO of Texas Capital Bancshares enabled him to build a vibrant bank in the aftermath of the great Texas banking crash of 1982–1992. Grant was respected for his expertise *and* his ability to build relationships. Both task and maintenance functions are important for successful groups and teams.

WORK TEAMS IN ORGANIZATIONS

Work teams are task-oriented groups, though in some organizations the term *team* has a negative connotation for unions and union members. Work teams make important and valuable contributions to the organization and are important to the member need satisfaction. For example, an idea to implement a simple change in packaging from a work team at Glenair, a UK-based aerospace and defense contractor, saved the company twenty-five minutes of packaging time per unit. Additionally, a job that used to take one worker half an hour to complete was reduced to only five minutes, freeing the worker to perform other work in the factory.[41]

Several kinds of work teams exist. One classification scheme uses a sports analogy. Some teams work like baseball teams with set responsibilities, other teams work like football teams through coordinated action, and still others work like doubles tennis teams with primary yet flexible responsibilities. In addition, crews are a distinct type of work team that can be studied using the concept of "crewness."[42] Although each type of team may have a useful role in the organization, the individual expert should not be overlooked.[43] That is, at the right time and in the right context, individual members must be allowed to shine.

Why Work Teams?

Teams are very useful in performing work that is complicated, complex, interrelated, and/or more voluminous than one person can handle. Harold Geneen, while chairman of ITT, said, "If I had enough arms and legs and time, I'd do it all myself." Obviously, people working in organizations cannot do everything because of the limitations of arms, legs, time, expertise, knowledge, and other resources. Individual limitations are overcome and problems are solved through teamwork and collaboration. World-class U.S. corporations, such as Motorola, Inc., are increasingly deploying work teams in their global affiliates to meet the competition and gain an

maintenance function

An activity essential to effective, satisfying interpersonal relationships within a team or group.

advantage.[44] Motorola's "Be Cool" team in the Philippines has a family atmosphere and may even begin a meeting with a prayer, yet is committed to improving individual and team performance. As we saw in Thinking Ahead, Toyota uses teamwork more broadly in its relationship with suppliers and customers too.

Teams make important contributions to organizations in work areas that lend themselves to teamwork. *Teamwork* is a core value at Hewlett-Packard. Complex, interdependent work tasks and activities that require collaboration particularly lend themselves to teamwork. Teams are appropriate where knowledge, talent, skills, and abilities are dispersed across organizational members and require integrated effort for task accomplishment. The recent emphasis on team-oriented work environments is based on empowerment with collaboration, not on power and competition. Teams with experience working together may produce valuable innovations, and individual contributions are valuable as well.[45] Larry Hirschhorn labels this "the new team environment" founded on a significantly more empowered workforce in the industrial sectors of the American economy. This new team environment is compared with the old work environment in Table 9.3. Beyond the new team environment is the emergence of virtual teams, such as those at BP PLC, Nokia Corporation, and Ogilvy & Mather as we see in The Real World 9.2.

That teams are necessary is a driving principle of total quality efforts in organizations. Total quality efforts often require the formation of teams—especially cross-functional teams composed of people from different functions, such as manufacturing and design, who are responsible for specific organizational processes. Former Eastman Kodak CEO George Fisher believed in the importance of participation and cooperation as foundations for teamwork and a total quality program. In a study of forty machine crews in a northeastern U.S. paper mill, organizational citizenship behaviors, specifically helping behavior and sportsmanship, contributed significantly to the quantity and quality of work group performance.[46]

Work Team Structure and Work Team Process

Work team effectiveness in the new team environment requires attention by management to both work team structure and work team process.[47] The primary structural issues for work teams are goals and objectives, operating guidelines,

TABLE A Comparison of the New Team Environment versus the Old Work Environment

New Team Environment	Old Work Environment
Person comes up with initiatives.	Person follows orders.
Team has considerable authority to chart its own steps.	Team depends on the manager to chart its course.
Members form a team because people learn to collaborate in the face of their emerging right to think for themselves. People both rock the boat and work together.	Members were a team because people conformed to direction set by the manager. No one rocked the boat.
People cooperate by using their thoughts and feelings. They link up through direct talk.	People cooperated by suppressing their thoughts and feelings. They wanted to get along.

SOURCE: *Managing in the New Team Environment*, by L. Hirschhorn, © 1991. Reprinted by permission of Prentice-Hall, Inc., Upper Saddle River, N.J.

teamwork
Joint action by a team of people in which individual interests are subordinated to team unity.

Rule of the Game in Virtual Teams at BP PLC, Nokia, and Ogilvy & Mather

BP PLC, Nokia, and Ogilvy & Mather are among the global companies that are benefiting from virtual teams. David Ogilvy, the late founder of advertising company Ogilvy & Mather, set the stage early for virtual teams with his investment in sharing knowledge through an internal IT-based community within the company. The in-depth case studies of successful virtual teams at Ogilvy & Mather, BP, and Nokia have led to ten golden rules.

1. Invest in an online resource where members can learn quickly about one another.

2. Choose a few team members who already know each other.

3. Identify "boundary spanners" and ensure that they make up at least 15 percent of the team.

4. Cultivate boundary spanners as a regular part of companywide practices and processes.

5. Break the team's work into modules so that progress in one location is not overly dependent on progress in another.

6. Create an online site where a team can collaborate, exchange ideas, and inspire one another.

7. Encourage frequent communication.

8. Assign only tasks that are challenging and interesting.

9. Ensure the task is meaningful to the team and the company.

10. When building a virtual team, solicit volunteers as much as possible.

These rules come from successful experience and any company implementing virtual teams should monitor the success and problems within their own work context.

SOURCE: L. Gratton, "Working Together . . . When Apart," *The Wall Street Journal* (June 16, 2007): R4.

performance measures, and the specification of roles. A work team's goals and objectives specify what must be achieved, while the operating guidelines set the organizational boundaries and decision-making limits within which the team must function. The goal-setting process was discussed in Chapter 6 and has applicability for work teams, too. In addition to these two structural elements, the work team needs to know what performance measures are being used to assess its task accomplishment. For example, a medical emergency team's performance measures might include the success rate in saving critically injured patients and the average number of hours a patient is in the emergency room before being transferred to a hospital bed. Finally, work team structure requires a clearly specified set of roles for the executives and managers who oversee the work of the team, for the work team leaders who exercise influence over team members, and for team members. These role specifications should include information about required role behaviors, such as decision making and task performance, as well as restrictions or limits on role behaviors, such as the limitations on managerial interventions in work team activities and decision making. Expectations as well as experience may be especially important for newcomer role performance in work teams.[48]

Work team process is the second important dimension of effectiveness. Two of the important process issues in work teams are the managing of cooperative behaviors and the managing of competitive behaviors. Both sets of behaviors are helpful in task accomplishment, and they should be viewed as complementary sets of behaviors. Cooperative teamwork skills include open communication, trust, personal integrity, positive interdependence, and mutual support. On the other hand, positive competitive teamwork skills include the ability to enjoy competition, play fair, be a good winner or loser; to have access to information for monitoring where the team and members are in the competition; and not to overgeneralize or exaggerate the results of any specific competition. In a study of reward structures in 75 four-member teams, competitive rewards enhanced speed of performance, while cooperative rewards enhanced accuracy of performance.[49]

Work team process issues have become more complex in the global workplace with teams composed of members from many cultures and backgrounds. This is enhanced by the presence of virtual work teams operating on the global landscape. Our discussions of diversity earlier in the text have particular relevance to multicultural work teams. In addition to the process issues of cooperation, competition, and diversity, three other process issues are related to topics we discuss elsewhere in the text. These are empowerment, discussed in the next major section of this chapter; team decision making, discussed in Chapter 10; and conflict management and resolution, discussed in Chapter 13.

Quality Teams and Circles

Quality teams and quality circles are part of a total quality program. Decision making in *quality teams* is discussed in detail in Chapter 10. Quality teams are different from QCs in that they are more formal and are designed and assigned by upper-level management. Quality teams are not voluntary and have formal power, whereas quality circles have less formal power and decision authority. Although less commonly used than a decade ago, quality circle principles continue to have value.

Quality circles (QCs) are small groups of employees who work voluntarily on company time—typically one hour per week—to address work-related problems such as quality control, cost reduction, production planning and techniques, and even product design. Membership in a QC is typically voluntary and is fixed once a circle is formed, although some changes may occur as appropriate. QCs are trained in various problem-solving techniques and use them to address the work-related problems.

QCs were popularized as a Japanese management method when an American, W. Edwards Deming, exported his thinking about QCs to Japan following World War II.[50] QCs became popular in the United States in the 1980s, when companies such as Ford, Hewlett-Packard, and Eastman Kodak implemented them. The Camp Red Cloud Garrison in South Korea saved $2 million by implementing the Six Sigma quality program that involved all garrison supervisors and looked at efficiencies from the customer's perspective. Some of the money saved from technology improvements has gone back to employees in an effort to improve safety equipment, work facilities, and employee recreation.

Quality teams and quality circles must deal with substantive issues if they are to be effective; otherwise, employees begin to believe the quality effort is simply a management ploy. QCs do not necessarily require final decision authority to be effective if their recommendations are always considered seriously and implemented when appropriate. One study found that QCs are effective for a period of time, and then their contributions begin to diminish.[51] This may suggest that quality teams and QCs must be reinforced and periodically reenergized to maintain their effectiveness over long periods of time.

Social Benefits

Two sets of social benefits are available to team or group members. One set accrues from achieving psychological intimacy. The other comes from achieving integrated involvement.[52]

Psychological intimacy is emotional and psychological closeness to other team or group members. It results in feelings of affection and warmth, unconditional

quality team
A team that is part of an organization's structure and is empowered to act on its decisions regarding product and service quality.

quality circle (QC)
A small group of employees who work voluntarily on company time, typically one hour per week, to address work-related problems such as quality control, cost reduction, production planning and techniques, and even product design.

(5) Identify the social benefits of group and team membership.

psychological intimacy
Emotional and psychological closeness to other team or group members.

positive regard, opportunity for emotional expression, openness, security and emotional support, and giving and receiving nurturance. Failure to achieve psychological intimacy results in feelings of emotional isolation and loneliness. This may be especially problematic for chief executives who experience loneliness at the top. Although psychological intimacy is valuable for emotional health and well-being, it need not necessarily be achieved in the work setting.

Integrated involvement is closeness achieved through tasks and activities. It results in enjoyable and involving activities, social identity and self-definition, being valued for one's skills and abilities, opportunity for power and influence, conditional positive regard, and support for one's beliefs and values. Failure to achieve integrated involvement results in social isolation. Whereas psychological intimacy is more emotion based, integrated involvement is more behavior and activity based. Integrated involvement contributes to social psychological health and well-being.

Psychological intimacy and integrated involvement each contribute to overall health. It is not necessary to achieve both in the same team or group. For example, while chief executive at Xerox Corporation, David Kearns was also a marathon runner; he found integrated involvement with his executive team and psychological intimacy with his athletic companions on long-distance runs.

Teams and groups have two sets of functions that operate to enable members to achieve psychological intimacy and integrated involvement. These are task and maintenance functions.

DIVERSITY AND CREATIVITY IN TEAMS

(6) Discuss diversity and creativity in teams.

Diversity and creativity are important, emerging issues in the study of teams and teamwork. Recent research in diversity has focused on the issue of dissimilarity and its effect within the team itself. This is often studied based on social identity theory and self-categorization theory. Later in the chapter, we specifically address the issue of multicultural diversity in upper echelons, or top management teams, in the global workplace. Creativity concerns new and/or dissimilar ideas or ways of doing things within teams. Novelty and innovation are creativity's companions. While creativity is developed in some detail in Chapter 10, we treat it briefly here in the context of teams.

Dissimilarity

We defined diversity in Chapter 1 in terms of individual differences. Recent relational demography research finds that demographic dissimilarity influences employees' absenteeism, commitment, turnover intentions, beliefs, workgroup relationships, self-esteem, and organizational citizenship behavior (OCB).[53] Thus, dissimilarity may have positive or negative effects in teams and on team members. In the accompanying Science feature, we see how structural diversity can enhance team performance. While value dissimilarity may be positively related to task and relationship conflict, it is negatively related to team involvement.[54] This highlights the importance of managing dissimilarity in teams, being open to diversity, and turning conflicts over ideas into positive outcomes.

Functional background is one way to look at dissimilarity in teams. One study of 262 professionals in thirty-seven cross-functional teams found that promoting functional background social identification helped individuals perform better as team members.[55] Another study of multifunctional management teams in a *Fortune* 100 company found that functional background predicted team involvement.[56] Finally, in a slightly different study of 129 members on twenty multidisciplinary project teams, informational dissimilarity had no adverse effects when there was member task and goal congruence.[57] Where there was incongruence, dissimilarity adversely affected team identification and OCBs.

integrated involvement
Closeness achieved through tasks and activities.

Structural "Holeyness" in Teams

This research examined diversity and performance of nineteen teams in a wood products company. The investigators were interested in demographic diversity among team members as well as the structural diversity of the team. Structural diversity concerns the number of structural holes within a work team. A structural hole in a team is a disconnection between two of its members. Is this disconnection good or bad for the team? What are the consequences of having more or fewer structural holes between team members? Neither race nor gender was a demographic factor that influenced the proportion of structural holes within a work team. However, age diversity significantly reduced the extent of structural holeyness. Hence, greater variance in age within a team leads to more member-to-member connections and fewer member-to-member disconnections. Teams with few structural holes may have problems with creativity, while teams with a high proportion of structural holes may have difficulty coordinating. These observations led the researchers to conclude that there is a curvilinear relationship between structural diversity, or structural holeyness, and team performance. The teams with moderate structural diversity achieve the best performance. This research is important because it points out that managers should look at the overall structure and network of relationships within their work teams in addition to the individual characteristics of team members in attempting to elicit the best performance from these teams.

SOURCE: F. Balkundi, M. Kilduff, Z. I. Barsness, and J. H. Michael, "Demographic Antecedents and Performance Consequences of Structural Holes in Work Teams," *Journal of Organizational Behavior* 28 (2007): 241–260.

Creativity

Creativity is often thought of in an individual context rather than a team context. However, there is such a thing as team creativity. In a study of fifty-four research and development teams, one study found that team creativity scores would be explained by aggregation processes across both people and time.[58] The investigators concluded that it is important to consider aggregation across time as well as across individuals when one is attempting to understand team creativity. In another study of creative behavior, a Korean electronics company found that individual dissimilarity in age and performance as well as functional diversity within the team positively affect individual employees' creative behavior.

Some think that the deck is stacked against teams as agents of creativity. Leigh Thompson disagrees and suggests that team creativity and divergent thinking can be enhanced through greater diversity in teams, brainwriting, training facilitators, membership change in teams, electronic brainstorming, and building a playground.[59] These practices can overcome social loafing, conformity, and downward norm setting in teams and organizations. Team members might exercise care in timing the insertion of their novel ideas into the team process so as to maximize the positive impact and benefits.[60]

EMPOWERMENT AND SELF-MANAGED TEAMS

Quality teams and quality circles, as we discussed earlier, are one way to implement teamwork in organizations. Self-managed teams are broad-based work teams that deal with issues beyond quality. Decision making in self-managed teams is also discussed in Chapter 10. On a dysfunctional note, employee resistance behavior can emerge in self-managed work teams. It is influenced by cultural values and can affect employee attitudes.[61] However, self-managed teams have an overall positive history and are increasingly used by U.S. multinational corporations in global operations.

Empowerment may be thought of as an attribute of a person or of an organization's culture.[62] As an organizational culture attribute, empowerment encourages participation, an essential ingredient for teamwork.[63] Quality action teams (QATs) at FedEx

(7) Discuss empowerment, teamwork, and self-managed teams.

are the primary quality improvement process (QIP) technique used by the company to engage management and hourly employees in four- to ten-member problem-solving teams.[64] The teams are empowered to act and solve problems as specific as charting the best route from the Phoenix airport to the local distribution center or as global as making major software enhancements to the online package-tracking system.

Empowerment may give employees the power of a lightning strike, but empowered employees must be properly focused through careful planning and preparation before they strike.[65]

You 9.2 includes several items from FedEx's survey-feedback-action (SFA) survey related to employee empowerment. Complete You 9.2 to see if you are empowered.

Empowerment Skills

Empowerment through employee self-management is an alternative to empowerment through teamwork.[66] Whether through self-management or teamwork, empowerment requires the development of certain skills if it is to be enacted effectively. Competence skills are the first set of skills required for empowerment. Mastery and experience in one's chosen discipline and profession provide an essential foundation for empowerment. This means that new employees and trainees should experience only limited empowerment until they demonstrate the capacity to accept more responsibility, a key aspect of empowerment.

Empowerment also requires certain process skills. The most critical process skills for empowerment include negotiating skills, especially with allies, opponents, and adversaries.[67] Allies are the easiest people to negotiate with because they agree with you about the team's mission, and you can trust their actions and behavior. Opponents require a different negotiating strategy; although you can predict their actions and behavior, they do not agree with your concept of the team's mission. Adversaries are dangerous, difficult people to negotiate with because they do not agree with your concept of the team's mission, and you cannot predict their actions or behaviors.

A third set of empowerment skills involves the development of cooperative and helping behaviors.[68] Cooperative people are motivated to maximize the gains for everyone on the team; they engage in encouraging, helpful behavior to bring about that end. The alternatives to cooperation are competitive, individualistic, and egalitarian orientations. Competitive people are motivated to maximize their personal gains regardless of the expense to other people. This can be very counterproductive from the standpoint of the team. Individualistic people are motivated to act autonomously, though not necessarily to maximize their personal gains. They are less prone to contribute to the efforts of the team. Egalitarian people are motivated to equalize the outcomes for each team member, which may or may not be beneficial to the team's well-being. Actually, the team members who need the most help often get the least because helping behaviors are frequently targeted to the most "expert" team members, a dynamic that actually compromises overall team performance.[69]

Communication skills are a final set of essential empowerment skills.[70] These include skills in self-expression and reflective listening. Empowerment cannot occur in a team unless members are able to express themselves effectively and listen carefully to one another.

Self-Managed Teams

Self-managed teams make decisions that were once reserved for managers. They are also called *self-directed teams* or *autonomous work groups*. Self-managed teams are one way to implement empowerment in organizations. Even so, managers have an important role in providing leadership and influence.[71] In doing so, there is strong support for the use of soft influence tactics in managers' communication with self-directed

self-managed team

A team that makes decisions that were once reserved for managers.

Are You an Empowered Employee?*

Read each of the following statements carefully. Then, to the right, indicate which answer best expresses your level of agreement (5 = strongly agree, 4 = agree, 3 = sometimes agree/sometimes disagree, 2 = disagree, 1 = strongly disagree, and 0 = undecided/do not know). Mark only one answer for each item, and respond to all items.

____ 1. I feel free to tell my manager what I think.	5 4 3 2 1 0
____ 2. My manager is willing to listen to my concerns.	5 4 3 2 1 0
____ 3. My manager asks for my ideas about things affecting our work.	5 4 3 2 1 0
____ 4. My manager treats me with respect and dignity.	5 4 3 2 1 0
____ 5. My manager keeps me informed about things I need to know.	5 4 3 2 1 0
____ 6. My manager lets me do my job without interfering.	5 4 3 2 1 0
____ 7. My manager's boss gives us the support we need.	5 4 3 2 1 0
____ 8. Upper management (directors and above) pays attention to ideas and suggestions from people at my level.	5 4 3 2 1 0

Scoring

To determine if you are an empowered employee, add your scores.

32–40: You are empowered! Managers listen when you speak, respect your ideas, and allow you to do your work.

24–31: You have *some* power! Your ideas are considered sometimes, and you have some freedom of action.

16–23: You must exercise caution! You cannot speak or act too boldly, and your managers appear to exercise close supervision.

8–15: Your wings are clipped! You work in a powerless, restrictive work environment.

*If you are not employed, discuss these questions with a friend who is employed. Is your friend an empowered employee?
SOURCE: *Survey-Feedback-Action (SFA)*, FedEx Corporation, Memphis, TN.

---

teams, which yields more positive results.[72] A one-year study of self-managed teams suggests that they have a positive impact on employee attitudes but not on absenteeism or turnover.[73] Evaluative research is helpful in achieving a better understanding of this relatively new way of approaching teamwork and the design of work. Research can help in establishing expectations for self-managed teams. For example, one study of autonomous work teams found that a key ingredient to enhancing organizational commitment and job satisfaction involves the perception that one has the required skills and abilities to perform well.[74] Further, there are risks, such as groupthink, in self-managing teams that must be prevented or managed if the team is to achieve full development and function.[75] Finally, one evaluation of empowerment, teams, and TQM programs found that companies associated with these popular management techniques did not have higher economic performance.[76]

Other evaluations of self-managed teams are more positive. Southwest Industries, a high-technology aerospace manufacturing firm, embarked on a major internal reorganization in the early 1990s that included the creation of self-managed teams to fit its high-technology production process. Southwest's team approach resulted in a 30 percent increase in shipments, a 30 percent decrease in lead time, a 40 percent decrease in total inventory, a decrease in machinery downtime, and almost a one-third decrease in production costs.[77] Self-managed teams were also the foundation for the miraculous resurrection of the former Chrysler (now DaimlerChrysler) Corporation's oldest plant in New Castle, Indiana, as the United Auto Workers' union and company management forged a partnership for success.[78]

A game called Learning Teams is available to help people create self-directed teams, learn cooperatively, and master factual information.[79] With no outside help, an engineering team in the Defense Systems and Electronics Group (DSEG), now part of Raytheon, developed themselves into a highly effective, productive, self-managed team. They then helped DSEG in its successful effort to win a Malcolm Baldrige National Quality Award.

UPPER ECHELONS: TEAMS AT THE TOP

(8) Explain the importance of upper echelons and top management teams.

Self-managed teams at the top of the organization—top-level executive teams—are referred to as *upper echelons*. Organizations are often a reflection of these upper echelons.[80] Upper echelon theory argues that the background characteristics of the top management team can predict organizational characteristics. Furthermore, upper echelons are one key to the strategic success of the organization.[81] Thus, the teams at the top are instrumental in defining the organization over time such that the values, competence, ethics, and unique characteristics of the top management team are eventually reflected throughout the organization. This ability to exert organization-wide power and influence makes the top management team a key to the company's success. This ability may be compromised if the top team sends mixed signals about teamwork and if executive pay systems foster competition, politics, and individualism.[82]

For example, when Lee Iacocca became CEO at the former Chrysler Corporation, his top management team was assembled to bring about strategic realignment within the corporation by building on Chrysler's historical engineering strength. The dramatic success of Chrysler during the early 1980s was followed by struggle and accommodation during the late 1980s. This raises the question of how long a CEO and the top management team can sustain organizational success.

upper echelon

A top-level executive team in an organization.

Hambrick and Fukutomi address this question by examining the dynamic relationship between a CEO's tenure and the success of the organization.[83] They found five seasons in a CEO's tenure: (1) response to a mandate, (2) experimentation, (3) selection of an enduring theme, (4) convergence, and (5) dysfunction. A summary of each season is shown in Table 9.4. All else being equal, this seasons model has significant implications for organizational performance. Specifically, organizational performance increases during a CEO's tenure to a peak, after which performance declines. This relationship is depicted in Figure 9.3. The peak has been found to come at about seven years—somewhere in the middle of the executive's seasons. As indicated by the dotted lines in the figure, the peak may be extended, depending on several factors, such as diversity in the executive's support team.

© KIMBERLY WHITE/REUTERS/LANDOV

Top-level executive teams are referred to as upper echelons. Google executives pictured here (L-R): Chief Executive Officer Eric Schmidt, Vice President of Global Communications and Public Affairs Elliot Schrage, Co-Founder & President of Products Larry Page, Co-Founder & President of Technology Sergey Brin, and Senior Vice President of Corporate Development David Drummond.

TABLE 9.4 The Five Seasons of a CEO's Tenure

Critical CEO Characteristics	1 Response to Mandate	2 Experimentation	3 Selection of an Enduring Theme	4 Convergence	5 Dysfunction
Commitment to a Paradigm	Moderately strong	Could be strong or weak	Moderately strong	Strong; increasing	Very strong
Task Knowledge	Low but rapidly increasing	Moderate; somewhat increasing	High; slightly increasing	High; slightly increasing	High; slightly increasing
Information Diversity	Many sources; unfiltered	Many sources but increasingly filtered	Fewer sources; moderately filtered	Few sources; highly filtered	Very few sources; highly filtered
Task Interest	High	High	Moderately high	Moderately high but diminishing	Moderately low and diminishing
Power	Low; increasing	Moderate; increasing	Moderate; increasing	Strong; increasing	Very strong; increasing

SOURCE: D. Hambrick and G. D. S. Fukutomi, "The Seasons of a CEO's Tenure," *Academy of Management Review*, 1991, p. 729. Permission conveyed through Copyright Clearance Center, Inc.

Diversity at the Top

From an organizational health standpoint, diversity and depth in the top management team enhance the CEO's well-being.[84] From a performance standpoint, the CEO's top management team can influence the timing of the performance peak, the degree of dysfunction during the closing season of the CEO's tenure, and the rate of decline in organizational performance. Diversity and heterogeneity in the top management team help sustain high levels of organizational performance at the peak and help maintain

FIGURE 9.3 Executive Tenure and Organizational Performance

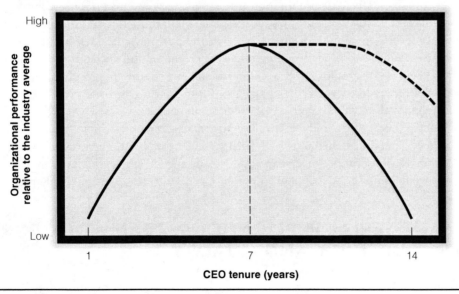

SOURCE: D. Hambrick, The Seasons of an Executive's Tenure, keynote address, the Sixth Annual Texas Conference on Organizations, Lago Vista, Texas, April 1991.

the CEO's vitality. The presence of a "wild turkey" in the top management team can be a particularly positive force. The wild turkey is a devil's advocate who challenges the thinking of the CEO and other top executives and provides a counterpoint during debates. If not shouted down or inhibited, the wild turkey helps the CEO and the team sustain peak performance and retard the CEO's dysfunction and decline. For example, President George W. Bush had his administration enhanced by the independent voice of Secretary of State Colin Powell. Often taking a more moderate position on policy issues than either the secretary of defense or the vice president, Powell brought variance and value to the voice of President Bush's administration. As we see in the Looking Back feature, Toyota is enhancing the diversity of its top management team.

No organization can succeed without a senior team that, collectively, captures a diversity of attributes: vision, task mastery, stewardship, and facilitation.[85] Leaders must evolve communication strategies to bring together a team that is functionally diverse, intellectually diverse, demographically diverse, temperamentally diverse, and so on, in order to complement each other. Dissimilarity develops strength, while similarity builds connections.

We can conclude that the leadership, composition, and dynamics of the top management team have an important influence on the organization's performance. In some cases, corporations have eliminated the single CEO. Current research has shown a dramatic increase in the number of co-CEO arrangements in both public and private corporations.[86] While more common in Europe than in the United States in the past, historical U.S. examples exist as well, such as when Walter Wriston created a three-member team when he was chairman at Citicorp (now part of Citigroup). At Southwest Airlines, the new top management team is emerging from the long shadow of legendary founder Herb Kelleher. This new top team led Southwest successfully through the terrorist crisis of September 2001.

Multicultural Top Teams

The backgrounds of group members may be quite different in the global workplace. Homogeneous groups in which all members share similar backgrounds are giving way to token groups in which all but one member come from the same background, bicultural groups in which two or more members represent each of two distinct cultures, and multicultural groups in which members represent three or more ethnic backgrounds.[87] Diversity within a group may increase the uncertainty, complexity, and inherent confusion in group processes, making it more difficult for the group to achieve its full, potential productivity.[88] On the positive side, Merck attributes its long-term success to its leadership model that promotes and develops the leadership skills of all Merck employees. Ray Gilmartin, former chairman, president, and CEO, valued diversity in Merck's top management team because he believed that diversity sparks innovation when employees with different perspectives work together to offer solutions. The design and function of top management teams in Great Britian, Denmark, and the Netherlands have been studied by international researchers.[89] The advantages of culturally diverse groups include the generation of more and better ideas while limiting the risk of groupthink, a subject to be discussed in Chapter 10.

MANAGERIAL IMPLICATIONS: TEAMWORK FOR PRODUCTIVITY AND QUALITY

Work groups and teams are important vehicles through which organizations achieve high-quality performance. The current emphasis on the new team environment, shown in Table 9.3, places unique demands on managers, teams, and individuals in leading,

FIGURE 9.4 The Triangle for Managing in the New Team Environment

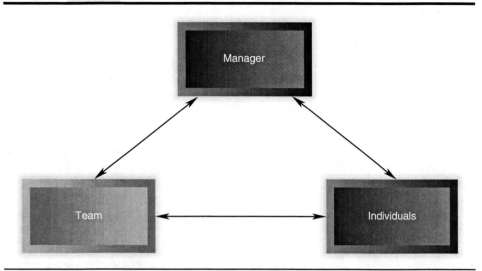

SOURCE: *Managing in the New Team Environment*, by L. Hirschhorn, © 1991. Reprinted by permission of Prentice-Hall, Inc., Upper Saddle River, N.J.

working, and managing. Managing these demands requires an understanding of individual diversity and the interrelationships of individuals, teams, and managers, as depicted in the triangle in Figure 9.4. Expectations associated with these three key organizational roles for people at work are different. The first role is as an individual, empowered employee. The second is as an active member of one or more teams. The third is the role of manager or formal supervisor. Earlier in the chapter, we discussed the foundations for teamwork, empowerment, and working in the new team environment. Individual empowerment must be balanced with collaborative teamwork.

The manager in the triangle is responsible for creating a receptive organizational environment for work groups and teams. This requires that she or he achieve a balance between setting limits (so that individuals and teams do not go too far afield) and removing barriers (so that empowered individuals and self-managed teams can accomplish their work). In addition, the manager should establish a flexible charter for each team. Once the charter is established, the manager continues to be available to the team as a coaching resource, as necessary. The manager establishes criteria for evaluating the performance effectiveness of the team, as well as the individuals, being supervised. In an optimum environment, this involves useful and timely performance feedback to teams that carries a sense of equity and fairness with it. The manager's responsibilities are different from the team leader's.

Effective team leaders may guide a work group or share leadership responsibility with their teams, especially self-managed teams. Team leaders are active team members with responsibility for nurturing the development and performance of the team.[90] They require skills different from those of the manager. Whereas the manager establishes the environment in which teams flourish, the team leader teaches, listens, solves problems, manages conflict, and enhances the dynamics of team functioning to ensure its success. It is the team leader's task to bring the team to maturity; help it work through interpersonal, task, and authority issues; and be skilled in nurturing a cohesive, effective team. A team leader requires the hands-on skills of direct involvement and full membership in the team. Flexibility, delegation, and collaboration are characteristics of healthy teams and their leaders. Increasing globalization requires team leaders to be skilled at forging teamwork among diverse individuals, whereas managers must be skilled at forging collaboration among diverse groups.

Diverse Duo Seals the Deal

Kerry Cannella and Selma Bueno are from two different worlds—literally. Cannella is from Rhode Island, while Bueno is from Brazil. Although they have different geographic and cultural backgrounds, Kerry and Selma are both bankers at Merrill Lynch; Cannella is a managing director; Bueno, a junior associate.

Earlier in the year, Merrill Lynch was involved in a deal potentially worth several million dollars. The firm had been representing Brazilian investors who were selling their stake in a multibillion-dollar Latin American company to potential U.S. investors. The deal was in process, but each side was moving slowly and cautiously. Merrill Lynch needed to do something to step up the pace of negotiations and close the deal.

Enter the team of Cannella and Bueno. The two bankers made frequent trips between New York and Brazil. Bueno analyzed financial papers and put together an offering document for investors in her native Portuguese. In addition, she selected hotels and restaurants and translated during negotiations, making both sides feel at ease. The result was a successful deal for Merrill Lynch worth hundreds of millions of dollars and one that met everyone's satisfaction. Cannella considers his partnership with Bueno "a perfect match." According to Cannella, "She [Bueno] bridged the gap between the U.S. party, the Brazilian party, and me."

1. Could Merrill Lynch have achieved similar success without having someone on the team with Selma Bueno's cultural background? Explain.
2. What risks and rewards can employers expect by placing representatives with diverse backgrounds on work groups and teams?

SOURCE: E. Iwata, "Companies Find Gold inside Melting Pot," *USA Today* (July 9, 2007): B1.

LOOKING BACK: TOYOTA

Diversity at the Top

James E. Press became the first non-Japanese member of Toyota's board of directors at age 60 while serving as president of the company's North American operations. He thus became a senior managing director of the corporation. The North American market is a large and important part of Toyota's overall business. About 34 percent of the company's overall sales volume, and 43 percent of its operating profit, comes from North America. In addition, Toyota exported about 50 percent of the cars it manufactures in Japan during 2007, an increase from the 38 percent that it exported during 2005. While the Japanese domestic car market—only one-third the size of the U.S. market—has remained flat, Toyota has enjoyed rising sales in the U.S. market, in part due to a spike in demand for its fuel-efficient cars.

There has been a deeper trend in diversity within Toyota that is apparently reflected in the new board appointment of Mr. Press. His appointment may be the tip of the iceberg. Other Americans hold top positions in Toyota divisions, such as in plant management and product development. There are also thousands of foreign employees within the company, so many that it opened a "Toyota Institute" outside Toyota City in order to teach them its corporate values. This initiative aims at establishing norms of behavior and building cohesion throughout the workforce. This deeper-level diversity trend within the employee population has increased to the extent that four foreigners held managing-officer positions by 2007. These key positions are just below the board level of the company.

At the top of every company or corporation sits its board of directors. Toyota had been publicly criticized for not having a non-Japanese executive on its 25-member board. The appearance was one of a glass ceiling for foreign employees, similar to the barriers many women have encountered within American companies and corporations. Toyota is now doing some top management team shuffling and expanding its board from 25 to 30 members, opening opportunities for outside senior-level executives. Diversity within this key team affords Toyota some distinct opportunities, advantages, and insights because it brings more direct and personal understanding into its important North American operations from a fellow board member. The key to taking advantage of this strategic opportunity is how fellow board members relate to their new and first non-Japanese member.[91]

Chapter Summary

1. Groups are often composed of diverse people at work. Teams in organizations are key to enhancing quality and achieving success.

2. Important aspects of group behavior include norms of behavior, group cohesion, social loafing, and loss of individuality.

3. Once a group forms, it generally goes through five stages of development. If successful, the group can function independently, with little interference from its leader.

4. Quality circles, originally popularized in Japan, and quality teams contribute to solving technological and quality problems in the organization.

5. Teams provide social benefits for team members, as well as enhancing organizational performance.

6. Functional and value dissimilarity may have positive or negative effects on teams. Managing dissimilarity

in teams and being open to diversity are highly important for promoting creativity.

7. Empowerment and teamwork require specific organizational design elements and individual psychological characteristics and skills.

8. Upper echelons and top management teams are key to the strategy and performance of an organization. Diversity and a devil's advocate in the top team enhance performance.

9. Managing in the new team environment places new demands on managers, teams, and individuals. Managers must create a supportive and flexible environment for collaborative teams and empowered individuals. Team leaders must nurture the team's development.

Key Terms

group (p. 290)
group cohesion (p. 291)
integrated involvement (p. 304)
loss of individuality (p. 292)
maintenance function (p. 300)
norms of behavior (p. 291)

psychological intimacy (p. 303)
quality circle (QC) (p. 303)
quality team (p. 303)
self-managed team (p. 306)
social loafing (p. 291)
status structure (p. 298)

task function (p. 299)
teamwork (p. 301)
upper echelon (p. 308)
work team (p. 290)

Review Questions

1. What is a group? A work team?

2. Explain four aspects of group behavior. How can each aspect help or hinder the group's functioning?

3. Describe what happens in each stage of a group's development according to Tuckman's Five-Stage Model. What are the leadership requirements in each stage?

4. Describe the four characteristics of mature groups.

5. Why are work teams important to organizations today? How and why are work teams formed?

6. Describe at least five task and five maintenance functions that effective work teams must perform.

7. Discuss diversity and creativity in teams.

8. Describe the necessary skills for empowerment and teamwork.

9. What are the benefits and potential drawbacks of self-managed teams?

10. What is the role of the manager in the new team environment? What is the role of the team leader?

Discussion and Communication Questions

1. Which was the most effective group (or team) of which you have been a member? What made that group (or team) so effective?

2. Have you ever felt peer pressure to act more in accordance with the behavioral norms of a group? Have you ever engaged in a little social loafing? Have you ever lost your head and been caught up in a group's destructive actions?

3. Name a company that successfully uses teamwork and empowerment. What has that company done that makes it so successful in this regard? Has its team approach made a difference in its performance? How?

4. Name a person you think is a particularly good team member. What makes him or her so? Name someone who is a problem as a team member. What makes this person a problem?

5. Think about your current work environment. Does it use quality circles or self-managed teams? What are the barriers to teamwork and empowerment in that environment? What elements of the environment enhance or encourage teamwork and empowerment?

(If you do not work, discuss this question with a friend who does.)

6. (*communication question*) Prepare a memo describing your observations about work teams and groups in your workplace or university. Where have you observed teams or groups to be most effective? Why? What changes might be made at work or in the university to make teams more effective?

7. (*communication question*) Develop an oral presentation about what the most important norms of behavior should be in an academic community and workplace. Be specific. Discuss how these norms should be established and reinforced.

8. (*communication question*) Interview an employee or manager about what he or she believes contributes to cohesiveness in work groups and teams. Ask the person what the conclusions are based on. Be prepared to discuss what you have learned in class.

9. Do you admire the upper echelons in your organization or university? Why or why not? Do they communicate effectively with groups and individuals throughout the organization?

Ethical Dilemma

Greg Towns and Michele Brown sat chatting. Michele had come to Greg's office to discuss the first meeting of the strategic planning team. Michele had found out only last week that she would be the team leader for this very important project. Recently, upper management discovered that many of their employees didn't feel that their needs, desires, or capabilities were being considered in the formation of company goals. In response, the president requested that a team of employees be formed to provide employee input for the new plan.

This would be Michele's first time in a leadership position. She was excited, especially since she had been handpicked by the president. She had come to Greg's office to ask for his support in the meetings. Michele did not have confidence in her leadership skills and wanted to know that she could count on someone to back her. Greg confidently assured Michele that she could count on him.

Everyone was excited as the meeting began. They were all happy to be working for a company that cared enough about its employees to create this committee. Michele began the meeting by reminding everyone why they were called together. She felt this was their time to shine for management. People began offering suggestions. Michele dismissed the first two as too broad. The third she called juvenile. The room fell silent. Michele was surprised by the silence and asked if everyone was out of suggestions. Allen Jamison finally spoke up. He told Michele that no one wanted to make suggestions if she was just going to shoot down every idea. Michele denied that she was discounting the others' ideas. She just wanted to be sure that they sent management their very best suggestions. Michele looked to Greg, waiting for the promised support.

Greg felt trapped. He agreed with Allen. Michele's behavior did not encourage input. She was acting like a dictator, not a team leader. He had promised to support her, but he never dreamt that she would act this way. Supporting her behavior went against his beliefs. But he had promised.

1. How would Greg's promise to support Michele still hold given her behavior?
2. Evaluate Greg's decision using consequential, rule-based, and character theories.

Experiential Exercises

9.1 Tower Building: A Group Dynamics Activity

This exercise gives you an opportunity to study group dynamics in a task-oriented situation. Each group must bring materials to class for building a tower. All materials must fit in a box no greater than eight cubic feet (i.e., 2 ft. × 2 ft. × 2 ft. or 1 ft. × 2 ft. × 4 ft.).

Step 1. Each group is assigned a meeting place and a workplace. One or two observers should be assigned in each group. The instructor may assign a manager to each group.

Step 2. Each group plans for the building of the paper tower (no physical construction is allowed during this planning period). Towers will be judged on the basis of height, stability, beauty, and meaning. (Another option is to have the groups do the planning outside of class and come prepared to build the tower.)

Step 3. Each group constructs its tower.

Step 4. Groups inspect other towers, and all individuals rate towers other than their own. See the evaluation sheet at the right. Each group turns in its point totals (i.e., someone in the group adds up each person's total for all groups rated) to the instructor, and the instructor announces the winner.

Step 5. Group dynamics analysis. Observers report observations to their own groups, and each group analyzes the group dynamics that occurred during the planning and building of the tower.

Step 6. Groups report on major issues in group dynamics that arose during the tower planning and building. Complete the tower building aftermath questionnaire as homework if requested by your instructor.

CRITERIA	GROUPS							
	1	2	3	4	5	6	7	8
Height								
Stability/Strength								
Beauty								
Meaning/Significance								
TOTALS								

Rate each criterion on a scale of 1–10, with 1 being lowest or poorest, and 10 being highest or best.

SOURCE: From *Organizational Behavior and Performance*, 5/e by Szilagyi/Wallace, © 1997. Reprinted by permission of Prentice-Hall, Inc., Upper Saddle River, N.J.

9.2 Design a Team

The following exercise gives you an opportunity to design a team. Working in a six-person group, address the individual characteristics, team composition, and norms for an effective group whose task is to make recommendations on improving customer relations. The president of a small clothing manufacturer is concerned that his customers are not satisfied enough with the company's responsiveness, product quality, and returned-orders process. He has asked your group to put together a team to address these problems.

Step 1. The class will form into groups of approximately six members each. Each group elects a spokesperson and answers the following questions. The group should spend an equal amount of time on each question.

a. *What characteristics should the individual members of the task team possess?* Members may consider professional competence, skills, department, and/or personality and behavioral characteristics in the group's discussion.

b. *What should the composition of the task team be?* Once your group has addressed individual characteristics, consider the overall composition of the task team. Have special and/or unique competencies, knowledge, skills, and abilities been considered in your deliberations?

c. *What norms of behavior do you think the task team should adopt?* A team's norms of behavior may evolve, or they may be consciously discussed and agreed upon. Take the latter approach.

Step 2. Each group will share the results of its answers to the questions in Step 1. Cross-team questions and discussion follow.

Biz Flix | Apollo 13

This superb film dramatically shows the NASA mission to the moon that had an in-space disaster. Innovative problem solving and decision making amid massive ambiguity saved the crew. *Apollo 13* has many examples of problem solving and decision making.

The scene from the film shows day 5 of the mission, about two-thirds of the way through *Apollo 13*. Earlier in the mission, Jack Swigert (Kevin Bacon) stirred the oxygen tanks at mission control's request. An explosion in the spacecraft happened shortly after this procedure, causing unknown damage to the command module. Before this scene takes place, the damage has forced the crew to move into the LEM (Lunar Exploration Module), which becomes their lifeboat for return to earth.

What to Watch for and Ask Yourself:

> What triggers the conflict in this scene?

> Is this intergroup conflict or intragroup conflict? What effects can such conflict have on the group dynamics on board *Apollo 13*?

> Does mission commander Jim Lovell (Tom Hanks) successfully manage the group dynamics to return the group to a normal state?

Workplace Video | Teamwork, Featuring Cold Stone Creamery

Freshly baked brownies and cones, handmade ice cream in an array of flavors, colorful tasty toppings—that's the "Ultimate Ice Cream Experience" at Cold Stone Creamery, and it's winning over customers in the United States and around the world.

Delivering Cold Stone's fun, flavorful "experience" to millions of customers takes teamwork, and the Scottsdale, Arizona-based ice-cream franchise uses many different kinds of teams to ensure that operations are as smooth as its cold, velvety treats. The company's vertical teams, which include members from the executive suite all the way down to the local managers, create plans and strategies that set the company in motion. Horizontal teams, which are comprised of employees of the same hierarchical level, work on daily prep, baking, and entertainment-oriented tasks. Special-purpose teams come together for a time to work on specific projects, such as boosting same-store sales. Self-directed teams form when multiskilled workers make group decisions normally reserved for managers.

Widespread excitement about Cold Stone Creamery has led to the development of another important team: the global team. Global teams collaborate across international boundaries to bring the Ultimate Ice Cream Experience to Japan, South Korea, China, and elsewhere. Because of the challenges of working across great distances, these groups function as virtual teams, relying on advanced telecommunications technologies to coordinate efforts.

All teams need effective leadership, and Cold Stone CEO Doug Ducey provides both the vision and resources necessary for his teams to succeed. Ducey and other top executives have set an ambitious company-wide goal that gives focus to the work of every employee: make Cold Stone Creamery the number-one-selling ice cream in the United States by 2010. The bar is high, but Ducey is confident that his franchisees can meet expectations if first-line managers and crew members are united in their efforts.

TAKE 2

Finally, while group-led initiative is helping Cold Stone achieve organizational success, it also is having a positive impact on individual workers. Teamwork at Cold Stone has increased employee satisfaction, expanded job knowledge, and augmented worker productivity. Most importantly, teams have created a culture of fun. Who would expect anything less from the maker of the ever-popular Birthday Cake Remix and the deliciously dirty Mud Pie Mojo?

Discussion Questions

1. What norms of behavior would you expect to find among team members working in a Cold Stone Creamery ice cream store?

2. What are some of the challenges involved in creating a global team at Cold Stone?

3. What characteristics of a team may influence group effectiveness, and what role does diversity play in team success?

Stryker's Use of Teamwork in Redesigning Surgical Equipment

The Stryker Corporation was built on innovation. "When Dr. Homer Stryker, an orthopedic surgeon from Kalamazoo, Michigan, found that certain medical products were not meeting his patients' needs, he invented new ones. As interest in these products grew, Dr. Stryker started a company in 1941 to produce them. The company's goal was to help patients lead healthier, more active lives through products and services that make surgery and recovery simpler, faster and more effective."[1]

Homer Stryker started Orthopedic Frame Company to sell devices for moving patients with spinal injuries.[2] A short time later he invented the first power tool for removing plaster casts after patients' broken bones had healed. After that the company began providing hospital beds. These early initiatives, but especially the oscillating cast saw, formed the foundation of what is now the Stryker Corporation, one of the leading companies in the worldwide market for orthopedic devices.[3] Stryker, headquartered in Kalamazoo, Michigan, employs over 15,000 people, with most of its operations being in the United States, Europe, and Japan. As a leading medical technology company and one of the largest in the $28.6 billion worldwide orthopedic market, Stryker manufactures replacement joints such as shoulders, knees, and hips; high-tech tools like imaging systems that help surgeons reconstruct body parts; and a variety of other medical devices and products, including surgical tools and hospital beds.[4]

One of Stryker's recent orthopedic innovations was a navigation system for hip replacement surgery that permitted surgeons to observe via a computer screen the precise positioning of a hip replacement prosthesis. Due to the nature of hip replacement, the navigation system had to have the capability of withstanding the various physical stresses put on the equipment, including pounding with a surgical hammer. In addition, the navigation system—especially its sophisticated electronics—had to survive repeated sterilization under 270-degree-Fahrenheit steam pressure. However, shortly after field testing of the hip replacement navigation system began, significant problems were discovered. Numerous complaints were received from surgeons, and the systems were returned to Stryker. Examination of the returned units revealed that the precision electronics of the system frequently failed and metal parts were broken or damaged.[5]

Finding a solution to the navigation system problems was assigned to Klaus Welte, vice president and plant manager for Stryker's Freiburg, Germany facility, which was acquired in 1998. Under its previous owner, Leibinger, the Freiburg facility had developed a magnetic imaging navigation system for use in neurosurgery. After the acquisition by Stryker, the Freiburg facility applied its navigation system technology and expertise to developing other surgical tools, including ones for orthopedics. Thus, the Freiburg facility was given the responsibility for solving the problems with the hip replacement navigation system.[6]

Welte's first challenge was assembling a team to work on solving the navigation system problem. Welte believed that the team's success "would require both a clear view of what had to be accomplished and a deep understanding of each team member's abilities."[7] Welte assembled a team of the best people at Freiburg in operations, computer-aided design, engineering, and research. One team member was talented in structural analysis, communication, and follow-through. Another member provided the "social glue" for the team and would never stop until all tasks were complete. Still another was an organizer who helped keep the team on task and from rushing ahead before it was ready. Yet another member was especially knowledgeable regarding how a product design will successfully survive the manufacturing process. Another person was noted for highly innovative—indeed visionary—product design ideas.[8]

Although each team member's abilities were important, how those abilities fit together was equally important. According to Welte, "Creating an effective team requires more than just filling all the job descriptions with someone who has the right talent and experience. . . . By no means can you substitute one engineer for another. There are really very, very specific things that they are good at . . . and how well the team members' abilities combine is as important as the abilities themselves."[9] How well the Stryker team jelled became evident in their approach to problem solving.

Due to the number of problems with the hip replacement navigation system, the Freiburg team addressed each problem separately, beginning with the most crucial issue and working down to the relatively minor problems. The solution for each problem was thoroughly tested before moving on to the next issue. Consequently, the team did not have a fully assembled prototype until all the problems were addressed. This approach proved successful, both in terms of the ultimate success of the prototype design and the team working effectively together as problem solvers. In the first nine months after the redesigned hip replacement navigation system was released, the company did not receive a single complaint from surgeons—an incredible achievement for complex surgical equipment.[10]

Discussion Questions

1. Using Table 9.1, discuss the extent to which the characteristics of well-functioning, effective groups accurately describe the Freiburg hip replacement navigation system team.

2. Explain why teamwork is important to effectively solve the problems revealed by field testing of the hip replacement navigation system.

3. Using Table 9.2, describe how the task functions and maintenance functions are operating within the Freiburg team.

4. Explain why diversity and creativity are important to the effective functioning of the Freiburg team.

SOURCE: This case was written by Michael K. McCuddy, The Louis S. and Mary L. Morgal Chair of Christian Business Ethics and Professor of Management, College of Business Administration, Valparaiso University.

Decision Making by Individuals and Groups

LEARNING OBJECTIVES

After reading this chapter, you should be able to do the following:

1 Explain the assumptions of bounded rationality.

2 Describe Jung's cognitive styles and how they affect managerial decision making.

3 Describe and evaluate the role of intuition and creativity in decision making.

4 Critique your own level of creativity and list ways of improving it.

5 Compare and contrast the advantages and disadvantages of group decision making.

6 Discuss the symptoms of groupthink and ways to prevent it.

7 Evaluate the strengths and weaknesses of several group decision-making techniques.

8 Explain the emerging role of virtual decision making in organizations.

9 Utilize an "ethics check" for examining managerial decisions.

THINKING AHEAD: GENENTECH, INC.

Good Decision Making Against All Odds

Genentech is the leading biotechnology firm in the pharmaceutical industry. As its competitors such as Pfizer continue to struggle, Genentech has repeatedly proven its ability to successfully develop and market drugs designed to fight a variety of diseases.

Recently, Genentech reported an increase in its earnings by 65 percent thanks to two new cancer-fighting drugs: Avastin and Tarceva. Genentech's CEO Arthur Levinson knows that the odds are one in 350 million that a new drug will be successful. Yet Genentech seems to be able to consistently beat those odds.

So, how does this biotechnology giant do it? They take a simple yet effective approach to decision making under great uncertainty. First, they have clearly defined short- and long-term goals that help everyone in the company rally around the same overarching objectives. Second, they let good science, rather than political behavior, drive all their decision making. Third, they have created a high employee involvement culture driven by team-based decision making. Finally, and perhaps most critically, Genentech is constantly seeking new domains of discovery. For example, they were investing money in research and development in cancer-fighting drugs some 25 years ago, when such investments were not even feasible for other companies. At the moment, they are embarking on ambitious research into immunology-related drugs even though it is entirely new territory for them.[1,2] In the Looking Back feature, you can read about Genentech's challenge one of their cancer drugs and their hope for the future.

THE DECISION-MAKING PROCESS

Decision making is a critical activity in the lives of managers. The decisions a manager faces can range from very simple, routine matters for which she or he has an established decision rule (*programmed decisions*) to new and complex decisions that require creative solutions (*nonprogrammed decisions*).[3] Scheduling lunch hours for one's work group is a programmed decision. The manager performs the decision activity on a daily basis, using an established procedure with the same clear goal in mind. In contrast, decisions like buying out another company are nonprogrammed. Genentech's decisions about which markets to penetrate and what areas to invest in for R&D purposes are examples of nonprogrammed decisions. The decision to acquire a company is another situation that is unique and unstructured and requires considerable judgment. Regardless of the type of decision made, it is helpful to understand as much as possible about how individuals and groups make decisions.

Decision making is a process involving a series of steps, as shown in Figure 10.1. The first step is recognition of the problem; that is, the manager realizes that a decision must be made. Identification of the real problem is important; otherwise, the manager may be reacting to symptoms and firefighting rather than dealing with the root cause of the problem. Next, a manager must identify the objective of the decision—in other words, determine what is to be accomplished by it.

The third step in the decision-making process is gathering information relevant to the problem. The manager must pull together sufficient information about why the problem occurred. This involves conducting a thorough diagnosis of the situation and going on a fact-finding mission.

The fourth step is listing and evaluating alternative courses of action. During this step, a thorough "what-if" analysis should also be conducted to determine the various factors that could influence the outcome. It is important to generate a wide range of options and creative solutions in order to be able to move on to the fifth step.

Next, the manager selects the alternative that best meets the decision objective. If the problem has been diagnosed correctly and sufficient alternatives have been identified, this step is much easier.

Finally, the solution is implemented. The situation must then be monitored to see whether the decision met its objective. Consistent monitoring and periodic feedback are essential parts of the follow-up process.

Decision making can be stressful. Managers must make decisions with significant risk and uncertainty, and often without full information. They must trust and rely on others in arriving at their decisions, but they are ultimately responsible. Sometimes the decisions are painful and involve exiting businesses, firing people, and

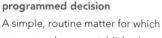

programmed decision

A simple, routine matter for which a manager has an established decision rule.

nonprogrammed decision

A new, complex decision that requires a creative solution.

© MICHAEL HALSBAND/LANDOV

The Blue Man Group has a history of making effective decisions. They have grown famous and successful by making sound business choices, even though none of the founders has any formal training in music, acting, or business.

FIGURE 10.1 The Decision-Making Process

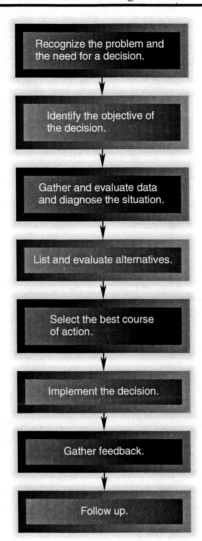

admitting wrong. Blue Man Group has a history of making effective decisions. Their theatrical productions are a creative combination of comedy, music, and multimedia in a type of entertainment that is totally unique. They have grown wildly famous and successful by making sound business choices, even though none of the founders has any formal training in music, acting, or business. The group turned down offers to sell credit cards, soft drinks, breath mints, and paint, all of course related to the color blue. With each new opportunity, the three founders use the same evaluation: "Okay, that's all well and good, that's a nice thought—but is it Blue Man?" They also have achieved what a lot of businesses want to do but never complete: a detailed 132-page operating manual. The founders make decisions by unanimous agreement.[4]

MODELS OF DECISION MAKING

The success of any organization depends on managers' abilities to make *effective decisions*. An effective decision is timely, is acceptable to the individuals affected by it, and meets the desired objective.[5] This section describes three models of decision making: the rational model, the bounded rationality model, and the garbage can model.

effective decision

A timely decision that meets a desired objective and is acceptable to those individuals affected by it.

Rational Model

Rationality refers to a logical, step-by-step approach to decision making, with a thorough analysis of alternatives and their consequences. The rational model of decision making comes from classic economic theory and contends that the decision maker is completely rational in his or her approach. The rational model has the following important assumptions:

1. The outcome will be completely rational.
2. The decision maker has a consistent system of preferences, which is used to choose the best alternative.
3. The decision maker is aware of all the possible alternatives.
4. The decision maker can calculate the probability of success for each alternative.[6]

In the rational model, the decision maker strives to optimize, that is, to select the best possible alternative.

Given its assumptions, the rational model is unrealistic. There are time constraints and limits to human knowledge and information-processing capabilities. In addition, a manager's preferences and needs change often. The rational model is thus an ideal that managers strive for in making decisions. It captures the way a decision should be made but does not reflect the reality of managerial decision making.[7]

Bounded Rationality Model

(1) Explain the assumptions of bounded rationality.

Recognizing the deficiencies of the rational model, Herbert Simon suggested that there are limits on how rational a decision maker can actually be. His decision theory, the bounded rationality model, earned a Nobel Prize in 1978.

Simon's model, also referred to as the "administrative man" theory, rests on the idea that there are constraints that force a decision maker to be less than completely rational. The bounded rationality model has four assumptions:

1. Managers select the first alternative that is satisfactory.
2. Managers recognize that their conception of the world is simple.
3. Managers are comfortable making decisions without determining all the alternatives.
4. Managers make decisions by rules of thumb or heuristics.

Bounded rationality assumes that managers *satisfice*; that is, they select the first alternative that is "good enough," because the costs of optimizing in terms of time and effort are too great.[8] Further, the theory assumes that managers develop shortcuts, called *heuristics*, to make decisions in order to save mental activity. Heuristics are rules of thumb that allow managers to make decisions based on what has worked in past experiences.

Does the bounded rationality model more realistically portray the managerial decision process? Research indicates that it does.[9] One of the reasons managers face limits to their rationality is that they must make decisions under risk and time pressure. The situation they find themselves in is highly uncertain, and the probability of success is not known.

rationality

A logical, step-by-step approach to decision making, with a thorough analysis of alternatives and their consequences.

bounded rationality

A theory that suggests there are limits to how rational a decision maker can actually be.

satisfice

To select the first alternative that is "good enough," because the costs in time and effort are too great to optimize.

heuristics

Shortcuts in decision making that save mental activity.

garbage can model

A theory that contends that decisions in organizations are random and unsystematic.

Garbage Can Model

Sometimes the decision-making process in organizations appears to be haphazard and unpredictable. In the *garbage can model*, decisions are random and unsystematic.[10]

FIGURE 10.2 The Garbage Can Model

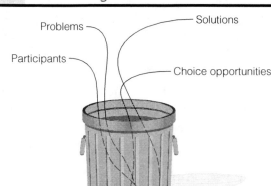

Problems — Solutions

Participants — Choice opportunities

SOURCE: From M. D. Cohen, J. G. March, and J. P. Olsen in *Administrative Science Quarterly* 17 (March 1972): 1–25. Reprinted by permission of the *Administrative Science Quarterly*.

Figure 10.2 depicts the garbage can model. In this model, the organization is a garbage can in which problems, solutions, participants, and choice opportunities are floating around randomly. If the four factors happen to connect, a decision is made.[11] The quality of the decision depends on timing. The right participants must find the right solution to the right problem at the right time.

The garbage can model illustrates the idea that not all organizational decisions are made in a step-by-step, systematic fashion. Especially under conditions of high uncertainty, the decision process may be chaotic. Some decisions appear to happen out of sheer luck.

On the high-speed playing field of today's businesses, managers must make critical decisions quickly, with incomplete information, and must also involve employees in the process.

DECISION MAKING AND RISK

Many decisions involve some element of risk. For managers, hiring decisions, promotions, delegation, acquisitions and mergers, overseas expansions, new product development, and other decisions make risk a part of the job.

Risk and the Manager

Individuals differ in terms of their willingness to take risks. Some people experience *risk aversion*. They choose options that entail fewer risks, preferring familiarity and certainty. Other individuals are risk takers; that is, they accept greater potential for loss in decisions, tolerate greater uncertainty, and in general are more likely to make risky decisions. Risk takers are also more likely to take the lead in group discussions.[12]

Research indicates that women are more averse to risk taking than men and that older, more experienced managers are more risk averse than younger managers. There is also some evidence that successful managers take more risks than unsuccessful ones.[13] However, the tendency to take risks or avoid them is only part of behavior toward risk. Risk taking is influenced not only by an individual's tendency but also by organizational factors. In commercial banks, loan decisions that require the assessment of risk are made every day.

risk aversion

The tendency to choose options that entail fewer risks and less uncertainty.

Upper-level managers face a tough task in managing risk-taking behavior. By discouraging lower-level managers from taking risks, they may stifle creativity and innovation. If upper-level managers are going to encourage risk taking, however, they must allow employees to fail without fear of punishment. One way to accomplish this is to consider failure "enlightened trial and error."[14] The key is establishing a consistent attitude toward risk within the organization.

When individuals take risks, losses may occur. Suppose an oil producer thinks there is an opportunity to uncover oil by reentering an old drilling site. She gathers a group of investors and shows them the logs, and they chip in to finance the venture. The reentry is drilled to a certain depth, and nothing is found. Convinced they did not drill deep enough, the producer goes back to the investors and requests additional financial backing to continue drilling. The investors consent, and she drills deeper, only to find nothing. She approaches the investors, and after lengthy discussion, they agree to provide more money to drill deeper. Why do decision makers sometimes throw good money after bad? Why do they continue to provide resources to what looks like a losing venture?

Escalation of Commitment

Continuing to support a failing course of action is known as *escalation of commitment*.[15] In situations characterized by escalation of commitment, individuals who make decisions that turn out to be poor choices tend to hold fast to them, even when substantial costs are incurred.[16] An example of escalation is the price wars that often occur between airlines. The airlines reduce their prices in response to competitors until at a certain stage, both airlines are in a "no-win" situation. Yet they continue to compete despite the heavy losses they are incurring. The desire to win is a motivation to continue to escalate, and each airline continues to reduce prices (lose money) based on the belief that the other airline will pull out of the price war. Another example of escalation of commitment is NASA's enormous International Space Station. Originally estimated to cost $8 billion, the Space Station has been redesigned five times and remains unfinished. Its estimated cost topped $30 billion, and some pundits speculate that the total bill may reach $130 billion for what physicist Robert Park describes as "the biggest technological blunder in history." Despite the station's drain on virtually every other NASA program, it remains a focal point of NASA's work and continues to consume vast resources.[17]

In the Real World 10.1, you can read about IBM's recent risky decision making that seemed like escalation of commitment at first, and how it seems to have paid off for the company.

Why does escalation of commitment occur? One explanation is offered by cognitive dissonance theory, as we discussed in Chapter 4. This theory assumes that humans dislike inconsistency, and that when there is inconsistency among their attitudes or between their attitudes and behavior, they strive to reduce the dissonance.[18]

Other reasons why people maintain a losing course of action are optimism and control. Some people are overly optimistic and overestimate the likelihood that positive things will happen to them. Other people operate under an illusion of control—that they have special skills to control the future that other people don't have.[19] In addition, sunk costs may encourage escalation. Individuals think, "Well, I've already invested this much . . . what's a few dollars more?" And the closer a project is to completion, the more likely escalation is to occur.[20]

Clinging to a poor decision can be costly to organizations. While most U.S. airlines (including United, American, and TWA) originally placed orders for the prestigious Mach 2 Concorde airliner during the 1960s, all U.S. orders for the plane were

escalation of commitment
The tendency to continue to support a failing course of action.

IBM Corporation: Challenging the Boundaries of Collaborative Research

IBM has long been a leading innovator in the computer hardware industry. Given the fierce competition and narrower profit margins, IBM has faced some rough times. In the latter half of 2003, IBM's chip-making division was in trouble. The company had pumped millions of dollars into research and development and the division was losing millions of dollars every year with no hope for the future.

This situation called for one of two decisions: IBM could either quit this course of action or it could take a novel approach to R&D. John Kelly, then head of the semiconductor division, called a meeting of top executives at IBM and suggested that they open the doors of their R&D division to key R&D partners. This proposal was met with fierce opposition as many feared it would reflect escalation of commitment. They also feared that almost ten years of their research might be in jeopardy if such open R&D collaborations went into effect. This decision also would mark a radical departure from

IBM's usual strategy with R&D, which was that if IBM couldn't build it, it probably wasn't good enough.

Yet after two hours of debate, Kelly convinced his executives that in the changing business environment, there would be great minds working outside IBM and it would help the company to collaborate. As a result, IBM adopted an open R&D collaboration with nine key partners including big names like Toshiba and Sony.

This decision paid off for IBM. Its partners have helped with the R&D costs, supplied much-needed brainpower, and IBM's chip-making division is turning a profit. This story reveals that it is sometimes very difficult to determine whether a risky decision will eventually pay off or not. IBM's decision highlighted key principles of innovative, outside-the-box decision making.

SOURCE: S. Hamm, "Radical Collaboration, Lessons from IBM's Innovation Factory," Special Report, *Business Week Online* (August 30, 2007), http://www.businessweek.com/innovate/content/aug2007/id20070830_258824.htm?chan=search.

eventually cancelled, leaving only British Airways and Air France as customers. While these two firms doggedly held onto their marginally profitable Concorde operations for almost three decades, a crash in 2000 led to closer scrutiny of the aging fleet, which was eventually retired in 2003. Industry insiders estimate that every customer who took the Concorde rather than a 747 cost British Airways more than $1,200 in profits.[21] Organizations can deal with escalation of commitment in several ways. One is to split the responsibility for decisions about projects. One individual can make the initial decision, and another can make subsequent decisions. Companies have also tried to eliminate escalation of commitment by closely monitoring decision makers.[22] Another suggestion is to provide individuals with a graceful exit from poor decisions so that their images are not threatened. One way of accomplishing this is to reward people who admit to poor decisions before escalating their commitment to them. A study also suggested that having groups, rather than individuals, make an initial investment decision would reduce escalation. Support has been found for this idea. Participants in group decision making may experience a diffusion of responsibility for the failed decision rather than feeling personally responsible; thus, they can pull out of a bad decision without threatening their image.[23]

We have seen that there are limits to how rational a manager can be in making decisions. Most managerial decisions involve considerable risk, and individuals react differently to risk situations.

JUNG'S COGNITIVE STYLES

In Chapter 3 we introduced Jungian theory as a way of understanding and appreciating differences among individuals. This theory is especially useful in pointing out that individuals have different styles of making decisions. Carl Jung's original theory

(2) Describe Jung's cognitive styles and how they affect managerial decision making.

identified two styles of information gathering (sensing and intuiting) and two styles of making judgments (thinking and feeling). You already know what each individual preference means. Jung contended that individuals prefer one style of perceiving and one style of judging.[24] The combination of a perceiving style and a judging style is called a *cognitive style*. There are four cognitive styles: sensing/thinking (ST), sensing/feeling (SF), intuiting/thinking (NT), and intuiting/feeling (NF). Each of the cognitive styles affects managerial decision making.[25]

STs rely on facts. They conduct an impersonal analysis of the situation and then make an analytical, objective decision. The ST cognitive style is valuable in organizations because it produces a clear, simple solution. STs remember details and seldom make factual errors. Their weakness is that they may alienate others because of their tendency to ignore interpersonal aspects of decisions. In addition, they tend to avoid risks.

SFs also gather factual information, but they make judgments in terms of how they affect people. They place great importance on interpersonal relationships but also take a practical approach to gathering information for problem solving. The SFs' strength in decision making lies in their ability to handle interpersonal problems well and to take calculated risks. SFs may have trouble accepting new ideas that break the organization's rules.

NTs focus on the alternative possibilities in a situation and then evaluate them objectively and impersonally. NTs love to initiate ideas, and they like to focus on the long term. They are innovative and will take risks. This makes NTs good at things like new business development.[26] Weaknesses of NTs include their tendencies to ignore arguments based on facts and to ignore the feelings of others.

NFs also search out alternative possibilities, but they evaluate the possibilities in terms of how they will affect the people involved. They enjoy participative decision making and are committed to developing their employees. However, NFs may be prone to making decisions based on personal preferences rather than on more objective data. They may also become too responsive to the needs of others.

Research supports the existence of these four cognitive styles and their influences on managerial decision making.[27] One study asked managers to describe their ideal organization, and the researchers found strong similarities in the descriptions of managers with the same cognitive style.[28] STs wanted an organization that relied on facts and details and that exercised impersonal methods of control. SFs focused on facts, too, but they did so in terms of the relationships within the organization. NTs emphasized broad issues and described impersonal, idealistic organizations. NFs described an organization that would serve humankind well and focused on general, humanistic values.

All four cognitive styles have much to contribute to organizational decision making.[29] Isabel Briggs Myers, creator of the MBTI, also developed the Z problem-solving model, which capitalizes on the strengths of the four separate preferences (sensing, intuiting, thinking, and feeling). By using this model, managers can use both their preferences and nonpreferences to make decisions more effectively. The Z model is presented in Figure 10.3.

According to this model, good problem solving has four steps:

1. *Examine the facts and details.* Use sensing to gather information about the problem.

2. *Generate alternatives.* Use intuiting to develop possibilities.

3. *Analyze the alternatives objectively.* Use thinking to logically determine the effects of each alternative.

4. *Weigh the impact.* Use feeling to determine how the people involved will be affected.

cognitive style

An individual's preference for gathering information and evaluating alternatives.

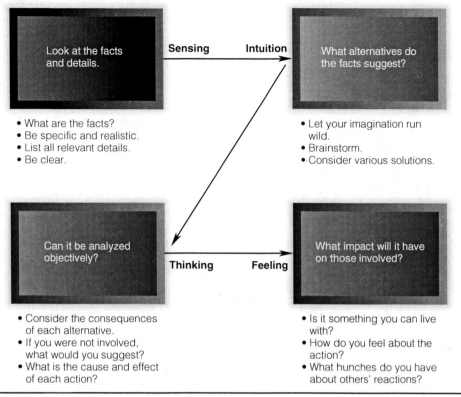

SOURCE: Excerpted from *Type Talk at Work* by Otto Kroeger and Janet M. Thuesen, 1992, Delacorte Press. Reprinted by permission of Otto Kroeger Associates.

Using the Z model can help an individual develop his or her nonpreferences. Another way to use the Z model is to rely on others to perform the nonpreferred activities. For example, an individual who is an NF might want to turn to a trusted NT for help in analyzing alternatives objectively.

OTHER INDIVIDUAL INFLUENCES ON DECISION MAKING

In addition to the cognitive styles just examined, many other individual differences affect a manager's decision making. Other personality characteristics, attitudes, and values, along with all of the individual differences variables that were discussed in Chapters 3 and 4, have implications for managerial decision making. Managers must use both their logic and their creativity to make effective decisions. Most of us are more comfortable using either logic or creativity, and we show that preference in everyday decision making. You 10.1 is an activity that will tell you which process, logic or creativity, is your preferred one. Take You 10.1 now, and then read on to interpret your score.

Brain hemispheric dominance is related to students' choices of college majors. Left-brained students gravitate toward business, engineering, and sciences, whereas right-brained students are attracted to education, nursing, communication, and literature.[30]

Our brains have two lateral halves (Figure 10.4). The right side is the center for creative functions, while the left side is the center for logic, detail, and planning. There are advantages to both kinds of thinking, so the ideal situation is to be "brain-lateralized" or to be able to use either logic or creativity or both, depending

Which Side of Your Brain Do You Favor?

There are no "right" or "wrong" answers to this questionnaire. It is more of a self-assessment than a test. Do not read the questions more than once. Don't overanalyze. Merely circle "a" or "b" to indicate which answer is more typical of you.

1. Typically, when I have a problem to solve,
   a. I make a list of possible solutions, prioritize them, and then select the best answer.
   b. I "let it sit" for a while or talk it over with someone before I attempt to reach a solution.

2. When I sit with my hands clasped in my lap (FOLD YOUR HANDS THAT WAY RIGHT NOW BEFORE GOING ON, THEN LOOK AT YOUR HANDS), the thumb that is on top is
   a. my right thumb.
   b. my left thumb.

3. I have hunches
   a. sometimes, but do not place much faith in them.
   b. frequently and I usually follow them.

4. If I am at a meeting or lecture, I tend to take extensive notes.
   a. True
   b. False

5. I am well organized, have a system for doing things, have a place for everything and everything in its place, and can assimilate information quickly and logically.
   a. True
   b. False

6. I am good with numbers.
   a. True
   b. False

7. Finding words in a dictionary or looking up names in a telephone book is something I can do easily and quickly.
   a. True
   b. False

8. If I want to remember directions or other information,
   a. I make notes.
   b. I visualize the information.

9. I express myself well verbally.
   a. True
   b. False

10. To learn dance steps or athletic moves,
    a. I try to understand the sequence of the steps and repeat them mentally.
    b. I don't think about it; I just try to get the feel of the game or the music.

Interpretation:

> Four, five, or six "a" answers indicate lateralization—an ability to use either hemisphere easily and to solve problems according to their nature rather than according to a favored manner.

> One, two, or three "a" answers indicate right-hemisphere dominance; corresponding traits include inventiveness, creativity, innovation, risk taking, whimsy, and an ability to see the "big picture."

> Seven, eight, or nine "a" answers indicate a left-hemisphere dominance—a tendency toward attention to detail, the use of logic, and traits of thoroughness and accuracy.

SOURCE: "Which Side of the Brain Do You Favor?" from *Quality Driven Designs*. Copyright 1992 Pfeiffer/Jossey-Bass. Reprinted by permission of Jossey-Bass, Inc., a subsidiary of John Wiley & Sons, Inc.

on the situation. There are ways to develop the side of the brain you are not accustomed to using. To develop your right side, or creative side, you can ask "what-if" questions, engage in play, and follow your intuition. To develop the left side, you can set goals for completing tasks and work to attain these goals. For managers, it is important to see the big picture, craft a vision, and plan strategically—all of which require right-brain skills. It is equally important to be able to understand day-to-day operations and flow chart work processes, which are left-hemisphere brain skills.

FIGURE 10.4 Functions of the Left and Right Brain Hemispheres

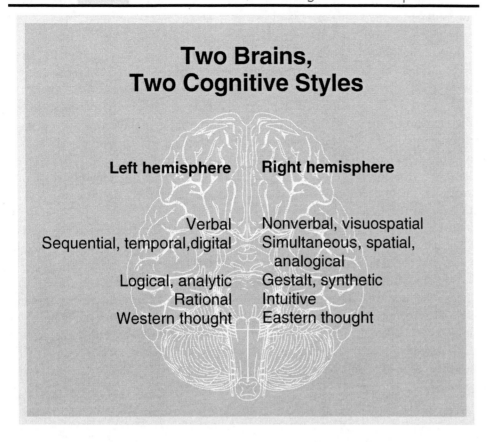

Two Brains,
Two Cognitive Styles

Left hemisphere	Right hemisphere
Verbal	Nonverbal, visuospatial
Sequential, temporal, digital	Simultaneous, spatial, analogical
Logical, analytic	Gestalt, synthetic
Rational	Intuitive
Western thought	Eastern thought

SOURCES: Created based on ideas from *Left Brain, Right Brain* by Springer and Deutsch, p. 272. © 1993 by Sally P. Springer and Georg Deutsch (New York: W. H. Freeman and Company, 1993). DILBERT reprinted by permission of United Feature Syndicate, Inc.

Two particular individual influences that can enhance decision-making effectiveness will be highlighted next: intuition and creativity.

The Role of Intuition

There is evidence that managers use their *intuition* to make decisions.[31] Henry Mintzberg, in his work on managerial roles, found that in many cases managers do not appear to use a systematic, step-by-step approach to decision making. Rather, Mintzberg argued, managers make judgments based on "hunches."[32] Daniel Isenberg

(3) Describe and evaluate the role of intuition and creativity in decision making.

intuition

A fast, positive force in decision making that is utilized at a level below consciousness and involves learned patterns of information.

studied the way senior managers make decisions and found that intuition was used extensively, especially as a mechanism to evaluate decisions made more rationally.[33] Robert Beck studied the way managers at BankAmerica (now Bank of America) made decisions about the future direction of the company following the deregulation of the banking industry. Beck described their use of intuition as an antidote to "analysis paralysis," or the tendency to analyze decisions rather than developing innovative solutions.[34]

Dr. Gary Klein, a renowned cognitive psychologist, has written a book on the power of intuition. Dr. Klein and his colleagues insist that skilled decision makers rely on patterns of learned information in making quick and efficient decisions. In a series of studies conducted with the U.S. Navy, firefighters, and the U.S. Army, they found that decision makers normally relied on intuition in unfamiliar, challenging situations. These decisions were superior to those made after careful evaluation of information and potential alternatives.[35]

Just what is intuition? In Jungian theory, intuiting (N) is one preference used to gather data. This is only one way that the concept of intuition has been applied to managerial decision making, and it is perhaps the most widely researched form of the concept of intuition. There are, however, many definitions of *intuition* in the managerial literature. Chester Barnard, one of the early influential management researchers, argued that intuition's main attributes were speed and the inability of the decision maker to determine how the decision was made.[36] Other researchers have contended that intuition occurs at an unconscious level, and that this is why the decision maker cannot verbalize how the decision was made.[37]

Intuition has been variously described as follows:

> The ability to know or recognize quickly and readily the possibilities of a situation.[38]

> Smooth automatic performance of learned behavior sequences.[39]

> Simple analyses frozen into habit and into the capacity for rapid response through recognition.[40]

Lee Iaccoca wrote in his autobiography, "To a certain extent, I've always operated by gut feeling."

© FRAN KITTEK/MCT/LANDOV

These definitions share some common assumptions. First, there seems to be a notion that intuition is fast. Second, intuition is utilized at a level below consciousness. Third, there seems to be agreement that intuition involves learned patterns of information. Fourth, intuition appears to be a positive force in decision making.

The use of intuition may lead to more ethical decisions. Intuition allows an individual to take on another's role with ease, and role taking is a fundamental part of developing moral reasoning. You may recall from Chapter 4 the role of cognitive moral development in ethical decision making. One study found a strong link between cognitive moral development and intuition. The development of new perspectives through intuition leads to higher moral growth, and thus to more ethical decisions.[41]

One question that arises is whether managers can be taught to use their intuition. Weston Agor, who has conducted workshops on developing intuitive skills in managers, has attained positive results in organizations such as the city of Phoenix and entertainment powerhouse Walt Disney Enterprises. After giving intuition tests to more than 10,000 executives, he has concluded that in most cases, higher management positions are held by individuals with higher levels of intuition. Just as the brain needs both hemispheres to work, Agor cautions that organizations need both analytical and intuitive minds to function at their peak. Consider Grant Tinker, former head of NBC. "Sometimes the boss has to go by his gut, hold his nose, and jump," Tinker writes in *Tinker in Television*. Lee Iacocca, in his autobiography, spends pages extolling intuition: "To a certain extent, I've always operated by gut feeling."[42] Agor suggests relaxation techniques, using images to guide the mind, and taking creative pauses before making a decision.[43] A review of the research on intuition suggests that although intuition itself cannot be taught, managers can be trained to rely more fully on the promptings of their intuition.[44]

Intuition is an elusive concept, and one with many definitions. There is an interesting paradox regarding intuition. Some researchers view "rational" methods as preferable to intuition, yet satisfaction with a rational decision is usually determined by how the decision feels intuitively.[45] Intuition appears to have a positive effect on managerial decision making, but it is not without controversy. Some writers argue that intuition has its place and that instincts should be trusted, but not as a substitute for reason. With new technologies, managers can analyze a lot more information in a lot less time, making the rational method less time-consuming than it once was.[46]

Creativity at Work

Creativity is a process influenced by individual and organizational factors that results in the production of novel and useful ideas, products, or both.[47] The social and technological changes that organizations face require creative decisions.[48] Managers of the future need to develop special competencies to deal with the turbulence of change, and one of these is the ability to promote creativity in organizations.[49]

Creativity is a process that is at least in part unconscious. The four stages of the creative process are preparation, incubation, illumination, and verification.[50] Preparation means seeking out new experiences and opportunities to learn, because creativity grows from a base of knowledge. Travel and educational opportunities of all kinds open the individual's mind. Incubation is a process of reflective thought and is often conducted subconsciously. During incubation, the individual engages in other pursuits while the mind considers the problem and works on it. Illumination occurs when the individual senses an insight for solving the problem. Finally, verification is conducted to determine if the solution or idea is valid. This is accomplished by thinking through the implications of the decision, presenting it to another person, or trying it out. Sleep is an important contributor to creative problem solving. Momentary quieting of the brain through relaxation can also increase "coherence" or the ability of different parts of the brain to work together.[51,52] Both individual and organizational influences affect the creative process.

Individual Influences Several individual variables are related to creativity. One group of factors involves the cognitive processes that creative individuals tend to use. One cognitive process is divergent thinking, meaning the individual's ability to generate several potential solutions to a problem.[53] In addition, associational abilities and the use of imagery are associated with creativity.[54] Unconscious processes such as dreams are also essential cognitive processes related to creative thinking.[55]

Personality factors have also been related to creativity in studies of individuals from several different occupations. These characteristics include intellectual and artistic values, breadth of interests, high energy, concern with achievement, independence of judgment, intuition, self-confidence, and a creative self-image.[56] Tolerance of ambiguity, intrinsic motivation, risk taking, and a desire for recognition are also associated with creativity.[57]

creativity

A process influenced by individual and organizational factors that results in the production of novel and useful ideas, products, or both.

There is also evidence that people who are in a good mood are more creative.[58] Positive affect is related to creativity in work teams because being in a positive mood allows team members to explore new ways of thinking.[59] Positive emotions enhance creativity by broadening one's cognitive patterns and resources. For example, repeated experiences of love, interest, courage, and gratitude cause one to discard old theories and automatic ways of doing things. Instead, these positive emotions initiate thoughts and actions that are novel and unscripted.[60, 61] Moreover, it is a cyclical process, because creative thoughts and incidents lead to more positive affect. You might say that thinking positively makes us more creative, and being more creative makes us think positively.[62] In tasks involving considerable cognitive demands, however, it has been found that people in negative moods perform better. When an individual experiences negative moods or emotions, it is a signal that all is not well, which leads to more attention and vigilance in cognitive activity. Positive moods signal that all is well with the status quo, which can lead to decreased performance on some decision-making tasks involving complex mental activity.[63,64]

Organizational Influences The organizational environment people work in can either support or impede creativity. Creativity killers include focusing on how work is going to be evaluated, being closely monitored while you are working, and competing with other people in win–lose situations. In contrast, creativity facilitators include feelings of autonomy, being part of a team with diverse skills, and having creative supervisors and coworkers.[65] High-quality, supportive relationships with supervisors are related to creativity.[66] High-quality social networks that are cohesive can have a positive impact on creative decision making. Such social networks encourage creative decision making by facilitating shared sense-making of relevant information and consensus building.[67] Flexible organizational structures and participative decision making have also been associated with creativity. An organization can also present impediments to creativity. These barriers include internal political problems, harsh criticism of new ideas, destructive internal competition, and avoidance of risk.[68] The physical environment can also hamper creativity. Companies like Oticon, a Danish hearing-aid manufacturer, and Ethicon Endo-Surgery, a division of Johnson & Johnson, use open-plan offices that eliminate office walls and cubicles so that employees interact more frequently. When people mix, ideas mix as well.[69]

Studies of the role of organizational rewards in encouraging creativity have mixed results. Some studies have shown that monetary incentives improve creative performance, whereas others have found that is not the case.[70] Still other studies have indicated that explicitly contracting to obtain a reward led to lower levels of creativity when compared with contracting for no reward, being presented with just the task, or being presented with the task and receiving the reward later.[71] Organizations can therefore enhance individuals' creative decision making by providing a supportive environment, participative decision making, and a flexible structure.

Individual/Organization Fit Research has indicated that creative performance is highest when there is a match, or fit, between the individual and organizational influences on creativity. For example, when individuals who desire to be creative are matched with an organization that values creative ideas, the result is more creative performance.[72]

A common mistaken assumption regarding creativity is that either you have it or you do not. Research refutes this myth and has shown that individuals can be trained to be more creative.[73] The Disney Institute features a wide range of programs offered to companies, and one of their best-sellers is creativity training. You 10.2 allows you to determine whether you prefer creative or logical problem solving.

Creative or Logical Problem Solving:
What Is Your Preference?

Try the following creative problem-solving challenge.

Each of the following problems is an equation that can be solved by substituting the appropriate words for the letters. Have fun with them!

Examples: 3F = 1Y (3 feet = 1 yard.)
4LC = GL (4 leaf clover = Good luck.)

1. M + M + NH + V + C + RI = NE.
2. "1B in the H = 2 in the B."
3. 8D − 24H = 1W.
4. 3P = 6.
5. HH & MH at 12 = N or M.
6. 4J + 4Q + 4K = All the FC.
7. S & M & T & W & T & F & S are D of W.
8. A + N + AF + MC + CG = AF.
9. T = LS State.
10. 23Y − 3Y = 2D.
11. E − 8 = Z.
12. Y + 2D = T.
13. C + 6D = NYE.
14. Y − S − S − A = W.
15. A & E were in the G of E.
16. My FL and South P are both MC.
17. "NN = GN."
18. N − P + SM = S of C.
19. 1 + 6Z = 1M.
20. "R = R = R."
21. AL & JG & WM & JK were all A.
22. N + V + P + A + A + C + P + I = P of S.
23. S + H of R = USC.

SOURCE: From *A Whack on the Side of the Head* by Roger Von Oech. Copyright © 1983, 1990, 1998 by Roger Von Oech. By permission of Warner Books.

Now try the following logical problem-solving exercise, entitled "Who Owns the Fish?", which is attributed to Albert Einstein.

There are five houses in a row and in five different colors. In each house lives a person from a different country. Each person drinks a certain drink, plays a certain game, and keeps a certain pet. No two people drink the same drink, play the same game, or keep the same pet.

> The Brit lives in a red house.
> The Swede keeps dogs.
> The Dane drinks tea.
> The green house is on the left of the white house.
> The green house owner drinks coffee.
> The person who plays tennis rears birds.
> The owner of the yellow house plays chess.
> The man living in the house right in the center drinks milk.

> The Norwegian lives in the first house.
> The man who plays poker lives next to the man who keeps cats.
> The man who keeps horses lives next to the one who plays chess.
> The man who plays billiards drinks beer.
> The German plays golf.
> The Norwegian lives next to the blue house.
> The man who plays poker has a neighbor who drinks water.

Question: Who owns the fish?

Answer: Your instructor can provide the solutions to this exercise.

SOURCE: By E. O. Welles, © 2004 Gruner + Jahr USA Publishing. "The Billionaire Next Door," first published in *Inc. Magazine*, 23 (6) (May 2001): pp. 80–85. Reprinted with permission.

Part of creativity training involves learning to open up mental locks that keep us from generating creative alternatives to a decision or problem. The following are some mental locks that diminish creativity:

> Searching for the "right" answer.

> Trying to be logical.

> Following the rules.

> Avoiding ambiguity.

> Striving for practicality.

> Being afraid to look foolish.

> Avoiding problems outside our own expertise.

> Fearing failure.

> Believing we are not really creative.

> Not making play a part of work.[74]

(4) Critique your own level of creativity and list ways of improving it.

Note that many of these mental locks stem from values within organizations. Organizations can facilitate creative decision making in many ways. Rewarding creativity, allowing employees to fail, making work more fun, and providing creativity training are a few suggestions. Also, companies can encourage creativity by exposing employees to new ideas. This can be done in several ways, including job rotation, which moves employees through different jobs and gives them exposure to different information, projects, and teams. Employees can also be assigned to work with groups outside the company, such as suppliers or consultants. Finally, managers can encourage employees to surround themselves with stimuli that they have found to enhance their creative processes. These may be music, artwork, books, or anything else that encourages creative thinking.[75]

We have seen that both individual and organizational factors can produce creativity. Creativity can also mean finding problems as well as fixing them. Recently, four different types of creativity have been proposed, based on the source of the trigger (internal or external) and the source of the problem (presented versus discovered). Responsive creativity means responding to a problem that is presented to you by others because it is part of your job. Expected creativity is discovering problems because you are expected to by the organization. Contributory creativity is responding to problems presented to you because you want to be creative. Proactive creativity is discovering problems because you want to be creative.[76]

3M consistently ranks among the top ten in *Fortune*'s annual list of most admired corporations. It earned this reputation through innovation: More than one-quarter of 3M's sales are from products less than four years old. Post-It Notes, for example, were created by a worker who wanted little adhesive papers to mark hymns for church service. He thought of another worker who had perfected a light adhesive, and the two spent their free time developing Post-It Notes. 3M has continued its tradition of innovation with Post-It Flags, Pop-Up Tape Strips, and Nexcare Ease-Off Bandages.

Leaders can play key roles in modeling creative behavior. Sir Richard Branson, founder and chairman of UK-based Virgin Group, believes that if you do not use your employees' creative potential, you are doomed to failure. At Virgin Group, the culture encourages risk taking and rewards innovation. Rules and regulations are not over-valued, nor is analyzing ideas to death. Branson says an employee can have an idea in the morning and implement it in the afternoon.[77]

Creativity is a global concern. Poland, for example, is undergoing a major shift from a centrally planned economy and monoparty rule to a market economy and Western-style democracy. One of the major concerns for Polish managers is creativity. Finding ingenious solutions and having the ability to think creatively can be a question of life or death for Polish organizations, which are making the transition to a faster pace of learning and change.[78]

Both intuition and creativity are important influences on managerial decision making. Both concepts require additional research so that managers can better understand how to use them, as well as how to encourage employees to use them to make more effective decisions.

PARTICIPATION IN DECISION MAKING

Effective management of people can improve a company's economic performance. Firms that capitalize on this fact share several common practices. Chief among them is participation of employees in decision making.[79] Many companies do this through highly empowered self-managed teams like the ones we discussed in Chapter 9. Even in situations where formal teams are not feasible, decision authority can be handed down to front-line employees who have the knowledge and skills to make a difference. At Hampton Inn hotels, for example, guest services personnel are empowered to do whatever is necessary to make guests happy—without consulting their superiors.

The Effects of Participation

Participative decision making occurs when individuals who are affected by decisions influence the making of those decisions. Participation buffers employees from the negative experiences of organizational politics.[80] In addition, participative management has been found to increase employee creativity, job satisfaction, and productivity.[81]

GE Capital believes in participation. Each year it holds dreaming sessions, and employees from all levels of the company attend strategy and budget meetings to discuss where the company is heading. As a result, young employees came up with e-commerce ideas like http://www.financiallearning.com and http://www.gefn.com, which were highly successful.[82]

As our economy becomes increasingly based on knowledge work, and as new technologies make it easier for decentralized decision makers to connect, participative decision making will undoubtedly increase.[83] Consider the city and county of San Francisco, a combined city/county government organization. When the city and county of San Francisco needed to adopt a single messaging system to meet the needs of more than 20,000 users, it faced a huge challenge in getting all the users to provide input into the decision. Technology helped craft a system that balanced the needs of all the groups involved, and IT planners developed a twenty-eight-page spreadsheet to pull together the needs and desires of all sixty departments into a focused decision matrix. Within two years, 90 percent of the users had agreed on and moved to a single system, reducing costs and complexity.[84]

Foundations for Participation and Empowerment

Organizational and individual foundations underlie empowerment that enhances task motivation and performance. The organizational foundations for empowerment include a participative, supportive organizational culture and a team-oriented work design. A supportive work environment is essential because of the uncertainty

participative decision making
Decision making in which individuals who are affected by decisions influence the making of those decisions.

that empowerment can cause within the organization. Empowerment requires that lower-level organizational members be able to make decisions and take action on them. As operational employees become empowered to make decisions, fear, anxiety, or even terror can be created among middle managers in the organization.[85] Senior leadership must create an organizational culture that is supportive and reassuring for these middle managers as the power dynamics of the system change. If not supported and reassured, the middle managers can become a restraining, disruptive force to participative decision-making efforts.

A second organizational foundation for empowerment concerns the design of work. The old factory system relied on work specialization and narrow tasks with the intent of achieving routinized efficiency.[86] This approach to the design of work had some economic advantages, but it also had some distressing disadvantages leading to monotony and fatigue. This approach to the design of work is inconsistent with participation, because the individual feels absolved of much responsibility for a whole piece of work. Team-oriented work designs are a key organizational foundation because they lead to broader tasks and a greater sense of responsibility. For example, Volvo builds cars using a team-oriented work design in which each person does many different tasks, and each person has direct responsibility for the finished product.[87] These work designs create a context for effective participation as long as the empowered individuals meet necessary individual prerequisites.

The three individual prerequisites for participation and empowerment are (1) the capability to become psychologically involved in participative activities, (2) the motivation to act autonomously, and (3) the capacity to see the relevance of participation for one's own well-being.[88] First, people must be psychologically equipped to become involved in participative activities if they are to be empowered and become effective team members. Not all people are so predisposed. For example, Germany has an authoritarian tradition that runs counter to participation and empowerment at the individual and group level. General Motors encountered significant difficulties implementing quality circles in its German plants, because workers expected to be directed by supervisors, not to engage in participative problem solving. The German initiatives to establish supervisory/worker boards in corporations are intended to change this authoritarian tradition.

A second individual prerequisite is the motivation to act autonomously. People with dependent personalities are predisposed to be told what to do and to rely on external motivation rather than internal, intrinsic motivation.[89] These dependent people are not effective contributors to decision making.

Finally, if participative decision making is to work, people must be able to see how it provides a personal benefit to them. The personal payoff for the individual need not be short term. It may be a long-term benefit that results in people receiving greater rewards through enhanced organizational profitability.

What Level of Participation?

Participative decision making is complex, and one of the things managers must understand is that employees can be involved in some, or all, of the stages of the decision-making process. For example, employees could be variously involved in identifying problems, generating alternatives, selecting solutions, planning implementations, or evaluating results. Research shows that greater involvement in all five of these stages has a cumulative effect. Employees who are involved in all five processes have higher satisfaction and performance levels. And all decision processes are not created equal. If employees can't be provided with full participation in all stages, the highest payoffs seem to come with involvement in generating alternatives, planning implementations, and evaluating results.[90] Styles of participation in decision making may need to change as the company grows or as its culture changes.

THE GROUP DECISION-MAKING PROCESS

Managers use groups to make decisions for several reasons. One is *synergy*, which occurs when group members stimulate new solutions to problems through the process of mutual influence and encouragement within the group. Another reason for using a group is to gain commitment to a decision. Groups also bring more knowledge and experience to the problem-solving situation.

Group decisions can sometimes be predicted by comparing the views of the initial group members with the final group decision. These simple relationships are known as *social decision schemes*. One social decision scheme is the majority-wins rule, in which the group supports whatever position is taken by the majority of its members. Another scheme, the truth-wins rule, predicts that the correct decision will emerge as an increasing number of members realize its appropriateness. The two-thirds-majority rule means that the decision favored by two-thirds or more of the members is supported. Finally, the first-shift rule states that members support a decision represented by the first shift in opinion shown by a member.

Research indicates that these social decision schemes can predict a group decision as much as 80 percent of the time.[91] Current research is aimed at discovering which rules are used in particular types of tasks. For example, studies indicate that the majority-wins rule is used most often in judgment tasks (that is, when the decision is a matter of preference or opinion), whereas the truth-wins rule predicts decisions best when the task is an intellective one (that is, when the decision has a correct answer).[92]

Advantages and Disadvantages of Group Decision Making

Both advantages and disadvantages are associated with group decision making. The advantages include (1) more knowledge and information through the pooling of group member resources; (2) increased acceptance of, and commitment to, the decision, because the members had a voice in it; and (3) greater understanding of the decision, because members were involved in the various stages of the decision process. The disadvantages of group decision making include (1) pressure within the group to conform and fit in; (2) domination of the group by one forceful member or a dominant clique, who may ramrod the decision; and (3) the amount of time required, because a group makes decisions more slowly than an individual.[93]

Given these advantages and disadvantages, should an individual or a group make a decision? Substantial empirical research indicates that whether a group or an individual should be used depends on the type of task involved. For judgment tasks requiring an estimate or a prediction, groups are usually superior to individuals because of the breadth of experience that multiple individuals bring to the problem.[94] On tasks that have a correct solution, other studies have indicated that the most competent individual outperforms the group.[95] This finding has been called into question, however. Much of the previous research on groups was conducted in the laboratory, where group members interacted only for short periods of time. Researchers wanted to know how a longer experience in the group would affect

(5) Compare and contrast the advantages and disadvantages of group decision making.

synergy
A positive force that occurs in groups when group members stimulate new solutions to problems through the process of mutual influence and encouragement within the group.

social decision schemes
Simple rules used to determine final group decisions.

decisions. Their study showed that groups who worked together for longer periods of time outperformed the most competent member 70 percent of the time. As groups gained experience, the best members became less important to the group's success.[96] This study demonstrated that experience in the group is an important variable to consider when evaluating the individual versus group decision-making question.

Research is just beginning on the role of trust and trustworthiness in team decision making. One study was conducted for six weeks on student teams that were involved in designing an information systems project. The teams' trust of each other and risk-taking actions were cyclical. When teams saw the other team as trustworthy, they took a risk; then the other team, based on their perception of the first team's trustworthiness, decided whether or not to take a risk, and so on. The study showed that the trust process works between teams much the same as it does between individuals.[97]

Given the emphasis on teams in the workplace, many managers believe that groups produce better decisions than do individuals, yet the evidence is mixed. It is clear that more research needs to be conducted in organizational settings to help answer this question.

Two potential liabilities are found in group decision making: groupthink and group polarization. These problems are discussed in the following sections.

Groupthink

(6) Discuss the symptoms of groupthink and ways to prevent it.

One liability of a cohesive group is its tendency to develop *groupthink*, a dysfunctional process. Irving Janis, the originator of the groupthink concept, describes groupthink as "a deterioration of mental efficiency, reality testing, and moral judgment" resulting from pressures within the group.[98]

Certain conditions favor the development of groupthink. One of the conditions is high cohesiveness. Cohesive groups tend to favor solidarity because members identify strongly with the group.[99] High-ranking teams that make decisions without outside help are especially prone to groupthink because they are likely to have shared mental models; that is, they are more likely to think alike.[100] And homogeneous groups (ones with little to no diversity among members) are more likely to suffer from groupthink.[101] Two other conditions that encourage groupthink are having to make a highly consequential decision and time constraints.[102] A highly consequential decision is one that will have a great impact on the group members and on outside parties. When group members feel that they have a limited time in which to make a decision, they may rush through the process. These antecedents cause members to prefer concurrence in decisions and to fail to evaluate one another's suggestions critically. A group suffering from groupthink shows recognizable symptoms. Table 10.1 presents these symptoms and makes suggestions on how to avoid groupthink.

An incident cited as a prime example of groupthink is the 1986 *Challenger* disaster, in which the shuttle exploded and killed all seven crew members. A presidential commission concluded that flawed decision making was the primary cause of the accident. Sadly, organizations often struggle to learn from their mistakes. In 2003, the shuttle *Columbia* exploded over Texas upon reentering the earth's atmosphere, killing all seven crew members. Within days of the *Columbia* disaster, questions began to surface about the decision-making process that led flight engineers to assume that damage caused to the shuttle upon take-off was minor and to continue the mission. Subsequent investigation led observers to note that NASA's decision-making process appears just as flawed today as it was in 1986, exhibiting all the classic symptoms of groupthink. The final accident report

groupthink
A deterioration of mental efficiency, reality testing, and moral judgment resulting from pressures within the group.

TABLE 10.1 Symptoms of Groupthink and How to Prevent It

Symptoms of Groupthink

- *Illusions of invulnerability.* Group members feel that they are above criticism. This symptom leads to excessive optimism and risk taking.
- *Illusions of group morality.* Group members feel they are moral in their actions and therefore above reproach. This symptom leads the group to ignore the ethical implications of their decisions.
- *Illusions of unanimity.* Group members believe there is unanimous agreement on the decisions. Silence is misconstrued as consent.
- *Rationalization.* Group members concoct explanations for their decisions to make them appear rational and correct. The results are that other alternatives are not considered, and there is an unwillingness to reconsider the group's assumptions.
- *Stereotyping the enemy.* Competitors are stereotyped as evil or stupid. This leads the group to underestimate its opposition.
- *Self-censorship.* Members do not express their doubts or concerns about the course of action. This prevents critical analysis of the decisions.
- *Peer pressure.* Any members who express doubts or concerns are pressured by other group members who question their loyalty.
- *Mindguards.* Some members take it upon themselves to protect the group from negative feedback. Group members are thus shielded from information that might lead them to question their actions.

Guidelines for Preventing Groupthink

- Ask each group member to assume the role of the critical evaluator who actively voices objections or doubts.
- Have the leader avoid stating his or her position on the issue prior to the group decision.
- Create several groups that work on the decision simultaneously.
- Bring in outside experts to evaluate the group process.
- Appoint a devil's advocate to question the group's course of action consistently.
- Evaluate the competition carefully, posing as many different motivations and intentions as possible.
- Once consensus is reached, encourage the group to rethink its position by reexamining the alternatives.

SOURCE: Irving L. Janis, *Groupthink: Psychological Studies of Policy Decisions and Fiascoes,* Second Edition. Copyright © 1982 by Houghton Mifflin Company. Used with permission.

blamed the NASA culture that downplayed risk and suppressed dissent for the decision.[103,104]

Consequences of groupthink include an incomplete survey of alternatives, failure to evaluate the risks of the preferred course of action, biased information processing, and a failure to work out contingency plans. The overall result of groupthink is defective decision making. This was evident in the *Challenger* situation. The group considered only two alternatives: launch or no launch. They failed to consider the risks of their decision to launch the shuttle, and they did not develop any contingency plans.

Table 10.1 presents Janis's guidelines for avoiding groupthink. Many of these suggestions center around the notion of ensuring that decisions are evaluated completely, with opportunities for discussion from all group members. This strategy helps encourage members to evaluate one another's ideas critically. Groups that are educated about the value of diversity tend to perform better at decision-making tasks. On the other hand, groups that are homogenous and are not educated about the value of diversity do not accrue such benefits in decision making.[105]

Janis has used the groupthink framework to conduct historical analyses of several political and military fiascoes, including the Bay of Pigs invasion, the Vietnam War, and Watergate. One review of the decision situation in the *Challenger* incident proposed that two variables, time and leadership style, are important to include.[106] When a decision must be made quickly, there is more potential for groupthink. Leadership style can either promote groupthink (if the leader makes his or her opinion known up-front) or avoid groupthink (if the leader encourages open and frank discussion).

There are few empirical studies of groupthink, and most of these involved students in a laboratory setting. More applied research may be seen in the future, however, as a questionnaire has been developed to measure the constructs associated with groupthink.[107] Janis's work on groupthink has led to several interdisciplinary efforts at understanding policy decisions.[108] The work underscores the need to examine multiple explanations for failed decisions. Teams that experience cognitive (task-based) conflict are found to make better decisions than teams that experience affective (emotion-based) conflict. As such, one prescription for managers has been to encourage cognitive conflict while minimizing affective conflict. However, these two forms of conflict can also occur together, and more research is needed on how one can be encouraged while minimizing the other.[109]

Group Polarization

Another group phenomenon was discovered by a graduate student. His study showed that groups made riskier decisions; in fact, the group and each individual accepted greater levels of risk following a group discussion of the issue. Subsequent studies uncovered another shift—toward caution. Thus, group discussion produced shifts both toward more risky positions and toward more cautious positions.[110] Further research revealed that individual group member attitudes simply became more extreme following group discussion. Individuals who were initially against an issue became more radically opposed, and individuals who were in favor of the issue became more strongly supportive following discussion. These shifts came to be known as *group polarization*.[111]

The tendency toward polarization has important implications for group decision making. Groups whose initial views lean a certain way can be expected to adopt more extreme views following interaction.

Several ideas have been proposed to explain why group polarization occurs. One explanation is the social comparison approach. Prior to group discussion, individuals believe they hold better views than the other members. During group discussion, they see that their views are not so far from average, so they shift to more extreme positions.[112] A second explanation is the persuasive arguments view. It contends that group discussion reinforces the initial views of the members, so they take a more extreme position.[113] Both explanations are supported by research. It may be that both processes, along with others, cause the group to develop more polarized attitudes.

Group polarization leads groups to adopt extreme attitudes. In some cases, this can be disastrous. For instance, if individuals are leaning toward a dangerous

group polarization

The tendency for group discussion to produce shifts toward more extreme attitudes among members.

decision, they are likely to support it more strongly following discussion. Both groupthink and group polarization are potential liabilities of group decision making, but several techniques can be used to help prevent or control these two liabilities.

TECHNIQUES FOR GROUP DECISION MAKING

Once a manager has determined that a group decision approach should be used, he or she can determine the technique that is best suited to the decision situation. Seven techniques will be briefly summarized: brainstorming, nominal group technique, Delphi technique, devil's advocacy, dialectical inquiry, quality circles and quality teams, and self-managed teams.

(7) Evaluate the strengths and weaknesses of several group decision-making techniques.

Brainstorming

Brainstorming is a good technique for generating alternatives. The idea behind *brainstorming* is to generate as many ideas as possible, suspending evaluation until all of the ideas have been suggested. Participants are encouraged to build on the suggestions of others, and imagination is emphasized. One company that benefits from brainstorming is Toyota. Despite its success with the baby-boomer generation, Toyota's executives realized that they were failing to connect with younger buyers, who viewed the firm as stodgy. In response, the company assembled a group of younger employees to brainstorm new products for this market. The result was the Toyota Echo, as well as the Scion, an entirely new line of boxy crossover vehicles aimed at young drivers.[114, 115, 116] Evidence suggests, however, that group brainstorming is less effective than a comparable number of individuals working alone. In groups, participants engage in discussions that can make them lose their focus.[117]

One recent trend is the use of electronic rather than verbal brainstorming in groups. Electronic brainstorming overcomes two common problems that can produce group brainstorming failure: production blocking and evaluation apprehension. In verbal brainstorming, individuals are exposed to the inputs of others. While listening to others, individuals are distracted from their own ideas.[118] This is referred to as production blocking. When ideas are recorded electronically, participants are free from hearing the interruptions of others; thus, production blocking is reduced. Some individuals suffer from evaluation apprehension in brainstorming groups. They fear that others might respond negatively to their ideas. In electronic brainstorming, input is anonymous, so evaluation apprehension is reduced. Studies indicate that anonymous electronic brainstorming groups outperform face-to-face brainstorming groups in the number of ideas generated.[119]

Nominal Group Technique

A structured approach to decision making that focuses on generating alternatives and choosing one is called *nominal group technique (NGT)*. NGT involves the following discrete steps:

1. Individuals silently list their ideas.
2. Ideas are written on a chart one at a time until all ideas are listed.
3. Discussion is permitted but only to clarify the ideas. No criticism is allowed.
4. A written vote is taken.

brainstorming
A technique for generating as many ideas as possible on a given subject, while suspending evaluation until all the ideas have been suggested.

nominal group technique (NGT)
A structured approach to group decision making that focuses on generating alternatives and choosing one.

NGT is a good technique to use in a situation where group members fear criticism from others.[120]

Delphi Technique

The *Delphi technique*, which originated at the Rand Corporation, involves gathering the judgments of experts for use in decision making. Experts at remote locations respond to a questionnaire. A coordinator summarizes those responses, and the summary is sent back to the experts. The experts then rate the various alternatives generated, and the coordinator tabulates the results. The Delphi technique is valuable in its ability to generate a number of independent judgments without the requirement of a face-to-face meeting.[121]

Devil's Advocacy

In the *devil's advocacy* decision method, a group or individual is given the role of critic. This devil's advocate has the task of coming up with the potential problems of a proposed decision. This helps organizations avoid costly mistakes in decision making by identifying potential pitfalls in advance.[122] As we discussed in Chapter 9, a devil's advocate who challenges the CEO and top management team can help sustain the vitality and performance of the upper echelon.

Dialectical Inquiry

Dialectical inquiry is a debate between two opposing sets of recommendations. Although it sets up a conflict, it is a constructive approach, because it brings out the benefits and limitations of both sets of ideas.[123] When using this technique, it is important to guard against a win–lose attitude and to concentrate on reaching the most effective solution for all concerned. Research has shown that the way a decision is framed (that is, win–win versus win–lose) is very important. A decision's outcome could be viewed as a gain or a loss, depending on the way the decision is framed.[124]

Quality Circles and Quality Teams

As you recall from Chapter 9, quality circles are small groups that voluntarily meet to provide input for solving quality or production problems. Quality circles are also a way of extending participative decision making into teams. Managers often listen to recommendations from quality circles and implement the suggestions. The rewards for the suggestions are intrinsic—involvement in the decision-making process is the primary one.

Quality circles are often generated from the bottom up; that is, they provide advice to managers, who still retain decision-making authority. As such, quality circles are not empowered to implement their own recommendations. They operate in parallel fashion to the organization's structure, and they rely on voluntary participation.[125] In Japan, quality circles have been integrated into the organization instead of added on. This may be one reason for Japan's success with this technique. In contrast, the U.S. experience is not as positive. It has been estimated that 60 to 75 percent of the quality circles have failed. Reasons for the failures have included lack of top management support and lack of problem-solving skills among quality circle members.[126]

Quality teams, in contrast, are included in total quality management and other quality improvement efforts as part of a change in the organization's structure.

Delphi technique

Gathering the judgments of experts for use in decision making.

devil's advocacy

A technique for preventing group-think in which a group or individual is given the role of critic during decision making.

dialectical inquiry

A debate between two opposing sets of recommendations.

Quality teams are generated from the top down and are empowered to act on their own recommendations. Whereas quality circles emphasize the generation of ideas, quality teams make data-based decisions about improving product and service quality. Various decision-making techniques are employed in quality teams. Brainstorming, flow charts, and cause-and-effect diagrams help pinpoint problems that affect quality.

Some organizations have moved toward quality teams, but Toyota has stuck with quality circles. The company has used them since 1963 and was the second company in the world to do so. Toyota's quality circles constitute a limited form of empowerment—and they like it that way. The members want to participate but not be self-directed. They would rather leave certain decisions to managers who are trusted to take good care of them. Toyota attributes its success with quality circles to the longevity of their use and to its view of them as true methods of participation.[127]

Quality circles and quality teams are methods for using groups in the decision-making process. Self-managed teams take the concept of participation one step further.

Self-Managed Teams

Another group decision-making method is the use of self-managed teams, which we also discussed in Chapter 9. The decision-making activities of self-managed teams are more broadly focused than those of quality circles and quality teams, which usually emphasize quality and production problems. Self-managed teams make many of the decisions that were once reserved for managers, such as work scheduling, job assignments, and staffing. Unlike quality circles, whose role is an advisory one, self-managed teams are delegated authority in the organization's decision-making process.

Many organizations have claimed success with self-managed teams. At Northern Telecom (now Nortel Networks), revenues rose 63 percent and sales increased 26 percent following the implementation of self-managed teams.[128] Research evidence shows that such teams can lead to higher productivity, lower turnover among employees, and flatter organization structure.[129]

Self-managed teams, like any cohesive group, can fall victim to groupthink. The key to stimulating innovation and better problem solving in these groups is welcoming dissent among members. Dissent breaks down complacency and sets in motion a process that results in better decisions. Team members must know that dissent is permissible so that they won't fear embarrassment or ridicule.[130] Before choosing a group decision-making technique, the manager should carefully evaluate the group members and the decision situation. Then the best method for accomplishing the objectives of the group decision-making process can be selected. If the goal is generating a large number of alternatives, for example, brainstorming would be a good choice. If group members are reluctant to contribute ideas, the nominal group technique would be appropriate. The need for expert input would be best facilitated by the Delphi technique. To guard against groupthink, devil's advocacy or dialectical inquiry would be effective. Decisions that concern quality or production would benefit from the advice of quality circles or the empowered decisions of quality teams. Moreover, recent research suggests that if individuals within a team are made accountable for the process of decision making (rather than for the end decision itself), then such teams are more likely to gather diverse information, share information, and eventually make better decisions.[131] Finally, a manager who wants to provide total empowerment to a group should consider self-managed teams.

DIVERSITY AND CULTURE IN DECISION MAKING

Styles of decision making vary greatly among cultures. Many of the dimensions proposed by Hofstede that were presented in Chapter 2 affect decision making. Uncertainty avoidance, for example, can affect the way people view decisions. In the United States, a culture with low uncertainty avoidance, decisions are seen as opportunities for change. In contrast, cultures such as those of Indonesia and Malaysia attempt to accept situations as they are rather than to change them.[132] Power distance also affects decision making. In more hierarchical cultures, such as India, top-level managers make decisions. In countries with low power distance, lower-level employees make many decisions. The Swedish culture exemplifies this type.

The individualist/collectivist dimension has implications for decision making. Japan, with its collectivist emphasis, favors group decisions. The United States has a more difficult time with group decisions because it is an individualistic culture. Time orientation affects the frame of reference of the decision. In China, with its long-term view, decisions are made with the future in mind. In the United States, many decisions are made considering only the short term.

The masculine/feminine dimension can be compared to the Jungian thinking/feeling preferences for decision making. Masculine cultures, as in many Latin American countries, value quick, assertive decisions. Feminine cultures, as in many Scandinavian countries, value decisions that reflect concern for others.

Managers should learn as much as possible about the decision processes in other cultures. NAFTA, for example, has eliminated many barriers to trade with Mexico. In Mexican organizations, decision-making authority is centralized, autocratic, and retained in small groups of top managers. As a consequence, Mexican employees are reluctant to participate in decision making and often wait to be told what to do rather than take a risk. Significant differences exist amongst Hispanic work-related ethics and non-Hispanic work-related ethics as well. These differences need be managed effectively by managers to help individuals make decisions that are aligned with organizational values and ethics.[133] In addition, joint ventures with family-owned *grupos* (large groups of businesses) can be challenging. It may be difficult to identify the critical decision maker in the family and to determine how much decision-making authority is held by the *grupo's* family board.[134] Mexican managers may be more likely to engage in escalation of commitment or continue to invest in a losing venture. However, because lower-level managers in Mexico have control over smaller amounts of resources, they tend to invest in smaller increments than do U.S. managers.[135]

Recent research examining the effects of cultural diversity on decision making has found that when individuals in a group are racially dissimilar, they engage in more open information sharing, encourage dissenting perspectives, and arrive at better decisions than racially similar groups.[136] Other kinds of diversity such as functional background have been studied as well. Top management teams that have members who come from a variety of functional backgrounds (for example, marketing, accounting, information systems) engage in greater debate in decision making that top management teams in which the members come from similar backgrounds. This diversity results in better financial performance for the firm.[137] Research also indicates than strategic decision making in firms can vary widely by culture. For example, one such source of variation stems from the differential emphasis placed on environmental scanning in different cultures. Furthermore, strategic decision making might appear rational but is also informed by firm level and national characteristics.[138]

TECHNOLOGICAL AIDS TO DECISION MAKING

Many computerized decision tools are available to managers. These systems can be used to support the decision-making process in organizations.

Expert Systems

Artificial intelligence is used to develop an expert system, which is a programmed decision tool. The system is set up using decision rules, and the effectiveness of the expert system is highly dependent on its design. Because expert systems are sources of knowledge and experience and not just passive software, the organization must decide who is responsible for the decisions made by expert systems. Organizations must therefore be concerned about the liability for using the recommendations of expert systems.

TriPath Imaging has found a way to automate a critical but tedious process: screening Pap smears for signs of cancer. Programmers developing this software, called FocalPoint, met with numerous pathologists to learn which criteria they look for, such as the color of a cell's nucleus. They then allowed the software to learn by "practicing" on slides that had already been examined by experts. Today, FocalPoint software screens about 10 percent of all Pap smear slides in the United States.[139]

Expert systems hold great potential for affecting managerial decisions. Thus, managers must carefully scrutinize the expert system rather than simply accepting its decisions.

Decision Support Systems

Managers use decision support systems (DSS) as tools to enhance their ability to make complex decisions. DSS are computer and communication systems that process incoming data and synthesize pertinent information for managers to use. One example is the Fire Management Information System (FMIS) developed by a team of five partners from companies representing four European countries. Fire managers who are in charge of emergencies are bombarded with information and stress as situations change. The team sought to design a system that would help the fire managers in their decision-making tasks during forest fires. Although emergencies can take different forms, managers do not require radically different plans for dealing with them. This makes it possible to develop and store skeletal plans that can be accessed using the DSS instead of starting from scratch with each forest fire.

The team combined five decision support services in putting together the system:

> Weather monitoring synthesized information from remote meteorological stations.

> Fire risk rating assessed risk using an expert system.

> Fighting adviser proposed plans for preventing and fighting the fire.

> Fire detection used a network of imaging sensors for early detection of fires.

> Fire modeling simulated the fire's pattern and spread, taking into account vegetation, topography, and weather.

The fire manager uses the system in two modes. In standby mode, the system constantly updates databases and maps. In operational mode, the fire manager navigates through different functions when an emergency arises. In this way, the FMIS integrates all the decision support tools the manager needs to make the quick decisions needed to fight forest fires.[140]

Group Decision Support Systems

Another tool for decision making focuses on helping groups make decisions. A group decision support system (GDSS) uses computer support and communication facilities to support group decision-making processes in either face-to-face meetings or dispersed meetings. The GDSS has been shown to affect conflict management within a group by depersonalizing the issue and by forcing the group to discuss its conflict management process.[141] Team decisions often improve by using a GDSS because members share information more fully when they use a GDSS.[142]

Shell Oil realized several years ago that its engineers were wasting time and money finding answers to questions when other people in the firm already had the solutions. To help leverage its internal knowledge, Shell devised a massive but simple system based on the familiar model of Web discussion groups. Within these "communities," engineers can pose questions to experts in other segments of the business. But perhaps more important, Shell indexes and archives the discussions from these boards, creating a living, growing knowledge base that future generations of engineers will rely on even more heavily. To date, Shell estimates that it has saved $200 for every dollar invested in the project.[143]

Northrop Grumman, a major defense contractor, works with a dazzling array of advanced technologies. But what happens when an aircraft engineer faces a decision involving an area with which he is unfamiliar, even though he is fairly sure that one of Grumman's other 10,000 employees probably knows the answer? Today, he can use a piece of decision support software called ActiveNet. ActiveNet digs through mountains of data, including employee profiles and internal documents—from e-mail to PowerPoint slides—to identify individuals whose interests or backgrounds might match the need. In some cases, the key people may be just down the hall; in others, they might be on another continent. By bringing workers together with other experts, ActiveNet helps them broaden their decision-making abilities by tapping the resources already present around them.[144]

The success of GDSS as an aid to decision making depends on a number of factors. Organizations in which people are open to change and in which managers attach importance to flexible and creative decision-making processes are more likely to benefit. Evidence also shows that a GDSS that encourages full participation and promotes raising questions and expressing concerns is more likely to be successful. Further, managers should carefully consider the group's size and the type of task in planning for a GDSS. In the initial stages of decision making, such as generating alternatives, larger groups may work well with a GDSS. For more complex problem solving and choice making, however, small groups (fifteen members or fewer) are more effective.[145]

The effects of GDSS need further investigation. In a study that involved making investment decisions, minority opinion holders expressed their views most frequently using a GDSS. However, these minority views were more influential under face-to-face communication. This means that GDSS may facilitate the expression of minority viewpoints, but GDSS may also diminish their influence on group decisions.[146]

DECISION MAKING IN THE VIRTUAL WORKPLACE

(8) Explain the emerging role of virtual decision making in organizations.

Managers today are working in flexible organizations—so flexible in fact that many workplaces are unconstrained by geography, time, and organizational boundaries. Virtual teams are emerging as a new form of working arrangement. Virtual teams are groups of geographically dispersed coworkers who work together using a combination of telecommunications and information technologies to

Virtual Goal Setting

Although technologies advance and offer several new media for communication, concerns associated with the effectiveness of such media have also arisen. For example, one common criticism of electronic communication is that it lacks the richness offered by face-to-face contact such as eye contact, gesturing, and body language.

Researchers in Germany conducted two experiments meant to contrast the effectiveness of face-to-face (FTF) goal-setting procedures with desktop videoconferencing systems (DCVS) goal setting. They hypothesized that FTF goal setting would result in better performance on a series of brainstorming tasks.

© JACK DABAGHIAN/REUTERS/LANDOV

Research has found that desktop videoconferencing systems can be just as effective as face-to-face interactions in successful goal setting. Here Philip Schiller, Apple senior vice president of worldwide product marketing, chats with three colleagues via multi-video conference.

The context of the study was a simulated advertising company, and participants were exposed to one of two forms of goal setting: do your best (DYB) versus setting specific difficult goals. Furthermore, they were also assigned to conditions of goal-setting interaction with their supervisor using either FTF or DCVS.

Researchers found that DCVS are just as effective as, if not more effective than, FTF interactions in successful goal setting. They also indicated that participative goal setting in the DCVS condition was the most effective technique of goal setting. In other words, when supervisors used a directive goal setting style in which DCVS was only used to communicate goals, they were not as effective as when they allowed workers to participate in setting the goals.

This research offers initial evidence for the use of DCVS as an effective managerial tool in participative goal-setting programs in organizations.

SOURCE: J. Wegge, T. Bipp, and U. Kleinbeck, "Goal Setting via Videoconferencing," *European Journal of Work & Organizational Psychology* 16 (2) (2007): 169–194.

accomplish a task. Virtual teams seldom meet face-to-face, and membership often shifts according to the project at hand.

How are decisions made in virtual teams? These teams require advanced technologies for communication and decision making. Many technologies aid virtual teams in decision making: desktop videoconferencing systems (DVCS), group decision support systems (GDSS), Internet/intranet systems, expert systems, and agent-based modeling.[147]

Desktop videoconferencing systems are the major technologies that form the basis for other virtual team technologies. DVCS recreate the face-to-face interactions of teams and go one step beyond by supporting more complex levels of communication among virtual team members. Small cameras on top of computer monitors provide video feeds, and voice transmissions are made possible through earpieces and microphones. High-speed data connections are used for communication. All team members can be connected, and outside experts can even be added. A local group can connect with up to fifteen different individuals or groups. Users can simultaneously work on documents, analyze data, or map out ideas. In the Science feature, you can read about the benefits of DVCS for goal setting as discussed in Chapter 5.

Managers use decision support systems (DSS) as tools to enhance their ability to make complex decisions. DSS are computer and communication systems that process incoming data and synthesize pertinent information for managers to use. Another tool for decision making focuses on helping groups make decisions. A group decision support system (GDSS) uses computer support and communication facilities to support group decision-making processes in either face-to-face meetings or dispersed meetings. The GDSS has been shown to affect conflict management within a group by depersonalizing the issue and by forcing the group to discuss its conflict management process.[148] Team decisions often improve by using a GDSS because members share information more fully when they use a GDSS.[149]

GDSS make real-time decision making possible in the virtual team. They are ideal systems for brainstorming, focus groups, and group decisions. By using support tools within the GDSS, users can turn off their individual identities and interact with anonymity, and can poll participants and assemble statistical information relevant to the decision being made. GDSS are thus the sophisticated software that makes collaboration possible in virtual teams.

Internal internets, or intranets, are adaptations of internet technologies for use within a company. For virtual teams, the Internet and intranets can be rich communication and decision-making resources. These tools allow virtual teams to archive text, video, audio, and data files for use in decision making. They permit virtual teams to inform other organization members about the team's progress and enable the team to monitor other projects within the organization.

By using DVCS, GDSS, and Internet/intranet technologies, virtual teams can capitalize on a rich communications environment for decision making. It is difficult, however, to duplicate the face-to-face environment. The effectiveness of a virtual team's decision making depends on its members' ability to use the tools that are available. Collaborative systems can enhance virtual teams' decision quality if they are used well.[150]

Agent-based modeling (ABM) is an agent-based simulation in which a computer creates thousands, even millions, of individual actors known as agents. Each of these virtual agents makes virtual decisions, thus providing an estimate of how each decision type might affect outcomes.[151]

Several organizations have adopted agent-based modeling to evaluate potential consequences of important decisions. For example, when Macy's was considering a major remodeling of their store space, they enlisted the services of PricewaterhouseCoopers to develop an ABM system that virtually modeled the changes in floor plans and consumer's responses to these changes. This simulation helped Macy's experiment with differing layout plans in cyberspace, thus predicting consumer behavior before it risked costly changes in the real world. You can see that for organizations like Macy's, ABM is a software simulation that can be very useful in making complex, nonroutine decisions involving some degree of uncertainty.

Decision making in the virtual workplace is characterized by the use of sophisticated technologies to assist in decision making. Some of these technologies, like videoconferencing, DSS, and GDSS, simply assist humans in making the decision. Others, like expert systems and some forms of agent-based modeling, play a greater role in making the decision. Regardless of the degree to which they play a role, all of these technologies make decision making in today's virtual workplace easier.

ETHICAL ISSUES IN DECISION MAKING

9 Utilize an "ethics check" for examining managerial decisions.

One criterion that should be applied to decision making is the ethical implications of the decision. Ethical decision making in organizations is influenced by many factors, including individual differences and organizational rewards and punishments.

Kenneth Blanchard and Norman Vincent Peale proposed an "ethics check" for decision makers in their book *The Power of Ethical Management*.[152] They contend that the decision maker should ponder three questions:

1. *Is it legal?* (Will I be violating the law or company policy?)
2. *Is it balanced?* (Is it fair to all concerned in the short term and long term? Does it promote win–win relationships?)
3. *How will it make me feel about myself?* (Will it make me proud of my actions? How will I feel when others become aware of the decision?)

General Dynamics, a major defense contractor that builds weapons ranging from submarines to fighter jets, faced charges of defrauding the government out of more than $2 billion on the Los Angeles class submarine project. While the company ultimately admitted no guilt, the scandal cost Admiral Hyman Rickover his career. And audiotapes of the firm's CEO and CFO discussing their plans to "screw the Navy," combined with revelations that a company vice president billed the Navy for the cost of kenneling his dog while he was out of town, started a long downhill slide that ultimately cost the two executives their jobs and cost General Dynamics its reputation.[153,154]

In summary, all decisions, whether made by individuals or by groups, must be evaluated for their ethics. Organizations should reinforce ethical decision making among employees by encouraging and rewarding it. Socialization processes should convey to newcomers the ethical standards of behavior in the organization. Groups should use devil's advocates and dialectical methods to reduce the potential for groupthink and the unethical decisions that may result. Effective and ethical decisions are not mutually exclusive. In recent times, almost all major businesses are paying attention to social and environmental issues in their decision-making processes. However, one major oil company and its CEO seem to take a different stand on such green business practices. Read about ExxonMobil CEO Rex Tillerson's viewpoints and decision-making strategy on such ethical issues in the Real World 10.2.

MANAGERIAL IMPLICATIONS: DECISION MAKING IS A CRITICAL ACTIVITY

Decision making is important at all levels of every organization. At times managers may have the luxury of optimizing (selecting the best alternative), but more often they are forced to satisfice (select the alternative that is good enough). And, at times, the decision process can even seem unpredictable and random.

Individuals differ in their preferences for risk, as well as in their styles of gathering information and making judgments. Understanding individual differences can help managers maximize strengths in employee decision styles and build teams that capitalize on strengths. Creativity is one such strength. It can be encouraged by providing employees with a supportive environment that nourishes innovative ideas. Creativity training has been used in some organizations with positive results.

Some decisions are best made by individuals and some by teams or groups. The task of the manager is to diagnose the situation and implement the appropriate level of participation. To do this effectively, managers should know the advantages and disadvantages of various group decision-making techniques and should minimize the potential for groupthink. Finally, decisions made by individuals or groups should be analyzed to see whether they are ethical.

ExxonMobil: Smarter Decision Making or Just Plain Profit Driven?

ExxonMobil is the largest energy company in the world. In an economy driven by concerns about global climate change and introduction of cleaner fuels and hybrid vehicles, one CEO stands tall—and alone—in his views on "greener" fuels. In his address at a major energy conference in 2007, Rex Tillerson reiterated Exxon's skepticism about global climate change issues. He commented that he wasn't 100 percent sure how global warming could or should affect industry activity. Some industry insiders speculate that such a stand could eventually hurt ExxonMobil, but for now, the tall Texan CEO is responding in a unique, and potentially risky, way.

He has invested in cutting down carbon dioxide emissions at Exxon's global facilities, an initiative claims has helped reduce carbon dioxide emissions equivalent to taking two million cars off the road. Exxon is also partnered with researchers at Stanford University to investigate complex biofuels. Thus, his strategy seems to be that Exxon will continue to invest in technological breakthroughs rather than adopting any other forms of green initiatives.

In spite of these initiatives, it is public knowledge that Tillerson does not yet support the idea that fossil fuels contribute to global warming or that alternative energy fuels are the answer. This position stands in stark opposition to other energy companies such as British Petroleum that are actively involved in reducing their footprint on the ecosystem. Only time will tell if Tillerson and ExxonMobil are truly ahead of the game and actually care about environmental issues. For now, there is a lot of speculation that the initiatives described above do not point in that direction and that they are just lip service to industry concerns with such issues.

SOURCE: C. Palmeri, "Exxon's Boss Is Cool on Green Policies," *Business Week Online* (February 14, 2007), http://www.businessweek.com/bwdaily/dnflash/content/feb2007/db20070214_217175.htm.

DIVERSITY DIALOGUE

Functional Diversity Comes Through in a Pinch

Jim Amoss is the editor of the *Times-Picayune* in New Orleans. Ordinarily, the newspaper's staffers would look to him or the senior editors to make the decisions. As the publication's leader, Amoss would be the most likely person to know what to do in case of an emergency. But on the morning of August 30, 2005, he did not know what to do. That was no ordinary day. It was the day that Hurricane Katrina struck New Orleans.

Like most organizations in the area, the staff at the *Times* had prepared for natural disasters. Extra generators were in place, and the staff had practiced emergency drills many times. In fact, the *Times* had even written articles detailing what to expect during a major hurricane. Unfortunately, all that planning literally went out the window during Hurricane Katrina. Water had flooded the generators and phones weren't working so no one could communicate. But this was the biggest story of their lives, and it had to be covered.

The staffers responded quickly without waiting for Amoss to hand out assignments. A functionally diverse team of about a dozen journalists, which included an editorial page editor, an art critic, and a religion writer, made the decision to return to the city's downtown area to gather supplies. They then went door to door searching for phone lines. The members of the team had never worked together before, but each of them went outside their comfort zones to make a decision that Amoss referred to as "an extraordinary moment of spontaneous leadership."

1. Discuss the effect of the team's functional heterogeneity on their decision to cover the Hurricane Katrina story.
2. What was Amoss' role in the team's ultimate decision?

SOURCE: J. Alexander, "Out of Disaster, Power in Numbers," *U.S. News & World Report* 141 (16), (October 30, 2006): 75–77.

LOOKING BACK: GENENTECH, INC.

Hope for the Future

Genentech recently added new research avenues to its existing R&D efforts and invested in eight new strategic collaborations. The biotech giant continues to surge forward, and its CEO Arthur Levinson remains committed to scientific excellence. He envisions a very hopeful future for Genentech based on new drug trials that have indicated positive results.

Genentech continues to build on its strategy of pioneering research in treatment of diseases that are scarcely researched in the industry. The road has not always been easy. In its published trials of the new cancer-fighting drug, Avastin, Genentech fared so poorly that stock analysts predicted the demise of the biotech superpower. However, through persistence in its R&D efforts, the company managed to turn the tide and now the investment in Avastin is paying off. This story shows how innovation and creative decisions might not always succeed in the short term, but there might be long-term benefits. In fact, one of Genentech's core strategies driving its decision making is a long-term focus on projects rather than blockbuster short-term miracle drugs. For now, this strategy seems to be working.[155, 156]

Chapter Summary

1. Bounded rationality assumes that there are limits to how rational managers can be.

2. The garbage can model shows that under high uncertainty, decision making in organizations can be an unsystematic process.

3. Jung's cognitive styles can be used to help explain individual differences in gathering information and evaluating alternatives.

4. Intuition and creativity are positive influences on decision making and should be encouraged in organizations.

5. Empowerment and teamwork require specific organizational design elements and individual characteristics and skills.

6. Techniques such as brainstorming, nominal group technique, Delphi technique, devil's advocacy, dialectical inquiry, quality circles and teams, and self-managed teams can help managers reap the benefits of group methods while limiting the possibilities of groupthink and group polarization.

7. Technology is providing assistance to managerial decision making, especially through expert systems and group decision support systems. More research is needed to determine the effects of these technologies.

8. Managers should carefully weigh the ethical issues surrounding decisions and encourage ethical decision making throughout the organization.

Key Terms

bounded rationality (p. 324)
brainstorming (p. 343)
cognitive style (p. 328)
creativity (p. 333)
Delphi technique (p. 344)
devil's advocacy (p. 344)
dialectical inquiry (p. 344)
effective decision (p. 323)

escalation of commitment (p. 326)
garbage can model (p. 324)
group polarization (p. 342)
groupthink (p. 340)
heuristics (p. 324)
intuition (p. 331)
nominal group technique (NGT) (p. 343)

nonprogrammed decision (p. 322)
participative decision making (p. 337)
programmed decision (p. 322)
rationality (p. 324)
risk aversion (p. 325)
satisfice (p. 324)
social decision schemes (p. 339)
synergy (p. 339)

Review Questions

1. Compare the garbage can model with the bounded rationality model. Compare the usefulness of these models in today's organizations.

2. List and describe Jung's four cognitive styles. How does the Z problem-solving model capitalize on the strengths of the four preferences?

3. What are the individual and organizational influences on creativity?

4. What are the organizational foundations of empowerment and teamwork? The individual foundations?

5. Describe the advantages and disadvantages of group decision making.

6. Describe the symptoms of groupthink, and identify actions that can be taken to prevent it.

7. What techniques can be used to improve group decisions?

Discussion and Communication Questions

1. Why is identification of the real problem the first and most important step in the decision-making process? How does attribution theory explain mistakes that can be made as managers and employees work together to explain why the problem occurred?

2. How can organizations effectively manage both risk taking and escalation of commitment in the decision-making behavior of employees?

3. How will you most likely make decisions based on your cognitive style? What might you overlook using your preferred approach?

4. How can organizations encourage creative decision making?

5. What are some organizations that use expert systems? Group decision support systems? How will these two technologies affect managerial decision making?

6. How do the potential risks associated with participating in quality circles differ from those associated with participating in quality teams? If you were a member of a quality circle, how would management's decisions to reject your recommendations affect your motivation to participate?

7. *(communication question)* Form a team of four persons. Find two examples of recent decisions made in organizations: one that you consider a good decision, and one that you consider a bad decision. Two members should work on the good decision, and two on the bad decision. Each pair should write a brief description of the decision. Then write a summary of what went right, what went wrong, and what could be done to improve the decision process. Compare and contrast your two examples in a presentation to the class.

8. *(comunication question)* Reflect on your own experiences in groups with groupthink. Describe the situation in which you encountered groupthink, the symptoms that were present, and the outcome. What remedies for groupthink would you prescribe? Summarize your answers in a memo to your instructor.

Ethical Dilemma

Slowly the managers of Beckman Services began arriving. An unexpected meeting had been called for 8:30 this morning and not everyone anticipated the news they were about to hear. Beckman was a financial services company that sold their services to individuals and companies. Since the terrorists' attacks on 9/11, Beckman had been experiencing financial difficulties. In order to boost sales, an incentive plan had been rolled out last December that management hoped would solve the problem. The plan challenged the sales force to increase sales by 15 percent. A daunting task, but the generous incentives made the challenge well worth the endeavor.

CEO Frank May opened the meeting by welcoming everyone to "one of the most difficult meetings he has ever had to call." Frank explained that although the incentive plan seemed to be working very well, the company's cash reserves were not as strong as they had hoped and delivering the promised bonuses would be more difficult than they had anticipated. He realized this was not going to be a popular decision, but he felt sure the salespeople would understand.

Richard Johnson, VP of human recourses sat quietly in the meeting. He could not believe what was happening. It was now early November, and the salespeople had been working hard for the last ten months. He knew many of the salespeople well, and they were counting on the promised bonuses. What message was the company sending if they cancelled this program at the last minute? He also knew he should say something, but disagreeing with Frank was never a good idea, especially when everyone else seemed to agree with the plan. Richard looked up and realized that the meeting was coming to an end. To challenge his boss in front of the team could be the end of his career at Beckman. But it couldn't be possible that everyone really agreed with Frank, could they? "Any questions or concerns about proceeding?" Frank asked. Richard needed to make a decision and make it fast.

Experiential Exercises

10.1 Making a Layoff Decision

Purpose

In this exercise, you will examine how to weigh a set of facts and make a difficult personnel decision about laying off valued employees during a time of financial hardship. You will also examine your own values and criteria used in the decision-making process.

The Problem

Walker Space Institute (WSI) is a medium-sized firm located in Connecticut. The firm essentially has been a subcontractor on many large space contracts that have been acquired by firms like Alliant Techsystems and others.

With the cutback in many of the National Aeronautics and Space Administration programs, Walker has an excess of employees. Stuart Tartaro, the head of one of the sections, has been told by his superior that he must reduce his section of engineers from nine to six. He is looking at the following summaries of their vitae and pondering how he will make this decision.

1. *Roger Allison*, age twenty-six, married, two children. Allison has been with WSI for a year and a half. He is a very good engineer, with a degree from Rensselaer Polytech. He has held two prior jobs and lost both of them because of cutbacks in the space program. He moved to Connecticut from California to take this job. Allison is well liked by his coworkers.

2. *Dave Jones*, age twenty-four, single. Jones is an African American, and the company looked hard to get him because of affirmative action pressure. He is not very popular with his coworkers. Because he has been employed less than a year, not much is known about his work. On his one evaluation (which was average), Jones accused his supervisor of bias against African Americans. He is a graduate of the Detroit Institute of Technology.

3. *William Foster*, age fifty-three, married, three children. Foster is a graduate of "the school of hard knocks." After serving in the Vietnam War, he

Questions

1. Who are the stakeholders in Beckman Services and what is Frank May's responsibility to them?

2. To whom does Richard Johnson have a responsibility?

3. Evaluate Johnson's decision using consequential, rule-based, and character theories.

started to go to school but dropped out because of high family expenses. Foster has worked at the company for twenty years. His ratings were excellent for fifteen years. The last five years they have been average. Foster feels his supervisor grades him down because he does not "have sheepskins covering his office walls."

4. *Donald Boyer*, age thirty-two, married, no children. Boyer is well liked by his coworkers. He has been at WSI five years, and he has a B.S. and M.S. in engineering from Purdue University. Boyer's ratings have been mixed. Some supervisors rated him high and some average. Boyer's wife is an M.D.

5. *Ann Shuster*, age twenty-nine, single. Shuster is a real worker, but a loner. She has a B.S. in engineering from the University of California. She is working on her M.S. at night, always trying to improve her technical skills. Her performance ratings have been above average for the three years she has been at WSI.

6. *Sherman Soltis*, age thirty-seven, divorced, two children. He has a B.S. in engineering from Ohio State University. Soltis is very active in community affairs: Scouts, Little League, and United Way. He is a friend of the vice president through church work. His ratings have been average, although some recent ones indicate that he is out of date. He is well liked and has been employed at WSI for fourteen years.

7. *Warren Fortuna*, age forty-four, married, five children. He has a B.S. in engineering from Georgia Tech. Fortuna headed this section at one time. He worked so hard that he had a heart attack. Under doctor's orders, he resigned from the supervisory position. Since then he has done good work, though because of his health, he is a bit slower than the others. Now and then he must spend extra time on a project because he did get out of date during the eight years he headed the section. His performance evaluations for the last two years have been above average. He has been employed at WSI for fourteen years.

8. *Robert Treharne*, age forty-seven, single. He began an engineering degree at MIT but had to drop out for financial reasons. He tries hard to stay current by regular reading of engineering journals and taking all the short courses the company and nearby colleges offer. His performance evaluations have varied, but they tend to be average to slightly above average. He is a loner, and Tartaro thinks this has negatively affected Treharne's performance evaluations. He has been employed at WSI for sixteen years.

9. *Sandra Rosen*, age twenty-two, single. She has a B.S. in engineering technology from the Rochester Institute of Technology. Rosen has been employed less than a year. She is enthusiastic, a very good worker, and well liked by her coworkers. She is well regarded by Tartaro.

Tartaro does not quite know what to do. He sees the good points of each of his section members. Most have been good employees. They all can pretty much do one another's work. No one has special training.

He is fearful that the section will hear about the downsizing and morale will drop. Work would fall off. He does not even want to talk to his wife about it, in case she would let something slip. Tartaro has come to you, Edmund Graves, personnel manager at WSI, for some guidelines on this decision—legal, moral, and best personnel practice.

Assignment

You are Edmund Graves. Write a report with your recommendations for termination and a careful analysis of the criteria for the decision. You should also carefully explain to Tartaro how you would go about the terminations and what you would consider reasonable termination pay. You should also advise him about the pension implications of this decision. Generally, fifteen years' service entitles you to at least partial pension.

SOURCE: W. F. Glueck, *Cases and Exercises in Personnel* (Dallas: Business Publications, 1978), 24–26.

10.2 Dilemma at 29,000 Feet

Purpose

Making ethical decisions often requires taking decisive actions in ambiguous situations. Making these decisions entails not just weighing options and making rational choices but making choices between competing but equally important demands. Managers must not only take action, they must also provide compelling reasons that make their choices rationally accountable to others. This exercise requires you to think through an ethical situation, take an action, and create a convincing justification for your action. The exercise is designed to encourage critical thinking about complex problems and to encourage thinking about how you might resolve a dilemma outside your area of expertise.

The Problem

Imagine you are the sole leader of a mountain-climbing expedition and have successfully led a group of three climbers to the mountain summit. However, on your descent, trouble sets in as a fierce storm engulfs the mountain and makes progression down nearly impossible. One climber collapses from exhaustion at 24,000 feet and cannot continue down the mountain. The two stronger climbers insist on continuing down without you because they know if they stay too long at high altitude death is certain. No one has ever survived overnight on the mountain. A rescue attempt is impossible because helicopters cannot reach you above 18,000 feet.

As the leader, you are faced with a difficult choice: abandon your teammate and descend alone or stay with your dying teammate and face almost certain death. On one hand, you might stay with your dying teammate in hopes that the storm might clear and a rescue party will be sent. However, you know that if you stay both of you will most likely die. On the other hand, you are still strong and may be able to make it down to safety, abandoning your teammate to die alone on the mountain.

Assignment

Your assignment is to make an argument for one of the actions: staying with your teammate or descending alone. The technical aspects of mountain climbing are not important, nor is it good enough to state that you would not get in this situation in the first place! What is important is that you provide a well-reasoned argument for your action. A good argument might address the following points:

1. A discussion of the pros and cons of each action: staying with your teammate or descending alone.

2. A discussion of the underlying values and assumptions of each action. For example, staying with the teammate implies that you have a particular obligation as the leader of a team; descending alone suggests that you may place a higher value on your own life.

3. A discussion of your own values and viewpoints on the topic. In other words, take a stand and justify your position. How, for example, might you justify to the family of the abandoned climber your decision to descend alone? How might you justify to

your own family your decision to stay with the ailing climber?

4. What prior experience, knowledge, or beliefs lead you to your conclusion?

5. How might this situation be similar to or different from the dilemmas faced in more typical organizations? For example, do leaders need to take actions that require them to make similar difficult decisions? Have you experienced any similar dilemmas that had no easy answer in the workplace, and how did you resolve them?

Final Thoughts

Remember, there is no right or wrong answer to this case. The point is to consider and make clear your own ethical choices by evaluating all relevant information, evaluating the underlying assumptions of each, and creating a clear and convicing argument for action. A quote by philosopher Martha Craven Nussbaum might act as a starting point for your study. She writes,

"Both alternatives make a serious claim on your practical attention. You might sense that no matter how you choose, you will be left with some regret that you did not do the other thing. Sometimes you may be clear about which is the better choice and yet feel pain over the frustration of the other significant concerns. It is extremely important to realize that the problem is not just one difficult decision but that conflicts arise when the final decision itself is perfectly obvious."

Good luck in your decision!

SOURCE: D. C. Kayes, "Dilemma at 29,000 Feet: An Exercise in Ethical Decision Making Based on the 1996 Mt. Everest Climbing Disaster," *Journal of Management Education* 26 (2002): 307–321. Reprinted by permission of Sage Publications.

Biz Flix | Dr. Seuss' How the Grinch Stole Christmas

Readers and lovers of the Dr. Seuss original tale may feel put off by Ron Howard's loose adaptation of the story. Whoville, a magical, mythical land, features the Whos who love Christmas and the Grinch (Jim Carrey) who hates it. Cindy Lou Who (Taylor Momsen) tries to bring the Grinch back to the Yuletide celebrations, an effort that backfires on all involved. Sparkling special effects will dazzle most viewers and likely distract them from the film's departures from the original story.

The selected scene is an edited version of the "Second Thoughts" sequence early in the film. Just before this scene, fearless Cindy Lou entered the Grinch's lair to invite him to be the Holiday Cheermeister at the Whobilation One-Thousand celebration. In typical Grinch fashion, he pulls the trap door on Cindy Lou, who unceremoniously slides out of his lair to land on a snowy Whoville street. The Grinch now must decide whether to accept the invitation. The film continues with the Cheermeister award ceremony.

What to Watch for and Ask Yourself:

> What are the Grinch's decision alternatives or options?

> What decision criteria does the Grinch use to choose from the alternatives?

> Describe the steps in the Grinch's decision-making process.

Workplace Video | Managerial Decision Making, Featuring McDonald's

McDonald's is the most recognized fast-food franchise in the world. In the sixty years since Dick and Mac McDonald first introduced the "Speedee Service System" at their San Bernardino, California, restaurant, the burger giant has grown to more than 30,000 locations in 118 countries, serving 50 million people daily.

The McDonald's story, which gained legendary status under the leadership of Ray Kroc and Fred Turner, weaves together many themes of business success—visionary leadership, mass-marketing genius, and groundbreaking business models. Yet one theme in the McDonald's success story is often overlooked: good decision making in turbulent times.

In 2001, cracks began appearing in the famed Golden Arches. Customer guest counts were down, profitability was on the decline, and rapid expansion of new stores wasn't producing financial results. As these internal problems raged, McDonald's found itself at the center of a politically charged obesity debate. The company finally hit bottom in 2004 when two consecutive CEOs died—a bizarre tragedy that made James Skinner the company's third chief in a single year.

To halt the slide, senior management began rethinking the company's decision-making process. First, McDonald's launched a formal probe to identify problems. Next, as part of its quantitative analysis, the company conducted market research aimed at identifying ongoing customer concerns. In addition, the company adopted a system of interdepartmental collaboration that encouraged managers from different areas of the organization to provide input and to propose fresh solutions.

After a period of evaluation and introspection, executives determined that short-term thinking was at the root of the company's sluggish growth. In particular, the company had spent too much time opening new restaurants and too little time improving existing ones. To remedy the situation, McDonald's created long-term plans and rallied leaders to promote comprehensive buy-in at the corporate, franchise, and customer levels.

Today McDonald's is back on top. Customers are responding positively to changes in the company's brand image, and gutsy decisions have refreshed the company mission. Even shareholders are feeling good again. Instead of expressing worries that franchises like Subway and Burger King will soon dominate the industry, McDonald's stakeholders are again feeling confident that the future of fast food lies beneath the Golden Arches.

Discussion Questions

1. Cite at least two ways in which McDonald's management followed the decision-making process during the company's big turnaround.

2. Were the decisions made by McDonald's management programmed or nonprogrammed? Explain.

3. What common decision-making errors could have caused even greater problems for McDonald's?

3M's Conundrum of Efficiency and Creativity

Innovative, successful companies, like Minnesota Mining and Manufacturing (3M), share at least four fundamental characteristics: (1) putting people and ideas at the heart of the management philosophy; (2) giving people opportunities and latitude to develop, try new things, and learn from their mistakes; (3) building a strong sense of openness, trust, and community throughout the organization; and (4) facilitating the mobility of talent within the organization.[1] 3M believes in the power of ideas and individual initiative, and "recognizes that entrepreneurial behavior will continue to flourish only if management is willing to accept and even applaud 'well-intentioned failure.'"[2] Innovation, the traditional hallmark of 3M's business operations and success, is "a process that thrives on multiple, diverse, independent and rapid experimentation, in a failure-tolerant environment that values and accommodates constructive conflict."[3]

The creative and innovative orientation of 3M—and in particular its tolerance for failure or defects or errors—came under serious attack in late 2000. When former General Electric executive James McNerney took over as CEO of 3M in December 2000, he immediately began implementing Six Sigma.[4] Management programs such as Six Sigma are designed to identify problems in work processes, and then use rigorous measurement to reduce variation, eliminate defects, and increase efficiency. When initiatives such as Six Sigma become embedded in a company's culture, as they did at 3M, creativity and innovation can easily get squelched.[5] In mid-2005, when McNerney departed 3M to take the CEO's job at Boeing, he left his successors with the difficult question of "whether the relentless emphasis on efficiency had made 3M a less creative company."[6]

According to management guru Tom Peters, McNerney's implementation of Six Sigma at 3M "more or less closed the lid on entrepreneurial behavior."[7] Vijay Govindarajan, a professor at Dartmouth's Tuck School of Business, observes that when more emphasis is placed on programs such as Six Sigma and Total Quality Management, the more likely it is that breakthrough innovations will be harmed.[8] Art Fry, the inventor of 3M's Post-It notes, says, "[y]ou have to go through 5,000 to 6,000 raw ideas to find one successful business," but the Six Sigma program would ask "why not eliminate all that waste and just come up with the right idea the first time?"[9] However, others have contended that Six Sigma should not be criticized indiscriminately. The program, they say, is very useful in reducing waste in virtually all processes where there is a known result that must be achieved.

Unfortunately, at 3M Six Sigma was deployed in an environment of innovation where the target was unknown.[10] "The problem is not with the methodology itself but rather with how it is applied and what specifically it is applied to . . . if managed effectively, Six Sigma can absolutely co-exist with innovation."[11] Six Sigma can eliminate mundane, repetitive, and tedious tasks that impede creative thinking and innovation.[12]

Six Sigma focuses on efficiency and quality in order to enhance profits, but the lifeblood of long-term profitability for most, if not all, businesses is innovation. Indeed, "to compete in the coming decades, creativity is one process that can't be left for later."[13] Still, "[t]urning ideas into commercial reality requires persistence and discipline, and overall effectiveness ultimately depends on top management being able to find the right balance between corporate creativity and efficiency."[14] Effective innovation "requires a delicate balancing act between play and discipline, practice and process, creativity and efficiency, where firms need to 'learn how to walk the fine line between rigidity—which smothers creativity—and chaos—where creativity runs amok and nothing ever gets to market.'"[15]

Robert Carter, a consultant at Raytheon, indicates that the Six Sigma process of define, measure, analyze, improve, control (DMAIC) can lead to overanalyzing the situation, which can be very detrimental when an idea begins to germinate.[16] "Six Sigma tries to replace subjectivity with objectivity and intuition with data wherever possible. While this is appropriate for some operations—like administration, logistics, and manufacturing—it's detrimental to exploratory research and design, which depend on subjectivity and intuition."[17] Creativity is seldom a logical process, and Six Sigma is not a panacea.[18]

Discussion Questions

1. How would you describe 3M's efficiency and creativity conundrum in terms of programmed and nonprogrammed decisions?

2. How would you describe 3M's efficiency and creativity conundrum in terms of the rational, bounded rationality, and garbage can models of decision making?

3. What role do intuition and creativity play in the decision making that is evident in 3M's efficiency and creativity conundrum?

SOURCE: This case was written by Michael K. McCuddy, The Louis S. and Mary L. Morgal Chair of Christian Business Ethics and Professor of Management, College of Business Administration, Valparaiso University.

CASE

Power and Political Behavior

After reading this chapter, you should be able to do the following:

1 Distinguish among power, influence, and authority.

2 Compare the interpersonal and inter-group sources of power.

3 Understand the ethical use of power.

4 Explain power analysis, an organizational-level theory of power.

5 Identify symbols of power and power-lessness in organizations.

6 Define organizational politics and understand the role of political skill and major influence tactics.

7 Develop a plan for managing employee–boss relationships.

8 Discuss how managers can empower others.

THINKING AHEAD: GOOGLE NAVIGATES POWER AND POLITICS

Google is one of the most successful firms in the technology world today. Every time stock analysts speculate that the company might crash, it has come out stronger than before. And it seems to be continuing in its ascent to the position of industry leader.

Yet Google's rapid rise has also brought its share of concerns and challenges for the Internet giant. For example, the company was involved in a major controversy with the Chinese government that restricted the kind of information Google could process in searches. As a result, in China Google now has to filter information and can only make publicly available information that does not violate government guidelines. In addition, Google has drawn considerable criticism for imitating Microsoft in certain monopolistic behaviors. The company plans to create and acquire software that profiles Internet users so that it can better customize its search services to individual preferences. This move is alarming to many because it enables Google to acquire and store massive amounts of personal data on Internet users—information that could be misused.

Some people even question whether actions such as signing a deal consenting to censorship by the Chinese government and monitoring Internet users are part of founders

Larry Page and Sergey Brin's monster ambitions to be the most powerful people on the Internet. Some also wonder how acts such as these square with Google's famous corporate mission, "Do No Evil."[1,2] We'll continue to examine Google's power controversy at the end of the chapter.

THE CONCEPT OF POWER

(1) Distinguish among power, influence, and authority.

Power is the ability to influence someone else. As an exchange relationship, it occurs in transactions between an agent and a target. The agent is the person using the power, and the target is the recipient of the attempt to use power.[3]

Because power is an ability, individuals can learn to use it effectively. *Influence* is the process of affecting the thoughts, behavior, and feelings of another person. *Authority* is the right to influence another person.[4] It is important to understand the subtle differences among these terms. For instance, a manager may have authority but no power. She may have the right, by virtue of her position as boss, to tell someone what to do. But she may not have the skill or ability to influence other people.

In a relationship between the agent and the target, there are many influence attempts that the target considers legitimate. Working forty hours per week, greeting customers, solving problems, and collecting bills are actions that, when requested by the manager, are considered legitimate by a customer service representative. Requests such as these fall within the employee's *zone of indifference*—the range in which attempts to influence the employee are perceived as legitimate and are acted on without a great deal of thought.[5] The employee accepts that the manager has the authority to request such behaviors and complies with the requests. Some requests, however, fall outside the zone of indifference, so the manager must work to enlarge the employee's zone of indifference. Enlarging the zone is accomplished with power (an ability) rather than with authority (a right).

Suppose the manager asks the employee to purchase a birthday gift for the manager's wife or to overcharge a customer for a service call. The employee may think the manager has no right to ask these things. These requests fall outside the zone of indifference; they're viewed as extraordinary, and the manager has to operate from outside the authority base to induce the employee to fulfill them. In some cases, no power base is enough to induce the employee to comply, especially if the employee considers the behaviors requested by the manager unethical.

Failures to understand power and politics can be costly in terms of your career. In the wake of the attacks on September 11, 2001, American Airlines CEO Donald Carty managed to wrest over a billion dollars from unions in concessions to keep the company from having to file bankruptcy. Unfortunately, on the same day the agreement was announced, it was disclosed that special pension trust funding and huge retention bonuses were given to American Airlines executives, including Carty—despite the fact that union workers had agreed to the steep pay cuts. Carty spent the next three-and-a-half weeks apologizing, even giving the money back, before falling on his sword. He may have lost his job because he lost the trust of his employees. This example illustrates that managers must learn as much as possible about power and politics to be able to use them effectively and to manage the inevitable political behavior in organizations.[6]

power

The ability to influence another person.

influence

The process of affecting the thoughts, behavior, and feelings of another person.

authority

The right to influence another person.

zone of indifference

The range in which attempts to influence a person will be perceived as legitimate and will be acted on without a great deal of thought.

FORMS AND SOURCES OF POWER IN ORGANIZATIONS

Individuals have many forms of power to use in their work settings. Some of them are interpersonal—used in interactions with others. One of the earliest and most influential theories of power comes from French and Raven, who tried to determine the sources of power managers use to influence other people.

② Compare the interpersonal and intergroup sources of power.

Interpersonal Forms of Power

French and Raven identified five forms of interpersonal power that managers use: reward, coercive, legitimate, referent, and expert power.[7]

Reward power is based on the agent's ability to control rewards that a target wants. For example, managers control the rewards of salary increases, bonuses, and promotions. Reward power can lead to better performance, but only as long as the employee sees a clear and strong link between performance and rewards. To use reward power effectively, then, the manager should be explicit about the behavior being rewarded and should make the connection clear between the behavior and the reward.

Coercive power is based on the agent's ability to cause the target to have an unpleasant experience. To coerce someone into doing something means to force the person to do it, often with threats of punishment. Managers using coercive power may verbally abuse employees or withhold support from them.

Legitimate power, which is similar to authority, is based on position and mutual agreement. The agent and target agree that the agent has the right to influence the target. It doesn't matter that a manager thinks he has the right to influence his employees; for legitimate power to be effective, the employees must also believe the manager has the right to tell them what to do. In some Native American societies, the chief has legitimate power; tribe members believe in his right to influence the decisions in their lives.

Referent power is based on interpersonal attraction. The agent has referent power over the target because the target identifies with or wants to be like the agent. Charismatic individuals are often thought to have referent power. Interestingly, the agent need not be superior to the target in any way. People who use referent power well are most often individualistic and respected by the target.

Expert power exists when the agent has specialized knowledge or skills that the target needs. For expert power to work, three conditions must be in place. First, the target must trust that the expertise given is accurate. Second, the knowledge involved must be relevant and useful to the target. Third, the target's perception of the agent as an expert is crucial. Using easy-to-understand language signals the target that the expert has an appreciation for real-world concerns and increases the target's trust in the expert.[8]

Which type of interpersonal power is most effective? Research has focused on this question since French and Raven introduced their five forms of power. Some of the results are surprising. Reward power and coercive power have similar effects.[9] Both lead to compliance. That is, employees will do what the manager asks them to, at least temporarily, if the manager offers a reward or threatens

reward power
Power based on an agent's ability to control rewards that a target wants.

coercive power
Power that is based on an agent's ability to cause an unpleasant experience for a target.

© PICTORIAL PRESS/ALAMY

Coercive power is based on the agent's ability to cause the target to have an unpleasant experience. In the 1972 film *The Godfather*, Marlon Brando's character used the threat of punishment to get others to do as he wished.

legitimate power
Power that is based on position and mutual agreement; agent and target agree that the agent has the right to influence the target.

referent power
An elusive power that is based on interpersonal attraction.

expert power
The power that exists when an agent has specialized knowledge or skills that the target needs.

The Power of Age and Experience

Several CEOs of successful organizations are young entrepreneurs like Sergey Brin and Larry Page of Google, and this might create the perception that young leaders can best lead firms. However, a comprehensive research study conducted among manufacturing and service firms might prove otherwise. This study included 632 small to medium-sized firms and reveals some interesting findings.

CEOs have a lot of power and influence within organizational settings, yet they have to gain approval from the board of directors or top management team (TMT) on key strategic decisions. One avenue for improving an organization's performance is through pursuit of new business directions, but this represents a certain level of risk for the firm. This study highlights the effects of CEO tenure with the firm as a key ingre-

dient in determining their influence in persuading the TMT to adopt risks. Specifically, researchers found that CEOs with 30-plus years of experience with the same firm have the most influence on the TMT in persuading them to take risks. This risk taking in turn led to better firm performance. The reason that CEOs with tenure are more influential is because they have in-depth knowledge of the technical aspects of the firm's products and capabilities, understand business contingencies, and develop deep social connections with members of the TMT. These results highlight the significance of expert power and legitimacy in the organization.

SOURCE: Z. Simsek, "CEO Tenure and Organizational Performance: An Intervening Model," *Strategic Management Journal* 28 (6) (2007): 653–662.

them with punishment. Reliance on these sources of power is dangerous, however, because it may require the manager to be physically present and watchful in order to apply rewards or punishment when the behavior occurs. Constant surveillance creates an uncomfortable situation for managers and employees and eventually results in a dependency relationship. Employees will not work unless the manager is present.

Legitimate power also leads to compliance. When told "Do this because I'm your boss," most employees will comply. However, the use of legitimate power has not been linked to organizational effectiveness or to employee satisfaction.[10] In organizations where managers rely heavily on legitimate power, organizational goals are not necessarily met.

Referent power, such as that of Oprah Winfrey, is based on interpersonal attraction.

© KEVIN DIETSCH/UPI/LANDOV

Referent power is linked with organizational effectiveness. It is the most dangerous power, however, because it can be too extensive and intensive in altering the behavior of others. Charismatic leaders need an accompanying sense of responsibility for others. The late disabled actor Christopher Reeve's referent power made him a powerful spokesperson for research on spinal injuries and stem cell research.

Expert power has been called the power of the future.[11] Of the five forms of power, it has the strongest relationship with performance and satisfaction. It is through expert power that vital skills, abilities, and knowledge are passed on within the organization. Employees internalize what they observe and learn from managers they perceive to be experts.

The results on the effectiveness of these five forms of power pose a challenge in organizations. The least effective power bases—legitimate, reward, and coercive—are the ones most likely to be used by managers.[12]

Managers inherit these power bases as part of the position when they take a supervisory job. In contrast, the most effective power bases—referent and expert—are ones that must be developed and strengthened through interpersonal relationships with employees. Marissa Mayer, vice president of search products and user experience at Google, is well respected and liked by her colleagues. She is described as someone with a lot of technical knowledge, and she is comfortable in social environments. This represents her expert power and referent power—she has an advanced degree in computer science from Stanford University and is known for her ability to connect with people. At 33 years old, she has had a very successful career at Google and is one of the most powerful female executives in the country.[13] Expert power and social networks help CEOs influence their top management teams in ways that are profitable for the firm, as you can see in the Science feature.

Using Power Ethically

Managers can work at developing all five of these forms of power for future use. The key to using them well is using them ethically, as Table 11.1 shows. Coercive power, for example, requires careful administration if it is to be used in an ethical manner. Employees should be informed of the rules in advance, and any punishment should be used consistently, uniformly, and privately. The key to using all five types of interpersonal power ethically is to be sensitive to employees' concerns and to communicate well.

(3) Understand the ethical use of power.

To French and Raven's five power sources, we can add a source that is very important in today's organizations. *Information power* is access to and control over important information. Consider, for example, the CEO's administrative assistant. He or she has information about the CEO's schedule that people need if they are going to get in to see the CEO. Central to the idea of information power is the person's position in the communication networks in the organization, both formal and informal. Also important is the idea of framing, which is the "spin" that managers put on information. Managers not only pass information on to subordinates; they interpret this information and influence the subordinates' perceptions of it. Information power occurs not only in the downward direction; it may also flow upward from subordinates to managers. In manufacturing plants, database operators often control information about plant metrics and shipping performance that is vital to managerial decision making. Information power can also flow laterally. Salespersons convey information from the outside environment (their customers) that is essential for marketing efforts.

Determining whether a power-related behavior is ethical is complex. Another way to look at the ethics surrounding the use of power is to ask three questions that show the criteria for examining power-related behaviors:[14]

1. *Does the behavior produce a good outcome for people both inside and outside the organization?* This question represents the criterion of *utilitarian outcomes*. The behavior should result in the greatest good for the greatest number of people. If the power-related behavior serves only the individual's self-interest and fails to help the organization reach its goals, it is considered unethical. A salesperson might be tempted to discount a product deeply in order to make a sale that would win a contest. Doing so would be in her self-interest but would not benefit the organization.

2. *Does the behavior respect the rights of all parties?* This question emphasizes the criterion of *individual rights*. Free speech, privacy, and due process are individual rights that are to be respected, and power-related behaviors that violate these rights are considered unethical.

information power
Access to and control over important information.

Guidelines for the Ethical Use of Power

Form of Power	Guidelines for Use
Reward power	Verify compliance.
	Make feasible, reasonable requests.
	Make only ethical requests.
	Offer rewards desired by subordinates.
	Offer only credible rewards.
Coercive power	Inform subordinates of rules and penalties.
	Warn before punishing.
	Administer punishment consistently and uniformly.
	Understand the situation before acting.
	Maintain credibility.
	Fit punishment to the infraction.
	Punish in private.
Legitimate power	Be cordial and polite.
	Be confident.
	Be clear and follow up to verify understanding.
	Make sure request is appropriate.
	Explain reasons for request.
	Follow proper channels.
	Exercise power consistently.
	Enforce compliance.
	Be sensitive to subordinates' concerns.
Referent power	Treat subordinates fairly.
	Defend subordinates' interests.
	Be sensitive to subordinates' needs and feelings.
	Select subordinates similar to oneself.
	Engage in role modeling.
Expert power	Maintain credibility.
	Act confident and decisive.
	Keep informed.
	Recognize employee concerns.
	Avoid threatening subordinates' self-esteem.

SOURCE: *Leadership in Organizations* by Gary A. Yukl. Copyright © 1981. Reprinted by permission of Prentice-Hall, Upper Saddle River, N.J.

3. *Does the behavior treat all parties equitably and fairly?* This question represents the criterion of *distributive justice*. Power-related behavior that treats one party arbitrarily or benefits one party at the expense of another is unethical. Granting a day of vacation to one employee in a busy week in which coworkers must struggle to cover for him might be considered unethical.

To be considered ethical, power-related behavior must meet all three criteria. If the behavior fails to meet the criteria, then alternative actions should be considered. Unfortunately, most power-related behaviors are not easy to analyze. Conflicts may exist among the criteria; for example, a behavior may maximize the greatest good for the

Murky Waters: The Abuse of Power by Conrad Black

People in positions of power are constantly faced with the pull of making decisions that benefit themselves and their own agendas rather than the organization's. The business world is replete with examples of such leaders, but the latest fall in ethical standards comes in the form of Conrad Black, a wealthy publisher and owner of Hollinger Inc. His company once owned newspapers such as the *Chicago Sun-Times*, the *National Post*, and the *Daily Telegraph* of London. The allegations against Black included charges of mail fraud, obstruction of justice, and pocketing money that should have gone to his shareholders.

Black sold major portions of his businesses starting in 1998 and entered into deals with the new owners which stated that his company would not compete against them. He diverted money from these deals to his personal account rather than paying shareholders. Furthermore, he was videotaped removing documents from his office that could potentially serve as evidence despite a court order against such actions. It was corrupt use of his position power that led to his conviction and he faces 35 years in prison and a penalty of $1 million.

The conviction of Conrad Black reflects a growing business concern with abuse of power. The justice system and the government have heightened their efforts in going after corporate offenders like Conrad Black with the hope that such convictions could serve as deterrents to the misuse of power within organizational settings.

SOURCE: Associated Press, "Ex-Media Mogul Black Convicted of Fraud," *MSNBC News*, http://www.msnbc.msn.com/id/19745657/.

---

greatest number of people but may not treat all parties equitably. Individual rights may need to be sacrificed for the good of the organization. A CEO may need to be removed from power for the organization to be saved. Still, these criteria can be used on a case-by-case basis to sort through the complex ethical issues surrounding the use of power. The ethical use of power is one of the hottest topics in the current business arena, due to the abuse of power by top executives at several firms such as Enron and Tyco International. Read about Conrad Black's fall from glory in The Real World 11.1.

Two Faces of Power: One Positive, One Negative

personal power
Power used for personal gain.

We turn now to a theory of power that takes a strong stand on the "right" versus "wrong" kind of power to use in organizations. David McClelland has spent a great deal of his career studying the need for power and the ways managers use power. As was discussed in Chapter 5, he believes there are two distinct faces of power, one negative and one positive.[15] The negative face of power is *personal power*—power used for personal gain. Managers who use personal power are commonly described as "power hungry." Dennis Koslowski's tenure as CEO of Tyco was marked by one of the most massive strings of acquisitions by any American firm, earning him the nickname "Deal-a-Month Dennis." But as questions began to mount about why Tyco continued to expand when many of its existing divisions were not profitable, Kozlowski simply dismissed them. Only later would it come to light that not only had Kozlowski mismanaged the firm, but he had also looted it for more than $240 million, which he spent on artwork, houses, yachts, and a $2 million birthday party for his wife.[16] People who approach

© SPENCER PLATT/GETTY IMAGES

Personal power is power used for personal gain. During Dennis Koslowski's tenure as CEO of Tyco, he mismanaged the firm and looted more than $240 million, which he spent on personal items.

relationships with an exchange orientation often use personal power to ensure that they get at least their fair share—and often more—in the relationship. They are most concerned with their own needs and interests. One way to encourage ethical behavior in organizations is to encourage principled dissent. This refers to valid criticism that can benefit the organization rather than mere complaints about working conditions. Much like whistle-blowers who can serve as checks on powerful people within the organization, dissenters can pinpoint wrongdoings, encourage employee voice in key issues, and create a climate conducive to the ethical use of power.[17]

Individuals who rely on personal power at its extreme might be considered Machiavellian—willing to do whatever it takes to get one's own way. Niccolo Machiavelli was an Italian statesman during the sixteenth century who wrote *The Prince,* a guide for acquiring and using power.[18] Among his methods was manipulating others, believing that it was better to be feared than loved. Machiavellians (or high Machs) are willing to manipulate others for personal gain, and are unconcerned with others' opinions or welfare.

The positive face of power is *social power*—power used to create motivation or to accomplish group goals. McClelland clearly favors the use of social power by managers. People who approach relationships with a communal orientation focus on the needs and interests of others. They rely on social power.[19] McClelland has found that managers who use power successfully have four power-oriented characteristics:

1. *Belief in the authority system.* They believe that the institution is important and that its authority system is valid. They are comfortable influencing and being influenced. The source of their power is the authority system of which they are a part.

2. *Preference for work and discipline.* They like their work and are very orderly. They have a basic value preference for the Protestant work ethic, believing that work is good for a person over and beyond its income-producing value.

3. *Altruism.* They publicly put the company and its needs before their own needs. They are able to do this because they see their own well-being as integrally tied to the corporate well-being.

4. *Belief in justice.* They believe justice is to be sought above all else. People should receive what they are entitled to and what they earn.

McClelland takes a definite stand on the proper use of power by managers. When power is used for the good of the group, rather than for individual gain, it is positive.

Intergroup Sources of Power

Groups or teams within an organization can also use power from several sources. One source of intergroup power is control of *critical resources*.[20] When one group controls an important resource that another group desires, the first group holds power. Controlling resources needed by another group allows the power-holding group to influence the actions of the less powerful group. This process can continue in an upward spiral. Groups seen as powerful tend to be given more resources from top management.[21]

Groups also have power to the extent that they control *strategic contingencies*—activities that other groups depend on in order to complete their tasks.[22] The dean's office, for example, may control the number of faculty positions to be filled in each department of a college. The departmental hiring plans are thus contingent on approval from the dean's office. In this case, the dean's office controls the strategic contingency of faculty hiring, and thus has power.

social power

Power used to create motivation or to accomplish group goals.

strategic contingencies

Activities that other groups depend on in order to complete their tasks.

Three factors can give a group control over a strategic contingency.[23] One is the *ability to cope with uncertainty*. If a group can help another group deal with uncertainty, it has power. One organizational group that has gained power in recent years is the legal department. Faced with increasing government regulations and fears of litigation, many other departments seek guidance from the legal department.

Another factor that can give a group control power is a *high degree of centrality* within the organization. If a group's functioning is important to the organization's success, it has high centrality. The sales force in a computer firm, for example, has power because of its immediate effect on the firm's operations and because other groups (accounting and servicing groups, for example) depend on its activities.

The third factor that can give a group power is *nonsubstitutability*—the extent to which a group performs a function that is indispensable to an organization. A team of computer specialists may be powerful because of its expertise with a system. It may have specialized experience that another team cannot provide.

The strategic contingencies model thus shows that groups hold power over other groups when they can reduce uncertainty, when their functioning is central to the organization's success, and when the group's activities are difficult to replace.[24] The key to all three of these factors, as you can see, is dependency. When one group controls something that another group needs, it creates a dependent relationship—and gives one group power over the other.

POWER ANALYSIS: A BROADER VIEW

Amitai Etzioni takes a more sociological orientation to power. Etzioni has developed a theory of power analysis.[25] He says that there are three types of organizational power and three types of organizational involvement, or membership, that will lead to either congruent or incongruent uses of power. The three types of organizational power are the following:

(4) Explain power analysis, an organizational-level theory of power.

1. *Coercive power*—influencing members by forcing them to do something under threat of punishment or through fear and intimidation.

2. *Utilitarian power*—influencing members by providing them with rewards and benefits.

3. *Normative power*—influencing members by using the knowledge that they want very much to belong to the organization and by letting them know that what they are expected to do is the "right" thing to do.

Along with these three types of organizational power, Etzioni proposes that we can classify organizations by the type of membership they have:

1. *Alienative membership*. The members have hostile, negative feelings about being in the organization. They don't want to be there. Prisons are a good example of alienative memberships.

2. *Calculative membership*. Members weigh the benefits and limitations of belonging to the organization. Businesses are good examples of organizations with calculative memberships.

3. *Moral membership*. Members have such positive feelings about organizational membership that they are willing to deny their own needs. Organizations with many volunteer workers, such as the American Heart Association, are examples of moral memberships. Religious groups are another.

Etzioni argues that the type of organizational power should be matched to the type of membership in the organization in order to achieve congruence. Figure 11.1 shows the matches in his power analysis theory.

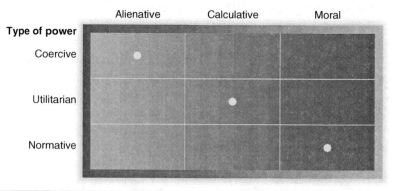

SOURCE: Adapted from Amitai Etzioni, *Modern Organizations* (Upper Saddle River, N.J.: Prentice-Hall, 1964), 59–61. Reprinted by permission of Pearson Education, Inc., Upper Saddle River, N.J.

In an alienative membership, members have hostile feelings. In prisons, for example, Etzioni would contend that coercive power is the appropriate type to use.

A calculative membership is characterized by an analysis of the good and bad aspects of being in the organization. In a business partnership, for example, each partner weighs the benefits from the partnership against the costs entailed in the contractual arrangement. Utilitarian or reward-based power is the most appropriate type to use.

In a moral membership, the members have strong positive feelings about the particular cause or goal of the organization. Normative power is the most appropriate to use because it capitalizes on the members' desires to belong.

Etzioni's power analysis is an organizational-level theory. It emphasizes that the characteristics of an organization play a role in determining the type of power appropriate for use in it. Etzioni's theory is controversial in its contention that a single type of power is appropriate in any organization.

SYMBOLS OF POWER

(5) Identify symbols of power and powerlessness in organizations.

Organization charts show who has authority but reveal little about who has power. We'll now look at two very different ideas about the symbols of power. The first comes from Rosabeth Moss Kanter. It is a scholarly approach to determining who has power and who feels powerless. The second is a semiserious look at the tangible symbols of power by Michael Korda.

Kanter's Symbols of Power

Kanter provides several characteristics of powerful people in organizations:[26]

1. *Ability to intercede for someone in trouble.* An individual who can pull someone out of a jam has power.

2. *Ability to get placements for favored employees.* Getting a key promotion for an employee is a sign of power.

3. *Exceeding budget limitations.* A manager who can go above budget limits without being reprimanded has power.

4. *Procuring above-average raises for employees.* One faculty member reported that her department head distributed 10 percent raises to the most productive

faculty members although the budget allowed for only 4 percent increases. "I don't know how he did it; he must have pull," she said.

5. *Getting items on the agenda at meetings.* If a manager can raise issues for action at meetings, it's a sign of power.

6. *Access to early information.* Having information before anyone else does is a signal that a manager is plugged into key sources.

7. *Having top managers seek out their opinion.* When top managers have a problem, they may ask for advice from lower-level managers. The managers they turn to have power.

A theme that runs through Kanter's list is doing things for others: for people in trouble, for employees, for bosses. There is an active, other-directed element in her symbols of power.

You can use Kanter's symbols of power to identify powerful people in organizations. They can be particularly useful in finding a mentor who can effectively use power.

Kanter's Symbols of Powerlessness

Kanter also wrote about symptoms of *powerlessness*—a lack of power—in managers at different levels of the organization. First-line supervisors, for example, often display three symptoms of powerlessness: overly close supervision, inflexible adherence to the rules, and a tendency to do the job themselves rather than training their employees to do it. Staff professionals such as accountants and lawyers display different symptoms of powerlessness. When they feel powerless, they tend to resist change and try to protect their turf. Top executives can also feel powerless. They show symptoms such as focusing on budget cutting, punishing others, and using dictatorial, top-down communication. Acting in certain ways can lead employees to believe that a manager is powerless. By making external attributions (blaming others or circumstances) for negative events, a manager looks as if he or she has no power.[27]

What can you do when you recognize that employees are feeling powerless? The key to overcoming powerlessness is to share power and delegate decision-making authority to employees.

Korda's Symbols of Power

Michael Korda takes a different look at symbols of power in organizations.[28] He discusses three unusual symbols: office furnishings, time power, and standing by.

Furniture is not just physically useful; it also conveys a message about power. Locked file cabinets are signs that the manager has important and confidential information in the office. A rectangular (rather than round) conference table enables the most important person to sit at the head of the table. The size of one's desk may convey the amount of power. Most executives prefer large, expensive desks.

Time power means using clocks and watches as power symbols. Korda says that the biggest compliment a busy executive can pay a visitor is to remove his watch and place it face down on the desk, thereby communicating "my time is yours." He also notes that the less powerful the executive, the more intricate the watch. Moreover, managers who are really secure in their power wear no watch at all, since they believe nothing important can happen without them. A full calendar is also proof of power. Personal planners are left open on the desk to display busy schedules.

Standing by is a game in which people are obliged to keep their cell phones, pagers, etc. with them at all times so executives can reach them. The idea is that

powerlessness

A lack of power.

the more you can impose your schedule on other people, the more power you have. In fact, Korda defines *power* as follows: There are more people who inconvenience themselves on your behalf than there are people on whose behalf you would inconvenience yourself. Closely tied to this is the ability to make others perform simple tasks for you, such as getting your coffee or fetching the mail.

While Kanter's symbols focus on the ability to help others, Korda's symbols focus on status—a person's relative standing in a group based on prestige and having other people defer to him or her.[29] By identifying powerful people and learning from their modeled behavior, you can determine the keys to power use in the organization.

POLITICAL BEHAVIOR IN ORGANIZATIONS

(6) Define organizational politics and understand the role of political skill and major influence tactics.

Like power, the term *politics* in organizations may conjure up a few negative images. However, *organizational politics* is not necessarily negative; it is the use of power and influence in organizations. Organizations are arenas in which people have competing interests, which effective managers must reconcile. Organizational politics are central to managing. As people try to acquire power and expand their power base, they use various tactics and strategies. Some are sanctioned (acceptable to the organization); others are not. *Political behavior* refers to actions not officially sanctioned by an organization that are taken to influence others in order to meet one's personal goals.[30] Sometimes personal goals are aligned with team or organizational goals, and they can be achieved in support of others' interests. But other times personal goals and the interests of others collide, and individuals pursue politics at the expense of others' interests.[31]

Politics is a controversial topic among managers. Some managers take a favorable view of political behavior; others see it as detrimental to the organization. Some workers who perceive their workplace as highly political actually find the use of political tactics more satisfying and report greater job satisfaction when they engage in political behavior. Some people may therefore thrive in political environments, while others may find office politics distasteful and stressful.[32]

Most people are also amazingly good at recognizing political behavior at all levels of the firm. Employees are not only keenly aware of political behavior at their level but can also spot political behavior at both their supervisor's level and the topmost levels of the organization.[33]

Many organizational conditions encourage political activity. Among them are unclear goals, autocratic decision making, ambiguous lines of authority, scarce resources, and uncertainty.[34] Even supposedly objective activities may involve politics. One such activity is the performance appraisal process. A study of sixty executives who had extensive experience in employee evaluation indicated that political considerations were nearly always part of the performance appraisal process.[35]

Marissa Mayer of Google is charged with the key task of approving new ideas at Google to be presented to founders Sergey Brin and Larry Page. She takes several steps to ensure that politicking does not occur in choice of ideas that move forward. For this purpose she has very clear criteria for objectively evaluating new ideas, holds meetings that allow ten minutes per idea with a timer ticking down, and has someone transcribe everything that is said in the meeting. She is also personally involved in the hiring process and conducts a summer trip abroad to stimulate creativity and build relationships with her design engineers.[36]

The effects of political behavior in organizations can be quite negative when such behavior is strategically undertaken to maximize self-interest. If people within the organization are competitively pursuing selfish ends, they're unlikely to be

organizational politics
The use of power and influence in organizations.

political behavior
Actions not officially sanctioned by an organization that are taken to influence others in order to meet one's personal goals.

attentive to the concerns of others. The workplace can seem less helpful, more threatening, and more unpredictable. People focus on their own concerns rather than on organizational goals. This represents the negative face of power described earlier by David McClelland as personal power. If employees view the organization's political climate as extreme, they experience more anxiety, tension, fatigue, and burnout. They are also dissatisfied with their jobs and are more likely to leave.[37] Not all political behavior is destructive. Constructive political behavior is selfless, rather than selfish, in nature. In this respect, it is similar to David McClelland's concept of social power. Constructive organizational politicians see the difference between ethical and unethical behavior, understand that relationships drive the political process, and use power with a sense of responsibility.[38]

Influence Tactics

Influence is the process of affecting the thoughts, behavior, or feelings of another person. That other person could be the boss (upward influence), an employee (downward influence), or a coworker (lateral influence). There are eight basic types of influence tactics. They are listed and described in Table 11.2.[39]

Research has shown that the four tactics used most frequently are consultation, rational persuasion, inspirational appeals, and ingratiation. Upward appeals and coalition tactics are used moderately. Exchange tactics are used least often, while pressure is the least effective tactic.

Influence tactics are used for impression management, which was described in Chapter 3. In impression management, individuals use influence tactics to control others' impressions of them. One way in which people engage in impression management is through image building. Another way is to use impression management to get support for important initiatives or projects.

Ingratiation is an example of a tactic often used for impression management. Ingratiation can take many forms, including flattery, opinion conformity, and subservient behavior.[40] Exchange is another influence tactic that may be used for impression management. Offering to do favors for someone in an effort to create a favorable impression is an exchange tactic.

Which influence tactics are most effective? It depends on the target of the influence attempt and the objective. Individuals use different tactics for different purposes, and for different people. Influence attempts with subordinates, for example, usually involve assigning tasks or changing behavior. With peers, the objective is often to request help. With superiors, influence attempts are often made to request approval, resources, political support, or personal benefits. Rational persuasion and coalition tactics are used most often to get support from peers and superiors to change company policy. Consultation and inspirational appeals are particularly effective for gaining support and resources for a new project.[41] Overall, the most effective tactic in terms of achieving objectives is rational persuasion. Pressure is the least effective tactic.

Influence tactics are often used on bosses in order to get them to evaluate the employee more favorably or to give the employee a promotion. Two tactics, rational persuasion and ingratiation, appear to work effectively. Employees who use these tactics receive higher performance evaluations than employees who don't.[42] When supervisors believe an employee's motive for doing favors for the boss is simply to be a good citizen, they are likely to reward that employee. However, when the motive is seen as brownnosing (ingratiation), supervisors respond negatively.[43] And, as it becomes more obvious that the employee has something to gain by impressing the boss, the likelihood that ingratiation will succeed decreases. So, how does one use ingratiation effectively? A study conducted among supervisors and subordinates of

TABLE 11.2   Influence Tactics Used in Organizations

Tactics	Description	Examples
Pressure	The person uses demands, threats, or intimidation to convince you to comply with a request or to support a proposal.	If you don't do this, you're fired. You have until 5:00 to change your mind, or I'm going without you.
Upward appeals	The person seeks to persuade you that the request is approved by higher management or appeals to higher management for assistance in gaining your compliance with the request.	I'm reporting you to my boss. My boss supports this idea.
Exchange	The person makes an explicit or implicit promise that you will receive rewards or tangible benefits if you comply with a request or support a proposal or reminds you of a prior favor to be reciprocated.	You owe me a favor. I'll take you to lunch if you'll support me on this.
Coalition	The person seeks the aid of others to persuade you to do something or uses the support of others as an argument for you to agree also.	All the other supervisors agree with me. I'll ask you in front of the whole committee.
Ingratiation	The person seeks to get you in a good mood or to think favorably of him or her before asking you to do something.	Only you can do this job right. I can always count on you, so I have another request.
Rational persuasion	The person uses logical arguments and factual evidence to persuade you that a proposal or request is viable and likely to result in the attainment of task objectives.	This new procedure will save us $150,000 in overhead. It makes sense to hire John; he has the most experience.
Inspirational appeals	The person makes an emotional request or proposal that arouses enthusiasm by appealing to your values and ideals or by increasing your confidence that you can do it.	Being environmentally conscious is the right thing. Getting that account will be tough, but I know you can do it.
Consultation	The person seeks your participation in making a decision or planning how to implement a proposed policy, strategy, or change.	This new attendance plan is controversial. How can we make it more acceptable? What do you think we can do to make our workers less fearful of the new robots on the production line?

SOURCE: First two columns from G. Yukl and C. M. Falbe, "Influence Tactics and Objectives in Upward, Downward, and Lateral Influence Attempts," *Journal of Applied Psychology* 75 (1990): 132–140. Copyright © 1990 by the American Psychological Association. Reprinted with permission.

a large state agency indicates that subordinates with higher scores on political skill used ingratiation regularly and received higher performance ratings, whereas individuals with lower scores on political skill who used ingratiation frequently received lower performance ratings.[44] Additionally, another research study demonstrated that supervisors rated subordinate ingratiation behavior as less manipulative if the subordinate was highly politically skilled.[45] These results indicate that political skill might be one factor that enables people to use ingratiation effectively. We'll describe political skill in more detail in the section of the chapter that follows.

Still, a well-disguised ingratiation is hard to resist. Attempts that are not obvious usually succeed in increasing the target's liking for the ingratiator.[46] Most people have trouble remaining neutral when someone flatters them or agrees with them. However, witnesses to the ingratiation are more likely to question the motive behind it. Observers are more skeptical than the recipients of the ingratiation.

There is evidence that men and women view politics and influence attempts differently. Men tend to view political behavior more favorably than do women. When both men and women witness political behavior, they view it more positively if the agent is of their gender and the target is of the opposite gender.[47] Women executives often view politics with distaste and expect to be recognized and promoted only on the merit of their work. A lack of awareness of organizational politics is a barrier that holds women back in terms of moving into senior executive ranks.[48] Women may have fewer opportunities to develop political skills because of a lack of mentors and role models and because they are often excluded from informal networks.[49]

Different cultures prefer different influence tactics at work. One study found that American managers dealing with a tardy employee tended to rely on pressure tactics such as "If you don't start reporting on time for work, I will have no choice but to start docking your pay." In contrast, Japanese managers relied on influence tactics that either appealed to the employee's sense of duty ("It is your duty as a responsible employee of this company to begin work on time.") or emphasized a consultative approach ("Is there anything I can do to help you overcome the problems that are preventing you from coming to work on time?").[50]

It is important to note that influence tactics do have some positive effects. When investors form coalitions and put pressure on firms to increase their research and development efforts, it works.[51] However, some influence tactics, including pressure, coalition building, and exchange, can have strong ethical implications. There is a fine line between being an impression manager and being seen as a manipulator.

How can a manager use influence tactics well? First, she or he can develop and maintain open lines of communication in all directions: upward, downward, and lateral. Then the manager can treat the targets of influence attempts—whether managers, employees, or peers—with basic respect. Finally, the manager can understand that influence relationships are reciprocal—they are two-way relationships. As long as the influence attempts are directed toward organizational goals, the process of influence can be advantageous to all involved.

Political Skill

Researchers at Florida State University have generated an impressive body of research on political skill.[52] *Political skill* is the ability to get things done through positive interpersonal relationships outside the formal organization. Researchers suggest that it should be considered in hiring and promotion decisions. They found that leader political skill has a positive effect on team performance and on trust and support for the leader.[53,54] Furthermore, it buffers the negative effects of stressors such as role conflict in work settings. These findings point to the importance of developing political skill for managerial success.[55] Politically skilled individuals have the ability to accurately understand others and use this knowledge to influence them in order to meet personal or organizational goals. Political skill is made up of four key dimensions: social astuteness, interpersonal influence, networking ability, and sincerity.

1. *Social astuteness* refers to accurate perception and evaluation of social situations. Socially astute individuals manage social situations in ways that present them in the most favorable light.

2. *Interpersonal influence* refers to a subtle and influential personal style that is effective in getting things done. Individuals with interpersonal influence are

Political skill

The ability to get things done through favorable interpersonal relationships outside of formally prescribed organizational mechanisms.

very flexible in adapting their behavior to differing targets of influence or differing contexts in order to achieve their goals.

3. *Networking ability* is an individual's capacity to develop and retain diverse and extensive social networks. People who have networking ability are effective in building successful alliances and coalitions, thus making them skilled at negotiation and conflict resolution.

4. *Sincerity* refers to an individual's ability to portray forthrightness and authenticity in all of their dealings. Individuals who can appear sincere inspire more confidence and trust, thus making them very successful in influencing other people.[56]

These four dimensions of political skill can each be learned. Several organizations now offer training to help develop this ability in their employees. And political skill is important at all levels of the organization. The biggest cause of failure among top executives is lack of social effectiveness.[57] High self-monitors and politically savvy individuals score higher on an index of political skill, as do individuals who are emotionally intelligent. You 11.1 helps you assess your political skill.

Military settings are particularly demanding in their need for leaders who can adapt to changing situations and maintain a good reputation. In such an environment, politically skilled leaders are seen as more sincere in their motives, can more readily perceive and adapt to work events, and can thus build a strong positive reputation among followers. In fact, political skill can be acquired through a social learning process and by having a strong mentor. Such a mentor then serves as a role model and helps the protégé navigate organizational politics and helps him/her learn the informal sources of power and politics in the organization.[58]

Managing Political Behavior in Organizations

Politics cannot and should not be eliminated from organizations. Managers can, however, take a proactive stance and manage the political behavior that inevitably occurs.[59]

Open communication is one key to managing political behavior. Uncertainty tends to increase such behavior, and communication that reduces the uncertainty is important. One helpful form of communication is to clarify the sanctioned and nonsanctioned political behaviors in the organization. For example, you may want to encourage social power as opposed to personal power.[60]

Another key is to clarify expectations regarding performance. This can be accomplished through the use of clear, quantifiable goals and the establishment of a clear connection between goal accomplishment and rewards.[61]

Participative management is yet another key. Often, people engage in political behavior when they feel excluded from decision-making processes in the organization. By including such people, you will encourage positive input and eliminate behind-the-scenes maneuvering.

Encouraging cooperation among work groups is another strategy for managing political behavior. Managers can instill a unity of purpose among work teams by rewarding cooperative behavior and by implementing activities that emphasize the integration of team efforts toward common goals.[62]

Managing scarce resources well is also important. An obvious solution to the problem of scarce resources is to increase the resource pool, but few managers have this luxury. Clarifying the resource allocation process and making the connection

Using the following 7-point scale, choose the number that best describes how much you agree with each statement about yourself.

1 = *strongly disagree*
2 = *disagree*
3 = *slightly disagree*
4 = *neutral*
5 = *slightly agree*
6 = *agree*
7 = *strongly agree*

1. _____ I spend a lot of time and effort at work networking with others.
2. _____ I am able to make most people feel comfortable and at ease around me.
3. _____ I am able to communicate easily and effectively with others.
4. _____ It is easy for me to develop good rapport with most people.
5. _____ I understand people very well.
6. _____ I am good at building relationships with influential people at work.
7. _____ I am particularly good at sensing the motivations and hidden agendas of others.
8. _____ When communicating with others, I try to be genuine in what I say and do.
9. _____ I have developed a large network of colleagues and associates at work who I can call on for support when I really need to get things done.
10. _____ At work, I know a lot of important people and am well connected.
11. _____ I spend a lot of time at work developing connections with others.
12. _____ I am good at getting people to like me.
13. _____ It is important that people believe I am sincere in what I say and do.
14. _____ I try to show a genuine interest in other people.
15. _____ I am good at using my connections and I network to make things happen at work.
16. _____ I have good intuition or savvy about how to present myself to others.
17. _____ I always seem to instinctively know the right things to say or do to influence others.
18. _____ I pay close attention to people's facial expressions.

A higher score indicates better political skill than a lower score.

between performance and resources explicit can help discourage dysfunctional political behavior.

Providing a supportive organizational climate is another way to manage political behavior effectively. A supportive climate allows employees to discuss controversial issues promptly and openly. This prevents the issue from festering and potentially causing friction among employees.[63]

Managing political behavior at work is important. The perception of dysfunctional political behavior can lead to dissatisfaction.[64] When employees perceive that there are dominant interest groups or cliques at work, they are less satisfied with pay and promotions. When they believe that the organization's reward practices are influenced by who you know rather than how well you perform, they are less satisfied.[65] In addition, when employees believe that their coworkers are exhibiting increased political behavior, they are less satisfied with their coworkers. Open communication, clear expectations about performance and rewards, participative decision-making practices, work group cooperation, effective management of scarce resources, and a supportive organizational climate can help managers prevent the negative consequences of political behavior.

MANAGING UP: MANAGING THE BOSS

(7) Develop a plan for managing employee–boss relationships.

One of the least discussed aspects of power and politics is the relationship between you and your boss. This is a crucial relationship, because your boss is your most important link with the rest of the organization.[66] The employee–boss relationship is one of mutual dependence; you depend on your boss to give you performance feedback, provide resources, and supply critical information. She depends on you for performance, information, and support. Because it's a mutual relationship, you should take an active role in managing it. Too often the management of this relationship is left to the boss; but if the relationship doesn't meet your needs, chances are you haven't taken the responsibility to manage it proactively.

Table 11.3 shows the basic steps to take in managing your relationship with your boss. The first step is to try to understand as much as you can about her. What are his goals and objectives? What kind of pressures does he face in the job? Many individuals naively expect the boss to be perfect and are disappointed when they find that this is not the case. What are the boss's strengths, weaknesses, and blind spots? Because this is an emotionally charged relationship, it is difficult to be objective; but this is a critical step in forging an effective working relationship. What is the boss's preferred work style? Does he prefer everything in writing or hate detail? Does he prefer that you make appointments or is dropping in at his office acceptable? The point is to gather as much information about your boss as you can and to try to put yourself in his shoes.

The second step in managing this important relationship is to assess yourself and your own needs in the same way you analyzed your boss's. What are your strengths, weaknesses, and blind spots? What is your work style? How do you normally relate to authority figures? Some of us have tendencies toward counterdependence; that

TABLE 11.3 Managing Your Relationship with Your Boss

Make Sure You Understand Your Boss and Her Context, Including:
Her goals and objectives.
The pressures on her.
Her strengths, weaknesses, and blind spots.
Her preferred work style.

Assess Yourself and Your Needs, Including:
Your own strengths and weaknesses.
Your personal style.
Your predisposition toward dependence on authority figures.

Develop and Maintain a Relationship That:
Fits both your needs and styles.
Is characterized by mutual expectations.
Keeps your boss informed.
Is based on dependability and honesty.
Selectively uses your boss's time and resources.

SOURCE: Reprinted by permission of *Harvard Business Review*. From "Managing Your Boss," by J. J. Gabarro and J. P. Kotter, (May–June 1993): p. 155. Copyright © 1993 by the Harvard Business School Publishing Corporation; all rights reserved.

is, we rebel against the boss as an authority and view him or her as a hindrance to our performance. Or, in contrast, we might take an overdependent stance, passively accepting the employee–boss relationship and treating him or her as an all-wise, protective parent. What is your tendency? Knowing how you react to authority figures can help you understand your interactions with your boss.

Once you have done a careful self-analysis and tried to understand your boss, the next step is to work to develop an effective relationship. Both parties' needs and styles must be accommodated. A fundraiser for a large volunteer organization related a story about a new boss, describing him as cold, aloof, unorganized, and inept. She made repeated attempts to meet with him and clarify expectations, and his usual reply was that he didn't have the time. Frustrated, she almost looked for a new job. "I just can't reach him!" was her refrain. Then she stepped back to consider her boss's style and her own. Being an intuitive-feeling type of person, she prefers constant feedback and reinforcement from others. Her boss, an intuitive thinker, works comfortably without feedback from others and has a tendency to fail to praise or reward others. She sat down with him and cautiously discussed the differences in their needs. This discussion became the basis for working out a comfortable relationship. "I still don't like him, but I understand him better," she said.

Another aspect of managing the relationship involves working out mutual expectations. One key activity is to develop a plan for work objectives and have the boss agree to it.[67] It is important to do things right, but it is also important to do the right things. Neither party to the relationship is a mind reader, and clarifying the goals is a crucial step.

Keeping the boss informed is also a priority. No one likes to be caught off guard, and there are several ways to keep the boss informed. Give the boss a weekly to-do list as a reminder of the progress towards goals. When you read something pertaining to your work, clip it out for the boss. Most busy executives appreciate being given materials they don't have time to find for themselves. Give the boss interim reports, and let the boss know if the work schedule is slipping. Don't wait until it's too late to take action.

The employee–boss relationship must be based on dependability and honesty. This means giving and receiving positive and negative feedback. Most of us are reluctant to give any feedback to the boss, but positive feedback is welcomed at the top. Negative feedback, while tougher to initiate, can clear the air. If given in a problem-solving format, it can even bring about a closer relationship.[68]

Finally, remember that the boss is on the same team you are. The golden rule is to make the boss look good, because you expect the boss to do the same for you.

SHARING POWER: EMPOWERMENT

Another positive strategy for managing political behavior is *empowerment*—sharing power within an organization. As modern organizations grow flatter, eliminating layers of management, empowerment becomes more and more important. Jay Conger defines *empowerment* as "creating conditions for heightened motivation through the development of a strong sense of personal self-efficacy."[69] This means sharing power in such a way that individuals learn to believe in their ability to do the job. The driving idea of empowerment is that the individuals closest to the work and to the customers should make the decisions and that this makes the best use of employees' skills and talents. You can empower yourself by developing your sense of self-efficacy. You 11.2 helps you assess your progress in terms of self-empowerment.

(8) Discuss how managers can empower others.

empowerment

Sharing power within an organization.

Are You Self-Empowered?

Circle to indicate how you usually are in these situations:

1. If someone disagrees with me in a class or a meeting, I
   a. immediately back down.
   b. explain my position further.
2. When I have an idea for a project, I
   a. typically take a great deal of time to start it.
   b. get going on it fairly quickly.
3. If my boss or teacher tells me to do something that I think is wrong, I
   a. do it anyway, telling myself he or she is "the boss".
   b. ask for clarification and explain my position.
4. When a complicated problem arises, I usually tell myself
   a. I can take care of it.
   b. I will not be able to solve it.
5. When I am around people of higher authority, I often
   a. feel intimidated and defer to them.
   b. enjoy meeting important people.
6. As I awake in the morning, I usually feel
   a. alert and ready to conquer almost anything.
   b. tired and have a hard time getting myself motivated.
7. During an argument I
   a. put a great deal of energy into "winning".
   b. try to listen to the other side and see if we have any points of agreement.
8. When I meet new people, I
   a. always wonder what they are "really" up to.
   b. try to learn what they are about and give them the benefit of the doubt until they prove otherwise.
9. During the day I often
   a. criticize myself on what I am doing or thinking.
   b. think positive thoughts about myself.
10. When someone else does a great job, I
    a. find myself picking apart that person and looking for faults.
    b. often give a sincere compliment.
11. When I am working in a group, I try to
    a. do a better job than the others.
    b. help the group function more effectively.
12. If someone pays me a compliment, I typically
    a. try not to appear boastful and I downplay the compliment.
    b. respond with a positive "thank you" or similar response.
13. I like to be around people who
    a. challenge me and make me question what I do.
    b. give me respect.
14. In love relationships I prefer the other person to
    a. have his/her own selected interests.
    b. do pretty much what I do.
15. During a crisis I try to
    a. resolve the problem.
    b. find someone to blame.
16. After seeing a movie with friends, I
    a. wait to see what they say before I decide whether I liked it.
    b. am ready to talk about my reactions right away.
17. When work deadlines are approaching, I typically
    a. get flustered and worry about completion.
    b. buckle down and work until the job is done.
18. If a job comes up I am interested in, I
    a. go for it and apply.
    b. tell myself I am not qualified enough.
19. When someone treats me unkindly or unfairly, I
    a. try to rectify the situation.
    b. tell other people about the injustice.
20. If a difficult conflict situation or problem arises, I
    a. try not to think about it, hoping it will resolve itself.
    b. look at various options and may ask others for advice before I figure out what to do.

Scoring:

Score one point for each of the following circled: 1b, 2b, 3b, 4a, 5b, 6a, 7b, 8b, 9b, 10b, 11b, 12b, 13a, 14a, 15a, 16b, 17b, 18a, 19a, 20b.

Analysis of Scoring

16–20 You are a take-charge person and generally make the most of opportunities. When others tell you something cannot be done, you may take this as a challenge and do it anyway. You see the world as an oyster with many pearls to harvest.

11–15 You try hard, but sometimes your negative attitude prevents you from getting involved in productive projects. Many times you take responsibility, but there are situations where you look to others to take care of problems.

0–10 You complain too much and are usually focused on the "worst case scenario." To you the world is controlled by fate, and no matter what you do, it seems to get you nowhere, so you let other people develop opportunities. You need to start seeing the positive qualities in yourself and in others and see yourself as the "master of your fate."

Four dimensions comprise the essence of empowerment: meaning, competence, self-determination, and impact.[70]

> *Meaning* is a fit between the work role and the employee's values and beliefs. It is the engine of empowerment that energizes employees about their jobs. If employees' hearts are not in their work, they cannot feel empowered.

> *Competence* is the belief that one has the ability to do the job well. Without competence, employees will feel inadequate and lack a sense of empowerment.

> *Self-determination* is having control over the way one does his or her work. Employees who feel they're just following orders from the boss cannot feel empowered.

> *Impact* is the belief that one's job makes a difference within the organization. Without a sense of contributing to a goal, employees cannot feel empowered.

Employees need to experience all four of the empowerment dimensions in order to feel truly empowered. Only then will organizations reap the hoped-for rewards from empowerment efforts. The rewards sought are increased effectiveness, higher job satisfaction, and less stress.

Empowerment is easy to advocate but difficult to put into practice. Conger offers some guidelines on how leaders can empower others.

First, managers should express confidence in employees and set high performance expectations. Positive expectations can go a long way toward enabling good performance, as the Pygmalion effect shows (Chapter 3).

Second, managers should create opportunities for employees to participate in decision making. This means participation in the forms of both voice and choice. Employees should not just be asked to contribute their opinions about any issue; they should also have a vote in the decision that is made. One method for increasing participation is using self-managed teams, as we discussed in Chapter 9.

Third, managers should remove bureaucratic constraints that stifle autonomy. Often, companies have antiquated rules and policies that prevent employees from managing themselves. An example is a collection agency where a manager's signature was once required to approve long-term payment arrangements for delinquent customers. Collectors, who spoke directly with customers, were the best judges of

FIGURE 11.2 Employee Empowerment Grid

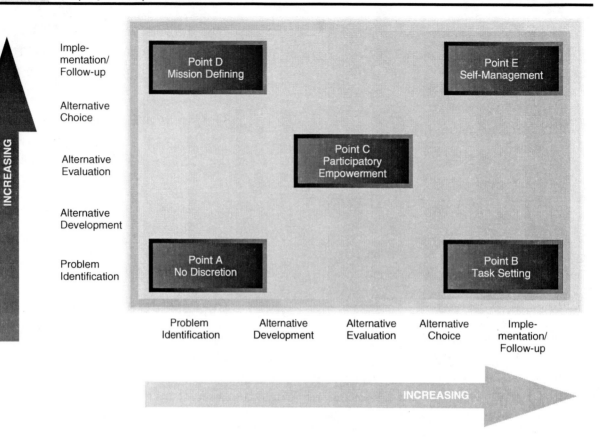

Decision-Making Authority over *Job Content*

whether the payment arrangements were workable, and having to consult a manager made them feel closely supervised and powerless. The rule was dropped and collections increased.

Fourth, managers should set inspirational or meaningful goals. When individuals feel they "own" a goal, they are more willing to take personal responsibility for it.

Empowerment is a matter of degree. Jobs can be thought of in two dimensions: job content and job context. Job content consists of the tasks and procedures necessary for doing a particular job. Job context is broader. It is the reason the organization needs the job and includes the way the job fits into the organization's mission, goals, and objectives. These two dimensions are depicted in Figure 11.2, the employee empowerment grid.

Both axes of the grid contain the major steps in the decision-making process. As shown on the horizontal axis, decision-making authority over job content increases in terms of greater involvement in the decision-making process. Similarly, the vertical axis shows that authority over job context increases with greater involvement in that decision-making process. Combining job content and job context authority in this way produces five points that vary in terms of the degree of empowerment.[71]

No Discretion (point A) represents the traditional, assembly-line job: highly routine and repetitive, with no decision-making power. Recall from Chapter 7 that if these jobs have a demanding pace and if workers have no discretion, distress will result.

Task Setting (point B) is the essence of most empowerment programs in organizations today. In this case, the worker is empowered to make decisions about the best way to get the job done but has no decision responsibility for the job context.

Participatory Empowerment (point C) represents a situation that is typical of autonomous work groups that have some decision-making power over both job content and job context. Their involvement is in problem identification, developing alternatives, and evaluating alternatives, but the actual choice of alternatives is often beyond their power. Participatory empowerment can lead to job satisfaction and productivity.

Mission Defining (point D) is an unusual case of empowerment and is seldom seen. Here, employees have power over job context but not job content. An example would be a unionized team that is asked to decide whether their jobs could be better done by an outside vendor. Deciding to outsource would dramatically affect the mission of the company but would not affect job content, which is specified in the union contract. Assuring these employees of continued employment regardless of their decision would be necessary for this case of empowerment.

Self-Management (point E) represents total decision-making control over both job content and job context. It is the ultimate expression of trust. One example is TXI Chaparral Steel (part of Texas Industries), where employees redesign their own jobs to add value to the organization.

Empowerment should begin with job content and proceed to job context. Because the workforce is so diverse, managers should recognize that some employees are more ready for empowerment than others. Managers must diagnose situations and determine the degree of empowerment to extend to employees. Recently, the management of change in organizations was identified as another area wherein empowerment can have a strong effect. Empowered employees are more likely to participate in and facilitate change processes in organizations as they feel more committed to the organizations' success.[72]

Robert Polet, the CEO of Gucci, seems to know how to get empowerment right. Read about his management style using empowerment in The Real World 11.2.

The empowerment process also carries with it a risk of failure. When you delegate responsibility and authority, you must be prepared to allow employees to fail; and failure is not something most managers tolerate well. At Merck, some say the CEO Ray Gilmartin empowered scientists too much and that their failures cost Merck its profitability and reputation as one of *Fortune*'s Most Admired Companies. One example of this empowerment involved a diabetes drug that early research showed caused tumors in mice. Scientists argued that despite early studies showing the drug wasn't viable, research should continue, and it did—until the drug was finally axed, costing the company considerably in terms of time and money.[73]

MANAGERIAL IMPLICATIONS: USING POWER EFFECTIVELY

Sydney Finkelstein, a professor at Dartmouth University, spends his time studying why executives fail. Interestingly, most of these failures involve the misuse of power and organizational politics. Here are several reasons why executives fail:

> *They see themselves and their companies as dominating their environments.* While confidence is helpful, the perception that a company is without peer is a recipe for failure. On a more personal level, CEOs who see themselves as uniquely gifted in comparison to their competitors and coworkers are generally ripe for a fall.

Gucci: Fine Fashion, Finer Management

When he took over as CEO of the Gucci Group, industry analysts wondered how Robert Polet, whose previous experience was in ice cream and frozen foods at Unilever, could handle the world of fine fashion and expensive leather. Besides, he was stepping into the uncomfortable role of having to manage Gucci's top designers and creative geniuses who are known for their temperamental personalities. Yet Gucci has done exceptionally well under Polet: income increased by 44 percent and some of the company's unprofitable brands are making a turnaround. So, what is the key to Polet's success?

Polet made changes to the management structure and style at Gucci. He strongly believes in empowering his design teams. Under his reign, each brand that Gucci owns operates largely autonomously. Each team is headed by a creative director who oversees the creative process of design, while a CEO for each team oversees the packaging and advertising part of the business. In addition, Polet set out a clear road map for where he expects Gucci to be in the future. This vision translated into clearly defined roles and responsibilities for key organizational players and roles, along with empowerment to carry out the responsibilities effectively. More than anything else, Polet seems adept at emphasizing the importance of the brand over the people associated with it, so that employees never lose sight of organizational goals. These acts of cooperation and empowerment have propelled Gucci towards success.

SOURCE: J. L. Yang, "Managing Top Talent at Gucci Group," *Fortune* (July 17, 2007). http://money.cnn.com/magazines/fortune/fortune_archive/2007/07/23/100135662/?postversion=2007071710

> *They think they have all the answers.* While decisive leadership and vision often lead to the executive suite, an unwillingness to admit ignorance or seek others' input is may trigger disaster. A reluctance to empower others leads to failure.

> *They ruthlessly eliminate anyone who isn't 100 percent behind them.* Business history is replete with leaders who culled the ranks of those who were willing to voice different opinions, only to find themselves blundering down the road to catastrophe without anyone to yell "Stop!"

> *They stubbornly rely on what worked for them in the past.* Like most of us, business leaders tend to fall back on what has worked before. Unfortunately, yesterday's solution is rarely an ideal fit for today's challenge, and successes of the past may well inhibit success in the future.

> *They have no clear boundaries between their personal interests and corporate interests.* As a top leader invests more time and effort in a firm, it's easy for him or her to become convinced that the firm is simply a reflection of his or her own enormous ego. Ironically, leaders who fail to make this distinction tend to be far less careful about spending corporate resources, leading to often embarrassing revelations of executive excess at employee and stockholder expense.[74]

While Finkelstein is quick to point out that corporate executives are, almost without exception, amazingly bright and talented individuals, they also tend to succumb to the same temptations as lesser mortals. Given the extreme power they wield, their failures tend to be much more visible, painful, and far-reaching than most. Corporate executives need accountability to help them avoid these mistakes.

In addition to learning from failure, there is research on how to use power successfully. John Kotter argues that managers need to develop power strategies to operate effectively.[75] Kotter offers the following guidelines for managing dependence on others and for using power successfully:

> *Use power in ethical ways.* People make certain assumptions about the use of power. One way of using the various forms of power ethically is by applying the criteria of utilitarian outcomes, individual rights, and distributive justice.

> *Understand and use all of the various types of power and influence.* Successful managers diagnose the situation, understand the people involved, and choose a compatible influence method.

> *Seek jobs that allow you to develop your power skills.* Recognize that managerial positions are dependent ones, and look for positions that allow you to focus on a critical issue or problem.

> *Use power tempered by maturity and self-control.* Power for its own sake should not be a goal, nor should power be used for self-aggrandizement.

> *Accept that influencing people is an important part of the management job.* Power means getting things accomplished; it is not a dirty word. Acquiring and using power well is a key to managerial success.

You can use these guidelines to enhance your own power skills. Mastering the power and politics within an organization takes respect and patience. When all people are empowered, the total amount of power within the organization will increase.

LOOKING BACK: IS GOOGLE "DOING NO EVIL"?

Google has recently suffered intense backlash from industry competitors for its wide-ranging power and influence. It has expanded from being an Internet search engine to being a giant in the advertising industry, thus scaring television and the print media. It has stepped on Microsoft's toes by offering an online office software package for a portion of Microsoft's Office software package. It also acquired the widely popular YouTube. Viacom sued Google for a whopping $1 billion for copyright infringements as users uploaded clips of popular TV shows like *The Colbert Report* and *South Park* on YouTube. Skeptics worry that Google has too much power in an industry where anything is possible thanks to the freedoms afforded by the Internet. One author even speculated that the company might pose a defense concern due to the vast amounts of information it has access to.

Yet Google seems to be navigating such allegations of a monopoly fairly well. It has done so by creating a strong company culture of employee commitment, empowerment, and cooperation. Ultimately, analysts point out, Google could survive concerns about its growing power and far-reaching influence by following its corporate mantra, "Do No Evil." Time will tell if Google can do so, but right now the outlook is good.[76]

Chapter Summary

1. Power is the ability to influence others. Influence is the process of affecting the thoughts, behavior, and feelings of others. Authority is the right to influence others.

2. French and Raven's five forms of interpersonal power are reward, coercive, legitimate, referent, and expert power. Information power is another form of interpersonal power.

3. The key to using all of these types of power well is to use them ethically.

4. McClelland believes personal power is negative and social power is positive.

5. Intergroup power sources include control of critical resources and strategic contingencies.

6. According to Etzioni's power analysis, the characteristics of the organization are an important factor in deciding the type of power to use.

7. Recognizing symbols of both power and powerlessness is a key diagnostic skill for managers.

8. Organizational politics is an inevitable feature of work life. Political behavior consists of actions not officially sanctioned that are taken to influence others in order to meet personal goals. Managers should take a proactive role in managing politics. Political skill is the ability to get things done through favorable interpersonal relationships outside of formally prescribed organizational mechanisms.

9. The employee–boss relationship is an important political relationship. Employees can use their skills to develop more effective working relationships with their bosses.

10. Empowerment is a positive strategy for sharing power throughout the organization.

Key Terms

authority (p. 364)
coercive power (p. 365)
empowerment (p. 381)
expert power (p. 365)
influence (p. 364)
information power (p. 367)

legitimate power (p. 365)
organizational politics (p. 374)
personal power (p. 369)
political behavior (p. 374)
political skill (p. 377)
power (p. 364)

powerlessness (p. 373)
referent power (p. 365)
reward power (p. 365)
social power (p. 370)
strategic contingencies (p. 370)
zone of indifference (p. 364)

Review Questions

1. What are the five types of power according to French and Raven? What are the effects of these types of power? What is information power?

2. What are the intergroup sources of power?

3. Distinguish between personal and social power. What are the four power-oriented characteristics of the best managers?

4. According to Rosabeth Moss Kanter, what are the symbols of power? The symptoms of powerlessness?

5. How do organizations encourage political activity?

6. Which influence tactics are most effective?

7. What are some of the characteristics of an effective relationship between you and your boss?

8. What are some ways to empower people at work?

Discussion and Communication Questions

1. Who is the most powerful person you know personally? What is it that makes the person so powerful?

2. Why is it hard to determine if power has been used ethically?

3. What kinds of membership (alienative, calculative, moral) do you currently have? Is the power used in these relationships congruent?

4. As a student, do you experience yourself as powerful, powerless, or both? On what symbols or symptoms are you basing your perception?

5. How does attribution theory explain the reactions supervisors can have to influence tactics? How can managers prevent the negative consequences of political behavior?

6. Are people in your work environment empowered? How could they become more empowered?

7. Chapter 2 discussed power distance as a dimension of cultural differences. How would empowerment efforts be different in a country with high power distance?

8. (communication question) Think of a person you admire. Write a newspaper feature analyzing the person's use of power in terms of the ideas presented in the chapter.

Ethical Dilemma

James Allen, a manager for a large retail department store, sat at his desk remembering how this whole thing began. He had called a meeting of his team in early June in which he had laid out his plan to increase productivity over the next six months. Between back to school and the holidays, July through December was always a busy time in retail, but this year needed to be exceptional. Just weeks before that meeting, James had been informed that the store manager was retiring and his successor would be appointed from within the organization. Specifically, the manager whose department was the most productive and efficient through the end of the year would be named the new general manager.

It was now October, and the evaluation period was half over. James felt confident that things were going well in his department. His concern at the moment was Tom Sharp's department. One of Tom's employees had confided that Tom was promising favors to his employees who helped him gain this promotion. Once promoted, he would be in a position to give raises or even promote those who had helped him advance. To help Tom accomplish his goals, the department employees were willing to do just about anything, even work overtime off the clock to reduce labor costs.

James knew that these practices were wrong and against the company's mission and policies. His concern was how to handle it. He felt confident that his department would be the best, so Tom's unethical practices would not affect the outcome. And if he were the new general manager, he could handle the problem then. However, was it right to let these behaviors continue for another three months? Was James sending the wrong signal to his own employees by keeping quiet? Was it enough to say that fair and just practices win in the end? If he did blow the whistle, would the people he would soon supervise think badly of him for being a snitch? James really wanted to do the right thing, but he just was not sure what that was.

Questions

1. Who are the stakeholders that would be affected by James's decision?

2. Does James have a responsibility to come forward with this information?

3. Using consequential, rule-based, and character theories, evaluate James's decision options.

Experiential Exercises

11.1 Social Power Role Plays

1. Divide the class into five groups of equal size, each of which is assigned one of the French and Raven types of power.

2. Read the following paragraph and prepare an influence plan using the type of power that has been assigned to your group. When you have finished your planning, select one member to play the role of instructor. Then choose from your own or another group a "student" who is to be the recipient of the "instructor's" efforts.

You are an instructor in a college class and have become aware that a potentially good student has been repeatedly absent from class and sometimes is unprepared when he is there. He seems to be satisfied with the grade he is getting, but you would like to see him attend regularly, be better prepared, and thus do better in the class. You even feel that the student might get really turned on to pursuing a career in this field, which is an exciting one for you. You are respected and liked by your students, and it irritates you that this person treats your dedicated teaching with such a cavalier attitude. You want to influence the student to start attending regularly.

3. Role-playing.

    a. Each group role-plays its influence plan.

    b. During the role-playing, members in other groups should think of themselves as the student being influenced. Fill out the following "Reaction to Influence Questionnaire" for each role-playing episode, including your own.

4. Tabulate the results of the questionnaire within your group. For each role-playing effort, determine how many people thought the power used was reward, coercive, and so on; then add up each member's score for item 2, then for items 3, 4, and 5.

5. Group discussion.

    a. As a class, discuss which influence strategy is the most effective in compliance, long-lasting effect, acceptable attitude, and enhanced relationships.

    b. What are the likely side effects of each type of influence strategy?

Reaction to Influence Questionnaire

Role-Play #1

1. Type of power used (mark one):

Reward—Ability to influence because of potential reward.

Coercive—Ability to influence because of capacity to coerce or punish.

Legitimate—Stems from formal position in organization.

Referent—Comes from admiration and liking.

Expert—Comes from superior knowledge or ability to get things done.

Role-Plays

1	2	3	4	5

Think of yourself on the receiving end of the influence attempt just described and record your own reaction with an "X" in the appropriate box.

2. As a result of this influence attempt I will . . .
    definitely not comply   definitely comply
         1 2 3 4 5

3. Any change that does come about will be . . .
    temporary   long-lasting
      1 2 3 4 5

4. My own personal reaction is . . .
    resistant   accepting
      1 2 3 4 5

5. As a result of this influence attempt, my relationship with the instructor will probably be . . .
    worse   better
      1 2 3 4 5

Role-Plays

1	2	3	4	5

SOURCE: Gib Akin, *Exchange* 3, No. 4 (1978): 38–39. Reprinted by permission of Gib Akin, McIntire School of Commerce, University of Virginia.

11.2 Empowerment in the Classroom

1. Divide the class into groups of six people.

2. Each group is to brainstorm ways in which students might be more empowered in the classroom. The ideas do not have to be either feasible or reasonable. They can be as imaginative as possible.

3. Each group should now analyze each of the empowerment ideas for feasibility, paying attention to administrative or other constraints that may hamper implementation. This feasibility discussion might include ideas about how the college or university could be altered.

4. Each group should present its empowerment ideas along with its feasibility analysis. Questions of clarification for each group should follow each presentation.

5. Discuss the following questions as a class:

   a. Who is threatened by the power changes caused by empowerment?

   b. Are there unintended or adverse consequences of empowerment? Explain.

T A K E 2

Biz Flix | Scarface

Cuban refugee Antonio "Tony" Montana (Al Pacino) comes to Miami to pursue the American dream. He quickly rises in power within the Miami drug world until life turns against him. This lengthy, punishing film will leave unforgettable images and thoughts with almost any viewer. It is a remake of the 1931 *Scarface*, a classic gangster film starring Paul Muni that set an early standard for films of this type.

The scene from *Scarface* comes from the "Shakedown" sequence that occurs about halfway through the film. The sequence takes place at a disco before Tony's confrontation with his sister Gina (Mary Elizabeth Mastrantonio) about the man she is dating.

Chief Detective of Narcotics Mel Bernstein (Harris Yulin) and Tony Montana discuss Mel's proposal to protect Tony's drug operation. After Mel says, "Thank you for the drink" and leaves, Tony goes to Elvira's (Michelle Pfeiffer) table. The film continues through more of Tony Montana's complex drug deals and to its well-known violent ending.

What to Watch for and Ask Yourself:

> What are Mel's sources or bases of power in this interaction with Tony Montana?

> What are Tony Montana's sources or bases of power?

> What type of power relationship forms between the two men?

Workplace Video | Managing in Turbulent Times, Featuring The Second City Theater

Since 1959, The Second City has been the nation's premier source of improvisational and sketch comedy. Originally founded as a cabaret revue staged by University of Chicago undergraduates, the theater troupe rose to fame in 1975 when owner Andrew Alexander produced the acclaimed comedy television series *SCTV*. Today Second City operates multiple entertainment divisions, including comedy clubs, improvisational training centers, national touring companies, and corporate communication workshops. The company's stage performances are a main attraction of big-city nightlife, delighting audiences from Chicago to Los Angeles.

From the beginning, Second City has been a launching pad for comedians, actors, directors, and others in show business. Mike Myers, Tina Fey, Bill Murray, and John Candy are just a few of the big stars whose careers developed under the watchful eye of Andrew Alexander and his Second City management team.

Planning, leading, and controlling a business based around creative talent requires creative leadership. Inartful leaders who use power coercively or merely for personal gain don't stand a chance in the theater world. For years Second City's managers have used authority and influence to forge creative partnerships with their diverse staff. Taking cues from the art form they promote, managers embrace improv's "yes-and" approach—an acting method in which one performer plays off another performer's ideas and adds to them. Like skilled improvisational actors on a stage, management at Second City encourage feedback from front-line employees and spontaneously parlay that information into new business opportunities.

The Second City has what it takes to direct a talented, diverse group of people. In a world of abusive bosses, Alexander and his team represent the positive face of power and authority. The chief's adroit use of social power to accomplish goals is fitting for a company whose product is people. As producer Robin Hammond says, the company is "all about the people on the stages—they are the heart and soul of The Second City."

Discussion Questions

1. Who has authority at Second City, and what forms of interpersonal power do these individuals possess by virtue of their formal positions?

2. Give an example of power in action at Second City.

3. In what ways does Second City's improvisational "yes-and" approach to management empower employees?

Power and Politics in the Fall and Rise of John Lasseter

John Lasseter grew up in a family heavily involved in artistic expression. Lasseter was drawn to cartoons as a youngster. Then as a freshman in high school he read *The Art of Animation*, a book about the making of the Disney animated film *Sleeping Beauty*. This proved to be a revelation for Lasseter. He discovered that people could earn a living by making cartoons. Lasseter started writing letters to The Walt Disney Company Studios regarding his interest in creating cartoons. Studio representatives, who corresponded with Lasseter many times, told him to get a great art education, after which they would teach him animation.[1]

When Disney started a Character Animation Program at the California Institute of Arts film school, the Disney Studio contacted Lasseter and he enrolled in the program. Classes were taught by extremely talented Disney animators who also shared stories about working with Walt Disney. During summer breaks, jobs at Disneyland further fueled Lasseter's passion for working as an animator for Disney Studios. Full of excitement, he joined the Disney animation staff in 1979 after graduation, but he was met with disappointment. According to Lasseter, "[T]he animation studio wasn't being run by these great Disney artists like our teachers at Cal Arts, but by lesser artists and businesspeople who rose through attrition as the grand old men retired." Lasseter was told, "[Y]ou put in your time for 20 years and do what you're told, and then you can be in charge." He continues, "I didn't realize it then, but I was beginning to be perceived as a loose cannon. All I was trying to do was make things great, but I was beginning to make some enemies."[2]

In the early 1980s, Lasseter became enthralled with the potential of using computer graphics technology for animation but found little interest among Disney Studio executives for the concept. Nonetheless, a young Disney executive, Tom Willhite, eventually allowed Lasseter and a colleague to develop a 30-second test film that combined "hand-drawn, two-dimensional Disney-style character animation with three-dimensional computer-generated back-grounds." Lasseter found a story that would fit the test and could be developed into a full movie. When he presented the test clip and feature movie idea to the Disney Studio head, the only question the studio head asked concerned the cost of production. Lasseter told him the cost of production with computer animation would be about the same as a regular animated feature, and Lasseter was informed, "I'm only interested in computer animation if it saves money or time."[3]

Lasseter subsequently discovered that his idea was doomed before he ever presented it to the studio head. Says Lasseter, "[W]e found out later that others poked holes in my idea before I had even pitched it. In our enthusiasm, we had gone around some of my direct superiors, and I didn't realize how much of an enemy I had made of one of them. I mean, the studio head had made up his mind before we walked in. We could have shown him anything and he would have said the same thing." Shortly after the studio head left the room, Lasseter received a call from the superior who didn't like him, informing him that his employment at Disney was being terminated immediately.[4]

Despite being fired, Lasseter did not speak negatively of the Disney organization, nor did he let others know anything other than that the project on which he was working had ended. His personal admiration and respect for Walt Disney and animation were too great to allow him to do otherwise.[5]

Lasseter was recruited to Lucasfilm by Ed Catmull to work on a project that "turned out to be the very first character-animation cartoon done with a computer."[6] Not long afterwards, Steve Jobs bought the animation business from George Lucas for $10 million and Pixar Animation Studios was born.[7] Lasseter became the chief creative genius behind Pixar's subsequent animated feature film successes like *Toy Story, Toy Story 2, A Bug's Life,* and *The Incredibles,* among others.[8]

In 2006, Disney CEO Robert Iger and Pixar CEO Steve Jobs consummated a deal for Pixar to become a wholly-owned subsidiary of Disney. Iger wanted to reinvigorate animation at Disney, and as the top creative executive at Pixar, John Lasseter was viewed a key figure in achieving this objective.[9] Lasseter ". . . is regarded by Hollywood executives as the modern Walt [Disney] himself [with capabilities]. . . that have made Pixar a sure thing in the high stakes animated world."[10] Former Disney Studios head Peter Schneider says Lasseter "is a kid who has never grown up and continues to show the wonder and joy that you need in this business."[11] Current Disney Studio chief Dick Cook says that Lasseter is like the famous professional basketball player Michael Jordan: "He makes all the players around him better."[12]

Lasseter now oversees development of movies at both Pixar's and Disney's animation studios.[13] Says Lasseter, "I can't tell you how thrilled I am to have all these new roles. I do what I do in life because of Walt Disney—his films and his theme park and his characters and his joy in entertaining. The emotional feeling that his creations gave me is something that I want to turn around and give to others."[14]

Discussion Questions

1. What forms of interpersonal power are evident in the case?

2. In what ways do the two faces of power appear in this case?

3. Do the firing of John Lasseter from Disney Studios and the events leading up to his firing demonstrate the ethical use of power? Explain your answer.

4. Did the firing of John Lasseter indicate the existence of political behavior in the Disney organization?

SOURCE: This case was written by Michael K. McCuddy, The Louis S. and Mary L. Morgal Chair of Christian Business Ethics and Professor of Management, College of Business Administration, Valparaiso University.

Leadership and Followership

After reading this chapter, you should be able to do the following:

1 Define *leadership* and *followership*.

2 Discuss the differences between leadership and management and between leaders and managers.

3 Evaluate the effectiveness of autocratic, democratic, and laissez-faire leadership styles.

4 Explain initiating structure and consideration, leader behaviors, and the Leadership Grid.

5 Evaluate the usefulness of Fiedler's contingency theory of leadership.

6 Compare and contrast the path–goal theory, Vroom–Yetton–Jago theory, the Situational Leadership® model, leader–member exchange, and the Substitutes for Leadership model.

7 Distinguish among transformational, charismatic, and authentic leaders.

8 Discuss the characteristics of effective and dynamic followers.

THINKING AHEAD: AMERICAN EXPRESS

Ken Chenault:
Leading with Kindness and Compassion

Ken Chenault is among the most unlikely competitors for the topmost position of a powerful American company. He is known as much for his kindness and gentlemanly side as he is for his business acumen. In a world crippled by ethical scandals, he is known for his honesty, integrity, and likeability. He has a law degree from Harvard and is known for his extremely good negotiating skills. More importantly, though, Chenault has consistently driven change at American Express, thus preparing it for changing business markets. In his reign at AMEX, Chenault has had to make several tough decisions, including cutting 16 percent of the workforce in order to survive in a post-9/11 environment. However, he succeeded in turning this tragic event into a defining learning moment for him personally and for AMEX. Through all the tough decisions, Chenault has received praise for his candor and fearlessness. He is also seen as a very charismatic leader who has helped the company survive several financial downswings and still come out on the top.[1]

① Define *leadership* and *followership*.

Leadership in organizations is the process of guiding and directing the behavior of people in the work environment. The first section of this chapter distinguishes leadership from management. *Formal leadership* occurs when an organization officially bestows on a leader the authority to guide and direct others in the organization. *Informal leadership* occurs when a person is unofficially accorded power by others in the organization and uses influence to guide and direct their behavior. Leadership is among the most researched but least understood social processes in organizations.

Leadership has a long, rich history in organizational behavior. In this chapter, we explore many of the theories and ideas that have emerged along the way in that history. To begin, we examine the differences between leaders and managers. Next, we explore the earliest theories of leadership, the trait theories, which tried to identify a set of traits that leaders have in common. Following the trait theories came behavioral theories, which proposed that leader behaviors, not traits, are what counts. Contingency theories followed soon after. These theories argue that appropriate leader behavior depends on the situation and the followers. Next, we present some exciting contemporary theories of leadership, followed by the exciting new issues that are arising in leadership. We end by discussing *followership* and offering some guidelines for using this leadership knowledge.

LEADERSHIP AND MANAGEMENT

② Discuss the differences between leadership and management and between leaders and managers.

leadership
The process of guiding and directing the behavior of people in the work environment.

formal leadership
Officially sanctioned leadership based on the authority of a formal position.

informal leadership
Unofficial leadership accorded to a person by other members of the organization.

followership
The process of being guided and directed by a leader in the work environment.

John Kotter suggests that leadership and management are two distinct yet complementary systems of action in organizations.[2] Specifically, he believes that effective leadership produces useful change in organizations and that good management controls complexity in the organization and its environment. Fred Smith, who founded Federal Express (FedEx) in 1971, has been producing constant change since the company's start. FedEx began with primarily high-dollar medical and technology shipments. The company recently bought Kinko's to extend its reach from the back office to the front.[3] Bill Gates has successfully controlled complexity—Microsoft has grown exponentially from early times when his company's sole product was DOS. Healthy organizations need both effective leadership and good management.

For Kotter, the management process involves (1) planning and budgeting, (2) organizing and staffing, and (3) controlling and problem solving. The management process reduces uncertainty and stabilizes an organization. Alfred P. Sloan's integration and stabilization of General Motors after its early growth years are an example of good management.

In contrast, the leadership process involves (1) setting a direction for the organization; (2) aligning people with that direction through communication; and (3) motivating people to action, partly through empowerment and partly through basic need gratification. The leadership process creates uncertainty and change in an organization. Donald Peterson's championing of a quality revolution at Ford Motor Company is an example of effective leadership. As noted in the opening feature, one reason why Ken Chenault is seen as a powerful business leader is that he has championed change at AMEX. Effective leaders not only control the future of the organization but also act as enablers of change. They disturb existing patterns of behaviors, promote novel ideas, and help organizational members makes sense of the change process.[4]

Abraham Zaleznik proposes that leaders have distinct personalities that stand in contrast to the personalities of a manager.[5] Zaleznik suggests that both leaders and managers make a valuable contribution to an organization and that each one's contribution is different. Whereas *leaders* agitate for change and new approaches, *managers* advocate stability and the status quo. There is a dynamic tension between leaders and managers that makes it difficult for each to understand the other. Leaders and managers differ along four separate dimensions of personality: attitudes toward goals, conceptions of work, relationships with other people, and sense of self. The differences between these two personality types are summarized in Table 12.1. Zaleznik's distinction between leaders and managers is similar to the distinction made between transactional and transformational leaders, or between leadership and supervision. Transactional leaders use formal rewards and punishment to engage in deal making and contractual obligations, which you will read about later in this chapter.

It has been proposed that some people are strategic leaders who embody both the stability of managers and the visionary abilities of leaders. Thus, strategic leaders combine the best of both worlds in a synergistic way. The unprecedented success of both Coca-Cola and Microsoft suggests that their leaders, the late Roberto Goizueta (of Coke) and Bill Gates, were strategic leaders.[6]

TABLE 12.1 Leaders and Managers

Personality Dimension	Manager	Leader
Attitudes toward goals	Has an impersonal, passive, functional attitude; believes goals arise out of necessity and reality	Has a personal and active attitude; believes goals arise from desire and imagination
Conceptions of work	Views work as an enabling process that combines people, ideas, and things; seeks moderate risk through coordination and balance	Looks for fresh approaches to old problems; seeks highrisk positions, especially with high payoffs
Relationships with others	Avoids solitary work activity, preferring to work with others; avoids close, intense relationships; avoids conflict	Is comfortable in solitary work activity; encourages close, intense working relationships; is not conflict averse
Sense of self	Is once born; makes a straightforward life adjustment; accepts life as it is	Is twice born; engages in a struggle for a sense of order in life; questions life

leader
An advocate for change and new approaches to problems.

manager
An advocate for stability and the status quo.

SOURCE: Reprinted by permission of *Harvard Business Review*. From "Managers and Leaders: Are They Different?" by A. Zaleznik (January 2004). Copyright © 2004 by the Harvard Business School Publishing Corporation; all rights reserved.

EARLY TRAIT THEORIES

The first studies of leadership attempted to identify what physical attributes, personality characteristics, and abilities distinguished leaders from other members of a group.[7] The physical attributes considered have been height, weight, physique, energy, health, appearance, and even age. This line of research yielded some interesting findings. However, very few valid generalizations emerged from this line of inquiry. Therefore, there is insufficient evidence to conclude that leaders can be distinguished from followers on the basis of physical attributes.

Leader personality characteristics that have been examined include originality, adaptability, introversion–extraversion, dominance, self-confidence, integrity, conviction, mood optimism, and emotional control. There is some evidence that leaders may be more adaptable and self-confident than the average group member.

With regard to leader abilities, attention has been devoted to such constructs as social skills, intelligence, scholarship, speech fluency, cooperativeness, and insight. In this area, there is some evidence that leaders are more intelligent, verbal, and cooperative and have a higher level of scholarship than the average group member.

These conclusions suggest traits leaders possess, but the findings are neither strong nor uniform. For each attribute or trait claimed to distinguish leaders from followers, there were always at least one or two studies with contradictory findings. For some, the trait theories are invalid, though interesting and intuitively of some relevance. The trait theories have had very limited success in being able to identify the universal, distinguishing attributes of leaders. Recent research investigated the effects of heritability among 178 fraternal and 214 identical female twins. Results indicated that genetic factors contribute to the motivation to occupy leadership positions among women leaders. Similarly, prior work experience also has a significant impact on the motivation to lead. Thus it seems that both personal factors and experience affect a person's desire to become a leader.[8]

BEHAVIORAL THEORIES

(3) Evaluate the effectiveness of autocratic, democratic, and laissez-faire leadership styles.

autocratic style

A style of leadership in which the leader uses strong, directive, controlling actions to enforce the rules, regulations, activities, and relationships in the work environment.

democratic style

A style of leadership in which the leader takes collaborative, responsive, interactive actions with followers concerning the work and work environment.

laissez-faire style

A style of leadership in which the leader fails to accept the responsibilities of the position.

Behavioral theories emerged as a response to the deficiencies of the trait theories. Trait theories told us what leaders were like, but didn't address how they behaved. Three theories are the foundations of many modern leadership theories: the Lewin, Lippitt, and White studies; the Ohio State studies; and the Michigan studies.

Lewin Studies

The earliest research on leadership style, conducted by Kurt Lewin and his students, identified three basic styles: autocratic, democratic, and laissez-faire.[9] Each leader uses one of these three basic styles when approaching a group of followers in a leadership situation. The specific situation is not an important consideration, because the leader's style does not vary with the situation. The *autocratic style* is directive, strong, and controlling in relationships. Leaders with an autocratic style use rules and regulations to run the work environment. Followers have little discretionary influence over the nature of the work, its accomplishment, or other aspects of the work environment. The leader with a *democratic style* is collaborative, responsive, and interactive in relationships and emphasizes rules and regulations less than the autocratic leader. Followers have a high degree of discretionary influence, although the leader has ultimate authority and responsibility. The leader with a *laissez-faire style* leads through nonleadership. A laissez-faire leader abdicates the authority and responsibility of the position, which often results in chaos.

Laissez-faire leadership also causes role ambiguity for followers by the leader's failure to clearly define goals, responsibilities, and outcomes. It leads to higher interpersonal conflict at work.[10]

Ohio State Studies

The leadership research program at The Ohio State University also measured specific leader behaviors. The initial Ohio State research studied aircrews and pilots.[11] The aircrew members, as followers, were asked a wide range of questions about their lead pilots using the Leader Behavior Description Questionnaire (LBDQ). The results using the LBDQ suggested that there were two important underlying dimensions of leader behaviors.[12] These were labeled initiating structure and consideration.

Initiating structure is leader behavior aimed at defining and organizing work relationships and roles, as well as establishing clear patterns of organization, communication, and ways of getting things done. *Consideration* is leader behavior aimed at nurturing friendly, warm working relationships, as well as encouraging mutual trust and interpersonal respect within the work unit. These two leader behaviors are independent of each other. That is, a leader may be high on both, low on both, or high on one while low on the other. The Ohio State studies were intended to describe leader behavior, not to evaluate or judge it.[12]

Michigan Studies

Another approach to the study of leadership, developed at the University of Michigan, suggests that the leader's style has very important implications for the emotional atmosphere of the work environment and, therefore, for the followers who work under that leader. Two styles of leadership were identified: production oriented and employee oriented.[14]

A production-oriented style leads to a work environment characterized by constant influence attempts on the part of the leader, either through direct, close supervision or through the use of many written and unwritten rules and regulations for behavior. The focus is clearly on getting work done.

In comparison, an employee-oriented leadership style leads to a work environment that focuses on relationships. The leader exhibits less direct or less close supervision and establishes fewer written or unwritten rules and regulations for behavior. Employee-oriented leaders display concern for people and their needs.

These three groups of studies—Lewin, Lippitt, and White; Ohio State; and Michigan—taken together form the building blocks of many recent leadership theories. What the studies have in common is that two basic leadership styles were identified, with one focusing on tasks (autocratic, production oriented, initiating structure) and one focusing on people (democratic, employee oriented, consideration). Use You 12.1 to assess your supervisor's task- versus people-oriented styles.

The Leadership Grid: A Contemporary Extension

Robert Blake and Jane Mouton's *Leadership Grid*, originally called the Managerial Grid, was developed with a focus on attitudes.[15] The two underlying dimensions of the grid are labeled Concern for Results and Concern for People. These two attitudinal dimensions are independent of each other and in different combinations form various leadership styles. Blake and Mouton originally identified five distinct managerial styles, and further development of the grid has led to the seven distinct leadership styles shown in Figure 12.1.

(4) Explain initiating structure and consideration, leader behaviors, and the Leadership Grid.

initiating structure

Leader behavior aimed at defining and organizing work relationships and roles, as well as establishing clear patterns of organization, communication, and ways of getting things done.

consideration

Leader behavior aimed at nurturing friendly, warm working relationships, as well as encouraging mutual trust and interpersonal respect within the work unit.

Leadership Grid

An approach to understanding a leader's or manager's concern for results (production) and concern for people.

How Does Your Supervisor Lead?

Answer the following sixteen questions concerning your supervisor's (or professor's) leadership behaviors using the seven-point Likert scale. Then complete the summary to examine your supervisor's behaviors.

	Not at All					Very Much	
	1	2	3	4	5	6	7

1. Is your superior strict about observing regulations? — 1 2 3 4 5 6 7
2. To what extent does your superior give you instructions and orders? — 1 2 3 4 5 6 7
3. Is your superior strict about the amount of work you do? — 1 2 3 4 5 6 7
4. Does your superior urge you to complete your work by the time he or she has specified? — 1 2 3 4 5 6 7
5. Does your superior try to make you work to your maximum capacity? — 1 2 3 4 5 6 7
6. When you do an inadequate job, does your superior focus on the inadequate way the job was done instead of on your personality? — 1 2 3 4 5 6 7
7. Does your superior ask you for reports about the progress of your work? — 1 2 3 4 5 6 7
8. Does your superior work out precise plans for goal achievement each month? — 1 2 3 4 5 6 7
9. Can you talk freely with your superior about your work? — 1 2 3 4 5 6 7
10. Generally, does your superior support you? — 1 2 3 4 5 6 7
11. Is your superior concerned about your personal problems? — 1 2 3 4 5 6 7
12. Do you think your superior trusts you? — 1 2 3 4 5 6 7
13. Does your superior give you recognition when you do your job well? — 1 2 3 4 5 6 7
14. When a problem arises in your workplace, does your superior ask your opinion about how to solve it? — 1 2 3 4 5 6 7
15. Is your superior concerned about your future benefits like promotions and pay raises? — 1 2 3 4 5 6 7
16. Does your superior treat you fairly? — 1 2 3 4 5 6 7

Add up your answers to Questions 1 through 8. This total indicates your supervisor's performance orientation:

Task orientation = _____

Add up your answers to Questions 9 through 16. This total indicates your supervisor's maintenance orientation:

People orientation = _____

A score above 40 is high, and a score below 20 is low.

SOURCE: Reprinted from "The Performance-Maintenance Theory of Leadership: Review of a Japanese Research Program" by J. Misumi and M. F. Peterson, published in *Administrative Science Quarterly* 30 (1985): 207. By permission of Administrative Science Quarterly © 1985.

The *organization man manager (5,5)* is a middle-of-the-road leader who has a medium concern for people and production. This leader attempts to balance a concern for both people and production without a commitment to either.

The *authority-compliance manager (9,1)* has great concern for production and little concern for people. This leader desires tight control in order to get tasks done efficiently and considers creativity and human relations unnecessary. Authority-compliance managers may become so focused on running an efficient organization that they actually use tactics such as bullying. Some authority-compliance managers may intimidate, verbally and mentally attack, and otherwise mistreat subordinates. This form of abuse is quite common, with one in six U.S. workers reporting that

organization man manager (5,5)
A middle-of-the-road leader.

authority-compliance manager (9,1)
A leader who emphasizes efficient production.

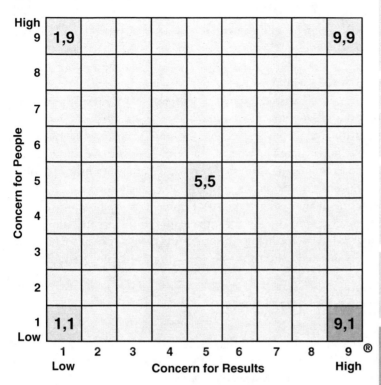

1,9 Country Club Management:
Thoughtful attention to the needs of the people for satisfying relationships leads to a comfortable, friendly organization atmosphere and work tempo.

9,9 Team Management:
Work accomplishment is from committed people; interdependence through a "common stake" in organization purpose leads to relationships of trust and respect.

5,5 Middle-of-the-Road Management:
Adequate organization performance is possible through balancing the necessity to get work out while maintaining morale of people at a satisfactory level.

1,1 Impoverished Management:
Exertion of minimum effort to get required work done is appropriate to sustain organization membership.

9,1 Authority-Compliance Management:
Efficiency in operations results from arranging conditions of work in such a way that human elements interfere to a minimum degree.

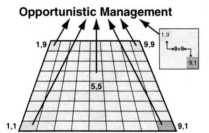

In Opportunisitic Management, people adapt and shift to any grid style needed to gain the maximum advantage. Performance occurs according to a system of selfish gain. Effort is given only for an advantage for personal gain.

9+9: Paternalism/Maternalism Management:
Reward and approval are bestowed to people in return for loyalty and obedience; failure to comply leads to punishment.

SOURCE: "The Leadership Grid®" figure, Paternalism figure, and Opportunism from *Leadership Dilemmas—Grid Solutions*, by Robert R. Blake and Anne Adams McCanse (formerly *The Managerial Grid* by Robert R. Blake and Jane S. Mouton). Houston: Gulf Publishing Company (Grid Figure: p. 29; Paternalism Figure: p. 30; Opportunism Figure: p. 31). Copyright 1991 by Blake and Mouton, and Scientific Methods, Inc. Reproduced by permission of the owners.

they have been bullied by a manager.[16] The *country club manager (1,9)* has great concern for people and little concern for production, attempts to avoid conflict, and seeks to be well liked. This leader's goal is to keep people happy through good interpersonal relations, which are more important to him or her than the task. (This style is not a sound human relations approach but rather a soft Theory X approach.)

The *team manager (9,9)* is considered ideal and has great concern for both people and production. This leader works to motivate employees to reach their highest levels of accomplishment, is flexible, responsive to change, and understands the need for change. The *impoverished manager (1,1)* is often referred to as a

country club manager (1,9)

A leader who creates a happy, comfortable work environment.

team manager (9,9)

A leader who builds a highly productive team of committed people.

impoverished manager (1,1)

A leader who exerts just enough effort to get by.

laissez-faire leader. This leader has little concern for people or production, avoids taking sides, and stays out of conflicts; he or she does just enough to get by. Two new leadership styles have been added to these five original leadership styles within the grid. The *paternalistic "father knows best" manager (9+9)* promises reward for compliance and threatens punishment for noncompliance. The *opportunistic "what's in it for me" manager (Opp)* uses the style that he or she feels will return the greatest self-benefits.

The Leadership Grid is distinguished from the original Ohio State research in two important ways. First, it has attitudinal overtones that are not present in the original research. Whereas the LBDQ aims to describe behavior, the grid addresses both the behavior and the attitude of the leader. Second, the Ohio State approach is fundamentally descriptive and nonevaluative, whereas the grid is normative and prescriptive. Specifically, the grid evaluates the team manager (9,9) as the very best style of managerial behavior. This is the basis on which the grid has been used for team building and leadership training in an organization's development. As an organizational development method, the grid aims to transform the leader in the organization to lead in the "one best way," which according to the grid is the team approach. The team style is one that combines optimal concern for people with optimal concern for results.

CONTINGENCY THEORIES

Contingency theories involve the belief that leadership style must be appropriate for the particular situation. By their nature, contingency theories are "if–then" theories: If the situation is ____, then the appropriate leadership behavior is ____. We examine four such theories, including Fiedler's contingency theory, path–goal theory, normative decision theory, and situational leadership theory.

Fiedler's Contingency Theory

(5) Evaluate the usefulness of Fiedler's contingency theory of leadership.

Fiedler's contingency theory of leadership proposes that the fit between the leader's need structure and the favorableness of the leader's situation determine the team's effectiveness in work accomplishment. This theory assumes that leaders are either task oriented or relationship oriented, depending on how the leaders obtain their primary need gratification.[17] Task-oriented leaders are primarily gratified by accomplishing tasks and getting work done. Relationship-oriented leaders are primarily gratified by developing good, comfortable interpersonal relationships. Accordingly, the effectiveness of both types of leaders depends on the favorableness of their situation. The theory classifies the favorableness of the leader's situation according to the leader's position power, the structure of the team's task, and the quality of the leader–follower relationships.

paternalistic "father knows best" manager (9+9)
A leader who promises reward and threatens punishment.

opportunistic "what's in it for me" manager (Opp)
A leader whose style aims to maximize self-benefit.

least preferred coworker (LPC)
The person a leader has least preferred to work with over his or her career.

The Least Preferred Coworker Fiedler classifies leaders using the Least Preferred Coworker (LPC) Scale.[18] The LPC Scale is a projective technique through which a leader is asked to think about the person with whom he or she can work least well (the *least preferred coworker*, or *LPC*).

The leader is asked to describe this coworker using sixteen eight-point bipolar adjective sets. Two of these sets follow (the leader marks the blank most descriptive of the least preferred coworker):

| Efficient | : | : | : | : | : | : | : | : | : | Inefficient |
| Cheerful | : | : | : | : | : | : | : | : | : | Gloomy |

Leaders who describe their least preferred coworker in positive terms (that is, pleasant, efficient, cheerful, and so on) are classified as high LPC, or relationship-oriented, leaders. Those who describe their least preferred coworker in negative terms (that is, unpleasant, inefficient, gloomy, and so on) are classified as low LPC, or task-oriented, leaders.

The LPC score is a controversial element in contingency theory.[19] It has been critiqued conceptually and methodologically because it is a projective technique with low measurement reliability.

Situational Favorableness The leader's situation has three dimensions: task structure, position power, and leader–member relations. Based on these three dimensions, the situation is either favorable or unfavorable for the leader. *Task structure* refers to the number and clarity of rules, regulations, and procedures for getting the work done. *Position power* refers to the leader's legitimate authority to evaluate and reward performance, punish errors, and demote group members.

The quality of *leader–member relations* is measured by the Group-Atmosphere Scale, composed of nine eight-point bipolar adjective sets. Two of these bipolar adjective sets follow:

| Friendly | : | : | : | : | : | : | : | : | : | Unfriendly |
| Accepting | : | : | : | : | : | : | : | : | : | Rejecting |

A favorable leadership situation is one with a structured task for the work group, strong position power for the leader, and good leader–member relations. In contrast, an unfavorable leadership situation is one with an unstructured task, weak position power for the leader, and moderately poor leader–member relations. Between these two extremes, the leadership situation has varying degrees of moderate favorableness for the leader.

Leadership Effectiveness The contingency theory suggests that low and high LPC leaders are each effective if placed in the right situation.[20] Specifically, low LPC (task-oriented) leaders are most effective in either very favorable or very unfavorable leadership situations. In contrast, high LPC (relationship-oriented) leaders are most effective in situations of intermediate favorableness. Figure 12.2 shows the nature of these relationships and suggests that leadership effectiveness is determined by the degree of fit between the leader and the situation. Recent research has shown that relationship-oriented leaders encourage team learning and innovativeness, which helps products get to market faster. This means that most relationship-oriented leaders perform well in leading new product development teams. In short, the right team leader can help get creative new products out the door faster, while a mismatch between the leader and the situation can have the opposite effect.[21]

What, then, is to be done if there is a misfit? That is, what happens when a low LPC leader is in a moderately favorable situation or when a high LPC leader is in a highly favorable or highly unfavorable situation? It is unlikely that the leader can be changed, according to the theory, because the leader's need structure is an enduring trait that is hard to change. Fiedler recommends that the leader's situation be changed to fit the leader's style.[22] A moderately favorable situation would be reengineered to be more favorable and therefore more suitable for the low LPC leader. A highly favorable or highly unfavorable situation would be changed to one that is moderately favorable and more suitable for the high LPC leader.

Fiedler's theory makes an important contribution in drawing our attention to the leader's situation. The following Science feature illustrates the importance of aligning leadership training with the context of the organization.

task structure
The degree of clarity, or ambiguity, in the work activities assigned to the group.

position power
The authority associated with the leader's formal position in the organization.

leader–member relations
The quality of interpersonal relationships among a leader and the group members.

FIGURE 12.2 Leadership Effectiveness in the Contingency Theory

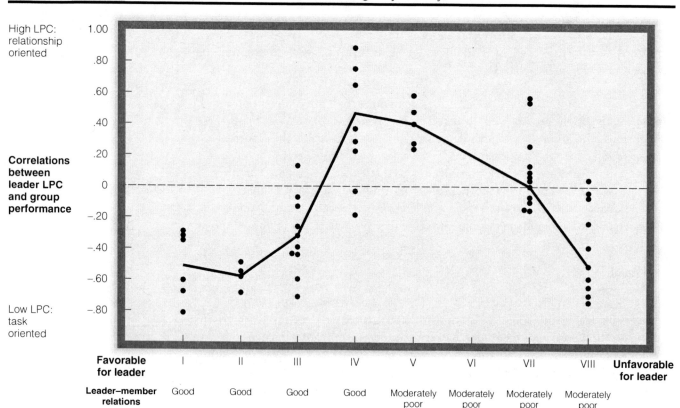

	I	II	III	IV	V	VI	VII	VIII	
Favorable for leader									**Unfavorable for leader**
Leader–member relations	Good	Good	Good	Good	Moderately poor	Moderately poor	Moderately poor	Moderately poor	
Task structure	Structured	Structured	Unstructured	Unstructured	Structured	Structured	Unstructured	Unstructured	
Leader position power	Strong	Weak	Strong	Weak	Strong	Weak	Strong	Weak	

SOURCE: F. E. Fiedler, *A Theory of Leader Effectiveness* (New York: McGraw-Hill, 1964). Reprinted with permission of the author.

Path–Goal Theory

⑥ Compare and contrast the path–goal theory, Vroom–Yetton–Jago theory, the Situational Leadership model, leader–member exchange, and the Substitutes for Leadership model.

Robert House developed a path–goal theory of leader effectiveness based on an expectancy theory of motivation.[23] From the perspective of path–goal theory, the basic role of the leader is to clear the follower's path to the goal. The leader uses the most appropriate of four leader behavior styles to help followers clarify the paths that lead them to work and personal goals. The key concepts in the theory are shown in Figure 12.3.

A leader selects from the four leader behavior styles, shown in Figure 12.3, the one that is most helpful to followers at a given time. The *directive style* is used when the leader must give specific guidance about work tasks, schedule work, and let followers know what is expected. The *supportive style* is used when the leader needs to express concern for followers' well-being and social status. The *participative style* is used when the leader must engage in joint decision-making activities with followers. The *achievement-oriented style* is used when the leader must set challenging goals for followers and show strong confidence in those followers.

In selecting the appropriate leader behavior style, the leader must consider both the followers and the work environment. A few characteristics are included in Figure 12.3. Let us look at two examples. In Example 1, the followers are

America's Leadership Factories: How They Do It

America's best-known companies seem to have perfected the art of grooming and producing exceptional leaders. Companies like General Electric, Johnson & Johnson, PepsiCo, and several others have strong leadership development programs in place that help them identify and groom employees for leadership positions. These leaders in turn are instrumental in guiding the organization to the goal of delivering on its promises. For example, Lexus is known for its tagline "The Pursuit of Perfection." Customers expect a certain degree of quality with a Lexus. The company's leadership translates this promise into reality by a strong emphasis on quality programs such as Six Sigma.

One research study examined the internal processes of leadership development across 150 of the top leader-producing firms and identified five key principles that were common to all the organizations. First, they identify leaders who are proficient at setting organizational strategy and identifying talent within the company. Second, they focus on customer expectations of the firm and ensure that leadership

never loses sight of those expectations. Third, leader performance and effectiveness are evaluated against these customer expectations. Fourth, leadership training at these firms includes skill development that is specific to meeting customer expectations. Fifth, the success of leadership development is periodically evaluated. An important aspect of this last principle is that customers are used for feedback and evaluation of company leadership. For example, this study illustrated a case in which the board of directors called on shareholders, important customers, and community leaders to evaluate and give feedback on CEO actions and accomplishments.

In sum, many organizations invest millions of dollars in leadership development, but many of these programs fail because they are very broad based and not tailored to the particular organization. By keeping the specific needs and characteristics of the organization in mind, these leadership development programs can produce high-quality, effective leaders.

SOURCE: D. Ulrich and N. Smallwood, "Building a Leadership Brand," *Harvard Business Review* 85 (7, 8) (2007): 92–100.

---

inexperienced and working on an ambiguous, unstructured task. The leader in this situation might best use a directive style. In Example 2, the followers are highly trained professionals, and the task is a difficult yet achievable one. The leader in this situation might best use an achievement-oriented style. The leader always chooses the leader behavior style that helps followers achieve their goals.

FIGURE 12.3   The Path–Goal Theory of Leadership

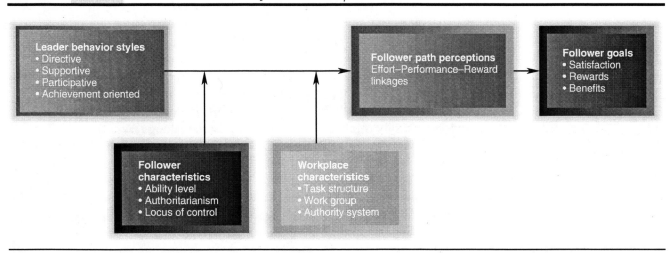

The path–goal theory assumes that leaders adapt their behavior and style to fit the characteristics of the followers and the environment in which they work. Actual tests of the path–goal theory and its propositions provide conflicting evidence.[24] The path–goal theory does have intuitive appeal and reinforces the idea that the appropriate leadership style depends on both the work situation and the followers. Research is focusing on which style works best in specific situations. For example, in small organizations, leaders who used visionary, transactional, and empowering behaviors, while avoiding autocratic behaviors, were most successful.[25]

Vroom–Yetton–Jago Normative Decision Model

The Vroom–Yetton–Jago normative decision model helps leaders and managers know when to have employees participate in the decision-making process. Victor Vroom, Phillip Yetton, and Arthur Jago developed and refined the normative decision model, which helps managers determine the appropriate decision-making strategy to use. The model recognizes the benefits of authoritative, democratic, and consultive styles of leader behavior.[26] Five forms of decision making are described in the model:

> *Decide.* The manager makes the decision alone and either announces it or "sells" it to the group.

> *Consult individually.* The manager presents the problem to the group members individually, gets their input, and then makes the decision.

> *Consult group.* The manager presents the problem to the group members in a meeting, gets their inputs, and then makes the decision.

> *Facilitate.* The manager presents the problem to the group in a meeting and acts as a facilitator, defining the problem and the boundaries that surround the decision. The manager's ideas are not given more weight than any other group member's ideas. The objective is to get concurrence.

> *Delegate.* The manager permits the group to make the decision within the prescribed limits, providing needed resources and encouragement.[27]

The key to the normative decision model is that a manager should use the decision method most appropriate for a given decision situation. The manager arrives at the proper method by working through matrices like the one in Figure 12.4. The factors across the top of the model (decision significance, commitment, leader expertise, etc.) are the situational factors in the normative decision model. This matrix is for decisions that must be made under time pressure, but other matrices are also available. For example, there is a different matrix managers can use when their objective is to develop subordinates' decision-making skills. Vroom has also developed a Windows-based computer program called Expert System that can be used by managers to determine which style to use.

Although the model offers very explicit predictions as well as prescriptions for leaders, its utility is limited to the leader decision-making tasks.

One unique study applied the normative decision model of leadership to the battlefield behavior of ten commanding generals in six major battles of the American Civil War. When the commanders acted consistently with the prescriptions of the Vroom–Yetton–Jago model, they were more successful in accomplishing their military goals. The findings also suggested that a lack of information sharing and consensus building resulted in serious disadvantages.[28]

TIME-DRIVEN MODEL

Instructions: The matrix operates like a funnel. You start at the left with a specific decision problem in mind. The column headings denote situational factors which may or may not be present in that problem. You progress by selecting High or Low (H or L) for each relevant situational factor. Proceed down from the funnel, judging only those situational factors for which a judgment is called for, until you reach the recommended process.

Problem Statement	Decision Significance	Importance of Commitment	Leader Expertise	Likelihood of Commitment	Group Support	Group Expertise	Team Competence	Result
	H	H	H	H	–	–	–	Decide
				L	H	H	H	Delegate
							L	Consult (Group)
						L	–	Consult (Group)
					L	–	–	Consult (Group)
			L	H	H	H	H	Facilitate
							L	Consult (Individually)
						L	–	Consult (Individually)
					L	–	–	Consult (Individually)
				L	H	H	H	Facilitate
							L	Consult (Group)
						L	–	Consult (Group)
					L	–	–	Consult (Group)
		L	H	–	–	–	–	Decide
			L	–	H	H	H	Facilitate
							L	Consult (Individually)
						L	–	Consult (Individually)
					L	–	–	Consult (Individually)
	L	H	–	H	–	–	–	Decide
				L	–	–	H	Delegate
							L	Facilitate
		L	–	–	–	–	–	Decide

SOURCE: Reprinted from *Organizational Dynamics, 28,* by V. H. Vroom, "Leadership and the Decision-Making Process," 82–94 (Spring 2000) with permission from Elsevier.

The Situational Leadership Model

The Situational Leadership model, developed by Paul Hersey and Kenneth Blanchard, suggests that the leader's behavior should be adjusted to the maturity level of the followers.[29] The model employs two dimensions of leader behavior as

FIGURE 12.5

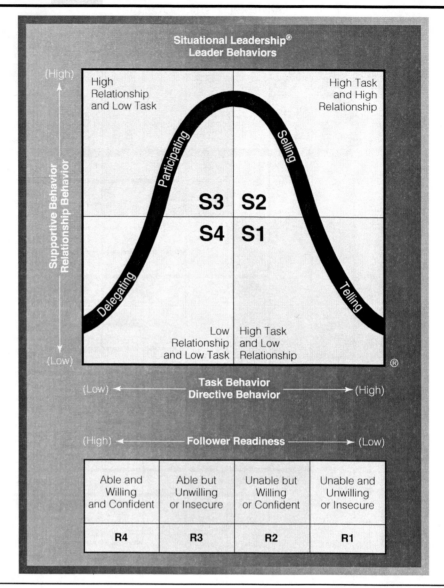

SOURCE: © 2006 Reprinted with permission of the Center for Leadership Studies, Inc., Escondido, CA 92025. All rights reserved.

used in the Ohio State studies; one dimension is task oriented, and the other is relationship oriented. Follower maturity is categorized into four levels, as shown in Figure 12.5. Follower readiness is determined by the follower's ability and willingness to complete a specific task. Readiness can therefore be low or high depending on the particular task. In addition, readiness varies within a single person according to the task. One person may be willing and able to satisfy simple requests from customers (high readiness) but less able or willing to give highly technical advice to customers (low readiness). It is important that the leader be able to evaluate the readiness level of each follower for each task. The four styles of leader behavior associated with the four readiness levels are depicted in the figure as well.

According to the Situational Leadership model, a leader should use a telling style (S1) when a follower is unable and unwilling to do a certain task. This style involves providing instructions and closely monitoring performance. As such, the telling style involves considerable task behavior and low relationship behavior. When a follower is unable but willing and confident to do a task, the leader can use the selling style (S2) in which there is high task behavior and high relationship behavior. In this case, the leader explains decisions and provides opportunities for the employee to seek clarification or help. Sometimes a follower will be able to complete a task but may seem unwilling or insecure about doing so. In these cases, a participating style (S3) is warranted, which involves high relationship but low task behavior. The leader in this case encourages the follower to participate in decision making. Finally, for tasks in which a follower is able and willing, the leader is able to use a delegating style (S4), characterized by low task behavior and low relationship behavior. In this case, follower readiness is high, and low levels of leader involvement (task or relationship) are needed.

One key limitation of the Situational Leadership model is the absence of central hypotheses that could be tested, which would make it a more valid, reliable theory of leadership.[30] However, the theory has intuitive appeal and is widely used for training and development in corporations. In addition, the theory focuses attention on follower maturity as an important determinant of the leadership process.

Leader–Member Exchange

Leader–member exchange theory, or LMX, recognizes that leaders may form different relationships with followers. The basic idea behind LMX is that leaders form two groups of followers: in-groups and out-groups. In-group members tend to be similar to the leader and given greater responsibilities, more rewards, and more attention. They work within the leader's inner circle of communication. As a result, in-group members are more satisfied, have lower turnover, and have higher organizational commitment. In contrast, out-group members are outside the circle and receive less attention and fewer rewards. They are managed by formal rules and policies.[31]

Research on LMX is supportive. In-group members are more likely to engage in organizational citizenship behavior, while out-group members are more likely to retaliate against the organization.[32] And the type of stress varies by the group to which a subordinate belongs. In-group members' stress comes from the additional responsibilities placed on them by the leader, whereas out-group members' stress comes from being left out of the communication network.[33] One surprising finding is that more frequent communication with the boss may either help or hurt a worker's performance ratings, depending on whether the worker is in the in-group or the out-group. Among the in-group, more frequent communication generally leads to higher performance ratings, while members of the out-group who communicate more often with the superior tend to receive lower performance ratings. Perhaps the out-group members get to talk to the boss only when something has gone wrong![34]

Employees who enjoy more frequent contact with the boss also have a better understanding of what the boss's expectations are. Such agreement tends to lead to better performance by the employee and fewer misunderstandings between employer and employee.[35]

In-group members are also more likely to support the values of the organization and to become models of appropriate behavior. If the leader, for example, wants to promote safety at work, in-group members model safe work practices, which leads to a climate of workplace safety.[36]

Substitutes for Leadership

Sometimes situations can neutralize or even replace leader behavior. This is the central idea behind the substitutes for leadership theory.[37] When a task is very satisfying and employees get feedback about performance, leader behavior is irrelevant, because the employee's satisfaction comes from the interesting work and the feedback. Other things that can substitute for leadership include high skill on the part of the employee, team cohesiveness, and formal controls on the part of the organization. Research on this idea is generally supportive, and other factors that act as substitutes are being identified.[38] Even a firm's customers can be a substitute for leadership. In service settings, employees with lots of customer contact actually receive significant leadership and direction from customer demands, allowing the firm to provide less formal supervision to these employees than to workers with little customer contact. This finding adds new weight to the old adage about the customer being boss.[39]

THE EMERGENCE OF INSPIRATIONAL LEADERSHIP THEORIES

Leadership is an exciting area of organizational behavior, one in which new research is constantly emerging. Three new developments are important to understand. These are transformational leadership, charismatic leadership, and authentic leadership. These three theories can be called inspirational leadership theories because in each one, followers are inspired by the leader to perform well.

Transformational Leadership

⑦ Distinguish among transformational, charismatic, and authentic leaders.

As we indicated earlier in the chapter, transactional leaders are those who use rewards and punishment to strike deals with followers and shape their behavior. In contrast, transformational leaders inspire and excite followers to high levels of performance.[40] They rely on their personal attributes instead of their official position to manage followers. There is some evidence that transformational leadership can be learned.[41] Transformational leadership consists of the following four sub dimensions: charisma, individualized consideration, inspirational motivation, and intellectual stimulation. We describe charisma in detail below. Individualized consideration refers to how much the leader displays concern for each follower's individual needs, and acts as a coach or a mentor. Inspirational motivation is the extent to which the leader is able to articulate a vision that is appealing to followers.[42] An extensive research study shows that transformational leadership predicts several criteria such as follower job satisfaction, leader effectiveness ratings, group or organizational performance, and follower motivation.[43] Transformational leadership research conducted in China, Kenya, and Thailand also showed that it had positive effects on employee commitment and negative effects on employee work withdrawal.[44]

As U.S. corporations increasingly operate in a global economy, there is a greater demand for leaders who can practice transformational leadership by converting their visions into reality[45] and by inspiring followers to perform "above and beyond the call of duty."[46] Howard Schultz, founder and chairman of Starbucks Coffee, is the transformational leader and visionary heart of Starbucks. He has grown his firm from a small specialty coffee bar into one of the best-known brands in the world. With the firm hoping to continue its rapid growth pace of 25–30 percent per year, Schultz's ability to develop new leaders within the firm (which helped Starbucks get where it is today) will be sorely tested. But given the enormous market for coffee worldwide (Starbucks currently has less than 10 percent of the market), the potential for further growth exists if the company can develop the people to tap it.[47]

Howard Schultz, right, founder and chairman of Starbucks Coffee, is the transformational leader and visionary heart of Starbucks.

Leaders can be both transformational and transactional.[48] Transformational leadership adds to the effects of transactional leadership, but exceptional transactional leadership cannot substitute for transformational leadership.[49] One reason the latter is effective is that transformational leaders encourage followers to set goals congruent with the followers' own authentic interests and values. Because of this, followers see their work as important and their goals as aligned with who they are.[50]

There is some evidence that transformational leadership may work in military organizations. One study showed that military leaders who practiced transformational leadership produced both greater development and better performance among their subordinates than leaders who used other leadership styles.[51]

Charismatic Leadership

Steve Jobs, the pioneer behind the Macintosh computer and the growing music download market, has an uncanny ability to create a vision and convince others to become part of it. This was evidenced by Apple's continual overall success despite its major blunders in the desktop computer wars. Jobs's ability is so powerful that Apple employees coined a term in the 1980s for it, the *reality-distortion field*. This expression is used to describe the persuasive ability and peculiar charisma of managers like Steve Jobs. This reality-distortion field allows Jobs to convince even skeptics that his plans are worth supporting, no matter how unworkable they may appear. Those close to these managers become passionately committed to seemingly impossible projects, without regard to the practicality of their implementation or competitive forces in the marketplace.[52] Similarly, people who have worked with Ken Chenault note that they admire him immensely and would do anything for him. He is known for chatting with executives and secretaries alike and is seen as someone who is free from the normal trappings of power.

Charismatic leadership results when a leader uses the force of personal abilities and talents to have profound and extraordinary effects on followers.[53] Some scholars see transformational leadership and charismatic leadership as very similar, but others believe they are different. *Charisma* is a Greek word meaning "gift"; the charismatic leader's unique and powerful gifts are the source of his or her great influence with followers.[54] In fact, followers often view the charismatic leader as one who possesses superhuman, or even mystical, qualities.[55] Charismatic leaders rely heavily on referent power, discussed in Chapter 11, and charismatic leadership is especially effective in times of uncertainty.[56] Charismatic leadership falls to those who are "chosen" (born with the "gift" of charisma) or who cultivate that gift. Some say charismatic leaders are born, and others say they are taught.

charismatic leadership
A leader's use of personal abilities and talents in order to have profound and extraordinary effects on followers.

Former presidents Bill Clinton and Ronald Reagan both used personal charisma to inspire followers.

© PAUL RICHARDS/AFP/GETTY IMAGES

Some charismatic leaders rely on humor as a tool for communication. Charismatic leadership carries with it not only great potential for high levels of achievement and performance on the part of followers but also shadowy risks of destructive courses of action that might harm followers or other people. Several researchers have attempted to demystify charismatic leadership and distinguish its two faces.[57] The ugly face of charisma is revealed in the personalized power motivations of Adolf Hitler in Nazi Germany and David Koresh of the Branch Davidian cult in Waco, Texas. Both men led their followers into struggle, conflict, and death. The brighter face of charisma is revealed in the socialized power motivations of U.S. President Franklin D. Roosevelt. Former presidents Bill Clinton and Ronald Reagan, while worlds apart in terms of their political beliefs, were actually quite similar in their use of personal charisma to inspire followers and motivate them to pursue the leader's vision. In each case, followers perceived the leader as imbued with a unique vision for America and unique abilities to lead the country there.

Authentic Leadership

Recently, a new form of leadership has started to garner attention thanks to the ethical scandals rocking the business world. In response to concerns about the potential negative side of inspirational forms of leadership, researchers have called for authentic leadership.[58] *Authentic leadership* includes transformational, charismatic, or transactional leadership as the situation demands. However, it differs from the other kinds in that authentic leaders have a conscious and well-developed sense of values. They act in ways that are consistent with their value systems, so authentic leaders have a highly evolved sense of moral right and wrong. Their life experiences (often labeled "moments that matter") lead to authentic leadership development, and allow authentic leaders to be their true selves.[59] Read about how such life experiences can lead to effective authentic leadership in The Real World 12.1. Authentic leaders arouse and motivate followers to higher levels of performance by building a workforce characterized by high levels of hope, optimism, resiliency, and self-efficacy.[60] Followers also experience more positive emotions and trust leadership as a result of transparency and a collective caring climate engendered by the leader. Researchers contend that this is the kind of leadership embodied by Gandhi, Nelson Mandela, and others like them throughout history. Only time and solid management research will tell if this approach can yield results for organizational leadership. One recent development in the identification of authentic leaders stems from the area of emotions. Emotions act as checks and balances that not only keep the ugly side of charisma in check but also provide certain cues to followers. For example, a leader who espouses benevolence (as a value) and does not display compassion (an emotion) might not be very authentic in followers' eyes.[61] Similarly, a leader who displays compassion when announcing a layoff may be seen by followers as more morally worthy and held in higher regard.[62]

authentic leadership

A style of leadership that includes transformational, charismatic, or transactional approaches as the situation demands.

View from the Top: Authentic Anne Mulcahy at Xerox

Leadership is an acquired skill. Organizations offer several leadership development and training programs to help groom employees for top positions. However, themes among all great business leaders are their willingness to step outside of their comfort zone and the ability to turn travesty into opportunity.

One such business leader is Anne Mulcahy, chairman and CEO of Xerox. When she took over Xerox in 2000, the company was drowning in debt to the tune of $18 million, and she was advised to file for bankruptcy. She had no background in finance and reached out to people in the company to tutor her. She started to ride with field salespeople to understand the business better. More than anything else, Mulcahy showed herself to be a consensus leader, seeking out several opinions and making decisions on the basis of consensus. Such tenacity, com-

The perception that Anne Mulcahy, chairman and CEO of Xerox, is an authentic leader, as well as her reputation as a consensus leader, has helped her overcome challenges at Xerox.

bined with a perception of Mulcahy as an authentic leader, has helped her overcome several challenges at Xerox. She managed to avert bankruptcy by cutting operating expenses.

Fortune magazine featured Mulcahy as one of the brightest minds and leaders in America in 2007. She has climbed the heights of the corporate world by staying true to the company's core values that stress employee engagement and citizenship toward employees, customers, and suppliers. Today, all her business decisions are guided by the same core values that were a part of Xerox almost thirty years ago when she first joined the company.

SOURCE: B. George, "What Is Your True North?" An excerpt from *True North* by Bill George, *Fortune* (March 19, 2007): 125–130.

CNNMoney.com, "How to Succeed in 2007?" http://money.cnn.com/popups/2006/biz2/howtosucceed/7.html

---

Despite the warm emotions charismatic leaders can evoke, some of them are narcissists who listen only to those who agree with them.[63] Whereas charismatic leaders with socialized power motivation are concerned about the collective well-being of their followers, charismatic leaders with a personalized power motivation are driven by the need for personal gain and glorification.[64]

Charismatic leadership styles are associated with several positive outcomes. One study reported that firms headed by more charismatic leaders outperformed other firms, particularly in difficult economic times. Perhaps even more important, charismatic leaders were able to raise more outside financial support for their firms than noncharismatic leaders, meaning that charisma at the top may translate to greater funding at the bottom.[65]

EMERGING ISSUES IN LEADERSHIP

Along with the recent developments in theory, some exciting issues have emerged of which leaders must be aware. These include emotional intelligence, trust, women leaders, and servant leadership.

Emotional Intelligence

It has been suggested that effective leaders possess emotional intelligence, which is the ability to recognize and manage emotion in oneself and in others. In fact, some researchers argue that emotional intelligence is more important for effective leadership than either IQ or technical skills.[66] Emotional intelligence is made up of several competencies, including self-awareness, empathy, adaptability, and self-confidence. While most people gain emotional intelligence as they age, not everyone starts with an equal amount. Fortunately, emotional intelligence can be learned. With honest feedback from coworkers and ongoing guidance, almost any leader can improve emotional intelligence, and with it, the ability to lead in times of adversity.[67]

Emotional intelligence affects the way leaders make decisions. Under high stress, leaders with higher emotional intelligence tend to keep their cool and make better decisions, while leaders with low emotional intelligence make poor decisions and lose their effectiveness.[68] Joe Torre, former manager of the New York Yankees, got the most out of his team, worked for a notoriously tough boss, and kept his cool. He was a model of emotional intelligence: compassionate, calm under stress, and a great motivator. He advocated "managing against the cycle," which means staying calm when situations are tough, but turning up the heat on players when things are going well.[69]

Trust

Trust is an essential element in leadership. Trust is the willingness to be vulnerable to the actions of another.[70] This means that followers believe that their leader will act with the followers' welfare in mind. Trustworthiness is also one of the competencies in emotional intelligence. Trust among top management team members facilitates strategy implementation; this means that if team members trust each other, they have a better chance of getting "buy-in" from employees on the direction of the company.[71] And if employees trust their leaders, they will buy in more readily.

How would you go about leading a team of people in different organizations, in different geographic locations around the world, who had never met? They would not have shared understandings of problems, norms, work distribution, roles, or responsibilities. This is a challenge that is becoming more common, and one that Boeing-Rocketdyne faced. What Boeing-Rocketdyne learned is that the leader of such teams needs to be the "spoke in the center of the wheel" in terms of coordination. The leader also needs to help the team create a common language and document results for the entire team.[72] Not surprisingly, Boeing's largest rival—Airbus Industries of Europe—has developed its own virtual teams. Called Elab, this network helps Airbus coordinate work by aerospace firms all over Europe, including British Aerospace, Rolls Royce, and Snecma. Using complex communications tools, including high-quality video, Elab allows these member firms to create complete working environments for groups of engineers scattered throughout the continent.[73] Leading virtual teams requires trust, because face-to-face interaction that is the hallmark of leadership is not possible. Leaders must not only come to trust their subordinates, but they must also express that trust. Research has shown that workers who believe their boss trusts them (called "felt trustworthiness") enjoy their work more, are more productive, and are more likely to "go the extra mile" at work and perform organizational citizenship behaviors.[74]

Effective leaders also understand both *who* to trust and *how* to trust. At one extreme, leaders often trust a close circle of advisors, listening only to them and gradually cutting themselves off from dissenting opinions. At the opposite extreme, lone-wolf leaders may trust nobody, leading to preventable mistakes. Wise leaders carefully evaluate both the competence and the position of those they trust, seeking out a variety of opinions and input.[75]

Gender and Leadership

An important, emergent leadership question is this: Do women and men lead differently? Historical stereotypes persist, and people characterize successful managers as having more male-oriented attributes than female-oriented attributes.[76] Although legitimate gender differences may exist, the same leadership traits may be interpreted differently in a man and a woman because of stereotypes. The real issue should be leader behaviors that are not bound by gender stereotypes.

Early evidence shows that women tend to use a more people-oriented style that is inclusive and empowering. Women managers excel in positions that demand strong interpersonal skills.[77] More and more women are assuming positions of leadership in organizations. Donna Dubinsky, founder and CEO of palmOne, cofounded Palm and Handspring and is known as the mother of the handheld computer. She wants to change the world so that PDAs outsell PCs. Interestingly, much of what we know about leadership is based on studies that were conducted on men. We need to know more about the ways women lead. Interestingly, recent research reports on the phenomenon of the *glass cliff* (as opposed to the *glass ceiling* effect discussed in Chapter 2). The *glass cliff* represents a trend in organizations of placing more women in difficult leadership situations. Women perceive these assignments as necessary due to difficulty in attaining leadership positions and lack of alternate opportunities combined with male in-group favoritism. On the other hand, men perceive that women are better suited to difficult leadership positions due to better decision making.[78]

Servant Leadership

Robert Greenleaf was director of management research at AT&T for many years. He believed that leaders should serve employees, customers, and the community, and his essays are the basis for today's view called servant leadership. His personal and professional philosophy was that leaders lead by serving others. Other tenets of servant leadership are that work exists for the person as much as the person exists for work, and that servant leaders try to find out the will of the group and lead based on that. Servant leaders are also stewards who consider leadership a trust and desire to leave the organization in better shape for future generations.[79] Although Greenleaf's writings were completed thirty years ago, many have now been published and are becoming more popular.

FOLLOWERSHIP

In contrast to leadership, the topic of followership has not been extensively researched. Much of the leadership literature suggests that leader and follower roles are highly differentiated. The traditional view casts followers as passive, whereas a more contemporary view casts the follower role as an active one with potential for leadership.[80] The follower role has alternatively been cast as one of self-leadership in which the follower assumes responsibility for influencing his or her own performance.[81] This approach emphasizes the follower's individual responsibility and self-control. Self-led followers perform naturally motivating tasks and do work that must be done but that is not naturally motivating. Self-leadership enables followers to be disciplined and effective, essential first steps if one is to become a leader.

An Engaged Workforce through Emotionally Intelligent Leadership

Johnson & Johnson (J&J) Medical Products in Canada is in the business of sales, marketing, and distribution of medical devices and diagnostic products. In this market, competition is intense and J&J implemented a leadership development program known as the "talent pool" to identify and develop leaders who could build a more engaged workforce. This initiative was driven by J&J's philosophy that an engaged workforce could help them outperform the competition. It was also directed at creating a culture of individual behavioral change and a shared language.

This program has resulted in several tangible benefits for the company and created a sustainable competitive advantage that is difficult for competitors to imitate. On the individual front, employee engagement increased from 29 percent to 59 percent since the inception of the program. These numbers are far higher than the average workforce engagement prevalent in the industry. J&J also reaped rewards related to organizational performance. For example, the market growth rate at J&J is three times the industry norm. Thus, individual engagement is tied to better organizational performance. J&J achieved these successes by assessing leaders using a 360-degree emotional intelligence inventory and by offering training in areas where managers were lacking. Moreover, this cycle of improvement is a continuous one at J&J with several short- and long-term action steps in place for employee development.

SOURCE: C. Cameron. "Johnson & Johnson Canada's Design, Development, and Business Impact of a Local Leadership Development Program," *Organization Development Journal* 25 (2) (2007): 65–70.

Organizational programs such as empowerment and self-managed work teams may be used to further activate the follower role.[82]

Types of Followers

(8) Discuss the characteristics of effective and dynamic followers.

Contemporary work environments are ones in which followers recognize their interdependence with leaders and learn to challenge them while at the same time respecting the leaders' authority.[83] Effective followers are active, responsible, and autonomous in their behavior and critical in their thinking without being insubordinate or disrespectful—in essence, they are highly engaged at work. Johnson & Johnson Medical Products instituted a leadership development program aimed at increasing engagement among followers. Read about it in The Real World 12.2.

Effective followers and four other types of followers are identified based on two dimensions: (1) activity versus passivity and (2) independent, critical thinking versus dependent, uncritical thinking.[84] Figure 12.6 shows these follower types.

Alienated followers think independently and critically, yet are very passive in their behavior. As a result, they become psychologically and emotionally distanced from their leaders. Alienated followers are potentially disruptive and a threat to the health of the organization. "Sheep" are followers who do not think independently or critically and are passive in their behavior. They simply do as they are told by their leaders. "Yes people" are followers who also do not think independently or critically, yet are very active in their behavior. They uncritically reinforce the thinking and ideas of their leaders with enthusiasm, never questioning or challenging the wisdom of the leaders' ideas and proposals. Yes people are the most dangerous to a leader because they are the most likely to give a false positive reaction and give no warning of potential pitfalls. Survivors are the least disruptive and the lowest risk followers in an organization. They perpetually sample the wind, and their motto is "better safe than sorry."

FIGURE 12.6 Five Types of Followers

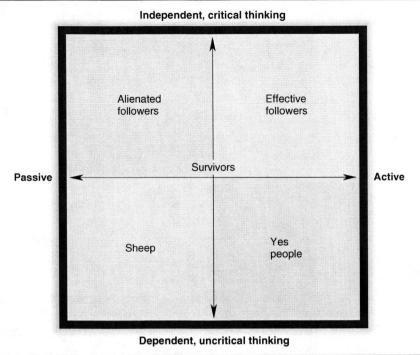

Independent, critical thinking

Alienated followers | Effective followers

Survivors

Passive ←————→ Active

Sheep | Yes people

Dependent, uncritical thinking

Effective followers are the most valuable to a leader and an organization because of their active contributions. Effective followers share four essential qualities. First, they practice self-management and self-responsibility. A leader can delegate to an effective follower without anxiety about the outcome. Second, they are committed to both the organization and a purpose, principle, or person outside themselves. Effective followers are not self-centered or self-aggrandizing. Third, effective followers invest in their own competence and professionalism and focus their energy for maximum impact. Effective followers look for challenges and ways in which to add to their talents or abilities. Fourth, they are courageous, honest, and credible. You 12.2 gives you an opportunity to consider your effectiveness as a follower.

Effective followers might be thought of as self-leaders who do not require close supervision.[85] The notion of self-leadership, or superleadership, blurs the distinction between leaders and followers. Caring leaders are able to develop dynamic followers.

The Dynamic Follower

The traditional stereotype of the follower or employee is of someone in a powerless, dependent role rather than in a potent, active, significant role. The latter, in which the follower is dynamic, is a more contemporary, healthy role.[86] The *dynamic follower* is a responsible steward of his or her job, is effective in managing the relationship with the boss, and practices responsible self-management.

The dynamic follower becomes a trusted adviser to the boss by keeping the supervisor well informed and building trust and dependability into the relationship. He or she is open to constructive criticism and solicits performance feedback. The dynamic follower shares needs and is responsible.

dynamic follower

A follower who is a responsible steward of his or her job, is effective in managing the relationship with the boss, and practices self-management.

Are You an Effective Follower?

To determine whether you are an effective follower, read the text section on "Types of Followers," look back at your self-reliance results in You 7.2, and work through the following four steps. Answer each question in the four steps yes or no.

Step 1. Self-Management and Self-Responsibility

_____ Do you take the initiative at work?

_____ Do you challenge the system at work when appropriate?

_____ Do you ask questions when you need more information?

_____ Do you successfully bring your projects to completion?

Step 2. Commitment beyond Yourself

_____ Are you committed to your boss's and company's success?

_____ Is there a higher purpose in life that you value deeply?

_____ Is there a principle(s) that you will not compromise?

_____ Is there a person at work or elsewhere you admire greatly?

Step 3. Self-Development

_____ Do you attend a professional development class annually?

_____ Do you have a program of self-study or structured learning?

_____ Do you take at least one class each semester in the year?

_____ Have you identified new skills to learn for your job?

Step 4. Courage and Honesty

_____ Have you disagreed with your boss twice this year?

_____ Have you taken two unpopular positions at work this year?

_____ Have you given critical feedback to someone, kindly?

_____ Have you taken one risk at work to do a better job?

Scoring:

Count the number of "yes" answers in Steps 1 through 4: _____

If you have 10 to 16 "yes" answers, this would suggest that you are an effective follower. If you have 7 or fewer "yes" answers, this may suggest that you fall into one of the other four categories of followers.

People who are self-reliant may also be effective followers, and effective followers may also be self-reliant. If you are an effective follower, were you also self-reliant in You 7.2? If you were not self-reliant in You 7.2, did you fall into a category other than the effective follower category?

SOURCE: Reprinted by permission of *Harvard Business Review*. From "In Praise of Followers" by R. E. Kelley, (November–December 1988). Copyright © 1988 by Harvard Business School Publishing Corporation; all rights reserved.

It takes time and patience to nurture a good relationship between a follower and a supervisor. Once this relationship has been developed, it is a valuable resource for both.

CULTURAL DIFFERENCES IN LEADERSHIP

The situational approaches to leadership would lead to the conclusion that a leader must factor in culture as an important situational variable when exercising influence and authority. Thus, global leaders should expect to be flexible enough to alter their approaches when crossing national boundaries and working with people from foreign cultures.[87]

We are beginning to learn more about how perspectives on effective leadership vary across cultures. You might assume that most Europeans view leadership in the same way. Research tells us instead that there are many differences among European countries. In Nordic countries like Finland, leaders who are direct and close to subordinates are viewed positively, while in Turkey, Poland, and Russia this is not the case. And leaders who give subordinates autonomy are viewed more positively in Germany and Austria than in the Czech Republic and Portugal.[88] There are even differences between the American view of transformational leadership and that found in the United Kingdom. The UK approach to transformational leadership is much closer to what we in the United States refer to as servant leadership. It involves more connectedness between leaders and followers and more vulnerability on the part of the leader.[89]

Ten years ago, a lot of people were talking about Denny's and race, as Denny's name became almost synonymous with racial tension. Today, people are still talking about Denny's and race, but in a different way. *Fortune* named Denny's one of the Best Companies for Minorities. What brought about the change?

Somebody had to lead the change. Former CEO of Denny's Jim Adamson believed that he had to find someone with a passion for diversity and the fire to make it happen. He knew that Ray Hood-Phillips had led Burger King toward an inclusive workplace, so he called her and asked for help. She agreed to consult for two or three days a week, getting up at 3:00 a.m. to commute from her home in Miami to Denny's headquarters in Spartanburg. After a few months of working eighteen-hour days, Hood-Phillips agreed to join Denny's.

Hood-Phillips's passion is diversity and inclusion. She led big changes at Denny's but was also a dynamic follower who didn't hesitate to challenge the boss (Adamson). Speaking to a group of executives, Adamson remarked, "You know, we need to be color-blind; we can't see color." Once they were out the door, Hood-Phillips pulled the CEO aside and took him to the woodshed. She told him that all humans have differences and that people from different racial and ethnic backgrounds also have different cultural and social references—people shouldn't be expected to think or act in the same ways. Adamson listened and credits Hood-Phillips with helping him see that Denny's could not pretend that everyone in the United States is the same. This distinction made all the difference.

Hood-Phillips has helped Denny's get diversity right. She monitors diversity progress in every area of the company's operations, including purchasing contracts, management positions, training and education, philanthropy, performance evaluations, and trade partnerships with minority groups. She has led the diversity charge at Denny's and is not afraid to be a dynamic follower in terms of challenging authority. Today, she is the company's chief diversity officer and also consults with other *Fortune* 500 firms that seek advice on diversity at work.[90, 91]

To be effective, leaders must understand other cultures. U.S. executives often perceive specific global regions as being made up of relatively homogenous individuals. For example, some U.S. leaders think that most of Latin America is populated with people of similar values and beliefs. But a recent study of more than 1,000 small-business owners in the region demonstrated that despite similarities, these business leaders are quite diverse in terms of their individual goals. Mexican and Brazilian leaders had values that were very different from leaders in other countries in the region. This means that we cannot stereotype people from Latin America as being totally similar.[92]

Whereas most American workers follow traditional Protestant work values, workers from other countries base their work values on very different sets of beliefs, drawing in some cases from multiple philosophies. China, for instance, draws from not one but three perspectives, as Buddhism, Taoism, and Confucianism harmonize to create work values such as trust, hierarchy, loyalty, and networks.[93] Across cultures, leaders vary widely in their orientation towards the future. This translates into focus on either short-term benefits or longer-term orientation toward employee development. For example, Singapore was the most future oriented of all cultures that were studied. This implies that leaders in Singapore are more focused on longer-term benefits such as delayed gratification, long-term planning, and investing in employee development with longer-term payoffs.[94]

GUIDELINES FOR LEADERSHIP

Leadership is a key to influencing organizational behavior and achieving organizational effectiveness. Studies of leadership succession show a moderately strong leader influence on organizational performance.[95] With this said, it is important to recognize that other factors also influence organizational performance. These include environmental factors (such as general economic conditions) and technological factors (such as efficiency).

Corporate leaders play a central role in setting the ethical tone and moral values for their organizations. While many corporate leaders talk about ethics, many never have to actually risk the firm's fortune on an ethical decision. In 1976, when James Burke, head of Johnson & Johnson, challenged his management team to reaffirm the company's historic commitment to ethical behavior, he had no idea he would be asked to demonstrate that commitment in action. But six years later, when poisoned packages of Tylenol appeared on store shelves, Burke did not hesitate to act on what he had pledged. The company pulled the product from the shelves at a cost of $100 million. It also offered a reward and revamped the product's packaging. In the end, Tylenol recovered and is once again the leading pain medication in the United States. Burke was recently recognized by *Fortune* as one of the ten greatest CEOs of all time, and Johnson & Johnson continues to be rated one of the best companies for which to work.[96]

Five useful guidelines have emerged from the extensive leadership research of the past sixty years:

> First, leaders and organizations should appreciate the unique attributes, predispositions, and talents of each leader. No two leaders are the same, and there is value in this diversity.

> Second, although there appears to be no single best style of leadership, there are organizational preferences in terms of style. Leaders should be chosen who challenge the organizational culture, when necessary, without destroying it.

> Third, participative, considerate leader behaviors that demonstrate a concern for people appear to enhance the health and well-being of followers in the work environment. This does not imply, however, that a leader must ignore the team's work tasks.

> Fourth, different leadership situations call for different leadership talents and behaviors. This may result in different individuals taking the leader role, depending on the specific situation in which the team finds itself.

> Fifth, good leaders are likely to be good followers. Although there are distinctions between their social roles, the attributes and behaviors of leaders and followers may not be as distinct as is sometimes thought.

White Males: Diversity Programs' Newest Leaders?

Keith Ruth was very surprised when he was approached by PricewaterhouseCoopers' chief diversity officer, Chris Simmons, to help lead the firm's corporate diversity effort. Why was he so surprised? Because Ruth is a white male, and it is common knowledge that diversity programs aren't designed for white males, right? Not according to Simmons.

When he became PwC's chief diversity officer in 2004, Simmons was given a directive by the U.S. chairman to move diversity "off the sidelines" and "into the mainstream." That meant fully integrating diversity into the firm's daily operations including client assignments and employee promotions. At the same time, diversity leaders were being named for PwC's four business units. Although Simmons is African American, he was concerned that none of the diversity leaders being named as a business unit diversity leader was a white male. He believed that having a Caucasian male champion diversity would be instrumental in helping to bring other white males on board. After all, he reasoned, they are still the majority of workers in most large firms. Frank McCloskey, Georgia Power's first white male head of diversity, insists that it would be difficult to create a sustainable diversity initiative if the majority of the workforce felt there was nothing in it for them.

Since becoming a PwC diversity leader, Keith Ruth has had much success reaching many people Chris Simmons admits he had had a difficult time reaching.

1. Do you believe recruiting white males to lead diversity programs is a good strategy for garnering support for diversity? Why or why not?

2. What leadership skills must Keith Ruth and other Caucasians use in order to be effective diversity leaders? Contrast them with skills that minority leaders must use.

SOURCE: E. White, "Diversity Programs Look to Involve White Males as Leaders," *The Wall Street Journal* (May 7, 2007): B4.

LOOKING BACK: AMERICAN EXPRESS

Ken Chenault addressed the Wharton Business School and talked about the driving principles of American Express. He noted that the key to success is adaptability through good leadership. He admits he has made mistakes in his career and is not afraid to correct them. He also noted that while compassion is an important part of being a good leader, one must also act decisively. Six attributes stand out in Chenault's mind while envisioning good leadership: integrity, courage, being a team player, emotional intelligence (as opposed to general intelligence), helping others succeed, and being proactive instead of reactive. These driving principles have taken American Express to the pinnacle of success in the corporate world while also creating a niche for Chenault as one of the most influential business leaders.[97]

Chapter Summary

1. Leadership is the process of guiding and directing the behavior of followers in organizations. Followership is the process of being guided and directed by a leader. Leaders and followers are companions in these processes.

2. A leader creates meaningful change in organizations, whereas a manager controls complexity. Charismatic leaders have a profound impact on their followers.

3. Autocratic leaders create high pressure for followers, whereas democratic leaders create healthier environments for followers.

4. The five styles in the Leadership Grid are manager, authority-compliance manager, country club manager, team manager, and impoverished manager.

5. According to Fiedler's contingency theory, task-oriented leaders are most effective in highly favorable or highly unfavorable leadership situations, and relationship-oriented leaders are most effective in moderately favorable leadership situations.

6. The path–goal theory, Vroom–Yetton–Jago theory, and Situational Leadership model say that a leader should adjust his or her behavior to the situation and should appreciate diversity among followers.

7. There are many developments in leadership. Emerging issues include emotional intelligence, trust, women leaders, and servant leadership.

8. Effective, dynamic followers are competent and active in their work, assertive, independent thinkers, sensitive to their bosses' needs and demands, and responsible self-managers. Caring leadership and dynamic followership go together.

Key Terms

authentic leadership (p. 414)

authority-compliance manager (9,1) (p. 402)

autocratic style (p. 400)

charismatic leadership (p. 413)

consideration (p. 401)

country club manager (1,9) (p. 403)

democratic style (p. 400)

dynamic follower (p. 419)

followership (p. 398)

formal leadership (p. 398)

impoverished manager (1,1) (p. 403)

informal leadership (p. 398)

initiating structure (p. 401)

laissez-faire style (p. 400)

leader (p. 399)

leader–member relations (p. 405)

leadership (p. 398)

Leadership Grid (p. 401)

least preferred coworker (LPC) (p. 404)

manager (p. 399)

opportunistic "what's in it for me" manager (Opp) (p. 404)

organization man manager (5,5) (p. 402)

paternalistic "father knows best" manager (9 + 9) (p. 404)

position power (p. 405)

task structure (p. 405)

team manager (9,9) (p. 403)

Review Questions

1. Define *leadership* and *followership*. Distinguish between formal leadership and informal leadership.

2. Discuss transformational, charismatic, and authentic leadership. Would you expect these styles of leadership to exist in all cultures? Differ across cultures?

3. Describe the differences between autocratic and democratic work environments. How do they differ from a laissez-faire workplace?

4. Define *initiating structure* and *consideration* as leader behaviors.

5. Describe the middle-of-the-road manager, authority-compliance manager, country club manager, team manager, and impoverished manager.

6. How does the LPC scale measure leadership style? What are the three dimensions of the leader's situation?

7. Describe the alternative decision strategies used by a leader in the Vroom–Yetton–Jago normative decision theory.

8. Compare House's path–goal theory of leadership with the Situational Leadership model.

9. Describe alienated followers, sheep, yes people, survivors, and effective followers.

Discussion and Communication Questions

1. Do you (or would you want to) work in an autocratic, democratic, or laissez-faire work environment? What might be the advantages of each? The disadvantages?

2. Is your supervisor or professor someone who is high in concern for production? High in concern for people? What is his or her Leadership Grid style?

3. What decision strategies does your supervisor use to make decisions? Are they consistent or inconsistent with the Vroom–Yetton–Jago model?

4. Discuss the similarities and differences between effective leadership and dynamic followership. Are you dynamic?

5. Describe the relationship you have with your supervisor or professor. What is the best part of the relationship? The worst part? What could you do to make the relationship better?

6. *(communication question)* Who is the leader you admire the most? Write a description of this person's characteristics and attributes that you admire. Note any aspects of this leader's behavior that you find less than wholly admirable.

7. *(communication question)* Refresh yourself on the distinction between leaders (also called transformational leaders) and managers (also called transactional leaders) in the text. Then read about four contemporary business leaders. Prepare a brief summary of each and classify them as leaders or managers.

8. *(communication question)* Interview a supervisor or manager about the best follower the supervisor or manager has worked with. Ask questions about the characteristics and behaviors that made this person such a good follower. Note in particular how this follower responds to change. Be prepared to present your interview results in class.

Ethical Dilemma

Sam Bennett has been president of Chateau Bank for the past thirty-five years. Next to his family, running the bank has been the focus of his life. When Sam took over as president, the bank was small and poorly run. Today, there are fifty branch offices across three counties, an accomplishment in which Sam takes great pride. Now Sam is almost seventy and is ready to retire. He has been preparing for this event for some time. Grooming his replacement is very important and something he has been working on for years.

For several years, Chris Hollister has been the heir apparent. Chris had caught Sam's eye when he first joined the bank. Sam has watched with great interest as Chris rose through the ranks. As Chris began moving into the upper echelons, Sam made it well known that Chris was his choice to succeed him as president. The problem Sam now faces is that Chateau is not the same bank. It has, and rightly so, become a bank of the twenty-first century. Computers run everything. But Chris is from the old school. He understands computers well enough, but moving the company into the future requires someone who understands that technology is the catalyst to do that.

Dana Heart might just be that person. Dana joined the company at the management level twelve years ago, straight from graduate school. She grew up in the technology era and knows how to use technology to her and the bank's advantage. Dana is not only good at what she does, but she also has a vision for the future. Sam likes Dana, but how can he turn his back on Chris?

Should his loyalty be with the man he has been grooming for so long or with the growth needs of the organization? Sam is sure that Chris could get the job done, but Dana would move the company forward.

Questions

1. Does Sam have an obligation to appoint Chris as the next president?

2. Evaluate each of Sam's alternatives, choosing Chris or Dana, using consequential, rule-based, and character theories.

Experiential Exercises

12.1 National Culture and Leadership

Effective leadership often varies by national culture, as Hofstede's research has shown. This exercise gives you the opportunity to examine your own and your group's leadership orientation compared to norms from ten countries, including the United States.

Exercise Schedule

1. Preparation (before class)

Complete the 29-item questionnaire.

2. Individual and Group Scoring

Your instructor will lead you through the scoring of the questionnaire, both individually and as a group.

3. Comparison of Effective Leadership Patterns by Nation

Your instructor leads a discussion on Hofstede's value system and presents the culture dimension scores for the ten countries.

In the questionnaire below, indicate the extent to which you agree or disagree with each statement. For example, if you strongly agree with a particular statement, circle the 5 next to the statement.

1 = strongly disagree
2 = disagree
3 = neither agree nor disagree
4 = agree
5 = strongly agree

QUESTIONNAIRE	STRONGLY DISAGREE				STRONGLY AGREE
1. It is important to have job instructions spelled out in detail so that employees always know what they are expected to do.	1	2	3	4	5
2. Managers expect employees to closely follow instructions and procedures.	1	2	3	4	5
3. Rules and regulations are important because they inform employees what the organization expects of them.	1	2	3	4	5
4. Standard operating procedures are helpful to employees on the job.	1	2	3	4	5
5. Instructions for operations are important for employees on the job.	1	2	3	4	5
6. Group welfare is more important than individual rewards.	1	2	3	4	5
7. Group success is more important than individual success.	1	2	3	4	5
8. Being accepted by the members of your work group is very important.	1	2	3	4	5
9. Employees should pursue their own goals only after considering the welfare of the group.	1	2	3	4	5
10. Managers should encourage group loyalty even if individual goals suffer.	1	2	3	4	5
11. Individuals may be expected to give up their goals in order to benefit group success.	1	2	3	4	5
12. Managers should make most decisions without consulting subordinates.	1	2	3	4	5
13. Managers should frequently use authority and power when dealing with subordinates.	1	2	3	4	5
14. Managers should seldom ask for the opinions of employees.	1	2	3	4	5
15. Managers should avoid off-the-job social contacts with employees.	1	2	3	4	5
16. Employees should not disagree with management decisions.	1	2	3	4	5
17. Managers should not delegate important tasks to employees.	1	2	3	4	5
18. Managers should help employees with their family problems.	1	2	3	4	5
19. Managers should see to it that employees are adequately clothed and fed.	1	2	3	4	5
20. A manager should help employees solve their personal problems.	1	2	3	4	5

(continued)

QUESTIONNAIRE

	STRONGLY DISAGREE				STRONGLY AGREE
21. Management should see that all employees receive health care.	1	2	3	4	5
22. Management should see that children of employees have an adequate education.	1	2	3	4	5
23. Management should provide legal assistance for employees who get into trouble with the law.	1	2	3	4	5
24. Managers should take care of their employees as they would their children.	1	2	3	4	5
25. Meetings are usually run more effectively when they are chaired by a man.	1	2	3	4	5
26. It is more important for men to have a professional career than it is for women to have a professional career.	1	2	3	4	5
27. Men usually solve problems with logical analysis; women usually solve problems with intuition.	1	2	3	4	5
28. Solving organizational problems usually requires an active, forceful approach, which is typical of men.	1	2	3	4	5
29. It is preferable to have a man, rather than a woman, in a high-level position.	1	2	3	4	5

SOURCES: By Peter Dorfman, *Advances in International Comparative Management*, vol. 3, pages 127–150, 1988. Reprinted by permission of JAI Press Inc. D. Marcic and S. M. Puffer, "Dimensions of National Culture and Effective Leadership Patterns: Hofstede Revisited," *Management International* (Minneapolis/St. Paul: West Publishing, 1994), 10–15. All rights reserved. May not be reproduced without written permission of the publisher.

12.2 Leadership and Influence

To get a better idea of what your leadership style is and how productive it would be, fill out the following questionnaire. If you are currently a manager or have been a manager, answer the questions considering "members" to be your employees. If you have never been a manager, think of situations when you were a leader in an organization and consider "members" to be people working for you.

Response choices for each item:

A = always   B = often   C = occasionally
D = seldom   E = never

A B C D E

1. I would act as the spokesperson of the group.
2. I would allow the members complete freedom in their work.
3. I would encourage overtime work.
4. I would permit the members to use their own judgment in solving problems.
5. I would encourage the use of uniform procedures.
6. I would needle members for greater effort.
7. I would stress being ahead of competing groups.

A B C D E

8. I would let the members do their work the way they think best.
9. I would speak as the representative of the group.
10. I would be able to tolerate postponement and uncertainty.
11. I would try out my ideas in the group.
12. I would turn the members loose on a job, and let them go on it.
13. I would work hard for a promotion.
14. I would get swamped by details.
15. I would speak for the group when visitors are present.
16. I would be reluctant to allow the members any freedom of action.
17. I would keep the work moving at a rapid pace.

	A B C D E
18. I would let some members have authority that I should keep.	
19. I would settle conflicts when they occur in the group.	
20. I would allow the group a high degree of initiative.	
21. I would represent the group at outside meetings.	
22. I would be willing to make changes.	
23. I would decide what will be done and how it will be done.	
24. I would trust the members to exercise good judgment.	
25. I would push for increased production.	
26. I would refuse to explain my actions.	

	A B C D E
27. Things usually turn out as I predict.	
28. I would permit the group to set its own pace.	
29. I would assign group members to particular tasks.	
30. I would act without consulting the group.	
31. I would ask the members of the group to work harder.	
32. I would schedule the work to be done.	
33. I would persuade others that my ideas are to their advantage.	
34. I would urge the group to beat its previous record.	
35. I would ask that group members follow standard rules and regulations.	

Scoring

People oriented: Place a check mark by the number if you answered either A or B to any of these questions:

Question # 2 ____   10 ____   22 ____
           4 ____   12 ____   24 ____
           6 ____   18 ____   28 ____
           8 ____   20 ____

Place a check mark by the number if you answered either D or E to any of these questions:

           14 ____ 16 ____ 26 ____ 30 ____

Count your check marks to get your total people-oriented score. ____

Task oriented: Place a check mark by the number if you answered either A or B to any of these questions:

           3 ____   7 ____   11 ____   13 ____
          17 ____   25 ____   29 ____   31 ____
          34 ____

Place a check mark by the number if you answered C or D to any of these questions:

           1 ____   5 ____   9 ____   15 ____
          19 ____   21 ____   23 ____   27 ____
          32 ____   33 ____   35 ____

Count your check marks to get your total task-oriented score. ____

Range	Range		
People 0–7;	Task 0–10	You are not involved enough in either the task or the people.	Uninvolved
People 0–7;	Task 10–20	You tend to be autocratic, a whip-snapper. You get the job done, but at a high emotional cost.	Task-oriented
People 8–15;	Task 0–10	People are happy in their work, but sometimes at the expense of productivity.	People-oriented
People 8–15;	Task 10–20	People enjoy working for you and are productive. They naturally expend energy because they get positive reinforcement for doing a good job.	Balanced

As a leader, most people tend to be more task oriented or more people oriented. Task orientation is concerned with getting the job done, while people orientation focuses on group interactions and the needs of individual workers.

Effective leaders, however, are able to use both styles, depending on the situation. There may be times when a rush job demands great attention placed on task completion. During a time of low morale, though, sensitivity to workers' problems would be more appropriate. The best managers are able to balance both task and people concerns. Therefore, a high score on both would show this balance. Ultimately, you will gain respect, admiration, and productivity from your workers.

Exercise Schedule

1. Preparation (before class)
Complete and score inventory.

2. Group discussion
The class should form four groups based on the scores on the Leadership Style Inventory. Each group will be given a separate task.

Uninvolved: Devise strategies for developing task-oriented and people-oriented styles.

Task-oriented: How can you develop a more people-oriented style? What problems might occur if you do not do so?

People-oriented: How can you develop a more task-oriented style? What problems might occur if you do not do so?

Balanced: Do you see any potential problems with your style? Are you a fully developed leader?

SOURCE: From Thomas Sergiovanni, Richard Metzcus, and Larry Burden, "Toward a Particularistic Approach to Leadership Style: Some Findings," *American Educational Research Journal*, vol. 6 (1), January 1969. Copyright 1969 The American Educational Research Association. Reprinted with permission of AERA.

Biz Flix | U-571

This action-packed World War II thriller shows a U.S. submarine crew's efforts to retrieve an Enigma encryption device from a disabled German submarine. After the crew gets the device, a German vessel torpedoes and sinks their submarine. The survivors must now use the disabled German submarine to escape from the enemy with their prize.

The *U-571* scene is an edited composite of the "To Be a Captain" sequence early in the film and the "A Real Sea Captain" sequence in about the middle of the film. A "chalkboard" (title screen) that reads, "Mr. Tyler, permission to speak freely?" separates the two parts. You can pause and separately study each part of the scene.

The first part occurs before the crew boards the disabled German U-boat. The second part occurs after the crew of survivors board the U-boat and try to return to England. Andrew Tyler (Matthew McConaughey), formerly the executive officer, is now the submarine's commander following the drowning death of Mike Dahlgren (Bill Paxton), the original commander. Just before this part of the scene, Tyler overheard some crewmen questioning his decision about taking a dangerous route to England. They also question why Chief Petty Officer Henry Klough (Harvey Keitel) is not the commander. The film continues with a German reconnaissance airplane circling their submarine and a crewman challenging Tyler's authority.

What to Watch for and Ask Yourself:

> What aspects of leadership does Dahlgren describe as important for a submarine commander?

> Which leadership behaviors or traits does Klough emphasize?

> Are these traits or behaviors right for this situation? Why or why not?

Workplace Video | Leadership, Featuring McDonald's

"Would you like to Supersize that?" This familiar phrase is heard by nearly 50 million people in more than 119 countries each day. Indeed McDonald's has become one of the most recognizable franchises in the world. The company's storied history, which gained legendary status under the leadership of Ray Kroc, weaves together many enduring themes of business success: visionary leadership, mass marketing, and groundbreaking business models.

Kroc, the iconic businessman credited with the rapid expansion of the McDonald's Corporation, was a franchising pioneer. The one-time distributor of Multimixer milk-shake makers was first to see the potential in replicating the McDonald's restaurant across the country. While visiting a McDonald's hamburger stand in California one day, Kroc noticed that the restaurant used eight Multimixers to serve a record number of customers. Knowing a good idea when he saw one, the young entrepreneur proposed opening several such restaurants. In 1955, Kroc opened the first McDonald's chain location in Des Plaines, Illinois. The rest is history.

Kroc is remembered as a leader who inspired many with his personal charisma and vision. Even so, he also was a methodical supervisor who possessed strong initiating structure. Kroc's clever quip "If you've got time to lean, you've got time to clean" reveals a goal-oriented approach that continues to guide managerial strategy at McDonald's today.

Although good leadership is concerned with goals and results, effective leaders must also show consideration for people. Top leaders at McDonald's demonstrate concern for their employees in various ways. "Plan-to-Win," the company's global strategy, lays out a comprehensive commitment to people that involves employee training, flexible scheduling, and career development. Moreover, managers promote job satisfaction by recognizing and rewarding the good effort of all employees. On the interpersonal level, supervisors treat subordinates as they themselves would want to be treated, acting more like coaches than chieftains.

Like many industry-leading corporations, McDonald's has achieved its greatness by showing equal concern for people and performance. That balance, though difficult to maintain, is as vital to the company's ongoing success as it was when Ray Kroc transformed a small hamburger stand into a franchising wonder.

Discussion Questions

1. Where does leadership at McDonald's fall on the Leadership Grid discussed in this chapter? Explain.

2. Which contingency model of leadership is utilized at McDonald's, according to the video?

3. Would you describe Ray Kroc as a transformational, charismatic leader? Why or why not?

Triumvirate Leadership at Google

In 1998, while they were doctoral students at Stanford University, Sergey Brin and Larry Page founded Google. In 2001, Brin and Page recruited Eric Schmidt to be Google's chief executive officer. Schmidt was charged with providing the organizational and operational expertise and leadership for Google, while Brin and Page provided the engineering, technological, and product development leadership.[1] As some pundits have said, Page and Brin knew they weren't professional managers or marketers or masters of strategy, so they brought in a "grown-up," Eric Schmidt, to operate the company.[2]

Google's success can be attributed to its triumvirate leadership of Brin, Page, and Schmidt, "who have managed to beat back rivals from Yahoo! to Microsoft."[3] However, one of Google's biggest mysteries is its three-man leadership and how it functions.[4] Page is president for products and is acknowledged as the company's thought leader and someone who gets involved in projects to make sure things get done. Brin is president of technology and assumes responsibility for advertising initiatives, which is the money-making part of Google.[5] "Conventional wisdom is that Schmidt's job is to break ties between Page and Brin and to communicate with Wall Street and the news media. Insiders say that underplays his role. He sets the company's overall agenda, gives direction on workaday issues the founders don't care to address, and more than occasionally reminds Page and Brin to behave themselves."[6] Schmidt is a skilled big-company executive, having had substantial experience at Novell and Sun Microsystems before being recruited to Google. He is a seasoned marketer and a renowned technology expert as well.[7] In April 2007, Schmidt was elected board chairman in addition to being CEO. Google had not had a chairman since it went public in 2004, although Schmidt effectively served in that role.[8] In commenting on the role Schmidt has played in Google's success, David Nadler, a renowned business consultant, says, "Page and Brin's handoff to Schmidt can be seen as a classic case of redesigning the management structure to complement the strengths of the top people."[9]

Nonetheless, Brin and Page seem to be the dominant forces in the company because their stock shares carry ten times as many votes as the ordinary stock shares. Moreover, Brin and Page "give themselves carte blanche to do what they like, buy what they like, diversify wherever they like and pay no dividends."[10]

The leadership triumvirate also has high expectations for Google employees. Google hires only class-A talent because Brin, Page, and Schmidt believe that hiring just one B-level person initiates a slide into mediocrity. The company has generous reward and award programs in order to ensure that employees with great ideas don't launch their own entrepreneurial ventures.[11] Moreover, Google essentially lets engineers run the show. Every Google employee divides his or her work time into three parts: 70 percent is devoted to Google's core businesses of search and advertising; 20 percent is targeted toward off-budget projects related to the core businesses; and 10 percent is allocated to the pursuit of far-out ideas.[12] The time allocation for off-budget projects and far-out ideas is more than a perk; "it's Google's seed corn for the future."[13]

Brin and Page do not see themselves as "infallible seers with a divine right to dictate Google's next strategy and the one after that." Instead, they have "created a Darwinian environment in which every idea must compete on its merits, not on the grandeur of its sponsor's title."[14] Encouraging creativity and innovation is a Google hallmark, and the company has implemented many policies, processes, and procedures to foster creativity and innovation. For instance, mechanisms are in place to share ideas, get input from peers, recruit people to work on project ideas, and generate support for change. This makes Google a highly transparent organization for insiders.[15]

But Google is not highly transparent for outsiders! The company seems to relish being secretive and opaque and confusing the competition.[16] This is nowhere more apparent than in the leadership triumvirate's deliberately confusing comments on transparency and corporate strategy. In describing the need for transparency in business, Schmidt says, "[w]ith all the headlines we're making, we don't want our announcements to surprise or confuse anyone. We don't want our partners to think we're competing against them." Schmidt continues, "[w]e try very hard to look like we're out of control. But in fact the company is very measured. And that's part of our secret."[17] Page adds, "[w]e don't generally talk about strategy . . . because it's strategic. I would rather have people think we're confused than let our competitors know what we're going to do."[18] Schmidt also says that he "intentionally propagated the perception of Google as a wacky place to allow the company to build up its business under the radar."[19]

Along with not being transparent to outsiders, Google has created some disharmony with them. By taking on Microsoft (desktop software), phone companies (a San Francisco Wi-Fi plan for free wireless Internet service), eBay (classified advertising), and others, Google has not been making friends.[20] The company even seems to be offending its paying customers, and in some "parts of the business community, it is acquiring the image of a somewhat sanctimonious bully."[21] This is an interesting anomaly, particularly given Google's famous slogan—"Don't Be Evil"—and its pro-consumer stance. Rather than

creating disharmony, Google should have been winning friends.[22]

Discussion Questions

1. In what ways are Sergey Brin, Larry Page, and Eric Schmidt managers? In what ways are they leaders?

2. Describe the nature of followership that Brin, Page, and Schmidt have sought to develop at Google.

3. Using the Leadership Grid and its underlying leader behaviors of initiating structure and consideration, explain the leadership orientations of Google's triumvirate.

4. Use the concepts of transactional, transformational, charismatic, and authentic leaders to describe the leadership of Brin, Page, and Schmidt.

5. What skills would you personally need to develop to become a leader like Brin, Page, and Schmidt? What could you do to develop or refine those skills?

SOURCE: This case was written by Michael K. McCuddy, The Louis S. and Mary L. Morgal Chair of Christian Business Ethics and Professor of Management, College of Business Administration, Valparaiso University.

Conflict and Negotiation

After reading this chapter, you should be able to do the following:

1 Diagnose functional versus dysfunctional conflict.

2 Identify the causes of conflict in organizations.

3 Identify the different forms of conflict.

4 Understand the defense mechanisms that individuals exhibit when they engage in interpersonal conflict.

5 Describe effective and ineffective techniques for managing conflict.

6 Understand five styles of conflict management, and diagnose your own preferred style.

THINKING AHEAD: GENENTECH, INC.

Conflict within One of the "Best Companies"

Only a select few ever make *Fortune*'s list of "100 Best Companies to Work For." For Genentech, making the esteemed list has become something of an annual tradition. In fact, the company's place on the 2007 list was number two—a slight drop from its 2006 ranking of number one. While all seems well inside the company, Genentech is in the business of pharmaceutical innovation, which brings with it some disputes and conflicts from time to time.

For example, Genentech has been hit by legal action for using research from another source without full permission. One such case came to light when a jury ordered it to hand over $300 million in unpaid royalties to City of Hope for the use of some of their patented methods of developing protein-based drugs that they had licensed to Genentech in 1976. City of Hope claimed that Genentech licensed these methods to other companies. City of Hope should have received royalties from this, but they claimed that Genentech had intentionally cheated them of their money. Ultimately, Genentech announced that they had been honest in all their transactions and had to take the hit for this one decision.[1]

THE NATURE OF CONFLICTS IN ORGANIZATIONS

All of us have experienced conflict of various types, yet we probably fail to recognize the variety of conflicts that occur in organizations. *Conflict* is defined as any situation in which incompatible goals, attitudes, emotions, or behaviors lead to disagreement or opposition between two or more parties.[2]

Today's organizations may face greater potential for conflict than ever before in history. The marketplace, with its increasing competition and globalization, magnifies differences among people in terms of personality, values, attitudes, perceptions, languages, cultures, and national backgrounds.[3] With the increasing diversity of the workforce, furthermore, comes the potential for incompatibility and conflict.

Importance of Conflict Management Skills for the Manager

Estimates show that managers spend about 21 percent of their time dealing with conflict.[4] That is the equivalent of one day every week. And conflict management skills are a major predictor of managerial success.[5] Emotional intelligence (EI) relates to the ability to manage conflict. It is the power to control one's emotions and perceive emotions in others, adapt to change, and manage adversity. Conflict management skills may be more a reflection of EI than of IQ. People who lack emotional intelligence, especially empathy or the ability to see life from another person's perspective, are more likely to be causes of conflict than managers of conflict.[6] EI seems to be valid across cultures. It is common among successful people not only in North America, but also in Nigeria, India, Argentina, and France.

Functional versus Dysfunctional Conflict

(1) Diagnose functional versus dysfunctional conflict.

Not all conflict is bad. In fact, some types of conflict encourage new solutions to problems and enhance creativity in the organization. In these cases, managers will want to encourage the conflicts. Thus, the key to conflict management is to stimulate functional conflict and prevent or resolve dysfunctional conflict. The difficulty, however, is distinguishing between dysfunctional and functional conflicts. The consequences of conflict can be positive or negative, as shown in Table 13.1.

Functional conflict is a healthy, constructive disagreement between two or more people. Functional conflict can produce new ideas, learning, and growth among individuals. When individuals engage in constructive conflict, they develop a better awareness of themselves and others. In addition, functional conflict can improve working relationships; when two parties work through their disagreements, they feel they have accomplished something together. By releasing tensions and solving problems in working together, morale is improved.[7] Functional conflict can lead to innovation and positive change for the organization.[8] Because it tends to encourage creativity among individuals, this positive form of conflict can translate into increased productivity.[9] A key to recognizing functional conflict is that it is often cognitive in origin; that is, it arises from someone challenging old policies or thinking of new ways to approach problems.

conflict

Any situation in which incompatible goals, attitudes, emotions, or behaviors lead to disagreement or opposition for two or more parties.

functional conflict

A healthy, constructive disagreement between two or more people.

Positive Consequences	Negative Consequences
• Leads to new ideas	• Diverts energy from work
• Stimulates creativity	• Threatens psychological well-being
• Motivates change	• Wastes resources
• Promotes organizational vitality	• Creates a negative climate
• Helps individuals and groups establish identities	• Breaks down group cohesion
• Serves as a safety valve to indicate problems	• Can increase hostility and aggressive behaviors

Dysfunctional conflict is an unhealthy, destructive disagreement between two or more people. Its danger is that it shifts the focus from the work to be done to the conflict itself and the parties involved. Excessive conflict drains energy that could be used more productively. A key to recognizing a dysfunctional conflict is that its origin is often emotional or behavioral. Disagreements that involve personalized anger and resentment directed at specific individuals rather than specific ideas are dysfunctional.[10] Individuals involved in dysfunctional conflict tend to act before thinking, and they often rely on threats, deception, and verbal abuse to communicate. In dysfunctional conflict, the losses to both parties may exceed any potential gain from the conflict.

Diagnosing conflict as good or bad is not easy. The manager must look at the issue, the context of the conflict, and the parties involved. The following questions can be used to diagnose the nature of the conflict a manager faces:

> Are the parties approaching the conflict from a hostile standpoint?

> Is the outcome likely to be a negative one for the organization?

> Do the potential losses of the parties exceed any potential gains?

> Is energy being diverted from goal accomplishment?

If the majority of the answers to these questions are yes, the conflict is probably dysfunctional. Once the manager has diagnosed the type of conflict, he or she can work either to resolve it (if it is dysfunctional) or to stimulate it (if it is functional).

It is easy to make mistakes in diagnosing conflicts. Sometimes task conflict, which is functional, can be misattributed as being personal, and dysfunctional conflict can follow. Developing trust within the work group can keep this misattribution from occurring.[11] A study of group effectiveness found that American decision-making groups made up of friends were able to more openly engage in disagreement than groups made up of strangers, allowing the friends' groups to make more effective decisions. When group members (friends) felt comfortable and trusting enough to express conflicting opinions, optimal performance resulted. But similar groups made up of Chinese friends and strangers exhibited both high levels of conflict *and* low levels of performance, suggesting that open disagreement in these groups was not helpful. This finding should serve as a cautionary tale for managers trying to apply one country's management style and techniques in another cultural setting.[12]

One occasion when managers should work to stimulate conflict is when they suspect their group is suffering from groupthink, discussed in Chapter 10.[13] When a group fails to consider alternative solutions and becomes stagnant in its thinking, it might benefit from healthy disagreements. Teams exhibiting symptoms of groupthink should be encouraged to consider creative problem solving and should

dysfunctional conflict

An unhealthy, destructive disagreement between two or more people.

appoint a devil's advocate to point out opposing perspectives. These actions can help stimulate constructive conflict in a group.

CAUSES OF CONFLICT IN ORGANIZATIONS

 Identify the causes of conflict in organizations.

Conflict is pervasive in organizations. To manage it effectively, managers should understand the many sources of conflict. They can be classified into two broad categories: structural factors, which stem from the nature of the organization and the way in which work is organized, and personal factors, which arise from differences among individuals. Figure 13.1 summarizes the causes of conflict within each category.

Structural Factors

The causes of conflict related to the organization's structure include specialization, interdependence, common resources, goal differences, authority relationships, status inconsistencies, and jurisdictional ambiguities.

Specialization When jobs are highly specialized, employees become experts at certain tasks. For example, one software company has one specialist for databases, one for statistical packages, and another for expert systems. Highly specialized jobs can lead to conflict, because people often have little awareness of the tasks that others perform.

A classic conflict of specialization may occur between salespeople and engineers. Engineers are technical specialists responsible for product design and quality. Salespeople are marketing experts and liaisons with customers. Salespeople are often accused of making delivery promises to customers that engineers cannot keep because the sales force lacks the technical knowledge necessary to develop realistic delivery deadlines.

Interdependence Work that is interdependent requires groups or individuals to depend on one another to accomplish goals.[14] Depending on other people to get work done is fine when the process works smoothly. When there is a problem, however, it becomes very easy to blame the other party, and conflict escalates. In a garment manufacturing plant, for example, when the fabric cutters get behind in their work, the workers who sew the garments are delayed as well. Considerable frustration may result when the workers at the sewing machines feel their efforts are being blocked by the cutters' slow pace, and their pay is affected because they are paid piece-rate.

FIGURE 13.1   Causes of Conflict in Organizations

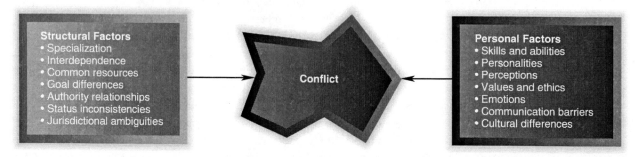

Common Resources Any time multiple parties must share resources, there is potential for conflict.[15] This potential is enhanced when the shared resources become scarce. For example, managers often share secretarial support. Not uncommonly, one secretary supports ten or more managers, each of whom believes his or her work is most important. This puts pressure on the secretary and leads to potential conflicts in prioritizing and scheduling work.

Goal Differences When work groups have different goals, these goals may be incompatible. For example, in one cable television company, the salesperson's goal was to sell as many new installations as possible. This created problems for the service department, because its goal was timely installations. With increasing sales, the service department's workload became backed up, and orders were delayed. Often these types of conflicts occur because individuals do not have knowledge of another department's objectives.

Authority Relationships A traditional boss–employee relationship is hierarchical in nature with a boss who is superior to the employee. For many employees, such a relationship is not a comfortable one, because another individual has the right to tell them what to do. Some people resent authority more than others, and obviously this creates conflicts. In addition, some bosses are more autocratic than others; this compounds the potential for conflict in the relationship. As organizations move toward the team approach and empowerment, there should be less potential for conflict from authority relationships.

Status Inconsistencies Some organizations have a strong status difference between management and nonmanagement workers. Managers may enjoy privileges—such as flexible schedules, reserved parking spaces, and longer lunch hours—that are not available to nonmanagement employees. This may result in resentment and conflict.

Jurisdictional Ambiguities Have you ever telephoned a company with a problem and had your call transferred through several different people and departments? This situation illustrates *jurisdictional ambiguity*—that is, unclear lines of responsibility within an organization.[16] The classic situation here involves the hardware/software dilemma. You call the company that made your computer, and they inform you that the problem is caused by the software. You call the software division, and they tell you it's the hardware . . . you get the idea.

The factors just discussed are structural in that they arise from the ways in which work is organized. Other conflicts come from differences among individuals.

Personal Factors

The causes of conflict that arise from individual differences include skills and abilities, personalities, perceptions, values and ethics, emotions, communication barriers, and cultural differences.

Skills and Abilities The workforce is composed of individuals with varying levels of skills and ability. Diversity in skills and abilities may be positive for the organization, but it also holds potential for conflict, especially when jobs are interdependent. Experienced, competent workers may find it difficult to work alongside new and unskilled recruits. Workers can become resentful when their new boss, fresh from college, knows a lot about managing people but is unfamiliar with the technology with which they are working.

jurisdictional ambiguity
The presence of unclear lines of responsibility within an organization.

Personalities Individuals do not leave their personalities at the doorstep when they enter the workplace. Personality conflicts are realities in organizations. To expect that you will like all of your coworkers, or vice versa, may be naive.

One personality trait that many people find difficult to deal with is abrasiveness.[17] An abrasive person ignores the interpersonal aspects of work and the feelings of colleagues. Abrasive individuals are often achievement oriented and hardworking, but their perfectionist, critical style often leaves others feeling unimportant. This style creates stress and strain for those around the abrasive person.[18]

Perceptions Differences in perception can also lead to conflict. For example, managers and workers may not have a shared perception of what motivates people. In this case, the reward system can create conflicts if managers provide what they think employees want rather than what employees really want.

Values and Ethics Differences in values and ethics can be sources of disagreement. Older workers, for example, value company loyalty and probably would not take a sick day when they were not really ill. Younger workers, valuing mobility, like the concept of "mental health days," or calling in sick to get away from work. This may not be true for all workers, but it illustrates that differences in values can lead to conflict.

Most people have their own sets of values and ethics. The extent to which they apply these ethics in the workplace varies. Some people have a strong desire for approval from others and will work to meet others' ethical standards. Some people are relatively unconcerned about approval from others and strongly apply their own ethical standards. Still others operate seemingly without regard to ethics or values.[19] When conflicts about ethics or values do arise, heated disagreement is common because of the personal nature of the differences.

Emotions The emotions of others can be a source of conflict in the workplace. Problems at home often spill over into the work arena, and the related moods can be hard for others to deal with.

Conflict by its nature is an emotional interaction,[20] and the emotions of the parties involved in conflict play a pivotal role in how they perceive the negotiation and respond to one another. In fact, emotions are now considered critical elements of any negotiation that must be included in any examination of the process and how it unfolds.[21]

One important research finding has been that emotion can play a problematic role in negotiations. In particular, when negotiators begin to act based on emotions rather than on cognitions, they are much more likely to reach an impasse.[22]

Communication Barriers Communication barriers such as physical separation and language can create distortions in messages, and these can lead to conflict. Another communication barrier is value judgment, in which a listener assigns a worth to a message before it is received. For example, suppose a team member is a chronic complainer. When this individual enters the manager's office, the manager is likely to devalue the message before it is even delivered. Conflict can then emerge.

Cultural Differences Although cultural differences are assets in organizations, sometimes they can be seen as sources of conflict. Often, these conflicts stem from a lack of understanding of another culture. In one MBA class, for example, Indian students were horrified when American students challenged the professor. Meanwhile, the American students thought the students from India were too passive. Subsequent discussions revealed that professors in India expected to be treated deferentially and with great respect. While students might challenge an idea vigorously, they would rarely challenge the professor. Diversity training that emphasizes education on cultural differences can make great strides in preventing misunderstandings.

GLOBALIZATION AND CONFLICT

Large transnational corporations employ many different ethnic and cultural groups. In these multiethnic corporations, the widely differing cultures represent vast differences among individuals, so the potential for conflict increases.[23] As indicated in Chapter 2, Hofstede has identified five dimensions along which cultural differences may emerge: individualism/collectivism, power distance, uncertainty avoidance, masculinity/femininity, and long-term/short-term orientation.[24] These cultural differences have many implications for conflict management in organizations.

Individualism means that people believe that their individual interests take priority over society's interests. Collectivism, in contrast, means that people put the good of the group first. For example, the United States is a highly individualistic culture, whereas Japan is a very collectivist culture. The individualism/collectivism dimension of cultural differences strongly influences conflict management behavior. People from collectivist cultures tend to display a more cooperative approach to managing conflict.[25]

Hofstede's second dimension of cultural differences is power distance. In cultures with high power distance, individuals accept that people in organizations have varying levels of power. In contrast, in cultures with low power distance, individuals do not automatically respect those in positions of authority. For example, the United States is a country of low power distance, whereas Brazil is a country with a high power distance. Differences in power distance can lead to conflict. Imagine a U.S. employee managed by a Brazilian supervisor who expects deferential behavior. The supervisor would expect automatic respect based on legitimate power. When this respect is not given, conflict would arise.

Uncertainty avoidance also varies by culture. In the United States, employees can tolerate high levels of uncertainty, whereas employees in Israel tend to prefer certainty in their work settings. A U.S.-based multinational firm might run into conflicts operating in Israel. Suppose such a firm is installing a new technology. Its expatriate workers from the United States would tolerate the uncertainty of the technological transition better than would their Israeli coworkers, and this might lead to conflicts among the employees.

Masculinity versus femininity illustrates the contrast between preferences for assertiveness and material goods versus preferences for human capital and quality of life. The United States is a masculine society, whereas Sweden is considered a feminine society. Adjustment to the assertive interpersonal style of U.S. workers may be difficult for Swedish coworkers.

Conflicts can also arise between cultures that vary in their time orientation of values. China, for example, has a long-term orientation; the Chinese prefer values that focus on the future, such as saving and persistence. The United States and Russia, in contrast, have short-term orientations. These cultures emphasize values in the past and present, such as respect for tradition and fulfillment of social obligations. Conflicts can arise when managers fail to understand the nature of differences in values.

An organization whose workforce consists of multiple ethnicities and cultures holds potential for many types of conflict because of the sheer volume of individual differences among workers. The key to managing conflict in a multicultural workforce is understanding cultural differences and appreciating their value.

FORMS OF CONFLICT IN ORGANIZATIONS

(3) Identify the different forms of conflict.

Conflict can take on any of several different forms in an organization, including interorganizational, intergroup, intragroup, interpersonal, and intrapersonal conflicts. It is important to note that the prefix *inter* means "between," whereas the prefix *intra* means "within."

Interorganizational Conflict

Conflict that occurs between two or more organizations is called *interorganizational conflict*. Competition can heighten interorganizational conflict. Corporate take-overs, mergers, and acquisitions can also produce interorganizational conflict. What about the interorganizational conflict between major league baseball's players' union and management, which is sometimes characterized as a battle between millionaires and multimillionaires. The players regularly go on strike to extract more of the profits from management, while management cries that it is not making a dime.

Conflicts among organizations abound. Some of these conflicts can be functional, as when firms improve the quality of their products and services in the spirit of healthy competition. Other interorganizational conflicts can have dysfunctional results.

Intergroup Conflict

When conflict occurs between groups or teams, it is known as *intergroup conflict*. Conflict between groups can have positive effects within each group, such as increased group cohesiveness, increased focus on tasks, and increased loyalty to the group. There are, however, negative consequences as well. Groups in conflict tend to develop an "us against them" mentality whereby each sees the other team as the enemy, becomes more hostile, and decreases its communication with the other group. Groups are even more competitive and less cooperative than individuals. The inevitable outcome is that one group gains and the other group loses.[26]

Competition between groups must be managed carefully so that it does not escalate into dysfunctional conflict. Research has shown that when groups compete for a goal that only one group can achieve, negative consequences like territoriality, aggression, and prejudice toward the other group can result.[27] Managers should encourage and reward cooperative behaviors across groups. Some effective ways of doing this include modifying performance appraisals to include assessing intergroup behavior and using an external supervisor's evaluation of intergroup behavior. Group members will be more likely to help other groups when they know that the other group's supervisor will be evaluating their behavior, and that they will be rewarded for cooperation.[28] In addition, managers should encourage social interactions across groups so that trust can be developed. Trust allows individuals to exchange ideas and resources with members of other groups and results in innovation when members of different groups cooperate.[29] Conflict often results when older employees fear that younger new-hires may take over their jobs. Social interaction can help reduce these perceived threats, creating trust and reducing the intergroup conflict in the process.[30] An emerging challenge identified by research in conflict management points at the intergenerational conflict brought about by the diversity in age in the U.S. workforce as discussed in Chapter 2. This type of intergenerational conflict can stem from the design of employee benefit packages that might appeal more to one age group than another. Organizations should design flexible employee benefit systems that

interorganizational conflict
Conflict that occurs between two or more organizations.

intergroup conflict
Conflict that occurs between groups or teams in an organization.

The Effects of Conflict on Trust in Self-Managed Teams

Task-focused conflict occurs when group members cannot agree on ideas, opinions, and decisions about group goal achievement. On the other hand, relationship conflict is based on interpersonal conflict driven by incompatibilities, and it shows up as annoyance, tension in the group, and other such behaviors.

One research study investigated the effects of task and relationship conflict on trust among team members. The participants in the study were MBA students who were organized as self-managed teams and worked together on a variety of projects and case simulations across eight courses in a four-month period. Each team was constructed to maximize diversity (gender, cultural, and functional background) and had total discretion in how they completed assigned tasks.

The results from this study indicated that relationship conflict reduced trust among team members. Reduced trust levels led to less individual autonomy.

Both types of conflict reduced the team members' interdependence on each other. Most importantly, this study revealed that high levels of each form of conflict led to lower team performance.

In summary, this research raises several interesting implications for the management of conflict in self-managed teams. One prescription is that perhaps organizations can impose restrictions on the structural factors in teams so that individual autonomy and team interdependence are preserved. Another prescription is that self-managed teams should be coached on prevention of conflict and how to implement resolution strategies. Otherwise, self-managed teams can fall prey to dysfunctional behaviors that hurt team performance.

SOURCE: C. W. Langfred, "The Downside of Self-Management: A Longitudinal Study of Conflict on Trust, Autonomy, and Task Interdependence in Self-Managing Teams," *Academy of Management Journal* 50 (4) (2007): 885–900.

have a broader appeal to a diverse age group to curtail this type of intergenerational conflict.[31]

Intragroup Conflict

Conflict that occurs within groups or teams is called *intragroup conflict*. Some conflict within a group is functional. It can help the group avoid groupthink, as we discussed in Chapter 10. Furthermore, recall that self-managed teams have a high degree of decision-making and implementation authority. One recent study reported in the Science feature above describes how conflict within a self-managed team can change its structure and lead to dysfunctional behaviors.

Even the newest teams, virtual teams, are not immune to conflict. The nuances and subtleties of face-to-face communication are often lacking in these teams, and misunderstandings can result. To avoid dysfunctional conflicts, virtual teams should make sure their tasks fit their methods of interacting. Complex strategic decisions may require face-to-face meetings rather than e-mails or threaded discussions. Face-to-face and telephone interactions early on can eliminate later conflicts and allow virtual teams to move on to use electronic communication because trust has been developed.[32]

Teams can experience many types of conflict. Using You 13.1, you can assess the types of conflict in a team you belong to, as well as design ways to manage those conflicts.

Interpersonal Conflict

Conflict between two or more people is *interpersonal conflict*. Conflict between people can arise from many individual differences, including personalities, attitudes, values, perceptions, and the other differences we discussed in Chapters 3 and 4. Later in this chapter, we look at defense mechanisms that individuals exhibit in interpersonal conflict and at ways to cope with difficult people.

intragroup conflict
Conflict that occurs within groups or teams.

interpersonal conflict
Conflict that occurs between two or more individuals.

Assess Your Team's Conflict

Think of a team you're a member of or one you were part of in the past. Answer the following eight questions regarding that team.

1. How much emotional tension was there in your team?

No tension				Lots of tension
1	2	3	4	5

2. How much conflict of ideas was there in your team?

No idea conflict				Lots of idea conflict
1	2	3	4	5

3. How often did people get angry while working in your team?

Never				Often
1	2	3	4	5

4. How different were your views on the content of your project?

Very similar views				Very different views
1	2	3	4	5

5. How much were personality clashes evident in your team?

No clashes evident				Personality clashes very evident
1	2	3	4	5

6. How much did you talk through disagreements about your team projects?

Never talked through disagreements				Always talked through disagreements
1	2	3	4	5

7. How much interpersonal friction was there in your team?

No friction				Lots of friction
1	2	3	4	5

8. How much disagreement was there about task procedure in your team?

No disagreement about procedure				Lots of disagreement about procedure
1	2	3	4	5

Total for items 2, 4, 6, and 8 = _____ indicating task conflict.

Total for items 1, 3, 5, and 7 = _____ indicating relationship conflict.

- Did your team experience higher relationship or task conflict?
- What actions can you take to better manage task conflict? Relationship conflict?
- Was there an absence of both, or either, types of conflict in your team? What does this indicate?

SOURCE: Adapted from K. Jehn, "A Multimethod Examination of the Benefits and Detriments of Intragroup Conflict," *Administrative Science Quarterly* 40 (1995): 256–282.

Advances in information technology, which allow employees to use office communications after hours, is associated with increased work-life conflict.

© DIGITAL RAILROAD

Intrapersonal Conflict

When conflict occurs within an individual, it is called *intrapersonal conflict*. There are several types of intrapersonal conflict, including interrole, intrarole, and person–role conflicts. A role is a set of expectations placed on an individual by others.[33] The person occupying the focal role is the role incumbent, and the individuals who place expectations on the person are role senders. Figure 13.2 depicts a set of role relationships.

Interrole conflict occurs when a person experiences conflict among the multiple roles in his or her life. One interrole conflict that many employees experience is work/home conflict, in which their role as worker clashes with their role as spouse or parent.[34] Work/home conflict has become even more common

FIGURE 13.2 An Organization Member's Role Set

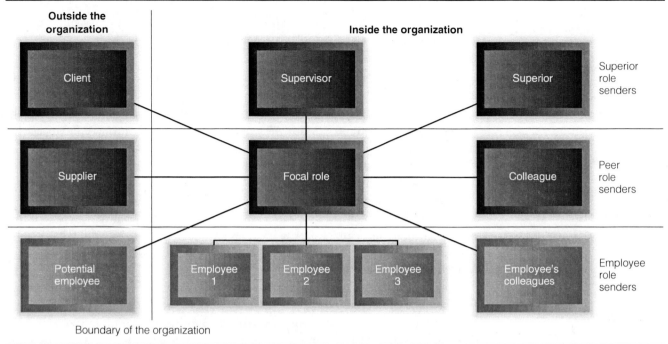

SOURCE: J. C. Quick, J. D. Quick, D. L. Nelson, and J. J. Hurrell, Jr., *Preventive Stress Management in Organizations*, 1997. Copyright © 1997 by the American Psychological Association. Reprinted with permission.

with the rise of work-at-home professionals and telecommuting because the home becomes the office, blurring the boundary between work and family life.[35] Recently, organizations are leveraging their use of information technology to gain a competitive edge. This has translated into ambitious and highly involved employees using office communications (for example, voice mail, e-mail, etc.) even after-hours. Such after-hours communication usage is associated with increased work-life conflict as reported by the employee and a significant other.[36]

Intrarole conflict is conflict within a single role. It often arises when a person receives conflicting messages from role senders about how to perform a certain role. Suppose a manager receives counsel from her department head that she needs to socialize less with the nonmanagement employees. She also is told by her project manager that she needs to be a better team member, and that she can accomplish this by socializing more with the other nonmanagement team members. This situation is one of intrarole conflict.

Person–role conflict occurs when an individual in a particular role is expected to perform behaviors that clash with his or her values.[37] Salespeople, for example, may be required to offer the most expensive item in the sales line first to the customer, even when it is apparent that the customer does not want or cannot afford the item. A computer salesman may be required to offer a large, elaborate system to a student he knows is on a tight budget. This may conflict with the salesman's values, and he may experience person–role conflict.

Intrapersonal conflicts can have positive consequences. Often, professional responsibilities clash with deeply held values. A budget shortfall may force you to lay off a loyal, hardworking employee. Your daughter may have a piano recital on the same day your largest client is scheduled to be in town visiting the office. In such conflicts, we often have to choose between right and right; that is, there's no correct response. These may be thought of as *defining moments* that challenge us to choose between two or more things in which we believe.[38] Character is formed in defining

intrapersonal conflict

Conflict that occurs within an individual.

interrole conflict

A person's experience of conflict among the multiple roles in his or her life.

intrarole conflict

Conflict that occurs within a single role, such as when a person receives conflicting messages from role senders about how to perform a certain role.

person–role conflict

Conflict that occurs when an individual is expected to perform behaviors in a certain role that conflict with his or her personal values.

moments because they cause us to shape our identities. They help us crystallize our values and serve as opportunities for personal growth.

INTRAPERSONAL CONFLICT

Intrapersonal conflict can be managed with careful self-analysis and diagnosis of the situation. Three actions in particular can help prevent or resolve intrapersonal conflicts.

First, when seeking a new job, you should find out as much as possible about the values of the organization.[39] Many person–role conflicts center around differences between the organization's values and the individual's values. Research has shown that when there is a good fit between the values of the individual and the organization, the individual is more satisfied and committed and is less likely to leave the organization.[40]

Second, to manage intrarole or interrole conflicts, role analysis is a good tool.[41] In role analysis, the individual asks the various role senders what they expect of him or her. The outcomes are clearer work roles and the reduction of conflict and ambiguity.[42] Role analysis is a simple tool that clarifies the expectations of both parties in a relationship and reduces the potential for conflict within a role or between roles.

Third, political skills can help buffer the negative effects of stress that stem from role conflicts. Effective politicians, as we discussed in Chapter 11, can negotiate role expectations when conflicts occur. All these forms of conflict can be managed. An understanding of the many forms is a first step. The next section focuses more extensively on interpersonal conflict because of its pervasiveness in organizations.

INTERPERSONAL CONFLICT

When a conflict occurs between two or more people, it is known as interpersonal conflict. To manage interpersonal conflict, it is helpful to understand power networks in organizations, defense mechanisms exhibited by individuals, and ways to cope with difficult people.

Power Networks

According to Mastenbroek, individuals in organizations are organized in three basic types of power networks.[43] Based on these power relationships, certain kinds of conflict tend to emerge. Figure 13.3 illustrates three basic kinds of power relationships in organizations.

The first relationship is equal versus equal, in which there is a horizontal balance of power among the parties. An example of this type of relationship would be a conflict between individuals from two different project teams. The behavioral tendency is toward suboptimization; that is, the focus is on a win–lose approach to problems, and each party tries to maximize its power at the expense of the other party. Conflict within this type of network can lead to depression, low self-esteem, and other distress symptoms. Interventions like improving coordination between the parties and working toward common interests can help manage these conflicts.

The second power network is high versus low, or a powerful versus a less powerful relationship. Conflicts that emerge here take the basic form of the powerful individuals trying to control others, with the less powerful people trying to become more autonomous. Conflict in this network can lead to job dissatisfaction, low organizational commitment, and turnover.[44] Organizations typically respond to these conflicts by tightening the rules. However, the more successful ways of managing these conflicts are to try a different style of leadership, such as a coaching and counseling style, or to change the structure to a more decentralized one.

FIGURE 13.3 Power Relationships in Organizations

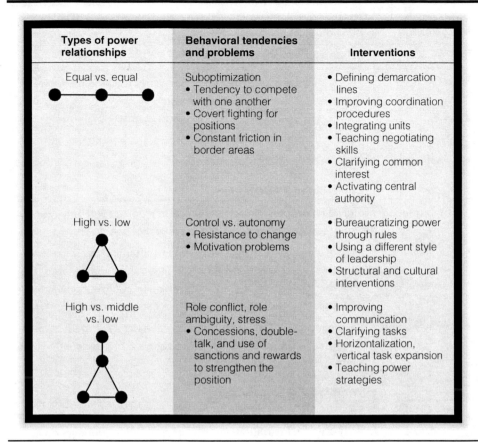

Types of power relationships	Behavioral tendencies and problems	Interventions
Equal vs. equal	Suboptimization • Tendency to compete with one another • Covert fighting for positions • Constant friction in border areas	• Defining demarcation lines • Improving coordination procedures • Integrating units • Teaching negotiating skills • Clarifying common interest • Activating central authority
High vs. low	Control vs. autonomy • Resistance to change • Motivation problems	• Bureaucratizing power through rules • Using a different style of leadership • Structural and cultural interventions
High vs. middle vs. low	Role conflict, role ambiguity, stress • Concessions, double-talk, and use of sanctions and rewards to strengthen the position	• Improving communication • Clarifying tasks • Horizontalization, vertical task expansion • Teaching power strategies

SOURCE: W. F. G. Mastenbroek, *Conflict Management and Organization Development*, 1987. Copyright John Wiley & Sons Limited. Reproduced with permission.

The third power network is high versus middle versus low. This power network illustrates the classic conflicts felt by middle managers. Two particular conflicts are evident for middle managers: role conflict, in which conflicting expectations are placed on the manager from bosses and employees, and role ambiguity, in which the expectations of the boss are unclear. Improved communication among all parties can reduce role conflict and ambiguity. In addition, middle managers can benefit from training in positive ways to influence others.

Knowing the typical kinds of conflicts that arise in various kinds of relationships can help a manager diagnose conflicts and devise appropriate ways to manage them.

Defense Mechanisms

When individuals are involved in conflict with another human being, frustration often results.[45] Conflicts can often arise within the context of a performance appraisal session. Most people do not react well to negative feedback, as was illustrated in a classic study.[46] In this study, when employees were given criticism about their work, over 50 percent of their responses were defensive.

When individuals are frustrated, as they often are in interpersonal conflict, they respond by exhibiting defense mechanisms.[47] Defense mechanisms are common reactions to the frustration that accompanies conflict. Table 13.2 describes several defense mechanisms seen in organizations.

Aggressive mechanisms, such as fixation, displacement, and negativism, are aimed at attacking the source of the conflict. In *fixation,* an individual fixates on

(4) Understand the defense mechanisms that individuals exhibit when they engage in interpersonal conflict.

fixation

An aggressive mechanism in which an individual keeps up a dysfunctional behavior that obviously will not solve the conflict.

TABLE 13.2   Common Defense Mechanisms

Defense Mechanism	Psychological Process
	Aggressive Mechanisms
• Fixation	Person maintains a persistent, nonadjustive reaction even though all the cues indicate the behavior will not cope with the problem.
• Displacement	Individual redirects pent-up emotions toward persons, ideas, or objects other than the primary source of the emotion.
• Negativism	Person uses active or passive resistance, operating unconsciously.
	Compromise Mechanisms
• Compensation	Individual devotes himself or herself to a pursuit with increased vigor to make up for some feeling of real or imagined inadequacy.
• Identification	Individual enhances own self-esteem by patterning behavior after another's, frequently also internalizing the values and beliefs of the other person; also vicariously shares the glories or suffering in the disappointments of other individuals or groups.
• Rationalization	Person justifies inconsistent or undesirable behavior, beliefs, statements, and motivations by providing acceptable explanations for them.
	Withdrawal Mechanisms
• Flight or withdrawal	Through either physical or psychological means, person leaves the field in which frustration, anxiety, or conflict is experienced.
• Conversion	Emotional conflicts are expressed in muscular, sensory, or bodily symptoms of disability, malfunctioning, or pain.
• Fantasy	Person daydreams or uses other forms of imaginative activity to obtain an escape from reality and obtain imagined satisfactions.

SOURCE: Timothy W. Costello and Sheldon S. Zalkind, adapted table from "Psychology in Administration: A Research Orientation" from *Journal of Conflict Resolution* III 1959, pp. 148–149. Reprinted by permission of Sage Publications, Inc.

displacement

An aggressive mechanism in which an individual directs his or her anger toward someone who is not the source of the conflict.

negativism

An aggressive mechanism in which a person responds with pessimism to any attempt at solving a problem.

compensation

A compromise mechanism in which an individual attempts to make up for a negative situation by devoting himself or herself to another pursuit with increased vigor.

identification

A compromise mechanism whereby an individual patterns his or her behavior after another's.

the conflict, or keeps up a dysfunctional behavior that obviously will not solve the conflict. An example of fixation occurred in a university, where a faculty member became embroiled in a battle with the dean because the faculty member felt he had not received a large enough salary increase. He persisted in writing angry letters to the dean, whose hands were tied because of a low budget allocation to the college. *Displacement* means directing anger toward someone who is not the source of the conflict. For example, a manager may respond harshly to an employee after a telephone confrontation with an angry customer. Another aggressive defense mechanism is *negativism,* which is active or passive resistance. Negativism is illustrated by a manager who, when appointed to a committee on which she did not want to serve, made negative comments throughout the meeting.

Compromise mechanisms, such as compensation, identification, and rationalization, are used by individuals to make the best of a conflict situation. *Compensation* occurs when an individual tries to make up for an inadequacy by putting increased energy into another activity. Compensation can be seen when a person makes up for a bad relationship at home by spending more time at the office. *Identification* occurs when one individual patterns his or her behavior after another's. One supervisor at a construction firm, not wanting to acknowledge consciously that she was not likely to be promoted, mimicked the behavior of her boss, even going so far as to buy a car just like the boss's. *Rationalization* is trying to justify one's behavior by constructing bogus reasons for it. Employees may rationalize unethical behavior like padding their expense accounts because "everyone else does it."

Withdrawal mechanisms are exhibited when frustrated individuals try to flee from a conflict using either physical or psychological means. Flight, withdrawal, conversion, and fantasy are examples of withdrawal mechanisms. Physically escaping a conflict is *flight*. When an employee takes a day off after a blowup with the boss is an example. *Withdrawal* may take the form of emotionally leaving a conflict, such as exhibiting an "I don't care anymore" attitude. *Conversion* is a process whereby emotional conflicts are expressed in physical symptoms. Most of us have experienced the conversion reaction of a headache following an emotional exchange with another person. *Fantasy* is an escape by daydreaming. In the Internet age, fantasy as an escape mechanism has found new meaning. A study conducted by International Data Corporation (IDC) showed that 30 to 40 percent of all Internet surfing at work is nonwork-related and that more than 70 percent of companies have had sex sites accessed from their networks, suggesting that employees' minds aren't always focused on their jobs.[48]

When employees exhibit withdrawal mechanisms, they often fake it by pretending to agree with their bosses or coworkers in order to avoid facing an immediate conflict. Many employees fake it because the firm informally rewards agreement and punishes dissent. The long-term consequence of withdrawal and faking it is emotional distress for the employee.[49]

Knowledge of these defense mechanisms can be extremely beneficial to a manager. By understanding the ways in which people typically react to interpersonal conflict, managers can be prepared for employees' reactions and help them uncover their feelings about a conflict.

CONFLICT MANAGEMENT STRATEGIES AND TECHNIQUES

The overall approach (or strategy) you use in a conflict is important in determining whether the conflict will have a positive or negative outcome.

These overall strategies are competitive versus cooperative strategies. Table 13.3 depicts the two strategies and four different conflict scenarios. The competitive strategy is founded on assumptions of win–lose and entails dishonest communication, mistrust, and a rigid position from both parties.[50] The cooperative strategy is founded on different assumptions: the potential for win–win outcomes, honest communication, trust, openness to risk and vulnerability, and the notion that the whole may be greater than the sum of the parts.

To illustrate the importance of the overall strategy, consider the case of two groups competing for scarce resources. Suppose budget cuts have to be made at an

rationalization

A compromise mechanism characterized by trying to justify one's behavior by constructing bogus reasons for it.

flight/withdrawal

A withdrawal mechanism that entails physically escaping a conflict (flight) or psychologically escaping (withdrawal).

conversion

A withdrawal mechanism in which emotional conflicts are expressed in physical symptoms.

fantasy

A withdrawal mechanism that provides an escape from a conflict through daydreaming.

TABLE 13.3 Win–Lose versus Win–Win Strategies

Strategy	Department A	Department B	Organization
Competitive	Lose	Lose	Lose
	Lose	Win	Lose
	Win	Lose	Lose
Cooperative	Win–	Win–	Win

insurance company. The claims manager argues that the sales training staff should be cut, because agents are fully trained. The sales training manager argues that claims personnel should be cut, because the company is processing fewer claims. This could turn into a dysfunctional brawl, with both sides refusing to give ground. This would constitute a win–lose, lose–win, or lose–lose scenario. Personnel cuts could be made in only one department, or in both departments. In all three cases, with the competitive approach the organization winds up in a losing position.

Even in such intense conflicts as those over scarce resources, a win–win strategy can lead to an overall win for the organization. In fact, conflicts over scarce resources can be productive if the parties have cooperative goals—a strategy that seeks a winning solution for both parties. To achieve a win–win outcome, the conflict must be approached with open-minded discussion of opposing views. Through open-minded discussion, both parties integrate views and create new solutions that facilitate productivity and strengthen their relationship; the result is feelings of unity rather than separation.[51]

In the example of the conflict between the claims manager and the sales training manager, open-minded discussion might reveal that there are ways to achieve budget cuts without cutting personnel. Sales support might surrender part of its travel budget, and claims might cut out overtime. This represents a win–win situation for the company. The budget has been reduced, and relationships between the two departments have been preserved. Both parties have given up something (note the "win–" in Table 13.3), but the conflict has been resolved with a positive outcome.

You can see the importance of the broad strategy used to approach a conflict. We now move from broad strategies to more specific techniques.

Ineffective Techniques

(5) Describe effective and ineffective techniques for managing conflict.

There are many specific techniques for dealing with conflict. Before turning to techniques that work, it should be recognized that some actions commonly taken in organizations to deal with conflict are not effective.[52]

Nonaction is doing nothing in hopes that the conflict will disappear. Generally, this is not a good technique, because most conflicts do not go away, and the individuals involved in the conflict react with frustration.

Secrecy, or trying to keep a conflict out of view of most people, only creates suspicion. An example is an organizational policy of pay secrecy. In some organizations, discussion of salary is grounds for dismissal. When this is the case, employees suspect that the company has something to hide. In The Real World 13.1, you can read about the drama between Hewlett-Packard and a former employee. This feature illustrates some of the potential harmful effects of secrecy. Secrecy may result in surreptitious political activity by employees who hope to uncover the secret![53]

Administrative orbiting is delaying action on a conflict by buying time, usually by telling the individuals involved that the problem is being worked on or that the boss is still thinking about the issue. Like nonaction, this technique leads to frustration and resentment.

Due process nonaction is a procedure set up to address conflicts that is so costly, time-consuming, or personally risky that no one will use it. Some companies' sexual harassment policies are examples of this technique. To file a sexual harassment complaint, detailed paperwork is required, the accuser must go through appropriate channels, and the accuser risks being branded a troublemaker. Thus, the company has a procedure for handling complaints (due process), but no one uses it (nonaction).

Character assassination is an attempt to label or discredit an opponent. Character assassination can backfire and make the individual who uses it appear dishonest

nonaction

Doing nothing in hopes that a conflict will disappear.

secrecy

Attempting to hide a conflict or an issue that has the potential to create conflict.

administrative orbiting

Delaying action on a conflict by buying time.

due process nonaction

A procedure set up to address conflicts that is so costly, time-consuming, or personally risky that no one will use it.

character assassination

An attempt to label or discredit an opponent.

Karl Kamb versus Hewlett-Packard

Karl Kamb Jr. was one of HP's wonder boys in 2002. In 2003, he made a presentation that convinced former CEO Carly Fiorina that HP should enter the lucrative flat panel television market. Fiorina liked the idea and a few months later, she announced that HP would indeed act on Kamb's suggestion. Just over a year later, Kamb was fired along with ten senior executives. HP sued him for $100 million, alleging he stole trade secrets and company funds to start his own flat panel television business.

In January 2007, Kamb filed a countersuit that was even more dramatic. He claimed that the money that HP was claiming went into his business was actually used to conduct illegal spying on its competitor Dell's upcoming business decisions in the printer market. He claimed that HP knew this money had gone there and even accused HP of pretexting or secretly reviewing his personal phone records.

While the legal decision on this saga as of 2007 is pending, analysts wonder why HP would bother spending so much in court costs in going after a case that might not even help them recover attorney fees if HP did win. HP states that going after past employees who might have violated company trust is a lesson in ethics and integrity and thus is important. The bigger question becomes: Why would a respected company like HP engage in questionable business practices, and why the secrecy?

SOURCE: N. Varchaver, "A Pretext for Revenge," *Fortune* (May 31, 2007), http://money.cnn.com/magazines/fortune/fortune_archive/2007/06/11/100060613/index.htm.

and cruel. It often leads to name-calling and accusations by both parties, both ending up losers in the eyes of those who witness the conflict.

Effective Techniques

Fortunately, there are effective conflict management techniques. These include appealing to superordinate goals, expanding resources, changing personnel, changing structure, and confronting and negotiating.

Superordinate Goals An organizational goal that is more important to both parties in a conflict than their individual or group goals is a *superordinate goal*.[54] Superordinate goals cannot be achieved by an individual or by one group alone. The achievement of these goals requires cooperation by both parties.

One effective technique for resolving conflict is to appeal to a superordinate goal—in effect, to focus the parties on a larger issue on which they both agree. This helps them realize their similarities rather than their differences.

In the conflict between service representatives and cable television installers that was discussed earlier, appealing to a superordinate goal would be an effective technique for resolving the conflict. Both departments can agree that superior customer service is a goal worthy of pursuit and that this goal cannot be achieved unless cables are installed properly and in a timely manner, and customer complaints are handled effectively. Quality service requires that both departments cooperate to achieve the goal.

Expanding Resources One conflict resolution technique is so simple that it may be overlooked. If the conflict's source is scarce resources, providing more resources may be a solution. Of course, managers working with tight budgets may not have this luxury. Nevertheless, it is a technique to be considered. In the example earlier in this chapter, one solution to the conflict among managers over secretarial support would be to hire more secretaries.

superordinate goal

An organizational goal that is more important to both parties in a conflict than their individual or group goals.

Changing Personnel In some cases, long-running severe conflict may be traced to a specific individual. For example, managers with lower levels of emotional intelligence have been demonstrated to have more negative work attitudes, to exhibit less altruistic behavior, and to produce more negative work outcomes. A chronically disgruntled manager who exhibits low EI may not only frustrate his employees but also impede his department's performance. In such cases, transferring or firing an individual may be the best solution, but only after due process.[55]

Changing Structure Another way to resolve a conflict is to change the structure of the organization. One way of accomplishing this is to create an integrator role. An integrator is a liaison between groups with very different interests. In severe conflicts, it may be best that the integrator be a neutral third party.[56] Creating the integrator role is a way of opening dialogue between groups that have difficulty communicating.

Using cross-functional teams is another way of changing the organization's structure to manage conflict. In the old methods of designing new products in organizations, many departments had to contribute, and delays resulted from difficulties in coordinating the activities of the various departments. Using a cross-functional team made up of members from different departments improves coordination and reduces delays by allowing many activities to be performed at the same time rather than sequentially.[57] The team approach allows members from different departments to work together and reduces the potential for conflict. However, recent research also suggests that such functional diversity can lead to slower informational processing in teams due to differences in members' perceptions of what might be required to achieve group goals. When putting together cross-functional teams, organizations should emphasize superordinate goals and train team members on resolving conflict. One such training technique could involve educating individual members in other functional areas so that everyone in the team can have a shared language.[58] In teamwork, it is helpful to break up a big task so that it becomes a collection of smaller, less complex tasks, and to have smaller teams work on the smaller tasks. This helps to reduce conflict, and organizations can potentially improve the performance of the overall team by improving the outcomes in each subteam.[59]

Confronting and Negotiating Some conflicts require confrontation and negotiation between the parties. Both these strategies require skill on the part of the negotiator and careful planning before engaging in negotiations. The process of negotiating involves an open discussion of problem solutions, and the outcome often is an exchange in which both parties work toward a mutually beneficial solution.

Negotiation is a joint process of finding a mutually acceptable solution to a complex conflict. Negotiating is a useful strategy under the following conditions:

> There are two or more parties. Negotiation is primarily an interpersonal or intergroup process.

> There is a conflict of interest between the parties such that what one party wants is not what the other party wants.

> The parties are willing to negotiate because each believes it can use its influence to obtain a better outcome than by simply taking the side of the other party.

> The parties prefer to work together rather than to fight openly, give in, break off contact, or take the dispute to a higher authority.

distributive bargaining
A negotiation approach in which the goals of the parties are in conflict, and each party seeks to maximize its resources.

There are two major negotiating approaches: distributive bargaining and integrative negotiation.[60] *Distributive bargaining* is an approach in which the goals of one party are in direct conflict with the goals of the other party. Resources are limited, and

Deutsche Telekom (DT): When Everyone Wants a Bigger Piece of the Pie

Deutsche Telekom is the largest telecom company in Germany. Recently there was a major dispute between the unionized workforce of DT and management. DT was planning on assigning 50,000 of its employees to work in subsidiary firms as a cost-cutting measure. The move would have resulted in these employees making substantially less money than they were making with DT. In response, the union threatened a strike, and 11,000 employees actually walked off the job in May 2007. Union negotiations leader Lothar Schröder said the strike was entirely due to management's refusal to consider any compromises offered by the union. Ironically, the man that he was up against in these negotiations was CEO René Obermann, whom he had helped into the top slot.

This strike and the impasse between DT and the union were seen as a massive showdown in the telecom industry. Analysts feared that the recovering German economy and the telecom industry in general would feel severe repercussions if the union carried out its strike for a long period. Obermann insisted

A strike between the unionized workforce and management at Deutsche Telekom, a German telecom company, ended only after major stakeholders and the German government got involved.

that the union was just interested in gaining all their demands and did not really care about the future of the company. DT employs about 160,000 employees and was also planning on major cutbacks in the future.

The strike ended after six weeks with major stakeholders and the German government getting involved. The union completely gave in to the demands of management and accepted pay cuts and longer working hours as a part of the settlement. Many analysts speculate that this was an unscrupulous power game as the German government controls 15 percent of DT's stocks. The union called the solution a "compromise" but some observers declared it a complete sellout.

SOURCE: *F. Dohmen, K. Kerbusk,* and *J. Tietz* , "DT Strikes a Battle for the Ages," *Business Week Online* (May 16, 2007), http://www .businessweek.com/globalbiz/content/may2007/gb20070516_ 600514.htm. Editorial Board Statement, "Germany: Union Sells Out Deutsche Telekom Strike—Agrees to Wage Cuts and Longer Working Hours" (June 25, 2007), http://www.wsws.org/ articles/2007/jun2007/tele-j25.shtml.

each party wants to maximize its share of the resources (get its part of the pie). It is a competitive or win–lose approach to negotiations. Sometimes distributive bargaining causes negotiators to focus so much on their differences that they ignore their common ground. In these cases, distributive bargaining can become counterproductive. The reality is, however, that some situations are distributive in nature, particularly when the parties are interdependent. If a negotiator wants to maximize the value of a single deal and is not worried about maintaining a good relationship with the other party, distributive bargaining may be an option. The Real World 13.2 illustrates the effects of such a tactic in one major German telecom company.

In contrast, *integrative negotiation* is an approach in which the parties' goals are not seen as mutually exclusive and in which the focus is on making it possible for both sides to achieve their objectives. Integrative negotiation focuses on the merits of the issues and is a win–win approach. (How can we make the pie bigger?) For integrative negotiation to be successful, certain preconditions must be present. These

integrative negotiation

A negotiation approach that focuses on the merits of the issues and seeks a win–win solution.

include having a common goal, faith in one's own problem-solving abilities, a belief in the validity of the other party's position, motivation to work together, mutual trust, and clear communication.[61]

Cultural differences in negotiation must be acknowledged. Japanese negotiators, for example, when working with American negotiators, tend to see their power as coming from their role (buyer versus seller). Americans, in contrast, view their power as their ability to walk away from the negotiations.[62] Neither culture understands the other very well, and the negotiations can resemble a dance in which one person is waltzing and the other doing a samba. The collectivism–individualism dimension (discussed in Chapter 2) has a great bearing on negotiations. Americans, with their individualism, negotiate from a position of self-interest; Japanese focus on the good of the group. Cross-cultural negotiations can be more effective if you learn as much about other cultures as possible.

Gender may also play a role in negotiation. There appears to be no evidence that men are better negotiators than women or vice versa. The differences lie in how negotiators are treated. Women have historically been discriminated against in terms of the offers made to them in negotiations.[63] Gender stereotypes also affect the negotiating process. Women may be seen as accommodating, conciliatory, and emotional (negatives in negotiations), and men may be seen as assertive, powerful, and convincing (positive for negotiations) in accordance with traditional stereotypes. Sometimes, when women feel they're being stereotyped, they exhibit stereotype reactance, which is a tendency to display behavior inconsistent with (or opposite of) the stereotype. This means they become more assertive and convincing. Alternatively, men may hesitate when they're expected to fulfill the stereotype, fearing that they might not be able to live up to the stereotype.

One way to help men and women avoid stereotyping each other is to promote shared, positive identities between the negotiators. This means recognizing similarities between the two parties; for example, recognizing each other as highly successful professionals. This results in more cooperation because of shared and equal status, as opposed to more competition because of gender stereotypes.[64]

CONFLICT MANAGEMENT STYLES

(6) Understand five styles of conflict management, and diagnose your own preferred style.

Managers have at their disposal a variety of conflict management styles: avoiding, accommodating, competing, compromising, and collaborating. One way of classifying styles of conflict management is to examine the styles' assertiveness (the extent to which you want your goals met) and cooperativeness (the extent to which you want to see the other party's concerns met).[65] Figure 13.4 graphs the five conflict management styles using these two dimensions. Table 13.4 lists appropriate situations for using each conflict management style.

Avoiding

Avoiding is a style low on both assertiveness and cooperativeness. Avoiding is a deliberate decision to take no action on a conflict or to stay out of a conflict situation. In recent times, Airbus, a European manufacturer of aircraft, has faced massive intra-organizational conflict stemming from major expansions that included French, German, Spanish, and British subsidiaries within the same parent company. Power struggles among executives, combined with massive changes in organizational structure, are believed to have led to this type of conflict. Airbus seems to be adopting the avoidance strategy in an effort to let these conflicts subside on their own.[66] Some relationship conflicts, such as those involving political norms and personal tastes, may

FIGURE 13.4   Conflict Management Styles

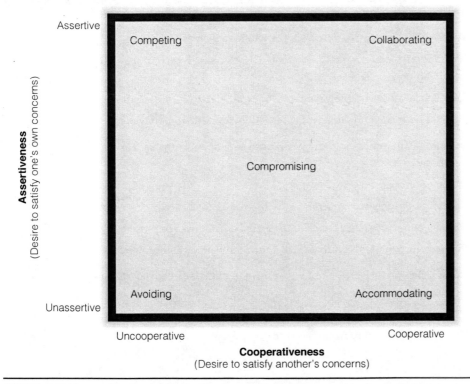

SOURCE: K. W. Thomas, "Conflict and Conflict Management," in M. D. Dunnette, *Handbook of Industrial and Organizational Psychology* (Chicago: Rand McNally, 1976), 900. Used with permission of M. D. Dunnette.

distract team members from their tasks and avoiding may be an appropriate strategy.[67] When the parties are angry and need time to cool down, it may be best to use avoidance. There is a potential danger in using an avoiding style too often, however. Research shows that overuse of this style results in negative evaluations from others in the workplace.[68]

Accommodating

Accommodating is a style in which you are concerned that the other party's goals be met but relatively unconcerned with getting your own way. It is cooperative but unassertive. Appropriate situations for accommodating include times when you find you are wrong, when you want to let the other party have his or her way so that that individual will owe you similar treatment later, or when the relationship is important. Overreliance on accommodating has its dangers. Managers who constantly defer to others may find that others lose respect for them. In addition, accommodating managers may become frustrated because their own needs are never met, and they may lose self-esteem.[69]

Competing

Competing is a style that is very assertive and uncooperative. You want to satisfy your own interests and are willing to do so at the other party's expense. In an emergency or in situations where you know you are right, it may be appropriate to put your foot down. For example, environmentalists forced Shell Oil Company (part of Royal Dutch/Shell Group) to scrap its plans to build a refinery in Delaware after a bitter "To Hell with Shell" campaign.[70] Relying solely on competing strategies is dangerous, though. Managers who do so may become reluctant to admit when they

TABLE 13.4   Uses of Five Styles of Conflict Management

Conflict-Handling Style	Appropriate Situation
Competing	1. When quick, decisive action is vital (e.g., emergencies).
	2. On important issues where unpopular actions need implementing (e.g., cost cutting, enforcing unpopular rules, discipline).
	3. On issues vital to company welfare when you know you are right.
	4. Against people who take advantage of noncompetitive behavior.
Collaborating	1. To find an integrative solution when both sets of concerns are too important to be compromised.
	2. When your objective is to learn.
	3. To merge insights from people with different perspectives.
	4. To gain commitment by incorporating concerns into a consensus.
	5. To work through feelings that have interfered with a relationship.
Compromising	1. When goals are important but not worth the effort or potential disruption of more assertive modes.
	2. When opponents with equal power are committed to mutually exclusive goals.
	3. To achieve temporary settlements to complex issues.
	4. To arrive at expedient solutions under time pressure.
	5. As a backup when collaboration or competition is unsuccessful.
Avoiding	1. When an issue is trivial or more important issues are pressing.
	2. When you perceive no chance of satisfying your concerns.
	3. When potential disruption outweighs the benefits of resolution.
	4. To let people cool down and regain perspective.
	5. When gathering information supersedes immediate decision.
	6. When others can resolve the conflict more effectively.
	7. When issues seem tangential or symptomatic of other issues.
Accommodating	1. When you find you are wrong—to allow a better position to be heard, to learn, and to show your reasonableness.
	2. When issues are more important to others than to yourself—to satisfy others and maintain cooperation.
	3. To build social credits for later issues.
	4. To minimize loss when you are outmatched and losing.
	5. When harmony and stability are especially important.
	6. To allow employees to develop by learning from mistakes.

SOURCE: K. W. Thomas, "Toward Multidimensional Values in Teaching: The Example of Conflict Behaviors," *Academy of Management Review* 2 (1977): 309–325.

are wrong and may find themselves surrounded by people who are afraid to disagree with them. In team settings, it has been noted earlier that task conflict and relationship conflict could occur together although task conflict is seen as functional, whereas relationship conflict is seen as dysfunctional for the team. In a recent study, pairs of participants were exposed to task-based conflict. One of the two members of the pairs was trained on using either the competing conflict handling style or the collaborative style. Results indicated that the competing style led to the most relationship conflict, whereas the collaborative style led to the least relationship conflict after the task conflict was resolved.[71]

Compromising

Compromising style is an intermediate style in both assertiveness and cooperativeness, because each party must give up something to reach a solution to the conflict. Compromises are often made in the final hours of union–management negotiations, when time is of the essence. Compromise may be an effective backup style when efforts toward collaboration are not successful.[72]

It is important to recognize that compromises are not optimal solutions. Compromise means partially surrendering one's position for the sake of coming to terms. Often, when people compromise, they inflate their demands to begin with. The solutions reached may only be temporary, and often compromises do nothing to improve relationships between the parties in the conflict.

Collaborating

Collaborating is a win–win style that is high on both assertiveness and cooperativeness. Working toward collaborating involves an open and thorough discussion of the conflict and arriving at a solution that is satisfactory to both parties. Situations where collaboration may be effective include times when both parties need to be committed to a final solution or when a combination of different perspectives can be formed into a solution. Collaborating requires open, trusting behavior and sharing information for the benefit of both parties. Long term, it leads to improved relationships and effective performance.[73]

Research on the five styles of conflict management indicates that although most managers favor a certain style, they have the capacity to change styles as the situation demands.[74] A study of project managers found that managers who used a combination of competing and avoiding styles were seen as ineffective by the engineers who worked on their project teams.[75] In another study of conflicts between R&D project managers and technical staff, competing and avoiding styles resulted in more frequent conflict and lower performance, whereas the collaborating style resulted in less frequent conflict and better performance.[76] Use You 13.2 to assess your dominant conflict management style.

Cultural differences also influence the use of different styles of conflict management. For example, one study compared Turkish and Jordanian managers with U.S. managers. All three groups preferred the collaborating style. Turkish managers also reported frequent use of the competing style, whereas Jordanian and U.S. managers reported that it was one of their least used styles.[77]

The human resources manager of one U.S. telecommunications company's office in Singapore engaged a consultant to investigate the conflict in the office.[78] Twenty-two expatriates from the United States and Canada and thirty-eight Singaporeans worked in the office. The consultant used the Thomas model (Figure 13.4) and distributed questionnaires to all managers to determine their conflict management styles. The results were not surprising: The expatriate managers preferred the competing, collaborating, and compromising styles, while the Asians preferred the avoiding and accommodating styles.

Workshops were conducted within the firm to develop an understanding of the differences and how they negatively affected the firm. The Asians interpreted the results as reflecting the tendency of Americans to "shout first and ask questions later." They felt that the Americans had an arrogant attitude and could not handle having their ideas rejected. The Asians attributed their own styles to their

What Is Your Conflict-Handling Style?

Instructions:

For each of the fifteen items, indicate how often you rely on that tactic by circling the appropriate number.

	Rarely	Always
1. I argue my case with my coworkers to show the merits of my position.	1—2—3—4—5	
2. I negotiate with my coworkers so that a compromise can be reached.	1—2—3—4—5	
3. I try to satisfy the expectations of my coworkers.	1—2—3—4—5	
4. I try to investigate an issue with my coworkers to find a solution acceptable to us.	1—2—3—4—5	
5. I am firm in pursuing my side of the issue.	1—2—3—4—5	
6. I attempt to avoid being "put on the spot" and try to keep my conflict with my coworkers to myself.	1—2—3—4—5	
7. I hold on to my solution to a problem.	1—2—3—4—5	
8. I use "give and take" so that a compromise can be made.	1—2—3—4—5	
9. I exchange accurate information with my coworkers to solve a problem together.	1—2—3—4—5	
10. I avoid open discussion of my differences with my coworkers.	1—2—3—4—5	
11. I accommodate the wishes of my coworkers.	1—2—3—4—5	
12. I try to bring all our concerns out in the open so that the issues can be resolved in the best possible way.	1—2—3—4—5	
13. I propose a middle ground for breaking deadlocks.	1—2—3—4—5	
14. I go along with the suggestions of my coworkers.	1—2—3—4—5	
15. I try to keep my disagreements with my coworkers to myself in order to avoid hard feelings.	1—2—3—4—5	

Scoring Key:

Collaborating		Accommodating		Competing		Avoiding		Compromising	
Item	**Score**	**Item**	**Score**	**Item**	**Score**	**Item**	**Score**	**Item**	**Score**
4.	___	3.	___	1.	___	6.	___	2.	___
9.	___	11.	___	5.	___	10.	___	8.	___
12.	___	14.	___	7.	___	15.	___	13.	___
Total = ___		Total = ___		Total = ___		Total = ___		Total = ___	

Your primary conflict-handling style is: _____
(The category with the highest total.)

Your backup conflict-handling style is: _____
(The category with the second highest total.)

SOURCE: Reprinted with permission of Academy of Management, PO Box 3020, Briar Cliff Manor, NY 10510-8020. *A Measure of Styles of Handling Interpersonal Conflict* (adaptation), M. A. Rahim, *Academy of Management Journal*, June 1983. Reproduced by permission of the publisher via Copyright Clearance Center, Inc.

cultural background. The Americans attributed the results to the stereotypical view of Asians as unassertive and timid, and they viewed their own results as reflecting their desire to "get things out in the open."

The process opened a dialogue between the two groups, who began to work on the idea of harmony through conflict. They began to discard the traditional stereotypes in favor of shared meanings and mutual understanding.

China is one of the biggest marketplaces in the world, and negotiating with the Chinese is very frustrating for Americans due to a lack of understanding of Chinese conflict management styles. One study indicated that compromising and avoiding are the most preferred conflict handling styles among the Chinese. Interestingly, the Chinese reported the most satisfaction with a business negotiation when accommodating and competing approaches were used by both parties.[79]

It is important to remember that preventing and resolving dysfunctional conflict is only half the task of effective conflict management. Stimulating functional conflict is the other half.

MANAGERIAL IMPLICATIONS: CREATING A CONFLICT-POSITIVE ORGANIZATION

Chinese and American businesspersons have begun to discard the traditional stereotypes in favor of shared meanings and mutual understandings.

Dean Tjosvold argues that well-managed conflict adds to an organization's innovation and productivity.[80] He discusses procedures for making conflict positive. Too many organizations take a win–lose, competitive approach to conflict or avoid conflict altogether. These two approaches view conflict as negative. A positive view of conflict, in contrast, leads to win–win solutions. Figure 13.5 illustrates these three approaches to conflict management.

Four interrelated steps are involved in creating a conflict-positive organization:

1. *Value diversity and confront differences.* Differences should be seen as opportunities for innovation, and diversity should be celebrated. Open and honest confrontations bring out differences, and they are essential for positive conflict.

2. *Seek mutual benefits and unite behind cooperative goals.* Conflicts have to be managed together. Through conflict, individuals learn how much they depend on one another. Even when employees share goals, they may differ on how to accomplish the goals. The important point is that they are moving toward the same objectives. Joint rewards should be given to the whole team for cooperative behavior.

FIGURE 13.5 Three Organization Views of Conflict

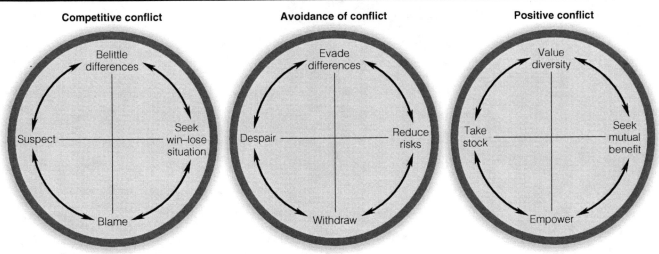

SOURCE: *The Conflict Positive Organization*, by Dean Tjsovold, © 1991. Reprinted by permission of Prentice-Hall, Inc., Upper Saddle River, N.J.

3. *Empower employees to feel confident and skillful.* People must be made to feel that they control their conflicts and that they can deal with their differences productively. When they do so, they should be recognized.

4. *Take stock to reward success and learn from mistakes.* Employees should be encouraged to appreciate one another's strengths and weaknesses and to talk directly about them. They should celebrate their conflict managment successes and work out plans for ways they can improve in the future.

Tjosvold believes that a conflict-positive organization has competitive advantages for the future.

A complimentary perspective comes from Peter J. Frost, who proposed that over time, organizational practices like poor conflict management can "poison" the organization as well as those who work within it. He describes how compassionate leaders can help reduce the effects of organizational toxins on their coworkers and how these toxin handlers should be rewarded for this crucial role in maintaining organizational health. Frost's position echoes Tjosvold's, as he calls for firms to become emotionally healthy workplaces for the good of their employees as well as for the good of their stockholders.[81]

Finally, don't overlook the importance of high emotional intelligence in the work of a good conflict manager. The ability to influence your own and others' emotions is not just a practical tool, but it can also serve as an important tactical asset, making you a better negotiator in a variety of situations and helping reduce conflict and increase productivity in your organization.[82]

LOOKING BACK: GENENTECH, INC.

Genentech: Lessons Learned from Many Conflicts

In Looking Ahead, we profiled the legal woes of Genentech and the huge fines it had to pay for unauthorized use of a patented protein drug development system. That was not the end of its legal troubles. In 1995, when current CEO Arthur Levinson took over, Genentech was in financial trouble and had just pleaded guilty to federal criminal charges of marketing a human growth hormone for uses not approved by the FDA. Genentech ended up paying $50 million in fines for this charge.

Next, in the 2002–2004 period, when its major cancer treatment drug Avastin was failing clinical trials, Levinson had to face crowds of angry investors urging him to suspend further research on Avastin. They also wanted Genentech to change its strategy of going after high-impact niche drugs such as cancer treatments and target mass medicinal drugs. Levinson, however, stood his ground because he believed in the power of Avastin in helping to fight cancer. Today, Avastin is one of the company's blockbuster drugs, already approved by the FDA for treatment of two types of cancer and awaiting decision on the treatment of breast cancer.

Levinson handled conflicts with investors by staying true to his values and staying involved with the R&D process. He also made sure that Genentech was less exposed to legal wrangling by requiring examination of all their sales information by their legal and regulatory departments.[83]

Chapter Summary

1. Conflict management skills are keys to management success. The manager's task is to stimulate functional conflict and prevent or resolve dysfunctional conflict.

2. Structural causes of conflict include specialization, interdependence, common resources, goal differences, authority relationships, status inconsistencies, and jurisdictional ambiguities.

3. Personal factors that lead to conflict include differences in skills and abilities, personalities, perceptions, or values and ethics; emotions; communication barriers; and cultural differences. The increasing diversity of the workforce and globalization of business have potential to increase conflict arising from these differences.

4. The levels of conflict include interorganizational, intergroup, interpersonal, and intrapersonal.

5. Individuals engaged in interpersonal conflict often display aggressive, compromise, or withdrawal defense mechanisms.

6. Ineffective techniques for managing conflict include nonaction, secrecy, administrative orbiting, due process nonaction, and character assassination.

7. Effective techniques for managing conflict include appealing to superordinate goals, expanding resources, changing personnel, changing structure, and confronting and negotiating.

8. In negotiating, managers can use a variety of conflict management styles, including avoiding, accommodating, competing, compromising, and collaborating.

9. Managers should strive to create a conflict-positive organization—one that values diversity, empowers employees, and seeks win–win solutions to conflicts.

Key Terms

administrative orbiting (p. 450)
character assassination (p. 450)
compensation (p. 448)
conflict (p. 436)
conversion (p. 449)
displacement (p. 448)
distributive bargaining (p. 452)
due process nonaction (p. 450)
dysfunctional conflict (p. 437)
fantasy (p. 449)

fixation (p. 447)
flight/withdrawal (p. 449)
functional conflict (p. 436)
identification (p. 448)
integrative negotiation (p. 453)
intergroup conflict (p. 442)
interorganizational conflict (p. 442)
interpersonal conflict (p. 443)
interrole conflict (p. 445)
intragroup conflict (p. 443)

intrapersonal conflict (p. 445)
intrarole conflict (p. 445)
jurisdictional ambiguity (p. 439)
negativism (p. 448)
nonaction (p. 450)
person–role conflict (p. 445)
rationalization (p. 449)
secrecy (p. 450)
superordinate goal (p. 451)

Review Questions

1. Discuss the differences between functional and dysfunctional conflict. Why should a manager understand conflict?

2. Identify the structural and personal factors that contribute to conflict.

3. Discuss the four major forms of conflict in organizations.

4. What defense mechanisms do people use in interpersonal conflict?

5. What are the most effective techniques for managing conflict at work? What are some ineffective techniques?

6. Identify and discuss five styles of conflict management.

Discussion and Communication Questions

1. What causes you the most conflict at work or school?

2. Identify the different intragroup, interrole, intrarole, and person–role conflicts that you experience.

3. Which defense mechanism do you see people exhibiting most frequently? Why do you think this is the case? How can you manage this type of reaction to a conflict?

4. Are you comfortable with your preferred conflict management style? Would you consider modifying it?

5. (communication question) Think of a person with whom you have had a recent conflict. Write a letter to this person, attempting to resolve the conflict. Use the concepts from the chapter to accomplish your objective. Be sure to address whether the conflict is functional or dysfunctional, what styles each party has used, effective strategies for resolving the conflict, and ineffective strategies that should be avoided.

Ethical Dilemma

Scott Davis sat at his desk anxiously waiting for the next few minutes to pass. It was almost time for the meeting he had scheduled between Debra Cronin and Ken Brown. Scott knew this meeting would be challenging for everyone. Debra and Ken had been at odds for quite some time. The problems started soon after Ken joined the company. At first Scott thought the conflict was healthy and would bring some much-needed change to the department. Scott soon learned that the disputes between Debra and Ken were more personal than professional.

Debra had been with the company for seven years. Scott had no complaints about her performance. She was a hard worker who got the job done. Unfortunately, Debra was also the source of a lot of conflict in the department. She always felt she knew the best way to do everything and freely shared that opinion with everyone, whether they wanted it or not. Scott has spent many hours listening to employees' complaints about Debra's insistence on showing them the "proper" way to do their jobs. Debra's interference had caused a fair amount of discontent in the department, but Scott never felt it was enough to consider termination. The meeting today might well change that opinion.

Ken Brown was new to the company. He had joined Scott's department just four months ago. He was young, with a lot of fresh ideas. Scott liked everything about Ken and thought he would be great for the department and the company. But like those before him, Ken found working with Debra difficult. She was set in her ways and was not going to change. Worse, she was undermining the other employees' interest in changing. Scott felt that he had done everything he could to resolve the conflict between the two, without success. He felt sure that today's meeting would end with one person leaving the company. His decision was which one: Debra, the longtime employee, or Ken, the newcomer with a vision for the future?

Questions

1. Does Scott have a greater responsibility to Debra than to Ken?

2. To whom does Scott owe the greatest responsibility?

3. Evaluate Scott's decision alternatives using consequential, rule-based, and character theories.

Experiential Exercises

13.1 Conflicts over Unethical Behavior

Many conflicts in work organizations arise over differences in beliefs concerning what constitutes ethical versus unethical behavior. The following questionnaire provides a list of behaviors that you or your coworkers might engage in when working for a company. Go over each item, and circle the number that best indicates the frequency with which you personally would (or do, if you work now) engage in that behavior. Then put an X over the number you think represents how often your coworkers would (or do) engage in that behavior. Finally, put a check mark beside the item (in the "Needs Control" column) if you believe that management should control that behavior.

	At Every Opportunity	Often	About Half the Time	Seldom	Never	Needs Control
1. Passing blame for errors to an innocent coworker.	5	4	3	2	1	_____
2. Divulging confidential information.	5	4	3	2	1	_____
3. Falsifying time/quality/quantity reports.	5	4	3	2	1	_____
4. Claiming credit for someone else's work.	5	4	3	2	1	_____
5. Padding an expense account by over 10 percent.	5	4	3	2	1	_____
6. Pilfering company materials and supplies.	5	4	3	2	1	_____
7. Accepting gifts/favors in exchange for preferential treatment.	5	4	3	2	1	_____
8. Giving gifts/favors in exchange for preferential treatment.	5	4	3	2	1	_____
9. Padding an expense account by up to 10 percent.	5	4	3	2	1	_____
10. Authorizing a subordinate to violate company rules.	5	4	3	2	1	_____

	At Every Opportunity	Often	About Half the Time	Seldom	Never	Needs Control
11. Calling in sick to take a day off.	5	4	3	2	1	_____
12. Concealing one's errors.	5	4	3	2	1	_____
13. Taking longer than necessary to do a job.	5	4	3	2	1	_____
14. Using company services for personal use.	5	4	3	2	1	_____
15. Doing personal business on company time.	5	4	3	2	1	_____
16. Taking extra personal time (lunch hour, breaks, early departure, and so forth).	5	4	3	2	1	_____
17. Not reporting others' violations of company policies and rules.	5	4	3	2	1	_____
18. Overlooking a superior's violation of policy to prove loyalty to the boss.	5	4	3	2	1	_____

Discussion Questions

1. Would (do) your coworkers seem to engage in these behaviors more often than you would (do)? Why do you have this perception?

2. Which behaviors tend to be most frequent?

3. How are the most frequent behaviors different from the behaviors engaged in less frequently?

4. What are the most important items for managers to control? How should managers control these behaviors?

5. Select a particular behavior from the list. Have two people debate whether the behavior is ethical or not.

6. What types of conflicts could emerge if the behaviors in the list occurred frequently?

SOURCE: From *Managerial Experience*, 3e by L. Jauch © 1983. Reprinted with permission of South-Western, a part of Cengage Learning: academic.cengage.com.

13.2 The World Bank Game: An Intergroup Negotiation

The purposes of this exercise are to learn about conflict and trust between groups and to practice negotiation skills. In the course of the exercise, money will be won or lost. Your team's objective is to win as much money as it can. Your team will be paired with another team, and both teams will receive identical instructions. After reading these instructions, each team will have ten minutes to plan its strategy.

Each team is assumed to have contributed $50 million to the World Bank. Teams may have to pay more or may receive money from the World Bank, depending on the outcome.

Each team will receive twenty cards. These cards are the weapons. Each card has a marked side (X) and an unmarked side. The marked side signifies that the weapon is armed; the unmarked side signifies that the weapon is unarmed.

At the beginning, each team will place ten of its twenty weapons in their armed position (marked side up) and the remaining ten in their unarmed position (marked side down). The weapons will remain in the team's possession and out of sight of the other team at all times.

The game will consist of *rounds* and *moves*. Each round will be composed of seven moves by each team. There will be two or more rounds in the game, depending on the time available. Payoffs will be determined and recorded after each round. The rules are as follows:

1. A move consists of turning two, one, or none of the team's weapons from armed to unarmed status, or vice versa.

2. Each team has one-and-a-half minutes for each move. There is a thirty-second period between each move. At the end of the one-and-a-half minutes, the team must have turned two, one, or none of its weapons from armed to unarmed status or from unarmed to armed status. If the team fails to move in the allotted time, no change can be made in weapon status until the next move.

3. The two-minute length of the period between the beginning of one move and the beginning of the next is unalterable.

Finances:

The funds each team has contributed to the World Bank are to be allocated in the following manner: $30 million will be returned to each team to be used as the team's treasury during the course of the game, and $20 million will be retained for the operation of the World Bank.

Payoffs:

1. If there is an attack:
   a. Each team may announce an attack on the other team by notifying the banker during the thirty seconds following any minute-and-a-half period used to decide upon the move (including the

seventh, or final, decision period in any round). The choice of each team during the decision period just ended counts as a move. An attack may not be made during negotiations.

b. If there is an attack by one or both teams, two things happen: (1) the round ends, and (2) the World Bank assesses a penalty of $2.5 million on each team.

c. The team with the greater number of armed weapons wins $1.5 million for each armed weapon it has over and above the number of armed weapons of the other team. These funds are paid directly from the treasury of the losing team to the treasury of the winning team. The banker will manage the transfer of funds.

2. If there is no attack:

At the end of each round (seven moves), each team's treasury will receive from the World Bank $1 million for each of its weapons that is at that point unarmed; and each team's treasury will pay to the World Bank $1 million for each of its weapons remaining armed.

Negotiations:

Between moves, each team will have the opportunity to communicate with the other team through its negotiations. Either team may call for negotiations by notifying the banker during any of the thirty-second periods between decisions. A team is free to accept or reject any invitation to negotiate.

Negotiators from both teams are required to meet after the third and sixth moves (after the thirty-second period following the move, if there is no attack).

Negotiations can last no longer than three minutes. When the two negotiators return to their teams, the minute-and-a-half decision period for the next move will begin once again.

Negotiators are bound only by (1) the three-minute time limit for negotiations and (2) their required appearance after the third and sixth moves. They are always free to say whatever is necessary to benefit themselves or their teams. The teams are not bound by agreements made by their negotiators, even when those agreements are made in good faith.

Special Roles:

Each team has ten minutes to organize itself and plan team strategy. During this period, before the first round begins, each team must choose persons to fill the following roles:

- A *negotiator*—activities stated above.
- A *representative*—to communicate the team's decisions to the banker.
- A *recorder*—to record the moves of the team and to keep a running balance of the team's treasury.

- A *treasurer*—to execute all financial transactions with the banker.

The instructor will serve as the banker for the World Bank and will signal the beginning of each of the rounds.

At the end of the game, each participant should complete the following questionnaire, which assesses reactions to the World Bank Game.

World Bank Questionnaire:

1. To what extent are you satisfied with your team's strategy?

   Highly   1 2 3 4 5 6 7   Highly
   dissatisfied   satisfied

2. To what extent do you believe the other team is trustworthy?

   Highly   1 2 3 4 5 6 7   Highly
   untrustworthy   trustworthy

3. To what extent are you satisfied with the performance of your negotiator?

   Highly   1 2 3 4 5 6 7   Highly
   dissatisfied   satisfied

4. To what extent was there a consensus on your team regarding its moves?

   Very little   1 2 3 4 5 6 7   A great deal

5. To what extent do you trust the other members of your team?

   Very little   1 2 3 4 5 6 7   A great deal

6. Select one word that describes how you feel about your team: _____.

7. Select one word that describes how you feel about the other team: _____.

Negotiators only:

   How did you see the other team's negotiator?

Phony and   1 2 3 4 5 6 7   Authentic
insincere   and sincere

At the end of the game, the class will reconvene and discuss team members' responses to the World Bank Questionnaire. In addition, the following questions are to be addressed:

1. What was each team's strategy for winning? What strategy was most effective?

2. Contrast the outcomes in terms of win–win solutions to conflict versus win–lose solutions.

SOURCE: Adapted by permission from N. H. Berkowitz and H. A. Hornstein, "World Bank: An Intergroup Negotiation," in J. W. Pfeiffer and J. E. Jones, eds., *The 1975 Handbook for Group Facilitators* (San Diego: Pfeiffer), 58–62. Copyright © 1975 Pfeiffer/Jossey-Bass. This material is used by permission of John Wiley & Sons, Inc.

WORLD BANK RECORD SHEET

		Round One		Round Two		Round Three		Round Four	
		Armed	Unarmed	Armed	Unarmed	Armed	Unarmed	Armed	Unarmed
	Move	10	10	10	10	10	10	10	10
	1								
	2								
	3								
Required Negotiation	4								
	5								
	6								
Required Negotiation	7								

Funds in Team Treasury	$30 million				
Funds of Other Treasury	$30 million				
Funds in World Bank	$40 million				

T A K E 2

Biz Flix | The Guru

"Deepak Chopra meets Dr. Ruth" is a possible alternate title or subtitle for this film. The film follows Ramu Gupta's (Jimi Mistry) journey from India to the United States where he wants to become a film star. Unlucky at keeping a job, Ramu is fired from a waiter's job and a pornographic film role. By closely following the advice of Sharrona (Heather Graham), his ex-pornographic co-star, Ramu becomes a highly acclaimed though mystical sex therapist.

The scene from *The Guru* appears in the final quarter of the film. It occurs after Ramu starts his performance at the Broadway Playhouse to a packed, enthusiastic audience. By this time in the film, he has become a renowned sex therapist who has moved from individual therapy to public performances. The film continues after this scene with self-appointed manager Vijay (Emil Marwa) bringing several beautiful women to Ramu's new apartment.

What to Watch for and Ask Yourself:

> What is the latent conflict (cause of conflict) that triggered this conflict event or episode?

> What conflict management style do Ramu and Sharrona use during this episode?

> Do they end the conflict with a clear conflict aftermath? Do you expect the conflict to continue? Why or why not?

Workplace Video | Managing in a Global Environment, Featuring Yahoo

Yahoo is a global-business success story. Launched as the hobby of two Stanford University graduate students in 1995, the search-engine portal has become one of the most trafficked Web sites in the world. Millions of netizens visit Yahoo for headline news and entertainment, and the site's loyal account members log on daily to check e-mail and use community services like Yahoo Groups and Yahoo Personals.

Attracting international audiences is a daunting task, and Yahoo uses various strategies to reach the world's billion-plus Internet users. For example, the company translates its Web properties and services into thirteen languages. In addition, the Sunnyvale, California-based company garners international interest through globally produced on-line events, such as Yahoo Time Capsule—a Web-based repository of personal musings posted by individuals in over 200 countries.

While access to billions of people creates enormous opportunity, having a global reach also puts strain on an organization. Managing conflict and overcoming international barriers is the job of Yahoo's offices in Europe, Asia-Pacific, Latin America, and Canada. These regional offices are generally effective in situating Yahoo's business within a local context outside the United States. They do not resolve all conflict, however, as opening offices overseas presents economic, political, and sociocultural challenges. Increasingly Yahoo looks to experienced global managers and teams to deal with such conflicts.

Despite its prestigious past, Yahoo maintains a forward-looking focus. Competitors like Google and MySpace threaten the relevance of Yahoo's services, and managing 11,000 employees worldwide requires twenty-first-century managerial thinking. Nevertheless, the continued strength of Yahoo's brand long after the dot-com bust seems a harbinger of future success. The company's management have shown they have both the global savvy and conflict-resolution skills necessary to lead the Internet to its next phase of growth.

Discussion Questions

1. What structural factors can lead to conflict at Yahoo and other global corporations?
2. What personal factors can lead to conflict at Yahoo?
3. How might Yahoo's managers diagnose if a specific conflict is functional or dysfunctional?

Molson Coors Brewing Company: Conflict Resolution in the Aftermath of a Merger

In the mid-1990s a dispute developed between rival factions of the Molson family for control of its business empire, including the Molson brewing business. Cousins Eric Molson and Ian Molson were pitted against one another in this struggle for control.[1] They clashed at board meetings, with their differences becoming increasingly intense and embittered. At a January 2003 board meeting, Eric announced a review of Molson's corporate governance. While a surprise to the board, the review was nonetheless conducted. The governance report recommended eliminating Ian's position as deputy chairman. Ian confronted Eric but nothing was resolved. At the following November board meeting, the recommendation to eliminate Ian's position was defeated. At the May 2004 meeting, three board members, including Ian, resigned in protest over Eric's leadership of the company. The remainder of the board chose to reaffirm Eric's status as chairman. At the company's annual meeting the following month, Ian and four other members of the family-controlled board refused to stand for re-election.[2]

Meanwhile, Molson Inc. and Adolph Coors Co. initiated merger talks. The two companies had been working together since 1998, with each distributing the other's products in its home territory. The major hurdle to the proposed merger was the feud between the two factions of the Molson family. Eric, who along with allied family members controlled more than half the voting shares, favored the merger. Ian, with approximately 10 percent of the voting shares, was against the merger. A shareholder agreement between Ian and Eric prevented either one from transferring or selling his voting shares without the consent of the other.[3] Eric maintained that he had found a legal way to circumvent the agreement. Ian, on the other hand, was preparing to offer as much as $4 billion to acquire Molson Inc. in order to prevent the merger with Coors.[4] On July 22, 2004, the two companies jointly announced the merger of Molson and Coors.[5] As a result, Molson Coors became the third-largest brewer in the United States and the fifth largest in the world,

operating primarily in three mature markets—Canada, the United States, and the United Kingdom.[6]

"At the time of the merger, bringing together the Molson and Coors families seemed like a recipe for disaster. One was Canadian. One was American. One was east. One was west. And they both built their businesses in different ways."[7] Even nearly three years afterwards, ". . . the merger is still a sore point with some, including Eric's cousin Ian Molson, who saw the 'merger of equals' as an outright takeover—and not an advantageous one for shareholders at that."[8] Nonetheless, just "[t]wo years after the highly publicized merger . . . the management problems anticipated by many analysts—most notably a power struggle between two long standing brewing families—have yet to come to pass. In fact, Molson Coors Brewing Co . . . is leveraging the strength of its family-based culture to strategically focus on brand building and growing its domestic and international beer business."[9]

How has Molson Coors Brewing avoided being decimated by conflict? CEO Leo Kiely, in describing how they were able to successfully merge two companies with strong cultures and traditions, cited two key factors. One factor involved investing local teams with the responsibility for their markets since the markets of the pre-merger Molson and Coors did not overlap much. The second factor was celebrating the two companies' common features—a strong family heritage and a passion for brewing beer.[10]

According to Kiely, the first priority after the merger was to get "a good balanced team in place."[11] After the merger of Molson and Coors, the senior management team was reorganized by drawing in people from both companies and both families and by establishing executive headquarters in both Denver and Montreal. Eric Molson serves as chairman of the board, and Peter Coors serves as vice chairman. Eric Molson works from Montreal, Canada, and CEO Kiely, from the Coors side, runs the merged company from Denver.[12] Other members of both the Molson and Coors families play active roles in the business.[13]

Another major factor in avoiding debilitating conflict was the similar business interests and heritage of the two companies. Geoff Molson, a seventh-generation family member working in the business, says "the thing outsiders don't understand is that the families' passion for brewing was 'really the essential ingredient' in getting the deal done." Molson continues, "In the past two years, we've had differences, identified them, and figured out a way to address them together with the interests of building the beer business at the same time."[14]

Although the merged company reflects twenty-first-century globalization and consolidation within the brewing industry, "each of the two companies is fighting to keep its identity, which is rooted in the past."[15] Regarding the Canadian side of the merger, Eric Molson says, "Since 1786, playing a part in the community has been the Molson tradition—a tradition that is woven into the cultural fabric of Molson and our family, and continues to thrive today. We are very proud to be part of this country, from coast to coast."[16] A similar perspective applies to the Coors traditions. Indeed, the family aspect and community involvement of both Molson and Coors define the separate histories of the companies as well as the present times of the merged Molson Coors Brewing.[17]

Will the two families of Molson Coors Brewing be able to continue working together amiably as they face an increasingly globalized and consolidated brewing industry? Addressing this dilemma became increasing more complicated on October 9, 2007 when Molson Coors and SABMiller PLC announced plans to merge their United States operations. The Molson and Coors families did not want to sell the entire brewing company to SABMiller, and consequently the company's operations in Canada and the United Kingdom will remain independent of SABMiller.[18]

Discussion Questions

1. From your perspective, were the consequences of the conflict between Eric Molson and Ian Molson positive or negative?

2. What *ineffective* techniques for managing conflict are evident in the case?

3. What *effective* techniques for managing conflict are evident in the case?

SOURCE: This case was written by Michael K. McCuddy, The Louis S. and Mary L. Morgal Chair of Christian Business Ethics and Professor of Management, College of Business Administration, Valparaiso University.

BP: The Dynamics of Leading a Large Global Organization

From its humble beginnings just over a century ago, BP has developed into a global energy giant employing over 96,000 people. On a daily basis, the company serves approximately 13 million customers in over 100 nations around the world.[1] BP has become the second-largest oil company in the world behind ExxonMobil.[2] A good deal of this phenomenal growth can be attributed to the leadership of John P. Browne, from his appointment as CEO in 1995 until his resignation from that position on May 1, 2007. At that time, Tony Hayward assumed the mantle of leadership as BP's CEO.

John Browne: CEO, 1995 to May 2007

John P. Browne, educated at Cambridge University in the United Kingdom, joined BP as a university apprentice in 1966. He eventually became head of BP's exploration unit, and then in 1995 became CEO.[3] Not long after that, Browne embarked on a strategic path that would significantly alter BP's stature in the oil industry. He reasoned that a limited world supply of oil and gas reserves meant that the best alternative for BP's future growth would be through the acquisition other oil companies.[4] This logic, coupled with the fact that world oil market prices were hovering close to $10 a barrel in the late 1990s, enabled Browne to convince BP's board of directors that acquisition of other oil companies and cost cutting were the only ways to survive.

The first acquisition occurred in 1998 when BP and Chicago-based Amoco Corporation merged. Interestingly, this merger set off numerous copycat deals within the oil industry.[5] The Amoco deal, worth $52 billion, turned BP, a midsize British company, into one of the world's energy giants. The deal put BP in a league with Royal Dutch/Shell and ExxonMobil. In conjunction with the Amoco acquisition, Browne promised he would slash $2 billion a year from expenses, half of which would come from the information technology area where there were overlapping systems and staffs.[6]

Subsequent to the Amoco merger, Browne engineered acquisitions of ARCO in 1999 and Burmah Castrol in 2000.[7] He also formed a partnership with the Russian company TNK to develop energy resources in Eastern Siberia.[8] BP's initiatives, as well as those of other oil companies, led to considerable consolidation within the oil industry. All these successes gave Browne his reputation as "an oilman's oilman."[9] In recent years, however, "critics have blamed the big spending cuts that accompanied the industry's consolidation for curtailing supply and contributing to today's super-high oil prices."[10]

Browne has also received accolades for being the first oilman to embrace the concept of global warming and emphasize environmental concerns. "As early as 1997, in a speech at Stanford Business School, he acknowledged the problem of climate change, the first leader of the oil industry to do so."[11] BP also became engaged in significant efforts to develop alternative energy sources, including biofuels, solar energy, and hydrogen fuels.[12] Then by 2003, BP had rebranded itself, with its initials now signifying *Beyond Petroleum*.[13]

After the Texas City, Texas, refinery explosion and fire, an investigative panel headed by James Baker found fault with the cost-cutting mentality associated with BP's culture. The Baker panel "determined that BP's management did not devote enough money or effort to ensuring safety at its American refineries."[14] Additionally, they commented on Browne's reputation as an advocate of reducing carbon dioxide emissions and promoting alternative fuels. In comparing his leadership on environmental and safety issues, the Baker panel observed, "[i]f Browne had demonstrated comparable leadership on and commitment to process safety, that leadership and commitment would likely have resulted in a higher level of process safety performance in BP's US refineries.'"[15] The Baker panel also noted that BP has "not adequately established process safety as a core value."[16]

Browne, however, "insists that there is no pattern to BP's various problems and no over-arching failure of management."[17] Yet other people believe BP's management is not assertive enough. Neil McMahon, with the Sanford Bernstein financial services firm, argues that BP should be reorganized in order to reduce the decentralized autonomy of its multiple units and to ensure more consistent policies and standards.[18]

Shortly before the Baker Panel's report was issued, Browne said that he would accelerate his scheduled retirement by seventeen months, to the end of July 2007. This announcement reinforced the growing perception "that something had gone badly wrong at BP and that a fresh start was needed to set the firm to rights."[19] Then on May 1, 2007, Browne abruptly resigned as BP's CEO.[20] Nigel Davis, a longtime observer of the oil industry, commented: "BP has lost its most influential leader and one of the most respected businessmen of his generation. Browne succeeded in areas where others could not. He transformed BP, indeed the oil world, with ground breaking deals with Amoco, Arco, Burmah Castrol, Veba Oel and Russia's TNK. The value of the company rocketed under his tenure. He has been called a businessman of intuition, vision and foresight. Yet those qualities appeared to leave him in his latter days as BP CEO."[21]

Tony Hayward: CEO, May 2007 to . . .

Browne's abrupt resignation did not catch the company unprepared. BP and the board of directors already had a succession plan in place for Tony Hayward. These preparations reflected, in part, efforts to deal with the accumulated safety and environmental problems from the past few years. As one observer noted, "the company seems to be gearing down and taking a close look at its operations, some of which have been troubled. BP may even be trying to ease the pressure on Hayward by lowering expectations."[22] Hayward probably will not change BP's strategy—at least very quickly. However, he has indicated he will put a new emphasis on safety given the series of operational problems that have occurred over the past two years.[23] Indeed, Hayward believes that in dealing with these operational problems, "BP's top brass were too imperious and failed to heed the concerns of the lower ranks."[24]

Hayward "spent his entire career at BP, much of it as . . . Browne's protégé, so he is steeped in its culture."[25] His knowledge of that culture can help him institute change. Yet he may be less inclined to initiate cultural—and structural—change *because* he has been so much a part of BP.

Initial indications are that Hayward may lead BP a bit differently than Browne did. Browne remained aloof from most BP staff members. Hayward is operating differently—for example, stopping by the basement cafeteria of BP's London headquarters. Moreover, "[o]n recent visits to the company's U.S. refineries, he spent hours talking to equipment operators rather than huddled with senior managers."[26]

Will the new leadership at the top of BP help in addressing the company's multiple challenges?

Discussion Questions

1. How would you describe John Browne's approach to leadership?

2. How would you describe Tony Hayward's approach to leadership?

3. How did Browne's approach to leadership affect communications and decision making at BP? How did his leadership approach reflect the use of power?

4. How might Tony Hayward's leadership approach affect work group dynamics within BP? How might his approach impact the resolution of conflict?

SOURCE: This case was written by Michael K. McCuddy, The Louis S. and Mary L. Morgal Chair of Christian Business Ethics and Professor of Management, College of Business Administration, Valparaiso University.

Glossary

A

adaptive culture An organizational culture that encourages confidence and risk taking among employees, has leadership that produces change, and focuses on the changing needs of customers.

adhocracy A selectively decentralized form of organization that emphasizes the support staff and mutual adjustment among people.

administrative orbiting Delaying action on a conflict by buying time.

advancement The second, high-achievement-oriented career stage in which the individual focuses on increasing competence.

affect The emotional component of an attitude.

affective commitment A type of organizational commitment based on an individual's desire to remain in an organization.

anthropocentric Placing human considerations at the center of job design decisions.

anthropology The science of the learned behavior of human beings.

anticipatory socialization The first socialization stage, which encompasses all of the learning that takes place prior to the newcomer's first day on the job.

artifacts Symbols of culture in the physical and social work environment.

assumptions Deeply held beliefs that guide behavior and tell members of an organization how to perceive and think about things.

attitude A psychological tendency expressed by evaluating an entity with some degree of favor or disfavor.

attribution theory A theory that explains how individuals pinpoint the causes of their own behavior and that of others.

authentic leadership A style of leadership that includes transformational, charismatic, or transactional approaches as the situation demands.

authority The right to influence another person.

authority-compliance manager (9,1) A leader who emphasizes efficient production.

autocratic style A style of leadership in which the leader uses strong, directive, controlling actions to enforce the rules, regulations, activities, and relationships in the work environment.

B

barriers to communication Aspects of the communication content and context that can impair effective communication in a workplace.

behavioral measures Personality assessments that involve observing an individual's behavior in a controlled situation.

benevolent An individual who is comfortable with an equity ratio less than that of his or her comparison other.

bounded rationality A theory that suggests there are limits to how rational a decision maker can actually be.

brainstorming A technique for generating as many ideas as possible on a given subject, while suspending evaluation until all the ideas have been suggested.

bridge employment Employment that takes place after retiring from a full-time position but before permanent withdrawal from the workforce.

C

career The pattern of work-related experiences that span the course of a person's life.

career anchors A network of self-perceived talents, motives, and values that guide an individual's career decisions.

career ladder A structured series of job positions through which an individual progresses in an organization.

career management A lifelong process of learning about self, jobs, and organizations; setting personal career goals; developing strategies for achieving the goals, and revising the goals based on work and life experiences.

career path A sequence of job experiences that an employee moves along during his or her career.

career plateau A point in an individual's career in which the probability of moving further up the hierarchy is low.

centralization The degree to which decisions are made at the top of the organization.

challenge The call to competition, contest, or battle.

change The transformation or modification of an organization and/or its stakeholders.

change agent The individual or group that undertakes the task of introducing and managing a change in an organization.

change and acquisition The third socialization stage, in which the newcomer begins to master the demands of the job.

character assassination An attempt to label or discredit an opponent.

character theory An ethical theory that emphasizes the character, personal virtues, and integrity of the individual.

charismatic leadership A leader's use of personal abilities and talents in order to have profound and extraordinary effects on followers.

classical conditioning Modifying behavior so that a conditioned stimulus is paired with an unconditioned stimulus and elicits an unconditioned response.

coercive power Power that is based on an agent's ability to cause an unpleasant experience for a target.

cognitive dissonance A state of tension that is produced when an individual experiences conflict between attitudes and behavior.

cognitive moral development The process of moving through stages of maturity in terms of making ethical decisions.

cognitive style An individual's preference for gathering information and evaluating alternatives.

collectivism A cultural orientation in which individuals belong to tightly knit social frameworks, and they depend strongly on large extended families or clans.

communication The evoking of a shared or common meaning in another person.

communicative disease The absence of heartfelt communication in human relationships leading to loneliness and social isolation.

communicator The person originating a message.

compensation A compromise mechanism in which an individual attempts to make up for a negative situation by devoting himself or herself to another pursuit with increased vigor.

compensation award An organizational cost resulting from court awards for job distress.

complexity The degree to which many different types of activities occur in the organization.

conflict Any situation in which incompatible goals, attitudes, emotions, or behaviors lead to disagreement or opposition for two or more parties.

consensus An informational cue indicating the extent to which peers in the same situation behave in a similar fashion.

consequential theory An ethical theory that emphasizes the consequences or results of behavior.

consideration Leader behavior aimed at nurturing friendly, warm working relationships, as well as encouraging mutual trust and interpersonal respect within the work unit.

consistency An informational cue indicating the frequency of behavior over time.

contextual variables A set of characteristics that influence the organization's design processes.

continuance commitment A type of organizational commitment based on the fact that an individual cannot afford to leave.

conversion A withdrawal mechanism in which emotional conflicts are expressed in physical symptoms.

counterdependence An unhealthy, insecure pattern of behavior that leads to separation in relationships with other people.

counter-role behavior Deviant behavior in either a correctly or incorrectly defined job or role.

country club manager (1,9) A leader who creates a happy, comfortable work environment.

creativity A process influenced by individual and organizational factors that results in the production of novel and useful ideas, products, or both.

cross-training A variation of job enlargement in which workers are trained in different specialized tasks or activities.

D

data Uninterpreted and unanalyzed facts.

defensive communication Communication that can be aggressive, attacking, and angry, or passive and withdrawing.

Delphi technique Gathering the judgments of experts for use in decision making.

democratic style A style of leadership in which the leader takes collaborative, responsive, interactive actions with followers concerning the work and work environment.

devil's advocacy A technique for preventing groupthink in which a group or individual is given the role of critic during decision making.

dialectical inquiry A debate between two opposing sets of recommendations.

differentiation The process of deciding how to divide the work in an organization.

discounting principle The assumption that an individual's behavior is accounted for by the situation.

disenchantment Feeling negativity or anger toward a change.

disengagement Psychological withdrawal from change.

disidentification Feeling that one's identity is being threatened by a change.

disorientation Feelings of loss and confusion due to a change.

displacement An aggressive mechanism in which an individual directs his or her anger toward someone who is not the source of the conflict.

distinctiveness An informational cue indicating the degree to which an individual behaves the same way in other situations.

distress The adverse psychological, physical, behavioral, and organizational consequences that may arise as a result of stressful events.

distributive bargaining A negotiation approach in which the goals of the parties are in conflict, and each party seeks to maximize its resources.

distributive justice The fairness of the outcomes that individuals receive in an organization.

diversity All forms of individual differences, including culture, gender, age, ability, religion, personality, social status, and sexual orientation.

divisionalized form A moderately decentralized form of organization that emphasizes the middle level and standardization of outputs.

dual-career partnership A relationship in which both people have important career roles.

due process nonaction A procedure set up to address conflicts that is so costly, time-consuming, or personally risky that no one will use it.

dynamic follower A follower who is a responsible steward of his or her job, is effective in managing the relationship with the boss, and practices self-management.

dysfunctional conflict An unhealthy, destructive disagreement between two or more people.

E

effective decision A timely decision that meets a desired objective and is acceptable to those individuals affected by it.

ego-ideal The embodiment of a person's perfect self.

eldercare Assistance in caring for elderly parents and/or other elderly relatives.

emotional contagion A dynamic process through which the emotions of one person are transferred to another either consciously or unconsciously through nonverbal channels.

emotions Mental states that typically include feelings, physiological changes, and the inclination to act.

empowerment Sharing power within an organization.

enacted values Values reflected in the way individuals actually behave.

encounter The second socialization stage in which the newcomer learns the tasks associated with the job, clarifies roles, and establishes new relationships at work.

engagement The expression of oneself as one performs in work or other roles.

engineering The applied science of energy and matter.

entitled An individual who is comfortable with an equity ratio greater than that of his or her comparison other.

environment Anything outside the boundaries of an organization.

environmental uncertainty The amount and rate of change in the organization's environment.

equity sensitive An individual who prefers an equity ratio equal to that of his or her comparison other.

ergonomics The science of adapting work and working conditions to the employee or worker.

escalation of commitment The tendency to continue to support a failing course of action.

espoused values What members of an organization say they value.

establishment The first career stage in which the person learns the job and begins to fit into the organization and occupation.

ethical behavior Acting in ways consistent with one's personal values and the commonly held values of the organization and society.

eustress Healthy, normal stress.

executive coaching A technique in which managers or executives are paired with a coach in a partnership to help the executive perform more efficiently.

expatriate manager A manager who works in a country other than his or her home country.

expectancy The belief that effort leads to performance.

expert power The power that exists when an agent has specialized knowledge or skills that the target needs.

expert system A computer-based application that uses a representation of human expertise in a specialized field of knowledge to solve problems.

extinction The attempt to weaken a behavior by attaching no consequences to it.

extraversion A preference indicating that an individual is energized by interaction with other people.

F

fantasy A withdrawal mechanism that provides an escape from a conflict through daydreaming.

feedback Information fed back that completes two-way communication.

feeling Making decisions in a personal, value-oriented way.

femininity The cultural orientation in which relationships and concern for others are valued.

first-impression error The tendency to form lasting opinions about an individual based on initial perceptions.

fixation An aggressive mechanism in which an individual keeps up a dysfunctional behavior that obviously will not solve the conflict.

flexible work schedule A work schedule that allows employees discretion in order to accommodate personal concerns.

flextime An alternative work pattern that enables employees to set their own daily work schedules.

flight/withdrawal A withdrawal mechanism that entails physically escaping a conflict (flight) or psychologically escaping (withdrawal).

followership The process of being guided and directed by a leader in the work environment.

formal leadership Officially sanctioned leadership based on the authority of a formal position.

formal organization The official, legitimate, and most visible part of the system.

formalization The degree to which the organization has official rules, regulations, and procedures.

functional conflict A healthy, constructive disagreement between two or more people.

fundamental attribution error The tendency to make attributions to internal causes when focusing on someone else's behavior.

G

garbage can model A theory that contends that decisions in organizations are random and unsystematic.

gateways to communication Pathways through barriers to communication and antidotes to communication problems.

general self-efficacy An individual's general belief that he or she is capable of meeting job demands in a wide variety of situations.

glass ceiling An intangible barrier that keeps women and minorities from rising above a certain level in organizations.

goal setting The process of establishing desired results that guide and direct behavior.

group Two or more people with common interests, objectives, and continuing interaction.

group cohesion The "interpersonal glue" that makes members of a group stick together.

group polarization The tendency for group discussion to produce shifts toward more extreme attitudes among members.

groupthink A deterioration of mental efficiency, reality testing, and moral judgment resulting from pressures within the group.

guanxi The Chinese practice of building networks for social exchange.

H

Hawthorne studies Studies conducted during the 1920s and 1930s that discovered the existence of the informal organization.

heuristics Shortcuts in decision making that save mental activity.

hierarchy of authority The degree of vertical differentiation across levels of management.

homeostasis A steady state of bodily functioning and equilibrium.

hygiene factor A work condition related to dissatisfaction caused by discomfort or pain.

I

identification A compromise mechanism whereby an individual patterns his or her behavior after another's.

impoverished manager (1,1) A leader who exerts just enough effort to get by.

impression management The process by which individuals try to control the impressions others have of them.

incremental change Change of a relatively small scope, such as making small improvements.

individual differences The way in which factors such as skills, abilities, personalities, perceptions, attitudes, values, and ethics differ from one individual to another.

individualism A cultural orientation in which people belong to loose social frameworks, and their primary concern is for themselves and their families.

inequity The situation in which a person perceives he or she is receiving less than he or she is giving, or is giving less than he or she is receiving.

influence The process of affecting the thoughts, behavior, and feelings of another person.

informal leadership Unofficial leadership accorded to a person by other members of the organization.

informal organization The unofficial and less visible part of the system.

information Data that have been interpreted, analyzed, and have meaning to some user.

Information Communication Technology (ICT) The various new technologies, such as e-mail, voice mail, teleconferencing, and wireless access, which are used for interpersonal communication.

information power Access to and control over important information.

initiating structure Leader behavior aimed at defining and organizing work relationships and roles, as well as establishing clear patterns of organization, communication, and ways of getting things done.

instrumental values Values that represent the acceptable behaviors to be used in achieving some end state.

instrumentality The belief that performance is related to rewards.

integrated involvement Closeness achieved through tasks and activities.

integration The process of coordinating the different parts of an organization.

integrative approach The broad theory that describes personality as a composite of an individual's psychological processes.

integrative negotiation A negotiation approach that focuses on the merits of the issues and seeks a win–win solution.

interactional psychology The psychological approach that says in order to understand human behavior, we must know something about the person and about the situation.

intergroup conflict Conflict that occurs between groups or teams in an organization.

interorganizational conflict Conflict that occurs between two or more organizations.

interpersonal communication Communication between two or more people in an organization.

interpersonal conflict Conflict that occurs between two or more individuals.

interrole conflict A person's experience of conflict among the multiple roles in his or her life.

intragroup conflict Conflict that occurs within groups or teams.

intrapersonal conflict Conflict that occurs within an individual.

intrarole conflict Conflict that occurs within a single role, such as when a person receives conflicting messages from role senders about how to perform a certain role.

introversion A preference indicating that an individual is energized by time alone.

intuition A fast, positive force in decision making that is utilized at a level below consciousness and involves learned patterns of information.

intuition Gathering information through "sixth sense" and focusing on what could be rather than what actually exists.

J

job A set of specified work and task activities that engage an individual in an organization.

Job Characteristics Model A framework for understanding person–job fit through the interaction of core job dimensions with critical psychological states within a person.

Job Diagnostic Survey (JDS) The survey instrument designed to measure the elements in the Job Characteristics Model.

job enlargement A method of job design that increases the number of activities in a job to overcome the boredom of overspecialized work.

job enrichment Designing or redesigning jobs by incorporating motivational factors into them.

job redesign An OD intervention method that alters jobs to improve the fit between individual skills and the demands of the job.

job rotation A variation of job enlargement in which workers are exposed to a variety of specialized jobs over time.

job satisfaction A pleasurable or positive emotional state resulting from the appraisal of one's job or job experiences.

job sharing An alternative work pattern in which more than one person occupies a single job.

Judging Preference Preferring closure and completion in making decisions.

jurisdictional ambiguity The presence of unclear lines of responsibility within an organization.

L

laissez-faire style A style of leadership in which the leader fails to accept the responsibilities of the position.

language The words, their pronunciation, and the methods of combining them used and understood by a group of people.

leader An advocate for change and new approaches to problems.

leader–member relations The quality of interpersonal relationships among a leader and the group members.

leadership The process of guiding and directing the behavior of people in the work environment.

Leadership Grid An approach to understanding a leader's or manager's concern for results (production) and concern for people.

leadership training and development A variety of techniques that are designed to enhance individuals' leadership skills.

lean production Using committed employees with ever-expanding responsibilities to achieve zero waste, 100 percent good product, delivered on time, every time.

learning A change in behavior acquired through experience.

least preferred coworker (LPC) The person a leader has least preferred to work with over his or her career.

legitimate power Power that is based on position and mutual agreement; agent and target agree that the agent has the right to influence the target.

locus of control An individual's generalized belief about internal control (self-control) versus external control (control by the situation or by others).

loss of individuality A social process in which individual group members lose self-awareness and its accompanying sense of accountability, inhibition, and responsibility for individual behavior.

M

Machiavellianism A personality characteristic indicating one's willingness to do whatever it takes to get one's own way.

machine bureaucracy A moderately decentralized form of organization that emphasizes the technical staff and standardization of work processes.

maintenance The third career stage in which the individual tries to maintain productivity while evaluating progress toward career goals.

maintenance function An activity essential to effective, satisfying interpersonal relationships within a team or group.

management The study of overseeing activities and supervising people in organizations.

management by objectives (MBO) A goal-setting program based on interaction and negotiation between employees and managers.

management by objectives (MBO) An organization-wide intervention technique that involves joint goal setting between employees and managers.

manager An advocate for stability and the status quo.

masculinity The cultural orientation in which assertiveness and materialism are valued.

meaning of work The way a person interprets and understands the value of work as part of life.

mechanistic structure An organizational design that emphasizes structured activities, specialized tasks, and centralized decision making.

medicine The applied science of healing or treatment of diseases to enhance an individual's health and well-being.

mentor An individual who provides guidance, coaching, counseling, and friendship to a protégé.

mentoring A work relationship that encourages development and career enhancement for people moving through the career cycle.

message The thoughts and feelings that the communicator is attempting to elicit in the receiver.

moral maturity The measure of a person's cognitive moral development.

motivation The process of arousing and sustaining goal-directed behavior.

motivation factor A work condition related to satisfaction of the need for psychological growth.

moving The second step in Lewin's change model, in which new attitudes, values, and behaviors are substituted for old ones.

Myers-Briggs Type Indicator (MBTI) instrument An instrument developed to measure Carl Jung's theory of individual differences.

N

need for achievement A manifest (easily perceived) need that concerns individuals' issues of excellence, competition, challenging goals, persistence, and overcoming difficulties.

need for affiliation A manifest (easily perceived) need that concerns an individual's need to establish and maintain warm, close, intimate relationships with other people.

need for power A manifest (easily perceived) need that concerns an individual's need to make an impact on others, influence others, change people or events, and make a difference in life.

need hierarchy The theory that behavior is determined by a progression of physical, social, and psychological needs, including lower-order needs and higher-order needs.

negative affect An individual's tendency to accentuate the negative aspects of himself or herself, other people, and the world in general.

negative consequences Results of a behavior that a person finds unattractive or aversive.

negativism An aggressive mechanism in which a person responds with pessimism to any attempt at solving a problem.

nominal group technique (NGT) A structured approach to group decision making that focuses on generating alternatives and choosing one.

nonaction Doing nothing in hopes that a conflict will disappear.

nondefensive communication Communication that is assertive, direct, and powerful.

nonprogrammed decision A new, complex decision that requires a creative solution.

nonverbal communication All elements of communication that do not involve words.

normative commitment A type of organizational commitment based on an individual's perceived obligation to remain with an organization.

norms of behavior The standards that a work group uses to evaluate the behavior of its members.

O

objective knowledge Knowledge that results from research and scientific activities.

one-way communication Communication in which a person sends a message to another person and no feedback, questions, or interaction follow.

operant conditioning Modifying behavior through the use of positive or negative consequences following specific behaviors.

opportunistic "what's in it for me" manager (Opp) A leader whose style aims to maximize self-benefit.

opportunities Favorable times or chances for progress and advancement.

organic structure An organizational design that emphasizes teamwork, open communication, and decentralized decision making.

organization development (OD) A systematic approach to organizational improvement that applies behavioral science theory and research in order to increase individual and organizational well-being and effectiveness.

organization man manager (5,5) A middle-of-the-road leader.

organizational behavior The study of individual behavior and group dynamics in organizations.

organizational citizenship behavior Behavior that is above and beyond the call of duty.

organizational commitment The strength of an individual's identification with an organization.

organizational (corporate) culture A pattern of basic assumptions that are considered valid and that are taught to new members as the way to perceive, think, and feel in the organization.

organizational design The process of constructing and adjusting an organization's structure to achieve its goals.

organizational life cycle The differing stages of an organization's life from birth to death.

organizational politics The use of power and influence in organizations.

organizational socialization The process by which newcomers are transformed from outsiders to participating, effective members of the organization.

organizational structure The linking of departments and jobs within an organization.

overdependence An unhealthy, insecure pattern of behavior that leads to preoccupied attempts to achieve security through relationships.

P

participation problem A cost associated with absenteeism, tardiness, strikes and work stoppages, and turnover.

participative decision making Decision making in which individuals who are affected by decisions influence the making of those decisions.

paternalistic "father knows best" manager (9+9) A leader who promises reward and threatens punishment.

people The human resources of the organization.

Perceiving Preference Preferring to explore many alternatives and flexibility.

perceptual screen A window through which we interact with people that influences the quality, accuracy, and clarity of the communication.

performance appraisal The evaluation of a person's performance.

performance decrement A cost resulting from poor quality or low quantity of production, grievances, and unscheduled machine downtime and repair.

performance management A process of defining, measuring, appraising, providing feedback on, and improving performance.

personal power Power used for personal gain.

personality A relatively stable set of characteristics that influence an individual's behavior.

personality hardiness A personality resistant to distress and characterized by commitment, control, and challenge.

person–role conflict Conflict that occurs when an individual is expected to perform behaviors in a certain role that conflict with his or her personal values.

phased retirement An arrangement that allows employees to reduce their hours and/or responsibilities in order to ease into retirement.

planned change Change resulting from a deliberate decision to alter the organization.

political behavior Actions not officially sanctioned by an organization that are taken to influence others in order to meet one's personal goals.

political skill The ability to get things done through favorable interpersonal relationships outside of formally prescribed organizational mechanisms.

position power The authority associated with the leader's formal position in the organization.

positive affect An individual's tendency to accentuate the positive aspects of himself or herself, other people, and the world in general.

positive consequences Results of a behavior that a person finds attractive or pleasurable.

power The ability to influence another person.

power distance The degree to which a culture accepts unequal distribution of power.

powerlessness A lack of power.

preventive stress management An organizational philosophy that holds that people and organizations should take joint responsibility for promoting health and preventing distress and strain.

primary prevention The stage in preventive stress management designed to reduce, modify, or eliminate the demand or stressor causing stress.

procedural justice The fairness of the process by which outcomes are allocated in an organization.

process consultation An OD method that helps managers and employees improve the processes that are used in organizations.

professional bureaucracy A decentralized form of organization that emphasizes the operating core and standardization of skills.

programmed decision A simple, routine matter for which a manager has an established decision rule.

projection Overestimating the number of people who share our own beliefs, values, and behaviors.

projective test A personality test that elicits an individual's response to abstract stimuli.

psychoanalysis Sigmund Freud's method for delving into the unconscious mind to better understand a person's motives and needs.

psychological contract An implicit agreement between an individual and an organization that specifies what each is expected to give and receive in the relationship.

psychological intimacy Emotional and psychological closeness to other team or group members.

psychology The science of human behavior.

punishment The attempt to eliminate or weaken undesirable behavior by either bestowing negative consequences or withholding positive consequences.

Q

quality circle (QC) A small group of employees who work voluntarily on company time, typically one hour per week, to address work-related problems such as quality control, cost reduction, production planning and techniques, and even product design.

quality program A program that embeds product and service quality excellence in the organizational culture.

quality team A team that is part of an organization's structure and is empowered to act on its decisions regarding product and service quality.

R

rationality A logical, step-by-step approach to decision making, with a thorough analysis of alternatives and their consequences.

rationalization A compromise mechanism characterized by trying to justify one's behavior by constructing bogus reasons for it.

realistic job preview (RJP) Both positive and negative information given to potential employees about the job they are applying for, thereby giving them a realistic picture of the job.

receiver The person receiving a message.

referent power An elusive power that is based on interpersonal attraction.

reflective listening A skill intended to help the receiver and communicator clearly and fully understand the message sent.

refreezing The final step in Lewin's change model, in which new attitudes, values, and behaviors are established as the new status quo.

reinforcement The attempt to develop or strengthen desirable behavior by either bestowing positive consequences or withholding negative consequences.

reinvention The creative application of new technology.

reward power Power based on an agent's ability to control rewards that a target wants.

richness The ability of a medium or channel to elicit or evoke meaning in the receiver.

risk aversion The tendency to choose options that entail fewer risks and less uncertainty.

robotics The use of robots in organizations.

role negotiation A technique whereby individuals meet and clarify their psychological contract.

rule-based theory An ethical theory that emphasizes the character of the act itself rather than its effects.

S

satisfice To select the first alternative that is "good enough," because the costs in time and effort are too great to optimize.

secondary prevention The stage in preventive stress management designed to alter or modify the individual's or the organization's response to a demand or stressor.

secrecy Attempting to hide a conflict or an issue that has the potential to create conflict.

selective perception The process of selecting information that supports our individual viewpoints while discounting information that threatens our viewpoints.

self-esteem An individual's general feeling of self-worth.

self-fulfilling prophecy The situation in which our expectations about people affect our interaction with them in such a way that our expectations are confirmed.

self-image How a person sees himself or herself, both positively and negatively.

self-interest What is in the best interest and benefit to an individual.

self-managed team A team that makes decisions that were once reserved for managers.

self-monitoring The extent to which people base their behavior on cues from other people and situations.

self-reliance A healthy, secure, *interdependent* pattern of behavior related to how people form and maintain supportive attachments with others.

self-report questionnaire A common personality assessment that involves an individual's responses to a series of questions.

self-serving bias The tendency to attribute one's own successes to internal causes and one's failures to external causes.

sensing Gathering information through the five senses.

simple structure A centralized form of organization that emphasizes the upper echelon and direct supervision.

Six Sigma A high-performance system to execute business strategy that is customer driven, emphasizes quantitative decision making, and places a priority on saving money.

skill development The mastery of abilities essential to successful functioning in organizations.

skills training Increasing the job knowledge, skills, and abilities that are necessary to do a job effectively.

social decision schemes Simple rules used to determine final group decisions.

social information-processing (SIP) model A model that suggests that the important job factors depend in part on what others tell a person about the job.

social learning The process of deriving attitudes from family, peer groups, religious organizations, and culture.

social loafing The failure of a group member to contribute personal time, effort, thoughts, or other resources to the group.

social perception The process of interpreting information about another person.

social power Power used to create motivation or to accomplish group goals.

social responsibility The obligation of an organization to behave in ethical ways.

sociology The science of society.

sociotechnical systems (STS) Giving equal attention to technical and social considerations in job design.

specialization The degree to which jobs are narrowly defined and depend on unique expertise.

standardization The degree to which work activities are accomplished in a routine fashion.

status structure The set of authority and task relations among a group's members.

stereotype A generalization about a group of people.

strain Distress.

strategic change Change of a larger scale, such as organizational restructuring.

strategic contingencies Activities that other groups depend on in order to complete their tasks.

stress The unconscious preparation to fight or flee that a person experiences when faced with any demand.

stressor The person or event that triggers the stress response.

strong culture An organizational culture with a consensus on the values that drive the company and with an intensity that is recognizable even to outsiders.

strong situation A situation that overwhelms the effects of individual personalities by providing strong cues for appropriate behavior.

structure The systems of communication, authority and roles, and workflow.

superordinate goal An organizational goal that is more important to both parties in a conflict than their individual or group goals.

survey feedback A widely used method of intervention whereby employee attitudes are solicited using a questionnaire.

synergy A positive force that occurs in groups when group members stimulate new solutions to problems through the process of mutual influence and encouragement within the group.

T

task An organization's mission, purpose, or goal for existing.

task environment The elements of an organization's environment that are related to its goal attainment.

task function An activity directly related to the effective completion of a team's work.

task revision The modification of incorrectly specified roles or jobs.

task structure The degree of clarity, or ambiguity, in the work activities assigned to the group.

task-specific self-efficacy An individual's beliefs and expectancies about his or her ability to perform a specific task effectively.

team building An intervention designed to improve the effectiveness of a work group.

team manager (9,9) A leader who builds a highly productive team of committed people.

teamwork Joint action by a team of people in which individual interests are subordinated to team unity.

technocentric Placing technology and engineering at the center of job design decisions.

technological interdependence The degree of interrelatedness of the organization's various technological elements.

technology The intellectual and mechanical processes used by an organization to transform inputs into products or services that meet organizational goals.

technology The tools, knowledge, and/or techniques used to transform inputs into outputs.

technostress The stress caused by new and advancing technologies in the workplace.

telecommuting Transmitting work from a home computer to the office using a modem.

terminal values Values that represent the goals to be achieved or the end states of existence.

tertiary prevention The stage in preventive stress management designed to heal individual or organizational symptoms of distress and strain.

Theory X A set of assumptions of how to manage individuals who are motivated by lower-order needs.

Theory Y A set of assumptions of how to manage individuals who are motivated by higher-order needs.

thinking Making decisions in a logical, objective fashion.

360-degree feedback A process of self-evaluation and evaluations by a manager, peers, direct reports, and possibly customers.

time orientation Whether a culture's values are oriented toward the future (long-term orientation) or toward the past and present (short-term orientation).

trait theory The personality theory that states that in order to understand individuals, we must break down behavior patterns into a series of observable traits.

transformational change Change in which the organization moves to a radically different, and sometimes unknown, future state.

transformational coping A way of managing stressful events by changing them into less subjectively stressful events.

transnational organization An organization in which the global viewpoint supersedes national issues.

triangulation The use of multiple methods to measure organizational culture.

two-way communication A form of communication in which the communicator and receiver interact.

Type A behavior pattern A complex of personality and behavioral characteristics, including competitiveness, time urgency, social status insecurity, aggression, hostility, and a quest for achievements.

U

uncertainty avoidance The degree to which a culture tolerates ambiguity and uncertainty.

unfreezing The first step in Lewin's change model, in which individuals are encouraged to discard old behaviors by shaking up the equilibrium state that maintains the status quo.

unplanned change Change that is imposed on the organization and is often unforeseen.

upper echelon A top-level executive team in an organization.

V

valence The value or importance one places on a particular reward.

values Enduring beliefs that a specific mode of conduct or end state of existence is personally or socially preferable to an opposite or converse mode of conduct or end state of existence.

virtual office A mobile platform of computer, telecommunication, and information technology and services.

W

whistle-blower An employee who informs authorities of the wrongdoings of his or her company or coworkers.

withdrawal The final career stage in which the individual contemplates retirement or possible career changes.

work Mental or physical activity that has productive results.

work simplification Standardization and the narrow, explicit specification of task activities for workers.

work team A group of people with complementary skills who are committed to a common mission, performance goals, and approach for which they hold themselves mutually accountable.

workaholism An imbalanced preoccupation with work at the expense of home and personal life satisfaction.

workplace deviance behavior Any voluntary counterproductive behavior that violates organizational norms and causes some degree of harm to organizational functioning.

Z

zone of indifference The range in which attempts to influence a person will be perceived as legitimate and will be acted on without a great deal of thought.